Incorporations

zone

Incorporations

Edited by Jonathan Crary and Sanford Kwinter

zone

ZONE Editors: Jonathan Crary, Michel Feher, Sanford Kwinter, Ramona Naddaff

Editors of this volume: Jonathan Crary and Sanford Kwinter

Managing Editor: Elizabeth Felicella

Design: Bruce Mau

Design Schema: Sanford Kwinter and Bruce Mau

Production: Ed Cleary, Alison Hahn, Vilip Mak, Kathleen Oginski,
Nigel Smith, Gregory Van Alstyne.

Image Research Coordinator: Elizabeth Felicella
with Naomi Jackson, Suzanne Jackson, Carole Naggar, Keith Seward,
Steve Snyder, Kristen Vallow, Timothy Wright

Manuscript Editor: Ted Byfield

Editorial Coordinators: Rennie Childress and Meighan Gale
with Suzanne Jackson, Linda Kelly, Rachel Robbins, Keith Seward,
Kristen Vallow, Thad Ziolkowski.

Translations: Randall Cherry, Mark Cohen, Robert Hurley, Martin Joughin,
Donald Leslie, Brian Massumi, Delphine Bechtel, Ted Byfield.

Fundraising and Advertising: Céline Cazals de Fabel

Initiating Projects Editor: Kerri Kwinter

Special Thanks: Brian Boigon, Lois Burke, Anne Dixon, Ed Epstein, Jason Greenberg,
Virginia Heckert, Barbara Hoffman, Christian Hubert, Alex Kessler, Gus Kiley, Andy
Levine, Kerry McCarthy at AP/World Wide, Melissa Mathis, Jeffrey Meikle, Erica
Meinhardt, Anne Mensior of CLAM, Guillaume Paris, Gilles Peress, Guy Poulin, Jackie
Raynal, Chris Rowat, Wendelin Scott, Carina Snyder, Susan Spiegel, Tim Sternberg,
Aiyemobisi Williams, Thomas Jean Yee; Aperture Magazine, Avery Library, CRT
Artificio, Museum of Modern Art Photography Department, Photofest, Telescope
Magazine, University of California at Riverside Photography Museum.

We gratefully acknowledge the generous support of the National Endowment for the
Arts, Tom Cugliani Gallery, Lorence Monk Gallery, Nahan Gallery, Marian Goodman
Gallery, Vincent Wapler, John Weber Gallery, Salvatore Ala Gallery, Leo Castelli
Gallery, Vrej Baghoomian, Sidney Janis.

Distributed by The MIT Press. Second printing June, 1995.
ISBN: 0·942299·29·9 (paper) 0·942299·30·2 (cloth)
Library of Congress Catalog Card Number: 88·051439

ZONE 6

zone

John Cage 1912–1992
Félix Guattari 1930–1992
In memoriam

Zone

zone

Contributors: **J. G. Ballard** is a novelist. His works include *The Crystal World, Crash, High-Rise, The Atrocity Exhibition* and *Concrete Island*. **Judith Barry** is an artist and writer who lives in New York City. She is represented by the Nicole Klagsbrun Gallery. **Ana Barrado** is a photographer whose work has been featured in international publications in the U.S. and Japan. A monograph of her work was published by Atelier Peytol in Tokyo. **Georges Canguilhem**, philosopher of science, is professor emeritus at the Sorbonne and is former director of the Institut d'Histoire des Sciences et des Techniques at the University of Paris. His works include *The Normal and Pathological, Connaissance de la vie* and *Ideology and Rationality: The History of the Life Sciences*. **Lisa Cartwright and Brian Goldfarb:** Lisa Cartwright teaches film and media studies at the University of Rochester and writes on cinema, science and technology. She is the author of *Physiological Modernity*. Brian Goldfarb is a computer graphics and video artist. He teaches multimedia art at the University of Rochester. **François Dagognet** is a philosopher and medical doctor who has taught at the universities of Lyon and Paris. He is the author of *La maîtrise du vivant, Philosophie de l'image,* and *Etienne-Jules Marey*. **Manuel DeLanda** is a film/video artist and author of *War in the Age of Intelligent Machines*. **Didier Deleule** is a philosopher and the author of *Le Corps productif* (with François Guéry) and *La Psychologie : Mythe scientifique*. **Gilles Deleuze** is a philosopher. Among his works are *Masochism, The Logic of Sense* and *Différence et répétition*. He co-authored (with Félix Guattari) *Anti-Oedipus* and *A Thousand Plateaus*. **Diller + Scofidio** is a collaborative team involved in cross-disciplinary work incorporating architecture, performing and visual arts. Elizabeth Diller is an Assistant Professor of Architecture at Princeton University. Ric Scofidio is Professor of Architecture at the Irwin S. Chanin School of Architecture, Cooper Union. **Peter Fend** is cofounder of Ocean Earth Construction and Development Corporation. He is represented by American Fine Arts Company in New York. **Leif Finkel** teaches in both the Department of Bioengineering and the Institute of Neurological Sciences at the University of Pennsylvania. **Susan L. Foster** is a choreographer, dancer, writer and Professor of Dance at the University of California, Riverside. She has published articles on semiotics and dance and is author of *Reading Dancing: Bodies and Subjects in Contemporary American Dance*. **Heidi Gilpin** teaches in the Department of Dance, University of California, Riverside. She is editor of *Parallax* and director of the Institute for New Dramaturgy. **Jean-Pierre Gorin** is a filmmaker, whose works include *Poto and Cabengo* and *Routine Pleasures*. He is co-director, with Jean-Luc Godard, of *Tout Va Bien* and was a member of the Dziga Vertov Group. He is currently teaching at University of California, San Diego. **Félix Guattari** is the author of *La Révolution moléculaire* and *Cartographies schizoanalytiques*. He co-authored (with Gilles Deleuze) *Anti-Oedipus* and *A Thousand Plateaus*. **Donna Haraway** is a professor in the History of Consciousness Board at the University of California, Santa Cruz, where she teaches feminist theory, technoscience studies, and women's studies. She is author of *Simians, Cyborgs, and Women: The Reinvention of Nature* and *Primate Visions: Gender, Race, and Nature in the World of Modern Science*. **Ronald Jones** teaches in the Yale School of Art and Architecture and is represented by Metro Pictures and the Sonnabend Gallery.

Leone & Macdonald is the collaborative team of Hillary Leone and Jennifer Macdonald. They are represented by the Joe Fawbush Gallery and have exhibited throughout the United States and in South America. **Ellen Lupton and J. Abbott Miller** are graphic designers and writers. Ellen Lupton is Curator of Contemporary Design at the Cooper-Hewitt National Museum of Design. J. Abbott Miller is principal of the studio Design Writing Research in New York. Both teach the history and theory of graphic design at Cooper Union. **Bill Krohn** is the Los Angeles correspondent for *Cahiers du Cinema* and a regular contributor to *Traffic* and *Modern Times*. **John O'Neill** is Distinguished Research Professor of Sociology at York University and author of *Plato's Cave: Desire, Power and the Specular Functions of the Media* and *Sociology as a Skin Trade: Essays Towards a Reflexive Sociology*. **Mark Poster** teaches at the University of California, Irvine. His recent books include *The Mode of Information*, *Critical Theory and Poststructuralism* and *Baudrillard: Selected Writings*. **Anson Rabinbach** teaches European History at Cooper Union. He is coeditor of *New German Critique* and author of *The Human Motor: Energy, Fatigue, and the Origins of Modernity*. **Paul Rabinow** is Professor of Anthropology at the University of California, Berkeley and is author of *French Modern: Norms and Forms of the Social Environment*. **Paul Rogers** is a Senior Lecturer in the Department of Peace Studies at Bradford University. He also writes for *The Guardian* and *The Observer* in London. **Nina Rosenblatt** is an art historian currently completing a study of the technologies and economies of French modernism in the 1920s and 1930s. **Elaine Scarry** teaches English at Harvard University and is the author of *The Body in Pain: The Making and Unmaking of the World* and *Resisting Representation*. **Hillel Schwartz** is a visiting scholar at the University of California at San Diego. He is author of *Century's End: A Cultural History of the Fin de Siècle from the 1890s through the 1990s* and *Never Satisfied: A Cultural History of Diets, Fantasies and Fat*. **Eve Kosofsky Sedgwick** is a Professor of English at Duke University and author of *Between Men: English Literature and Male Homosocial Desire* and *The Epistemology of the Closet*. **Gilbert Simondon** is a philosopher and was a professor at the Sorbonne. He is the author of *Du mode d'existence des objets techniques* and *L'individu et sa genèse physico-biologique*. **Alluquère Roseanne Stone** teaches in the department of Sociology at the University of California, San Diego. She is director of the Group for the Study of Virtual Systems at the Center for Cultural Studies at the University of California, Santa Cruz. **Klaus Theweleit** is a freelance writer working in West Germany. He is the author of *Male Fantasies*. **Frederick Turner** is Founders Professor of Arts and Humanities at the University of Texas, Dallas. He is author of *Beauty: The Value of Values*, *Rebirth of Value* and *Tempest, Flute and Oz*. **Paul Virilio** has been Director of the Ecole Spéciale d'Architecture and is a founding member of the Center for Interdisciplinary Research in Peace Studies and Military Strategy. His books include *Speed and Politics*, *La Machine de vision*, and *War and Cinema: The Logistics of Perception*. **Francisco J. Varela** is Director of Research at the Institute of Neurosciences of the CNRS in Paris. His books include *Principles of Biological Autonomy*, *The Tree of Knowledge: The Biological Roots of Human Understanding* (with Humberto Maturana), and *The Embodied Mind: Cognitive Science and Human Experience*.

Foreword

Incorporations outlines a complex motif central to the understanding of our contemporary world, one inseparable from the
myriad forces through which humans have continually sought to
make and remake themselves modern. This title encompasses at
once themes of integration — the integration of human life forces
into the larger-than-human systems of social and technical organization; as well as the finer-grained processes of embodiment —
those strategies through which human life combines with, and
assimilates, the minute, shifting, often invisible patterns and
rhythms of the concrete historical milieus within which it unfolds.

   In the first category may be included all those processes —
economic, ergonomic, scientific and social — that evolved from
the new managerial and disciplinary techniques introduced
within the great state bureaucracies and industrial assemblages of
the later nineteenth century. This turning point was marked by
the first systematic transfer of the human will to mastery away
from the non-human world of nature to the knowledge, management and control of a human nature as well. The flux and energy
of human life became increasingly reduced to finite quantities of
force and sensation, allowing it to be evermore efficiently subsumed and deployed in schools, factories, hospitals and house-
holds by the productivist and rationalizing imperatives of a
capitalist megamachine.

   With the second category we mean to conceive of the individual's practical relation to its milieu as a dynamic system of local,

interdependent, self-updating movements, perceptions and gestures. Such a system would proceed through the capture of, and adaptation to, specific socially and technically generated patterns and effects, for example, the way new industrial speeds and rhythms were adopted at the turn of the century alongside new fluid models of human movement, kinaesthetics and energy.

Our book then, is a dynamical map of the pathways, accidents and strategic evolutions out of which the very problem of "life" itself first arose as a specific and autonomous concept, and how life, in its simultaneously quotidian, menacing and delirious concreteness, became what it is within twentieth-century modernity. Our topic is the problem of life itself, understood as a complex, labile, overtone structure, neither dependent upon, nor reducible to, an organic substrate or historical object — in short, to what contemporary habit too knowingly calls "the body." Rather, this volume addresses the forces — aesthetic, technical, political, sexual — with which things combine in order to form novel aggregates of pattern and behavior. In still other ways, moreover, it is about these processes of formation themselves, understood as a larger fundamental evolutionary process to which we humans belong as a central though otherwise unprivileged part. For this reason it is no coincidence that a number of essays in this volume contain the prefix bio- in their titles, indeed many others could have. But if a specifically biological modality has become operative here, it is an indication of the vast transformations in techniques of knowledge that continue to occur since the demise of the mechanical model of explanation in the nineteenth century.

The modern problem of life then, is unthinkable apart from another set of figures, that of the organism and the machine. Although profound and nearly invisible processes of economic subsumption have never ceased effecting the convergence of the biological and mechanical spheres of existence, what is changing today, and what our book in a partial way attempts to chart, is how the classical processes of the mechanization of life are giving way to a new and unprecedented vitalization of the machine. This development in no way signals a monolithic historical shift but rather a proliferation at a variety of levels of new virtual pathways and historical countermovements which have the potential to be used or activated in diverse and opposing ways. Though many of these tendencies are either already stabilized in familiar social arrangements or deeply embedded in the inexorable movements of contemporary regimes of power and production, there are others that remain volatile, paradigm-resisting forces, full of unknown and unforeseeable capacities for cognitive and cultural transformation.

The book develops along two axes: one traverses certain features of our own contemporaneity, here represented by works of philosophers, neuroscientists, architects, filmmakers, artists and others; the other axis is historical, tracing lines of development from the late nineteenth century to the present. The choice to elaborate these two axes simultaneously underscores how current transformations of biological and technological arrangements are neither the result nor the sign of some recent shift in cultural paradigms, but instead are part of ongoing processes of modernization traceable to the second half of the nineteenth century at least.

One of the aims of this book, then, is to outline the ways in which overlapping "biotechnic" arrangements have throughout the twentieth century brought about continuous transformations of a "lifeworld." Though the same relentless processes of modernization and rationalization continue today unabated, they have become increasingly and inseparably linked to the positive production of such generalized lifeworlds or ambient milieus as sites of invention and transformation. Neither human subjects nor the conceptual or material objects among which they live are any longer thinkable in their distinctness or separation from the dynamic, correlated, multipart systems within which they arise. Every thing, and every individual emerges, evolves and passes away by incorporating and being incorporated into, other emerging, evolving or disintegrating structures that surround and suffuse it. Indeed, incorporation may well be the name of the new primary logic of creation and innovation in our late modern world.

— Jonathan Crary and Sanford Kwinter

Regimes, Pathways, Subjects
Félix Guattari

Classical thought distanced the soul from matter and separated the
essence of the subject from the cogs of the body. Marxists later set up
an opposition between subjective superstructures and infrastructural
relations of production. How then ought we talk about the production
of subjectivity today? Clearly, the contents of subjectivity have become
increasingly dependent on a multitude of machinic systems. No area
of opinion, thought, images, affects or spectacle has eluded the invasive
grip of "computer-assisted" operations, such as databanks and telematics. This leads one to wonder whether the very essence of the subject
— that infamous essence, so sought after over the centuries by Western
philosophy — is not threatened by contemporary subjectivity's new
"machine addiction." Its current result, a curious mix of enrichment
and impoverishment, is plainly evident: an apparent democratization
of access to data and modes of knowledge, coupled with a segregative
exclusion from their means of development; a multiplication of anthropological approaches, a planetary intermixing of cultures, paradoxically
accompanied by a rising tide of particularisms, racisms and nationalisms; and a vast expansion in the fields of technoscientific and aesthetic investigation, taking place in a general atmosphere of gloom and
disenchantment. Rather than joining the fashionable crusades against
the misdeeds of modernism, or preaching a rehabilitation of worn-out
transcendent values, or indulging in the disillusioned indulgences of
postmodernism, we might instead try to find a way out of the dilemma
of having to choose between unyielding refusal or cynical acceptance of
this situation.

The fact that machines are capable of articulating statements and
registering states of fact in as little as a nanosecond, and soon in a pico-
second,[1] does not in itself make them diabolical powers that threaten

Agecroft Power Station, Pendlebury, Salford, Greater Manchester, 1983.
John Davies

to dominate human beings. People have little reason to turn away from machines; which are nothing other than hyperdeveloped and hyperconcentrated forms of certain aspects of human subjectivity, and emphatically not those aspects that polarize people in relations of domination and power. It will be possible to build a two-way bridge between human beings and machines and, once we have established that, to herald new and confident alliances between them.

In what follows, I shall address the following problem: that today's information and communication machines do not merely convey representational contents, but also contribute to the fabrication of new *assemblages* of enunciation, individual and collective.

Before going any further, we must ask whether subjectivity's "entry into the machine" — as in the past, when one "entered" a religious order — is really all that new. Weren't precapitalist or archaic subjectivities already engendered by a variety of initiatory, social and rhetorical machines embedded in clan, religious, military and feudal institutions, among others? For present purposes, I shall group these machines under the general rubric of *collective apparatuses* [equipment] *of subjectification*. Monastic machines, which passed down memories from antiquity to the present day, thereby enriching our modernity, are a case in point. Were they not the computer programs, the "macroprocessors," of the Middle Ages? The neoplatonists, in their own way, were the first programmers of a processuality capable of spanning time and surviving periods of stasis. And what was the Court of Versailles, with its minutely detailed administration of flows of power, money, prestige and competence, and its high-precision etiquette, if not a machine deliberately designed to churn out a new and improved aristocratic subjectivity — one far more securely under the yoke of the royal State than the seignorial aristocracy of the feudal tradition, and entertaining different relations of subjection to the values of the rising bourgeoisie?

It is beyond the scope of this article to sketch even a thumbnail history of these collective apparatusess of subjectification. As I see it, neither history nor sociology is equal to the task of providing the analytical or political keys to the processes in play. I shall therefore limit myself to highlighting several fundamental paths/voices [*voie/voix*] that these apparatuses have produced, and whose crisscrossing remains the basis for modes and processes of subjectification in contemporary Western societies. I distinguish three series:

First: Paths/voices of *power* circumscribing and circumventing human groupings from the outside, either through direct coercion of, and panoptic grip on, bodies, or through imaginary capture of minds.

Second: Paths/voices of *knowledge* articulating themselves with technoscientific and economic pragmatics from within subjectivity.

Third: Paths/voices of *self-reference* developing a processual subjectivity that defines its own coordinates and is self-consistent (what I have discussed elsewhere under the category of the "subject-group"), but can nevertheless establish transversal relations to mental and social stratifications.

(1) Power over exterior territorialities, (2) deterritorialized modes of knowledge about human activities and machines, and (3) the creativity proper to subjective mutations: these three paths/voices, though inscribed in historical time and rigidly incarnated in sociological divisions and segregations, are forever entwining in unexpected and strange dances, alternating between fights to the death and the promotion of new figures.

I should note in passing that the "schizoanalytic" perspective on the processes of subjectification I am proposing will make only very limited use of dialectical or structuralist approaches, systems theory or even genealogical approaches as understood by Michel Foucault. In my view, all systems for defining models are in a sense equal, all are tenable, but only to the extent that their principles of intelligibility renounce any universalist pretensions, and that their sole mission be to help map real existing territories (sensory, cognitive, affective and aesthetic universes) — and even then only in relation to carefully delimited areas and periods. This relativism is not in the least embarrassing, epistemologically speaking: it holds that the regularities, the quasi-stable configurations, for which our immediate experiences first emerge are precisely those systems of self-modeling invoked earlier as self-reference, the third path/voice. In this kind of system, discursive links, whether of expression or of content, obey ordinary logics of larger and institutional discursive ensembles only remotely, against the grain, or in a disfiguring way. To put it another way: at this level, absolutely anything goes — any ideology, or even religion will do, even the most archaic: all that matters is that it be used as the raw material of existence.[2]

The problem is to situate appropriately this third path/voice, of creative, transforming self-reference, in relation to the first two, modes of power and modes of knowledge. I have said both that self-reference is the most singular, the most contingent path/voice, the one that anchors human realities in finitude, and that it is the most universal one, the one that effects the most dazzling crossings between heterogeneous domains. I might have used other terms: it is not so much that this path/voice is "universal" in the strict sense, but that it is the richest in what may be called *universes of virtuality*, the best endowed with lines of processuality. (I ask the reader here not to begrudge me my plethora of qualifiers, or the meaning-overload of certain expressions, or even the vagueness of their cognitive scope: there is no other way to proceed!)

The paths/voices of power and knowledge are inscribed in external referential coordinates guaranteeing that they are used extensively and that their meaning is precisely circumscribed. The Earth was once the primary referent for modes of power over bodies and populations, just as capital was the referent for economic modes of knowledge and mastery of the means of production. With the figureless and foundationless Body without Organs of self-reference we see spreading before us an entirely different horizon, that of a new machinic processuality considered as the continual point of emergence of all forms of creativity.

I must emphasize that the triad territorialized power–deterritorialized knowledge–processual self-reference has no other aim than to clarify certain problems — for example, the current rise of neoconservative ideologies and other, even more pernicious archaisms. It goes without saying that so perfunctory a model cannot even claim to begin to map concrete processes of subjectification. Suffice it to say that these terms are instruments for a speculative cartography that makes no pretense of providing a universal structural foundation or increasing

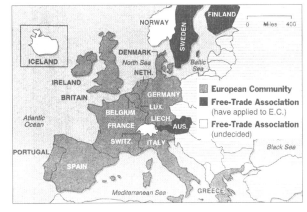

Carolingian Empire.

European Community, 1992.

on-the-ground efficiency. This is another way of saying, by way of a reminder, that these paths/voices have not always existed and undoubtedly will not always exist (at least, not in the same form). Thus, there may be some relevance in trying to locate their historical emergence, and the thresholds of consistency they have crossed in order to enter and remain in the orbit of our modernity.

It is safe to assume that their various consistencies are supported by collective systems for "memorizing" data and modes of knowledge, as well as by material apparatuses of a technical, scientific and aesthetic nature. We can then, attempt to date these fundamental subjective mutations in relation, on the one hand, to the historical birth of large-scale religious and cultural collective arrangements, and on the other, to the invention of new materials and energies, new machines for crystallizing time and, finally, to new biological technologies. It is not a question of material infrastructures that directly condition collective subjectivity, but of components essential for a given setup to take consistency in space and time as a function of technical, scientific and artistic transformations.

These considerations have led me to distinguish three zones of historical fracture on the basis of which, over the last thousand years, the three fundamental capitalist components have come into being: *the age of European Christianity,* marked by a new conception of the relations between the Earth and power; *the age of capitalist abstraction or deterritorialization of knowledge and technique,* founded on principles of general equivalence; and *the age of planetary computerization,* creating the possibility for creative and singularizing processuality to become the new fundamental point of reference.

With respect to the last point, one is forced to admit that there are very few objective indications of a shift away from oppressive mass-media modernity toward some kind of more liberating postmedia era in which subjective assemblages of self-reference might come into their own. Nevertheless, it is my guess that it is only through "remappings" of the production of computerized subjectivity that the path/voice of self-reference will be able to reach its full amplitude. Obviously, nothing is a foregone conclusion — and nothing that could be done in this domain could ever substitute for innovative social practices. The only point I am making is that, unlike other revolutions of subjective emancipation — Spartacus and other slave rebellions, peasant revolts during the Reformation, the French Revolution, the Paris Commune and so on — individual and social practices for the self-valorization and self-organization of subjectivity are now within our reach and, perhaps for the first time in history, have the potential to lead to something more enduring than mad and ephemeral spontaneous outpourings — in other words, to lead to a fundamental repositioning of human beings in relation to both their machinic and natural environments (which, at any rate, now tend to coincide).

The Age of European Christianity
In Western Europe, a new figure of subjectivity arose from the ruins of the late Roman and Carolingian empires. It can be characterized by a double articulation combining two aspects: first, the relatively autonomous base territorial entities of ethnic, national or religious character, which originally constituted the texture of feudal segmentary, but have survived in other forms up to the present day; and second, the deterritorialized subjective power entity transmitted by the Catholic Church and structured as a collective setup on a European scale.

Unlike earlier formulas for imperial power, Christianity's central figure of power did not assert a direct, totalitarian-totalizing hold over the base territories of society and of subjectivity. Long before Islam, Christianity had to renounce its desire to form an organic unity. However, far from weakening processes for the integration of subjectivity, the disappearance of a flesh-and-blood Caesar and the promotion of a deterritorialized Christ (who cannot be said to be a substitute for the former) only reinforced them. It seems to me that the conjunction between the partial autonomy of the political and economic spheres proper to feudal segmentarity and the hyperfusional character of Christian subjectivity (as seen in the Crusades and the adoption of aristocratic codes such as the Peace of God, as described by Georges Duby) has resulted in a kind of fault line, a metastable equilibrium favoring the proliferation of other equally partial processes of autonomy. This can be seen in the schismatic vitality of religious sensibility and reflection that characterized the medieval period; and of course in the explosion of aesthetic creativity, which has continued unabated since then; the first great "takeoff" of technologies and commercial exchange, which is known to historians as the "industrial revolution of the eleventh century," and was a correlate of the appearance of new figures of urban organization. What could have given this tortured, unstable, ambiguous formula the surfeit of consistency that was to see it persist and flourish through the terrible historical trials awaiting it: barbarian invasions, epidemics, never-ending wars? Schematically, one can identify six series of factors:

First: The promotion of a monotheism that would prove in practice to be quite flexible and evolutionary, able to adapt itself more or less successfully to particular subjective positions — for example, even those of "barbarians" or slaves. The fact that flexibility in a system of ideological reference can be a fundamental asset for its survival is a basic given, which can be observed at every important turning point in the history of capitalist subjectivity (think, for example, of the surprising adaptive abilities enabling contemporary capitalism literally to swallow the so-called socialist economies whole). Western Christianity's consolidation of new ethical and religious patterns led to two parallel markets of subjectification: one involves the perpetual reconstitution of the base territorialities (despite many setbacks), and a redefinition of filiation suzerainty and national networks; the other involves a predisposition to the free circulation of knowledge, monetary signs, aesthetic figures, technology, goods, people and so forth. This kind of market prepared the ground for the deterritorialized capitalist path/voice.

Second: The cultural establishment of a disciplinary grid onto Christian populations through a new type of religious machine, the original base for which was the parish school system created by Charlemagne, but which far outlived his empire.

Third: The establishment of enduring trade organizations, guilds, monasteries, religious orders and so forth, functioning as so many "databanks" for the era's modes of knowledge and technique.

Fourth: The widespread use of iron, and wind and water mills; the development of artisan and urban mentalities. It must be emphasized, however, that this first flowering of machinism only implanted itself in a somewhat parasitic, "encysted" manner within the great human assemblages on which the large-scale systems of production continued essentially to be based. In other words, a break had not yet been made with the fundamental and primordial relation of human being to tool.

Fifth: The appearance of machines operating by much more advanced subjective integration: clocks striking the same canonical hours throughout all of Christendom; and the step-by-step invention of various forms of religious music subordinated to scripture.

Sixth: The selective breeding of animal and plant species, making possible a rapid quantitative expansion of demographic and economic parameters, and therefore leading to a rescaling of the assemblages in question.

In spite or because of the colossal pressures — including territorial restrictions but also enriching acculturations — associated with the Byzantine Empire, then Arab imperialism, as well as with nomadic and "barbarian" powers (which introduced, most notably, metallurgical innovations), the cultural hotbed of protocapitalist Christianity attained a relative (but long-term) stability with respect to the three fundamental poles governing its relations of power and knowledge: peasant, religious and aristocratic subjectification. In short, the "machinic advances" linked to urban development and the flowering of civil and military technologies were simultaneously encouraged and contained. All this constitutes a kind of "state of nature" of the relation between human being and tool, which continues to haunt paradigms of the "Work, Family, Fatherland" type even today.

zone

The Age of Capitalist Deterritorialization
of Modes of Knowledge and Technique

The second component of capitalist subjectivity begins effectively in the eighteenth century. It is marked above all by a growing disequilibrium in the relations of human being to tool. Human beings also witnessed the disappearance and eradication of social territorialities that, until then, were thought to be permanent and inalienable. Their landmarks of social and physical corporeality were profoundly shaken. The universe of reference for the new system of generalized exchange was no longer territorial segmentarity, but rather capital as a mode of semiotic reterritorialization of human activities and structures uprooted by machinic processes. Once, a real Despot or imaginary God served as the operational keystone for the local recomposition of actual territories. Now, though, that role would be played by symbolic capitalization of abstract values of power bearing on economic and technological modes of knowledge indexed to newly deterritorialized social classes, and creating a general equivalence between all valorizations of goods and human activities. A system of this sort cannot preserve its historical consistency without resorting to a kind of endless headlong race, with a constant renegotiation of the stakes. The new "capitalist passion" would sweep up everything in its path, in particular the cultures and territorialities that had succeeded to one degree or another in escaping the Christian steamroller. The principal consistency factors of this component are the following:

First: The general spread of the printed text into all aspects of social and cultural life, correlated with a certain weakening of the performative force of direct oral communication; by the same token, capabilities of accumulating and processing knowledge are greatly expanded.

Second: The primacy of steam-powered machines and steel, which multiplied the power of machinic vectors to propagate themselves on land, sea and air, and across every technological, economic and urban space.

Third: The manipulation of time, which is emptied of its natural rhythms by: chronometric machines leading to a Taylorist rationalization of labor power; techniques of economic semiotization, for example, involving credit money, which imply a general virtualization of capacities for human initiative and a predictive calculus bearing on domains of innovation — checks written on the future — all of which makes possible an unlimited expansion of the imperium of market economies.

Fourth: The biological revolutions, beginning with Pasteur's discoveries, that have linked the future of living species ever more closely to the development of biochemical industries.

Human beings find themselves relegated to a position of quasi-parasitic adjacency to the machinic phyla. Each of their organs and social relations are quite simply repatterned in order to be reallocated, overcoded, in accordance with the global requirements of the system. (The most gripping and prophetic representations of these bodily rearrangings are found in the work of Leonardo da Vinci, Brueghel and especially Arcimboldo.)

The paradox of this functionalization of human organs and faculties and its attendant regime of general equivalence between systems of value is that, even as it stubbornly continues to invoke universalizing perspectives, all it ever manages to do historically is fold back on itself, yielding reterritorializations of nationalist, classist, corporatist, racist and nationalist kinds. Because of this, it inexorably returns to the most conservative, at times caricatured, paths/voices. The "spirit of enlightenment," which marked the advent of this second figure of capitalist subjectivity, is necessarily accompanied by an utterly hopeless fetishization of profit — a specifically bourgeois libidinal power formula. That formula distanced itself from the old emblematic systems of control over territories, people and goods by employing more deterritorialized mediations — only to secrete the most obtuse, asocial and infantilizing of subjective groundworks. Despite the appearance of freedom of thought that the new capitalist monotheism is so fond of affecting, it has always presupposed an archaistic, irrational grip on unconscious subjectivity, most notably through hyperindividuated apparatuses of responsibility- and guilt-production, which, carried to a fever pitch, lead to compulsive self-punishment and morbid cults of blame — perfectly repertoried in Kafka's universe.

Solaris, 1972, directed by Andrei Tarkovsky.

The Age of Planetary Computerization

Here, in the third historical zone, the preceding pseudo-stabilities are upset in an entirely different way. The machine is placed under the control of subjectivity — not a reterritorialized human subjectivity, but a new kind of machinic subjectivity. Here are several characteristics of the taking-consistency of this new epoch:

First: Media and telecommunications tend to "double" older oral and scriptural relations. It is worth noting that in the resulting polyphony, not only human but also machinic paths/voices link into databanks, artificial intelligence and the like. Public opinion and group tastes are developed by statistical and modelizing apparatuses, such as those of the advertising and film industries.

Second: Natural raw materials are replaced by a multitude of new custom-made, chemically produced materials (plastics, new alloys, semiconductors and so on). The rise of nuclear fission, and perhaps soon nuclear fusion, would seem to augur a considerable increase in energy resources — providing, of course, that irreparable pollution disasters do not occur! As always, everything will depend on the new social assemblages' capacity for collective reappropriation.

Third: The temporal dimensions to which microprocessors provide access allow enormous quantities of data and huge numbers of problems to be processed in infinitesimal amounts of time, enabling the new machinic subjectivities to stay abreast of the challenges and issues confronting them.

Fourth: Biological engineering is making possible unlimited remodeling of life forms; this may lead to a radical change in the conditions of life on the planet and, consequently, to an equally radical reformulation of all of its ethological and imaginary references.

The burning question, then, becomes this: Why have the immense processual potentials brought forth by the revolutions in information processing, telematics, robotics, office automation, biotechnology and so on up to now led only to a monstrous reinforcement of earlier systems of alienation, an oppressive mass-media culture and an infantilizing politics of consensus? What would make it possible for them finally to usher in a postmedia era, to disconnect themselves from segregative capitalist values and to give free rein to the first stirrings, visible today, of a revolution in intelligence, sensitivity and creativity? Any number of dogmatisms claim to have found the answer to these questions in a violent affirmation of one of the three capitalist paths/voices at the expense of the others. There are those who dream of returning to the legitimated powers of bygone days, to the clear circumscription of peoples, races, religions, castes and sexes. Paradoxically, the neo-Stalinists and social democrats, both of whom are incapable of conceiving of the socius in any terms other than its rigid insertion into State structures and functions, must be placed in the same category. There are those whose faith in capitalism leads them to justify all of the terrible ravages of modernity — on people, culture, the environment — on the grounds that in the end they will bring the benefits of progress. Finally, there are those whose fantasies of a radical liberation of human creativity condemn them to chronic marginality, to a world of false pretense, or who turn back to take refuge behind a facade of socialism or communism.

Our project, on the contrary, is to attempt to rethink these three necessarily interwoven paths/voices. No engagement with the creative phyla of the third path/voice is tenable unless new existential territories are concurrently established. Without hearkening back to the post-Carolingian pathos, they must nevertheless include protective mechanisms for the person and the imaginary and create a supportive environment. Surely the mega-enterprises of the second path/voice — the great collective scientific and industrial adventures, the administration of knowledge markets — still have legitimacy: but only on the condition that they redefine their goals, which remain today singularly deaf and blind to human truths. Is it still enough to claim profit as the only goal? In any case, the aim of the division of labor, and of emancipatory social practices, must be redirected toward a *fundamental right to singularity,* toward an ethic of finitude that is all the more demanding of individuals and social entities, because its imperatives are *not* founded on transcendent principles. It has become apparent in this regard that ethicopolitical universes of reference now tend to institute themselves as extensions of aesthetic universes, which in no way authorizes the use of such terms as "perversion" or "sublimation." It will be noted that not only the existential operators pertaining to these ethicopolitical matters but the aesthetic operators as well inevitably reach the point at which meaning breaks down, entail irreversible processual engagements whose agents are, more often than not, incapable of accounting for anything (least of all themselves) — and are therefore exposed to a panoply of risks, including madness. Only if the third path/voice takes consistency in the direction of self-reference — carrying us from the consensual media era to the dissensual postmedia era — will each be able to assume his or her processual potential and, perhaps, transform this planet — a living hell for over three quarters of its population — into a universe of creative enchantments.

I imagine that this language will ring false to many a jaded ear, and that even the least malicious will accuse me of utopianism. Utopia, it is true, gets bad press these days, even when it acquires a charge of realism and efficiency, as it has with the Greens in Germany. But let there be no mistake: these questions of subjectivity production do not only concern a handful of illuminati. Look at Japan, the prototypical model of new capitalist subjectivities. Not enough emphasis has been placed on the fact that one of the essential ingredients of the miracle mix showcased for visitors to Japan is that the collective subjectivity produced there on a massive scale combines the highest of "high-tech" components with feudalisms and archaisms inherited from the mists of time. Once again, we find the reterritorializing function of an ambiguous monotheism — Shinto-Buddhism, a mix of animism and universal powers — contributing to the establishment of a flexible formula for subjectification going far beyond the triadic framework of capitalist Christian paths/voices. We have a lot to learn!

For now, though, consider another extreme, the case of Brazil. There, phenomena involving the reconversion of archaic subjectivities have taken an entirely different turn. It is common knowledge that a considerable proportion of the population is mired in such extreme poverty that it lives outside the money economy, but that does not prevent Brazil's industry being ranked sixth among Western powers. In this society, a dual society if there ever was one, there is a double sweep of subjectivity: on the one hand, there is a fairly racist Yankee wave

Over: Kowloon Walled City, Hong Kong.
Ryuji Miyamoto

(like it or not) beamed in on one of the most powerful television transmitting networks in the world, and on the other, an animist wave involving religions like *candomblé*, passed on more or less directly from the African cultural heritage, which are now escaping their original ghettoization and spreading throughout society, including the most well-connected circles of Rio and São Paulo. It is interesting that, in this case, mass-media penetration is preceding capitalist acculturation. What did President Sarney do when he wanted to stage a decisive coup against inflation, which was running as high as 400 percent per year? He went on television. Brandishing a piece of paper in front of the cameras, he declared that from the moment he signed the order he held in his hand everyone watching would become his personal representative and would have the right to arrest any merchant who did not respect the official pricing system. It seems to have been surprisingly effective — but at the price of considerable regression in the legal system.

Capitalism in permanent crisis (Worldwide Integrated Capitalism) is at a total subjective impasse. It knows that paths/voices of self-reference are indispensable for its expansion, and thus for its survival, yet it is under tremendous pressure to efface them. A kind of superego — that booming Carolingian voice — dreams only of crushing them and reterritorializing them onto archaic images. Let us attempt to find a way out of this vicious circle by resituating our three capitalist paths/voices in relation to the geopolitical coordinates — First, Second and Third Worlds — commonly used to establish a hierarchy of the major subjective formations. For Western Christian subjectivity, everything was (and, unconsciously, remains) quite simple: it has no restrictions in latitude and longitude. It is the transcendent center around which everything is deemed to revolve. The paths/voices of capital, for their part, have continued their onward rush — first westward, toward elusive "new frontiers," more recently toward the East, in conquest of what remains of the ancient Asiatic empires (Russia included). However, this mad race has reached the end of the road, from one direction in California, from the other in Japan. The second path/voice of capital has closed the circle; the world has buckled, the system is saturated. Henceforth, the North–South axis will perhaps function as the third path/voice of self-reference. This is what I call "the barbarian compromise." The old walls marking the limits of "barbarism" have been torn down, deterritorialized once and for all. The last shepherds of monotheism have lost their flocks, for it is not in the nature of the new subjectivity to be herded. Moreover, capitalism itself is now beginning to shatter into animist and machinic polyvocity. What a fabulous reversal, if the old African, pre-Columbian and aboriginal subjectivities became the final recourse for subjective reappropriation of machinic self-reference! The very same blacks, Indians, even South Sea islanders whose ancestors chose death over submission to Christian and capitalist ideals of power: first slavery, then the exchange economy.

I hope that my last examples are not faulted for being overly exotic. Even in Old World countries such as Italy there has been a proliferation of small family enterprises in symbiosis with cutting-edge sectors of the electronics industry and telematics; this has happened over the last few years in the northeast–center triangle of Italy. If an Italian Silicon Valley develops there, it will be founded on a reconversion of subjective archaisms originating in the country's antiquated patriarchal structures. Some futurologists, who are in no way crackpots, predict that certain Mediterranean countries — Italy and Spain, in particular — will overtake the great economic centers of northern Europe in a few decades' time. So when it comes to dreaming and utopia, the future is wide open! My wish is that all those who remain attached to the idea of social progress — all those for whom the social has not become an illusion or a "simulacrum" — look seriously into these questions of subjectivity production. The subjectivity of power does not fall from the sky. It is not written into our chromosomes that divisions of knowledge and labor must necessarily lead to the hideous segregations humanity now suffers. Unconscious figures of power and knowledge are not universals. They are tied to reference myths profoundly anchored in the psyche, but they can still swing around toward liberatory paths/voices. Subjectivity today remains under the massive control of apparatuses of power and knowledge, thus consigning technical, scientific and artistic innovations to the service of the most reactionary and retrograde figures of sociality. In spite of that, other modalities of subjective production — processual and singularizing ones — are conceivable. These alternate forms of existential reappropriation and self-valorization may in the future become the *reason for living* for human collectivities and individuals who refuse to give in to the deathlike entropy characterizing the period we are passing through.

NOTES

1. A nanosecond is 10^{-9} seconds; a pico-second is 10^{-12}. On the futurological themes touched on here, see the special issue of *Science et technique* entitled "Rapport sur l'état de la technique," ed. Thierry Gaudin.

2. The immediate aim of their expressive chains is no longer to denote states of fact or to embed states of sense in significational axes but — I repeat — to activate existential crystallizations operating, in a certain way, outside the fundamental principles of classical reason: identity, the excluded middle, causality, sufficient reason, continuity.... The most difficult thing to convey is that these materials, which can set processes of subjective self-reference in motion, are themselves extracted from radically heterogeneous, not to mention heteroclite, elements: rhythms of lived time, obsessive refrains, identificational emblems, transitional objects, fetishes of all kinds.... What is affirmed in this crossing of regions of being and modes of semiotization are traits of singularization that date — something like existential postmarks — as well as "event," "contingent" states of fact, their referential correlates and their corresponding assemblages of enunciation. Rational modes of discursive knowledge cannot fully grasp this double capacity of intensive traits to singularize and transversalize existence, enabling it, on the one hand, to persist locally, and on the other, to consist transversally (giving it transconsistency). It is accessible to apprehension only on the order of affect, a global transferential grasp whereby that which is most universal is conjoined with the most highly contingent facticity: the loosest of meaning's ordinary moorings becomes anchored in the finitude of being-there. Various traditions of what could be termed "narrow rationalism" persist in a quasi-militant, systematic incomprehension of anything in these metamodelizations pertaining to virtual and incorporeal universes, fuzzy worlds of uncertainty, the aleatory and the probable. Long ago, narrow rationalism banished from anthropology those modes of categorization it considered "prelogical," when they were in reality metalogical or paralogical, their objective essentially being to give consistency to individual and/or collective assemblages of subjectivity.

What we need to conceptualize is a continuum running from children's games and the makeshift ritualizations accompanying attempts at psychopathological recompositions of "schizoid" worlds, through the complex cartographies of myth and art, all the way to the sumptuous speculative edifices of theology and philosophy, which have sought to apprehend these same dimensions of existential creativity (examples are Plotinus's "forgetful souls" and the "unmoving motor" which, according to Leibniz, preexists any dissipation of potential).

Translated from the French by Brian Massumi

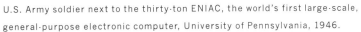

U.S. Army soldier next to the thirty-ton ENIAC, the world's first large-scale, general-purpose electronic computer, University of Pennsylvania, 1946.

Stalking Cancer

ONCOMOUSE™ shortens the path to knowledge in carcinogenesis

ONCOMOUSE™/*ras* transgenic animal is the first *in vivo* model to contain an activated oncogene. Each OncoMouse carries the *ras* oncogene in all germ and somatic cells. This transgenic model, available commercially for the first time, predictably undergoes carcinogenesis. OncoMouse reliably develops neoplasms within months...and offers you a shorter path to new answers about cancer. Available to researchers only from Du Pont, where better things for better living come to life.

For more information about OncoMouse and monoclonal antibodies for specifically detecting the activated *ras* oncogene protein, call 1-800-551-2121.

Better things for better living

When Man™ Is on the Menu

Donna Haraway

In its April 27, 1990 ad for OncoMouse™ in *Science* magazine, DuPont Corporation presents its fully commodified rodent, "the first *in vivo* model to contain an activated oncogene" that results in reliable tumor production, under the title "Stalking Cancer."[1] Produced by genetic engineering, this fine transgenic mouse is "available to researchers only from DuPont, where better things for better living come to life."[2] The mouse is a weapon in the war on cancer, a conflict that sustains empires of technoscience and biotechnology. In the strongest possible sense, OncoMouse™ is a technological product whose natural habitat and evolutionary future are fully contained in that world-building space called "the laboratory." Denizen of the wonderful realms of the undead (where better things for better living come to life), this little murine smart bomb is also, in the strongest possible sense, a cultural actor. A tool-weapon for stalking cancer, the bioengineered mouse is simultaneously a metaphor and a technology. This is the normal state of the entities in technoscience cultures, including ourselves. In science, as Nancy Stepan pointed out for nineteenth-century studies of sex and race, a metaphor may become a research program.[3]

"A Few Words About Reproduction From A Leader In The Field" is the advertising slogan for Logic General Corporation's software duplication system in the May 1, 1983 issue of *Science*. The immediate visual and verbal impact of Logic General's advertising image insists on the absurdity of separating the technical, organic, mythic, textual and political threads in the semiotic fabric of technoscience culture. Under the unpromising orange-to-yellow rainbow of the earth-sun logo of Logic General, a biological white rabbit has its (her? sex and gender are not so settled in this reproductive system) back to us. Its paws are on a keyboard, that inertial, old-fashioned residue of the typewriter that lets our computers feel natural to us, user-friendly, as it were. But the keyboard is misleading; no letters are transferred by a mechanical key to a waiting solid surface. The computer–user interface works differently: even if s/he doesn't understand the implications of her duplicitous keyboard, the white rabbit is, like her mouse cousin, in her natural home — s/he is fully artifactual. Like fruit flies, yeast, transgenic mice and the humble nematode worm, *Caenorhabditis elegans*, this rabbit's evolutionary story transpires in the lab; the lab is its proper niche, its true habitat. Both material system and sign for the measure of fecundity, this kind of rabbit occurs in no other nature than the lab, that preeminent scene of replication practices in our hypermodern world of rationalized copying practices. Figures in stories of enlightenment, the bunnies, worms, mice and men of technoscience are simultaneously research models, cultural metaphors and potent jokes — jokes with the power to remake worlds and the subjects who inhabit them.

As with DuPont's OncoMouse™, which climbs toward the blindingly bright, open shutter of a camera, the rabbit is also peering at a luminous icon of technoscientific illumination; but with Logic General we are not in a biological laboratory. Looking into the screen of a video display terminal the organic rabbit peers at its image, but the image is not her reflection, indeed, *especially* not her reflection. This is not Lacan's world of mirrors: primary identification and maturing metaphoric substitution will be produced with other techniques, other writing technologies. The white rabbit will be translated, her potencies and competences relocated radically. The guts of the computer produce a kind of visual product other than distorted, self-birthing reflections. The simulated bunny inside the computer screen peers out at us face first. It is s/he who locks her gaze with us. S/he also has her paws on a grid, one just barely reminiscent of a typewriter, but more reminiscent of an older icon of technoscience — the Cartesian coordinate system that maps the

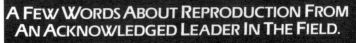

world into the imaginary spaces of rational modernity and enlightenment.

In her natural electronic habitat, the virtual rabbit is on a grid that insists on the world as a game played on a chesslike board made up of a square array of floppy disks. This rabbit insists that the truly rational actors will replicate themselves in a virtual world where the best players will not be Man, though he may linger like the horse-drawn carriage that gave its form to the railroad car or the typewriter that gave its illusory shape to the computer interface. The functional privileged signifier in this system will not be so easily mistaken for any primate male's urinary and copulative organ. Metaphoric substitution and other circulations in the very material symbolic domain will be more likely to be effected by a competent mouse. The vague femaleness of both the rabbits, of course, gives no confidence that the new players other to Man will be women. More likely, the rabbit that is interpellated into the World in this non-mirror stage, this diffracting moment of subject constitution, will be literate in a quite different grammar of gender.

Like OncoMouse™, both the rabbits in the Logic General ad are cyborgs — compounds of the organic, technical, mythic, textual and political — and they call us, interpellate us, into a world in which we are reconstituted as subjects. Interpolated — that is, inserted — thus into the matrices of techno-scientific maps, we may or may not wish to take shape there. But, literate in the reading and writing practices proper to the technical-mythic territories of the laboratory, we have little choice. We inhabit these narratives, and they inhabit us. The figures and the stories of these ads haunt us, literally. The reproductive stakes in the texts of Logic General and DuPont — and, in general, in the inscription practices of the laboratory — are future life forms and ways of life for humans and unhumans.

If these are the zones in which those who respond to DuPont's and Logic General's call take shape, then such shaping highlights our need for stories of shape-changers. We need stories for imagining how to be responsible within and for the zones in which we find ourselves. Most important obligations and passions in the world are unchosen; "choice" has always been a desperately inadequate political metaphor for resisting domination and for inhabiting a livable world. Interpellation is not about choice; it is about insertion. It is past time to put our reading practices into action. My question, rooted in a reading of the technoscience text in the world, is a political one: If technological products are cultural actors, and if "we," whoever that problematic invitation to inhabit a common space might include, are technological products at deeper levels than we have yet comprehended, then what kind of cultural action will forbid the evolution of OncoMouse™ into Man™? The question has a historical antecedent from the olden times of historical narrative, when revolution was not a bad joke: What is to be done?

Notes

1. This short intervention is revised from a section of a paper-in-progress, "Of OncoMouse™ and Man™," for a book to be edited by Carl Cranor, *Genes 'R' Us, So Who's That?*, which grew out of a residential study group sponsored by the University of California Humanities Research Institute, winter 1990, at U.C. Irvine. I wish to thank the uchri and all the participants in the study group.

2. Those who follow the commercial circuits of biotechnology will know that DuPont became DuPont-Merck shortly after the "stalking cancer" advertising series appeared. The slogan, "better things for better living," seems to have passed from the Earth. But, like the words from the introduction to "Star Trek," "to boldly go where no man has gone before," millions of earthlings have paid DuPont's slogan the compliment of incorporating it into a most refractory unconscious, where it will be compost for future advertising copy.

3. Nancy Stepan, "Race and Gender: The Role of Analogy and Science," *Isis* 77 (1986), pp. 261–77.

China, 1958.
Henri Cartier-Bresson/Magnum Photos

Machine and Organism

Georges Canguilhem

The relationship between machine and organism has generally been studied in only one way. Nearly always, the organism has been explained on the basis of a preconceived idea of the structure and functioning of the machine; but only rarely have the structure and function of the organism been used to make the construction of the machine itself more understandable. Even though mechanistic theory sparked some very impressive technical research, the fact remained that the very notion of an "organology," as well as its basic premises and methodology, remained undeveloped.[1]

Philosophers and mechanistic biologists approached the machine as a set of data, or else made it into a problem that they could solve purely through mental application. To do this, they called on the engineer, who was for them a scientist in the truest sense. Misled by the ambiguities of their view of mechanics, they saw machines only as theorems in concrete form. The operations necessary to construct machines were only secondary considerations when compared with the all-important idea that the machine revealed their theories *in concreto*. To see this, one needed only to acknowledge what science could accomplish, and from there it was simply a matter of the confident application of that knowledge. However, I do not believe that it is possible to treat the biological problem of the "living machine" by separating it from the technological problem it supposedly resolves — namely, the problem of the relationship between technology and science. This problem is normally resolved by starting with the idea that, logically and chronologically, knowledge precedes application. What I want to show is that the construction of machines can indeed be understood by virtue of certain truly biological principles, without having at the same time to examine how technology relates to science.

I shall address the following topics in successive order: what it means to compare an organism to a machine; the relationship between mechanical processes, and the results that might be achieved by using them; and the historical reversal of the traditional relationship between the machine and the organism and the philosophical consequences of this reversal.

For those who have carefully studied living beings and the forms they take, it is rare — and only in the case of the vertebrates — that one notices any truly mechanical attributes, at least in the sense that the term is commonly understood by scientists. In *La Pensée technique*, for example, Julien Pacotte notes that movements of the joints and the eyeball can be paralleled with what mathematicians call a "mechanism."[2] A machine can be defined as a man-made, artificial construction, which essentially functions by virtue of mechanical operations. A mechanism is made of a group of mobile solid parts that work together in such a way that their movement does not threaten the integrity of the unit as a whole. A mechanism therefore consists of movable parts that work together and periodically return to a set relation with respect to each other. It consists of interlinking parts, each of which has a determinable degree of freedom of movement: for example, both a pendulum and a cam valve have one degree of freedom of movement, whereas a threaded screw has two. The fact that these varying degrees of freedom of movement can be quantified means that they can serve as tangible guides for measuring, for setting limits on the amount of movement that can be expected between any two interacting solid objects. In every machine, then, movement is a function, first, of the way the parts interact and, second, of the mechanical operations of the overall unit.[3]

Mechanics is governed by the principle that every movement of a machine is geometric and measurable. What is more, every such movement regulates and transforms the forces and energy imparted to it. Mechanics, though, does not work in the same way that a motor does: in mechanics, movements are simply propagated, not created. A rather simple example of how this transformation of movement takes place can be seen in several devices — a wheel crank or an eccentric crank, for example — that are set into motion by an initial lateral movement but eventually produce reciprocating, rotary movement. Of course, mechanical operations can be combined, either by superimposing them or adding them together. It is even possible to take a basic mechanical device, modify it and make it capable of performing a variety of other mechanical operations. This is exactly what happens when a bicycle freewheel clutch is released or stopped.[4]

What constitutes the rule in human industry is the exception in the structure of organisms and the exception in nature, and I must add here that in the history of technology and the inventions of man *assembled* configurations are not the most primitive. The oldest known tools are made of a single piece. The construction of axes or of arrows made by assembling a flint and a handle, or the construction of nets or fabrics, are so many signs that the primitive stage has been passed.

This brief overview of some elementary principles of kinematics helps to give a fuller sense of the problem without losing sight of a central paradox: Why was it necessary to turn to the theory of mechanism, as outlined above, in order to explain the living organism? The answer can be found, it seems, in the fact that this mechanical model of living organisms does not rely on kinematics alone. A machine, as defined above, is not totally self-sufficient: it must receive and then transform energy imparted to it from an outside source. To be represented in movement it must be associated with an energy source.[5]

For a long time, kinematic mechanisms were powered by humans or animals. During this stage, it was an obvious tautology to compare the movement of bodies to the movement of a machine, when the machine itself depended on humans or animals to run it. Consequently, it has been shown that mechanistic theory has depended, historically, on the assumption that it is possible to construct an automaton, meaning a mechanism that is miraculous in and of itself and does not rely on human or animal muscle power.

This is the general idea put forth in the following well-known text:
Examine carefully the physical economy of man: What do you find? The jaws are armed with teeth, which are no more than pincers. This stomach is nothing but a retort, or heat chamber; the veins, the arteries and indeed the entire vascular system are simply hydraulic tubes; the heart, a pump; the viscera, nothing but filters and sieves; the lungs, a pair of bellows; and what are muscles if not a system of cables and ropes. What is the oculomotor nerve, if not a pulley? And so on. Try as they will, chemists cannot explain nature and set up a separate philosophy simply by coining a new vocabulary around words like "fusion," "sublimation" and "precipitation"; for this does not at all address either the incontrovertible laws of equilibrium or the laws governing the workings of the wedge, cables, pumps as elements of mechanical theory.

This text is not where we might think to find it, but in fact comes from the *Praxis medica*, written by Baglivi in 1696, an Italian doctor belonging to the iatromechanical school. This school, founded by Borelli, had apparently been influenced by Descartes, although for reasons of national prestige, the Italians prefer to attribute it to Galileo.[6] This text is interesting because it treats the wedge, the rope, the cable and the pump as if they could be seen in the same terms for formulating explanatory principles. It is clear, however, that from the mechanistic point of view there is a difference between these devices: a cable essentially transmits a given movement, whereas a pump transforms a given movement and is also a motor — admittedly, a motor that returns whatever energy it receives; but, at certain intervals, it apparently has a degree of independence of movement. In Baglivi's text, the heart is the *primum movens* — the central pump that serves as the motor for the whole body.

Therefore, a crucial element behind the mechanical explanation of bodily movement is that, in addition to machines that perform as kinematic devices, there are also machines that act as motors, deriving their energy, at the moment it is utilized, from a source other than animal muscle. And this is why, although Baglivi's text seems linked to Descartes, the idea of the body-as-machine actually goes back to Aristotle. When dealing with the Cartesian theory of the animal-machine, it is often difficult to decide whether or not Descartes had any precursors for this idea. Those who look for Descartes's predecessors here usually cite Gomez Pereira, a Spanish doctor of the second half of the sixteenth century: Pereira suggested, before Descartes, that he could demonstrate that animals were wholly machines and that they do not possess that sensitive soul so frequently attributed to them.[7] But in other respects, it is unquestionably Aristotle who saw the congruity between animal movements and automatic mechanical movements, like those observed in instruments of war, especially catapults. This idea is treated rather extensively by Alfred Espinas, who discusses the connection between the problems dealt with by Aristotle in *De Motu animalium* and those in his compilation of *Quaestiones mechanicae*.[8] Aristotle draws a clear parallel between the organs of animal movement and "*organa*," or parts of war machines, like the arm of a catapult about to launch a projectile. Thus catapults, typical automatic machines of the period, seemed to be articulated like a human limb, as they were poised and made to release their great stores of pent-up energy. In the same work, Aristotle carries the analogy even further by comparing the movement of our limbs to mechanisms; and he makes his case in much the same way that Plato did when, in the *Timaeus*, he compared the movement of vertebrates to hinges or pivots.

It is true that in Aristotle the theory of movement is somewhat different from what it would become in Descartes. According to Aristotle, the soul is the principle of all movement. All movement first presupposes immobility and then requires a prime mover or some motivating force. Desire moves the body, and desire is explained by the soul, just as potentiality is explained by an act. Despite their differing explanations of movement, for Aristotle as for Descartes later, the comparison of the body with a machine presupposes that man is composed of automated mechanical parts reliant on an energy source that produces motor effects over time and continue to do so well after the original (human or animal) energy has dissipated. It is this discrepancy between the storage of energy to be released by the mechanism and the moment of release that allows us to forget the relation of dependence between the effects of the mechanism and the actions of a body. When Descartes looks to machines to explain how organisms work, he invokes spring-operated and hydraulic automata. As a result, he owes a great intellectual debt to the ideas behind the technical creations of his own time, including clocks and watches, water mills and church organs of the early seventeenth century. We can say, then, that as long as the concept of the human and animal body is inextricably "tied" to the machine, it is not possible to offer an explanation of the body in terms of the machine. Historically, it was not possible to conceive of such an explanation until the day that human ingenuity created mechanical devices that not only imitated organic movements — as in the launching of a projectile or the back-and-forth movement of a saw — but also required no human intervention except to construct them and set them going.

In two instances, I have asserted that an explanation cannot be formulated without the existence of certain conditions. Is this tantamount to attributing a historical necessity to scientific explanation? How do I explain the abrupt appearance in Descartes of a lucid mechanistic interpretation of biological phenomena? This theory is clearly related to modifications that occurred in the economic and political structure of Western society, but the nature of this relation remains obscure.

This problem has been treated in depth by P.-M. Schuhl, who has shown that in ancient philosophy the opposition of science and technique paralleled the opposition of freedom and servitude and, at a deeper level, of art and nature.[9] Schuhl supports this parallel with Aristotle's assertion that natural and violent movement are opposed — a violent movement occurs when mechanisms are used against nature, and its characteristics are that it exhausts itself rapidly and never becomes habitual — which is to say, a permanent tendency to reproduce itself never obtains.

Here I must turn to the difficult problem of the history of civilization and the philosophy of history. With Aristotle, the hierarchy of freedom and servility, of theory and practice, of nature and art, is paralleled by an economic and political hierarchy in the cities, namely, the relations of freemen and slaves. The slave, according to Aristotle in the *Politics*, is an animated machine.[10] This is the crux of the problem to which Schuhl only alludes in passing: Did the Greek conception of the dignity of science lead to their disdain for technique and the resultant paucity of inventions? And did this in turn lead to the difficulty of applying the results of technical activity to the explanation of nature? Or, rather, did the Greeks' high regard for purely speculative science and detached contemplation explain the absence of technical invention? Did their disregard for work cause slavery, or did the abundance of slaves due to military supremacy explain their low regard for work? Are we obliged to explain the ideology in terms of the socioeconomic structure or, rather, the socioeconomic structure in terms of the ideology? Did the ease of exploiting human beings make it easier to disdain the techniques that would allow them to exploit nature? Does the arduousness of exploiting nature justify the exploitation of man by man? Is there a causal relationship at work here? And if so, in which direction does it go? Or are we dealing with a global structure having reciprocal relations and influences?

A similar problem is presented by Father Lucien Laberthonnière, who contrasts the physics of an artist or an aesthete to that of an engineer and an artisan.[11] Laberthonnière suggests that the determining factor here is ideas, given that the Cartesian transformation in the philosophy of technique presupposes Christianity. It was necessary to conceive of man as a being who transcends nature and matter in order to then uphold his right and his duty to exploit matter ruthlessly. In other words, man had to be valorized so that nature could be devalorized. Next it was necessary to conceive of men as being radically and originally equal so that, as the exploitation of humans by each other was condemned on political grounds, there were increased technical means to exploit nature and a growing sense of duty to do so. This analysis permits Laberthonnière to speak of a Christian origin for Cartesian physics. However, he qualifies his own claim: the physics and technique supposedly made possible by Christianity came, for Descartes, well after Christianity had been founded as a religion. Moreover, humanist philosophy, which saw man as master and proprietor of nature, was in direct opposition to Christianity as humanists saw it: the religion of salvation, of escape into the hereafter, inspired by a contempt for the things of this life and unconcerned with whatever fruits technology might win for mankind in this world below. Laberthonnière asserts that "time does not enter into the question," but this is by no means certain. In any case, several classic texts have demonstrated that certain technical inventions that transformed the use of animal motor power — for example, the horseshoe and the shoulder harness — accomplished more for the emancipation of slaves than did the countless preachings of abolitionists.

In *Der Übergang vom feudalem zum bürgerlichen Weltbild*, Franz Borkenau argues that there is a causal relationship between mechanistic philosophy and the totality of social and economic conditions in which it arises.[12] He claims that at the start of the seventeenth century the qualitative philosophy of antiquity and the Middle Ages was eclipsed by mechanistic ideas. The success of these new ideas was, on the level of ideology, an effect of the economic fact of the new organization and expansion of manufacturing. For Borkenau, the division of artisanal labor into separate, simplified operations requiring little skill produced the concept of abstract social labor. Once labor had been decomposed into simple, identical and easily repeatable movements, price and wages could be determined simply by comparing the hours worked — and the result was a process that, previously qualitative, had become quantifiable.[13] Calculating work in purely quantitative terms that can be treated mathematically is claimed to be the basis and the starting point for a mechanistic conception of the life world. It is therefore by reducing all value to economic value, "to cold hard cash," as Marx puts it in *The Communist Manifesto*, that the mechanistic view of the universe is supposed to be fundamentally a Weltanschauung of the bourgeoisie. Finally, Borkenau claims that the animal-machine gives rise to the norms of the nascent capitalist economy. Descartes, Galileo and Hobbes are thus the unwitting heralds of this economic revolution.

Borkenau's theses have been analyzed and criticized more forcefully by Henryk Grossmann.[14] According to him, Borkenau ignores five hundred years of economic and ideological history by seeing mechanistic theory as coinciding with the rise of manufacturing at the beginning of the seventeenth century: Borkenau writes as if Leonardo da Vinci had never existed. Referring to Pierre Duhem's *Les Origines de la statique* (1905), and the publication of Leonardo's manuscripts (Herzfeld, 1904; Gabriel Séailles, 1906; Péladan, 1907), Grossmann agrees with Séailles that with the publication of Leonardo's manuscripts it became clear that the origins of modern science could be pushed back by more than a century. The quantification of the notion of work occurs first within mathematics, well before its economic rationalization. The norms of the capitalist evaluation of production, moreover, had been defined by the Italian bankers even in the thirteenth century. Relying on Marx, Grossmann reminds us that although in general there was no division of labor in manufacturing properly speaking, manufacturing at its inception meant the gathering together in the same place of skilled artisans who had previously worked independently. According to Grossmann, then, it is not the calculation of cost per hour of work, but the evolution of mechanization that is the real cause of the mechanical view of the universe. The development of mechanization begins during the Renaissance.[15] It is, therefore, more accurate to say that Descartes had consciously rationalized a mechanistic technique than that he had unconsciously expressed the imperatives of a capitalist economy. For Descartes, mechanics is a *theory of machines* that presupposes a spontaneous invention which science must then consciously promote and develop.

Which machines did the most to modify the relationship between man and nature before the time of Descartes, far beyond the wildest imaginations of the ancients — and did most to justify and rationalize the hopes men had vested in machines? Above all there were firearms, which hardly interested Descartes except in terms of the problem of the projectile.[16] On the other hand, Descartes was very interested in clocks and watches, in lifting machines, in water-driven machines and other related devices. As a result, one should say that Descartes made a human phenomenon — the construction of machines — into an integral part of his philosophy; and one should avoid saying that he transposed the social phenomena of capitalist production into ideology. The key question becomes: How does Cartesianism account for an internal principle of goal-directed activity in mechanisms, as is implied in the comparison of a machine with an organism?

The theory of the animal-machine is inseparable from "I think therefore I am." The radical distinction between the soul and the body, between thought and extension, requires the affirmation that matter, whatever form it adopts, and thought, whatever function it fulfills, are each an undivided substance.[17] Because the only function of the soul is judgment, it is impossible to admit the existence of a soul in animals, since we have no proof that animals judge, incapable as they are of language or invention.[18]

For Descartes, though, the refusal to attribute a soul — that is, reason — to animals, does not necessarily lead to the conclusion that animals are not alive (since not much more than a warm, beating heart is at issue); nor must animals be denied sensibility, to the extent that such sensibility is solely a function of their organs.[19]

In the same discussion, a moral foundation for the animal-machine theory comes to light. Descartes views the animal as Aristotle had viewed the slave, devalorizing it in order to justify man's using it to serve his own purposes: "My opinion is no more cruel to animals than it is overly pious toward men, freed from the superstitions of the Pythagorians, because it absolves them of the hint of crime whenever they eat or kill animals."[20] And it comes as no small surprise to find the same argument in reverse in a passage of Leibniz: "if we are compelled to view the animal as being more than a machine, we would have to become Pythagorians and renounce our domination of animals."[21] And so we confront an attitude typical of Western thought. On the theoretical level, the mechanization of life only considers animals to the extent that they serve man's technological ends. Man can only make himself the master and proprietor of nature if he denies any natural finality or purpose; and he must consider the whole of nature, including all life forms other than himself, as solely a means to serve his purposes.

This is how the mechanical model of the living organism, including the human body, was legitimized; for already in Descartes the human body, if not man's entire self, is seen as a machine. As I have already noted, Descartes based his mechanical model on automata, that is, on moving machines.[22]

In order to see the full implications of Descartes's theory, I now intend to look at the beginning of his "Treatise on Man," which was published for the first time in Leyden in 1662. He wrote there:

These men will be composed, as we are, of a soul and a body. First I must describe the body on its own, then the soul, again on its own; and finally I must show how these two natures would have to be joined and united in order to constitute men who resemble us.

I suppose the body to be nothing but a statue or machine made of earth, which God forms with the explicit intention of making it as much as possible like us. Thus God not only gives it externally the colors and shapes of all the parts of our

Animal testing, c. 1970.

bodies, but also places inside it all the parts required to make it walk, eat, breathe, enabling it to imitate all those functions which seem to proceed from matter and to depend solely on the interacting movements of our organs.

We see clocks, artificial fountains, water mills and other such machines which, although only man-made, seem to move of their own accord in various ways; but I am supposing this machine to be made by the hands of God, and so I think you may reasonably think it capable of a greater variety of movements than I could possibly imagine in it, and of exhibiting more artistry than I could possibly ascribe to it.[23]

Were we to read this text as naively as possible, the theory of the animal-machine would seem to make sense only if we put forward two important and often-neglected postulates. The first is the existence of a God who builds things, and the second that living bodies are given in essence before machines are constructed. In other words, to understand the machine-animal, it is necessary to see it as being preceded, logically and chronologically, by God, who is an efficient cause, and by a preexisting living model after which it is to be modeled or imitated, which is a formal and final cause. With all this in mind, I propose to take the animal-machine theory, which is usually seen as a departure from the Aristotelian concept of causality, and show how all of Aristotle's types of causality are nonetheless found in it, but not always in the same place or simultaneously.

If we read the text more closely, we see that in order to construct the living machine[24] it is necessary to imitate a preexisting living model. The construction of a mechanical model presupposes a living original (Descartes is perhaps closer here to Plato than to Aristotle). The platonic Demiurge copies the ideas, and the Idea is the model of which the natural object is a copy. The Cartesian God, the *Artifex maximus*, works to produce something equivalent to the living body itself. The model for the living machine is that body itself. Divine art imitates the Idea — but the Idea is the living body. What is more, in the same way that a regular polygon is inscribed in a circle, and that one must pass an infinite distance to deduce one from the other, there is something of the machine in every aspect of life; but to pass from one to the other would require crossing over an infinite gap, one that only God can close. This is the idea brought out at the end of the text: "but I am supposing this machine to be made by the hands of God, and so I think you may reasonably think it capable of a greater variety of movements than I could possibly imagine in it, and of exhibiting more artistry than I could possibly ascribe to it." The theory of the animal-machine would, therefore, have the same relation to life that a set of axioms has to geometry, that is, nothing more than a rational reconstruction. Thus, the theory operates by deception: it pretends to ignore the concrete existence of what it must represent, and it denies that what it actually produces comes only after it has been rationally legitimized.

This aspect of Cartesian theory, moreover, was accurately assessed by a contemporary anatomist, the noted Nicolaus Steno, in the *Dissertation on the Anatomy of the Brain* delivered in Paris in 1665, a year after the "Treatise on Man" had appeared. While paying homage to Descartes (which was remarkable, since anatomists had not always been very accepting of Cartesian anatomy), he notes that Descartes's man was man reconstituted by Descartes with God as a foil, but that this was not man as the anatomist understands him. One can therefore say that by substituting the body for the machine, Descartes removed teleology from life, but in appearance only, because he has concentrated it in its entirety at the point at which life begins. A dynamic structure is replaced by an anatomical one; but since this form is produced by technique, all possible sense of teleology has been confined to the technique of production. In fact, it appears that mechanical theory and purposiveness cannot be placed in opposition, nor can mechanism and anthropomorphism. If the functioning of a machine can be explained by relations of pure causality, the construction of a machine cannot be understood without taking two things into consideration: a specific goal-directed activity and man himself. A machine is made by man and for man, to achieve specific ends, to produce a given series of effects.[25]

The positive element, then, in Descartes's attempt to explain life mechanically is that he eliminates the need to tie mechanism to finality in its anthropomorphic aspect. However, it seems that in doing this, one anthropomorphism has been substituted for another. A technological anthropomorphism has been substituted for a political anthropomorphism.

In "Description of the Human Body and All of Its Functions," a short treatise written in 1648, Descartes addresses the question of voluntary movement in man: he offers, in terms so lucid that they were to dominate the entire theory of reflex and automatic movements up until the nineteenth century, the explanation that the body obeys the soul only on condition that the body is primed mechanically to do so. For the soul to decide to move is not a sufficient condition to induce the body to move. "The soul," writes Descartes "cannot produce any movement without the appropriate disposition of the bodily organs which are required for making the movement. On the contrary, when all the bodily organs are appropriately disposed for some movement, the body has no need of the soul in order to produce that movement."[26] Descartes means that when the soul moves the body it does not act like a king or a general commanding his subjects or his troops as is popularly conceived. Rather, by viewing the body as a clock mechanism he envisions each organ driving the other like interlocking cogwheels. So Descartes substitutes for the image of the political chain of command — where commands are passed by signals or spoken orders, through a type of magical causality — the technological image of "control," in which a desired series of operations is activated by a controlling device or coordinated by a series of mechanical linkups.

Descartes takes the exact opposite position of Claude Bernard who, in his critique of vitalism, in *Leçons sur les phénomènes de la vie communs aux animaux et aux végétaux*, refuses to admit that a vital force could have a separate existence because it "cannot do anything" — but he does admit, surprisingly, that it can "direct phenomena that it does not produce."[27] In other words, Bernard replaces the notion of a vital-force-as-worker with the idea of vital-force-as-legislator or guide. This is a way of admitting that one can direct events without taking action — which borders on a kind of magical concept of direction, implying that the overall operation transcends the execution of individual operations. On the contrary, according to Descartes, a mechanical operation replaces the power of direction and command, but God has fixed the direction once and for all: the constructor includes the guide-controls within the mechanical process itself.

In short, with the Cartesian explanation, it might appear that we have not moved beyond the idea of finality or inner purposiveness. The reason for this is that if we limit ourselves to the workings of the machine, everything can be explained by the theory of mechanism; but the theory cannot account for the construction of the machine itself. Machines do not construct other machines, and it could even be said that, in a sense, explaining organs or organisms through mechanical models amounts to explaining the organ by means of itself. At bottom, then, we are dealing with a tautology; for it can be shown — and I shall indeed try to justify this view — that *machines can be considered as organs of the human species*.[28] A tool or a machine is an organ, and organs are tools or machines. And so it is hard to see how mechanism can be distinguished from purposiveness. No one doubts that a mechanism is needed to ensure that a given operation is carried out successfully; and, conversely, every mechanism must follow a precisely determined sequence toward performing some particular task, since a mechanism cannot depend on randomness or chance. Therefore, the opposition would be between those mechanisms whose purpose is manifest and those whose purpose remains latent. In the case of a lock or a watch, their function is apparent, while the pincers of the crab, often considered a marvel of adaptation, have a latent purpose. As a result, it seems impossible to deny that certain biological mechanisms serve a set purpose. Let us consider an oft-cited example, which mechanistic biologists use to argue their case; namely, that of the woman's pelvis, which enlarges just before she gives birth. To deny that this enlargement might not in someway be the fulfillment of a fundamental, purposive activity, we need only view the question in another way: given that the largest-sized fetus exceeds the maximum size of the pelvis by 1 or 1.5 cm, it would be impossible to give birth were it not for a loosening of the symphyses and a gradual rocking movement toward the sacrococcygien bone which increases the diameter ever so slightly beyond its maximum. It is understandable that one would not want to believe that an act with such a specific biological purpose is allowed to occur only by virtue of a mechanism with no real biological function. And "allow" is indeed the word that applies here, since without this mechanism the act simply could not take place. It is well known that, when dealing with an unknown mechanism, we have to make certain that it is in fact a mechanism — that is, we have to know what ultimate purpose or function it is intended to serve. We can come to no conclusions about how it is to be used, simply on the basis of its form or its structure, unless we already know how the machine or similar machines are used. As a result, it is necessary first to see the machine at work before attempting to deduce the function from the structure.

We are now at the point where we can see the historical reversal of the Cartesian relationship between the machine and the organism. It is a well-known fact — and so need not be belabored — that in all organisms we observe the phenomena of autoconstruction, automaintenance, autoregulation and autorepair. In the case of the machine, its construction is beyond its power and depends on the skill of the mechanic. Its maintenance requires the constant attention and watchfulness of the machinist; for we all know how the complex workings of a machine can be irremediably damaged due to inattention and carelessness. As for maintenance and repair, they demand the same periodic intervention of human action. While there are machines that are self-regulating, these are in fact machines that man has grafted onto another machine. The construction of servomechanisms or electronic automata merely displaces the question of the man–machine relationship without changing it in any fundamental way.

Further, in the case of the machine there is a strict adherence to rational, economical rules. The whole is rigorously the sum of its parts. The final effect depends on the ordering of the causes. What is more, a machine functions within narrowly defined limits, and these limits become all the more rigid with the practice of standardization. Standardization leads to the simplification of basic models and spare parts, and to unified standards of measurement and quality, which allows for the interchangeability of parts. Any individual part can be exchanged for any other part meant for the same place — within, of course, a margin of tolerance determined by manufacturing constraints.

Now that the properties of a machine have been defined in relation to those of an organism, can one say that there is more or less purposiveness in a machine than in an organism?

One would surely agree that there is more purposiveness in machines than in organisms, since a machine seems to move uniformly, unidirectionally toward completing a particular activity. A machine cannot replace another machine. The more specific the end-result desired, the more the margin of tolerance is reduced, and the more the machine's directiveness seems concentrated, focused on a particular end. It is well known that functions in the organism are substitutable, organs are polyvalent. Although this substitutability of functions and polyvalence of organs is not absolute, in comparison with the same qualities in the machine, it is so considerable that any comparison is quite obviously absurd.[29] As an example of the substitutability of functions, I can give a very simple and well-known case, that of aphasia in children. A hemiplegia on the right side of the child's brain is almost never accompanied by aphasia, because the other areas of the brain ensure the continuance of the linguistic functions. In the case of the child who is less than nine months old, any existing aphasia disappears very quickly.[30] As for the problem of the polyvalent organs, I need simply note the fact that for a majority of organs, which we have traditionally believed to serve some definite function, the truth is that we have no idea what other functions they might indeed fulfill. This is the reason that the stomach is said to be, in principle at least, an organ of digestion. However, it is a fact that after a gastrectomy performed to treat an ulcer, there are fewer problems with digestion than with those we observe with hematopoiesis. It was finally discovered that the stomach behaves like an internal secretive gland. And I might also cite yet another example — and not at all to be taken as some sort of miracle — which came to light during a recent experiment performed by the biologist Courrier, at the Collège de France. Courrier made an incision in the uterus of a pregnant rabbit, extracted a placenta from the uterus and placed it in the peritoneal cavity. This placenta grafted itself onto the intestine and fed itself normally. When the graft was performed, the rabbit's ovaries were ablated — meaning that the function fulfilled by the corpus luteum during pregnancy was suppressed. At that moment, all the placentas present in the uterus were aborted and only the placenta situated in the peritoneal cavity came to term. Here is an example of the intestine behaving like a uterus, and perhaps, one might even say, more successfully.

In this case, then, it is tempting to reverse one of Aristotle's formulations in his *Politics*: "For nature is not stingy, like the smith who fashions the Delphian knife for many uses; she makes each thing for a single use, and every instrument is best made when intended for one and not for many uses."[31] On the contrary, it seems that this definition of finality or purposiveness would be more applicable to a machine than to an organism. One must be willing to acknowledge, ultimately, that in an organism, a given organ can accommodate a diversity of functions. Clearly, an organism has a greater range of activity than a machine. It is less bound by purposiveness and more open to potentialities.[32] Every aspect and every movement of the machine is calculated; and the working of the machine confirms how each calculation holds up to certain norms, measures or estimates; whereas the living body functions according to experience. Life is experience, meaning improvisation, acting as circumstances permit; life is tentative in every respect. Hence the overwhelming but often misunderstood fact that life permits monstrosities. There are no monstrous machines. There is no mechanical pathology, as Xavier Bichat noted in 1801 in his *General Anatomy, Applied to Physiology and Medicine*.[33] Whereas monsters are still living things, there is no way to distinguish between the normal and the pathological in physics and mechanics. Only among living beings is there a distinction between the normal and the pathological.

Above all, it is work in experimental embryology that has led to the abandoning of such mechanistic representations when interpreting living phenomena, primarily by demonstrating that once the embryo starts to develop, it does not contain any kind of "specific mechanism" intended to produce automatically one organ or another. There can be no doubt that this was Descartes's conception as well. In his "Description of the Human Body," he wrote: "If we had a good knowledge of what makes up the semen of some species of animal in particular, for example man, then we would be able to deduce from this alone, using certain and mathematical reasoning, the complete shape and conformation of each of its members, and likewise, reciprocally, if we knew many particularities about this conformation, it would be possible to deduce from that what the semen is."[34] However, as Paul Guillaume remarks, it seems that the more we compare living beings to automatic machines, the more we seem to understand their functions but the less we understand their genesis.[35] If the Cartesian conception were accurate, that is, if the living organism were both preformed in the embryo and developed mechanistically, any modification made in the earliest stages would tend to disrupt the development of the egg or prevent development altogether.

However, this is hardly the case. According to a study in potential egg development, based on research by Driesch, Hörstadius, Speman and Mangold, it was shown that embryonic development cannot be reduced to a mechanical model without running into anomalies. Let us take the example of the experiments conducted by Hörstadius on the egg of a sea urchin. He cut an egg A from a sea urchin at stage sixteen so that each part of the egg maintained a horizontal symmetry, and then he cut egg B, with each part being vertically symmetrical. He joined half of A with half of B and the egg developed normally. Driesch took the sea urchin egg at stage sixteen and pressed the egg between two thin layers of cells, while modifying the reciprocal position of the cells at the two poles; still, the egg developed normally. The results of these two studies allow us to conclude that the same effect is achieved regardless of how conditions are varied.

There is an even more striking experiment, in which Driesch took blastomeres from the sea urchin egg at stage two. By removing the blastomeres, either mechanically or chemically in sea water lacking calcium salts, the result was that each of the blastomeres gave birth to a larva which was perfectly normal down to the smallest detail. Here, then, the result is the same regardless of how the characteristics of a factor are changed. The quantitative change in a given factor does not lead to a qualitative change in the result. Conversely, when two sea urchin eggs are joined they result in a single larva that is larger than normal. This is yet another confirmation that the result is unaffected by the quantitative change in one of the factors. Whether the factors are multiplied or divided, the experiment yields the same results.

I should add that the development of all eggs cannot be reduced to this schema. For quite some time there was a problem in knowing whether there were two different kinds of eggs at issue: regulated eggs, like the eggs of sea urchins, and mosaic eggs, like those of frogs, whose first blastomeres develop in exactly the same way, whether they are dissociated or remain together. Most biologists have recently come around to admitting that what distinguishes the two phenomena is simply that determination occurs earlier in the so-called mosaic eggs. On the one hand, the regulated egg starts to act like a mosaic egg at a certain stage; on the other hand, at stage two the blastomere of the frog egg yields a complete embryo, as does a regulated egg, if it is reversed.[36]

Thus, it is illusory to deny the idea of purposiveness in organisms and to attribute it to automatic functions, however complex we might imagine these to be. As long as a machine cannot construct itself, and as long as an organism is not equal to the sum of its parts, it might seem legitimate to think that biological organization is the basis and the necessary condition for the existence and purpose of a machine. From the philosophical point of view, it is less important to explain the operation of a machine than to understand it. And to understand it means to inscribe it in human history by inscribing human history in life — not overlooking the fact that with the advent of man there appeared a culture that was no longer entirely reducible to natural causes. And so we arrive at the point where the machine is seen as a *fact of culture,* expressed in mechanisms that are themselves nothing more than *an explainable fact of nature.* In a celebrated text in "Principles of Philosophy," Descartes writes, "It is certain that all the rules of mechanics belong to physics, *to the extent that all artificial things are thereby natural.* Since, for example, when a watch counts the hours, by using the cogs from which it is made, this is no less natural for it than it is for a tree to produce fruit."[37] But, from our point of view, we can and must reverse the relationship of the watch to the tree and say that the cogs and generally all the components that make up a watch are designed to produce a desired effect: all the parts of the mechanism are products of imagination, each piece fulfilling some final purpose or design that at one time was only imagined or dreamed of; they are thus the direct or indirect products of a technical activity that is as authentically organic as the flowering of trees. And, on a more fundamental level, the process works with great efficiency even though there is no more conscious observance of the rules and laws of physics than there might be within vegetal life. Although the construction of a machine might presuppose at some stage the understanding of the logics of physics, it should not and cannot be forgotten that, as a matter of chronology and biology, construction of machines took place well before there was any understanding of physics.

However, another author has asserted, contrary to Descartes, that living organisms cannot be reduced to a machine and, similarly, art cannot be reduced to science. The author in question is Kant, in his *Critique of Judgment*. While it is true that the French have not tended to look to Kant as a philosopher of technique, it is no less true that German authors greatly interested in this question, especially after 1870, *have* done so.

In the "Critique of Teleological Judgment," Kant distinguishes between the machine and the organism, while drawing on Descartes's favorite example of the watch. In a machine, he states, each part exists for the other but not because of the other: no part produces another part; no one part is produced by the entire unit; nor does one part produce another part of similar kind. There is no watch that makes other watches. No part can replace itself. And no machine can replace one of its own missing parts. And so, while a machine possesses motor power, it has no transformational energy that might propagate itself or be transmitted to an object outside the machine itself. Kant draws a distinction between human skill and technology, which are marked by intentionality, as opposed to involuntary life processes. But in an important passage of the "Critique of Aesthetic Judgment," Kant defines the originality of human skill as it relates to knowledge:

> Art, regarded as human skill, differs from science (as ability differs from knowledge) in the same way that a practical aptitude differs from a theoretical faculty, as technique differs from theory. What one is capable of doing, as soon as we merely know what ought to be done and therefore are sufficiently cognizant of the desired effect, is not called art. Only that which a man, even if he knows it completely, may not therefore have the skill to accomplish belongs to art. Camper describes very exactly how the best shoes must be made, but he certainly could not make one.[38]

This text is cited by Paul Krannhals in *Der Weltsinn der Technik*, and, following Kant, he acknowledges that all technique is essentially primordial, meaning that it cannot be reduced to a simple question of rationality.[39] Indeed, we tend to see the skilled hand that adjusts a machine or the mind that carefully orchestrates a production process as examples of "ingenuity," having their basis in instinct; but these are in fact as difficult to explain as the production of mammalian eggs outside the ovary, even in the event that the physiochemical composition of protoplasm and of sexual hormones had been made entirely clear to us.

This is why the work of anthropologists (and not engineers) seems to shed more light, however faint, on the question of the construction of machines.[40] Currently in France, ethnologists have come closest to creating a philosophy of technique in which the philosophers themselves seem to have lost interest, their main concern having been chiefly the philosophy of science. On the contrary, the ethnographers have generally focused their attention on the relationship between the production of the earliest tools, the first instruments that were used to act upon and modify nature, and the ways these tools were assembled or grouped together. The only philosopher in France I know to have posed these questions is Alfred Espinas, in his classic text on *Les Origines de la technologie*.[41] This work includes an appendix, the outline for a course taught at the Faculté des Lettres at Bordeaux around 1890, which dealt with the will, and in which Espinas addressed, under the guise of will, the question of practical human behavior and especially the invention of tools. By borrowing the theory of organic extension from the German writer Ernst Kapp, Espinas was able to explain the construction of the first tools. Kapp first made his theories known in 1877.[42] According to the theory of extension, whose philosophical bases go back to Hartmann's *The Philosophy of the Unconscious* and further back still to Schopenhauer, the earliest tools were simply extensions of moving human organs. The flint, the club and the lever extend and magnify the organic movement of the arm and its ability to strike. This theory, like all theories, has its limits and runs into certain stumbling blocks, especially when it is used to explain fundamental inventions, such as fire and the wheel. In these cases, we would search in vain for the body movements and the organs that fire and the wheel are supposed to prolong or extend; but the explanation certainly works for instruments like the hammer or the lever and all such related tools. In France, then, it was the ethnographers who sought out and compiled not only the facts but also the hypotheses from which a biological philosophy of technique could be constituted. The philosophical path was laid out by the Germans[43] — for example, the theory of the development of inventions based on the Darwinian notion of variation and natural selection, as advanced by Alard Du Bois-Reymond in his *Erfindung und Erfinder* (1906), or again, by Oswald Spengler in *Der Mensch und die Technik*, which presented the theory that machines are constructed as a "life tactic"[44] — and is taken up again, independently it seems, by André Leroi-Gourhan in his book *Milieu et techniques*. Leroi-Gourhan attempts to explain the phenomenon of the construction of tools by comparing it to the movement of the amoeba, which extends substances out beyond its mass so that it might seize and capture an object it wishes to digest:

> If we are drawn to view the act of percussion as the fundamental technical activity, it is because we witness an act of touch or contact in almost every technological process; but even though the amoeba's expansion always leads its prey through the same digestive process, there is no one way of explaining the working of that process — whether we view the material being digested or whether we approach the question from any given view of technology — since our view must change according to the circumstances, just as the digestive process itself might be like the various specialized grasping or striking organs.[45]

In the last chapters of this work one finds a theory of machine that is altogether different from the traditional theories that, for lack of a better term, I shall classify as Cartesian — where technical invention amounted to the application of a given system of knowledge.

Traditionally, the locomotive is presented as a classic example of a "marvel of science." However, the construction of the steam engine is only understandable when placed in light of theoretical knowledge that preceded it, as the culmination of an age-old problem, and a specifically technological one at that — how to pump water out of mines. And so it would be necessary to understand the natural history of the development of the pump, and to know about the fire pump (which at first did not rely at all on vapor but produced a vacuum via condensation under the pistons, thereby allowing the atmospheric pressure acting as a motor to lower the piston) in order to see that the essential "organ" in a locomotive is a cylinder and a piston.[46]

Tracing a similar progression of ideas, Leroi-Gourhan goes even further, pointing back to the wheel as one of the locomotive's ancestors, in the biological sense of the word. "It is machines like the wheel," he states, "that gave rise to steam engines and modern-day motors. All of the highest technological achievements of the most inventive minds of our time can be grouped around the circular movements of the crank, the pedal, the drive belt."[47] He then goes on to add: "The way inventions influenced each other has not been studied sufficiently and we don't seem to take note of the fact that, without the wheel, we would not have the locomotive."[48] Further on:

> At the beginning of the nineteenth century no one had yet recognized how to make use of the elemental forms that would later give birth to the locomotive, the automobile and the airplane. The underlying principles of mechanics were spread throughout twenty applications which had been known for many centuries. It is here we find the principle that explains invention, but the defining characteristic is that it in someway manifests itself spontaneously.[49]

In light of these remarks, we see how science and technique must be considered as two separate areas; that is, they do not graft onto each other but, rather, each takes from the other either its solutions or its problems. It is the rationalizing and ordering imposed by technology that makes us forget that machines have their origin in the irrational. In this area as in all others, it is necessary to know how to accommodate the irrational, even when — and especially when — we want to defend rationalism.[50]

It must be added that the reversal of the relationship between the machine and the organism, brought about by a systematic understanding of technical inventions as if they were extensions of human behavior or life processes, is in someway confirmed by the belief that the generalized use of machines has slowly imposed contemporary industrialized society on man. George Friedmann has shown very clearly the steps by which "body" gradually became a first-order term in the human machine-body equation.[51] With Frederick Taylor and the first technicians to make scientific studies of work-task movements, the human body was measured as if it functioned like a machine. If we see their aim as the elimination of all unnecessary movement and their view of output as being expressed only in terms of a certain number of mathematically determined factors, then rationalization was, for all intents and purposes, a mechanization of the body. But the realization that technologically superfluous movements were biologically necessary movements was the first stumbling block to be encountered by those who insisted on viewing the problem of human-body-as-machine in exclusively technological terms. From here on, the systematic examination of certain physiological, psychotechnological and even some psychological conditions (since a consideration of values leads inevitably to questions at the very center of the origin of human personality) finally culminated in a reversal, called an inevitable revolution by Friedmann, in which technology would adapt machines to the human body. As Friedmann saw it, this industrial technology appeared to take the form of a scientific rediscovery of the same entirely empirical procedures through which primitive peoples had always sought to have their tools meet the highest organic norms: that is, their tools had to carry out a given action effectively while maintaining a biological economy; and this occurred at the optimum level, when it most closely approximated the movement of the body at work, as when the body defends itself spontaneously from becoming exclusively subordinate to the mechanical.[52] In this way, Friedmann could speak, without irony or paradox, of the legitimacy of considering the industrial development of the West from an ethnographic point of view.[53]

In summary, by considering technology as a universal biological phenomenon[54] and no longer simply as an intellectual operation to be carried out by man, I am led to the following conclusions: on the one hand, the creative autonomy of the arts and skilled crafts in relation to all forms of knowledge that are capable of annexing them or expanding on them; and, on the other hand, to inscribe the mechanical into the organic. It is no longer then, a question of determining the extent to which an organism can be thought of as a machine, whether by virtue of its structure or of its functions. But it is necessary to find the reasons that gave rise to the opposite view, the Cartesian one. I have attempted to shed light on this problem, suggesting that the mechanistic conception of the body was no less anthropomorphic, despite appearances, than a teleological conception of the physical world. The answer I am tempted to offer would insist on showing that technology allows man to live in continuity with life, as opposed to a solution that would see humankind as living in a state of rupture for which we ourselves are responsible because of science. There is no doubt that this answer appears to lend credence to the list of accusations that all too many writers have offered up nostalgically from time to time, with no apparent regard to their lack of originality, as they point out the faults of technology and progress. I have no intention of rushing to support their cause. It is clear that if human society has embraced the idea of a technology based on a mechanistic model, the implications are enormous, and the whole question cannot easily be treated lightly or recalled on demand. But that model is *altogether different* from the one just examined.

Notes

1. After having been dogmatically accepted by biologists for many years, the mechanistic theory of the organism is now considered narrow and inadequate by those scientists who call themselves dialectical materialists. But the fact that they still concern themselves with formulating a philosophical position could easily support the rather widespread idea that philosophy does not possess its own domain, that it is a poor relation of speculation, and must clothe itself in the hand-me-downs scientists have used and then discarded. It will be my aim to show that the problem of machine and organism is much broader in scope and more philosophically important than is commonly thought; and that it is far more than a theoretical and methodological dispute among biologists.

2. Julien Pacotte, *La Pensée technique* (Paris: Alcan, 1931).

3. One example of the fundamental principles of a general theory of mechanisms understood in this way can be found in Franz Reuleaux's *Theoretische Kinematik: Grundzüge einer Theorie des Maschinwesen* (Braunschweig: Vieweg, 1875).

4. For everything concerning machines and mechanisms, see Pacotte, *La Pensée technique*, ch. 3.

5. According to Marx, a tool is moved by human power while the machine is moved by a natural force; see his *Capital*, trans. Samuel Moore and Edward Aveling (New York: International Publishers, 1967), vol. 1, pp. 374–79.

6. For more on this, see Charles Victor Daremberg, *Histoire des sciences médicales* (Paris: Baillière, 1870), vol. 2, p. 879.

7. Gomez Pereira, *Antoniana Margarita: Opus physicis, medicis ac theologis non minus utile quam necessarium* (Medina del Campo, 1555–58).

8. Alfred Espinas, "L'Organisation ou la machine vivante en Grèce au IVe siècle avant J.-C.," *Revue de métaphysique et de morale* (1903), pp. 702–15.

9. P.-M. Schuhl, *Machinisme et philosophie* (Paris: Alcan, 1938).

10. *Aristotle's Politics*, trans. Hippocrates G. Apostle and Lloyd P. Gerson (Grinnel, Iowa: Peripatetic Press, 1986), bk. 1, ch. 2, secs. 4–7.

11. Lucien Laberthonnière, *Les Etudes sur Descartes* (Paris: Vrin, 1935), especially the appendix to volume 2: "La Physique de Descartes et la physique d'Aristote."

12. Franz Borkenau, *Der Übergang vom feudalem zum bürgerlichen Weltbild* (Paris: Alcan, 1934).

13. Jean de la Fontaine's fable, "The Cobbler and the Businessman" (in *La Fontaine: Selected Fables*, trans. Jamie Michie [New York: Viking, 1979], pp. 188–91) is an excellent illustration of the two different conceptions of work and its remuneration.

14. Henryk Grossmann, "Die gesellschaftlichen Grundlagen der mechanistischen Philosophie und die Manufaktur," *Zeitschrift für Sozialforschung*, 4th ser., vol. 2 (1935), pp. 161–231.

15. "Mechanization" here means the generalized use of machines to replace human labor. However, it was also used to describe Descartes's theory of animals as machines before the nineteenth century when the above usage was in force — TRANS.

16. In Descartes's "Principles of Philosophy" (4.187 [AT 8A.314], *Descartes: Selected Philosophical Writings*, trans. John Cottingham, Robert Stoothoff and Dugald Murdoch [New York: Cambridge University Press, 1988], pp. 199–200), there are a few passages that reveal Descartes to be equally interested in gunpowder, but he did not look for an analogous explanatory principle for the animal organism in the explosion of gunpowder as a source of energy. It was an English doctor, Thomas Willis, who explicitly formulated a theory of muscular movement based on the analogy with what occurs when the powder explodes in a harquebus. In the seventeenth century, Willis compared the nerves to powder lines in a manner that remains valid today in some quarters — most notably, W. M. Bayliss comes to mind. Nerves are a sort of Bickford cord. They produce a spark that will set off, in the muscle, an explosion that, in Willis's view, is the only thing capable of accounting for the phenomena of spasm and prolonged contraction observed by the doctor.

17. "For there is within us but one soul, and this soul has within it no diversity of parts: it is at once sensitive and rational too, and all its appetites are volitions" ("The Passions of the Soul" 47, in *Selected Philosophical Writings*, p. 236).

18. "Discourse on Method" 5 (AT 6.56ff.), in ibid., p. 44ff. Letter to the Marquis of Newcastle, Nov. 23, 1646.

19. Letter to Morus, Feb. 21, 1649, in Descartes, *Correspondance*, ed. Charles Adam and Gérard Milhaud (Paris: P.U.F., 1963), vol. 8, pp. 121–39. In order to understand

adequately the relationship of sensibility to the arrangement of the organs, we must be familiar with the Cartesian theory of the degrees of sense; on this subject, see Descartes, "Author's Replies to the Sixth Objections" 9 (AT 7.436–39), in *The Philosophical Writings of Descartes*, trans. John Cottingham, Robert Stoothoff and Dugald Murdoch (Cambridge, Eng.: Cambridge University Press, 1984), vol. 2, pp. 294–96.

20. Descartes, Letter to Morus, Feb. 21, 1649, in *Correspondance*, vol. 8, p. 138.

21. Letter to Conring, March 19, 1678, in *Gottfried Wilhelm Leibniz: Sämtliche Schriften und Briefe* (Darmstadt: Reichl, 1926), 2d ser., vol. 1, pp. 397–401. Leibniz's outline of criteria in particular, which would allow us to distinguish an animal from an automaton, should be compared to the analogous arguments adduced by Descartes, and also the profound reflections of Edgar Allan Poe on the same subject in his "Maelzel's Chessplayer." On the Leibnizian distinction between the machine and the organism, see "A New System of the Nature and the Communication of Substances" 10, in *Leibniz: Philosophical Papers and Letters*, trans. and ed. Leroy Loemker (Chicago: University of Chicago Press, 1956), vol. 2; and "Monadology" 63–66, in *Monadology and Other Philosophical Essays*, trans. Paul Schrecker and Anne Martin Schrecker (New York: Macmillan, 1985).

22. It is important to point out that Leibniz was no less interested than Descartes in the invention and construction of machines, as well as in the problem of automatons. See especially his correspondence with Duke John of Hanover (1676–1679) in the *Sämtliche Schriften und Briefe* (Darmstadt: Reichl, 1927), 1st ser., vol. 2. In a text of 1671, *Bedenken von Aufrichtung einer Academie oder Societät in Deutschland zu Aufnehmen der Kunste und Wissenschaften*, Leibniz exalts the superiority of German art, which has always strived to produce works that move (watches, clocks, hydraulic machines, and so on), over Italian art, which has always attached itself exclusively to the fabrication of lifeless objects made to be contemplated from without (ibid. [Darmstadt: Reichl, 1931], 4th ser., vol. 1, p. 544). This passage is cited by Jacques Maritain in his *Art and Scholasticism and the Frontiers of Poetry*, trans. Joseph W. Evans (New York: Scribners, 1962), p. 156.

23. "Treatise on Man" (AT XI. 119–20), in *The Philosophical Writings of Descartes*, trans. John Cottingham, Robert Stoothoff and Dugald Murdoch (Cambridge, Eng.: Cambridge University Press, 1985), vol. 1, p. 99.

24. This phrase is a traditional equivalent of "the human body," especially in the eighteenth century — TRANS.

25. Moreover, Descartes can only express the meaning of God's construction of animal-machines in terms of finality: "considering the machine of the human body as having been formed by God in order to have in itself all the movements usually manifested there" ("Sixth Meditation," in *Philosophical Works of Descartes* [1913], trans. Elizabeth S. Haldane and G. R. T. Ross [New York: Cambridge University Press, 1967], vol. 1, p. 83). [Here the wording of the older translation is more literal than is the translation of Cottingham et al., *Philosophical Writings of Descartes*, vol. 2, pp. 50–62 — TRANS.]

26. "Description of the Human Body and All of Its Functions" 1 (AT II. 225), in *Philosophical Writings of Descartes*, vol. 1, p. 315.

27. Claude Bernard, *Leçons sur les phénomènes de la vie communes aux animaux et aux végétaux: 1878–1879* (Paris: Masson, 1936).

28. For more on this idea, see Raymond Ruyer, *Eléments de psycho-biologie* (Paris: P.U.F., 1946), pp. 46–47.

29. "Artificial means what is aimed at a definite goal. And is opposed therefore to *living*. Artificial or human or anthropomorphic are distinguished from whatever is only living or vital. Anything that succeeds in appearing in the form of a clear and finite goal becomes artificial and this is what tends to happen as consciousness grows. It is also true of man's work when it is intended to imitate an object or a spontaneous phenomenon as closely as possible. Thought that is conscious of itself makes itself into an artificial system.... If life had a goal, it would no longer be life" (Paul Valéry, *Cahier B* [Paris: Gallimard, 1910]).

30. See Ed. Pichon, *Le Développement psychique de l'enfant et de l'adolescent* (Paris: Masson, 1936), p. 126; and Paul Cossa, *Physiopathologie du système nerveux* (Paris: Masson, 1936), p. 845.

31. *Politics*, bk. 1, ch. 1 (1252b), in *The Basic Works of Aristotle*, ed. Richard McKeon (New York: Random House, 1941), p. 1128.

32. Max Scheler, in his *Man's Place in Nature* [1928] (trans. Hans Meyerhoff [Boston: Beacon, 1961], pp. 75–81), has remarked that it is those living things that are the least specialized that are the most difficult to explain by the mechanistic idea, *pace* the mechanists, because in their case all functions are carried out by the whole organism. It is only with the growing differentiation of functions and the increased complexity of the nervous system that structures which resemble a *machine in some fashion tend to appear.*

33. *General Anatomy, Applied to Physiology and Medicine*, trans. George Hayward (Boston: Richardson and Lord, 1822).

34. "Description du corps humain" 1 (AT II. 225), in Charles Adam and Paul Tannery, eds., *Ouevres de Descartes* (Paris: Vrin, 1974), vol. 11, p. 225. [This pasage is omitted from the English translation of "Description of the Human Body and of All of Its Functions" — TRANS.]

35. Paul Guillaume, *La Psychologie de la forme* (Paris: Flammarion, 1937), p. 131.

36. Pierre Grassé and Max Aron, *Précis de biologie animale* (2d ed., Paris: Flammarion, 1947), p. 647ff.

37. 4.203, in *Philosophical Writings of Descartes*, p. 288. See also my study "Descartes et la technique," *Travaux du Congrès International de Philosophie*, vol. 2: Etudes cartesiennes (Paris: Hermann, 1937), p. 77ff.

38. "An organized being is not a mere machine, for that has merely moving *power*, but it possesses in itself formative power of a self-propagating kind which it communicates to its materials though they have it not of themselves; it organizes them, in fact, and this cannot be explained by the mere mechanical faculty of motion" (*Critique of Judgment*, trans. J. H. Bernard [New York: Hafner, 1951], p. 22).

39. Krannhals, *Der Weltsin der Technik* (Munich and Berlin: Oldenbourg, 1932), p. 68.

40. The starting point for these works must be sought in Darwin, *The Descent of Man* — whose ideas Marx saw clearly as immensely significant.

41. Alfred Espinas, *Les Origines de la technologie* (Paris: Alcan, 1897).

42. Ernst Kapp, *Grundlinien einer Philosophie der Technik* (Braunschweig: Westermann, 1877). This work, which was a classic in Germany, has remained so misunderstood in France that certain psychologists who took up the problem of how animals utilize tools, and animal intelligence, and who took the research of Köhler and Guillaume as their starting point, attributed this theory of projection to Espinas himself, without noting that Espinas states explicitly, at numerous junctures, that he borrowed it from Kapp. I am alluding here to the excellent little book by Gaston Viaud, *L'Intelligence: Son evolution et ses formes* (Paris: P.U.F., 1946).

43. See Eberhard Zschimmer's *Deutsche Philosophen der Technik* (Stuttgart: Enke, 1937).

44. Alard Du Bois-Reymond, *Erfindung und Erfinder* (Berlin: Springer, 1906); and Oswald Spengler, *Der Mensch und die Technik* (Munich: Beck, 1931). Alain outlined a Darwinian interpretation of technical constructions in a fine remark (*Les Propos d'Alain* [Paris: N.R.F., 1920], vol. 1, p. 60), preceded and followed by some others that are most pertinent to our problem. The same idea is referred to many times in the *Système des Beaux-Arts*, concerning the making of the violin (4.5), furniture (6.5), houses in the countryside (6.3, 6.8).

45. André Leroi-Gourhan, *Evolution et technique*, vol. 2: *Milieu et techniques* (Paris: Michel, 1945).

46. The double-acting engine, in which the steam acted on the upper and lower sides of the piston alternately, was perfected by Watt in 1784. Sadi Carnot's *Réflexions sur la puissance motrice du feu* dates from 1824, and we know that it was ignored until the middle of the nineteenth century. On this subject, see Pierre Ducasse, *Histoires des techniques* (Paris: P.U.F., 1945), which stresses that technique precedes theory.

On the subject of the empirical succession of the various organs and uses of the steam engine, consult Arthur Vierendeel's *Esquisse d'une histoire de la technique* (Brussels and Paris: Vromant, 1921), which summarizes Thurston's extensive work, *History of the Steam Engine*. For more about the history of Watt's work as an engineer read the chapter entitled "James Watt ou Ariel ingénieur," in Pierre Devaux's *Les Aventures de la science* (Paris: Gallimard, 1943).

47. Leroi-Gourhan, *Milieu et techniques*, p. 100. The same view can be found in an article by A. Hadricourt on "Les Moteurs animés en agriculture" (*Revue de botanique appliquée et d'agriculture tropicale* 20 [1940], p. 762): "We must not forget that we owe our inanimate motors to irrigation: the noria is at the origin of the hydraulic mill, just as the pump is at the origin of the steam engine." This excellent study sets out the principles for explaining tools from the perspective of their relationship to organic commodities and the traditional ways they were used.

48. Leroi-Gourhan, *Milieu et techniques*, p. 104.

49. Ibid., p. 406.

50. In his *The Two Sources of Morality and Religion* (trans. R. Ashley Andra and Cloudesley Brereton [New York: Holt, 1949]), Henri Bergson thinks very explicitly that the spirit of mechanical invention, although it is fed by science, remains distinct from it and can even, if necessary, be separated from it (pp. 329–30). The fact is that Bergson is also one of the rare French philosophers, if not the only one, who has considered mechanical invention as a biological function, an aspect of the organization of matter by life: *Creative Evolution* (trans. Arthur Mitchell [New York: Modern Library, 1944) is, in some sense, a treatise of general organology.

On the subject of the relationship between explanation and action see also Paul Valéry, "L'Homme et la coquille" and "Discours aux chirurgiens," in *Variété V* (Paris: Gallimard, 1945), and his description of boat building in *Eupalinos*.

And, finally, read the admirable "In Praise of Hands" in Henri Focillon, *The Life of Forms in Art* (New York: Zone Books, 1989), pp. 157–84.

51. George Friedmann, *Problèmes humains du machinisme industrielle* (Paris: Gallimard, 1946).

52. Ibid., p. 96, note.

53. Ibid., p. 369.

54. This attitude is one that has begun to be familiar among biologists. In particular, see L. Cuénot, *Invention et finalité en biologie* (Paris: Flammarion, 1941); and Andrée Tétry, *Les Outils chez les êtres vivants* (Paris: Gallimard, 1948) — especially the latter's reflections on "Adaptation and Invention" (p. 120ff.). It is impossible to mistake the impetus given to these treatments by the ideas of Teilhard de Chardin.

A new discipline, Bionics, which emerged around ten years ago in the United States, studies biological structures and systems able to be utilized as models or analogues by technology, notably by builders of systems for detection, direction and equilibration meant for equipping planes or missiles. Bionics is the extremely subtle art of information that has taken a leaf from natural life. The frog, with its eye capable of selecting information that is instantly usable, the rattlesnake, with its thermoceptor which traces the blood of its prey at night, the common fly, balancing itself in flight by means of two vibratile filaments, have all furnished models for this new breed of engineers. In many American universities, special training in Bioengineering is available, for which the Massachusetts Institute of Technology seems to have been the instigator. See the article by J. Dufrenoy, "Systèmes biologiques servant de modèles à la technologie," *Cahiers des ingénieurs agronomes* (June–July, 1962), p. 21.

Translated from the French by Mark Cohen and Randall Cherry

November 9, Road from Nice to Peira-Cava.

Jacques-Henri Lartigue

Torque: The New Kinaesthetic of the Twentieth Century
Hillel Schwartz

Between 1840 and 1930 the dance world in Europe and the United States had, by seduction and then concussion, suffered a shift in attitudes toward physical movement. The date 1840 is not chosen haphazardly, for by that year François Delsarte had begun his lectures in Paris, a *Cours d'esthétique appliqué*. Delsarte taught a system of relating gesture to expression, expression to the soul. There were Orders and Laws of Movement, and a Law of Correspondence: "To each spiritual function responds a function of the body; to each grand function of the body corresponds a spiritual act." Delsarte's system was religiously colored and highly trinitarian, and its later exponents made heroic efforts either to explain the intrinsic psychic connection between his theology and his original science of gesture, or to divorce the two entirely.[1]

Delsarte's lectures, designed to help actors, singers and musicians understand the relationship between gestures, sentiments and the senses, were as catholic and enlightened as they were French and Catholic. He drew implicitly upon Enlightenment and early Romantic critiques of eighteenth-century actors perambulating through sequences of consciously histrionic, unfelt postures on a badly framed, poorly composed stage. Like Diderot, Rousseau and Goethe, Delsarte meant to reinvigorate theatrical — especially operatic — convention so that, as in the very best of political and pulpit oratory, voice and movement would together become an integral expression of that newly furnished entity, the self.[2]

More the exuberant Illuminist (and illusionist) than the dispassionate *illuminé*, a young American named Steele MacKaye was drawn to study with the Old Master shortly before his death in 1871. The American became a favored disciple, scheduled to appear under Delsarte's auspices at the Théâtre Français, an honor never before granted to a foreigner — and honored only in the breach, the Franco-Prussian War intervening. The disciple had however the fortune to attend the Old Master's last set of classes, in which, according to a visitor, Delsarte depicted "the various passions and emotions of the human soul, by means of expression and gesture only, without uttering a single syllable.... You were forced to admit that every gesture, every movement of a facial muscle, had a true purpose — a *raison d'être*." MacKaye returned to the United States to produce and stage plays where "each incident lived in the memory as a vivid picture," where "the tempo and flux of [a revolutionary mob's] rhythmic sound-surges" were vital but dialogue almost incidental, gesture and theatrical machinery all. He would patent a sliding stage, an elevator stage, a floating stage, and he would, literally, electrify his theaters. At the (premature) end of his life, he conceived a vastly kinematic Spectatorium with twenty-five telescopic stages on six miles of railroad track, in full view of nine thousand people watching a six-act historical drama, *The Great Discovery, or the World Finder*, performed essentially without spoken words, for the Columbian Exposition in Chicago in 1893. Unfinished, the Spectatorium was compromised into a small Scenitorium and passed away with MacKaye himself in 1894, but others did follow through on one of MacKaye's less magniloquent projects — his Harmonic Gymnastics, a series of Delsartean exercises "to so train and discipline the body that it would become a responsible and expressive instrument through which fluid movement could pass without the obstacles of stiff and unyielding joints and muscles."[3]

That last quotation is from Ted Shawn, who, with Isadora Duncan and Ruth St. Denis, pioneered modern dance in the United States. Shawn had studied with Mrs. Richard Hovey, a pupil of Delsarte's other favored disciple, his son Gustave. The mothers of Duncan and St. Denis had also studied with disciples of the Frenchman. In 1898 Duncan herself lauded Delsarte as "the master of all principles of flexibility, and lightness of body," who "should receive universal thanks for the bonds he removed from our constrained members."[4]

Ignoring his rigid equations of specific gestures with specific meanings, American dancers took from Delsarte his concern for the absolute integrity of gesture, his attention to the expressive power of the torso and his desire for movements liberated from highly mannered codes of motion. Duncan called for the initiation of movement from the lower torso, from some physical/spiritual center akin to the solar plexus, and for the free elaboration of movement out of that center — uninhibited by corsets, heavy skirts and narrow shoes. One used the whole foot, the whole torso, the whole body to move. Gertrude Colby, among the first of modern dance instructors, later wrote, "The arm positions grow out of the body movements and follow the life and sway of the body. They do not move independently but grow out of and continue the trunk movements." Helen Moller, western tomboy turned modern dancer, insisted in 1918 that

Isadora Duncan died in Nice, September 14, 1927 while test driving a Bugatti she planned to buy. Her trailing scarf caught in the wheel in its first revolution and broke her neck.

"All true physical expression has its generative centre in the region of the heart....Movements flowing from any other source are aesthetically futile." Katharane Edson, national director of the Denishawn schools, would conclude, "The art of gesture must come first to a dancer because his gesture represents himself as a whole." She too had studied with Mrs. Richard Hovey, the Delsartean.[5]

As Duncan and a long line of more modest Epigoni returned to Greek models, as St. Denis and Shawn looked farther east, they began to foster a new kinaesthetic. This kinaesthetic demanded sincerity, the loving accommodation of the force of gravity, fluid movement flowing out of the body center, freedom of invention and natural transitions through many fully expressive positions.[6]

Eurythmy

About the time that Duncan, Shawn and St. Denis were releasing the human torso that had been so rigorously confined by the costume and choreography of stylized ballet, another European master arose, a Professor of Harmony at Geneva, Emile Jaques-Dalcroze. In 1910 in a village outside of Dresden, he established his own college of Eurythmy, of "music made visible." At Hellerau ("bright meadow"), "they taught you an alphabet and a grammar of movements. With your arms you kept the time; a set of movements for three-part time, another for four, and so on. With your feet and body you indicated the duration of notes. It was a kind of rhythmic gymnastics," wrote Sinclair Lewis in *World's End*, and it was "not only beautiful but healing, a way to train the young in grace and happiness, in efficiency and co-ordination of body and mind." Rhythm was all important; sensitivity to one's personal physical rhythms was necessarily prior to the mastery of musical rhythms, but ultimately one sought a classical "Grecian" grace and its complementary spiritual measure. "The special merit of gymnastics based on rhythm," claimed Jaques-Dalcroze, "is that it unites the body and soul in education.... What is rhythm? Is it spiritual or corporeal? Assuredly it is both."[7]

Americans first read about Jaques-Dalcroze in an article by an English devotee in 1911, but much more influential were two students of, and rebels from, the master: Mary Wigman and Rudolf Laban. Wigman spent years with Jaques-Dalcroze but eventually felt oppressed by his strict emphasis upon the melodic line in physical responses to music; she, like another young Dalcroze teacher, Suzanne Perrottet, was "looking for dissonance, in order to express my character, and that was not possible with [Jaques-Dalcroze's] altogether harmonious structure." Perrottet in 1912 transferred her allegiances — and her love — to the seductive Laban, a man of aristocratic bearing who, after spending the year of 1899 in officer training at the behest of his military father, had left for sophisticated Paris only to become enamored of mysterious landscapes, country folk, and incantatory, whirling dervish dances. From Paris to Munich, where Laban orchestrated pageants and festivals, culminating in a "sorcerer's apprentice" vision which would have aroused the envy of Steele MacKaye: eight hundred performers costumed as giants, witches and demons transfusing a big-city Witches' Sabbath with the spirit and spirits of "unmodified nature." Mary Wigman, desperate to express her own unmodified nature, met Laban through the wife of the painter Emile Nolde, whose canvases were beset by human bodies of extreme nervous compression. Wigman would soon recreate his images of motion, beginning with her *Hexentanz* ("Witch Dance") of 1913 performed at Monte Verita, the Mountain of Truth, above Ascona. Laban was spending his summers now at that extraordinary countercultural settlement in Italian Switzerland; there he urged Perrottet, Wigman and other exuberant dancers to speak with their entire "festive being." Meanwhile, between 1914 and 1917, he worked as Jaques-Dalcroze's assistant, shaping a *Eukinetik* more spacious and more irregular than Dalcroze eurythmics, making use of rhythm by its dialectics of tension and relaxation, strain and impulse, with movements unwound and outflung from the center of the body/soul. The work of Laban and Wigman (and Perrottet at the Laban school in Zurich) reached the United States in two forms: first, as a dance discipline demanding high energy and focus — adapted by Hanya Holm and by Martha Graham, a Denishawn graduate; later, refined and subdued, as a system of dance notation (Labanotation) whose categories of movement continue today to determine ideas about dance instruction and improvisation.[8]

The "cultured" Dalcroze emphasis upon personal and dynamic rhythms, energized by the Dionysiac bursts of Laban and Wigman, was compatible with other aspects of the emerging kinaesthetic of modern dance — itself at once an outgrowth of, and reaction to, ballet. Formal ballet had begun in the late sixteenth century as a courtly demonstration of grand manners, which proceeded from one straight-spined elegant posture to the next through, soon enough, the five standard positions of the feet. Leaving behind the masks and hooped dresses of aristocratic amateurs, professional ballerinas of the eighteenth century worked for greater elevation (on the halftoe), greater agility and more expressive visages. Once out of fashionable high heels and caught up in the throes of an arabesque, romantic, storytelling nineteenth century, ballerinas moved quickly from heelless slippers into wooden-wedged toe shoes, encouraged toward full linear extension and the fantasy of apparently effortless flight, lighter than air.[9] Still, this ballet remained essentially a

Hexentanz, Mary Wigman, Monte Verita, 1913.

74

dance of faces, arms, wrists, fingers, ankles and toes, a spectacle of pirouettes, overhead lifts, set mimetic attitudes, statuesque positions and plane geometries. The center of the body remained tightly corseted; the torso, from pelvic girdle to shoulder blades, was fitted to an enduringly classical tradition of calm.

Now, at the turn of the century, with the advent of powered flight, dancers (the Diaghilev troupe within the ballet world, the modern dancers beyond) became enamored of torsion. A generation earlier, glider pilots had sent themselves carefully aloft from the tops of slopes and dunes, assuming a single considered position for the length of the flight. These flights were in effect isolated gestures, poses taken through space, comparable to the performances of young women practicing Delsartean or Harmonic Gymnastics

Four rhythmicians — Annie Beck, Clara Brooke, Suzanne Perottet and Jeanne Alleman. Geneva, 1913.

during the 1880s. Like the men hanging from canvas wings and pushing off from soft promontories, Delsarteans knew enough to follow the natural momentum of their initial impulse; like the glider pilots, too, their performances were customarily short and self-consciously dramatic. But when Wilbur Wright in 1904 banked slowly over an Ohio field in his spindly biplane and — for the first time — returned full circle to his point of departure, he was the skyborn herald of a new kinaesthetic. Holding a wing-warping lever linked to a movable rudder in one organic system of control, Wilbur's command came from the peculiarly sensitive center of the structure, whose lateral balance was decided by a helical twist across its cambered wings.[10]

Such dynamic balance and torsion broke the seal, in the realm of heavier-than-air machines, to the same kinaesthetic toward which pathbreaking modern dancers were headed in their heavier-than-air bodies. Modern dancers insisted on effort, on weight and torque, and they consistently dissented from the balletic "delusion that the law of gravitation does not exist for them." Indeed, Laban with his Effort/Shape studies, St. Denis with the sensuous pulsing/writhing of her bare midriff, Duncan with her earthward stamping, spinning gestures, and Graham with her contractions and releases together established a model of motion as a spiral at whose radiant center was a mystical solar plexus and at whose physical axis was the preternaturally flexible spine, bound link by vertebral link to the earth as to the heavens. Dancing, one bent one's whole body to the whole music; like Duncan or St. Denis,

Orville Wright, Wilbur Wright and Dan Tate, 1902.

one did not dance to single beats but to the phrase or the center line out of which flowed the rest of the music. Movement unfolded from the center of the body in the same way that music expanded (for Laban most explicitly) from the middle note of the octave, from one's personal middle C.[11]

From Delsarte to the Bennington School inaugurated in 1934, dancers of "the modern dance" had come to insist upon a grounded human body moving nonetheless fluidly, rhythmically, naturally and, in the sense that any part of the body could be called upon, freely. Its chief pattern was the spiral; its deepest resource was torsion (from the Latin *torsio*, a wringing of the bowels). For Duncan, for the "Greek" dancers, barefoot dancers, natural dancers, and *Seelentänzer* or "soul dancers" who followed in her wake, for St. Denis and Shawn (who abandoned the ministry for dance), as for Delsarte, Jaques-Dalcroze, Wigman and Laban, physical movement was a crucial means of human expression, a form of worship. If we can find that God-Within, wrote Shawn, we can return to the primitive sources of dance, which were "the flowering of man's full self-consciousness." Wrote St. Denis: "To dance is to live life in its finer and higher vibrations, to live life harmonized, purified, controlled." A successful dance found the means to be an eloquent prayer.[12]

Prayer transforms. Dance was not only an expression, it was a reflexive experience. What happened in the century between Delsarte's public lectures and the modern dance of the 1930s was the elaboration of a kinaesthetic in which, above all, movement transforms. As early as 1856, Mathias Roth in his *Handbook of the Movement Cure* had defined "kinesiatrics" as the treatment of diseases by means of gymnastics or muscular activity. Known also as "kinesipathy" or "kinesitherapy," the treatment was ancestor to our occupational and physical therapies. The distinction between the outlook of the kinesitherapist and the modern dancer was that the former sought to treat physical diseases; for the modern dancer, dance worked upon character.[13]

Delsarte had insisted that if one moved wisely, gesture would be a true reflection of the self (or of the role portrayed, or of the lyrics sung). He had also implied that moving wisely would benefit one spiritually: to be attuned to the nuances of a raised arm or a tilted head, one had to be personally in tune. For the modern dancers, the release of the torso from the prison of classical ballet was a spiritual release as well. In their dances they often expressed this release in a flight from plot to painting, from telling a story to the music to telling the story of the music itself — what Jaques-Dalcroze called "music made visible" and what St. Denis called "music visualization." Since emotion and movement were to be intrinsically related (rather than customary and formal, as in much of classical ballet), and since there was to be high drama in movement itself, the dance must be a process of character transformation. Movement was at the same time expressive and operative.[14]

Script

Delsarte's system had involved an elaborate attempt to specify the absolute meanings of various gestures. An arm extended forward, palm up, meant "It is"; an arm extended downward at a 45-degree angle from the torso, palm up, meant "It is improbable," and so forth. This was analogous to the fixed-sign system of Abbé Jean-Hippolyte Michon, author of the seminal *La Méthode pratique de graphologie* of 1878. Michon had found that physical motions, whose residue were written words, had meanings and some syntax of their own related to the personality of the scribe. In the same way that Delsarte matched gesture with inner meaning, Michon matched particular letter forms directly and absolutely with character traits, emotional dispositions and psychological states.[15]

The successor to Michon, Jules Crépieux-Jamin, took a more holistic approach to handwriting. Like Jaques-Dalcroze, he stressed the importance of rhythm — spacing in and between words, variation in sizes of letters, angle of slant across the page. Graphological signs were relative, not absolute, and must be deciphered within the full context of a person's writing. Complex qualities such as jealousy showed up only as resultants of several simple qualities, and trained intuition was required to construct the psychographic equations. With Alfred Binet, Crépieux-Jamin sought to determine scientifically the predictive possibilities of graphology. At century's turn they found that handwriting did not disclose the age or sex of an individual, but it did reveal the intelligence of the writer — which, to Binet, said as much about moral fiber as it did about mental faculties. Somehow (it was not clear how), motor behavior as recorded in script was an expression of the personality, hence consistent and reliable.[16]

William Preyer, Georg Meyer and then Ludwig Klages studied in fine the relationship between handwriting and psychomotor functioning. Klages, the most influential of the German school of graphologists in the early twentieth century, looked at the entire outlooming motion of handwriting, determined its *Formniveau* or general form-quality, its harmonies and rhythm. Like Wigman and Laban, he identified impulse with expression and constructed a theory based on dynamic oppositions. Handwriting, Klages believed, is the clearest record we have of the personal human contest between

Graphology sample from Abbé Jean Hippolyte Michon.

Graphology sample from Ludwig Klages.

a restraining mind and a liberating soul. The written line is expressive both of psychological state and of spiritual conflict.[17]

Martha Graham might well have appreciated this, just as Isadora Duncan might well have appreciated the fact that most if not all graphologists interpreted divergence from standardized letter forms (school forms) as a sign of vitality and individuality.[18] After the publication in 1919 of June Downey's book on the psychology of handwriting, Americans may have been receptive to the idea that handwriting, like dance, was evidence of an interactive link between physical motion and inner states. But the major impact of graphology was not felt in the United States until 1933, with the publication

of *Studies in Expressive Movement*. Steeped in German gestaltist psychology, the authors Gordon Allport and Philip E. Vernon included a chapter by Edwin Powers on "matching sketches of personality with script." The authors concluded that character was revealed by motions of all kinds, including script, and that physical behavior was not distant from inner states. In script there were no isomorphic or constant relationships between particular letter forms and personality traits, but rhythm, direction, density and scale of writing were important indices to character.[19]

Graphological theories between 1870 and 1930 had undergone the same series of changes as theories about dance. With less forthrightness than the modern dancers, graphologists had also fashioned a similar kinaesthetic. Robert Saudek, for example, in his major work *Experiments with Handwriting* (1929), listed the adult signs of an unnatural (unappealing or disingenuous) penmanship: slow speed of execution; subsequent "touching-up" of letters; frequent change of grip; wavering or interrupted pen strokes; marked changes in angle of writing; complexity of initial stroke adjustment; use of the "ornamental fashion of a bygone age." To write naturally (genuinely) was to write under an "elementary sentence-impulse," in other words, to write from somewhere suspiciously close to the solar plexus, with the unimpeded sweep of an emotion or explosion of an idea. The positive values of Saudek's kinaesthetic were fluidity (which implied sincerity), rhythm (vitality), freedom of expression (honesty and spontaneity), naturalness of transitions between letter forms (innocence) and an emphasis upon the full phrase (wholeheartedness).[20]

Saudek's kinaesthetic was as common to other graphologists as it was to the modern dancers. Less common but nonetheless present by 1930 was the graphological assumption that handwriting was not only expressive but operative, that if one changed one's handwriting, one might through the change in motor habits change one's character. Dr. Edgar Berillon had discussed *la psychothérapie graphique* as early as 1908, and by 1932 Charles-Louis Julliot was reporting on a series of achievements in the field. Milton N. Bunker, who founded the International Graphoanalysis Society in Chicago in 1929, would assure his American readers that "*you can change your character* by changing your writing." If you were failing in business or on the brink of romantic defeat, a new script could effect a new and more successful person.[21]

By the thirties, dancers and graphologists had proposed a kinaesthetic that valued motion as much for its operative as for its expressive properties. If genuine movements reflected the inner passions, struggles and joys of being human, integrated and centered rhythmic movements could in turn recreate the human being.

On the surface of things, neither the operative nor the expressive aspects of this kinaesthetic were new. At the end of the eighteenth century but recalling ancient rhetorical theory, the English orator Edmund Burke had described how the assumption of a physical posture typical of a specific emotional state would produce that state to striking effect in a skilled speaker. The Reverend Gilbert Austin, in his *Chironomia* of 1806, had advocated that natural, sincere, fluid gestures accompany all oratory. Swiss educational reformer Johann Heinrich Pestalozzi and his followers in the United States, admiring the sensationalist epistemology of Condillac and the German idealism of Fichte, emphasized the strengthening of sense impressions through natural play, gymnastics and psychophysical exercises in observation and attention. Ethical lessons began not with the catechistic "What is God?" but with the question "Do you have hands?" — in answer to which students would gradually lay claim to their physical (and public) persons. Alluding perhaps to contemporary experiments with the "Wild Boy of Aveyron," Pestalozzi in 1807 wrote that one young girl, "who had been little better than a savage, by keeping her head and body upright, and not looking about [when in his classroom], made more progress in her moral education than anyone would have believed possible." The willful habit of carrying oneself well could work wonders.[22]

Yet, from the perspective of the modern dancers, there was in practice much of an unnatural muchness to this ancestry. Burke's own gestures as a speaker, for example, were "angular and awkward," and his fellow orator William Pitt "used to saw the air with his arms like a windmill." Irish patriot Daniel O'Connell, famous for his oratory, "threw himself into a great variety of attitudes…now he stands bolt upright, like a grenadier; then he assumes the port and bearing of a pugilist." Across the Atlantic, Daniel Webster used "the gestures of enforcing rather than of describing; the pointing finger, the vigorous bringing down of the arm, the easy sidewise wave of all, these were much his variety." As late as the first decade of the twentieth century, an orator's manual would present sixteen pages of charts on the specific meanings of various gestures, and a young man from Missouri would be "drilled to bring the arm up in a graceful curve, to make a classical swing with the wrist and then to unfold the forefinger first, the second finger next, and the little one last." That young man, Dale Carnegie, modern salesman par excellence, found the whole performance "wooden and affected. There was nothing sensible or honest about it…. There was no attempt whatever to get me to put my own individuality into my movements; no attempt to spur me on to feeling like gesturing; no endeavour to get the flow and blood of life in the process, and make it natural and unconscious and inevitable; no urging me to let go, to be spontaneous, to break through my shell of reserve, to talk and act like a human being." And where the orators struck attitudes, Pestalozzi's students, despite the liberating theory, were often drilled into marching order, asked to repeat statements and proofs "over and over" like good automata, taught to spell by heart before learning their alphabets, then to multiply "thousands by tens of thousands, promptly, without slate or pencil."[23]

What gave force, distinction and novelty to the kinaesthetic of the modern dancers and graphologists was late nineteenth-century work in anthropology and neurophysiology. Through this work, the new kinaesthetic became the nodal point of a powerful theory about education and the origins of culture.

For many anthropologists, "primitive" societies were physical cultures; "savages" were more likely to respond emotionally and physically than intellectually. Indeed, "savages" were barely speaking animals, and anthropologists therefore scrutinized them for clues to the original meanings of physical gestures. Since "savages" were somehow the living ancestors of modern civilized people, anthropologists also looked to them for clues to the origins of culture itself. In the 1890s, Karl Groos and Karl Bücher put the clues together: the element common to all "savage" tribes was rhythm, from which culture sprang in expansive physical play and ritual dance. Rhythm was the energy behind primitive economy and religion.[24]

While Groos and Bücher were enjoying considerable continental fame for their synthetic work on the essential physicality of culture, American physiologists and psychologists were laying bare the overwhelming importance of rhythm within the physical person. Studying reflex arcs, cardiovascular and circulatory mechanisms and the relationship of brain to muscle motions and nerve impulses, they announced that the human body was, above all, "a device for producing rhythm." Moreover, motion seemed crucial to sensation, growth and — possibly — intelligence. As the physician Luther Gulick wrote in 1898, "Muscular contraction appears to be closely related to the genesis of all forms of psychic activity. Not only do the vaso-motor and muscular systems express the thinking, feeling, and willing of the individual, but the muscular apparatus itself appears to be a fundamental part of the apparatus of these psychical states."[25]

This was but one version of the motor theory of consciousness, a theory expressed in different forms by William James, by John Broadus Watson and other behaviorists, by Pavlov and other animal objectivists. By 1913, psychologist G. V. N. Dearborn could write confidently that "Kinesthesia is about…to come into its own as the primary and essential

Classroom exercise in group response to simple rhythmic patterns.

sense.... The very meaning of protoplasm, physically speaking, is motion."[26]

Married quickly to genetic psychology, the theory of rhythm and the motor theory of consciousness engendered a pedagogical theory — to wit, that the subject of instruction during each period of individual personal growth should conform to the cultural products of the race in its comparable epoch. Since rhythmic movement was natural and primitive, mastery of rhythm must precede mastery of more "civilized" forms of expression. Like "savages," children were primarily physical beings whose intellectual faculties had not fully developed. One should begin their education by encouraging their play in the direction of rhythmic activities and the vigorous exercise of large muscles.[27]

Such pedagogy was more than a stealthy way of introducing songs and dances. It was good neurophysiology. As the graphologist William Preyer explained in his widely admired book on *The Mind of the Child*, repetitive (rhythmic) motions made passable the nerve paths between muscles and brain. Other experts would go so far as to claim that physical activity was responsible for the laying of those paths. G. Stanley Hall, whose work in genetic psychology served as the underpinning for much subsequent child study, praised Preyer for his

The Alexander principle, developed by Frederick Matthias Alexander (1869–1955). Students of the technique build up a new body grammar by correlating muscular use to a corresponding mental pattern imprinted through repeated sequences of words.

double emphasis upon will and kinaesthesia. Early on, Hall had been excited by the study of motor functions vis-à-vis mental function. Education, in the sense of the cortical development of the brain, might very well be a physical process. The child begins by responding with her entire body; slowly motor specificity is established, slowly she coordinates muscles, slowly she gains the ability to execute complex serial physical maneuvers.[28]

Play, therefore, must be the child's work, the means by which the neural network was fixed. Rhythmic play would facilitate learning, which must begin with the large (or fundamental) muscles and pass carefully to the small, finer, accessory muscles.[29]

John Dewey was delighted: "The manual-training movement has been greatly facilitated by its happy coincidence with the growing importance attached in psychological theory to the motor element." Dewey had been insisting upon an active, physical, manual education, and himself promoted Alexander technique, a system for postural and personal alignment founded on a presumption of mind–body unity. The Englishman who developed the technique, Frederick Matthias Alexander, like the

Frenchman Delsarte, had originally set out on a stage career; also like Delsarte, he had been besieged by voice and throat problems which led him to the study of the body and motor habits. His *Use of the Self* (1932) attracted physiologists, genetic psychologists, the comparative anatomist Raymond A. Dart, pianists, violinists, thespians and an ailing Aldous Huxley. As with Alexander's fiercely manipulative orthopedics, a kind of muscular chiropractic disabused of its neurology, Dewey's "learning by doing" philosophy was justified because, in fact, doing *was* learning.[30]

The kinaesthetic of the small population of graphologists and modern dancers was carried into larger American (and later, European) society through widespread reforms in the motor training of young children, based upon rhythmic play and large-muscle activity. The graphologists' positive evaluation of natural, full-bodied rhythms and flow in handwriting was reflected in a penmanship instruction that emphasized the writing of whole letters, whole words, rather than the rote repetition of artificially designated constituent strokes. The modern dancers' insistence upon a free torso and fluid motions in long rhythmic phrases was reflected throughout the years of schooling, from the wholesome uninterrupted play of nursery school and the encouragement of individual expression in primary grades to collegiate training in natural gymnastics rather than rigidly uniform calisthenics.

The pedagogy of one form of expression, handwriting, evolved in cultural tandem with graphological theories. Penmanship instruction during the nineteenth century concentrated upon drill in the movements specific to each alphabet letter, then upon the general movements requisite to shaping any letter form, finally upon letters in context. Instruction gradually departed from the copybook to the chalkboard and the large pencil on soft paper. By 1930, American students no longer practiced the standard 48-degree slant of 1870s Spencerian script; slant would come naturally, would vary with the individual, and, according to the major pedagogues, would be congruent with the rhythm of the handwriting. Rhythm and ease were the foremost considerations, especially in the first grades, where students were still struggling to coordinate finger movements. Penmanship supervisors constantly redesigned school desks and chairs to afford younger children freer arm motions and better posture, so that writing could flow, as it were, from the center of their beings. In the classroom teaching of writing ("a very complex muscular movement involving the use of some five hundred or more muscles altogether"), instructors stressed legibility rather than strict imitation of forms. They used singsong chants, metronomes and the new Waterman split-feed fountain pen to help children toward a fluid, simple, rhythmic, centered script.[31]

The changing pedagogy in penmanship entailed a changed script. Austin N. Palmer, who died a millionaire after promoting his penmanship system for thirty years, wrote at the start of his career in 1896 that "the masses have no use for ornate penmanship; the people do not ask for it and do not want it.... I would define practical writing for the people as a style devoid of all superfluous lines; made up of letters that can, to the greatest possible extent, be formed without lifting the pen, or checking the motion; an unshaded style, executed with medium pointed or coarse pen."[32]

But even he did not anticipate the introduction, in the mid-twenties, of the form most devoid of all superfluous lines: manuscript writing or, as we now call it in the United States, printing. Printing was easier. The children themselves liked it in the early grades because without much training they could produce legible words. They printed more rapidly and fluently than they could write in cursive, and they appeared to have no difficulty switching to the (faster) cursive in later grades. Printing required mostly downstrokes, strokes bringing the hand in toward the body, and physiologists agreed that arm motions toward the body could be executed with less strain than the outflung motions demanded in most cursive forms. Rhythm was not lost (even in cursive, *pace* Palmer, the good writer lifted the pen from the paper at rhythmic intervals), and the child gained a sense of personal accomplishment which had often eluded youngsters well into their practice with cursive.[33]

Reforms in penmanship instruction were not limited to a few progressive schools. They spread throughout American schoolrooms and resulted in a significantly different set of motor experiences for many young children. Consider the amount of time children spent writing: in 1926, for example, Ameri-

6. Curve fingers.
   Close the thumbs and fingers of both hands until the corners of the nails of the first fingers touch the

balls of the thumbs about an eighth of an inch from their extreme ends. (To secure a natural curvature.)

29

Penmanship technique. Excerpt from the seventeen discrete excercises that precede the actual commitment of pen to paper, according to Albert Kirby's 1916 rhythmic method.

can students in grades one through six received direct penmanship instruction for seventy to eighty minutes each week, on the average. If spelling practice, arithmetic, art and drawing be taken into account, weekly writing or equivalent manual practice occupied an average of more than four hours in first grade, more than seven hours at its peak in fourth grade.[34] The figures must be immediately supplemented, of course, by the incidental writing practice in subjects such as grammar, geography, history and the social sciences. Indeed, penmanship supervisors advised teachers to introduce writing as an integral part of tasks in all areas of the curriculum.

"The Crying of the Being To Be"

Like penmanship, drawing had been undergoing a similar pedagogical change during the same period. The reform in drawing instruction was particularly noticeable in Kimon Nicolaides' *The Natural Way to Draw* (1941). Nicolaides, who finished the initial draft of his book in 1936 after decades as an instructor at the Art Students League, advocated a drawing pedagogy perfectly parallel to the notions of movement in modern dance: start with the core, the imagined center of the form; start with the impulse and not the position; remember with your own muscles the movements of the model; think of gesture as dynamic and outward bound. Drawing reforms, however, proceeded more slowly and narrowly than reforms in penmanship instruction, since fewer schools could afford specially trained art instructors.[35]

Behind the momentum of the reforms lay not only a desire for practical penmanship in an age of typewriters, or a desire to train the eye in mechanical prospects, or a desire to entrain the muscles in proper order. There was also that other element in the emerging kinaesthetic, the operative quality of *motion*. Colonel Francis W. Parker's lectures of 1891 were reprinted in 1937, and the implicit argument he made against the old penmanship teaching stood behind much of the urgency of all the reforms: "The imperative rule for an adequate act of expression is that the whole body, every muscle and fiber, is concentrated upon the act; a person should sing, write, speak, by means of the freest action of the entire physical organism. When agents are isolated by premature attempts at precision before poise and ease of body become habitual, the inevitable knotting and tension of muscles react, cripple the body, and constrain the mind."[36] If graphologists could read one's character in one's script, then penmanship (and drawing) instructors were partly responsible for the true expression — and the healthy formation — of character.

Across-the-board penmanship and drawing training normally ceased with the coming of puberty or secondary education, but the kinaesthetic promoted by modern dancers did not: it reached beyond grammar school to physical education in high school and college, and outside of grammar school to children on playgrounds, in nurseries, at home manipulating a toy.

"I do not know what research has been made as to the exact correspondence of body structure to mental and psychic condition, but from general observation I hazard a guess that there must be a close relation between motion and emotion; that failure or inhibition of movement, especially of movements which (so to speak) answer the call of the muscle for action, bespeaks decadence. On the other hand, can we not premise that with the discovery of new and more subtle rhythms and movements, new and fuller experience of life is attainable?" So speculated Ruth St. Denis in 1932 in an article for the *Journal of Health and Physical Education*. Seventeen years earlier, in his wildly influential book, *Play in Education*, Joseph Lee had written, "Play is the child. In it he wreaks himself. It is the letting loose of what is in him, the active projection of the force he is, the becoming of what he is to be.... And rhythm is the method of the soul's progression, the natural manner — not indeed the ruling motive, but the gait and habit — of the human spirit."[37] To physical education instructors who had been fighting since 1880 for creative play rather than military drill, these were key statements. As with changes in the teaching of small-muscle movements in penmanship, changes in the teaching of large-muscle movements depended upon the growing recognition of a congruence between psychological health and fluent, rhythmic, spontaneous, centered movements. First came the emblematic change in names, from physical "training" to physical "education." Chautauqua University sponsored the first North American classes to prepare physical "education" teachers in 1886; by 1891, there were 130 graduates of the program, many of whom had studied with Emily Bishop, whose Americanized Delsarte system of dance sought to "make the body a temple for the indwelling soul." Next came Melvin Ballou Gilbert's "esthetic calisthenics," taught at Harvard from 1894 onward, with the approval of the physical education director, Dudley Allen Sargent. This too derived from Delsarte. Then there was "educational gymnastics," defended by Lura W. Sanborn, who quoted from John Dewey: "I believe that consciousness is essentially motor or impulsive; that conscious states tend to project themselves in action." By 1930, in *Athletics and Education*, Jesse F. Williams and William Leonard Hughes could ask the leading question, "Is physical education an education of the physical [or]...an education through the physical?" By 1930, too, like formalist nineteenth-century ballet, traditional gymnastics with its classical and military heritage had come to seem not only antique but highly technical, a species of work consciously directed and mechanically systematic, promoting not autonomy but automata. Its modern opposite

Chicago playground, c. 1910.

was physical play, free and spontaneous, pleasurable and unspecialized, centered happily within the individual, engaging the whole body and the whole person.[38]

The new kinaesthetic was most congenial to nursery school and kindergarten teachers. Edna Dean Baker, president of the National Kindergarten and Elementary College, wrote in 1922: "In this very wonderful provision of movement in response to stimulus, a continuous reaction of the organism to environing conditions, lies the possibility of education." The active, playing child was a learning child. Alice Corbin Sies, a professor of childhood education, was even more outspoken in that same year: "Movement is 'the cry of the being to be,' the I AM of the human organism." She called for a progressive use of the intuitive and nearly perpetual motion of children, for more playgrounds and for more tolerance of spontaneous play.[39]

She would get them. Through Dr. Arnold Gesell's Yale campaign for nursery schools and kindergartens, teachers were made aware of the applications of genetic psychology and physiology. Although the kindergarten owed its inspiration to the German educator Friedrich Froebel, whose work early in the nineteenth century favored play as a means of education, kindergartens did not burrow into major American school systems until teachers linked play with character on a physiological and then on a genetic-psychological model.[40] Kindergarten reforms begun in the 1890s included the redesigning of Froebelian activities to compensate for the small-muscle imprecision of younger children. Soon, physical tasks such as handwriting were carefully age-graded; correlations between nutritive needs and common growth curves were studied by school hygienists; manufacturers and retailers began to advertise their children's toys and games by specific age ranges. Through the Playground and Recreation Association of America (founded 1906), the number of public playgrounds was multiplied fivefold by 1929, and new pieces of commercially designed equipment — slides, jungle gyms — became a familiar part of the landscape of childhood.[41]

Children were to be independent, mobile, natural, spontaneous, fluent, supple and, of course, rhythmic. In the kindergarten one could promote independence and refine the rhythmic sense by employing the theories of genetic psychology, modern dance and Jaques-Dalcroze eurythmy.[42] At the very least, one could give children opportunities to develop large-muscle coordination and (thereby) to express themselves fully.

This very least was fingerpainting. Uniting the new kinaesthetic of penmanship reforms, drawing reforms and child's free play movement, fingerpainting was meant explicitly to be the ideal form of recorded expression for a playing child. Ruth Faison Shaw invented children's fingerpaints in 1931; she had been seeking a medium for expression that would eliminate the small-muscle strain of holding brushes, chalk, pens or pencils. Actually, "fingerpainting" was a misnomer: according to Shaw, "When a child begins to finger paint, his whole body contributes to the rhythmic movements which register characteristic arcs and swirls of extraordinary grace in color. As one small boy put it, 'I paint with the spot in the middle of my

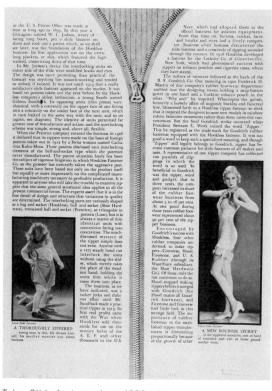

Talon Slide fastener from 1932 editorial.

back.'" Had she questioned the boy more closely, I suspect that the spot in the back would have been the modern dancer's center of movement — the solar plexus of Isadora Duncan, the nexus of tension and release in the Martha Graham torso. For Ruth Shaw, the fingerpainting child was dancing and painting at the same time, and the result was startling: fingerpainting began as an honest, integral expression of "inmost fancies," but became supremely therapeutic. "Once ['problem children'] were given direct means of free expression for the impulses smothering inside them, the 'problems' solved themselves."[43]

The Slide Fastener

"Few locked doors can resist that master key of rhythm," wrote Shaw, who found that she could apply that key to "the affliction sometimes described as 'oral constipation'" or stammering. In an earlier essay, I took that selfsame key into the world of children's clothing, to demonstrate how thoroughly issues of constipation (corporeal stuttering), small-muscle training, mobility, free play and personal expression were wound into the marketing of a new device paradigmatic of the new kinaesthetic — the slide fastener or, as we have known it since the twenties, the zipper.[44] I argued there that the zipper was one of a set of mechanical inventions between 1877 and 1913 — *before* World War I — that made possible a significantly different sense of physical movement. The escalator yielded the rhythm of motion along a stairway. The motion picture camera, preceded by Etienne-Jules Marey's photographic gun,[45] recorded movement so well that people could begin the concerted study of the anatomy of a man jumping, a woman dressing. The Ford assembly line produced automobiles so cheaply that the middle-class consumer might do more than dream of imperial mobility, and wealthier customers could eventually drive streamlined, expensively fluid cars. For the working class, the roller coaster (1885) was almost solely kinaesthetic in its appeal, and for the leisured few the spiral track of the phonograph (1877) brought the vaulting rhythms of great symphonies into the home in tandem, often,

88

with the ragtime of player-piano rolls. By repeating operations along a continuous track, the escalator, the motion picture camera and projector, the central conveyor belt, the roller-coaster and the phonograph integrated series of elements into products that had, it seemed, a rhythm of their own.

Escalator, projector, conveyor belt, phonograph, these all lay within the realm of Dalcroze eurythmy: bodies could be made (or made to appear) whole and mobile if only one understood the principles of rhythm. In order to improve the escalator, one had to smooth out the rhythm of the moving stairs. To improve the projector, one had to take into account the optical rhythm of afterimages. To improve the assembly line, one transformed the rhythms of the worker on the basis of "time-and-motion studies," which reflected the new kinaesthetic in their own transition from the original stopwatch techniques of Frederick W. Taylor to the polished cinematics of the efficiency experts Frank and Lillian Gilbreth. To improve the phonograph, one had to adjust the prime movers, cams and gearing so that nothing interfered with the spoken and musical rhythms already inscribed on the cylinders or discs. In each case, one sought a natural, fluid transition from step to step, frame to frame, task to task, bar to bar.

When Whitcomb L. Judson in 1893 patented his "clasp locker or unlocker for automatically engaging and disengaging an entire series of clasps by a single continuous movement," he slid into another kinaesthetic world. The pull of the movable guide brought into being and

Otis Elevator Company built the first escalators in its Yonkers factory in 1899 and introduced them to the public at the Paris Exposition of 1900. A few years later escalators were installed in the New York City subway system and in Bloomingdale's and Gimbel's department stores. The early Reno-type escalator was an endless conveyor loop with a series of inclined cleats. Escalators and moving walkways carry heavy traffic in a continuous flow across vistas of merchandise.

— this was the trick — then dissolved the track on which the guide moved. In other words, motion did not simply follow a track, nor was motion (as it was earlier with the motion picture camera, escalator, assembly line, roller-coaster, phonograph) the result of the track; instead, motion gave meaning to the series of clasps. Motion brought all elements together. The zipper came amazingly close to one formulation of the ideal in (Americanized) Delsarte gesture theory: "Love, fear, anger, hate, surprise, are all indicated by a movement of the shoulder, which translates itself along the arm from joint to joint until it reaches the tips of the fingers.... Now these movements, from joint to joint should, as it were, overlap each other, slide into each other, and make a graceful gesture."[46] It is this graceful gesture I will follow

Thunderbolt Coaster, Rockaway Beach, New York.

here, rather than the slide fastener itself, whose impact upon adult life in the United States before 1930 was generally limited to tobacco pouches, heavy-duty overalls and galoshes (or B. F. Goodrich Mystik Zipper Boots, whence the generic name "zipper"). Having established some of the patterns of impact of the new kinaesthetic on the motor training and corporeal apprenticeship of children in the first three decades of this century, I wish to suggest that while very young Americans were being coaxed into, and coached toward, the new kinaesthetic by playground supervisors, nursery school teachers, penmanship instructors, physical culturists, child psychologists and clothing manufacturers, their parents themselves were hardly less susceptible to parallel changes in the ways they handled themselves as believable bodies in the modern world.

Impulses

After all, François Delsarte had devoted himself primarily to realigning the gestures of fully operatic bodies with the passionate lyrics sung by voices in their maturity, inclining toward the most soulful of harmonies. Over the next century, between 1840 and 1940, children and adults alike would slowly be rehearsed into a habit of gesturing and a repertoire of "streamlined" gestures central to the new kinaesthetic — clean, fluid, curvilinear gestures moving from the center of the body outward through uninterrupted but muscularly well-controlled rhythmic impulses. Like pulpit oratory in churches or political debate on senate podiums, rhetoric in the schools would be cut away from its medieval (*trivial*) root-companions, logic and grammar, only to be firmly transplanted to the quadrivial realm of music and geometry, bound to the voice as an instrument and the body as an increasingly theatrical property. In the process, rhetoric would come to connote simply (and to any late medieval mind, barely) speech, and speech would be divested of the Delsartean isomorphisms that fixed each sentiment or statement to a single gestural position. In company with manifestos for more "naturalistic" acting, the new kinaesthetic demanded that gestures arise not out of the public need to conform to conventionally meaningful attitudes, but out of the personal desire to give true expression to a private impulse that might otherwise be smothered. As Dale Carnegie concluded after listening to some 150,000 speeches in his international campaign to educate adults in public speaking, "Any gesture that is gotten out of a book is very likely to look like it. The place to get it is out of yourself, out of your heart, out of your mind…out of your own impulses. The only gestures that are worth one, two, three, are those that are born on the spur of the instant."[47]

Gestures, then, were expressive *releases* rather than practiced achievements — or so they must always seem to be, in casual conversation as in the most defiant of harangues or meditative of dances. If they were true releases, gestures were also true confessions and would, it was presumed, be socially intelligible. The difference between this theory of gesture and that on which, for example, much nineteenth-century melodrama operated, was subtle but remarkable: one read not merely the attitude but the entire stretch of the outlooming motion of which the last position struck was just the finishing touch.

What then of that late nineteenth-century epidemic of apparently uncontrollable gesture — an epidemic of tics, choreas, convulsions, aphasias and strangely impermanent but recurrent paralyses that left so many women of all classes invalids? It was with the new theory of gesture under his belt that Sigmund Freud would reconsider the etiology of hysteria and examine hysterical patients, whose repetitive gesticulations and sudden hemiplegias seemed to arise out of nowhere. Indeed, Freud would observe that "In his [more often, her] paralyses and other manifestations, the hysteric acts as if anatomy did not exist, or as if the hysteric had no awareness of anatomy." The twitches, seizures and paralyses did not make any physiological sense; instead, they were mapped onto the body as the layperson might draw it, superficially, by skin and skeleton rather than by neurological pathways. And yet, hysterical attacks were theatrically intelligible: "A part of the striking motor manifestations evinced by Frau von N. was simply an emotional expression, and easily recognized in this significance; thus, the extension of the hand with the spread and curved fingers as an expression of fear." If there was no correctly articulated neural path from an inner physiological center to the hysteric's outer ex-scription (or paralytic conscription) of impulse, there had to be a psychic path from some inner center to account for an outwardly symbolic pantomime. "Pantomime" was the word Freud used as he began to develop his theory of the hysterical conversion of psychic energy to somatic innervation. No longer content to read a hysteric's gestures as formally extravagant attitudes, Freud proposed in 1895 that his patients' "pantomimes" were giving true expression to private anguish otherwise and harmfully smothered. A past trauma had not been effectively "abreacted," so now the hysteric was acting *out* both her response to the horrible scene (convulsions, hallucinations) and the subsequent suppression of feelings (paralysis, loss of sensation or analgesia).[48]

Neither Freud nor his feuding disciples would pursue the theme of the pantomime, preferring instead to work with recall by way of words, anamnesis by way of words, abreaction by way of words. But if psychoanalysis became a kind of bass-ackwards speech therapy, turn-of-the-century physiologists were proving the existence of physiological feedback mechanisms and extensive connections between autonomic nervous system, emotions and mental states. By the twenties, Charles H. Woolbert's popular textbook, *Fundamentals of Speech*, would bespeak not only kinaesthetic sets and the beauty of curvilinear gesture but also the therapeutic effects of fluent movement upon halting speech, incomplete ideas,

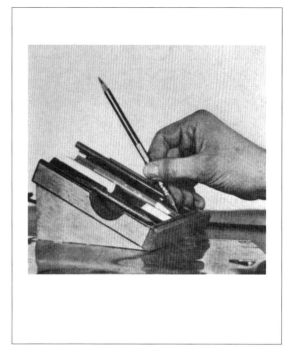

"Very few people realize that the working girl should be measured for her working chair in which she spends one-half of the time that she is awake during her entire working life. For this purpose we have had testing chairs of varying heights made for the girls to sit in, and then have made a chair for each girl, particularly adapted to her and her work. The correct height of chair is determined much quicker and fits much more accurately than does an adjustable chair.

"This chair is of type one, devised for doing work that has always been considered sitting work, either standing or sitting. In this case an ordinary chair has been boosted so that a worker can sit at a work-bench made exactly the right height for standing work. The chair is provided with ball-bearing casters, so that it can be pushed out of the way or pulled into position with little effort. This device helped make it possible to divide each hour into work periods and rest periods — thus not only eliminating unnecessary fatigue, but providing an efficient means for recovery from necessary fatigue."

"This picture shows a 'one-motion' pencil rack. This is one of the many little devices that we have used to cause every one throughout the plant to think in terms of elementary and least fatiguing motions. This pencil rack was devised little by little, suggestions coming from different employees. For example, one suggestion was that a deep horizontal groove be added, that the fingers might go around the pencil at the exact place where used when in the position of writing. The slant of the rack is that slant whereby the pencil will surely slide down by gravity to the stop at the bottom of the pencil rack, but not slide with force enough to break even the most delicate point.

"Such a device alone saves very little time or fatigue, but it represents one of many kinds of devices that make for habits that cause less fatigue."

The captions accompanying these images are those provided by Frank Gilbreth in his 1916
Fatigue Study: The Elimination of Humanity's Greatest Unnecessary Waste.

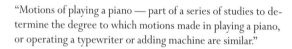

"Motions of playing a piano — part of a series of studies to determine the degree to which motions made in playing a piano, or operating a typewriter or adding machine are similar."

"This photograph shows a typical 'motion-studied' desk. This desk is cross-sectioned, so that standards can be made as to the placing of those things that are constantly required for work. The only drawer containing any permanent materials is pulled out at the left. It contains duplicate supplies of our standard forms, so arranged that a man will not run out of supplies at his desk, as the holder in which the reserve supply is placed is a notification to the desk supply boy that supplies in addition to the weekly furnishings are wanted immediately."

inarticulate emotion. George H. Mead in the United States and a variety of eclectic behaviorists and phenomenological philosophers in Europe would, in the thirties, have gesture itself redound upon thought, as if by "going through the motions" one might (wordlessly) discover and redefine oneself. This, of course, was an essential pivot in the semantics of the new kinaesthetic, as it moved from the expressive to the operative, and from the operative to the transformative.[49]

The Body of the Text

¶   One good example of the play of the new kinaesthetic in that perpetually gray area between gesture and thought was the re-creation of the paragraph. A prime determinant of the pattern of gestures accompanying speeches read from written texts, and of the larger rhythms of scribes and typesetters, penmen and typists, the paragraph had achieved no formal recognition until late in the seventeenth century and was generally ignored by rhetoricians until Alexander Bain's *English Composition and Rhetoric* of 1866. Bain, an Aberdeen philosopher whose earlier books on *The Senses and the Intellect* (1855) and *The Emotions and the Will* (1859) would be held in high esteem by William James, had developed a sophisticated associationalist psychology whose laws he applied to the structure of writing. Since thinking and writing must be more than kissing cousins, Bain drew from the Laws of Similarity, Contiguity, and Compound Association a systematic theory in which paragraph structure should be anticipatable from sentence structure (Similarity), thoughts within a paragraph should flow from one sentence to the next (Contiguity) and, together, the concordance of sentences should yield a powerful resultant (Compound Association). In other words, a paragraph truly expressive of one's thoughts should have Unity, Coherence and Mass (Emphasis).

¶   Today, high school students with their teachers worship at the altar of the Topic Sentence in the Temple of the Paragraph, oblivious to the relatively recent context out of which Bain's sacred architecture came. In 1860, for example, the average English sentence had half the words of an Elizabethan sentence. Through and beyond the century's turn, the penny press and tabloid journalism would further shorten the sentences most people read most frequently. No story longer than 250 words, guest editor Alfred Harmsworth demanded for the January 1, 1901, issue of Joseph Pulitzer's newspaper *The World*, and "All the News in Sixty Seconds." It was all the more likely, then, in this modern world, that sentences would be hanging about in unhealthy anomic crowds or going astray, unattended. Given that few had the Johnsonian wherewithal to shape each sentence as a self-sufficient epigram, the grammarian and the psychologist had best do something with parallelism, proportion, coherence and logic so as to effect "a collection of sentences with unity of purpose."

¶   Thus, Bain's definition of the paragraph — an entity later termed "organic," by which

Bain's successors meant something very much akin to what modern dancers meant when demonstrating truly expressive movement. The paragraph (flowing from mind through pen to paper, or from mind through voice to audience) must travel from its central thought outward, in natural transitions from phrase to phrase, sentence to associated sentence, toward an emphatic conclusion which, again, would lead through the rhythms of association to the next full sweep of thought. "If we have given up the great sentences of Hooker and Milton and Clarendon," wrote John Earle in his 1890 *English Prose: Its Elements, History, and Usage*, "we have a good compensation for it, and a real equivalent for the advantages of it, in our more developed sense of the function of the paragraph."[50]

¶   It had taken hundreds of years to shake England loose from the gospel of great sentences; it took forty years or less to convert American textbook writers into evangelists for the organic paragraph. John S. Hart, Professor of Rhetoric at the College of New Jersey, dedicated sixty pages to Sentences in his 1870 *Manual of Composition and Rhetoric* with nary a line to the structure of paragraphs, which made their appearance solely amidst advanced problems in the punctuation of quotations. John F. Genung, Professor of Rhetoric at Amherst, did devote seventeen pages to the Paragraph in his *Outlines of Rhetoric* of 1893, but his paragraph was "virtually an expanded sentence" on one topic. In 1902, however, Charles Sears Baldwin, Assistant Professor of Rhetoric at Yale, would produce *A College Manual of Rhetoric* that began with the Composition as a Whole and moved immediately to the Paragraph, which had to be unified, emphatic and coherent, proceeding "in natural sequence without break or jar." The paragraph was itself entirely natural: "So soon as an essay is developed beyond a certain length, it falls naturally into paragraphs." By 1916, William D. Lewis, a high school principal, and James F. Hosic, instructor at Chicago Normal College, were explaining in their *Practical English for High Schools* that a paragraph is "a unit of thought. When you think logically, you must think in paragraphs." The same for speaking: "The speaker who makes his audience understand and feel, speaks in paragraphs." Writing in paragraphs was at once the organic statement of coherent ideas and a training toward clear thought.[51]

¶   This organic paragraph was no mere rhetorical gambit for the late Victorian essayist or Edwardian schoolmistress. Rather, it stood in trust of the link between mental activity and physical movement, and it was implicitly intended to be as operative as it was expressive. Writing in paragraphs could organize thought just as thoughts should naturally (organically) appear on the page in the form of paragraphs, following not only the laws of associationalist psychology but also of psychophysiology, a new experimental field toward which Alexander Bain looked with especial fascination. In his earliest published essay in the *Westminster Review* (1842), Bain had discoursed "On Toys," praising their extraordinary virtues as instruments for the development of motor skills, kinaesthetic pleasures and associated ideas and memories: "The passion for handling is not duly appreciated," he wrote. "Handling has led youth over a much larger range of thought than the mere sight [of ornamental objects]." He argued on behalf of jointed, transformable, movable, manipulable toys with the same spirit and toward the same ends as he would much later, in *Mind and Body* (1872), argue on behalf of the importance of muscular effort to mental states. The physical and the mental were, in his own italics, "*a double-faced unity*."[52]

¶   Assumptions of "an intimate relation and dependence of mind and body all through" surely lay behind Bain's reform of the complex act of composition. Much as he would oppose his notion of an actively unified mind to a Victorian psychology that divided the mind into independent faculties, so he would oppose his paragraph to a rhetoric of individual sentences and tropes. His paragraph was meant to be more than a literary model. It was a physiological tracing of a psychological moment, a marker of the passage of mind and body in motion together, unfolding from a center fluid, expansive, transformable, genuine.[53]

Attitudes

Should such evidence for the cultural pervasiveness of the new kinaesthetic seem too distant from actual sinewed bodies, we can gather equally impressive evidence from the close confines of popular theater. Although Diderot in the mid-eighteenth century had been critical of the superficial, self-conscious gestures of actors, his solution for the theater had been neither Method Acting nor Naturalism but a series of well-composed but seemingly accidental *tableaux vivants*, as absorbing as the best of paintings, with gesture and countenance emotionally, visibly true. The German diplomat Friedrich Melchior Grimm, who had by 1765 seen "select companies, gathered in the country during autumn evenings,… imitating compositions of well-known paintings," considered this "excellent for forming taste, especially for young people, and for teaching them to grasp the most delicate nuances of characters and passions." Well into the next century, such entertainments would be constant favorites in middle- and upper-class parlors during the fall and winter. Intermixed with *poses plastiques* (imitations of statuary) and pantomimic charades that proceeded by dumbshow rebus — a man at an INN + a woman gesturing NO + a boy finding a CENT = INNOCENT — were *tableaux vivants* carefully arranged behind large wooden frames to "resemble, as closely as possible, painted pictures." With extensive costuming, makeup, props, mirrors, side lighting and gauze screens, adults and children collaborated in recreating scenes from dramatic literature, sentimental episodes from archetypal life ("Waiting for the Verdict," "Sitting for a Picture," "The Dancing Lesson"), little morality plays or actual paintings and sculptures of groups of figures. As Sarah Annie Frost Shields reminded the readers of her books filled with scenarios, verses, proverbs and phrases to be enacted at home, "The great requirement on the part of the performer is, of course, to remain perfectly still — a feat which may be acquired to a wonderful degree by practicing before a mirror," yet still demanding half a dozen rehearsals to manage "a look of strained anxiety," "a despairing expression and imploring gesture," "a pretty attitude of entreaty."[54]

Like these homely but often elaborate amateur theatricals, professional theater and semi-professional pantomime in Europe and North America through to the late nineteenth century regularly relied upon a set of stock attitudes, a stereotypical language of whole-body and half-body gestures. The language was itself a creature of necessity in France, where most actors had been forbidden by fiat, on and off since 1697, to speak or exiled behind gauze screens. They could on occasion sing, and certainly they could laugh, cry, shout, squawk, but they had to (or had come to) use their faces and bodies in that hyperbolic manner we now associate with silent-movie slapstick and melodrama, which indeed descended directly from pantomime and penny theaters.[55]

However, while Delsarte at the Opéra Comique was losing his beautiful singing voice and turning instead to the mastery of dramatic gesture, Parisian heads were being turned by a different sort of mime, one who covered his features with flour so that the compelling expressiveness of the face could be more persuasively complemented by the subtler movements of a flexible, eloquent body. Jean-Gaspard Deburau's Pierrot and Arlequin appeared in human comedies whose music and song came from the raucous Boulevard du Temple, but whose movements reflected a unique synthesis of gymnastics, acrobatics, ballet, tightrope walking, the commedia dell'arte, operatic dance and the masked (but mute) Greek actor. A theatergoer who saw Deburau in action found him remarkable "above all for his exquisite finesse and extreme sobriety of gesture" — so fine that he could manage a pantomime of the theosophy of Emanuel Swedenborg! "Never did he strike a pose so that his own efforts might be admired. Far from assuming that annoying posture of self-importance common to those actors who draw attention to each of their gestures, Deburau on the boards moved as if he were preoccupied with real life."[56]

Although Deburau's son Charles continued, quite literally and far more silently, in the ancestral footsteps after his father's death in 1846, most subsequent pantomimists in France, England and Italy did not maintain Deburau père's sinuous, full-bodied connections between motion and emotion. Just as many of those who practiced the Delsarte exercises of reaction and recoil traduced them into classical *poses plastiques* or sentimental flourishes, so silent mime and (the more vocal) pantomime had by century's end evidently become an art (once again) of the extremities (the hands, the face, the feet) and of static postures — against which the mime Charles Aubert in 1901 would rail, "It is not enough to make gestures and grimaces. For the registration of an emotion to be complete, the body and all its members must cooperate. The grace, definiteness, and power of an actor depend on the harmonious participation of the whole organism." A transitional figure who adored Deburau but proclaimed that "pantomimes shall be animated pictures, our characters living statues," Aubert would emphasize that "dramatic movements express only verbs, nothing but verbs," yet state grandly that

> Acting should consist
>> Always in attitudes.
>>> Often in facial expressions.
>>> Rarely in gesticulations.[57]

Jacques Copeau, born in 1879, student at the prestigious Lycée Condorcet and the Sorbonne, French teacher in Copenhagen, failed ironworks manager, clerk in the Georges Petit art gallery, Parisian drama critic, cofounder in 1909 (with André Gide and Antonin Artaud, among others) of the *Nouvelle Revue Française* — he hated *cabotinage*. He had seen enough of ham acting, of gesticulations, grimaces, attitudes, living statues, and he was purist enough, classicist enough, theocrat enough to establish in October 1913 his own theater, the Vieux Colombier, dedicated to "corporeal mime." The spoken word, he urged, must be "the culmination of a thought felt by the actor in all his being, and the blossoming of both his interior state and of the bodily expression which translates it." Copeau began therefore to retrain and restrain actors to concentrate upon their nearly nude bodies, faces hidden first in scarves, later by expressionless masks. When World War I intervened, Copeau visited Jaques-Dalcroze, had colloquies with theater visionaries Gordon Craig and Adolph Appia, toured in the United States (directing fifty Greek plays at the Garrick Theater in New York City), studied Noh drama and returned in 1919 to eliminate the proscenium, the footlights, the scenery and furniture of traditional European theater. He devised some of the first overhead theater lights, so that the body rather than the face would be best illuminated by rays that came as if from the sun, spreading across a naked stage.[58]

On this stage, shortly after World War I, and then at Copeau's school in Burgundy, the new kinaesthetic of the twentieth century was joined with what we now understand to be mime. Copeau and his collaborator Suzanne Bing trained, among others, Etienne Decroux, who in 1931 mythopoetically prescribed a thirty-year training for actors: the first twenty years would be soundless, then five years of cries, five years of invented words. It was not that Copeau or Bing or Decroux detested spoken language; rather, they wanted a language that came from the center of the being, in the context of the most truthful body. Face and hands were (as customarily used) "instruments of falsehood, henchmen of gossip"; the limbs, the extremities, should not "shoot out like individual syllables" but move only "on the condition that they extend the line of force initiated by the trunk." Corporeal mime had two principles:

1. The trunk is more important than the arms and legs.
2. When the attitude changes, it should change smoothly.[59]

The manner of the mime, then, "resembled the slow motion of film," but it was "the slow production of one gesture in which many others were synthesized." So wrote Decroux, who

himself never totally abandoned intelligible words and indeed made a number of movies between 1925 and 1945. Most influential of these was *Les Enfants du paradis*, a film about the
bohemian life of mid-nineteenth-century Paris, inspired by an anecdote about (who else?)
Gaspard Deburau. The great mime had, after great provocation, killed a drunkard. "What
made the incident enthralling," said Marcel Carné, the film's director, "was this: that all Paris
attended the trial at the Assizes Court *just to hear Deburau speak*. The idea bowled us over."[60]

Decroux also played in that film, as did another of Copeau's students, Jean-Louis Barrault,
who would import his background as a mime wholesale into the cinema, even as he spoke:
"The man who walks is a moving WHOLE. Walking is centred neither in the toe nor in the
heel. It is centred at the level of the chest. It is the chest, carried on the supple spinal column,
that should express a will to motion. And beneath this will to motion the legs coast along."
The first thing in a person to move is that "hollow magical box" of the thoracic cage, and
"every gesture originates in the spinal column" with "the focal point lying at the centre of
the stomach, the navel."[61]

Barrault called this mime "subjective mime," by which he meant "the study of states of
the soul translated into bodily expression."[62] Bound as it was to movement arising from the
trunk of the body and particularly from that area between spine and navel known to dancers,
of course, as the solar plexus, Barrault's acting was the culmination in the realm of mime of
the same pattern of changes that we have seen in oratory, dance, graphology, drawing instruction, handwriting forms and literary composition. On its way to the new kinaesthetic, mime
had shifted from

> static isolated exaggerated gestures
> postures poses whose single meanings were
> conveyed primarily by the face and hands

> to sets of more fluent less stereotypical attitudes
> emphasizing the extremities and countenance
> but prompted from a heartfelt center

> to whole-body movements flowing out of a soulful solar
> plexus in smooth natural progressions whose drama lay in
> the torque and dynamic balance achieved in the course of the
> full sweep of an idea or emotion.

And along the way, the new kinaesthetic as expressed in mime made its way through film to
us, the audience. In the shift from the *tableau vivant* to the photographic sitting to the snap-

shot and then to those ratcheted sets of snapshots called "movies," the technology of the image colluded with modern dancers and corporeal mimes (as it was colluding with industrial time-and-motion experts and scientific physiologists) to redefine the nature of physical grace and the manner by which we expect our bodies to tell the truth about our innermost selves. If motion pictures as technology were a metaphor for the new kinaesthetic's concern with fluid motion along a natural path, motion pictures as theater were literally instrumental in reeducating old and young alike in posture, gesture and gracious or efficacious movement. Psychologist G. Stanley Hall, impressed by the power of gesture in silent films, hoped in 1921 for the revival of Delsartean classes. Silent-movie stars such as Lillian and Dorothy Gish, Ina Claire and Myrna Loy had studied at Denishawn studios. Charlie Chaplin and Stan Laurel came from an active pantomime tradition in England. For Hollywood as for the English, German and French cinemas, it was modern dancers, pantomimists and corporeal mimes who not only performed in but also choreographed some of the most bountiful productions. Few would ever be apprenticed to modern dancers or corporeal (or spiritual) mimes, yet the indirect impact of their shared kinaesthetic upon audiences sitting year after year in front of the silver screen must have been enormous.[63]

Motion pictures, like modern dance, corporeal mime and, soon, the schools of naturalistic or Stanislavskian acting, demanded much more than a simple reading of one discrete attitude after another. They demanded a reading of the body in motion and an appreciation of the full impulse of that motion. As directors learned the tricks of the close-up and the dissolve, the quick cut and the wipe, movie audiences learned to presume continuity between positions, to require more than mere "attitudinizing," to watch for those subtler motions of face, shoulder, rib cage and pelvis that reflected inner states but had been scarcely visible from the distant galleries and boxes of "legitimate" theater, vaudeville or burlesque.

Although the photographic still and the old pantomimic spectacle continued to influence the staging of early films through to the twenties, bad movie acting came to be called "wooden" and "stiff," and the glamour of the stars came to be equated with a dynamism that drew on the new kinaesthetic — from the dynamic balance of a Chaplin and the abdominal motivations of a poker-faced Keaton to the menacing torque of villains, the slowly unfolding grief of tragic heroines and the seductive spirals of vamps. This dynamism transcended the celluloid of the motion picture: adolescents and adults learned to make love to the rhythms of their favorite film inamoratas and inamoratos, in the theater balcony or in the back seats of (by 1927) "streamlined" Model A cars; fashion models imitated the carriage of film stars; women's and men's fashions had at last a lightness, elasticity and ease of

Lillian Gish.

fastening that allowed for and (by way of magazine advertisements) encouraged those very sorts of full-bodied movements choreographed on the silver screen.[64]

Wooden Legs and Phantom Limbs
Could the new kinaesthetic come no closer to the adult body than this, this world of fantasies?

It could.

Much closer. Too close, perhaps, for comfort.

After the Civil War, and because of the carnage of that war, in which 5 percent of all white males aged 18 to 45 were wounded, the United States became a leading innovator in the production and fitting of artificial limbs. These would subsequently be adapted and improved by the English, French and Germans during World War I.[65] Between the years 1865 and 1920, changes in the design of artificial limbs followed with surprising exactness the pattern of changes that elsewhere were yielding the new kinaesthetic — from the conventional (sometimes exclusively cosmetic) modeling of the extremities, to an interest in joints and hinges, to a primary concern with the central impulses of movement and their prosthetic progressions.

The anonymous author of the article on wooden arms and legs in Diderot and d'Alembert's *Encyclopédie* had described devices that supposedly fulfilled the functional demands of lost limbs as suitably as they filled their physical place, but the vast majority of such devices until late in the nineteenth century were monolithic or poorly articulated wood-and-leather replicas of missing hands, arms, legs or feet. As replicas or as peglegs, they were more often comic than tragic. In Victorian literature and verse, cartoon and caricature, they were disengaged appendages, sometimes gallant, sometimes efficient, never of a piece or at peace with the person. When Miss Kilmansegg's left leg was amputated, she had it replaced, according to the poet Thomas Hood, with a golden substitute, and

She was gold, all gold, from her little gold toe

To her organ of Veneration!

Her greedy husband murdered her "not only *for*, but *with*" the leg:

And they brought it in as Felo de Se

"Because her own Leg had killed her!"[66]

With Dr. Silas Weir Mitchell's still-masterful report on phantom limbs in *Injuries of Nerves and Their Consequences* (1872), amputations (many of which he had performed himself during the Civil War) could henceforth never be considered perfectly clean cuts. Willy-nilly, the body extended its lines of force toward the lost extremities, and movements in phantom limbs were often experienced by amputees as normal, requiring voluntary effort. In addition to the tender youth of many of the recent amputees, the cultural image of the phantom limb undergirded, I suspect, the revival of interest in machining prostheses that accommodated a wider variety and greater fluidity of movement. The well-balanced wooden leg articulated at

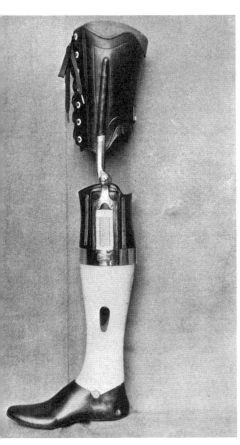

Prosthetic leg.

knee and ankle with a sponge-rubber foot, the wooden arm articulated at elbow and wrist with a rubber hand cast from the mold of an actual hand, adjusted swivel cups and slip-sockets at the stumps — these were fitted to many young men during and after the Civil War.[67]

Then came the second wave of industrialization in the United States, and forty years later George E. Marks could claim that "The mowing machine and the reaper have cut off more limbs than the scythe..., dynamite has mutilated the human body more than the black powder of former days." Marks *would* know, for the company founded by his father, A. A. Marks of New York City, was the leading business house "in the world" for prosthetics, with one hundred thousand customers and correspondents. They wrote to tell him how pleased they were with their purchases. "My artificial arm is so natural," wrote John Burkley, dance instructor in Ohio, "that the dancing people do not know which is the artificial one until I tell them — which I don't do very often." F. J. Bernier, a professional *prestidigitateur*, testified that "When I appear on the stage my steps are elastic and never betray the fact that I wear an artificial leg."[68]

For the firm of A. A. Marks as for its loyal customers, women as well as men, the success of the prosthetic disguise was proportional to the grace and strength of the physical movements the artificial limbs and arms made possible. We can see in the Marks *Manual of Artificial Limbs* (1905) a relatively novel emphasis upon considerations of weight-bearing joints, of lightweight materials (aluminum and sponge rubber), and of the need to keep the body in motion with its prosthesis. Indeed, the first chapter of the manual is a disquisition on "How We Walk," informed by kinetoscopic photography revealing how knee-flexing varies with speed, and how propulsion results from rising on the ball of the rear foot. Someone wearing an artificial leg must walk naturally, without excessive caution, "propped from the pelvis instead of from the shoulders" so that the torso be undistorted. A. A. Marks reduced the deadweight of artificial limbs to reasonable numbers (3–7 lbs. for legs, 1–2½ lbs. for arms), advised the stimulation of muscles in stumps to put an end to phantom pains "associated with inactivity" and discoursed at length upon the virtues of exercise to prevent neuralgia and muscle atrophy. The prosthetic ideal was now no longer preponderantly cosmetic but kinaesthetic, and that kinaesthetic was centered at the pelvis, concerned with the flow of movement outward from an unconstricted torso through undeniably weight-bearing joints (or stumps) to light and durable extremities.[69]

All this without any extraordinary advances in the surgical reconnection of nerves or the rebuilding of muscle tissue. A. A. Marks never promised to restore the sense of touch or any "mental sympathy" between the amputated nerves and the brain. Nor could the biomechanical engineers of World War I promise tactility as they devised artificial hands with movable fingers and thumbs to enable wounded veterans to return to skilled work.[70] But prosthetics research would thenceforth take as its directive the complete integration of artificial limbs with the neuromuscular movements prompted, however weakly, from what remained at the center of the body.

Kinestructs and Kinecepts

We might well go on from here to the historical origins of the distinction between the bodiliness one *is* and the body one *has*, between the cultural constructs that maintain the body and the proprioceptive systems that maintain its physical posture.[71] And it would seem only natural to speak of the history of phenomenology, which has made of the sensation of movement the *fons et origo* of personhood....

But I have brought us to this point, from the original gestures of a man who had lost his singing voice to the gestures of men and women who had lost their original arms, with malice aforethought. For as I have been putting in historical order the elements of the new kinaesthetic, it must have seemed as though I was contradicting the received wisdom about movement and the body during the twentieth century. Current wisdom maintains that modern life, with its essentially industrial momentum, has processed our world and our bodies into dissociated, fetishized, ultimately empty and machinable elements; most perversely, I have been positing the emergence of a new kinaesthetic that insists upon rhythm, wholeness, fullness, fluidity and a durable connection between the bodiliness of the inner core and the outer expressions of the physical self.

Lest I be accused of taking too lightly the current wisdom, let me briefly (and without attribution) make clear how finely knitted its reasoning may be:

President Herbert Hoover signing the Unemployment Relief Bill, 1930 — the first flashbulb news photograph. A noiseless and smokeless version of the flash was adopted by news photographers immediately after its introduction in the late 1920s. The tripod-mounted "open flash" method — in which the shutter was held open until the flash could be manually set off — soon gave way to the fully mobile unit, in which the shutter release was mechanically synchronized with the discharge of electric current, allowing both camera and flash to be hand-held.

The West entered the twentieth century in the company of assembly lines, time clocks, scientific management, time-and-motion studies, flashbulb photography, silent films, ragtime music and Cubism. These conspired not only to make people intensely aware of isolated moments but also to isolate their own movements, to fractionate them into multiple perspectives, infinite exposures. Like snapshots and headline journalism, the rhythm of life in the new century has been as staccato, syncopated or jerky as most popular dances. At the factory, in the designer kitchen, in commercial elevators and business offices, on the escalators of department stores and the moving sidewalks of international airports, people have begun to carry themselves like "robots" (from the Czech word for drudgery and slavery, in Karel Čapek's 1921 play *RUR*). No wonder that such theater visionaries as Gordon Craig, the Futurists, the Dadaists and later performance artists would call for a marionetted or mechanized (nonhuman) stage. Perhaps shocking, this was certainly congruent with a scientific worldview that has tended increasingly to treat human behavior as patterns of stimuli and responses, reducing mind to brain and brain to electrochemical impulses, and treating organs as interchangeable parts. Rather than the classically harmonious body as the ruling metaphor of good government, the commanding image is now the machine: the well-oiled machine, the corrupt machine, the broken-down machine, the totalitarian juggernaut, the scrap heap. Our bodies themselves have been configured into machinehood: they run smoothly or break down, compute or go haywire. We lead monotonic lives punctuated by obsessions with an impossible perfection (mechanization) of the body in sport, in sexual congress and in childrearing. We are uncomfortable with anything less than a streamlined figure, flawless, odorless, detached and detachable. While we pay our respects to a psychology that labors to (re)integrate the body, we spend far more on weapons designed to shatter the body with fragments, and become fascinated with pastiches and diversely multiple personalities. The modern kinaesthetic, embarrassed by modern dancers and graphologists, is really that which has moved away from fluent cursive handwriting to the staccato press-and-slap of manual typing and the verticals of manuscript (printed) characters; away from elegant, spiraling flourishes of arm and pen to simple taps on an electronic keyboard. That is, broadly, the progression we have witnessed in most other manual tasks as also in the painting of portraits, the styling of household goods, the cooking of food. All in all, we have managed speed but not coherence, repetition but not meaning, isolation but not independence, juxtaposition but not integrity. So runs the current wisdom. And yet, this essay has been neither so perverse nor so contrary as might appear, for the current wisdom is at last a critique — a critique founded upon, and grounded in, nothing less than the new kinaesthetic. The ideals of movement embedded within the assumptions of that critique are precisely the ideals of the new kinaesthetic.

There is, to be sure, a difference between kinaesthetic ideals (or kinestructs) and central kinaesthetic experiences (kinecepts).[72] Was the new kinaesthetic a protest, setting its kinestructs against the kinecepts (and technology) of our century, as the mannered attacks of current wisdom would imply? Or was the new kinaesthetic promoting kinestructs in creative tandem with changes in kinecepts?[73]

Dudley Sargent, Harvard's director of physical education, wrote in 1909, "This demand for rhythmic exercises is felt all the more keenly at the present day, because the introduction of steampower, electricity, and labor-saving machinery has taken this factor out of our lives.... What wonder that ragtime music (which is all rhythm) has been taken up by the best society." Sargent's premise was that a kinestruct had been set against the ruling kinecept. Social dance forms were not consistent with, but rebelled against, the kinecept of working life. Perhaps, then, the childrearing and educational kinestructs of the new kinaesthetic were counterbalances to the (unpleasant) kinecept controlling most working adults. If so, it might well be profitable to consider modern "adolescence" as a stage during which youths revolt against a disjunct kinecept they must eventually accommodate.[74]

The flow of my argument, however, has been toward demonstrating that the movement ideals of the new kinaesthetic were indeed incorporated into most if not all of the central movement experiences of this century, from nursery school play and grammar school penmanship on through organized sports[75] to adult gymnastics and beyond, to the design of prosthetic devices. The training of large- and small-muscle movements was regularly if not always allied to the new kinaesthetic in both its expressive and operative aspects, with which technology was often concordant.[76]

More specifically, I would tentatively suggest that the kinestruct of the new kinaesthetic evolved to the accompaniment of a kineceptual (and technological) transition from the push to the pull-and-slide. Elizabeth Selden, writing in 1930 on *Elements of the Free Dance*, distinguished classical (pre-1900) ballet from modern dance in these five ways:

> The main action for speed in ballet was the kick, in modern dance the swing;
>
> Ballet was a technique of thrust, modern dance a technique of winding and unwinding;
>
> Ballet dancers worked to the beat, modern dancers to the phrase, legato;
>
> Ballet was composed of a disjointed series of highly articulated motions, modern dance of integrated motions of pull and release;
>
> Ballet artists made quick changes in direction, modern dancers worked along the path of the motion.[77]

Selden was overstating her case, but her contrasts were paradigmatic of the rhetoric by which the new kinaesthetic made its pitch, and also of the kinds of movement experiences introduced through advocates of the new kinaesthetic. Teachers influenced by modern dance and physiological theory likely led their students in exercises of pull-and-swing more often than in exercises of push or press. I find this in books on games and rhythmic movement for middle-class children in the twenties. I find this in the most popular new playground equipment: the jungle gym, the backyard swingset, the metal slide.[78]

Among adults, I find evidence in typing, where speed-typists emphasized rhythm, continuous flow of motion and stroking rather than striking the keys, just as piano teachers began to insist upon the stroke rather than the strike of the ticklish ivories. Early twentieth-century concert pianist Ethel Leginska, educated in the high-finger, rigid-wrist school of Beethoven, Czerny and Leschetizky, did not yet believe "in the so-called finger stroke"; nonetheless, she observed in 1915 that "It was not the fashion of [the late nineteenth century] to play with the relaxed freedom, with the breadth and depth of style which we demand of artists to-day. In those days relaxation had not received the attention it deserved, therefore we should probably find the playing of the greatest artists of a former generation stiff and angular." She herself did believe "in absolute freedom in every part of the arm anatomy," and in the natural weight and pressure exerted by fingers closer to the keyboard than her masters might have allowed. Tobias Matthay, whose books on piano technique and whose *Muscular Relaxation Studies* would be far more influential than the words of his contemporary Leginska, described in the same year the important rotary motion of the forearm, and advised that "You must never hit a key down, nor hit at it. The finger-tip may fall on the key, and in gently reaching the key you may follow up such fall by acting against the key," in perfect miniature of the fall-sweep-and-rise of the early modern dancers. And then there was Anton Rubinstein in the twenties: "Instead of sitting bolt upright as the pictures in most instruction books would have the pupils do, he is inclined decidedly toward the keyboard. In all his forte passages he employed the weight of his body and shoulders." Which was congruent with Beryl Rubinstein's *Outline of Piano Pedagogy*, emphasizing in 1929 a continuous, never-spasmodic flow of power from the shoulders down into the fingers. By the fifties, teachers of classical piano were even willing to admit into the heart of their system that very rhythm and swing only jazz pianists had cultivated before. "In the 1890s," noted Frank Merrick, "young girls were instructed that it was vulgar to swing their arms as they walked…. These self-same vulgar movements, carried back and forward, parallel with the line of your footsteps, exactly produce the looseness [at the shoulder] advocated in [my *Practising the Piano*]." The culmination was at Juilliard with Abby Whiteside, who had taught since the twenties and would at last announce that "It is the body *as a whole* which transfers the *idea* of music into the actual production of music," from the torso through the shoulder — girdle to the arms and fingers — that is, from center to extremity, just as (she wrote) a dancer moves.[79]

The Poetry of Motion

Admittedly, people had been pulling on doorknobs before Delsarte, and they would push on bicycle pedals after Duncan and Jaques-Dalcroze. But, as bicycle-shop owners Wilbur and Orville Wright well knew, the kinaesthetic experience people associated with the bicycle since the improvements of the 1880s and 1890s — tubular-steel frame, ball bearings, chain-gear drive and rubber tires the same size front and rear — had more to do with slide-lift-and-pull than with a simple push. Downhill, the bicycle was like a sled, and one could "glide away toward the base." On the flat, one sped along, in command from the center of one's own body and moving always forward, outward. Exhilarated, "lifted out" of himself, "up, up from the body that drags," a trainee at an indoor cycling school in New York City would exclaim, "I was going round and round the place, not pushing pedals, but flying. My world took on a new aspect. I was master, or about to become master, of the poetry of motion."[80]

That, in the end, is what this essay has been about: our world taking on a new aspect through the incorporation of a poetry of movement. Laying to one side the cultural history of kinestruct and kinecept, I am convinced from my own experience as a modern dancer, as a teacher of dance improvisation, as a bicyclist, as a longtime student of t'ai chi, that people have not begun to move like machines. Nor do they admire mechanical motion in others, except perhaps to applaud the patience and phenomenal physical control of those performers who imitate penny-arcade automata and repeat a stilted series of isolated movements extremely difficult to learn. If women, men and children these days experience themselves as off-balance, gawky, clumsy, stiff, they also share a vision and experience of flowing movement spiraling outward from a soulful center. That vision and experience may be soon transformed by a powerful literary and cinematic mythology of androids, cyborgs and free-fall, or by an art of amazing puppets and marionettes. There may soon enough be a very different notion of what it is to move or move well. In the meantime, we may say grace.

Notes

1. Genevieve Stebbins, "Delsarte's Address Before the Philotechnic Society of Paris," in Genevieve Stebbins, ed., *Delsarte System of Expression* (New York: E. S. Werner, 1902 [1885]), p. 67; Abbé Delaumosne, *Delsarte System of Oratory* (4th ed., New York: E. S. Werner, 1893 [1882]); and Angélique Arnaud, *François Del Sarte* (Paris, 1882).

2. On these critiques, see esp. Michael Fried, *Absorption and Theatricality: Painting and Beholder in the Age of Diderot* (Berkeley: University of California Press, 1980), pp. 77–82, 95–97, 101–104. The relatively static, "inoffensive" system of gesticulations practiced by many actors, preachers and orators during the eighteenth century was itself a reaction against mid-seventeenth-century "Phanatacism and Foppery," as the English translator wrote in his preface to Michel Le Faucheur's *An Essay upon the Action of an Orator, as to His Pronunciation and Gesture* (London, 1680? [1657]). Le Faucheur, for example, frowned on "fickle Agitation" (p. 178), the shrugging of the shoulders (p. 193) and the use of the left hand alone, which "can make no motion of itself but what is unhandsome and disagreeable" (p. 198). See also attacks upon the enthusiastic style of an early eighteenth-century public speaker who was personally opposed to "still-life" lectures: Graham Midgley, *The Life of Orator Henley* (Oxford: Clarendon Press, 1973), p. 97ff.

3. Francis A. Durivage, "Delsarte," *Atlantic Monthly* 27 (1871), pp. 613–14; and Ted Shawn, *Every Little Movement: A Book about François Delsarte* (2d ed., Pittsfield, Mass.: Eagle Print and Binding, 1963 [1910]), p. 49 (for quotes). On MacKaye, see Claude L. Shaver, "Steele MacKaye and the Delsartian Tradition," in Karl R. Wallace, ed., *History of Speech Education in America* (New York: Appleton-Century-Crafts, 1954), pp. 202–18; S. S. Curry, "Delsarte and MacKaye," *The Voice* 7 (March 1885), pp. 42–44; Percy MacKaye, *Epoch: The Life of Steele MacKaye*, 2 vols. (New York: Boni and Liveright, 1927), vol. 1, pp. 132–67, and vol. 2, pp. 145–46 (for quote); David F. Burg, *Chicago's White City of 1893* (Lexington: University Press of Kentucky, 1976), pp. 227–28; A. Nicholas Vardac, *Stage to Screen: Theatrical Origins of Early Film, David Garrick to D. W. Griffith* (Cambridge, Mass.: Harvard University Press, 1949), pp. 135–51 (quote on p. 136); and William R. Alger, "The Aesthetic Gymnastics of Delsarte," *Werner's Magazine* (formerly *The Voice*) 16 (Jan. 1894), pp. 3–4.

4. Duncan's statement, in an interview given to the *New York Herald* (Feb. 20, 1898), was reprinted in *The Director* (March 1898), p. 110, where also was reprinted an interview with Mrs. Hovey (Sept. 1898). As late as 1926, a Denishawn dancer would comment that "most of what I did copy down [from Ruth St. Denis's lectures] were her quotations from Delsarte, whom she greatly admired and respected": Jane Sherman, *Soaring: The Diary and Letters of a Denishawn Dancer in the Far East, 1925–1926* (Middletown, Conn.: Wesleyan University Press, 1976), p. 23.

5. Isadora Duncan, *The Art of the Dance,* ed. Sheldon Cheney (New York: Theater Arts, 1970 [1928]), pp. 48, 54–55, 100, 129, 136–37; Gaspard Etscher, "The Renaissance of the Dance: Isadora Duncan," *Forum* 46 (1911), p. 326; Irma Duncan, *The Technique of Isadora Duncan* (New York: Dance Horizons, 1970 [1937]), pp. 11–13; Isadora Duncan, *My Life* (New York: Boni and Liveright, 1927), pp. 75–77; Elizabeth S. Selden, *Elements of the Free Dance* (New York: A. S. Barnes, 1930), pp. 54–61; Gertrude K. Colby, *Natural Rhythms and Dances* (New York: A. S. Barnes, 1933 [1922]), p. 13; Helen Moller, *Dancing with Helen Moller*, ed. Curtis Dunham (New York: John Lane, 1918), p. 96; and Katharane Edson, "The Art of Gesture," *Denishawn Magazine* 1.1 (1924), pp. 153–56. See also Joseph E. Marks III, *America Learns to Dance* (New York: Exposition Press, 1957), pp. 77–105.

The solar plexus, as "a kind of common centre of action and sympathy, to the whole system of organic nerves" (Sylvester Graham, *A Lecture on Epidemic Diseases* [1833; new ed., Boston, 1838], p. 10), had assumed its politico-anatomical place at the pit of the stomach early in the nineteenth century with the investigations of French physiologists; its centrality was, I suspect, further if inadvertently strengthened by the later neurophysiological investigations of David Ferrier (1876, 1886) on "spinally organized synergies" and of Charles Scott Sherrington on *The Integrated Action of the Nervous System* (New Haven, Conn.: Yale University Press, 1906); see also Richard E. Talbott, "Ferrier, the Synergy Concept, and the Study of Posture and Movement," in Talbott and Donald R. Humphrey, eds., *Posture and Movement* (New York: Raven Press, 1977), pp. 1–12.

6. Although this essay focuses upon movement and movements in the North Atlantic ecumene, and especially within the United States, which offered arguably the least resistance to the new kinaesthetic,

that kinaesthetic did not have exclusively Western roots. West African, South Indian, Sufi, Balinese and Japanese movement forms (from the Noh dramas and martial arts) were central inspirations not only for dancers but for actors and mimes on stage and in silent pictures. In this context, it is notable that alongside judo (redesigned by Jigoro Kano in 1882 and brought to the favorable attention of the West in the 1890s), a "new" system of Japanese weaponless self-defense was made public in 1910 by Morihei Uyeshiba, hereditary successor to the secret Takeda family tradition of *daitoryu-aiki-ju-jutsu*, or aikido. The kinaesthetic of aikido — maintaining the flow of the *ki* (life force), centered a little above the pelvis and in front of the spine; initiating circular or spiral motions from the torso outward; matching movement and rhythm to that of one's opponent; stepping forward with feet sweeping along the ground; acknowledging the full force of gravity and mastering *ukemi* (the art of falling) — was nearly identical to the kinaesthetic bespoken by many a modern dancer. See Senta Yamada and Alex Macintosh, *The Principle and Practice of Aikido* (New York: Arco, 1966), esp. pp. 15, 18, 23, 26, 29; and John Stevens, *Abundant Peace: The Biography of Morihei Uyeshiba, Founder of Aikido* (Boston: Shambhala, 1987).

7. Sinclair Lewis, *World's End* (New York: Viking, 1940), pp. 5, 6; Emile Jaques-Dalcroze, "Eurythmics and Its Implications," *Musical Quarterly* 16 (1930), p. 360; idem, *Rhythm, Music and Education*, ed. Harold F. Rubinstein (New York: Arno, 1976 [1921]); Erma Brunet-Lecomte, *Jaques-Dalcroze, sa vie, son oeuvre*

Emile Jaques-Dalcroze
1865–1950.

(Geneva: Jeheber, 1950); Alberto Langlade, *Recherche sur les origines, l'intégration et l'actualité de la gymnastique moderne* (Paris: Federation française de gymnastique educative et de gymnastique volontaire, 1966), pp. 40–45.

8. Charles B. Ingham, "Music and Physical Grace: The New Rhythmic Gymnastics," *Good Housekeeping* 52 (1911), pp. 14–17; Lincoln Kirstein, *Dance: A Short History of Classic Theatrical Dancing* (Brooklyn: Dance Horizons, 1969 [1935]), pp. 303–305; Brunet-Lecomte, *Jaques-Dalcroze*, p. 114; Martin Green, *Mountain of Truth: The Counterculture Begins, Ascona, 1900–1920* (Hanover, N.H.: University Press of New England, 1986), ch. 3 (quotes at pp. 86–87, 90, 92, 96, 101); John Martin, *America Dancing* (New York: Dodge Publishing, 1968 [1936]), pp. 96–98, 180–205; Mary Wigman, *The Mary Wigman Book*, ed. and trans. Walter Sorrell (Middletown, Conn.: Wesleyan University Press, 1975), pp. 25–54, 67–68, 81–85; Ann Hutchinson Guest, *Labanotation* (rev. ed., New York: New Directions, 1970), pp. 2–4; Rudolf Laban, *Choreutics*, ed. Lisa Ullmann (London: Plays, Inc., 1966), pp. 3–9; and Irmgard Bartenieff, "Effort/Shape in Teaching Ethnic Dance," in Tamara Comstock, ed., *New Dimensions in Dance Research: Anthropology and Dance* (New York: Committee on Research in Dance, 1974), pp. 176–78.

9. I am condensing here the analytical narrative supplied most interestingly by Philip E. Hammond and Sandra N. Hammond, "The Internal Logic of Dance: A Weberian Perspective on the History of Ballet," *Journal of Social History* 12 (1979), pp. 591–608.

10. For his analysis of the particular achievement of the Wright brothers, I am heavily indebted to

Tom D. Crouch, *A Dream of Wings: Americans and the Airplane, 1875–1905* (New York: Norton, 1981), esp. pp. 13–15, 235, 252. On Americanized Delsarte, see also Nancy Lee Ruyter, *Reformers and Visionaries: The Americanization of the Art of Dance* (New York: Dance Horizons, 1979), ch. 2.

11. Margaret Naumberg, "The Dalcroze Idea: What Eurhythmics Is and What It Means," *Outlook* 106 (1914), pp. 127–31; Ruth St. Denis, "Music Visualization," *Denishawn Magazine* 1.3 (1925), pp. 5, 15; and Green, *Mountain of Truth*, pp. 96, 98. See also Elizabeth Kendall, *Where She Danced* (New York: Knopf, 1979), esp. part 1, which stresses the origins of modern dance in the "new kind of American body — tall, with naturally weighted movement" (p. 41) — but draws upon American popular theater and physical culture to explain the particular syntheses achieved by St. Denis and Duncan.

12. Duncan, *Art of the Dance*, pp. 52, 79; idem, *My Life*, 75, 85 and passim; Moller, *Dancing with Helen Moller*; St. Denis, "The Dance as Life Experience," *Denishawn Magazine* 1.1 (1924), pp. 1–3; and Ted Shawn, "The History of the Art of Dancing, Part I," ibid., pp. 4–6. See also S. A. Kriegsman, *Modern Dance in America: The Bennington Years* (Boston: G. K. Hall, 1981). This spiritual and transformative aspect of the modern dance may be seen especially clearly in the responses to, and writings of, Loie Fuller, a dancer whose important career as "*la voyante de l'infini*" and "*révélatrice du réel*" was devoted to proving that "motion and not language is truthful." Although a progenitrix of the spiraling movements of modern dance, Fuller was more entranced by the motion of fabrics and the manipulation of light than she was dedicated to the techniques or experiences of the body itself, and so I have omitted her from my accounting. See, however, the fine essay by Frank Kermode, "Poet and Dancer Before Diaghilev," *Salmagundi* 33/34 (1976), pp. 23–47, from which (pp. 44–45) I have drawn the quotations immediately above.

13. There were French precedents: C. J. Tissot, *Gymnastique médicinale et chirurgicale* (Paris, 1780); and Nicolas Dally, *Prophylaxie et curation du choléra par le mouvement* (2d ed., Paris, 1856 [1855]). See also "Bally (N. et Eugène)," *Dictionnaire de biographie française* (Paris: Letouzey et Ané, 1965), vol. 10, p. 6.

14. Stebbins, *Delsarte System of Expression*, pp. 439–43, 480–86; Emily Montague Bishop, *Self-Expression and Health: Americanized Delsarte Culture* (9th ed., Chautauqua, N.Y.: E. Bishop, 1901 [1892]), pp. 26, 185–86; Ruth St. Denis with William H. Bridge, "The Dance in Physical Education," *Journal of Health and Physical Education* 3 (Jan. 1932), pp. 11–14, 61; Ted Shawn, "Principles of Dancing for Men," ibid. 4 (Dec. 1933), pp. 27–29, 60–61; Brunet-Lecomte, *Jaques-Dalcroze*, pp. 82–83; Rudolf Steiner, *Eurhythmy as Visible Speech*, trans. V. and J. Compton-Burnett (2d ed., London, 1944 [1931]), p. 14 — Steiner's theosophical variation upon Jaques-Dalcroze; and Selma Jeanne Cohen, ed., *Dance as a Theatre Art* (New York: Dodd, Mead, 1974), pp. 118–53 (for statements by St. Denis, Graham, Duncan, Wigman and Doris Humphrey). An early direct reference to dance transforming character was made by Mrs. Alfred Webster, "Dancing as It Affects the Mind," *The Director* (Oct.–Nov. 1898), pp. 269–70.

15. Claude Savart, *L'Abbé Jean-Hippolyte Michon, 1806–1881* (Paris: Les Belles Lettres, 1971), pp. 233–54; Philippe Berthelot, "Graphologie," *La Grande encyclopédie* (Paris: H. Lamirault, 1886–1902), vol. 19, pp. 220–35; and Emilie de Vars, *Histoire de la graphologie* (Paris, 1874). For a fine example in English of the Michon system, see Cora Linn Daniels and C. M. Stevans, "Graphology," *Encyclopaedia of*

Superstitions, Folklore, and the Occult Sciences of the World (Chicago and Milwaukee: J. H. Yewdale, 1903), vol. 3, pp. 1682–699.

16. J. Héricourt, "La Graphologie," *Revue philosophique de la France et de l'étranger* 20 (1885), pp. 499–512, critical of Michon; Gabriel Tarde, "La Graphologie," ibid. 44 (1897), pp. 337–63, reviewing Crépieux-Jamin's *L' Ecriture et le caractère* (4th ed., Paris, 1896 [1889]), which was freely translated by John A. Schooling as *Handwriting and Expression* (London, 1892) and more carefully, by L. K. Given-Wilson, as *The Psychology of the Movements of Handwriting* (London: Routledge, 1926); Jules Crépieux-Jamin, *ABC de la graphologie* (4th ed., Paris: P.U.F., 1970 [1929]); Arsène Aruss, *La Graphologie simplifiée* (2d ed., Paris, 1899 [1891]), popularizing Crépieux-Jamin's system and condemning the plagiarism by Italian criminologist Cesare Lombroso in his *Manuale Hoepli grafologia* (Milan: Hoepli, 1895); and Alfred Binet, *Les Révélations de l'écriture d'après un contrôle scientifique* (Paris: Alcan, 1906).

17. Ludwig Klages, *Handschrift und Charakter* (Leipzig: J. A. Barth, 1917); idem, *Ausdrucksbewegung und Gestaltungskraft*, trans. by W. H. Johnston as *The Science of Character* (Cambridge, Mass.: Sci-Art Publishers, 1932) from the 5th and 6th German editions (1928 [1st Ger. ed., 1913]); William Preyer, *Zur Psychologie des Schreibens* (Leipzig, 1895); and Klara Roman, "Graphology, History of," in Rose Wolfson and Maurice Edwards, eds., *Encyclopedia of the Written Word* (New York: F. Ungar, 1968), pp. 174–79. Brief accounts of the system and wide influence of Klages appear in Wladimir Eliasberg, "Graphology and Medicine," *Journal of Nervous and Mental Diseases* 100 (1944), pp. 381–401; John Bell, *Projective Techniques* (New York: Longmans, Green, 1948), pp. 291–94; Robert Saudek, "Writing Movements as Indicators of the Writer's Social Behavior," *Journal of Social Psychology* 2 (1931), pp. 337–40; and see Hayden V. White, "Klages, Ludwig (1872–1956)," *Encyclopedia of Philosophy* (New York: Macmillan, 1967), vol. 4, pp. 343–44. Klages later became a leading ideologist for the Nazis.

Ludwig Klages
1872–1956.

18. Certain divergences, however, were judged to be unhealthy by criminologists who, for example, identified pasty handwriting with suppressed sensuality or depraved sexuality; this moralizing scientism lingers today in much of the training literature for handwriting analysis.

19. On the criminological bent, see Renée Rubin's review of material in "Handwriting as a Diagnostic Aid in Mental Illness," M.A. Thesis in criminology, University of California at Berkeley, 1952. For the rest, see June E. Downey, *Graphology and the Psychology of Handwriting* (Baltimore: Warwick and York, 1919); and Gordon Allport and Philip E. Vernon, *Studies in Expressive Movement with a Chapter on Matching Sketches of Personality with Script* (New York and London: Haffner, 1967 [1933]), pp. 185–248, with follow-up study by H. Cantril, H. A. Rand and Allport, "The Determination of Personal Interests by Psychological and Graphological Methods," *Character and Personality* 2 (Dec. 1933), pp. 134–43, with comment by Jan Meloun, pp. 144–51. Adelle H. Land, "Graphology: A Psychological Analysis," *University of Buffalo Studies* 3 (1923–24), pp. 81–114, provides an excellent methodological critique and overview of graphological assumptions. Good reviews of research since 1933 appear in Fritz A. Fluckiger et al., "A Review of Experimental Research in Graphology, 1933–1960," *Perceptual and Motor Skills* 12 (1961), pp. 67–90; International Graphological Society,

An Annotated Bibliography of Studies in Handwriting Analysis Research (Chicago: International Graphoanalysis Society, 1970); and Virgil E. Herrick, *Handwriting and Related Factors 1890–1960* (Washington, D.C.: Handwriting Foundation, 1963), sec. 13.

20. Robert Saudek, *Experiments with Handwriting* (New York: Morrow, 1929), pp. 23–24, 30–31, 128, 227, 277–87.

21. Charles-Louis Julliot, "La Graphologie et la médecine," *La Presse médicale* 40 (1932), pp. 188–90, 803–805; Paul de Sainte Colombe, *Graphotherapeutics* (Hollywood, Calif.: Laurida Books, 1966), pp. 13–14; and Milton N. Bunker, *Handwriting Analysis: The Science of Determining Personality by Graphoanalysis* (Chicago: Nelson-Hall, 1974 [1959]), pp. 9–13. In the context of the discussion that follows, it is important to note that Bunker's first work was *Physical Training for Boys* (Boston: Lothrop, Lee and Shepard, 1916).

22. Edmund Burke, *A Philosophical Enquiry into the Origin of Our Ideas of the Sublime and Beautiful* (5th ed., London, 1767 [1757]), pp. 249–52; Gilbert Austin, *Chironomia or a Treatise on Rhetorical Delivery*, eds. Mary M. Robb and Lester Thonssen (Carbondale: Southern Illinois University Press, 1966 [1806]), esp. ch. 22; Roger de Guimps, *Pestalozzi: His Life and Work*, trans. from 2d French ed. by J. Russell (New York, 1896 [1st Fr. ed., 1874]), pp. 105 (on Fichte), 160 (for quote); Gerald Lee Gutek, *Joseph Neef: The Americanization of Pestalozzianism* (Tuscaloosa: University of Alabama Press, 1978), esp. pp. 17–25, 75–76 (quote on p. 117); Lewis F. Anderson, ed., *Pestalozzi* (Westport, Conn.: Greenwood Press, 1974 [1931]), esp. pp. 61, 147; and Ralph E. Billot, "Evidence of Play and Exercise in Early Pestalozzian and Lancastrian Elementary Schools in the United States," *Research Quarterly* 23 (1952), pp. 127–35. On the Wild Boy of Aveyron, see Roger Shattuck, *The Forbidden Experiment* (New York: Farrar, Straus, Giroux, 1980). Physician Itard's concern with the boy had less to do with training his body, already strong and well coordinated, than with eliciting speech, proof of *human* intelligence. Their travails together belong more properly to the history of approaches to the deaf and dumb, an avenue I leave unexplored in this essay, excepting the related subject of mime, for which see below.

23. David Efron, *Gesture, Race and Culture* (The Hague: Mouton, 1972 [1941]), pp. 49–50, citing accounts of the orators by Earl Curzon of Kedleston, *Modern Parliamentary Eloquence* (London: Macmillan, 1914) and David A. Harsha, *The Most Eminent Orators...* (New York: Scribners, 1864); George L. Raymond, *The Orator's Manual* (Freeport, N.Y.: Books for Libraries Press, 1972 [1910]), pp. 125–51; Dale Carnegie, *Public Speaking and Influencing Men in Business* (24th printing, New York: Association Press, 1937 [1926]), pp. 240–41; de Guimps, *Pestalozzi*, p. 167; Thomas A. Barlow, *Pestalozzi and American Education* (Boulder, Colo.: Este Es Press, 1977), p. 20; and Gutek, *Joseph Neef*, pp. 26–27, 74, 110, and 24 (for quote, from C. D. Gardette, "Pestalozzi in America," *The Galaxy* 4 [Aug. 1867], p. 437).

24. Hoffman Reynolds Hays, *From Ape to Angel: An Informal History of Social Anthropology* (New York: Knopf, 1960), pp. 18–20, 183–85, 197–203; Anya Peterson Royce, *The Anthropology of Dance* (Bloomington: Indiana University Press, 1977), pp. 17–26; Wilfred Dyson Hambly, *Tribal Dancing and Social Development* (New York: Macmillan, 1927); Alfred R. Radcliffe-Brown, *The Andaman Islanders* (New York: Free Press, 1964 [1922, but written 1908–1909]), pp. 247–53; E. E. Evans-Pritchard, "The Dance," *Africa* 1 (1928),

pp. 457, 459; Karl Groos, *The Play of Man*, trans. Elizabeth L. Baldwin (New York: D. Appleton, 1908 [1898]), pp. 20–25; and Karl Bücher, *Arbeit und Rhythmus* (Leipzig, 1897). Havelock Ellis soon constructed an influential aesthetic upon the same basis: *The Dance of Life* (Boston: Grosset and Dunlap, 1923); see Paul Souriau, *L' Esthétique du mouvement* (Paris, 1889), pp. 50–54. Shattuck's *Forbidden Experiment* (note 22, above) is an account of the study of a "savage" isolated within civilized society. At the same time that Itard was completing his second report on the Wild Boy of Aveyron, the Scottish anatomist Charles Bell was issuing his *Anatomy of Expression* (1806), dealing with questions earlier raised by Johann Kaspar Lavater about the innateness of gesture, questions later pursued by Duchenne de Boulogne in *Mécanisme de la physionomie humaine* (1862) and by Charles Darwin in *The Expression of the Emotions in Man and Animals* (1872). By the start of the twentieth century, a person's repertoire of gestures was generally considered by anthropologists, physiologists and psychologists to be a complex mix of autonomic reflexes, racial inheritance, cultural conditioning and idiosyncratic experience. Exactly where one lay the burden of the expressive or the operative aspects of the new kinaesthetic depended (I suspect) upon one's political position, an issue which begs for study. See, for starters, Roger Cooter, "The Power of the Body: The Early Nineteenth Century," in Barry Barnes and Steven Shapin, eds., *Natural Order* (Beverly Hills: Sage Publications, 1979), pp. 73–95.

25. Thaddeus L. Bolton, "Rhythm," *American Journal of Psychology* 6 (1894), pp. 163–64; C. R. Squire, "A Genetic Study of Rhythm," ibid. 12 (1901), pp. 492–589; P. F. Swindle, "On the Inheritance of Rhythm," ibid. 24 (1913), pp. 180–213; Christian A. Ruckmich, "A Bibliography of Rhythm," ibid. 24 (1913), pp. 508–19; R. H. Stetson, "A Motor Theory of Rhythm and Discrete Succession, I and II," *Psychological Review* 12 (1905), pp. 250–70, 293–350; T. Graham Brown, "On the Nature of the Fundamental Activity of the Nervous Centres…," *Journal of Physiology* 48 (1914), pp. 18–46; and see Herbert Spencer, *First Principles* (4th ed., New York, 1898 [1864]), pt. 2, ch. 10; Luther Gulick, "Some Psychical Aspects of Muscular Exercise," *Popular Science Monthly* 53 (1898), p. 797; and Edward Drinker Cope, *The Primary Factors of Organic Evolution* (Chicago, 1896), pp. 246–384, 496–516.

One outcome of this phenomenal interest in physiological rhythms was the careful study of fertility cycles and the promotion of a more reliable rhythm method of contraception: Leo J. Latz, *The Rhythm of Sterility and Fertility in Women* (Chicago: Latz Foundation, 1932).

26. H. Charlton Bastian, "On the 'Muscular Sense' and on the Physiology of Thinking," *British Medical Journal* (May 1–June 5, 1869), pp. 394–96, 437–39, 461–63, 509–12; George H. Lewes, "Motor Feelings and the Muscular Sense," *Brain* 1 (1878), pp.14–28; Theodule A. Ribot, "Contribution à la psychologie des mouvements," *Revue philosophique de la France et de l' étranger* 16 (1883), pp. 188–200; Eugene Gley, "Le 'Sens musculaire' et les sensations musculaires," ibid. 20 (1885), pp. 601–10; Charles H. Judd, "Movement and Consciousness," *Psychological Review* 7 (1905), monograph supp. 29;

Ivan Petrovich Pavlov, 1849–1936.

B. Pillsbury, "The Place of Movement in Consciousness," ibid. 18 (1911), pp. 83–99; Margaret F. Washburn, *Movement and Mental Imagery: Outlines of a Motor Theory of the Complexer Mental Processes* (Boston: Houghton Mifflin, 1916); Carl Georg Lange and William James, *The Emotions* (New York: Hafner, 1967 [1922]); Walter B. Cannon, *Bodily Changes in Pain, Hunger, Fear and Rage* (New York and London: D. Appleton, 1915; very rev. ed., 1929); idem, "The James–Lange Theory of Emotions: A Critical Examination and an Alternate Theory," *American Journal of Psychology* 39 (1927), pp. 106–24; John B. Watson, *Behaviorism* (rev. ed., New York: W. W. Norton, 1930 [1924–25]); Louis W. Max, "An Experimental Study of the Motor Theory of Consciousness," *Journal of Genetic Psychology* 11 (1934), pp. 112–25, and ibid. 13 (1935), pp. 159–75; Abraham A. Roback, *Behaviorism at Twenty-Five* (Cambridge, Mass.: Sci-Art Publishers, 1937); and G. V. N. Dearborn, "Kinesthesia and the Intelligent Will," *American Journal of Psychology* 24 (1913), pp. 204–25.

27. See especially Lilian E. Appleton, *A Comparative Study of Play Activities of Adult Savages and Civilized Children* (Chicago: University of Chicago Press, 1910), which is somewhat critical of this culture-epoch theory of education. For the theory in its most basic form, see Alexander F. Chamberlain, *The Child: A Study in the Evolution of Man* (London and New York: Scribners, 1901).

28. William Preyer, *The Mind of the Child*, trans. E. W. Brown, 2 vols. (New York, 1890–93 [1881]), vol. 1, p. 339; G. Stanley Hall and Joseph Jastrow, "Studies of Rhythm, I" *Mind* 11 (1886), pp. 55–62; and Dorothy Ross, *G. Stanley Hall: The Psychologist as Prophet* (Chicago: University of Chicago Press, 1972), pp. 279–308.

29. Frederic Burk, "From Fundamental to Accessory in the Development of the Nervous System and of Movements," *Pedagogical Seminary* 6 (1898), pp. 5–64; Everett Shepardson, "A Preliminary Critique of the Doctrine of Fundamental and Accessory Movements," ibid. 14 (1907), pp. 101–16; George E. Johnson, *Education by Play and Games* (Boston: Ginn, 1907), p. 24; and Edward L. Thorndike and Arthur I. Gates, *Elementary Principles of Education* (New York: Macmillan, 1931), esp. pp. 273–74.

30. John Dewey, "The Place of Manual Training in the Elementary Course of Study (1901)," in *The Middle Works, 1899–1924*, ed. Jo Ann Boydston, 2 vols. (Carbondale: Southern Illinois University Press, 1976), vol. 1, pp. 231–32; idem, *Art as Experience* (New York: Minton, Balch, 1934), pp. 162–71, waxing hyperbolic on the value of rhythm; Frederick Matthias Alexander, *The Use of the Self* (3d ed., London: Chaterson, 1946 [1932]), pp. 1-10; and idem, *The Resurrection of the Body*, ed. Edward Maisel (New York: Dell, 1969) with Dewey's various prefaces to Alexander's books, pp. 169–84.

31. To follow this evolution, see Platt R. Spencer, *Spencerian Key to Practical Penmanship* (New York, 1872); H. C. Kinne, "The Writing Exercise," *California Teacher and Home Journal* 2 (1883), pp. 114–16; Annie E. Hills, "Vertical Writing," *National Education Association Proceedings* [hereafter *N.E.A. Proceedings*] 35 (1896), pp. 541–53; Charles H. Judd, *Genetic Psychology for Teachers* (New York: D. Appleton, 1903), ch. 6; Harry Houston, "Penmanship Foundations," *Journal of Education* 69 (1909), pp. 668–69; Brenelle Hunt, "Arm Movement Penmanship in the Lower Grades," ibid. 77 (1913), p. 236; Jane A. Stewart, "Teaching Tots To Read and Write," ibid. 80 (1914), pp. 46–47; Harry Houston, "Pedagogical Principles in Teaching Penmanship," ibid. 83 (1916), pp. 241–42; Mary E. Thompson, *Psychology and Pedagogy of*

Writing (Baltimore: Warwick and York, 1911), p. 49 (for quote); A. N. Palmer, "Penmanship," *N.E.A. Proceedings* 53 (1915), pp. 888–93; H. W. Nutt, "Rhythm in Handwriting," *Elementary School Journal* 17 (1917), pp. 432–45; Frank N. Freeman, *The Handwriting Movement: A Study of the Motor Factors of Excellence in Penmanship* (Chicago: University of Chicago Press, 1918); Frank N. Freeman and Mary L. Dougherty, *How To Teach Handwriting: A Teacher's Manual* (Boston: Houghton Mifflin, 1923); Harry Houston, "A Turning Point in Penmanship Instruction," *Normal Instructor and Primary Plans* (in three parts): 33.1 (1923), pp. 30, 81; 33.2 (1923), pp. 28, 73; 33.3 (1924), pp. 30, 81; Oscar E. Hertzberg, *A Comparative Study of Different Methods Used in Teaching Beginners To Write* (New York: Columbia University Press, 1926); Joseph S. Taylor, *Supervision and Teaching of Handwriting* (Richmond, Va.: Johnson Publishing, 1926); F. F. Gaither, "The 'Life' Way of Penmanship," *Educational Review* 74 (1927), pp. 209–12; Paul V. West, *Changing Practice in Handwriting Instruction*, Educational Research Monographs 9 (Bloomington, Ill.: Public School Publishing, 1927), ch. 6; and Beulah P. Beale, "Principles Underlying the Supervision and Teaching of Handwriting," *Educator* 38.10 (1933), pp. 17–18.

On desks and chairs, see C. Victor Campbell, "Desks That Fit," *Child-Study Monthly* 6 (1900), pp. 141–45; Henry E. Bennett, "A Study of School Posture and Seating," *Elementary School Journal* 26 (1925), pp. 50–57; and Prudence Maufe, "Make the Furniture Fit the Child," *New Era in Home and School* 13 (1932), pp. 312–14.

The invention of the Waterman split-feed was the basis for the new fountain pen of the turn of the century. Although generally too expensive to be used widely in grammar schools, it was considered by educa-

tors to be complementary to the pedagogy of fluent handwriting. See "Waterman, Lewis Edson," *National Cyclopaedia of American Biography* (1893), vol. 1, p. 372; Ethelind M. Phelps, "The Handwriting Lesson and the 'Other' Subjects," *Elementary School Journal* 33 (1932), p. 146; Mary Doyle, "Writing," *Educator* 38.9 (1933), p. 9; advertisement for Esterbrook pens, "Rhythm in writing for smoothness," *Grade Teacher* 49 (1932), p. 736; and see advertisement for Dixon's Beginner's Pencil, "Give Us Liberty," *American Childhood* 13.10 (1928), p. 56. The ballpoint pen, first commercially produced in 1895, was not very practical until redesigned in 1938 by the Biro brothers in Hungary and accompanied by a quick-drying ink developed by Austrian chemist Fran Seech; it would play a part in the new kinaesthetic only after World War II.

For physiological research referring explicitly to penmanship pedagogy, see Floyd N. McAllister, "Researches on Movements Used in Writing," *Studies from the Yale Psychological Laboratory* 8 (1900), pp. 21–63; "Experimental Study of the Mechanism of Writing," *Nature* 95 (April 15, 1915), pp. 185–87; and Beth Wellman, *The Development of Motor Coordination in Young Children* (Iowa City: University of Iowa, 1926).

32. Austin N. Palmer, "Practical Writing — A Course for Colleges and Public Schools To Answer the Needs of the People," *N.E.A. Proceedings* 35 (1896), pp. 825–26; "Austin N. Palmer Dies; Was Noted Penman," *New York Times* (Nov. 17, 1927), 25:4; and ibid. (Dec. 6, 1927), 53:2. On the actual state of adult penmanship, see John G.

The Waterman split-feed fountain pen.

Kirk, "Handwriting Survey To Determine Grade Standards," *Journal of Educational Research* 13 (1926), pp. 181–88, 259–72.

33. Marjorie Wise, "Manuscript Writing," *Teachers College Record* 26 (Jan. 1924), pp. 26–38; Arthur I. Gates and Helen Brown, "Experimental Comparisons of Print-Script and Cursive Writing," *Journal of Educational Research* 20 (June 1929), pp. 1–14; Olive G. Turner, "The Comparative Legibility and Speed of Manuscript and Cursive Handwriting," *Elementary School Journal* 30 (1930), pp. 780–86; Harry Houston, "Large or Small Writing for Beginners?" ibid. 30 (1930), pp. 693–99; William H. Gray, "An Experimental Comparison of the Movements in Manuscript Writing and Cursive Writing," *Journal of Educational Psychology* 21 (1930), pp. 259–72; Jean Corser, *Manuscript Writing* (Cleveland: Harter Publishing, 1931); S. Lucia Keim, "The Present Status and Significance of Manuscript Writing," *Journal of Educational Research* 24 (1931), pp. 115–26; Jennie Wahlert, "Manuscript Writing," *Childhood Education* 8 (1932), pp. 517–21; Edith U. Conard, *Trends in Manuscript Writing* (New York: Columbia University Press, 1936); and idem, *Data on Manuscript Writing for Parents and Teachers with a Bibliography* (New York: A. N. Palmer, 1937).

34. Carleton H. Mann, *How Schools Use Their Time* (New York: Columbia University Press, 1928), pp. 20, 25, 86–87, tables 42–47. Compare Taylor, *Supervision and Teaching of Handwriting*, p. 52, citing Principal Joseph T. Griffin: "Children write on an average three hours per day" — most of that time in subjects other than penmanship. On the prevalence of penmanship (and drawing) instruction in primary grades, see Charles H. Judd, "Education," in President's Research Committee on Social Trends, *Recent Social Trends in the United States* (New York: McGraw-Hill, 1933), pp. 334, 336.

35. See Peter C. Marzio, *The Art Crusade: An Analysis of American Drawing Manuals 1820–1860* (Washington, D.C.: Smithsonian Institution Press, 1976); H. G. Fitz, "Freehand Drawing in Education," *Popular Science Monthly* 51 (1897), pp. 755–65; Chamberlain, *The Child*, pp. 199–211; Harold Rugg and Ann Shumaker, *The Child-Centered School* (Yonkers-on-Hudson, N.Y.: World Book Company, 1928), ch. 15; J. B. Smith, "Trends of Thought in Art Education," *School Review* 41 (1933), pp. 266–77; and Kimon Nicolaides, *The Natural Way To Draw*, ed. Mamie Harmon (Boston: Houghton Mifflin, 1941). Contrast the highly geometric, highly industrial drawing classes introduced by the Ferry reforms in France, 1883–1909, which had interesting repercussions on modern art: Molly Nesbit, "Ready-Made Originals: The Duchamp Model," *October* 37 (summer 1986), pp. 53–63.

36. Colonel Francis W. Parker, *Talks on Pedagogics*, ed. Elsie A. Wygant and Flora J. Cooke (New York: Johns Day, 1937), p. 205.

37. Ruth St. Denis with William H. Bridge, "The Dance in Physical Education," *Journal of Health and Physical Education* 3 (Jan. 1932), p. 12; and Joseph Lee, *Play in Education* (New York: National Recreation Association, 1942 [1915]), pp. viii, 165.

38. On changes in physical education theory, see especially Peter C. McIntosh, *Physical Education in England Since 1800* (rev. ed., London: Bell, 1968); Deobold B. Van Dalen and Bruce L. Bennett, *A World History of Physical Education* (2d ed., Englewood Cliffs, N.J.: Prentice Hall, 1971) pt. 4; Harvey Green, *Fit for America* (New York, 1986); Peter J. Wosh, "Sound Minds and Unsound Bodies: Massachusetts

Schools and Mandatory Physical Training," *New England Quarterly* 55 (1982), pp. 39–60, arguing that creative play reformers at mid-century lost out to drill sergeants in the immediate aftermath of the Civil War — analogous to the French school system's embrace of military drill after the defeats of the Franco-Prussian War, for which see Marcel Spivak, "Le Développement de l'éducation physique et du sport français de 1852 à 1914," *Revue d'histoire moderne et contemporaine* 24 (1977), pp. 28–48 — but contrast the extensive gymnastics programs in Germany, Wolfgang Eichel, ed.-in-chief, *Geschichte der Körperkultur in Deutschland 1789–1917* (Berlin: Sportverlag, 1973); Hillel Schwartz, *Never Satisfied: A Cultural History of Diets, Fantasies and Fat* (New York: Anchor Books, 1990 [1986]), pp. 65–68 and notes thereto on Dioclesian Lewis, a figure transitional between drill and play; Fernand Lagrange, "Free Play in Physical Education," *Popular Science Monthly* 42 (1893), pp. 813–20; Nils Posse, *The Special Kinesiology of Educational Gymnastics* (Boston, 1894); John T. McManis, "Reciprocal Relation between Physical and Mental Education," *Educational Bi-Monthly* 3 (1909), pp. 226–33; Wilbur P. Bowen and Elmer D. Mitchell, *The Theory and Practice of Organized Play*, 2 vols. (New York: A. S. Barnes, 1926–28), vol. 1, pp. 302–304, 308; Paul Klapper, *Contemporary Education: Its Principles and Practice* (New York: D. Appleton, 1929), pp. 96–100; Lee Vincent, "Physical Education's Contribution to the Mental Health of Students," *Journal of Health and Physical Education* 4 (March–April 1933), p. 37; and Harriet O'Shea, "The Mental Hygiene Significance of Physical Education," ibid. 4 (March–April 1933), pp. 14–16, 78–79.

On the integration of modern dance into physical education theory and curricula, see George W. Beiswanger, "Physical Education and the Emergence of the Modern Dance," ibid. 7 (1936), pp. 413–16, 463; Harold L. Ray, "Chautauqua: Early Showcase of Physical Education," ibid. 33 (Nov. 1962), pp. 37–41, 69; Dudley A. Sargent, "Useful Dancing from the Standpoint of Physical Training," *Educational Bi-Monthly* 3 (1909), pp. 191–200; William J. Davison, *Gymnastic Dancing* (New York: Young Men's Christian Association Press, 1912); Mary Lou Remley, "The Wisconsin Idea of Dance: A Decade of Progress, 1917–1926," *Wisconsin Magazine of History* 58 (spring 1975), pp. 179–95; Alan M. Hawkins, *Modern Dance in Higher Education* (New York: Columbia University Press, 1954), pp. 3–23; Margaret N. H'Doubler, *A Manual of Dancing* (Madison, Wis.: Tracy and Kilgore, 1921); and Agnes L. Marsh and Lucille Marsh, *The Dance in Education* (New York: A. S. Barnes, 1930 [1924]), esp. Foreword by Jesse F. Williams. Final quotes here are taken from Lura W. Sanborn, "Physical Training in the Public Schools," *Child-Study Monthly* 6 (1900), p. 218; John Dewey, *My Pedagogic Creed* (Chicago: A. Flanagan, 1910); and Jesse F. Williams and William Leonard Hughes, *Athletics in Education* (Philadelphia: W. B. Saunders, 1930), p. 66.

39. Edna Dean Baker, *Parenthood and Child Nurture* (New York: Macmillan, 1922), p. 23; and Alice Corbin Sies, *Spontaneous and Supervised Play in Childhood* (New York: Macmillan, 1922), pp. 209 (for quote), 11, 214 and see 273–74, which relies upon the work of Jaques-Dalcroze.

40. See Arnold Gesell, *The Guidance of Mental Growth in Infant and Child* (New York: Macmillan, 1930), esp. pp. 3–12; idem, *The Kindergarten and Health* (Washington, D.C.: Washington Govt. Print., 1923), pp. 13–15; idem, *The Mental Growth of the Pre-School Child* (New York: Macmillan, 1925); Ada Hart Arlitt, *Psychology of Infancy and Early Childhood* (New York: McGraw-Hill, 1928), esp. pp. 184–90; Beth L. Wellman,

"Physical Growth and Motor Development and Their Relations to Mental Development in Children," in *A Handbook of Child Psychology*, ed. C. Murchison (Worcester, Mass.: Clark University Press, 1931), pp. 242–77; Margaret Mead and Frances Cooke MacGregor, *Growth and Culture* (New York: Putnam, 1951), pp. 10–13, 20, on the American popularization of child-study principles; and Dominick Cavallo, "From Perfection to Habit: Moral Training in the American Kindergarten, 1860–1920," *History of Education Quarterly* 16 (1976), pp. 147–61.

On the kindergarten itself, see Friedrich Froebel, *The Education of Man*, trans. W. N. Hailmann (New York and London, 1887 [1826]), esp. Hailmann's own comments, pp. 18–19, 36–39, 55–60, 103, 107; Kate D. Wiggins and Nora A. Smith, *Froebel's Occupations* (Boston and New York, 1899), pp. 34–39, 57, 94–96; Francis E. Cook, "The Relation of the Kindergarten to Primary Education," *Transactions of the Illinois Society for Child-Study* 4.2 (1899), pp. 41–55; Nina C. Vandewalker, *The Kindergarten in American Education* (New York: Macmillan, 1971 [1908]), esp. pp. 212–213, 220–23 (on reforms of the 1890s in teaching art and introducing physical education), 234–35 (on influence of genetic psychology); President's Research Committee, *Recent Social Trends*, pp. xliv–xlv, 706, 754–55, 763, 784–88, 792, 796–98; William G. Carr, "The Status of the Kindergarten," *Childhood Education* 10 (1934), pp. 283–85, 374–76, 425–28; and Olga Adams, "The Present Crisis in Kindergarten Education," ibid. 10 (1934), pp. 421–24. Although the kindergarten lost ground during the Depression, by the thirties many of its philosophies and activities had already been imported into the primary grades. See also Evelyn Weber, *The Kindergarten: Its Encounter with Educational Thought in America* (New York: Teachers College Press, 1969), esp. p. 85; and Elizabeth D. Ross, *The Kindergarten Crusade* (Athens: Ohio University Press, 1976), esp. p. 71.

41. See Sadie American, "The Movement for Small Playgrounds," *American Journal of Sociology* 4 (1898), pp. 159–70; G. T. W. Patrick, "The Psychology of Play," *Pedagogical Seminary* 21 (1914), pp. 469–84; Henry S. Curtis, *The Play Movement and Its Significance* (New York: Macmillan, 1917); Luther H. Gulick, *A Philosophy of Play* (New York and Boston: Scribners, 1920); Joseph R. Fulk, *The Municipalization of Play and Recreation* (University Place, Nebr.: McGrath, 1922); Clarence E. Rainwater, *The Play Movement in the United States* (Chicago: University of Chicago Press, 1922); Robert S. Lynd and Helen M. Lynd, *Middletown in Transition* (New York: Harcourt, Brace, 1937), pp. 248, 290–91, and see 220–25; Bernard Mergen, "The Discovery of Children's Play," *American Quarterly* 27 (1975), pp. 399–420; and Dominick Cavallo, *Muscles and Morals: Organized Playgrounds and Urban Reform, 1880–1920* (Philadelphia: University of Pennsylvania Press, 1981).

On age-graded toys, see Miriam Brubaker, "A Century of Progress in Toys," *Childhood Education* 10 (1934), pp. 177–80; Marion L. Faegre, "Playthings That Help Children Grow," *Ladies Home Journal* (Dec. 1933), p. 36; "Puzzled Parents Offered a 5-Year Toy Plan," *Business Week* 60 (Nov. 18, 1931), p. 8; "The Merchant to the Child," *Fortune* 4 (Nov. 1931), pp. 108–10; and Elizabeth F. Boettiger, *Children's Play, Indoors and Out* (New York: E.P. Dutton, 1938). On playground equipment, see the issue on "Play and Play Materials," *Child Study* 10 (Dec. 1932); "Progress in Public Recreation, 1909–1929," *Playground and Recreation* 24 (April 1930), p. 59; Virginia W. Marx, "Play Equipment That Keeps Children Outdoors," *Parents Magazine* 8 (April 1933), pp. 28, 48; and see note 78, below.

42. On children and eur(h)ythmy, see Ernest Groves and Gladys H. Groves, *Wholesome Childhood* (Boston: Houghton Mifflin, 1924), pp. 10–11; Lawrence P. Jacks, *Education through Recreation* (New York: Harper, 1932), p. 60; Grace L. Enders, "The Place of Dalcroze Eurhythmics in Physical Education," in *Dance: A Basic Educational Technique*, ed. Frederick R. Rogers (New York: Macmillan, 1941), pp. 268–82; and Fanny E. Lawrence, "Rhythm in the Nursery School," *American Childhood* 13 (Nov. 1927), pp. 31–32. Physical culturists in England had been particularly impressed by Jaques-Dalcroze methods: see the *Hibbert Journal*, esp. A Headmistress, "An Experience in Educating the Mind through the Body," 31 (Jan. 1933), pp. 217–23.

Walter Damrosch, American conductor, opera director and, from 1927, music counselor for the National Broadcasting Company, wrote (in a foreword to Jo Pennington's *The Importance of Being Rhythmic* [New York: Putman, 1925], p. iv) that if Jaques-Dalcroze's teachings "were accepted and taught to the children of the entire world it would effect a revolution, and a finer, a nobler race would be the result." Meanwhile, Rudolf Bode, early student of Jaques-Dalcroze and avid reader of the works of Ludwig Klages, was developing a spiritual-nationalist theory of gymnastics, based upon rhythm, which lay behind much of the Nazi preoccupation with physical culture. See Rudolf Bode, *Expression-Gymnastics*, trans. S. Forthal and E. Waterman (New York: A. S. Barnes, 1931 [1922]), pp. 11–48; and Hans E. Schröder, *Der Rhythmus als Erzieher: Festschrift zum 60. Geburtstag von Rudolf Bode* (Berlin-Lichterfelde: Widukind-Verlag, 1941).

43. Ruth Faison Shaw, *Finger Painting: A Perfect Medium for Self-Expression* (Boston: Little, Brown, 1934), pp. 14, 22, 30–32, 38. See also Edward A. Jewell, "Children's Finger Paintings, Shown at McClelland's, Present Striking Method of Training," *New York Times* (March 11, 1933), 16:2; G. G. Telfer, "Fingers Were Made before Brushes," *Horn Book* 10 (1934), pp. 313–15; "Finger Painting," *Fortune* 11 (May 1935), p. 52; and Ilse Forest, *The School for the Child from Two to Eight* (Boston and New York: Ginn, 1935), p. 163.

44. Hillel Schwartz, "The Zipper and the Child," in Norman Cantor and Nathalia King, eds., *Notebooks in Cultural Analysis* (Durham, N.C.: Duke University Press, 1985), vol. 2, pp. 1–31. I thank Duke University Press for allowing me to draw liberally from this essay.

45. Marey, author of *La Machine animale* (Paris, 1873) and of *Movement*, trans. Eric Pritchard (New York, 1895 [1894]), was president of the French Commission of Gymnastics and advocate of exercises based on a Swedish rather than a military model. He also worked on the recording of motion tracks on revolving cylinders and designed the first convenient sphygmograph for recording pulse waves in reading blood pressure. This work, combined with investigations by physiologists, served as the basis for another technological innovation paradigmatic of both the expressive and operative aspects of the new kinaesthetic — the polygraph or "lie detector," whose capacity for truth-telling rested squarely upon presumptions that those (im)pulses coming from the center of the body cannot lie, and that arrhythmic (im)pulses in response to questions must indicate a central disturbance or constipation otherwise identifiable as deceit. See François Dagognet, *Etienne-Jules Marey: A Passion for the Trace*, trans. Robert Galeta (New York: Zone Books, forthcoming); Christopher Lawrence, "Physiological Apparatus in the Wellcome Museum: 1. The Marey Sphygmograph," *Medical History* 22 (1978), pp. 196–200; Matthew N. Chappell, "Blood Pressure Changes in Deception," *Archives of Psychology* 105 (1929); Leonarde Keeler, "A Method for Detecting Deception," *American Journal*

of Police Science 1 (1930), pp. 38–51; and John A. Larson with George W. Henry and Leonarde Keeler, *Lying and Its Detection* (Chicago: University of Chicago Press, 1932).

46. Cora Linn Daniels, "Delsarte Philosophy at Lunch," *The Voice* 6 (Dec. 1884), p. 207.

47. On changes in "speech" education, see Joseph C. Frobisher, *A New and Practical System of the Culture of Voice and Action* (New York, 1868), pp. 123–32, which still lists positions for the passions; discussions in the trade journal, *The Voice*, esp. Thomas M. Balliet, "Delsarte Philosophy a Branch of Aesthetics," 5 (May 1883), p. 71, and Sarah L. Arnold, "The Delsarte Gymnastics in the Public Schools," 9 (1887), p. 175; E. N. Kirby, *Vocal and Action-Language* (Boston, 1888), pp. 123–26; T. Earl Pardoe, "Language of the Body," *Quarterly Journal of Speech Education* 9 (1923), pp. 252–57; Giles W. Gray, "Problems in the Teaching of Gesture," ibid. 10 (1924), pp. 238–52; and Dale Carnegie, *Public Speaking and Influencing Men in Business*, p. 242 (for quote).

48. See Edward Shorter, "Paralysis: The Rise and Fall of a 'Hysterical' Symptom," *Journal of Social History* 19 (1986), pp. 549–82, which concentrates on disorders of gait; Jeffrey M. Masson, ed. and trans., *The Complete Letters of Sigmund Freud to Wilhelm Fliess, 1887–1904* (Cambridge, Mass.: Belknap Press, 1985), pp. 22n–23n (for quote and discussion); Joseph Breuer and Sigmund Freud, *Studies in Hysteria*, trans. A. A. Brill (Boston: Beacon, 1937 [1895]), p. 65 (for quote); and Monique David-Menard, *L'Hystérique entre Freud et Lacan: Corps et langage en psychanalyse* (Paris: Editions Universitaires, 1983), pp. 9, 16. Compare Pierre Janet, *The Major Symptoms of Hysteria* (2d ed., New York: Hafner, 1965 [1907, 1920]), noting that hysteric patients coming out of a somnambulistic state would often "indulge in some odd and perfectly regular gymnastics" (p. 121).

49. John C. Burnham, "The Mind–Body Problem in the Early Twentieth Century," *Perspectives in Biology and Medicine* 20 (1977), pp. 271–84; Charles H. Woolbert, *The Fundamentals of Speech* (rev. ed., New York: Harper, 1927 [1920]); and George H. Mead, *Mind, Self and Society from the Standpoint of a Social Behaviorist*, ed. Charles W. Morris (Chicago: University of Chicago Press, 1934).

50. I am heavily indebted here to Paul C. Rodgers, Jr., "Alexander Bain and the Rise of the Organic Paragraph," *Quarterly Journal of Speech* 51 (1965), pp. 399–408; and Ned A. Shearer, "Alexander Bain and the Genesis of Paragraph Theory," ibid. 58 (1972), pp. 408–17. For the English publisher Harmsworth, see Reginald Pound and Geoffrey Harmsworth, *Northcliffe* (New York: Praeger, 1959), pp. 264–67.

51. John S. Hart, *A Manual of Composition and Rhetoric* (Philadelphia, 1874 [1870]); John F. Genung, *Outlines of Rhetoric* (Boston, 1893), p. 221; Charles Sears Baldwin, *A College Manual of Rhetoric* (New York: Longmans, Green, 1902), pp. 9, 10; and William D. Lewis and James F. Hosic, *Practical English for High Schools* (New York: American Book, 1916), pp. 29, 30.

52. William L. Davidson, "Bain, Alexander," *Encyclopaedia Britannica* (11th ed., 1922), vol. 3, pp. 221–22; Alexander Bain, "On Toys," *Westminster Review* 37 (1842), pp. 97–121 (quotes at pp. 97, 98); and idem, *Mind and Body* (New York, 1873 [1872]), p. 196, also quoted in Jagdish N. Hattiangadi, "Bain, Alexander," *Dictionary of Scientific Biography* (New York: Scribners, 1970), vol. 1, pp. 403–404. On Bain's connections to physical culture through psychophysiology, see Bruce Haley, *The Healthy Body and Victorian Culture*

(Cambridge, Mass.: Harvard University Press, 1978), pp. 37–44.

53. Bain, *Mind and Body*, p. 2; and H. N. MacCracken and Helen E. Sandison, *Manual of Good English* (New York: Macmillan, 1917), pp. 143, 147.

54. Fried, *Theatricality and Absorption*, pp. 78–79, 82 and 208 (for quote from Grimm); and Sarah Annie Frost (Shields), *The Book of Tableaux and Shadow Pantomimes* (New York, 1869), pp. 9, 11, 12, 24–27, 37, 65–66, 111, 146.

55. Thomas Leabhart, *Modern and Post-Modern Mime* (New York: St. Martin's Press, 1989), pp. 4–6; Paul Hugounet, *Mimes et pierrots* (Paris, 1889), p. 47ff.; and Paul Sheridan, *Penny Theatres of Victorian London* (London: Dobson, 1981), esp. p. 23, on twenty-minute abridgments of *Hamlet, MacBeth, Richard III, Othello,* which must have been done primarily through large, stereotyped gesticulation, similar to photographic stereotypes — for which, see *An Album of Stereographs, Or, "Our Country Victorious and Now a Happy Home,"* from the Collections of William Culp Darrah and Richard Russack (Garden City, N.Y.: Doubleday, 1977).

56. Paul Hippeau, "Etude sur la pantomime," in Gaspard and Charles Deburau, *Pantomimes*, trans. Emile Goby (Paris, 1889), pp. xiii–xxxi; Jean Dorcy, *The Mime*, trans. Robert Speller and Pierre de Fontnouvelle (New York: R. Speller, 1961), p. 36; and Jules Fleury, *Souvenirs et portraits de jeunesse* (Geneva: Slatkine Reprints, 1970 [1872]), pp. 64–65 — my own (free) translation.

57. Charles Aubert, *The Art of Pantomime*, trans. Edith Sears (New York: Holt, 1970 [1901]), pp. 8, 9, 10–13, 96, 153.

58. Leabhart, *Modern and Post-Modern Mime*, ch. 1 (quote on p. 26); and Frederick Brown, *Theater and Revolution: The Culture of the French Stage* (New York: Viking Press, 1980), ch. 6.

59. Etienne Decroux, *Words on Mime*, trans. Mark Piper from 2d French ed. (Claremont, Calif.: Claremont College, 1985 [1977]), pp. 4, 26–27, 38, 39, 68, 94, 126.

60. Ibid., p. 4; and Brown, *Theater and Revolution*, pp. 436–37 (quote from Carné on pp. 436–37).

61. Jean-Louis Barrault, *Reflections on the Theater*, trans. Barbara Wall (London: Rockliff, 1951), pp. 24, 26, 114; and Brown, *Theater and Revolution*, ch. 11.

62. Leabhart, *Modern and Post-Modern Mime*, p. 63 (for quote). Leabhart, in his chapter (4) on Marcel Marceau, astutely points out that his Bip, created in 1947, returns him to the nineteenth century of classical vignettes performed on a footlit stage, but it is still the case that Marceau's "objective mime" makes use of the torso in a manner fully informed by the new kinaesthetic.

63. G. Stanley Hall, "Gesture, Mimesis, Types of Temperament, and Movie Pedagogy," *Pedagogical Seminary* 28 (1921), pp. 171–201; Gregorio Marañon, "The Psychology of Gesture," *Journal of Nervous and Mental Disease* 112 (1950 [article written before 1939]), pp. 469–97; Kendall, *Where She Danced*, ch. 8; and Lynd and Lynd, *Middletown in Transition*, pp. 260–63.

64. See A. Nicholas Vardac, *Stage to Screen* (Cambridge, Mass.: Harvard University Press, 1949), esp. ch. 11; and Anne Hollander, *Seeing through Clothes* (New York: Viking Press, 1978), pp. 339–44. On streamlining, see Donald J. Bush, *The Streamlined Decade* (New York: Braziller, 1975).

65. For a concise survey, see E. Muirhead Little, "Modern Artificial Limbs and Their Influence upon

Methods of Amputation," *British Medical Journal* (Oct. 27, 1917), pp. 550–55.

66. "Jambe de bois," *Encyclopédie, ou dictionnaire raisonné des sciences, des arts et des métiers* (Paris, 1751–80), vol. 8, p. 442; Vernon R…, "In Pursuit of the Wooden Leg," *New Statesman* (Nov. 9, 1918), pp. 111–12; and Margaret Doody, "If a Body Meet a Body," *University Publishing* 3 (winter 1978), pp. 1–2, 14 (with quotations from Hood).

67. Julius Hoffmann, "Phantom Limb Syndrome: A Critical Review of the Literature," *Journal of Nervous and Mental Disease* 119 (1954), pp. 261–70; G. Murdoch, "Amputation Revisited," *Prosthetics and Orthotics International* 8 (1984), pp. 8–15; George E. Marks, *Manual of Artificial Limbs…An Exhaustive Exposition of Prosthesis* (New York: A. A. Marks, 1905), pp. 20, 59, 188, 241 and passim.

68. Marks, *Manual of Artificial Limbs*, pp. 179–80, 265, 272; "Marks, Amasa A.," *National Cyclopaedia of American Biography* (New York: James T. White, 1901), vol. 11, p. 386.

69. Marks, *Manual of Artificial Limbs*, pp. 16–20, 25, 32–33, 59, 141–42, 149, 152 (for quote), 185–86.

70. Ibid., p. 181; and "Man and His Machines: Ingenious Devices by Which Men Injured in the War Are Being Rendered Capable of Doing Useful Work," *World's Work* 36 (June 1918), pp. 221–24.

71. See C. A. van Peursen, *Body, Soul, Spirit*, trans. Hubert H. Hoskins (London: Oxford University Press, 1966), pp. 120–41, on bodiliness, as also F. J. J. Buytendijk, *Prolegomena to an Anthropological Physiology*, trans. Anneke J. Orr (Pittsburgh: Duquesne University Press, 1974), pp. 3, 46, 53, 228–41.

72. I borrow this distinction from Eleanor Metheny, *Connotations of Movement in Sport and Dance* (Dubuque, Iowa: W. C. Brown, 1965), pp. 58–60. The distinction is occasionally implicit in the work of Marx, Canguilhem, Foucault and Baudrillard, but these philosophers are no éminences grises to this essay; their concerns have been generally metacorporeal, whereas I have been trying to close in on our bodies themselves. See however, Bryan S. Turner, *The Body and Society* (Oxford: Basil Blackwell, 1984) for Marx, Foucault and Freud on the body.

73. There have been fewer studies of kinecepts than of kinestructs, and fewer still of relationships between kinecepts, kinestructs and technology. On kinestructs, see especially Joann Kealiinohomoku, "Hopi and Polynesian Dance," *Ethnomusicology* 11 (1967), pp. 343–57; Ray L. Birdwhistell, *Kinesis and Context: Essays on Body Motion Communication* (Philadelphia: University of Pennsylvania Press, 1970); Gregory Bateson, *Steps to an Ecology of Mind* (San Francisco: Chandler, 1972), pp. 107–27; Martha Davis, *Towards Understanding the Intrinsic in Body Movement* (New York: Arno Press, 1975); Jonathan Benthall and Ted Polhemus, eds., *The Body as a Medium of Expression* (London: Allen Lane, 1975); Stephen Kern, *Anatomy and Destiny: A Cultural History of the Human Body* (Indianapolis: Bobbs-Merrill, 1975); and "Le Corps… entre illusions et savoirs," *Esprit* series 2.2 (Feb. 1982).

Studies of kinecepts have generally remained within psychological frameworks, beginning notably with Wilhelm Reich, *Character Analysis* (New York: Orgone Institute Press, 1949 [1933]), but see also Geoffrey Gorer, "The Function of Different Dance Forms in Primitive African Communities," *Salmagundi* 33/34 (spring/summer 1976 [1935]), pp. 175–92; Margaret Mead, "The Swaddling Hypothesis: Its Reception," *American Anthropologist* 56 (1954), pp. 395–409; Gordon W. Hewes, "The Anthropology of Posture,"

Scientific American 196 (Feb. 1957), pp. 123–32; Peggy Harper, "Dance in Nigeria," *Ethnomusicology* 13 (1969), pp. 280–95; Robert F. Thompson, *African Art in Motion: Icon and Art* (Los Angeles: University of California Press, 1974); Georges Vigarello, *Le Corps redressé: Histoire d'un pouvoir pédagogique* (Paris: Delarge, 1978), a chapter of which, "Les Préalables de la civilité," trans. by Ughetta Lubin as "The Upward Training of the Body from the Age of Chivalry to Courtly Civility," in *Zone 4, Fragments for a History of the Human Body*, pt. 2, ed. Michel Feher with Ramona Naddaff and Nadia Tazi (1989), pp. 148–99; and a very provocative article by Jerre Levy and Marylou Reid, "Variations in Writing Posture and Cerebral Organization," *Science* 194 (1976), pp. 337–39.

Three valuable methodological discussions are Marcel Mauss, "Techniques of the Body" (1934), reprinted in this volume, pp. 454–479; Franz Boas, ed., *The Function of Dance in Human Society* (New York: Boas School, 1944), pp. 17–18, 46–52; and Luc Boltanski, "Les Usages sociaux du corps," *Annales: Economies, sociétés, civilisations* 26 (1971), pp. 205–33.

On the relationship of kinecept, kinestruct and technology, see Siegfried Giedion, *Mechanization Takes Command* (New York: Oxford University Press, 1948); André Leroi-Gourhan, *Le Geste et la parole*, 2 vols. (Paris: A. Michel, 1964–65); Alan Lomax et al., *Folk Song Style and Culture* (Washington, D.C.: American Association for the Advancement of Science, 1968); Edward T. Hall, *The Hidden Dimension* (Garden City, N.Y.: Doubleday, 1969); Edmund Carpenter, *Oh What a Blow That Phantom Gave Me!* (New York: Holt, Rinehart and Winston, 1973); and Stephen Kern, *The Culture of Time and Space, 1880–1918* (Cambridge, Mass.: Harvard University Press, 1983), ch. 5 (on speed).

This paper has neglected the contributions of art historians as it has skirted the intricate problems of the visual arts and architecture in relationship to the new kinaesthetic. A provocative entry point, given the concern here with pedagogy, is Edgar Kaufmann, Jr., "'*Form* Became *Feeling*,' a New View of Froebel and Wright," *Journal of the Society of Architectural Historians* 402 (1981), pp. 130–33.

74. Dudley Sargent, "Useful Dancing from the Standpoint of Physical Training," *Educational Bi-Monthly* 3 (1909), p. 194. Similar statements appeared in Gustav Stickley, "The Relation of Dancing to a Commercial Age," *The Craftsman* 26 (1914), p. 241; Hugh Hartshorne, *Childhood and Character* (Boston: The Pilgrim Press, 1919), pp. 205–206; and more recently in Eugen Weber, "Gymnastics and Sports in Fin-de-Siècle France: Opium of the Classes?" *American Historical Review* 76 (1971), pp. 70–98. The complex relationships between fashions in social dancing and the development of the new kinaesthetic (from the waltz on) must be left unexamined here, but for comparison see a fine study by Adrienne L. Kaeppler, "Preservation and Evolution of Form and Function in Two Types of Tongan Dance," in Genevieve A. Highland et al., *Polynesian Culture History* (Honolulu: Bishop Museum Press, 1967), pp. 503–36; and a provocative work by Julie M. Taylor, "Tango: Theme of Class and Nation," *Ethnomusicology* 20 (1976), pp. 273–91. On adolescence, technology and kinecepts, see Erik H. Erikson, "Environment and Virtues," in Gyorgy Kepes, ed., *Arts of the Environment* (New York: Braziller, 1972), pp. 74, 76.

75. There is a growing literature concerning notions of competitive sport as critical to the shaping, principally, of male character. The literature generally centers upon the Baron de Coubertin's speech at a dinner

at the 1894 Congress he organized to reestablish the Olympic Games: "In the last resort, man is not composed of two parts, body and soul, but of three: body, mind, and character; it is not the mind that forms the character, but principally the body" (quotation from Peter C. McIntosh, *Sport in Society* [London: C. A. Watts, 1963], p. 91). Rarely, however, do the scholarly works deal with changes in the *quality* of movement in various sports — as, for example and most noticeably, in professional boxing with the turn-of-the-century advent of the corkscrew punch, the redirected aim at the solar plexus and an emphasis upon ambidexterity and a flexible rather than a stolid body — all compatible with the new kinaesthetic (see, e.g., Robert Cantwell, *The Real McCoy: The Life and Times of Norman Selby* [Princeton: Auerbach Publishers, 1971], early chs.). Nor do these works assess the enduring kinceptual import of the rise of basketball, volleyball and other essentially twentieth-century street or beach sports which, to oversimplify, have encouraged a sense of dynamic balance and a mastery of torsion.

76. More than twenty years ago, cultural anthropologist Robert F. G. Spier argued that work posture was not absolutely "tool bound," and that tools were more often fitted to habitual cultural postures than vice versa — in other words, that technology was not necessarily the prime determinant of kincept. See his "Work Habits, Postures and Fixtures," in Carroll L. Riley and Walter W. Taylor, eds., *American Historical Anthropology: Essays in Honor of Leslie Spier* (Carbondale: Southern Illinois University, 1967), pp. 197–220.

77. Selden, *Elements of the Free Dance*, pp. 54–85.

78. See Mary S. Shafer, *Rhythms for Children* (New York: A. S. Barnes, 1938 [1921]); Sies, *Spontaneous and Supervised Play in Childhood*; Marsh and Marsh, *The Dance in Education*; and advertisement for the jungle gym, patented 1923, in *Parents Magazine* 6 (July 1931), p. 54. Slides, first as boards and later as mass-produced metal forms, were scarcely mentioned as playground equipment until the twenties. The model playgrounds of 1895 to 1900, for example, contained many swings but no slides. See Johnson, *Education by Play and Games*, pp. 94–95, with rare picture of "An Artificial Slide"; Henry S. Curtis, *Play and Recreation for the Open Country* (Boston and New York: Ginn, 1914), pp. 19, 46, encouraging the use of slides sold by Marshall Field and Co. — not available from the Sears Roebuck or Montgomery Ward catalogues until the mid-twenties; and Ilse Forest, *The School for the Child from Two to Eight*, pp. 143–44: "Slides of various heights have of recent years become a familiar bit of lower-school equipment. They are always great favorites. Fairly durable and not overwhelmingly expensive, they are perhaps the best single gymnasium equipment for children from two to five years old."

79. Margaret B. Owen, *The Secret of Typewriting Speed* (Chicago: Forbes, 1917); Shaw, *Finger Painting*, pp. 136–38, on Leona Clarkson Grugan's stroking of the piano keys; Harriette Brower, *Piano Mastery: Talks with Master Pianists and Teachers* (New York: Frederick A. Stokes, 1915), pp. 49–51 (Leginska), 87–89 (Matthay); Tobias Matthay, *Muscular Relaxation Studies* (London and New York: Bosworth, 1908), esp. pp. 5, 65; Theodore Widmer, "Have We Lost Something through Over-Relaxation in Piano Study?" *Etude* 50 (Nov. 1932), p. 775; Josef Lhevine, *Basic Principles in Pianoforte Playing* (New York: Dover, 1972 [1924]), p. 29 (on Anton Rubinstein); Beryl Rubinstein, *Outline of Piano Pedagogy* (rev. ed., New York: C. Fisher, 1947 [1929]), p. 21; Frank Merrick, *Practising the Piano* (London, 1958), p. 68; Abby Whiteside, *Indispensables*

of Piano Playing (New York, 1961 [1955]), pp. 3, 14–16; and see József Gát, *The Technique of Piano Playing* (3d ed., London: Collet's, 1965) for the "swing stroke" and a history of gymnastic exercises preparatory to piano playing. I thank Steve Prussing for his help here.

80. Quotations from Richard Harmond, "Progress and Flight: An Interpretation of the American Cycle Craze of the 1890s," *Journal of Social History* 5 (1971–72), pp. 242, 247. See also David Rubinstein, "Cycling in the 1890s," *Victorian Studies* 21 (1977), pp. 47–71.

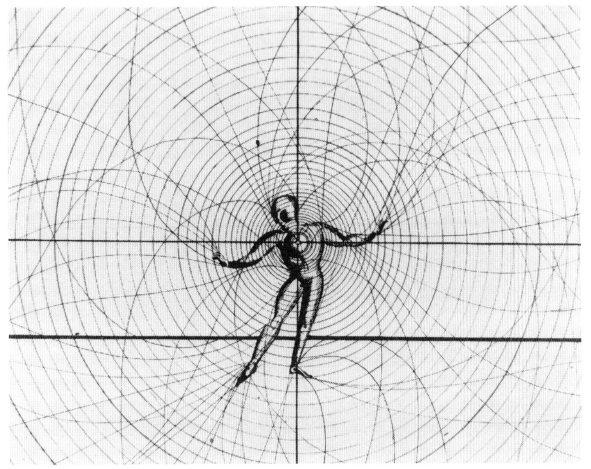

Drawing by Oskar Schlemmer.

Nonorganic Life

Manuel DeLanda

According to Thomas Kuhn's well-known theory, scientific revolutions are triggered by a "paradigm-induced gestalt switch." A traditional way of conducting scientific research is replaced by a new one (a new paradigm is implemented), and scientists come to perceive phenomena that previously were "invisible." Kuhn gives the Copernican revolution as one example of such a shift. Unlike Chinese astronomers, who had been able to observe the occurrence of sunspots centuries before Galileo simply because their cosmological beliefs did not preclude celestial change, early Western astronomers were unable to "see" changes in the cosmos. Sunspots, for example, remained "invisible" — that is, insignificant and anomalous — until Copernicus's ideas changed the ways in which European astronomers could look at the heavens.[1]

The last thirty years have witnessed a similar paradigm shift in scientific research. In particular, a centuries-old devotion to "conservative systems" (physical systems that, for all practical purposes, are isolated from their surroundings) is giving way to the realization that most systems in nature are subject to flows of matter and energy that continuously move through them. This apparently simple paradigm switch is, in turn, allowing us to discern phenomena that, a few decades ago, were, if they were noticed at all, dismissed as anomalies.

For example, when we approach systems as if they were conservative — that is, artificially isolate them (experimentally or analytically) from ambient fluxes of energy and matter — we are led to expect that these systems will eventually reach a point of steady-state equilibrium. However, when we acknowledge that these fluxes necessarily flow through the system, a new possibility emerges — a *dynamic* equilibrium. One of the most striking examples of this is the spontaneous assembly of a "chemical clock." In a "normal" chemical reaction, the interacting molecules simply collide randomly, transforming one another when the energy generated by their collisions passes a certain threshold. If we imagine the substances involved as, say, "red" and "blue," we would expect their random interactions to result in a "violet" mixture. Indeed, a conservative model would almost certainly preclude any other expectation.

Reality, however, is full of surprises: under certain conditions, some chemical reactions behave in a most counterintuitive way. The reactants, rather than reaching a steady-state equilibrium (a violet mixture), suddenly turn completely red, then blue, and back to red, according to a perfectly regular rhythm. In order to perform such a feat, the billions of interacting molecules must somehow act in concert, since only by coordinating their movements could they produce rhythmic motions with such precision. According to the old paradigm, this spontaneous "cooperation" among molecules was so unlikely that, until very recently, it was thought to defy the laws of classical thermodynamics. Indeed, while the reign of the previous paradigm lasted, such chemical clocks were for all practical purposes invisible:

> [The chemical clock effect was] first reported in 1921 by William Bray, in the decomposition of hydrogen peroxide into water and oxygen, with an iodine catalyst. But chemists then believed — wrongly — that the laws of thermodynamics forbid oscillations. Instead of following up Bray's discovery, they concentrated on explaining it away, on the grounds that his experimental method must have been at fault — an attitude that set them back nearly forty years. In 1958 the Russian chemist B. P. Belousov observed periodic oscillations in the colour of a [chemical reaction]. Ilya Prigogine had by then shown that far from thermodynamic equilibrium, the usual laws of thermodynamics don't hold, and people were more prepared to take the results seriously.[2]

In a sense, we could say that the contributions of Prigogine and others have made visible this and other self-organizing chemical reactions. What were formerly rare phenomena, irritants to be explained away, began, under the new paradigm, to appear everywhere and in every form:

> Only a few years ago a chemical reaction was supposed to have a decent reaction order and not much more. But now, such a reaction is of low standing if it does not include a few of the following items among its properties: bifurcations, bistability, catastrophe, chaos, dissipative structures, echo waves, multistability oscillations, superchaos, symmetry breaks, trigger waves, etc. Our fascination with such phenomena in chemical systems is due to the fact that we believe they are the fundamental elements of dynamics which may integrate to form life.[3]

The spontaneous emergence of temporal patterns (chemical clocks) or spatial patterns (chemical waves and spirals) has many profound consequences for theories of evolution. These phenomena could elucidate how the right conditions for the emergence of life came about in the so-called primeval soup. Prigogine, for instance, calls attention to the special thermodynamic conditions necessary for the emergence of order out of chaos. At equilibrium, he says, matter is blind, but in these "far-from-equilibrium" conditions, as he calls them, it becomes capable of "perceiving" weak gravitational and magnetic fields.[4]

In other words, at the onset of a process of self-organization (when a chemical clock begins to assemble, for example), the mechanisms involved become extremely sensitive to minor fluctuations in the environment. A small change in external conditions, one that in thermodynamic equilibrium would have had negligible consequences — caused perhaps by a relatively weak gravitational or magnetic field — is amplified and directs the kind of chemical clock that is assembled (the period of its oscillations, for example), thereby "naturally selecting" one self-assembly pattern over another. Thus, because of their extreme sensitivity to initial conditions, spontaneously emerging chemical patterns in the primeval soup could have become beneficiaries of the pruning process of a prebiotic natural selection.

This idea has been developed by Peter Decker, a German researcher of self-organizing phenomena. Decker calls any chemical system sensitive to small fluctuations during its self-assembly a "bioid," which he defines as an open system capable of generalized Darwinian evolution. Unlike the chemical reactions used by Prigogine as examples of self-organization, which have been criticized for the rather artificial conditions under which they occur,[5] Decker's could have *actually* occurred in certain reactions that were present in the primeval atmospheric conditions on Earth. The onset of one such reaction (the formal reaction) and the self-organizing processes to which it might have given rise represent, according to Decker, the acquisition of the very first bit of evolutionary information on the planet.[6]

Of course, the kind of information that may be generated by chemical oscillations is rather meager and repetitive when compared with even the most primitive organisms. Yet, according to other recent findings, the same systems that pulsate regularly under some conditions are, under other conditions, capable of oscillating in extremely intricate patterns. Because these patterns make the behavior of the chemical system essentially unpredictable, they have often been described as "chaotic." For our purposes, what matters is that these chaotic oscillations, under the right conditions, could have generated the complexity we observe in the living world. Prigogine, for example, invites us to imagine a chaotic chemical reaction in which, at certain points, some of the chemicals precipitate or diffuse outside the reaction space. If we also imagine that these chemicals accumulate on a "tape" — some kind of natural storage device, like a self-replicating macromolecule — the spatial patterns generated will be as asymmetric and information-rich as those we observe in organic life.[7]

Another class of self-organizing phenomena, very different from those just discussed but also instrumental in reshaping how we understand the richness of expression of the material world, is called "solitary waves." Differing from ordinary waves in that they do not quickly dissipate as they move, they maintain their shape for a relatively long period of time. When, as happens, a solitary wave maintains its exact identity after interacting with other waves, it becomes a "soliton."[8] As with chemical oscillations, various forms of this phenomenon have been observed for a long time — over a century and a half — but they were relegated to the realm of anomalies. The first person to study these phenomena was John Scott Russell, a Scottish engineer and ship designer. In 1834, he witnessed the spontaneous emergence of a soliton in the surface of a canal near Edinburgh, and after chasing the coherent mass of water for several miles, he became convinced he had seen something extremely important. But science was not ready for this discovery, even though a mathematical explanation for it was available as early as 1892 (the Kortweg–de Vries equation).[9] As the components of a new scientific paradigm began to consolidate in the 1960s, solitons were recognized everywhere. In the ocean, for instance, they are called "tsunamis":

> Tsunamis are formed when a strong seismic shock occurs in the ocean floor. The wave, only a few inches or feet high, can travel intact across the ocean for many thousands of miles.... The human problem begins when the tsunami reaches the continental shelf. In shallower waters, nonlinear effects at the sea bed act to shorten the wavelength of the wave and increase its height. The result is awesome. From a soliton a few inches or feet high, the tsunami becomes a 100-foot mountain of water crashing into coasts and harbors. The tsunami that killed thousands in Lisbon in 1775 caused many writers in the age of Enlightenment to question the existence of a benevolent God. In 1702 a tsunami in Japan drowned over 100,000 people, and in the seismic soliton created by the volcanic explosion of Krakatoa Island in 1882 thousands died.[10]

Solitons can occur at much greater scales than tsunamis. In the atmosphere of Jupiter, for instance, there exists a soliton (the famous Red Eye) with a diameter roughly equal to the distance from the Earth to the Moon. On the other hand, solitons have also been found at extremely small scales: for example, this is the way in which electrons traveling through solid objects form charge-density waves. Indeed, *anything* that flows in regular waves (electricity, sound, heat, light) can give rise to solitons. Not surprisingly, the laws of classical thermodynamics would seem to forbid such coherent waves from arising spontaneously: if a given amount of energy is introduced into a flowing medium, the energy should diffuse evenly throughout the components of the medium. And indeed, this *does* normally happen; but in special circumstances, the energy can form into a pulselike wave and retain its

Zinc oxide smoke.

coherent identity over time — and in some cases, even after collisions with other solitons.

Chemical clocks (periodic and chaotic) and solitons exist within our bodies. An important chemical reaction in our own metabolism, which serves to transform glucose into useful energy (glycolysis), has been shown to generate spontaneously rhythmic oscillations.[11] Chaotic oscillations, on the other hand, occur in neural activity associated with the control of the heartbeat and the secretion of some hormones. (Apparently, nonperiodic oscillations are more adaptable and flexible than rigidly periodic ones, lending them, perhaps, a functional advantage.[12]) Solitons, for their part, are helpful in understanding how energy is conveyed throughout the human body: since regular waves dissipate their energy too rapidly to be of any metabolic use, coherent pulses that maintain their identity could explain how energy produced in one part of the body fuels processes in another, distant part. Solitons traveling along the "backbone" of certain proteins could be the answer to this puzzle.[13] Similarly, electrical signals travel through the nervous system too fast to be accounted for by the traditional understanding of "incoherent" waves; thus, solitons have been proposed as the most likely mechanism for neural signal transmission, and in this regard they have been described as constituting the "elementary particles of thought."[14] In short, it seems that our bodies are inhabited as much by the phenomena of "nonorganic life" as by the more familiar phenomena of organic life.

Chaos and solitons have become the yin and yang of the new physics.[15] At one extreme, there are relatively simple systems (a chemical clock, a mechanical pendulum), which can generate bewilderingly complex behavior; at the other, there are extremely complicated systems (oceanic and atmospheric motion), which can generate simple and coherent structures (pulselike solitons, or more generally, fronts, shock waves and bubbles). When the two are combined — by adding "friction" to a soliton-bearing equation, for instance — the result is the formation and competition of spatial patterns of great complexity and beauty. Indeed, what the study of chaos and solitons was to the 1980s, the study of pattern formation may be to the 1990s.[16] What is important for our purposes, though, is that both periodic and nonperiodic oscillations and coherent structures are among the unexpected possible behaviors of "inert" matter, behaviors of which we have only recently become aware. Matter, it turns out, can "express" itself in complex and creative ways, and our awareness of this must be incorporated into any future materialist philosophy.

One may well wonder why it has taken so long for these material effects to be recognized. Of the many possible explanations, one undoubtedly deserves special mention: our "mathematical technology" was simply incapable of modeling self-organizing phenomena. The kind

of equation most abundant in science (both classical and quantum), the
"linear" equation, is extremely useful for modeling physical systems —
not so much because this mathematical form captures all the relevant
aspects of behavior, but because it provides a workable approximation,
easily solved, and thus adequate in its predictive ability. Nonlinear equations, on the other hand, were not so easily solved, at least not before
the advent of digital computers; even if they gave us a more realistic
representation of reality, they were useless for practical applications. As
a result, nonlinearities (like friction and air drag) were eliminated as
much as possible from mathematical models, making nonlinear effects
like chaos and solitons "invisible" (that is, visible only as anomalies to be
eliminated). According to one mathematician:

> So docile are linear equations, that classical mathematicians were willing to
> compromise their physics to get them. [Consequently,] the classical theory
> deals with shallow waves, low-amplitude vibrations, small temperature gra-
> dients [that is, eliminates nonlinearities]. So ingrained became the linear
> habit that by the 1940's and 1950's many scientists and engineers knew lit-
> tle else.... Linearity is a trap. The behaviour of linear equations...is far
> from typical [in nature]. But if you decide that only linear equations are
> worth thinking about, self-censorship sets in.... Your textbooks fill with
> triumphs of linear analysis, its failures buried so deep that the graves go
> unmarked and the existence of the graves goes unremarked. [17]

Thus, one of the main causes of the paradigm shift that has allowed
us to "see" matter as capable of self-organization is an advance in the
technology that materially supports mathematics, and with it mathematical technology. Needless to say, this will not be an overnight replacement, and much of science (classical and quantum) will remain
linear. But nonlinear science has begun to reveal new and startling facts
about matter, in particular, that the behavior of entirely different material systems can exhibit "universal features." Physicists, for example,
have known for some time that phase transitions in matter (from liquid
to solid, from magnetic to nonmagnetic, from conductor to supercon-
ductor) display a common mathematical structure despite the diversity
of their actual physical mechanisms. More recently, it was found that
the onset of turbulence in a flowing liquid (a self-organizing process) is
also closely related to such phase transitions, as well as to the onset of
coherence in laser light. In a very important sense, then, all these transitions may be said to be "mechanism independent": one and the same
"mathematical mechanism" can account for all these events that would
seem otherwise to be wholly unrelated. [18]

Similarly, the onset of rhythmic behavior in a chemical reaction is
identical to many other processes in which equilibrium systems suddenly
begin to oscillate — a well-documented example is the spontaneous
aggregation of slime mold amoebas, in which one individual amoeba

functions as a "clock" that regulates the assembly of other separate cells into one large multicellular organism. Nonlinear oscillations have been observed in fields as diverse as electronics, economics and ecological relations (such as predator–prey systems). Soliton phenomena, as we saw, occur at every scale, from Jupiter's Red Eye to tsunamis, to atomic charge-density waves, and in every kind of energy flow (heat, light, sound). This startling universality of the mathematics of self-organization is one of the most revolutionary elements of these new theories:

> "There is no better, there is no more open door by which you can enter into the study of natural philosophy," Michael Faraday has written, "than by considering the physical phenomena of a candle." Although the wisdom of this remark lay unrecognized for well over a century, it is now rather widely understood that the study of nonlinear diffusion in a candle…is closely related to the dynamics of nerve impulse propagation, the spread of contagious disease, and the beating of the human heart…. The same equation that solid state physicists and electrical engineers use to describe the propagation of magnetic flux quanta (called "fluxons")…is also employed by theoretical physicists as a model for elementary particles. Similarly, the soliton on an optical fibre…is closely related to suggested mechanisms for the transport and storage of biological energy in protein.[19]

In mathematical terminology, the events at the onset of self-organization are called "bifurcations." Bifurcations are mutations that occur at critical points in the "balance of power" between physical forces — temperature, pressure, speed and so on — when new configurations become energetically possible, and matter spontaneously adopts them. It is as though "inert" matter, confronted with a problem stated in terms of a balance of forces, spontaneously generates a machinelike solution by drawing from a "reservoir" of abstract mathematical mechanisms. For instance, in the case of chemical self-organization, two distinct forces are at work: the rate at which the substances diffuse and the rate at which they react with each other. When the balance of power is dominated by diffusion, the result is a steady-state equilibrium, but the moment reaction rates begin to dominate, the chemical substances are suddenly confronted with a new problem, and they must respond to the challenge by adopting a configuration that meets the new energetic requirements. In this case, the new stable solution to the problem is to enter into an oscillatory equilibrium, and it is in this way that chemical clocks are born. But, again, more important than the self-assembly of these clocks is the fact that essentially the same solution is available to other systems, like populations of electronic circuits or of economic agents, which involve balances of power between forces of a completely different kind.

Gilles Deleuze and Félix Guattari have suggested that this abstract reservoir of machinelike solutions, common to physical systems as diverse as clouds, flames, rivers and even the phylogenetic lineages of living creatures, be called the "machinic phylum"[20] — a term that would indicate how nonlinear flows of matter and energy spontaneously generate machinelike assemblages when internal or external pressures reach a critical level, which only a very few abstract mechanisms can account for. In short, there is a single machinic phylum for all the different living and nonliving phylogenetic lineages.

The machinic phylum remained largely invisible until the advent of digital computers; or rather, considering how pervasive nonlinear behavior is throughout nature (it could hardly have escaped everyone's attention), we had to learn to recognize it.[21] Bifurcating sequences leading to complex behavior *had* been "observed" by mathematicians such as Henri Poincaré as early as the 1890s — although those early glimpses into the wild spaces of the machinic phylum horrified most who saw them. Those passing glimpses have, with the proliferation of computers in mathematical investigations (giving rise to "experimental mathematics"), opened onto vast landscapes — computer screens becoming our "windows" onto the machinic phylum in more than a figurative sense.

If computers have emerged as windows onto this world, it is because the nonlinear mathematical models of bifurcation processes can be given a visual representation, a "phase portrait." The first step in creating a phase portrait is to identify the relevant aspects of the behavior of the physical system to be modeled. It is impossible, for example, to model an oven by considering each and every atom of which it is composed, but one *can* consider the single aspect of the oven that matters: its temperature. Similarly, in modeling the behavior of a pendulum, only its velocity and position are important. In technical terms, the oven has "one degree of freedom," its change in temperature; the pendulum, in turn, has two degrees of freedom. A bicycle, on the other hand — taking into account the coordinated motion of its different parts (handlebars, front and back wheels, right and left pedals) — is a system with approximately ten degrees of freedom.

The next step is to create an abstract space (called "phase space") that has as many dimensions as the system to be modeled has degrees of freedom.[22] In this way, everything that matters about the system at any given moment in time can be condensed into a single point: a point in one-dimensional space (a line) for the oven, a point in two-dimensional space (a plane) for the pendulum or a point in ten-dimensional space for the bicycle. Moreover, as the system changes in time (the oven heats up or the bicycle makes a turn), this point in phase space will also change, thus describing a trajectory. This trajectory, in essence, will contain all the information that matters about the history of the modeled system. For example, if the system under study tends to oscillate between two extremes, like a driven pendulum, its trajectory in phase

Liquid crystals.

space will form a closed loop, which represents a system whose "movement" consists of a repetitive cycle. A free pendulum, on the other hand, which eventually comes to a standstill, appears in a phase portrait as a spiral. More complex systems will be represented by more complex trajectories in phase space.

Now, it is one thing to model a system with a set of equations, but quite another to solve those equations. Sometimes, when the equations modeling a system are so complex that they cannot be solved — that is, when they are nonlinear — scientists can nevertheless learn something about the system's behavior by looking at its phase portrait. They cannot make precise quantitative predictions about the system, but they can use the phase portrait to elicit qualitative insights about the general traits governing the system's long-term tendencies. In particular, there are certain special spots in phase space that tend to attract or repel all nearby trajectories; that is, regardless of where a trajectory begins, it will tend to drift toward certain points (called "attractors"), or to move away from certain others (called "repellors").

Because these trajectories represent the behavior of real physical systems, the attractors and repellors in a phase portrait represent the long-term tendencies of a system. For instance, a ball rolling downhill will always "seek" the lowest point. If it is pushed up a little, it will roll down to this lowest point again. Its phase portrait will contain a "point attractor": small fluctuations (the ball being pushed up a little) will move the trajectory (representing the ball) away from the attractor, but then the trajectory will naturally return to it. Other systems will have two point attractors or more. A well-made light switch, for example, whose resting states are "on" and "off," has two attractors — and if it is delicately set between them, chances are good that it will spontaneously snap into either position. Its phase portrait can't tell us *when* it will do so — that is, provide a precise quantitative prediction, which implies that the equation has been solved — but it can describe the system's long-term tendency to snap into one of its points of equilibrium. In fact, the specific form of the nonlinear equation modeling the system will reveal this before its specific trajectory has been calculated.

Attractors, though, do not necessarily appear as points. For example, an attractor with the shape of a closed loop (called a "periodic attractor" or "limit cycle") will force all trajectories passing nearby to wrap around it, to enter into an oscillating state, like a pendulum. If the phase portrait of a physical system has a periodic attractor embedded in it, we know that no matter how we manipulate the behavior of the system, it will tend toward an oscillation between two extremes.

These two attractors, points and closed loops, were the only types known before computer screens opened windows onto phase space. What followed was the discovery of a much wilder array of creatures inhabiting phase space: among them were attractors with strangely tangled shapes, called "strange" or "chaotic" attractors, representing turbulent behavior in nature, and the incredibly complex, chaotic boundaries separating "basins of attraction" (a simple attractor's sphere of influence in phase space). Far more startling, though, was the discovery that an attractor can spontaneously mutate into a different attractor. These spontaneous transformations are known as "bifurcations." For instance, a physical system that originally tended toward a steady-state equilibrium (a point attractor) can suddenly begin to oscillate between two extremes (a limit cycle); this would describe the self-assembly of a chemical clock. Spontaneous self-organization can take other forms as well: the onset of turbulence in a flowing liquid appears in phase space as a cascade of bifurcations that takes a circle (limit cycle) and, through successive doublings, transforms it into a strange attractor. Roughly, we could say that phenomena of self-organization occur whenever a bifurcation takes place: when a new attractor appears on the phase portrait of a system, or when the system's attractors mutate in kind.

We have, then, three distinct entities inhabiting phase space: specific trajectories (corresponding to systems in the actual world), attractors (corresponding to the long-term tendencies of these systems) and bifurcation events (corresponding to the emergence in these systems of new structural tendencies). Bifurcation events are brought about by changes in certain "control parameters," which represent the more or less constant conditions affecting physical objects; temperature, pressure, gravity and so on. As the value of a parameter shifts through certain ranges, the attractors of the physical system represented will usually change subtly; at certain critical points, though, a bifurcation will take place, and the attractors will transform themselves.

As I said earlier, because essentially the same attractors and bifurcations are available for many different physical systems, they may be seen as *virtual* or *abstract mechanisms* that are "incarnated" in different concrete physical mechanisms. This is not to say that attractors and bifurcations exist in some platonic realm waiting to be realized — rather, *they are intrinsic features of the dynamics of physical systems, and they have no independent existence outside of those physical systems.* Yet, attractors and bifurcations do constitute an abstract reservoir of resources available to nonlinear flows of matter and energy — a condition that applies as much to the beating of hearts as to earthquakes, flames and clouds, tsunamis and amoebas. And it is in this respect that I introduce the term "machinic phylum" to designate a single phylogenetic line cutting through *all* matter, "living" or "nonliving," a single source of spontaneous order for all of reality. More specifically, the attractors define the more or less stable and permanent features of this reality (its long-term tendencies), and bifurcations constitute its source of creativity and variability. Or to put it more philosophically, attractors are veritable "figures of destiny," for they define the future of many systems.

For instance, when the dynamics of a physical system are governed by a periodic attractor, it is as if the very flows of matter and energy rushing through the system were binding it, or destining it, to an oscillatory future. And yet, for several reasons, this iron-clad determinism should not be given too mechanistic an interpretation. For one thing, the phase portraits of most systems usually contain more than one attractor, which means that the system in question has a "choice" between several destinies. Then, there is the "freedom" built in to chaotic attractors. When a system's dynamics are caught in a strange attractor (deterministic chaos), that system is "bound to be creative," that is, to explore all the possibilities of a small region of phase space. Furthermore, even if we are destined to follow the attractors guiding our dynamical behavior, there are also bifurcations, critical points at which we may be able to change our destiny (that is, modify our long-term tendencies). And because minuscule fluctuations in the environment in which a bifurcation occurs may decide the exact nature of the resulting attractors, one can hardly conclude that all actions we undertake — as individuals or collectively — are irrelevant in the face of these deterministic forces. Bifurcations may not be a "guarantee of freedom," but they certainly do provide a means of experimenting with — and perhaps even modifying — our destinies:

> From the physicist's point of view this involves a distinction between states of the system in which all individual initiative is doomed to insignificance on one hand, and on the other, bifurcation regions in which an individual, an idea, or a new behaviour can upset the global state. Even in those regions, amplification obviously does not occur with just any individual, idea, or behaviour, but only with those that are "dangerous" — that is, those that can exploit to their advantage the nonlinear relations guaranteeing the stability of the preceding regime. Thus we are led to conclude that the same nonlinearities may produce an order out of the chaos of elementary processes and still, under different circumstances, be responsible for the destruction of the same order, eventually producing a new coherence beyond another bifurcation.[23]

Although attractors and bifurcations appear *only* in the phase portraits of systems that are "dissipative" (those in which energy is not conserved), even conservative systems show a partitioning of phase space into regions, some of which define systemic long-term tendencies. Such a phase space may be seen as an "energy landscape," with peaks and valleys that correspond to maxima and minima of free energy. These valleys serve as attractors in the sense that these systems will spontaneously adopt a physical configuration that minimizes the amount of free energy — in other words, their trajectories will tend toward low-energy valleys. Despite the important distinction between dissipative and conservative systems, in both cases a feature of their phase portraits constitutes a "figure of destiny" — and for that reason, I shall simply refer to these as "attractors."[24]

A similarly important distinction exists between equilibrium and nonequilibrium phase transitions. Although the former — illustrated by the transition from gaseous to liquid or to solid states of matter — is a bifurcation that involves the generation of a new energy landscape in phase space, the latter case — the transition from calm ("laminar") to turbulent flow in fluids — involves the creation of a new set of attractors. Again, though, in *both* cases a critical point in the balance of power between physical forces brings about the alteration of the system's long-term tendencies — and so I shall refer to both as "bifurcations." A more complete theory of the machinic phylum would have to address these issues in detail, but this rough picture of the mathematics of self-organization will suffice for our purposes here: defining the concept of nonorganic life and the theories that connect it to our own organic bodies.

Let us consider a few hypothetical scenarios of how "reality" as we know it could emerge from the interplay of attractors and bifurcations — in other words, how more or less permanent physical structures (from organisms to entire planets) could be created by the machinic phylum, by the "mere" nonlinear flow of matter and energy. Let's begin with an impossibly simple case, that of a "crystal planet" made entirely of a single element. We can imagine this planet as it exists at the moment of its birth, that is, as it precipitates from a protostar, a ball of superhot plasma (which at a very high temperature is an electrically charged cloud of subatomic particles). As the plasma cools, it increasingly acquires form: atomic nuclei appear, then the naked nuclei acquire electrons, forming atoms, which then form molecules (precipitating a gas), which condenses into a liquid — from which, eventually, there crystallizes a solid, our planet.[25]

The plasma, at its highest temperature, may be regarded as formless — there are not even atomic nuclei, only flows of subatomic matter and energy. The *possible* bifurcations, on the other hand, the critical temperatures at which new forms arise, are already "there," in the sense that for any given element these points are very precisely defined. As the plasma crosses these temperature thresholds, these bifurcations are actualized.[26] The actualization of a bifurcation, as noted, involves the creation of new attractors (or of new energy landscapes), which define the stable configurations that the components of the plasma may adopt. These attractors, in turn, must be actualized for those configurations to become real. Thus, the naked atomic nuclei of the cooling plasma precipitate a whole set of new attractors, which specify the virtual orbits that electrons may occupy. The passing electrons that become trapped in them are, in a sense, actualizations of these virtual orbits. When all of these orbits are filled — that is, when all the attractors have been incarnated — the result is a stable form: an atom. Thus, form emerges out of formless matter, order emerges out of chaos, through the incarnation of bifurcations (critical temperatures) and the actualization of the resulting attractors.[27]

Although this hypothetical crystal planet would hardly look like a real planet, even at this stage, the simple cooling process in the plasma could give rise to complex patterns. Control parameters, other than the one I have described (temperature) as driving the bifurcations, would complicate the emerging forms; pressure and volume are two obvious factors. Because these would vary over the surface of the planet, they would disrupt the formation of a homogeneous crystal, producing instead regions of gas, liquid and solid in different parts of the planet (and perhaps even areas where all three phases coexist). Moreover, the possible paths to solidification would depend on which element we chose: some elements (for example, silicon) have a "choice" of solidifying either as crystal (quartz) or as a glass (opal, an amorphous solid). The result that is actualized, the path taken, will depend on how fast the bifurcation is crossed in any given area: if the solidification is rapid (a process called "quenching"), the result will be a glass, but if it is slow ("annealing"), it will be a more or less perfect crystal.[28]

Obviously, a more realistic scenario would involve a planet made of more than a single element. This would allow a vast increase in complexity, even if we assume only a limited number of elements. (On Earth, only ninety-two elements occur naturally; others, like plutonium, are too unstable to occur spontaneously, although they can be created under laboratory conditions.) With this addition, new phase transitions are created, like those at the onset of chemical reactivity. In other words, the different elements will begin to interact and form new substances. Furthermore, the gas, liquid and solid phases of the materials may enter into complex mixtures called "colloids" — examples of which are a solid and a gas (an aerosol), a solid and a liquid (gel), or any other, more complex combination. The colloidal state of matter is indeed very common.[29]

Clearly, if we admit enough such additions to our original scenario, the result will be a more realistic planet. Any extra details we add will simply increase the number of possible bifurcations available to matter — as, for instance, the novel phase transitions of the colloid state (like the bizarre mutations from solid to liquid we observe in quicksand — a bifurcation actualized through a small shock). Yet the planet that would result from such a process would simply be a collage of states of matter

Chladni figure. Grains of fine sand settling on plate agitated by a sound wave.

interacting with one another. A *real* planet, on the other hand, has mountains, valleys and other geological formations. Were we to peer inside
the mountains, for example, we would find folded layers of different
types of stone. In short, we would observe a historical structure — *not*
a collage of states of matter.

On Earth, the main historical process responsible for the formation
of mountains and other structures, is called the "geological cycle."
Briefly put: Erosion and weathering create the raw materials for the
cycle (stones, pebbles, grains), which rivers, through a process known
as "hydraulic sorting," sort out and deposit as sediment at the bottom
of the ocean. The sediment already has a structure, since the sorting
process causes matter to deposit in distinct layers. When these layers
are buried under further deposits, they undergo a transformation: the
pebbles and grains that form these layers are cemented together into
sedimentary rock (for example, sandstone or limestone). When these
rock layers are folded under the pressure of movements of the Earth's
crust, mountains emerge — which are then sculpted by erosion, and so
on ad infinitum.[30]

Self-organizing processes drive the geological cycle. The tectonic
forces behind the burial and folding of sediment are driven by molten
rock flowing up from beneath the crust in convection cells, a coherent
flow arising after a temperature bifurcation, constituting a kind of
self-assembled conveyor belt. The rivers that sort out the pebbles and
grains that make up the layers of sediment, can be seen as self-organized
"hydraulic computers." The dynamics of a river's flow at different
points in its course are governed by different attractors, turbulent flow
from strange attractors, and coherent pulses (solitons) from weaker
forms of nonlinear stabilization. It is these different "regimes of flow"
that give the river its capability of sorting raw materials by grain size,
shape and even composition.[31] Finally, the processes of erosion and
weathering also act as "filters" or "sieves," sorting out materials by their
degree of stability. Mountains are worked over by these processes,
removing those components that are not fully stable, and leaving behind
those are strongly locked into their attractors. (For this reason,
granite, a highly stable crystalline configuration, is typically found on
high ground.[32])

Thus, adding these historical processes changes our simple picture
of the birth of a planet. Instead of a simple sequence of bifurcations
taking us from a plasma to crystal, here the formation of hardened
structures involves attractors and bifurcations engaged in more complex interactions. The self-organized machinic assemblages they create
(conveyor belts, hydraulic computers) provide the labor needed to generate geological constructions in a two-step process: first, the raw materials are selected and sorted (sedimentation), then they are consolidated

into permanent structures (cementation or hardening). Because the end result of these two operations is geological strata, this process of double articulation has been given the name of "stratification."[33]

According to Deleuze and Guattari, processes of stratification occur not only in the world of geology but in every sphere of reality. In other words, any sphere of reality — the hydrosphere, the biosphere and so on — can be defined in terms of flows of matter and energy and the reservoirs driving those flows. At any given point in time, portions of these flows will be involved in any number of actively self-organizing processes; other portions of the flows, however, will have sedimented or hardened into more or less stable structures. Thus, we can describe a given region of the planet at a given moment by specifying which of the three possible states of these flows predominates: freely self-organizing, loosely bound or rigidly bound. But because these states are neither irreversible nor exclusive, we can speak of various components in terms of the "degrees of stratification" they exhibit.

For instance, a rock may seem to us the archetypal example of permanence and stability, but when one takes the long view, even *rocks* flow: their atoms migrate along grain borders (self-diffusion), dislocation boundaries within grains move, cracks and fissures propagate. In this sense, the flow of rocks is very viscous; they constantly change, but at extremely slow speeds. Furthermore, under extreme heat and pressure, rocks may undergo a bifurcation (limestone, a sedimentary rock, metamorphoses into marble).[34] Alternatively, rock may be melted into lava and reincorporated into the convection flows driving plate tectonics. Stratification, then, is in no way a terminal state: free matter and energy stratify, and the stratified destratifies.

Moreover, hydrological strata (rain belts, ice caps, rivers), atmospheric strata (pressure systems, wind patterns) and organic strata (food chains, dominance hierarchies) can also be understood as complexes of matter and energy flows that are stratified to different degrees.

What we have, then, is a kind of "wisdom of the rocks," a way of listening to a creative, expressive flow of matter for guidance on how to work with our own organic strata.[35]

Organic stratification, which gives rise to our own bodies (among other things), unfolds through chemical reactivity — that is, the onset of a reaction transforming one set of substances into another. This, too, can be considered a phase transition because these reactions involve "activation thresholds," the minimum amounts of energy necessary for chemical processes to begin. The control parameters determining these processes, however, are by no means fixed: catalysts — substances capable of manipulating these activation thresholds without themselves being affected — can raise the thresholds or lower them, and in this way can either inhibit or enhance a reaction.

In a very literal sense, catalysts are the first form of matter that can affect directly the control parameters driving bifurcations, either preventing or accelerating their actualization. (More precisely, catalysts push systems away from their attractors and toward the border of their basin of attraction, where small fluctuations can push them into the domain of a different attraction.[36]) In some cases, a substance can catalyze its own production (autocatalysis); in others, two or more substances can "cooperate" with one another by catalyzing each other's reactions (cross-catalysis). Chemical clocks arise only in these kinds of reactions. Among all the elements, the most powerful catalysts are metals, and for this reason metals have been said to bear a privileged status in the machinic phylum:

> [W]hat metal and metallurgy bring to light is a life proper to matter, a vital state of matter as such, a material vitalism that doubtless exists everywhere but is ordinarily hidden or covered, rendered unrecognizable.... [M]etal is coextensive with the whole of matter, and the whole of matter to metallurgy. Even the waters, the grasses and varieties of wood, the animals are populated by salts or mineral elements. Not everything is metal, but metal is everywhere. Metal is the conductor of all matter. The machinic phylum is metallurgical, or at least has a metallic head, as its itinerant probe-head or guidance device.[37]

This special capability of catalysts to intervene in the dynamics of other processes is the necessary precondition for life to begin. Indeed, the catalysts involved in living processes, called "enzymes," are far more specific than metals in their dynamic effects, allowing for much more detailed control of chemical reactions. The instructions for building each enzyme are stored in DNA, and this allows particular enzyme "designs" to be not only inheritable, but also capable of being fine-tuned for specific functions through the action of natural selection. Because the translation of sequences of DNA into enzymes is itself an activity regulated by enzymes, we seem to have here a classic chicken-or-egg dilemma.

Recent theories of how a machine as complicated as DNA and its translation operations came to be assembled begin with networks of cooperating nucleic acids and enzymes. One suggested precursor, called a "hypercycle," might have been a self-replicating molecule (nucleic acid) coded to produce an enzyme that enhanced the production of a second nucleic acid, which, in turn, coded for an enzyme that enhanced the production of the first — a dynamical cross-catalytic system governed by attractors and subject to bifurcations.[38]

Such a cooperating network might have been the mechanism through which the machinic phylum gave rise to organic life. Organic

Cathode-ray ocilloscope pattern.

strata, however, differ from geological strata in that they have enveloped within their sphere of operations the control parameters driving bifurcations. In the case of our hypothetical crystal planet, the forces determining the control parameters (temperature, pressure, volume) had not yet been integrated into, nor harnessed by, the mountains and rocks they gave rise to. The latter simply emerged as the flows of matter and energy underwent bifurcations, but these structures had little or no effect on which bifurcations occurred. With organic strata, on the other hand, the stratified structures — in particular, DNA — also drive the control parameters, and are thereby able to determine which bifurcations are actualized.

For our purposes, we can treat living systems as made of two kinds of components: those that function more or less independently of the rate and flow of matter and energy, and those that depend critically on these rates of flow (that is, on degrees of viscosity or stratification). The bifurcations of the latter occur only at critical points in the rate of flow of matter and energy, whereas the instructions stored as genetic information for the assembly of enzymes are completely stratified and rate independent. In this sense, DNA and its enzymes can be seen as a complex parallel computer regulating the relative "viscosities" of different flows so as to permit the actualization of certain bifurcations but not others. This is, in essence, the hypothesis proposed by philosopher Howard Patee, who calls information-based structures like DNA "symbol systems":

> [S]ymbol systems exist as rate-independent (nonintegrable) constraints....
> [They do not] depend, within wide limits, on the rate of reading or writing, or on the rate of energy or matter flow in the symbol-manipulating hardware. On the other hand, the effect...of symbols functioning as instructions is exerted through the selective control of rates. For example, the rate of reading or translating a gene does not affect the determination of which protein is produced. However, the synthesis of the protein as instructed by the gene is accomplished through the selective control, by enzymes, of the rates of individual reactions.[39]

These separate roles played by DNA and nonlinear, self-organizing processes can perhaps be best illustrated by looking at the way in which the genetic information contained in a fertilized egg is slowly converted into a fully developed individual of a given species. This is the process known as "embryogenesis." Roughly speaking, during embryogenesis two kinds of processes occur: those mediated by DNA, thus subject to genetic control, and those governed by attractors and bifurcations, thus constrained but not created by genetic information.

An egg consists of a nucleus (containing genetic information) and cytoplasm. Traditionally, the latter was regarded simply as a source of energy and nutrients for the developing embryo, but it is now known to play a much more fundamental role. As a rule of thumb, we should look for manifestations of nonorganic life in those processes in the developing embryo where the nucleus is not involved *as a source of informational constraints*. This qualification is necessary because the nucleus may be involved in the emergence of bifurcations, though not by virtue of its genetic material. For example, its position in the egg can create an initial "polarity" between different zones of the egg. This initial polarity, established during the formation of the egg (oogenesis), has been found to constitute a fundamental source of asymmetry guiding the development of the first few stages in embryogenesis. Even when the genetic activity of the nucleus has been inhibited, an egg will undergo certain early bifurcations due to its global dynamics:

> Self-assembly during [the early stages of] embryonic development is not mediated by direct gene intervention. When all the transcriptions have been prevented [through the use of an inhibitor] the regular cleavage patterns are retained. However, the polarity of molecular organization of both the egg's cytoplasm and its nucleus (chromatic) are essential for normal development. Hence the main features of [early] embryogenesis — cell differentiation, induction, determination of pattern formation — all stem from the oogenetically originated, spatial distribution of preformed informational macromolecules. The initial condition of embryogenesis is oogenesis. The epigenetics of embryonic development is built on the topological self-organization and orientation of macromolecules of the total egg.[40]

In later stages of embryo development, the emergence of the patterns forming various organs and structures — an eye, a leg and so on — similarly involves events directly mediated by DNA and those resulting from the global dynamics of interacting cells. Historically, the study of embryogenesis has shifted in the importance attributed to each of these factors. A century ago, there were two main theories of embryogenesis: one positing that organs are somehow preformed in the egg, and another positing that organs arise out of the dynamics of development. The first approach held that, as an egg cell divides, each cell would contain half of the total organism and so on throughout the course of embryogenesis. This has, of course, been proven false, for the destiny of a cell is not rigidly predetermined but, rather, is *regulated* during development:

> The classical demonstration of [the phenomenon of regulation] was provided in the 1890s in H. Driesch's experiments on sea-urchin embryos. When one of the cells of a very young embryo at the two-celled stage was killed, the remaining cell gave rise not to half a sea-urchin, but to a small but complete sea-urchin. Similarly, small but complete organisms developed after the destruction of any one, two or three cells of embryos at the four-celled stage. Conversely, the fusion of two young sea-urchin embryos resulted in the development of one giant sea-urchin.[41]

Several hypotheses have been proposed to explain the regulation of cell differentiation, the process through which a group of essentially similar cells — for example, an egg after the first few divisions — gives rise to incredibly diverse tissues. Following the discovery of DNA, it was thought that differentiation was entirely genetic — that as cells differentiated, their DNA changed as well, guiding the development of various sets of proteins and enzymes for various cell types. It was found, however, that DNA remains essentially the same in cells of totally different types.

What, then, accounts for cell differentiation? One general hypothesis holds that during embryogenesis certain chemical patterns emerge and guide cells to produce specific proteins at specific times. There are, in fact, several theories about exactly how chemical patterns accomplish this task, which differ mainly in the importance they attribute to genetic information in the guidance of these processes. On the one hand, the "positional information" hypothesis asserts that simple gradients of chemical concentrations are interpreted by differentiating cells according to a very complex genetic code. On the other, the "prepattern" hypothesis asserts that chemical patterns are very complex, and the genetic code with which the cells interpret them is very simple.[42] Clearly, there is a trade-off here: the greater the complexity one attributes to a self-organizing chemical pattern, the less the genetic information one need postulate for its interpretation, and vice versa.

For a long time, the latter hypothesis was favored because a mechanism for spontaneously forming simple chemical patterns seemed much more likely than one for complex patterns. But, as I suggested at the beginning of this essay, this situation is changing rapidly: chemical reactions are now viewed as capable of undergoing several kinds of bifurcations that result in the self-assembling chemical clocks, traveling waves, spirals and other complex patterns previously thought impossible. So the hypothesis of a prepattern is becoming accepted more widely, and with it an increased role for nonorganic life in the creation of organic structures.[43]

Regulation and regeneration were what first prompted scientists to postulate forces in embryogenesis other than genetic information. At particular stages in the development of an embryo, groups of cells interact and thereby develop along specific paths. These paths, though, do not seem to be wholly determined by genetic control: if a group of cells in a developing embryo is transplanted from one region to another, they will develop, not into the structure emerging in the first area, but into the structure corresponding to the second. These stable paths of development that guide or "canalize" cell behavior have been called "chreods."[44] Confronted with such self-organizing phenomena, one scientist has felt the need to postulate the existence of physical forces unknown to ordinary physics, which are supposed to act in a nonenergetic way, independently of space and time.[45] I see no need, however, for postulating mysterious agents to account for chreods: the attractors guiding the global dynamics of interacting cells suffice to account for their canalized behavior, and the bifurcations arising in those dynamical interactions adequately account for the emergence of the attractors themselves. More specifically, the enzymes produced by the expression of genetic information enter into "chemical reaction networks" whose dynamics are guided by attractors. Each type of cell (bone, muscle, nerve) is now thought to arise from a different attractor, with the DNA simply pushing cells from one basin of attraction to another.[46] This description has the advantage of explaining the spontaneous emergence of new patterns by invoking only intrinsic features of the global dynamics of cell populations, without postulating additional forces with mysterious properties.

Roughly speaking, then, the belief that all embryological events involve direct genetic supervision is giving way to a new vision: the egg begins as an undifferentiated field that undergoes a series of bifurcations, each of which produces a new set of attractors that form the chreods guiding development until the next bifurcation. One scheme for classifying attractors and bifurcations, known as "catastrophe theory," presents a taxonomy of seven elementary morphogenetic (that is, form-producing) events. To each of these sets of attractors and bifurcations corresponds a different process of self-organization in cell groups: in the right conditions, these will tend spontaneously to form a pleat or a fold, a pocket, a spike or a furrow.[47]

The more self-organizing processes scientists discover, the smaller the domain of DNA's control appears to be. Rather than including a complete blueprint for the construction of an entire individual, DNA must include only enough constraints to harness self-organizing processes in the creation of the structures that characterize a particular species. Mathematical analysis has established (for now) that the attractors and bifurcations guiding these dynamics are relatively few in number, so organic processes of stratification are themselves constrained by dynamical forces. In other words, morphogenesis — for example, the spontaneous emergence of form in a relatively formless egg — is limited by the available attractors and bifurcations. Hence, DNA constraints can only operate within these limits. In the words of one biologist:

There are several consequences of this view of morphogenesis. First, it is evident that morphology is generated in a hierarchical manner, from simple to complex, as bifurcations result in spatially ordered asymmetries and periodicities, and non-linearities give rise to fine local detail. Since there is a limited set of simple broken symmetries and patterns that are possible (e.g., radial, bilateral, periodic), and since developing organisms must start off laying down these elements of spatial order, it follows that these basic forms will be most common among all species. On the other hand, the

Crystal of virus.

finer details of pattern will be most variable between species, since the pattern-generating process results in a combinatorial richness of terminal detail, and specific gene products in different species stabilize trajectories leading to one or another of these.... The fact that virtually all the basic organismic body plans were discovered and established during an early evolutionary period, the Cambrian, is often remarked with surprise, but it is just what one would expect on the basis of the above argument. "Ancient" and "recent" morphological characters are secondary consequences of the hierarchical nature of morphogenesis and the exploration of its potential in time.[48]

The idea of an undifferentiated egg slowly developing into a full organism as it crosses bifurcations corresponds to our earlier image of a formless plasma giving rise to a crystal planet as it cools down and undergoes phase transitions. But as we saw before, we must also bring into play the action of historical processes of stratification in order to complete the picture. Like volcanoes in the lithosphere or hurricanes in the atmosphere, creatures in the biosphere must meet strict matter and energy budgets. The flow of flesh (biomass) through food chains constitutes the main form of energy circulation in organic strata — that is, energy budgets are met by all living creatures by eating and avoiding being eaten. In all ecosystems, planets are at the bottom of these food chains, constituting a reservoir of solar energy stored chemically (through photosynthesis). On top of this layer of primary productivity come several layers of consumers (herbivores, carnivores). The specific job that an animal or plant performs in an ecosystem (what is called its "niche") is defined by its position in one of these circuits for the circulation of biomass. So in this sense, organic strata are, like any other strata, composed of temporary coagulations of matter (the bodies of plants and animals), themselves the product of the ceaseless flow of energy through ecosystems.[49] And yet, animals and plants are unique in that they must also meet a second budget, a genetic budget that compels them to try to spread their genes as far and wide as possible. For these creatures, meeting their energy–matter budget is, in a sense, of secondary importance. They must eat and avoid being eaten only to endure until the mating season, when the main objective of their lives is revealed: the continuation of a genetic line, the preservation of the portion of the gene pool they encapsulate. The gene pool of a species may be seen as a veritable reservoir driving flows of genetic material through the bodies of its individual members. More specifically, a gene pool supplies the raw materials for the pruning process of natural selection. It contains the stored "experience" of the species over many generations, the "knowledge" of how to survive successfully in a given environment. Individual animals and plants are like temporary "experiments" with which gene pools probe current environmental conditions to make sure that past successes are still viable (in other words, that energy–matter budgets can still be met as before).[50]

Although gene pools are designed to replicate themselves very accurately (and thereby preserve past experience intact) random copy-error (mutations) and sexual shuffling of gene groups (recombination) generate enough variation so that these genetic reservoirs can respond to new environmental challenges. In short, thanks to variation, gene pools can evolve and be submitted to historical processes of stratification. Roughly speaking, mutation and recombination play the role of erosion and weathering — that is, they provide the raw materials for the sorting process of natural selection. In the simplest case, for example in the case of selection by climatic conditions, this process merely sorts out the fit from the unfit, or more generally, the stable from the unstable. And yet, like the hydraulic computers mentioned above, selection pressures are also patterned by nonlinearities. For instance, some pressures may add some directionality to evolution, as in the case of natural arms races: a thickening of the armor in a prey species directly provokes a sharpening of the claws and teeth in its predatory counterpart, which in turn puts pressure on armor designs to get even thicker. Similar catalytic loops occur between parasites and hosts, or between male decorations and female sexual choice.[51] In other cases, when the fitness of a particular trait or behavior is nonlinear (that is, when selection pressures depend on how frequent that behavior is exhibited in a population), behavioral patterns come to be stabilized by attractors (the so-called evolutionary stable strategies).[52]

Thus, selection pressures of many kinds play the same role that processes of sedimentation perform in the case of rocks. They select the stable from the unstable, and then sort out what's left into the layers of a food chain. The analogy does not end there. Like patterns in the sedimentary deposits that form at the bottom of the ocean, the accumulated patterns of adaptive traits and behaviors brought about by natural selection are very ephemeral. They slowly sediment over many generations but they can be wiped out by a single large-scale bifurcation, like the onset of the ice age. So what then corresponds here to the process of cementing together loosely accumulated pebbles into hardened sedimentary rock? The answer, according to the discipline of macroevolutionary dynamics, is the process of "speciation," that is, the birth of a new species. When a portion of a population becomes reproductively isolated from its parent group, the information contained in its gene pool becomes permanently injected into the larger phylogenetic lineage to which both groups belong. Speciation acts like a ratchet, preventing accumulated adaptations from being eroded away. In this form, what was a loosely bonded set of anatomical and behavioral traits is now hardened into the more or less permanent structure of a particular species.[53]

Thus, the simple images of developing eggs and cooling plasmas, though good illustrations of the action of self-organizing processes, must always be complemented by a description of the actual historical processes of stratification that have determined how attractors and bifurcations have been actualized. These images are also misleading in another sense. On the one hand, eggs and plasmas are good metaphors for the machinic phylum, which I defined as a destratified, nonlinear flow of matter-energy. In both cases, matter and energy originally exist in a more or less formless state in which actual forms and structures exist only virtually as the various bifurcations that eggs and plasmas are capable of undergoing. On the other hand, these images could seduce us into thinking that the machinic phylum is something that exists only initially, and that it gradually disappears as concrete forms and structures emerge.

As the extreme example of limb regeneration indicates, though, the phylum does not "vanish" or become irrelevant in the aftermath of the system's early development. On the contrary, as with the nonorganic systems described above, the phylum remains immanent throughout the organism's development: it can be found whenever a process of self-organization occurs — whenever a phase transition takes place or an internal chemical reaction undergoes a bifurcation. Indeed, the dynamics of the complex networks of chemical reactions that make up our own metabolic processes are guided by bifurcations and attractors that guide the system between stable, or homeostatic, states:

> Homeostasis refers to the relative constancy of the internal environment with respect to variables such as blood sugar, blood gases, electrolytes, osmolarity, blood pressure, and pH. The physiological concept of homeostasis can be associated with the notion of steady states in mathematics. Steady states refer to a constant solution of a mathematical equation [a point attractor].... Although the mean blood pressure is maintained relatively constant, as we all know, the contractions of the heart are approximately periodic.... Likewise...with the rhythms of heartbeat, respiration, reproduction, and the normal sleep–awake cycle. Less obvious, but of equal physiological importance, are oscillations in numerous other systems — for example, release of insulin and luteinizing hormone, peristaltic waves in the intestine and ureters, electrical activity of the cortex and autonomic nervous system, and constrictions in peripheral blood vessels and the pupil. Physiological oscillations are associated with periodic solutions of mathematical equations [periodic attractors].[54]

Perhaps the best example of these processes is the internal physiological cycles involving waking, sleeping, temperature and so on, the so-called circadian rhythms. "Circadian," which literally means "about a day," refers to the fact that this internal rhythm has a period of roughly twenty-*five* hours. Consequently, as our internal "clock" adapts to the external day–night cycle, it undergoes a bifurcation every day. Because our circadian rhythms are dynamical processes — they are guided by periodic attractors — they are capable of synchronizing or "entraining" to an external rhythm. Although entrainment to the light–dark cycle of the regular Earth day, for example, can by desynchronized (as in jet lag), the same dynamic flexibility that allows self-organizing clocks to adjust to the external environment also allows them to undergo other kinds of bifurcations. Thus, a flash of light at a critical moment (of bifurcation) can send one's clock into a totally different period or stop it altogether. A whole range of pathological phenomena has been associated with the occurrence of bifurcations and has received the name "dynamical diseases."[55]

The phenomenon of entrainment — the spontaneous phase synchronization of different oscillating entities — is common in nature. One well-known example is the slime mold amoeba: in normal circumstances, a group of these amoebas will behave as unrelated individuals, but when the level of environmental nutrients reaches a critically low value, they assemble themselves into a coherent colony with differentiated "organs." Entrainment also occurs in laser light, which differs from ordinary light in that the photons oscillate "in phase" (that it, they are synchronized), resulting in the emission of a coherent beam. Entrainment takes place in so many physical systems that it is, in a sense, a mechanism-independent process:

> Populations of crickets entrain each other to chirp coherently. Populations of fireflies come to coherence in flashing. Yeast cells display coherence in glycolytic oscillation. Populations of insects show coherence in their cycles of eclosion (emergence from the pupal to the adult form).... Populations of women living together may show phase entrainment of their ovulation cycles. Populations of secretory cells, such as the pituitary, pancreas, and other organs, release their hormones in coherent pulses.[56]

In phase space, entrainment appears as a torus-shaped attractor, which the trajectories of different systems (the oscillating entities) come to wrap around. The transition from nonsynchronized to synchronized oscillations can be understood as a bifurcation in which a set of separate limit cycles transform themselves into a single attractor. Entrainment is common in living systems because periodic attractors are their main form of organization. Indeed, one crucial difference between geological and organic strata is the former's tendency to develop around points of static equilibrium (minima of energy, point attractors), as opposed to the latter's tendency to make use of forms of dynamic equilibrium (periodic and even chaotic attractors). Were one to track the flow of matter around the planet, one would see how it becomes stratified along these lines. For example, although the key element of life, carbon, is for the most part locked in rocks, some of it — notably in the form of carbon dioxide — moves freely through the biosphere; some of this, in

Dielectric in the process of breakdown.

turn, is trapped cyclically by plants (through photosynthesis), captured in their biomass and released when their leaves fall in autumn.

There is a sense, then, in which we are all inhabited by processes of nonorganic life. We carry in our bodies a multiplicity of self-organizing processes of a definite physical and mathematical nature — a set of bifurcations and attractors that could be determined empirically, at least in principle. Yet, is there any way *to experience* this nonorganic life traversing us (for example, through the use of meditation techniques or psychedelic chemicals to "destratify" ourselves)?[57] As noted above, there *is* a "wisdom of the rocks" from which we can derive an ethics involving the notion that, ultimately, we too are flows of matter and energy (sunlight, oxygen, water, protein and so on). At any moment in these flows, we can distinguish some portions that are more viscous (hardened, stratified) than others. An ethics of everyday life, in these terms, would involve finding the relative viscosities of our flows, and giving some fluidity to hardened habits and making some fleeting ideas more viscous — in short, finding, through experimentation, the "right" consistency for our flows (the "right" mixture of rigid structures, supple structures and self-organizing processes).

Clearly, though, it is impossible to derive ethical lessons from the machinic phylum without considering processes of self-organization and stratification at the level of society. Animal and human societies, like individual organic bodies, are also "crossed" by the machinic phylum. For example, a particular population of animals is regulated by a simple equation concerning its birth and death rates and the reservoir of its environmental resources. This simple equation has been shown to undergo bifurcations: a population that for many years tended toward a steady-state equilibrium may suddenly begin to oscillate between two extremes. Similarly, the respective biomasses of two populations (one prey, the other predator) are also linked by equations susceptible to bifurcation.[58]

Phalanx of soldiers.

Elaborating on the observation that phase transitions and other bifurcations occur at the level of animal populations, Arthur Iberall has proposed a model of human society in terms that emphasize self-organizing processes. In his view, societies function as an ensemble of flows and the reservoirs driving those flows: water, metabolic energy, bonding pressures, action modes, population, trade, technology and so on. In doing so, Iberall is not out to replace standard accounts of human development but "to stress the role of flows and phase transitions in determining social field stability." He goes on to say:

> I view the discontinuous social change manifested by the appearance of food-producing societies (e.g., from hunting-gathering to horticulture to

settled agriculture) as evidence of internal rearrangements, new associations and configurations, and a new phase condensation — as if a gaslike phase of matter were becoming liquidlike or solid state–like.... At his beginning, modern man apparently lived in hunting–gathering groups operating in a range appropriate to human size and metabolism.... If, as is appropriate to his size, man had the typical mammalian metabolism and roaming range of about 25 miles/day, cultures separated on the order of 50 miles would have little interaction.... The 70- to 100-mile separation of populations, as empirically found, is highly suggestive of a system of weak force, "gaslike" interactions.... [D]ecreases in the levels of the required potentials (temperature, water, food) cause condensation [liquification] of small bands on fixed centers of population.... The nature of the social phase condensation, however, depends on the amplifying capability of the technological potential. Associated with those two chief potentials — water supply and technology (tools) — came changes in modes of living, improvement in the use of water resources, and localized social development through the domestication of plants and animals....[59]

Eventually, these "fluidlike" social formations "crystallized" into stratified civilizations. Based on the archaeological record, Iberall concludes,

civilizations began when there was extensive trade (convective flow) among population concentrations (condensations). The urban centers held cumulative populations greater than 2500 and were composite groups. The threshold size can be estimated from the absence of complex cultures of smaller population.[60]

This picture of social evolution corresponds in many ways to the creation scenario of our hypothetical crystal planet. Clearly though, if a simple liquid solution can harden into crystal or glass, ice or snowflake, depending on the multiplicity of nonlinearities shaping the solidification process, human societies — which have a wider range of attractor types — have far more leeway in how they develop stable configurations. And while there is much to be learned from analyzing in detail the actual processes of stratification and destratification that have occurred in different societies at different times, even a picture as simple as this already points to certain principles of a "geological ethics." Notably, society cannot be understood as climbing a ladder of "progress," as though hunter–gatherers, agriculturalists and "civilized" communities were stages on a path toward ever-increasing perfection. Rather, understanding these transformations as phase transitions would imply that a State apparatus is not essentially better than a "primitive" society, since after all, there is nothing intrinsically better about a solid than a liquid.

From the viewpoint of a geological ethics, early societies may even have achieved a better consistency among their flows, a viscosity more in tune with their ecosystems than our own. Indeed, it seems that some early societies may have sensed the approach of social solidification and developed mechanisms to prevent actualizing such a bifurcation.[61] This, of course, is not to say that we should return to some lost paradise of a "savage state," a bygone era of greater innocence and harmony. Rather, we must work on the society in which we find ourselves, tracking the flows of matter and energy, destratifying hardened institutions, setting into flux human practices that have sedimented — in short, we must find the right viscosity for our fluxes, the exact consistency that would allow humanity to self-organize without the need for coercion and war.

Iberall pictures the flow of goods along trade routes as an example of convective flow, as though precapitalist markets were indeed self-organizing structures creating order out of chaos. We may have to discover in the history and present of human practices those institutions that realize best the workings of the machinic phylum, or, more precisely, the degrees of stratification of each of its components: those flowing more or less freely, those sedimented into more or less supple structures and those rigidified into permanent institutions (entrenched political hierarchies, inflexible belief systems). The geological strata teach us that even the seemingly most rigid structures can flow (however slowly), mutate (metamorphic rocks) or even be reincorporated into self-organizing processes (convection flows of lava).

Part of such an effort would involve creating "maps" showing the attractors that govern the dynamical behavior of social flows, and more important, the bifurcation regions where — to paraphrase Prigogine — a "dangerous idea" can amplify itself by taking advantage of the nonlinearities that guarantee the stability of a given social system. The work of Deleuze and Guattari is exemplary for the creation of such maps: they show how our lives may be viewed as a composite of rigid structures (family, school, military service, office, marriage), supple structures (temporary alliances, transitory love affairs, loosely knit groups) and, finally, "lines of flight," the bifurcations that could allow us to change our destinies as defined by those two types of structures.[62] In every area of human reality (art, politics, love), they attempt to "measure" the degrees of stratification of the flows of matter and energy at work in these domains. For example, after showing how music originates from the expressive powers of matter itself (in particular, the self-organizing processes of animal territories that give rise to bird songs), they argue that music has a greater capacity to "destratify" than does painting. It is as though the modulated flows of air that we experience as music have a greater capacity to set our emotions and thoughts into flux than do the more viscous, spatial flows of form and color found in painting.[63]

It follows, then, that the kind of "stratometers" that could perform these measurements of relative viscosity in various material and energy flows need not all be mathematically based. A great novel can, for a given society, capture the coexistence and interactions of rigid structures and

Marching formation at Nazi rally.

sedimented habits, as well as the active and creative forces driving a society to undergo bifurcations. That there is plenty of room for intuition and experimentation in tracking the machinic phylum in no way obviates the need for, or possibilities of, stratometers of a more mathematical kind. Some might be computer programs capable of creating complex phase portraits of interacting dynamical systems, and of detecting their various elements — those operating linearly in equilibrium conditions (rigid structures), those that are nonlinear in near equilibrium conditions (supple structures) and, finally, those operating nonlinearly far from equilibrium. (Only the latter allows the flows of matter and energy to express themselves.)

In order to visualize better the uses to which we could put these stratometers, consider as examples two kinds of human institution operating at different degrees of stratification: the marketplace and the State. As noted, cities and towns may be seen as composed of a series of reservoirs (water, protein, labor and so on) driving a variety of flows and, in the process, giving rise to the institutions that channel, amplify or control these flows. On the one hand, the more or less fluid structures of markets arise from the spontaneous interaction of many agents, without any central organ directing the process of assembly. On the other, the more rigid hierarchical structure of State institutions comes to life not spontaneously but through the goal-directed activities of an elite.

Mainstream economic science, however, fails to capture the fluid nature of market dynamics: the operation of markets is treated as though it resembled the growth of perfect crystalline structures, that is, as though it were governed by a tendency to move toward a single point of equilibrium (where supply meets demand) — a point of optimal efficiency, from the viewpoint of society as a whole (full employment equilibrium). In order to obtain this well-behaved dynamics from their models, though, economists must rely on two unwieldy assumptions: first, that there exists perfect competition among all economic agents (that is, no monopolies or oligopolies manipulating prices); and second, that these agents have perfect information about market conditions as well as an unbounded rationality to act on that information, so that each is able to negotiate the deals that maximize the agent's benefit (utility).[64] But when these unrealistic assumptions are relaxed, the dynamics of the market begin to resemble in many respects those of self-organizing structures in liquids, from the controlled flow of a convective cell to the wild patterns of turbulence or even solitons. If, alternatively, the relatively long-lasting and stable structures of some markets are understood as suggesting that a "solid" metaphor were appropriate, market behavior would resemble, among all solids, that of glass — which is guided by multiple equilibria — more than that of a crystal with a single equilibrium. The more amorphous structure of glass results precisely

Liquid crystals.

Cloverleaf intersection.

from the conflicting constraints imposed by many attractors (local energy minima) and from the possibility of being "trapped" by an attractor that prevents the optimal use of energy. Markets function like glass in that, in the presence of imperfect conditions (imperfect decision making), they can be trapped in suboptimal equilibria — like a supply–demand equilibrium with high unemployment — as has been well known since Keynes's work in the 1930s.[65]

As Joseph Schumpeter showed around the same time, moreover, the equilibrium on which a market settles need not be a stationary state: more likely than not it will be a cycle instead. The upswing of a cycle will bring prosperity, and the downswing a period of recession and high unemployment. This behavior has been accounted for by models that generate these nonlinear dynamics through a periodic attractor: Kondratieff cycles, for example, in which prices and interest rates follow a fifty-two-year long-wave motion — which has been operating for at least two centuries — have been explained as resulting from positive feedback loops forming in specific areas of the economy (specifically, in the capital goods sector, which produces the machinery needed to generate consumer goods). By amplifying small fluctuations in the relevant sector, these positive feedback loops drive the economy away from equilibrium and trigger a Hopf bifurcation, transforming a steady-state equilibrium into a stable oscillatory motion.[66]

Modeling markets as self-organizing structures has nothing to do with the famous "invisible hand" that, according to some economists, guides a market toward optimal levels of efficiency when left to its own devices. On the contrary, the presence of nonlinear effects throughout the economy — from multiplier–accelerator effects in investment and finance to the multiplicity of delays, bottlenecks, surpluses and shortages stemming from the limited rationality of economic agents — means that real markets must be able to cope with life far from equilibrium, and indeed, to create special buffering structures (inventories, retail stores, banks) for this purpose.[67] In short, to the extent that markets emerge and operate spontaneously, they are incapable of achieving optimal equilibria on their own. Other kinds of human organizations, on the other hand — the State, sedentary armies, large corporations — are more capable of goal-directed optimization; these latter can be treated as crystallizations in the flows of matter and energy.

And yet, not even these are perfect crystalline structures, for just as the dynamics permitting actual formation of crystals is complicated by the Earth's real conditions — by gravity, notably — so are the dynamics of human institutions. If one wants to grow "pure" crystals, one must do so (for now) aboard a space shuttle, where the single point of equilibrium guiding their formation is artificially isolated from other influences. Should one attempt to do so on Earth, crystals require special nonequilibrium structures, "dislocations," which trap energy locally to allow a crystal to overcome limitations to its growth. Iberall has compared the role of dislocations to that of human elites in the development of State institutions: these elites operate, for example, by monopolizing a surplus of grain that allows the State to extend its regular structure over the more amorphous agricultural villages around it.[68] And these organizations, precisely because of their hierarchical nature permitting the controlled application of reason and power, are more capable than "pure" markets of reaching more or less optimal solutions to social problems.

Great Wall of China.

If hierarchies have this advantage over markets, though, they present other dangers of their own. Robert Crosby has described these in terms appropriate to this analysis: the goals of the elite often tend to diverge from those of lower hierarchical levels, and when this occurs ever-greater amounts of energy must be diverted to the task of making the lower levels comply with official goals — rules multiply, enforcement units proliferate, punitive means increase.[69] According to Crosby, we may have to search for the right mixture of fluid market structures and more stratified hierarchical organizations: a hybrid system combining the resilience and adaptability of markets with the goal-seeking behavior of hierarchies.[70] Ideally, such a hybrid would be able to avoid the dangers of markets (like the formation of monopolies due to economies of scale, or the disregard of "external" effects and costs, like pollution), as well as the need to exercise that eternal temptation of command structures: too much control.

Is it possible to design stratometers capable of performing the necessary measurements to give this hybrid the right consistency and viscosity? In a sense, yes. For example, among the considerations involved in such a design could be that of creating a new conception of control. Crosby suggests that if we could manage to map the attractors and bifurcations governing the dynamics of a given human community, we could then articulate a new "philosophy of control" in a few policy rules: if a local sector of a hybrid system were trapped in a nonoptimal attractor, then moving this sector toward a more efficient attractor might be prohibitively costly, so the best policy would be to exercise no control at all; if, on the other hand, this sector were near a bifurcation (or near the border of a basin of attraction), then the proper role of control would be to guide it toward the most favorable outcome (the most favorable available attractor).[71] Such a philosophy, of course, would imply accepting modest gains and accepting suboptimality as a fact of life; but in return, it could allow society to track the machinic phylum, to follow the more natural paths of development, those allowing for a greater consistency or adequacy in our relationships with each other and the environment.

There are, in fact, many proposals as to how to utilize knowledge of self-organizing processes for the purpose of formulating policies, or more generally, strategies of life. Ecologist C. S. Holling, for example, distinguishes between the notions of "stability" (defined as being locked into an attractor) and "resiliency" (defined as existing at the border of a basin of attraction). In his view, ecosystems (whether natural or human-made) are not so much stable as resilient. In other words, the ability to maintain a steady or cyclic state is not considered by him to be as important as the ability to switch rapidly between stable states (attractors), thus allowing more responsiveness to environmental changes. He claims that if mechanisms existed for maintaining a position at the border of several attractors, that is, for achieving resiliency, very little effort would be needed to choose between alternative stable states. If Holling's hypothesis is correct, it means that government policies that attempt to drive, say, the economy toward stability may be approaching the problem in the wrong way and that economic policies should be designed to achieve resiliency instead.[72]

A similar but more radical approach is suggested by the work of scientists like Stuart Kauffman and Christopher Langton. These authors recommend that systems should be located not at the border of a basin of attraction, but rather in the vicinity of certain bifurcations. Through careful exploration of the dynamics of a wide variety of systems, they have found a "magic region" of phase space where self-organizing effects are maximized, that is, where spontaneous self-organization reaches a peak in complexity. This region is reached, they say, by avoiding attractors. In their view, point and limit-cycle attractors are too rigid and predictable to generate anything novel, while chaotic attractors are too wild to produce anything viable. At the frontier between the two (at a bifurcation from periodic to chaotic, for instance), magic happens, and so Kauffman and Langton claim that natural evolution may have in fact selected for mechanisms designed to keep organisms "poised at the edge of chaos."[73]

Another way of thinking about such "poised systems" is in terms of phase transitions in matter. The solid state would represent the existence of too much order, and the gaseous state that of too much chaos. It is well known that the liquid state has more interesting dynamics than the other two states since it can, for example, give rise to vortices and solitons (and other coherent structures). The state at the edge of chaos exists in the vicinity of the solid–liquid bifurcation. It is a state that is not too liquid, but not too solid either, that is, a state with the right viscosity or consistency. Matter in this magic state, according to Langton, acquires spontaneous "computational abilities," almost as if complex computational devices could self-assemble at the frontier with chaos.[74] If this is indeed true, it will have serious consequences for economic policy. In market economies, prices serve as transmitters of information (and incentive), and for this reason economic systems can be seen as complex computers, the sum of the decision-making abilities of many micro-economic agents (consumers and producers). Mainstream economics regards these agents as perfectly rational, so the computational abilities of the economy as a whole are seen simply as a reflection of this underlying rationality. But if nonlinear economics is right, if agents are essentially limited in their rationality as well as in their access to information, then the economy as a whole may have to acquire its power of computation dynamically, that is, by operating poised at the edge of chaos.

Because the problems raised by hybrid systems involve both dealing with flows of matter and energy and studying the stratifications that form in those flows, we might do well to learn from the experiences of those who were the first to track the machinic phylum — artisans and metallurgists. Before the advent of modern methods, they did this by using their instincts and the empirical know-how accumulated through the ages. They had to track everything from stratified ore deposits to a metal's melting and crystallization points, and then to experiment with different ways of crossing those bifurcations through forging techniques; they had to look for their own hybrids, that is, synergistic combinations of metals in which the whole spontaneously becomes more than the sum of its parts (alloys), and to allow the materials to have their own say in the final form produced. All of this involved following a given material's local accidents and imperfections, rather than imposing a rigid, pre-planned form on it.

According to metallurgist Cyril Stanley Smith, this know-how had been developed well before the Greeks began to apply formal reasoning to these problems, and it was therefore mostly of a sensual nature.[75] These artisans, in a sense, developed a special ability to follow the phylum, to track the machinic effects created by nonlinear phenomena in nature, and it is this ability that we must acquire again if we are to help social hybrid structures evolve. (As *sensual* knowledge, this know-how would constitute yet another stratometer, one built into our own bodies.)

Artisans and metallurgists, though, are not the only source of insight for such a project: the Earth itself has been dealing with flows of matter and energy for millennia, and herein lies the wisdom of the rocks from which we might derive our inspiration. In geological, hydrological and organic strata (as well as in the two other strata that bind us, intentionality and language[76]), we can always find some elementary components that are not only less stratified, less bound to their attractor, but that are also capable of destratifying their own and other systems' components by pushing them away from their attractors, toward the border of their basin of attraction, where small fluctuations can then tip the system into a completely new regime. In the lithosphere, for example, this role is played by metallic catalysts: by interacting with various other elements and thereby allowing them to transform each other chemically,

Polyhedral salt crystals.

they enable inert matter to explore the space of possible chemical combinations, in a nonconscious search for new machinelike solutions to problems of matter and energy flow. It is as though catalysts were, to use Deleuze and Guattari's term, the Earth's own "probe heads," its own built-in device for exploration; and indeed, to the extent that autocatalytic loops and hypercycles were part of the machinery involved in the "discovery" of life, these probe heads allowed physicochemical strata to transform themselves and their milieus into completely new worlds.

We ourselves must become this kind of probe head in our own strata, and allow society to explore and experiment with the possible machinic solutions to its own problems. We must create stratometers of every kind — mathematical *and* nonmathematical — and get to work mapping the attractors that define our local destinies and the bifurcations that could allow us to modify these destinies. And though this is undoubtedly an enterprise fraught with dangers, we can derive some comfort from the hints of the machinic phylum that have recently become visible to us and seem to indicate there may be ways of evading our currently doomed environmental destiny.

NOTES

1. Thomas Kuhn, *The Structure of Scientific Revolutions* (Chicago: University of Chicago Press, 1970), p. 116.

2. Ian Stewart, *Does God Play Dice? The Mathematics of Chaos* (Oxford: Basil Blackwell, 1989), p. 186.

3. Hans Degn, Lars Olsen and John Perram, "Bistability, Oscillation and Chaos in an Enzyme Reaction," in Okan Gurel and Otto Rossler, eds., *Bifurcation Theory and Applications in Scientific Disciplines* (New York: New York Academy of Sciences, 1979), p. 623.

4. Ilya Prigogine and Isabelle Stengers, *Order out of Chaos* (New York: Bantam, 1984), p. 14.

5. See, for example, Philip W. Anderson and Daniel L. Stein, "Broken Symmetry, Emergent Properties, Dissipative Structures, Life: Are They Related?" in Eugene Yates, ed., *Self-Organizing Systems* (New York: Plenum, 1987), p. 454.

6. Peter Decker, "Spatial, Chiral and Temporal Self-Organization through Bifurcation in 'Bioids': Open Systems Capable of Generalized Darwinian Evolution," in Gurel and Rossler, eds., *Bifurcation Theory*, p. 236.

7. Gregoire Nicolis and Ilya Prigogine, *Exploring Complexity* (New York: Freeman, 1989), p. 187.

8. David Campbell, "Nonlinear Science: From Paradigms to Practicalities," in Necia Grant Cooper, ed., *From Cardinals to Chaos* (Cambridge, Eng.: Cambridge University Press, 1989), p. 225.

9. John Briggs and F. David Peat, *Turbulent Mirror* (New York: Harper and Row, 1989), p. 121.

10. Ibid., p. 123.

11. Prigogine and Stengers, *Order out of Chaos*, p. 155.

12. Ary L. Goldberger, David R. Rigney and Bruce J. West, "Chaos and Fractals in Human Physiology," *Scientific American* 262.2 (Feb. 1990), p. 42.

13. Alwyn C. Scott, "Solitons in Biological Molecules," in David Pines, ed., *Emerging Syntheses in Science*, Santa Fe Institute Studies in the Sciences of Complexity (Reading, Mass.: Addison-Wesley, 1988).

14. Briggs and Peat, *Turbulent Mirror*, p. 123.

15. Alwyn C. Scott, "Introduction," in Peter Christiansen and R. D. Parmentiert, eds., *Structure, Coherence and Chaos in Dynamical Systems* (Manchester, Eng.: Manchester University Press, 1989), p. 2.

16. David Campbell, "Introduction to Nonlinear Dynamics," in Daniel Stein, ed., *Lectures in the Sciences of Complexity*, Santa Fe Institute Studies in the Sciences of Complexity (Reading, Mass.: Addison-Wesley, 1989), p. 90.

17. Stewart, *Does God Play Dice?*, p. 83.

18. Hermann Haken, "Synergetics and Bifurcation Theory," in Gurel and Rossler, eds., *Bifurcation Theory*, p. 365.

19. Scott, "Introduction," in Christiansen and Parmentiert, eds., *Structure, Coherence and Chaos*, p. 1.

20. "We always get back to this definition: the machinic phylum is materiality, natural or artificial, and both simultaneously; it is matter in movement, in flux, in variation, matter as conveyor of singularities and traits of expression" (Gilles Deleuze and Félix Guattari, *A Thousand Plateaus: Capitalism and Schizophrenia*, trans. Brian Massumi [Minneapolis: University of Minnesota Press, 1987], p. 409). Here, the term "singularities" refers to phase transitions and other bifurcations; "traits of expression" are the "emergent properties" that arise in material systems when their global behavior is guided by attractors; and "emergent properties" are those synergistic properties that distinguish a whole as being more than the sum of its parts (properties that cannot be deduced from the components' properties, but only from their interactions).

21. Many may well have "seen" nonorganic life long before the advent of computers: Deleuze, for example, credits several philosophers (from the ancient Stoics to Spinoza, Nietzsche and Bergson) with having "tracked" the machinic phylum in various ways.

Ralph Abraham divides the historical study of bifurcations into three periods, according to the instrument of study used: "The period of direct observation may be much older than we think, but let us say that it begins with the musician Chladni, contemporary of Beethoven, who observed bifurcations of thin plate vibrations.... Analogous phenomena discovered in fluids by Faraday are still actively studied. These experiments, so valuable because the medium is real, suffer from inflexibility — especially in choosing initial conditions.... The next wave of bifurcation experiments, which I shall call the analog period, begins with the triode oscillator. The pioneering work of van der Pol (in the 1920's)...produced a flexible analog computer, and institutionalized the subharmonic bifurcations.... The development of the early computing machines ushered in the digital period. Well-known numerical methods were implemented from the start, and graphical output began to appear in the literature. The pioneering papers of Lorenz, and Stein and Ulam, are still studied" ("Dynasim: Exploratory Research in Bifurcations Using Interactive Computer Graphics," in Gurel and Rossler, eds., *Bifurcation Theory*, p. 676).

22. Useful introductions to phase space can be found in: Stewart, *Does God Play Dice?*, ch. 5; James Gleick, *Chaos: Making a New Science* (New York: Viking, 1987), pp. 49–52; and Ralph Abraham and Christopher Shaw, *Dynamics: The Geometry of Behavior*, The Visual Mathematics Library (Santa Cruz, Cal.: Aerial Press, 1985), vol. 1.

23. Prigogine and Stengers, *Order out of Chaos*, p. 206.

24. See Campbell, "Introduction to Nonlinear Dynamics," in Stein, ed., *Lectures in the Sciences of Complexity*, p. 26.

25. A more detailed account of phase transitions from plasma to crystal can be found in Hans Gutbrod and Horst Stocker, "The Nuclear Equation of the State," *Scientific American* 265.5 (Nov. 1991), p. 61.

26. Although the transition from plasma to gas is not in fact "sharp" in the same way that those from gas to liquid or from liquid to solid are, this does not substantially affect this example.

27. According to quantum physics, the virtual orbits around naked nuclei are not attractors but minima of free energy — that is, the equations of quantum physics are linear, and hence do not give rise to self-organization as nonlinear equations do. Many of the pioneers of quantum physics, though — Enrico Fermi, Werner Heisenberg, Louis de Broglie, John von Neumann — envisioned a future in which their discipline would become nonlinear. Various methods have since been proposed that would permit elementary particles to be described in terms of attractors. In *Toward a General Science of Viable Systems* (New York: McGraw Hill, 1972), p. 33, Arthur Iberall offers a nonlinear theory of matter and energy (ranging from atoms to human societies) relying exclusively on limit cycle attractors (which tends to make it mechanistic at points). Iberall challenges received quantum theory, arguing that it provides only a "statistical algorithm" that undoubtedly gives the right results but no conceptual structure with which to understand them (an ad hoc "numerology"); he proposes that it be replaced with a theory that characterizes the eigenvalues (fundamental parameters) of a field in terms of nonlinear limit cycles.

28. Richard Palmer, "Broken Ergodicity," in Stein, ed., *Lectures in the Sciences of Complexity*, p. 275.

29. "The clothes you wear, be they wool, cotton, or silk, are animal or plant gels. They are dyed with colors, which in many instances…are colloid in type…. The leather in your shoes is an animal gel, closely related to the prototype of the colloids, gelatin…. The wood of the chairs in which you rest is made of cellulose, which in all its various forms is colloid in nature…. [They] are held together by glue or by steel nails and steel is a colloid solid solution…. The paper upon which you write…[and] the ink in your fountain pens [are] probably also colloid…. [C]olloid, too, is the hard rubber of your pen holders, prepared from that notoriously colloid mother substance, soft rubber" (Wolfgang Ostwald quoted in Milton

Gottlieb, Max Garbuni and Werner Emmerich, *Seven States of Matter* [New York: Walker, 1966], p. 92).

30. Harvey Blatt, Gerard Middleton and Raymond Murray, *The Origin of Sedimentary Rock* (Englewood Cliffs, N.J.: Prentice Hall, 1972), p. 20.

31. Ibid., p. 300.

32. Michael Bisacre, Richard Carlisle, Deborah Robertson and John Ruck, eds., *The Illustrated Encyclopedia of Natural Resources* (New York: Simon and Schuster, 1984), p. 77.

33. Deleuze and Guattari, *A Thousand Plateaus*, p. 40. Hardening, whether soft or rigid, is in no way limited to the form of the example here: for example, soft structures may result from forms of statistical accumulation quite different from sedimentary sorting. These two modes of stratification may also occur simultaneously rather than sequentially.

34. Bisacre et al., eds., *The Illustrated Encyclopedia of Natural Resources*, p. 79.

35. My essay may be seen as expanding on the philosophical insights of Deleuze and Guattari found in the following quote: "The Earth ... is a body without organs. This body without organs is permeated by unformed, unstable matters, by flows in all directions, by free intensities or nomadic singularities [i.e., bifurcations], by mad or transitory particles [e.g., solitons].... [But] there simultaneously occurs upon the earth a very important, inevitable phenomenon that is beneficial in many respects and unfortunate in many others: stratification. Strata are Layers, Belts. They consist of giving form to matters, of imprisoning intensities or locking singularities into systems of resonance and redundancy, of producing upon the body of the earth molecules large and small and organizing them into molar aggregates.... The strata are judgments of God; stratification in general is the entire system of judgments of God (but the earth, or the body without organs, constantly eludes that judgment, flees and becomes destratified, decoded, deterritorialized)" (*A Thousand Plateaus*, p. 40). Deleuze and Guattari call the ethics we might derive from this process "the geology of morals."

36. Arthur Iberall and Harry Soobak, "A Physics for Complex Systems," in Yates, ed., *Self-Organizing Systems*, p. 509.

37. Deleuze and Guattari, *A Thousand Plateaus*, p. 411.

38. Peter Schuster and Karl Sigmund, "Self-Organization of Macromolecules," in Yates, ed., *Self-Organizing Systems*, p. 75.

39. Howard H. Patee, "Instabilities and Information in Biological Self-Organization," in Yates, ed., *Self-Organizing Systems*, p. 334.

40. Vladimir Glisin, Ana Savic, Radomir Crykvenjakov, Sabera Ruzdijic and Neveenka Bajkovic-Moskov, "Molecular Biology in Embryology: The Sea-Urchin Embryo," in Yates, ed., *Self-Organizing Systems*, p. 163.

41. Rupert Sheldrake, *A New Science of Life: The Hypothesis of Formative Causation* (Los Angeles: J. P. Tarcher, 1981), p. 19.

42. V. French, "Pattern Formation in Animal Development," in C. F. Graham and P. F. Wareing, eds., *Developmental Control in Animals and Plants* (Oxford: Basil Blackwell, 1984), p. 242.

43. Hans Meinhardt, "The Random Character of Bifurcations and the Reproducible Processes in Embryonic Development," in Gurel and Rossler, eds., *Bifurcation Theory*, p. 188.

44. C. H. Waddington, *New Patterns in Genetic Development* (New York: Columbia University Press, 1964), pp. 44–45.

45. Sheldrake, *A New Science of Life*, p. 71.

46. Stuart A. Kauffman, "Principles of Adaptation in Complex Systems," in Stein, ed., *Lectures in the Sciences of Complexity*, pp. 621, 651.

47. P. T. Sounders, *An Introduction to Catastrophe Theory* (New York: Cambridge University Press, 1986), pp. 118–19.

48. Brian C. Goodwin, "The Evolution of Generic Form," in J. Maynard Smith and G. Vida, eds., *Organizational Constraints on the Dynamics of Evolution* (Manchester, Eng.: Manchester University Press, 1990), pp. 114–15.

49. I. G. Simmons, *Biogeography: Natural and Cultural* (London: Edmund Arnold, 1979), pp. 58–62. Further, "The flows of energy and mineral nutrients through an ecosystem manifest themselves as actual animals and plants of a particular species" (p. 79).

50. Many aspects of the reproductive budget (including parental investment and battles of the sexes and the generations) are treated in Richard Dawkins, *The Selfish Gene* (Oxford: Oxford University Press, 1989), chs. 7, 8, 9.

51. A good discussion of catalytic loops in evolutionary arms races and male decorations can be found in Richard Dawkins, *The Blind Watchmaker* (New York: W. W. Norton, 1987), chs. 7, 8.

52. John Maynard Smith, "Evolution and the Theory of Games," in *Did Darwin Get It Right? Essays on Games, Sex and Evolution* (New York: Chapman Hall, 1989), pp. 206–207.

Evolutionary stable strategies, according to Maynard Smith, are those that are optimal for a given context and cannot therefore be invaded by a mutant strategy. To this extent, they are not stabilized nonlinearly by attractors, but rather linearly, like a crystal. The idea that evolution optimizes is becoming more and more frequently the target of nonlinear science. The arguments are similar to those I use below for the case of human economics (basically, the existence of mutually incompatible constraints). For a criticism and a version of these concepts in terms of attractors, see Kauffman, "Principles of Adaptation," pp. 687–95.

53. Niles Eldrige, *Macro-Evolutionary Dynamics: Species, Niches and Adaptive Peaks* (New York: McGraw Hill, 1989), p. 151.

54. Leon Glass and Michael C. Mackey, *From Clocks to Chaos* (Princeton: Princeton University Press, 1990), pp. 114–15.

55. Ibid., ch. 9.

56. Alan Garfinkel, "The Slime Mold Dictyostelium as a Model of Self-Organizing Systems," in Yates, ed., *Self-Organizing Systems*, p. 200.

57. See Deleuze and Guattari, *A Thousand Plateaus*, ch. 6: "How Do You Make Yourself a Body without Organs?"

58. Gleick, *Chaos*, pp. 59–77; R. M. May, "Chaos and Dynamics of Biological

Populations," in *Dynamical Chaos* (London: Royal Society, 1987); and Manfred Peshel and Werner Mende, *The Predator–Prey Model: Do We Live in a Volterra World?* (Vienna: Springer, 1986).

59. Arthur Iberall, "A Physics for the Study of Civilizations," in Yates, ed., *Self-Organizing Systems*, pp. 531–33.

60. Ibid., p. 533.

61. See Pierre Clastres, *Society against the State*, trans. Robert Hurley (New York: Zone Books, 1987), p. 189ff. "Societies against the State" have also been termed "anticivilizations" to stress their effective resistance to crystallization into a stratified society: see Gordon W. Hewes, "Agriculture and Civilization," in Matthew Melko and Leighton R. Scott, eds., *The Boundaries of Civilization in Space and Time* (Landham, Md.: University Press of America, 1987), p. 199.

62. See, for example, Gilles Deleuze, "Politics," *Semiotext(e)* 8 (1978), pp. 154–63.

63. Deleuze and Guattari, *A Thousand Plateaus*, ch. 11: "The Refrain."

64. In some mathematical models, periodic and even strange attractors can result if we maintain these two assumptions: in other words, even if the model allows markets to clear perfectly (supply always exactly satisfying demand), and the agents are given perfect foresight, cycles and chaos can result if we include nonlinear financial constraints (for example, limited access to borrowing). See Michael Woodford, "Finance, Instability and Cycles," in Willi Semmler, ed., *Financial Dynamics and Business Cycles: New Perspectives* (Armonk, N.Y.: M. E. Sharpe, 1989).

65. On the phenomenon of "locking in" suboptimal equilibria, see W. Brian Arthur, "Self-Reinforcing Mechanisms in Economics," in Philip W. Anderson, Kenneth J. Arrow and David Pines, eds., *The Economy as an Evolving Complex System* (Reading, Mass.: Addison-Wesley, 1988).

66. A recent nonlinear model of Kondratieff cycles can be found in: J. D. Sterman, "Nonlinear Dynamics in the World Economy: The Long Wave," in Christiansen and Parmentiert, eds., *Structure, Coherence and Chaos*. Also of note is the pioneering work of Richard Goodwin, who has been using nonlinear models since the 1950s: see his *Essays in Nonlinear Economic Dynamics* (Frankfurt: Peter Lang, 1989). There are many models of Kondratieff cycles, both linear and nonlinear; for a survey, see Christopher Freeman, ed., *Long Waves in the World Economy* (Stoneham, Mass.: Butterworth, 1983).

67. Richard H. Day, "Adaptive Economics," in Robert Crosby, ed., *Cities and Regions as Non-Linear Decision Systems* (Washington, D.C.: AAAS, 1983), p. 10.

68. On the role of dislocation structures in real crystals, see Allan Bennet, "The Importance of Imperfections," in Sharon Banigan, ed., *Crystals, Perfect and Imperfect* (New York: Walker, 1965), p. 85. On human elites as dislocations, see Iberall, *Toward a General Science*, p. 208.

69. Robert Crosby, "Asking Better Questions," in Crosby, ed., *Cities and Regions*, p. 10.

70. Ibid., p. 12.

71. Ibid., p. 21.

72. C. S. Holling, "Resilience and Stability in Ecosystems," in Erich Jantsch and Conrad H. Waddington, eds., *Evolution and Consciousness* (Reading, Mass.: Addison-Wesley, 1976), p. 87.

73. Stuart A. Kauffman, "Antichaos and Adaptation," *Scientific American* 265.2 (Aug. 1991), p. 82; and Christopher Langton, "Life at the Edge of Chaos," in Langton, Charles Taylor, J. Doyne Farmer and Steen Rasmussen, eds., *Artificial Life* (Reading, Mass.: Addison-Wesley, 1992), p. 85.

74. Langton, "Life at the Edge," p. 82. If as Langton and Kauffman think, poised systems are where complexity and variety peak (i.e., are "crossed" in the most intense form by the machinic phylum), then we may imagine a different set of policies (or even philosophies of everyday life). We would have to track these special zones, for example, by destratifying ourselves (that is, by pushing our "solid" components a little, but only a little, toward the "liquid" state). Just exactly how much to "liquify" should be established through careful experimentation, since there are dangers if one goes too far (one may be swallowed up by a chaotic attractor). This is how Deleuze and Guattari put it: "You don't reach the [machinic phylum] by wildly destratifying.... If you free it with too violent an action, if you blow apart the strata without taking precautions, then instead of [tapping into the phylum] you will be killed, plunged into a black hole, or even dragged toward catastrophe. Staying stratified — organized, signified, subjected — is not the worst that can happen; the worst that can happen is if you throw the strata into demented or suicidal collapse, which brings them back down on us heavier than ever. This is how it should be done: Lodge yourself on a stratum, experiment with opportunities it offers, find an advantageous place on it, find potential movements of deterritorialization, possible lines of flight, experience them, produce flow conjunctions here and there, try out continuums of intensities segment by segment, have a small plot of new land at all times" (*A Thousand Plateaus*, pp. 160–61).

75. Cyril Stanley Smith, *A Search for Structure* (Cambridge, Mass.: MIT Press, 1982), p. 113.

76. Intentional strata correspond to the world of beliefs and desires as they exist in the animal kingdom, past a certain level of complexity of informational flow. The sedimentations and hardenings that make up these strata grow "on top" of the organic stratum (they use the brain as their substratum). They, in turn, provide the raw materials for the emergence in humans of linguistic strata. Deleuze and Guattari offer theories on these two strata, which they call "subjectification" and "signifiance." I shall produce a more detailed exposition of these topics in my forthcoming book *Chaos and the Millennium*.

Angular Momentum
Ana Barrado

Plates

1. Hydra Maniac
   Wet 'n Wild, Orlando, Florida, 1991
2. Rocket Garden
   Kennedy Space Center, Florida, 1988
3. Chairs at the Quay Beach Club
   Key Largo, Florida, 1990
4. Sundial at Disney Team
   Arata Isozaki, architect
   Lake Buena Vista, Florida, 1991
5. Flash Flood
   Wet 'n Wild, Orlando, Florida, 1991
6. Family Outing
   Spaceport USA, 1991
7. Discovery Cove
   Sea World, Orlando, Florida, 1991
8. Der Stuka
   Wet 'n Wild, Orlando, Florida, 1991
9. Lazy River
   Wet 'n Wild, Orlando, Florida, 1991

zone

zone

Neurasthenia and Modernity
Anson Rabinbach

"Men, like batteries, need a reserve force, and men, like batteries, need to be measured by the amount of this reserve, and not by what they are compelled to expend in ordinary daily life."[1] With this analogy, the New York physician George Miller Beard identified the modernity of "neurasthenia." In his pioneering work *American Nervousness* (1881), Beard claimed that "nervous diseases are far greater here than in any other nation of history." Americans were especially prone to the lack of nerve force required for "brain-toil" and the "punctuality" necessary to "keep the lamps actively burning." Beard believed, paradoxically, that because of their superior mental capacity, the scientific and technological genius of Americans made them less resilient to the shocks inflicted on them by their own mighty civilization.

Beard's contention that neurasthenia was a product of the culture of modernity remained a staple of theorizing for decades. However, as I shall make clear in this essay, among European physicians and physiologists, the relationship between neurasthenia and modernity did not remain fixed. It was transformed during three decades of debate, ultimately revealing a remarkable secret — that neurasthenia could also account for the triumph of modernity.

As Beard's term swept the continent during the 1880s, European physicians challenged his social etiology and his insistence that neurasthenia was an "American nervousness." Augustin Morel's theory of degeneration and Jean-Martin Charcot's emphasis on the hereditary origins of nervous disorders, for example, competed with the view that neurasthenia had social causes. Critics of Beard also observed nervous illness in the ancient world, and some experts argued that in Europe the shock of confrontation between the old and the new exaggerated such effects.[2]

The standard textbook on neurasthenia in fin-de-siècle France, *L'Hygiène du neurasthénique*, was co-authored by Dr. Achille-Adrien Proust, father of the greatest literary neurasthenic of the age. The elder Proust was a prominent Paris physician and epidemiologist who served in the French Ministry of Public Health.[3] Like Beard, Proust saw neurasthenia as a disorder "least dependent on heredity," pointing to its "predominance in towns, among the middle and upper classes, in a word, in all circumstances where intellectual culture or commercial and industrial traffic are carried to their highest degree of intensity."[4]

But if neurasthenia could be ascribed to the social pressures of modern life, for Proust it also approached a modernist text in its virtual maze of shifting and unreliable "objective" symptoms, and the even more unreliable "subjective" monologues produced by the afflicted. Neurasthenia often took the form of "stigmata" that appeared to be physiological — headache, rachialgia, neuromuscular asthenia, dyspepsia, insomnia and sensitivity of the skin — yet for which no organic causes or "lesions" could be found. The chief sign of neurasthenia was the "perpetual sensation of fatigue" (muscular, energetic, mental), and patients complained of exhaustion similar to the effects of fatiguing mental activity. Frequently, neurasthenics showed a distinctive but inexplicable "aboulia" or lack of will.

Neurasthenia was not simply a malady, but a kind of incessant orchestration of analogies to other maladies. In fact, neurasthenic patients produced symptoms that were so close to "real" disorders that misdiagnosis was extremely common. Neurasthenia resembled both hysteria and melancholia, but was far more elusive and shrewdly deceptive in its plethora of physical disorders. Freud commented on this aspect when he noted that hysteria and neurasthenia were often combined "either when people whose hysterical disposition is almost exhausted become neurasthenic, or when exasperating impressions provoke both neuroses simultaneously."[5] This similitude, combined with a frequent alteration of mental and physical states, accounts for what physicians referred to as "cyclical or circular neurasthenia," in which hyperactivity alternated with moments of complete fatigue and immobility.[6]

Extreme confusion, even the lack of ability to remember their own symptoms, was widely reported to be a universal characteristic of neurasthenics. Proust noticed that even his most intelligent patients gave an "incoherent and diffuse" description of their disorder. Charcot applied the revealing bon mot "*l'homme du petit papier*" to those neurasthenic patients who frequently appeared in his consulting room with slips of paper or manuscripts with an endless list of their ailments.[7] Otto Binswanger, the leading German expert, noted that neurasthenics demonstrated a lack of attentiveness and disturbances in memory, especially in more complicated thought patterns: "If you question the patient more closely, so you will find, that at the outset of this memory disturbance the memory image of an earlier occurring sensation is not lost, nor are simple thought sequences."[8] One writer referred to "fatigue-anesthesia" as the state of being too tired to remember to feel tired.[9]

In the presence of symptoms almost completely lacking in consistency and reliability, the physician has no other means of information than the statements and lamentations of the invalid: "There are few patients whose examination demands so much patience and tact as that of neurasthenia." Like the critic confronted with a disjointed and elliptical narrative, the physician relies only on his or her interpretive authority to stabilize the chaos of appearances produced by the patient:

> By proceeding thus with methodical inquiries, prudently directed and often repeated, the physician will be able little by little to check the statements of the patient, separate the true from the false, and arrange the symptoms according to their clinical importance, disentangling those of leading importance from those that are secondary.[10]

As allegories of the "real," neurasthenic symptoms derive their power entirely from the amplification of other illnesses. These symptoms are elusive, fleeting and immediately lost unless invested with meaning by becoming part of a larger interpretive matrix — a phenomenon that Walter Benjamin once explained as the shock required by all allegorical representation. The meaning that such images reveal is at once quickly exhausted, leaving only a melancholic deadness in its wake.[11] We may call this allegorical aspect the second order of modernity in neurasthenia, a modernity of symptom and narrative in the "physiognomy of the disease."

The treatment of neurasthenia proved even more difficult than diagnosis, since social milieu played an important role in any cure. Proust and Ballet observed that neurasthenia

Dystopia ∞ No. 0037, 1986.
Black and white photograph, 24 x 20 inches.
Orsolya Drozdik
Courtesy of Tom Cugliani Gallery

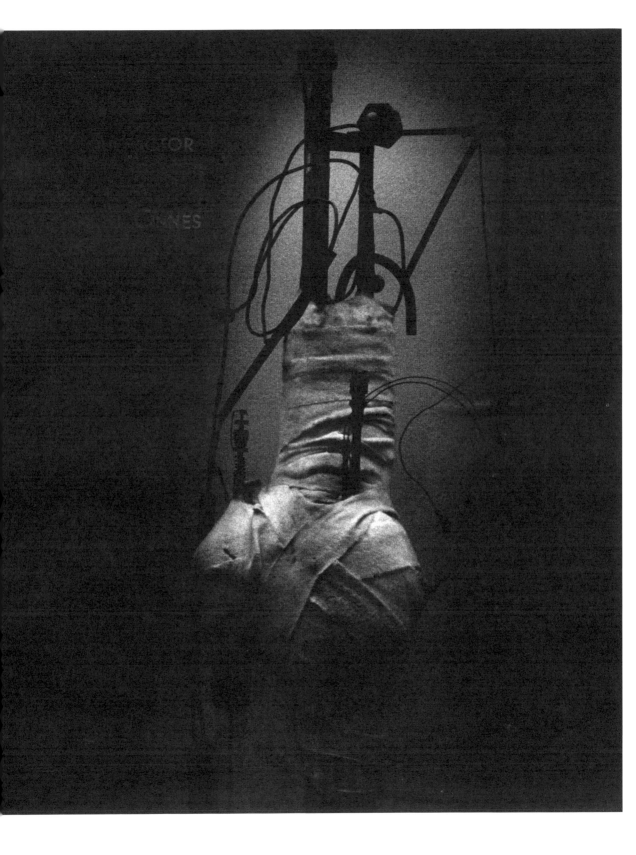

could be treated by "the observance of a large number of hygienic measures dealing with environment, alimentation and physical exercises." They singled out boarding schools as an "evil" for those children especially prone to neurasthenia and viewed as "the most serious danger" incubated there the "exaggerated development of the sexual instincts between the ages of twenty and thirty giving rise to debauchery and lubricity." Proust and Ballet counseled that the child must be "habituated to *will*," and if this fails, there "may give rise in him that moral paralysis that is called *aboulia*." [12]

Proust discounted the American physician Silas Weir Mitchell's "rest cure," which demanded complete withdrawal from the demands of society, as well as Beard's famous "electrotherapy," "hydrobaths" and a host of popular cures. These, he claimed, were secondary to the more basic "suggestion" of the physician: "the moral action exerted on the neurasthenic by the physician and his surroundings constitutes one of the most powerful therapeutic agents that can be employed." [13]

Although neurasthenics were plagued by fatigue, there was little consensus on what precisely was the root cause of their notorious lack of energy. Charles Féré, a student of Charcot, observed that at La Salpêtrière patients with hysterical disorders demonstrated during their intense periods of "automatism" a kind of extreme physical fatigue equivalent to the experience of arduous labor in normal individuals. Féré took this fact to be evidence that neurasthenia was not without organic origin, and that the "derangements of the mind" were produced by some form of extreme nervous excitation or "*irritabilité*." [14] Neurasthenia could sometimes be detected by a device called an "audiometer" — a measure of reaction to almost inaudible sounds — which permitted researchers to compare the "states of distraction" of neurasthenics with normal "lazy" subjects. [15]

With its unreliable and analogic symptoms, its absence of lesions and the confounding behaviors of sufferers, neurasthenia seemed to defy the laws of physiology. By the early nineteen hundreds, several prominent French psychologists began to despair of the ambiguities associated with the multiple symptoms and causes of neurasthenia, and proposed the new classification of "asthenia" to distinguish the specific "maladies of energy" or "diseases of the will" from neurasthenia *tout court*. These materialist physicians believed it was necessary to separate loss of energy and inability to act from neurasthenia's confusing and secondary proliferation of symptoms. "Today, the domain of '*la neurasthénie*' is so vast, so imprecise, that it is necessary to undertake a work of revision," wrote Albert

Deschamps in his 1908 *Les Maladies de l'énérgie*. "In this 'vast forest,'" he continued, "it is necessary to mark out a path to separate that which is 'simple nervousness' [*névropathie simple*], from hysteria, from degeneracy, and from psychasthenia [*psychasthénie*], and to show that neurasthenia is not singular, and that there is no one neurasthenia, but the *asthenias*" — which he defined as a series of responses to "a defective organization in the reservoir of energy."[16] Closely following the German physiologist Hermann von Helmholtz, Deschamps theorized that energy was carried along its pathways by "nervous waves" (*l'onde nerveuse*) analogous to electromagnetic waves, which created a "perpetual circulation of energy in the organism," but which might become impaired by either insufficient or excessive expenditure.

Deschamps was hardly alone in his attempt to place neurasthenia on a firmer physiological basis. At the beginning of the century, Théodule Ribot, editor of the influential *Revue philosophique*, the central organ of philosophical materialism in fin-de-siècle France, carried on a virtual campaign to provide the "diseases of the will" with a materialist foundation. For the leading "psychophysiological" psychologists — which included Ribot, Charles Richet and Wilhelm Wundt — "desires, passions, perceptions, images and ideas" were the product of bodily sensation. The "I will" wrote Ribot, "has no efficacy" without the complex "psycho-physiological mechanism, in which alone resides the power to act or restrain."[17] It followed, therefore, that all irrational beliefs could be attributed to the defects of the will. Ribot dedicated his major 1884 treatise on *Les Maladies de la volonté* to exposing the connection between reactionary religious or political ideas and disturbances in the will. Like Charcot, who also drew a parallel between the psychic states experienced by hysterics and those experienced by religious mystics, Ribot traced these experiences to an "annihilation of the will."[18] Religious "ecstasy," in which all energy is concentrated and the will seems to evaporate, was seen as being analogous to somnambulism or hypnotic trance, in which consciousness is temporarily abolished. These atavisms recalled an earlier and "automatic" stage in the evolution of the will, while the conscious will, the highest stage of physiological *and* moral development, was held to be a shield against these primitive states of mind.

The pathological will is evident, Ribot contended, in "two great classes," *impaired* and *extinguished*. The impaired will might exhibit "morbid inertia," usually accompanied by intense feelings of fatigue. The extinguished will is characterized by aboulia, or, as Ribot explains, the "'I will' does not transform itself into impelling volition." These patients "know how to will interiorly, mentally, according to the dictates of reason. They may experience the desire to do something, but are powerless *to act* accordingly."[19] If the treatment of neurasthenia required the careful disentangling of physical analogies and mental representations, so too the "diseases of the will" required that mental ephemera be distinguished from the material foundations of the disorder. The pathologies of the will — pessimism, irresolution, morbid fear of action and above all the refusal to engage in any productive activity or work — are not states of consciousness but consciousness of an inner state of depletion.

Characteristically, materialist physiology prescribed work or energy as a therapy as opposed to the moral or "suggestive" treatment of Proust and Ballet. Weir Mitchell's "rest cure" merely capitulated to the disorder's demands. Patients who withdrew from their demanding lives into the infantile passivity of "Dr. Diet and Dr. Quiet" did not, as a rule, return to their former pursuits. Theodor Dunin, a German physician noted that neurasthenia was an "aversion to work" (*Unlust zur Arbeit*) and that "activity was the greatest enemy of neurasthenia." The neurasthenic's proclivity to "do nothingness" was exacerbated by the "lifestyle" of the "higher classes," and was even more serious among wealthy women who "had no preoccupation and could find none."[20] Though neurasthenia could be found equally among men, Proust and Ballet, following Weir Mitchell (who treated women almost exclusively), considered the "neurasthenia of women" especially intense: "The dominant feature of this neurasthenic state is profound discouragement, powerlessness to exert the will, in one word *aboulia*, joined to a degree of *muscular asthenia* that is hardly ever seen except in this form."[21]

Ribot's analysis of aboulia touches on an aspect of neurasthenia not immediately evident to those early investigators like Beard who simply equated its onset with the social pressures of modernity. Neurasthenia now appears as an inverted work ethic, a resistance to work, productivity and modernity in all its forms.[22] The cumulative effect of mental fatigue was to create a society lacking in "inhibitive power."[23] The diagnosis of "asthenia" à la Ribot or Deschamps inverted its etiology: whereas Beard or Proust and Ballet saw excessive social and moral pressure as the source of inhibition, Ribot and Deschamps placed primary emphasis on the inhibiting power of the will as a material force. Neurasthenia was responsible for what might be called a traditionalism of the psyche, a profoundly conservative inertia that threatened all progress. Yet Ribot's theory also gave credence to an alternative possibility — to wit, that neurasthenia, rather than resisting modernity's enormous energies, actually *contributed* to their success. The long-forgotten debate over "inertia" in French ethnography reveals that Ribot was ultimately won over to this view.

In his classic treatise *La Fatica* (1891), the Turin physiologist Angelo Mosso demonstrated that the course of fatigue could be objectively charted by means of an ingenious invention he called the "ergograph." Mosso's experiments showed, moreover, that fatigue even performed an invaluable function by ensuring an optimal state of equilibrium in which the body's energy economy was syncretic with the imperatives of civilization.[24] According to the "law of least effort," first discovered by Helmholtz, all organic life sought the shortest path to its goal. The body's natural rhythms — for example, the course of fatigue, pulse and heart rate — determined the pace of work and eliminated waste in human labor. Fatigue governed the expenditure of labor power, as a governor mechanism prevents a machine from exceeding its efficient speed. From this perspective, fatigue is indispensable in restoring the equilibrium of the body and allows the human motor to operate at optimum efficiency. For adherents of a psychophysical approach to pedagogy and psychology, it was thought that fatigue research might even profitably apply its insights to the factory, the school and a variety of other social domains.[25]

In 1894, the noted Italian anthropologist and psychologist Guillaume Ferrero published a sensational article entitled "Les Formes primitives du travail" in the *Revue scientifique*. Ferrero claimed that recent ethnological research proved that in primitive cultures idleness or "inertia" was the natural state of the human species.[26] The "horror of mental and volitional effort," the "repugnance" that savages display toward work confirmed that the major portion of humankind did not engage in social labor without constraint or force. Even in the modern world, entire social groups — thieves, vagabonds, prostitutes — were motivated solely by the avoidance of productive labor. Modernity was a violation of human nature. The only question, Ferrero concluded, is "why does mankind progress at all, why does inertia not rule the species, eliminating all incentives to progress, productivity, and civilization?"

Two years later, the German economist and musicologist Karl Bücher published *Arbeit und Rhythmus*, an extraordinarily popular book which challenged Ferrero's conclusion that the primitive was a prisoner of idleness and inertia. It was not work per se that the primitive avoided, but rather "tense, regular work." In fact, the labor of primitives was "extraordinarily toilsome," accomplished with inadequate technical means and often achieved with extreme artistry. Primitive labor, Bücher observed, was governed by its own natural rhythm — for example, the beat of a blacksmith's hammer or the work song or chant. The body's tempo guaranteed "thrifty energy use." This natural order, however, was considered to be inverted by civilization, which systematically destroys the rhythmic element in work, making it *externally imposed*. Rhythm — the source of all economy in work — not external constraint, was at the origin of both culture and production.[27]

Seizing on Bücher's work, Ribot argued that Ferrero had confused the pathological asthenia investigated by Deschamps and by the psychologist Pierre Janet with the normal state of mankind.[28] Rather, society's *asthéniques* demonstrated the pathological form of the law of least effort in their obsessive desire to avoid activity and to sleep and rest. Janet had noted this "horrible exhaustion" and "aversion to all novelty" in his asthenic patients, a pathological traditionalism he called "*misonéisme*," an opposition to anything new.[29] Rather than contributing to a pathological avoidance of labor, Ribot held that the law of least effort was socially adaptive, leading to greater efficiency, simplicity and productivity. Indeed, social life was unthinkable without the kind of "shorthand" ubiquitous in the arrangements of society — language, morals, daily life, political institutions, religious belief, science and art — which benefited from "inaction or the minimum of action."[30] Linguistics, for example, has long understood that there is a kind of "principle of laziness" (*principe de paresse*), which gradually eliminates excessive sounds, at work in phonetics. Similarly, the history of religion shows that the law of least effort brings about tolerance, since the fanaticism dividing hostile beliefs ultimately "surrenders to the analogy" that can be found between all systems of belief.[31] Ribot thus claimed to have discovered the productive side of *misonéisme*, the disposition of the psyche to find the shortest path in any endeavor. The pathology of neurasthenia revealed the paradoxical secret of progress, efficiency and the order of productivity.

The modernity of neurasthenia is not simply the effect of excessive pressure, but rather the *misonéisme* inherent in all analogy — not unlike the propensity of neurasthenics to produce analogic symptoms as a kind of visible shorthand of their pathological fatigue. The pathological resistance to modernity of the energy-afflicted and the primitive are, ontogenetically and phylogenetically, evidence of an atavistic stage in the evolution of the

will. These pathologies expose the secret of modernity: if *misonéisme* signaled anxiety in the face of change, modernity depended on it to bring about a "rupture with habit." Because the human will was characterized by "mediocre perseverance and vigor," because of its rapid fatigue, *misonéisme* is the protective instinct of the species to reduce excessive action, to regulate physical and mental activity and to find new means to achieve its ends. The law of least effort produced not inertia but innovation.

If, at the outset, neurasthenia was identified by Beard and his European followers as the inability of mind and body to resist the onrush of modernity's stimuli, Ribot and Bücher made fatigue indispensable for the great achievements of modern civilization. Only in its most pathological forms — neurasthenia and psychasthenia — did the will exhibit an impairment or extinction inimical to rationality and social progress. In normal circumstances, though, just as survival of the fittest was the mechanism that explained the emergence of new and viable species, *misonéisme* guaranteed that the law of least effort functioned as the regulator of economy and efficiency in mind, body and society. Anxiety about fatigue was misplaced in the modern era, the materialists reassuringly concluded, since normal fatigue did not threaten modernity but defined the threshold of excessive labor and energy expenditure. Insofar as it "presupposes a balance between debits and receipts, between useful activity and rest," fatigue conserves energy and regulates its movements according to the law of least effort. Fatigue does not threaten civilization — it ensures its triumph.

NOTES

1. George Miller Beard, *American Nervousness: Its Causes and Consequences* (New York: Putnam's, 1881), p. 12.

2. See Robert A. Nye, *Crime, Madness, and Politics in Modern France: The Medical Concept of National Decline* (Princeton: Princeton University Press, 1984), pp. 148–54.

3. Bernard Straus, "Achille-Adrien Proust, M.D.: Doctor to River Basins," *Bulletin of the New York Academy of Medicine* 50 (1974), pp. 833–36; idem, *The Maladies of Marcel Proust: Doctors and Disease in His Life and Work* (New York and London: Holmes and Meier, 1980), pp. 81–102.

4. Achille-Adrien Proust and Gilbert Ballet, *L'Hygiène du neurasthénique* (Paris: Masson, 1887) [*The Treatment of Neurasthenia*, trans. Peter Campbell Smith (New York: Edward R. Pelton, 1903), p. 7].

5. Sigmund Freud, "Hysteria," in James Strachey, ed., *Standard Edition* (London: Hogarth, 1966 [1888]), vol. 1, p. 53.

6. M. Potel, "Neurasthénie," *La Grande encyclopédie* (Paris: Lamirault, 1886), p. 987.

7. Proust and Ballet, *The Treatment of Neurasthenia*, p. 33.

8. Otto Binswanger, *Die Pathologie und Therapie der Neurasthenie: Vorlesungen für Studierende und Ärtze* (Jena: Fisher, 1896), p. 110.

9. Edward Cowles, *The Mental Symptoms of Fatigue* (New York, 1893), p. 22.

10. Proust and Ballet, *The Treatment of Neurasthenia*, p. 33.

11. Walter Benjamin, *The Origin of German Tragic Drama*, trans. John Osborne (London: New Left Books, 1977), p. 183.

12. Proust and Ballet, *The Treatment of Neurasthenia*, p. 96.

13. Ibid., p. 34.

14. Alfred Binet and Charles Féré, "Recherche expérimentale sur la physiologie des mouvements chez les hystériques," *Archive de physiologie* 10 (1887), p. 320.

15. Nicole Vaschide and Claude Vurpas, "Contribution à l'étude de la fatigue mentale des neuras-théniques," *Société de biologie* (March 7, 1903), p. 296.

16. Albert Deschamps, *Les Maladies de l'énergie, thérapeutique générale* (Paris, 1890), pp. 46, 47.

17. Théodule Ribot, *The Diseases of the Will*, trans. Merwin Marie Snell (Chicago: Open Court, 1896), p. 2; on Ribot, see M. Reuchlin, "The Historical Background of National Trends in Psychology: France," *Journal of the History of the Behavioral Sciences* 1/2 (1965), pp. 115–22.

18. See Jan Goldstein, "The Hysteria Diagnosis in Nineteenth Century France," *Journal of Modern History* 54 (June 1982), pp. 209–39.

19. Ribot, *Diseases of the Will*, pp. 27, 28.

20. Theodor Dunin, *Grundsätze der Behandlung der Neurasthenie und Hysterie* (Berlin: Hirschwald, 1902), pp. 32, 33.

21. Proust and Ballet, *Treatment of Neurasthenia*, p. 73.

22. The connection between "inhibition to action" (*Handlungshemmung*) in melancholia and in labor was first explored by Wolf Lepenies in *Melancholie und Gesellschaft* (Frankfurt: Suhrkamp, 1972), pp. 207–13.

23. Ribot, *Diseases of the Will*, p. 10.

24. Angelo Mosso, *La Fatica* (Milan: Fratelli Treves, 1921 [1891]). On Mosso's influence, see Anson Rabinbach, *The Human Motor: Energy, Fatigue and the Origins of Modernity* (New York: Basic Books, 1990), chs. 5, 6.

25. *International congrès d'Hygiène et de Demographie, tenu à Bruxelles du 3 au 8 Septembre 1903,*

compte-rendus du congrès, bk. 5, sec. 4, Hygiène industrielle et professionnelle (Brussels: Congrès International d'Hygiène et de Démographie, 1903), p. 72.

26. M. G. Ferrero, "Les Formes primitives du travail," *Revue scientifique* 45.11 (March 7, 1896), pp. 331–35.

27. Karl Bücher, *Arbeit und Rhythmus* (Leipzig: Teubner, 1899 [1897]), pp. 8–10, 358.

28. Théodule Ribot, "Le Moindre effort en psychologie," *Revue philosophique* (July–Dec. 1910), p. 364.

29. Pierre Janet, *Les Obsessions et psychasthénie* (Paris: Alcan, 1911), vol. 1, p. 335. According to Ribot, the term originated with Césare Lombroso.

30. Ribot, "Le Moindre effort," p. 374.

31. Ibid., p. 376.

Radiography, Cinematography and the Decline of the Lens
Lisa Cartwright and Brian Goldfarb

Tome 1: 1920

Having long given up on his well-known work on the mechanics of the cinema, photochemist Louis Lumière publishes an account of a new technology for still photography, which he calls "*photo-stéréo-synthèse*" (*Compte Rendu des Séances de l'Académie des Sciences 171*, 1920). Subjecting the camera lens and photographic plate to proportional, axial movement around the profilmic object (a man's head), Lumière creates photographs in which only a specified plane within the space of the object remains in a fixed relation to the plate during a single exposure. This fixed point or plane of the object registers as the sole area of focus on the photographic plate; the remainder of the object appears blurred due to the relative movement of the apparatus. Shifting the apparatus by increments perpendicularly "into" the space of the object with each successive shot, Lumière exposes a series of plates until every designated plane of the object is recorded. Printing a faint negative from each plate, he then stacks these prints in succession, reconstructing the space of the object in a laminated visual composite. The claim is that this composite of images offers a precise geometric register of the contained space of

Plates from a series produced by Lumière in his method of *photo-stéréo-synthèse* (*Revue d'optique*, June 1923).

Demonstration of the Lumière Cinématographe at a meeting of the French Society for the Encouragement of National Industry.
First public Edison and Lumière screenings.
Publication of Roentgen's first communication on the X-ray.
First X-ray photography of body (Frau Roentgen's hand).

1896

1895

The Lumières investigate X-ray imaging of opaque bodies.
Edison attempts to produce X-ray image of the brain.
The Lumières investigate X-ray sensitivity of photographic emulsions.
Edison markets X-ray focus tubes and fluoroscopic screen.

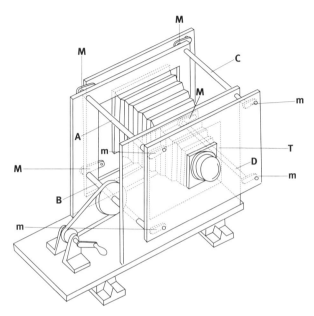

Description of plates: Lumière's technique of photo-stéréo-synthèse employs a simple manually driven mechanical apparatus (left) to pivot the camera lens and the negative plate around the focal axis. Note that **M** is longer than **m**, and thus the photographic plate is propelled along a greater radius than the lens to a degree proportional to the focal length. Lumière's diagram (below) describes the geometric theory behind this apparatus. **O** is the originating position of the lens. **P** is the point in focus. **p** is the distance between the lens and point **P**, and so on. When the lens is displaced to **O′**, the plate is displaced such that

$$\frac{h}{H} = \frac{p}{p+p'}$$

the profilmic object, whereas a single image of the same object shot with greater depth of field offers only a pictorial sensation of depth.

While the cinema, used as an instrument of measurement, may analytically segment movement of objects through space into equal temporal units, *photo-stéréo-synthèse* measures the movement of the apparatus itself through the static interior space of its object. A decade after Lumière's death, radiologists Joseph Duhamel and Jean-Claude Roques point out that the filmmaker had found for himself a problem identical to that of the radiologist: the problem of charting an object, in a highly precise manner, according to its volumetric space – for Lumière, a problem consisting in obtaining photographic images of dimensional object-space without succumbing to the imprecisions of lenticular geometry ("Louis Lumière et les

origines photographiques de la tomographie," *La Presse medicale*, October 3, 1959). If this project can be traced back to Lumière's place at the origins of the cinema in 1895, it is only through a consideration of what amounted to a rejection of lenticular optics in that same year: Roentgen's introduction of the X-ray as an imaging technology in 1895 is critical not only to Lumière's 1920 process of *photo-stéréo-synthèse*, but to the undercutting of the cinematic space born in that same year.

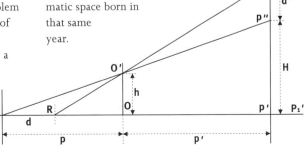

Tome 2: 1921

As a medical officer in the French army, André-Edmund-Marie Bocage had been assigned to a radiological unit, where he practiced what he called "direct analytical radiography." In 1921, he patents an X-ray apparatus based on this method, which is designed to image the body in a series of shallow planes. Although he would be unable to put this apparatus into operation until 1938, his patent would be regarded as the earliest practicable plan for a system of tomography. The patent reads as follows:

> The focus of the radiographic tube is put in motion, as also is the sensitive plate; the plate is only able to receive motion of translation. Both are connected by a mecha-

nism in such a way that their primary displacements are always synchronous, parallel, of opposite direction and in a ratio of constant magnitude.

Under these conditions there exists between them, in space, a single fixed plane [within the profilmic object], in which each point always has a corresponding image point on the plate; hence, only the organs contained in this plane are in focus. The other organs form only diffuse shadows, being able to partly change the intensity of the primary image, but without adding to it new lines, because the farther away from the plane, the more extensive are the movements of the tube, and the more displaced are the images of the points on the plate. (Patent 536464, trans. James D. Bricker, in André J. Bruwer, ed.,

André-Edmund-Marie Bocage rendered in computer-assisted simulation of *photo-stéréo-synthèse*.

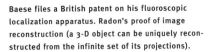

Baese files a British patent on his fluoroscopic
localization apparatus. Radon's proof of image
reconstruction (a 3-D object can be uniquely reconstructed from the infinite set of its projections).

1915

1917

Baese files an Italian patent for fluoroscopic localization of foreign bodies
(used to locate bullets in the bodies of war casualties).

Classic Descriptions of Roentgenology, vol. 2 [Springfield,
Mass.: Charles C. Thomas, 1964])

Duhamel and Roques point out that Bocage's
method corresponds precisely to Lumière's process
of *photo-stéréo-synthèse*. Both methods attempt to map
the space of the body in planar projections, each
plane constituted as the sum of a multiple set of geometric projections. In both processes, the extreme
reduction of the focal field counteracts the spatial
imprecisions introduced by standard photographic
perspective. It can be argued that *photo-stéréo-synthèse*
does not simply correct perspectival space, but introduces an entirely new model of spatial representation.
The stereo-synthetic image is less a pictorial record of
appearances than a means of measuring an abstract,
nonvisible property of a body: volume. Similarly,
radiography measures a physical property: density.
More than an advance on photographic space, stereo-
synthetic and radiographic space effectively break
with the logic of conventional pictorial space, encoding the photographic image as a graphic register of
nonvisible properties.

Rejecting the projection of three-dimensional
objects onto a two-dimensional plane, Lumière incorporates the lens into an optical system meant virtually
to replicate the volume of the object rather than its
appearance. Ultimately, the individual images produced in *photo-stéréo-synthèse* would be laminated so as
to form a photographic block proportionate to the
object. This dimensional model is important not
because it reproduces the object, but because it facilitates the precise measurement of, and the location of
points within, a space that cannot otherwise be seen
or photographed from any single vantage point.
Replacing the lens with the radiographic tube, Bocage
outlines a nearly identical method in which the movement of an apparatus serves to segment an object into
measurable planes of interior space. Because it elimi-

nates the lens and the light ray altogether, the radiographic image goes a step further than *photo-stéréo-synthèse*
in negating the logic of the photographic image.

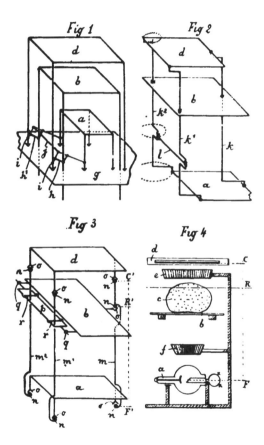

Figures 1, 2 and 3 represent three different types of
apparatus intended to achieve coordinated movements
of the plate and the tube, these types being determined by the way the tube is displaced. Figure 4 represents schematically the whole of the apparatus of the
anti-diffusion screens indicated [in the drawing] above
[it]. (Bocage 1921 patent, in Bruwer 1964)

Louis Lumière introduces *photo-stéréo-synthèse*, applied to the head.

Cummings introduces cinematic concept of "seeingaround" (U.S.).
Lumière patents *photo-stéréo-synthèse*.

1921

1920

1925–1926

Bocage files a French patent on a tomographic apparatus.
Portes and Chausse file a French patent on a tomographic apparatus.

Tome 3: 1925

In his correspondence of 1925, poet e.e. cummings sends physician and filmmaker James Sibley Watson, Jr., some sketches of shooting sets and directions for filming dimensional objects – a doll, a heart. Having little concern with "subjectmattering" a film text, cummings, like Lumière a few years earlier, is interested in using the camera lens to reconstruct the volume of objects without relying on the pictorial conventions of perspective and foreshortening. His interest in cinematography is based largely on the idea that camera movement establishes the interior volume of an object. Movement as a perceptual experience (speed, object displacement, duration) is of little consequence. Cummings uses the term "seeingaround" to describe his method: "such is the strict idiom which seems to me to constitute the aesthetic foundation of the 'moving picture'." According to cummings, the language that employs this idiom "is concentric. It suggests to me Dr F's Repetition Compulsion." The movement of cummings's proposed moving pictures is concentrated in the function of the apparatus. It describes the form of the "~~object~~ subject," which is included in the apparatus as a mobile unit in the articulation of its own volumetric space.

Cummings's outline for a cinematic idiom of "seeingaround," described in the following quotations and diagrams, closely parallels Lumière's 1920 process of *photo-stéréo-synthèse* and Bocage's 1921 method for tomography. In all three cases, movement functions

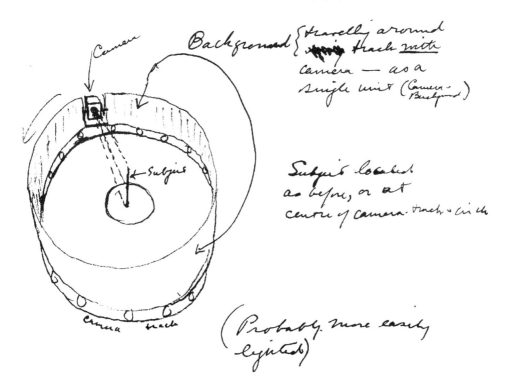

Vallebona introduces stratigraphy (a tomographic method),
applied to the study of the skull (Italy).

1931

1930

Ziedses des Plantes introduces planigraphy (a tomographic
method), applied to the study of the skull (Holland).

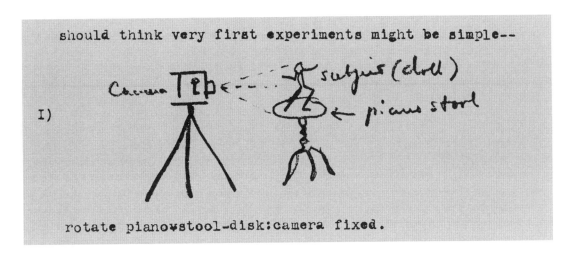

should think very first experiments might be simple--

I)

rotate piano-stool-disk:camera fixed.

to describe space according to the property of volume. As in tomography, blur is a critical factor in the establishment of volumetric space: "I think blurs of which you write should be valuable rather than the reverse," writes cummings in response to Watson's concern about the effect of moving the apparatus.

While Watson did not employ this idiom of "seeingaround" in his avant-garde films of the 1920s and 1930s, cummings's ideas correspond remarkably to the three-dimensional cine-radiographic films Watson would produce after World War II – films entirely dependent on the factor of blur so central to tomographic movement. It is the work of Watson that Duhamel and Roques single out as cutting-edge radiography in 1959.

Diagrams (above and facing): e.e. cummings, proposals for film-shooting patterns, 1925. Diagrams and quotations on this and facing page from papers of James Sibley Watson, Jr., anonymous private collection, copyright e.e. cummings Trust.

Cummings's plans are as follows:

Number 1 arrangement: OR (the) solidity (of a)...: OR – seeingaround

a) I should consider this "arrangement" a formula, comparable to the "3 dimensions" formula in painting (i.e. to paint a subject so as to give the illusion of behindNess, so as to make the spectator feel that the a-little-less-than-half-of a subject (arm, woman, tree) which he does not see (in terms of paint) IS – the camera formula being based, however, on NONillusion or better, on DISillusion.... In the Number 1 arrangement or formula, "moving" on the part of the camera actually means, or constitutes, "solidity" on the part of the subject. b) The above applies, strictly speaking, to one voyage of the camera around a stationary ~~object~~ subject, or semi-voyages of camera & subject in opposite directions, or a single revolution of a subject before a fixed lens. (Camera (on track) encircling ~~object~~ subject – camera on track half-encircling ~~object~~ subject which makes half revolution in opposite direction (~~object~~ subject on turntable) – camera stationary, shooting ~~object~~ subject on turntable which revolves once).

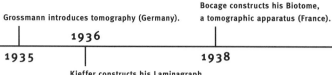

Grossmann introduces tomography (Germany).

1936

1935

Kieffer constructs his Laminagraph,
a tomographic apparatus (U.S.).

Bocage constructs his Biotome,
a tomographic apparatus (France).

1938

Tome 4: 1930

Radiologist Allesandro Vallebona proposes two techniques for the radiographic analysis of volumetric form as a series of quantifiable planes or strata. He cites as his model systems used in World War I to locate foreign objects in wounded bodies. His method, called "stratigraphy," follows precisely the rotational and revolutionary formulas for seeingaround proposed by cummings:

> Let us suppose that the film and the roentgen tube are joined in a rigid system capable of rotating about an adjustable axis, of the type designed by Baese which was used during the war to localize missiles. During the exposure, this rigid system undergoes rotation about its axis. The plane which corresponds to this axis will have a clear radiographic image while the others will be blurred. Alternatively, during the exposure the skull could undergo a slight rotation about an axis corresponding to the desired plane. (Bruwer, p. 1420)

Vallebona follows the second, object-rotational, system — a process paralleling cummings's turntable method. Like cummings, his goal is to undercut the effects of perspective and other techniques for depth rendering by abstracting the object into dimensionless planes. He notes that, prior to his own method, stereoradiography had been the only X-ray technique for locating a lesion in volumetric space. In the stereoradiographic image, any single focused plane is always partially obscured by shadow images of planes of the body extraneous to the organ or region of interest. Stratigraphy eliminates this problem: the rotation of the apparatus effectively causes all planes but the one at the locus of rotation to register as a diffuse blur. Paradoxically, stratigraphy makes possible depth measurement of the body by rendering the body as a series of planes that are dimensionless in themselves (see figure on facing page). Depth is computed as an absence, a nonvisible differential between two images, two positions.

This exclusion of sight from the spatial field is brought about by the absence of the optical lens in the radiographic process. Vallebona cites the incommensurability of the X-ray and the photographic lens as a drawback to the aims of imaging internal dimensional

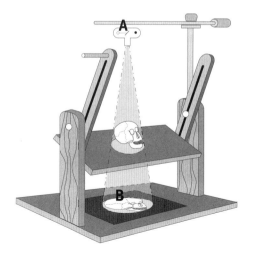

Vallebona's first apparatus is a simple mechanism for pivoting the subject so that one internal plane remains in a fixed relation to the tube and the film plate. Like cummings, Vallebona also describes a system in which the tube (A) and the plate (B) revolve around the subject in a fixed relationship.

The subject of Vallebona's first set of images was a dry skull (facing page). These early stratigraphs showed internal structures that would have been obstructed from view in conventional X-ray images.

Holography introduced.
First electronic on-line digital computer.
Metzker investigates ultrasound as therapeutic technique (Germany).
Engstrom introduces commercial photomultiplier.

1948

1947

Death of Louis Lumière.
First scintillation counters.
Invention of the transistor.

space: "If we could use lenses and mirrors for roentgen rays in the same way that we do for light rays the problem would be resolved, for as in microscopy or photography we could focus on only one definite plane" (Bruwer, pp. 1419–20). The high power of the microscopic lens and, more importantly, the light-permeability of the microscopic specimen suggest a situation parallel to that of radiography: the microscopic specimen is rendered as a permeable field of varying density rather than as a modulated surface or field of contained objects. Applied to objects viewed at a microscopic scale, light can be made to take on the relative intensity of the X-ray. By optically limiting the focal field, a virtually dimensionless plane of activity can be isolated inside the shallow depths of the specimen. This project clearly parallels that of stratigraphic imaging.

While stratigraphy and microscopy may share this project of delimiting a shallow plane of space, their methods are radically different. Vallebona suggests that stratigraphy is limited in that it cannot rely on optical properties to isolate a field of focus; however, it was this "limitation" that led to an innovation that foreclosed on the perspectival representation of depth altogether, necessitating a complete shift in optical paradigms.

Although Vallebona lamented his inability to employ lenticular optics, he introduced a method undercutting its very logic. Like *photo-stéréo-synthèse*, which addressed the perceived imprecisions of lenticular optics from within optics itself, stratigraphy introduced a method of visual analysis surpassing the optical laws that informed prior visual practices. In stratigraphy, as in *photo-stéréo-synthèse*, it is a superimposition of multiple exposures taken from a multiplicity of positions, and not the optical limitation of a focal field from a single vantage point, that isolates a single plane.

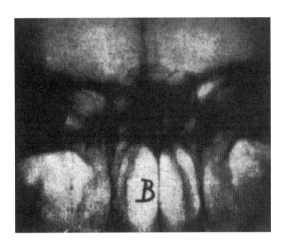

In the absence of a lens, movement across an infinite range of subject positions serves to isolate a single, static graphic strata. This does not imply that movement comes to occupy a central position historically (as for Bergson, Futurism); movement in tomography and *photo-stéréo-synthèse* is always the movement of seeingaround, a fixed relation of change or a mobile geometry at the service of the arbitrary and infinite abstraction of objects/space according to degrees of density. Movement simply facilitates the rise of differential analysis, the position of the viewing subject as well as the meaning of stratigraphy resting in the nonvisible space between two stratigraphic images, or between two vantage points within the apparatus. Similarly, pathology is no longer identified by way of surface symptom; it is now located in the differential between the multiple surfaces constituting the depth field of the body. The skin is no longer the body's privileged signifying surface. This factor has immediate consequences for a logic of appearances: the gaze directed toward the body's surface is no longer markedly significant. It is reduced to one factor in an equation directed toward the measurement of nonvisible space.

Watson et al. announce 3-D X-ray motion picture process.

1954

1953

Death of Auguste Lumière.

Tome 5: 1953

Five years after Louis Lumière's death, an entry in the March *Journal of Medical Education* announces Watson's development of a successful apparatus for three-dimensional radiographic motion pictures. Echoing one version of the procedure for seeingaround outlined by cummings three decades earlier, Watson's process of 3-D cinefluorography is based, like Vallebona's stratigraphy, on the principle of rotational movement on the part of the object imaged.

Cinefluorography must be distinguished from cineradiography. In the latter process, a succession of still X-ray exposures are joined together and projected as a motion picture. In cinefluorography, the image is registered first in real time on a fluoroscopic screen: this empirically visible moving image is then recorded with a standard cinematic camera. By the mid-1950s,

cinefluorography had already proven itself useful in clinical imaging and analysis of bodily functions (the circulatory system, the digestive tract), and was commonly used in the hospital setting to screen incoming patients. Watson's use of cinefluorography is not unique; numerous radiologists during this period record the real-time fluoroscopic image on motion picture film for repeated viewing and analysis. Nor is his 3-D method unique.

Roques and Duhamel suggest that Watson's process is a critical move in the direction of a tomographic organization of space because it attempts to make measurable the interior volume of form. In 3-D cinefluorography, rapid viewing of sequential images allows for an illusion of dimensional space; however, examination of individual frames as separate entities provides no more information about dimensionality

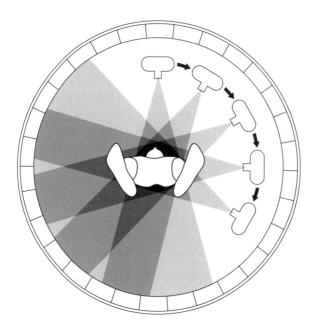

Computed Axial Tomography (CAT) relies on electronic X-ray sensors to record data from multiple projections through each plane of the subject. This data correlates to projections that are roughly equivalent to the frames of the rotating subject in the cinefluoroscopy of Janker (right) and Watson. While cinefluoroscopy dictates that dimensionality is empirically observed, reading the CAT scan entails a computation of differentials to arrive at a static, planar (and nondimensional) model of the subject.

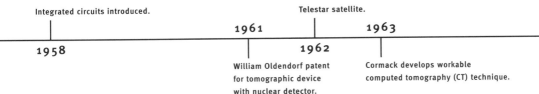

Integrated circuits introduced.

Telestar satellite.

1961

1963

1958

1962

William Oldendorf patent
for tomographic device
with nuclear detector.

Cormack develops workable
computed tomography (CT) technique.

than a conventional X-ray image. The perception of
3-D cinefluorography is dependent on the reading of
a differential between frames. The introduction of
the cinematic lens to record the fluoroscopic image
would suggest that Watson reincorporates the illu-
sionistic space of perspective – the very optical system so effectively displaced by direct radiography and
tomography.

The introduction of perspectival depth to the radiographic image makes it impossible to derive new
quantitative data from the image field. Though visually compelling, the 3-D cinefluorographic moving
image is no more valuable diagnostically than the
standard radiograph. Ultimately, cummings's seeingaround must repudiate the lenticular optics on which
it is based if it is to get beyond the visual barrier of
skin and other intervening bodily masses. The introduction of lenticular optics to the radiographic image
reintroduces the outmoded logic of perspectival
space that radiography had done away with so effectively. Why this retrograde move? One explanation
might be found in the appeal of the 3-D movie in the
popular cinema during the mid-1950s. Watson's films
appear during the same period that 3-D movies become a popular novelty in the entertainment cinema.
However, they find their exact model in the 3-D cine-
fluoroscopic films produced in the 1930s by radiologists in Nazi Germany. Using these films as a model
for his own studies, Watson carries Nazi medicine's
logic of space over into postwar U.S. medical research.

Even as Watson works, medical imaging is undergoing another major transition. Electronic media
introduces a new phase of imaging even more radically divorced than tomography from the sensory act
of seeing and the phenomenal. The graphic codes
of ultrasound and computed tomography undercut
the empirical force of the short-lived 3-D cinefluoro-
scopic image.

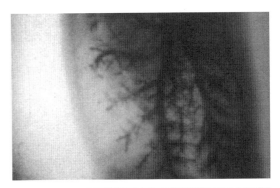

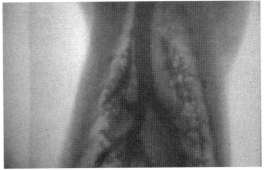

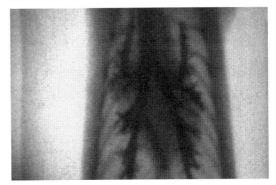

Frame enlargement from c. 1933 cinefluoroscopy of a cat
torso by Robert Janker. Cat's lungs are filled with contrast
medium to facilitate radiography viewing (Janker, *History
of Cineradiography*, Germany, c. 1960).

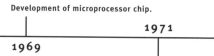

Tome 6: 1964

Just as Watson gives up on X-ray cinematography, radiologist James Bricker makes a case for tomography as a process with a lively future by using the cinema as a point of comparison:

> In some regions of the country [tomography] is used little, and in some regions of the body it is used little, but like cine "moving pictures" it is here to stay!
>
> (Bruwer, p. 1410)

Bricker recognizes the appeal of moving pictures in the cinema; though tomography involves movement of a different type, its pictures will also guarantee a certain appeal. However, by the late 1960s, the image as such will no longer be a part of the tomographic process. With the advent of computed tomography, object space will be described according to numerical registers of density, rather than according to the laws of perspectival space. The pictorial field will be reduced from a visual image to be seen to a graphic register to be mechanically decoded. The move from tomography to computed tomography (CT) signals a critical step in the historical repudiation of sight in the field of scientific knowledge.

Within this repudiation of sight, the visual retains its primacy nonetheless, functioning now as graphic register. Within a decade, the numerical data of the CT

Auguste and Louis Lumière imaged with average reflective values represented in each quadrant of an arbitrarily imposed grid.

scan derived from the pictorial image will be able to be transformed back into a tonally rendered visual display. But this belated return to the image will not carry with it a return to the standards of lenticular optics. The post-1978 CT image will function as a salutary measure; it will satisfy a desire for visibility without lending credibility to the image as such. And yet, the desire to read the visual display as a picture will persist for a long time. It will be necessary for the radiological technician to militate against his or her own outmoded desire to view the tomographic image as a picture:

> As physicists, we cannot emphasize strongly enough that the basis of the CT is absorption measurement, and that the image is actually only a visual model. We can only hope that the medical profession does not forget…that we have renounced the qualitative assessment of image shadows for the display of quantitative absorption value. (K. Ungerer, in *Clinical Computer Tomography*, ed. A. Baert et al. [Springer, 1978])

The modernist repudiation of lenticular optics begun around 1920 with tomographic and stereo-synthetic space has been implemented fully in CT and related technologies (MRI, PET and ultrasound). These techniques all share a nonperspectival method of representing spatial dimensions. The organization of these images can be traced back to the planar geometry of *photo-stéréo-synthèse*, to tomography, and to the modernist idiom of seeingaround. In the seventy years since 1920, lenticular optics has been challenged persistently from within the diverse institutions in which it functioned most centrally. The technician's disassembling of lenticular optics constitutes a challenge to the empirical gaze and the sight-based epistemologies informing Western culture. The institutional and technological bases of this challenge deserve further examination not only from the standpoint of institutions of popular culture and media, but from the perspective of the demarcated profes-

sional spheres of scientific imaging. Incorporated across all of these spheres, the technology of Louis Lumière blurs institutional lines of demarcation even as it dismantles the very system of vision-based knowledge upon which it is grounded.

178	174	183	184	170	174	175	172	152	186
184	195	177	133	181	186	194	197	194	189
203	128	020	041	049	130	186	200	200	189
203	013	111	186	188	172	128	161	184	167
170	049	181	144	156	184	120	092	081	141
184	153	033	055	156	189	163	045	020	058
189	108	120	105	158	170	178	163	034	056
183	108	108	066	153	167	102	091	056	064
194	170	069	086	91	047	025	109	055	047
191	178	070	100	127	139	034	047	075	020
170	125	081	083	025	001	001	034	063	039
134	097	084	081	072	031	001	002	063	119
011	103	086	041	070	113	125	113	147	136
001	027	066	059	041	088	117	116	136	097
028	005	001	005	084	063	059	097	114	109
186	016	001	001	019	041	086	113	114	116
195	181	158	006	001	001	001	070	119	124
184	191	197	086	001	001	001	001	001	102
181	181	192	191	170	056	001	001	001	014

Numerical values in the illustration above represent the reflective properties of given quadrants within the rectilinear segment of the image on the facing page. In computed tomography, diagnostic images are generated from computed density values.

Sound localization experiment, 1890s.

The Living Machine: Psychology as Organology

Didier Deleule

Husserl created a myth and baptized it "Galileo." The myth can essentially be described as "substituting idealized nature for the prescientific nature of sense perception."[1] The consequences are well known: what Husserl calls the "cloak of ideas" or the "veil of symbols" becomes, by a great trick, a self-true "Nature." In short, pure method is substituted for the living thing itself. What made this deception so successful was that it was simultaneously a discovery (that is, a laying bare) and a concealment (as if, out of modesty, the body had somehow to be dressed in ideas): the body was stripped down to its pure, mathematical essence and, in the same operation, fitted with new clothing to hide it from the indiscretions of immediate perception. This careful fitting was crucial: "Sense perceptions are merely and only *subjective*,"[2] and so, by the same stroke, everything concerning prescientific life is "devalued." The logical consequence of this line of thinking was that the subject's personal, sensate experience was no longer a primary concern; nor were what Husserl called the "cultural properties associated with objects over the course of human activity."[3] Hence, there was a complete split between the world of nature, on the one hand, and a subjective-cultural world, on the other. Essentially, this split was introduced by Cartesianism through its "naturalization of the psychic," which was to leave an indelible mark on the modern era. Maurice Merleau-Ponty pursued the effects of the myth: according to him, the psychologists had missed the bandwagon; the demotion of the body to the status of one object among so many others, in a flat and uniform world, meant that the body could not be a means of communication with the outside world. At the same time, this meant that the world had to be seen as a sum of discrete objects and not at all as a "latent horizon of our experience."[4]

It would seem, then, that for psychology there was a kind of original sin — as became apparent with the emergence of scientific psychology in the second half of the nineteenth century. Even as the domain of psychological investigation expanded dramatically, psychology placed itself under its own rather formidable limitations: the psychic object, having now been reduced to a second-order reality, could be subjected to a kind of scientific analysis; and, by the magic of this approach itself, that object could be invested with a certain objectivity. Although it lost its singularity, it now had a dignified place in the universality of being. That's where it belonged. Its rightful place was in the realm of objective knowledge — however much that place may have cost it in terms of the particularity and complexity of its specific character. What was lost (for the researcher) was, of course, the subject's experience. What psychology sought above all else was the identity of a being who could be represented, quantified and, in effect, mastered. To appreciate the consequences of this devaluation of corporeal experience, Merleau-Ponty stated that by treating bodily experience in this way, psychologists were unaware that they were merely using science to avoid an inevitable dilemma.[5] It was probably not entirely the fault of the psychologists themselves. Their mistakes were, in certain ways, the inevitable outcome of the *lato sensu* success of their discourse. This also meant that their errors could be seen as a predictable result of their aesthetic surgery: in order to purify the body and present it in a more manageable form, they replaced its messy, invasive subjectivity with a marvelously intelligible and finely tuned machine whose working parts could easily be interchanged. In short, they subscribed to the old Socratic ideal — this time through an industrial aesthetic.

The Galilean revolution was not simply an outgrowth of a brutal subversion of medieval values.[6] Rather, it developed as a simplified image of the complex body: denying vital forces any epistemological validity became the very condition for constructing the epistemological framework itself. More precisely, this set the conditions for a certain body of scientific knowledge that was itself seen as laying down the conditions for acquiring power over all things — over nature in general, which had been reduced to a "mechanical toy."[7]

Of course, this effort at rationalizing nature affected the way the body was represented: corporeal experience was entirely excluded from the domain of epistemology; and in tandem with this, the body could only be considered as an imaginary object (a central theme of the theory of the organic machine). On the other hand, the body was seen as the locus of vital experience, as the privileged site of desire, but also of illusions and deceptions that had to be held in check by the guiding life force.[8] But to say that the reality of subjective experience is somehow overtaken by imaginary representation would make it virtually impossible to get past Descartes's "First Meditation."[9] Nonetheless, what is being separated analytically is not the body's soul, as if the soul were sovereign over the body; on the contrary, there is the de facto union of the soul and the body in keeping with Descartes's idea of the "composite," which, as a primary but problematic phenomenon, makes it possible to conceive of the potential separation-abstraction of the body into nothing but a machine that is subject to the basic laws of mechanics. In point of fact, then, the body is always linked with the soul; but that union, being empirical, points up the many other ambiguities surrounding the body.[10] Only a juridical viewpoint allows us to take the body apart, like a machine, and treat it as an autonomous entity. That juridical separation is at the core of Cartesianism.

One point needs to be made clear: Life does not imitate the machine, nor is it reduced to a mechanical construct. It is the machine itself that actually simulates life.[11] This is what permitted the unintelligible, even scandalous, displacement to the level of language: witness, for example, the importance placed on the *adaptation* of the machine to man. Although modeling life after the machine seems like a representational distortion — yet another step toward exploiting the living machine — the real perversion is that the humanists pointed it out only to denounce it. In fact, the representational perversion first takes on its full meaning when it makes a bid for power in order to confer a mechanistic structure to the image of life: the body, having become an imaginary object, projects its vital energy into a totally mechanistic structure so that no surprises are possible; and second, this projection is maintained by virtue of the fact that the organism must be understood as an imitative object designed to carry out complex productive activities. But what is obtained through this metamorphosis is, first and foremost, an excess of power — and *this* fact is the key to the mystery of the entire process. The idea, in effect, is not that the machine might replace the life process — the machine is not capable of such an act of conquest — but, rather, that *life* is essentially conquest; as fulfills its function, it must facilitate the larger, general movement of the living organism.[12] The fact that this simulation remains simulation (that is, an approximation and not fusion) changes nothing. The organic machine is driven both by life force (as is affirmed in the movement to dominate the environment) and by machine, insofar as the machine is called on to develop maximum efficiency or to ensure functional movement.[13] Thus, we are not simply dealing with a descriptive tool; nor is it only a matter of agreeing on standard terminology or of simplifying for other pedagogical reasons. Rather, this model challenges the notion that, in the face of the forces of "nature," vital energy occupies a central, privileged place as a point of application and as a means of mastery and conquest. At the same time, the model provides a way of undertaking the never-ending task of conquest: even though the organic machine owes its very conception to the life process, the machine reclaims some of the life process that it simulates. The organic machine theory thus appears, in a single, unifying movement as an updating of, and return to, the very essence of technology: in order to visualize this "machinery," the life process had to be reduced conceptually to a machine — a machine modeled on the image of life itself. In this way, the machine revealed itself for what it was, namely, *an extension* of the life process (albeit via inanimate forces). In truth, then, life should be seen as part of the same sphere of technology and not as a term in opposition to it. [14]

Similarly, the machine is not a substitute for the life process, even though advances in cybernetics might have us believe otherwise. Nor was the machine ever intended to take over life's work tasks or to alleviate the problems of work overload in "imperfect societies." In spite of all the arguments, we still hear about "labor-saving" machines or production processes that allow for more leisure time. These all misrepresent the fundamental character of Western civilization. The fact is, machines were not built in order to free humans from servile tasks. The function of machines is to increase the power of life itself, to enhance life's capacity for mastery and conquest. The machine does not in any sense replace life. [15]

We can now look, for example, at what Engels called "the victory of mechanical work over manual labor," by which he meant the equation of manual labor with mechanical work. [16] This was the *feedback* [17] that came about as a result of the gradual destruction of the independent manufacturer under proletarianization. Without taking anything away from the life model, Marxism set up a certain economic model to explain and, in turn, to take the blame for, the reversal in the workers' situation: the revolt of human labor against the dead labor that sought to supplant it, the refusal of life to submit to death. Yet there were subtle indications that a kind of homogeneity was at work: the machine entered into competition with workers in the same way that workers competed against each other on the labor market. The former process aggravated the latter, and competition became even fiercer as women and children began entering the labor force. [18] However, as people and their labor were subjugated to machines, their lives were devalued, diminished and sapped of vitality by rhythmic and repetitive tasks. But that scenario was not without its contradictions: the machine participates in a certain life "project," the biological body is considered a tool within a mechanical process (which indeed it is, but only by virtue of a reversed image). It was a contradiction that revolutionary strategists and tacticians were able to promote alternately or even simultaneously throughout the history of workers' movements.

In the mechanistic view of the biological body, the life process is seen as constituting work activities. Life is perceived as purely work intensive, freed from the defects of subjectivity; hence, leisure and idleness became incarnations of social evil. The organic machine is destined to be productive, not because the machine is more productive than the body, but because the life process itself must be presented as a productive force in keeping with its mission to conquer; and the machine is an extension of that life activity. And so, if the life process must be machinelike, it is because the machine acquires all the capacities attributed to life itself while, to all appearances, making effective use of vital energy. It is as if, through that apparent economy, one could speak of work energy as a free, untapped bodily energy that might somehow be "freed up" for nonproductive tasks (rest is required only as a means of recuperation). Hence, there are two extremes as far as the use of bodily energy and vital, productive forces are concerned: either they are used up as in a "sweatshop," or, through the now much-vaunted antidote, this pent-up energy is subjected to an intensive sports or exercise program (yet another kind of asceticism and sustained program of mutilation). What the organic machine implies, then, is the progressive reduction of manual labor to a mechanical process. But it follows that mechanical activity itself amounts to the simplest expression of a complex skill and the simulation of living work.[19] Still, that implication is justified only by the historical "effects" that the image supports, but it has no real sound theoretical basis.

Thus, the significance of the organic machine theory is hardly the apparent reduction of the life process to the status of machine: it is this, to be sure, but such an image is produced only by virtue of a deception; for the two processes are in fact one. And that is what gives them their exemplary character. Production involves bodily organs (and not the soul, which thus will not concern us here) in a particular way at a given moment. Thus, automation is also an "act of nature."[20] For that matter, death can be seen as the moment of total mechanical failure (again, the soul does not enter the picture), and the shutdown of the life processes can be viewed as the final breakdown of the mechanical system. However, it is precisely because the destruction of the machine has such specific consequences for the life/machine process that one inevitably thinks that the last movements of the working parts are still somehow not a process like others that the machine performs.[21] When Cartesian mechanics is viewed in the context of the living machine, it sheds light on a process inherent in technology: divesting the life process of its natural and immediate finality in order to transfer it secretly to a level that is foreign to life itself.

The construction of the productive body is possible because of the juridical separation between the body/machine. The real increment of power taken away is related to the radical reorientation of the assumed relations between the living organism and nature; and at the same time, it is this reorientation that requires an intelligible homogeneity of the powers that are brought face to face. After all, it is

only to make the body more *understandable*, and not so much to discipline and control it, that it is subjected to a mechanistic treatment.[22] What is really at issue is
a certain kind of bio-power: the forces of mechanical nature correspond to the
strength of the body-machine. Thus, the homogeneity of the treatment corresponds
not so much to some kind of cosmological fusion as to the setup of an antagonistic
scenario: face to face, viewed in the same mechanistic terms, the organic machine
confronts the world-machine. However, homogeneity does not necessarily imply
equilibrium; the surpluses of the mission to conquer eventually lead to a disequilibrium between what constitutes the role of humanity in the life process. The
model realized for the living machine or the animal-machine, even if it is the telos
of intelligibility of the man-machine, remains a real deprivation (that is, at the same
time language and calculation: it has a set, thought-out objective).[23]

In order for the productive body to reveal itself, the theory of the organic machine arises, in this respect, beyond the project of
an overriding intelligibility in which it plays a part, as recognition and exploitation
of an original characteristic of life: life as conquest and domination of nature; and
simultaneously, the organic machine is exactly the trick to transfer finality so as to
exclude life from the project. In this way, it is always possible to view the productive body as a consequence of a complete overthrow or undoing of man's relation
to nature — man as a "breaking and entering" of nature — following a plan that
constantly implicates him.[24]

In order for the productive body to reveal itself, the biological body must be dis-
sected, viewed in parts. Its lost unity can only be retrieved epistemologically, while
also accounting for the division of labor, separation of task. Productive activity has
to be extracted from the body itself, from living labor, and relocated within the
parcelization of physical motion, which is most meaningful and at its most efficient
when an organ is attributed a specific and unique function as a guarantee of its
infallibility. Yet, it is included in a general mechanistic plan whose meaning is not
entirely understood by the actor-participant and which, as it is carried out, leaves
a mark on the body — as in Menenius Agrippa's fable, by allowing the individual to
portray himself metonymically, through an image in which a fragment of the body
becomes the entire body.

Now it remains to show how, by taking things to their logical extreme, this image
is refined and enriched by a new discipline dealing specifically with it: a productive
body centered within a psychological science. This recognition of a new concept of
life implies a new kind of collaborative enterprise in which tasks are broken down
into individual operations and are regulated by an automated control center. This
is the pure image of the productive body, forced to sustain the illusion of a lost but
nonetheless hoped-for collaboration.

Psychology as "Organology" or the Living
Machine and Its Contradictions

Let us imagine an encyclopedia or catalog showing how each of the body's systems carries out a productive activity. Under the listing for the sense of touch, for example, we would find that this sense is the most direct medium of contact with the outside world, and that the skin is the organ par excellence of manipulation and tactility. There would be an entry pointing out how most investigation and systematic inquiry on the senses begins with the sense of touch, thus reaffirming an idea with a long philosophical tradition. Still, for some of us, many questions would remain: What happens when we touch or are touched? What touches what? Of course, we might answer that we touch other objects. This is true, but objects change and are therefore constantly open to reinterpretation: they exhibit resistance, have weight, expand, contract, are sometimes hot, sometimes cold.[25] These and other qualities make it possible for the senses to misevaluate other objects or perhaps even one's own body. So we must proceed, then, by stretching out the entire skin surface and pinning it to a laboratory slide, as we might do with a mouse. But we shall settle for probing and testing our human subject with an esthesiometer. (By passing over the skin with a pair of compass ends covered with cork, we shall attempt to determine the distance between the two arms of the compass at which our subject senses each point of contact as being distinctly separate.) After applying this test to the skin and certain mucous membranes, such as the tongue and the lips, we can expect the following results: the most sensitive regions, where the ends are felt most distinctly, are located at the tip of the tongue, the edges of the lips and on the fingertips. Sensitivity would diminish gradually as we move away from the extremities and toward the torso, until we reached the area with the poorest capacity for sensory discrimination: the back. We would find that the endpoints of the compass are felt most distinctly when each is applied to the skin surface one after the other, not simultaneously. And whenever the subject moves the finger that has been attached to the esthesiometer, he or she would be able to distinguish each endpoint faster than usual; and, in general, there would be a noticeable improvement in the movement of all organs of touch. Finally, to sense the separate points of contact, the endpoints would have to be separated a minimum distance of one millimeter when testing the tongue, and two millimeters on the fingertip.

Such results would seem to support the hypothesis that tactile sensitivity is identical for everyone and that different organisms obey laws of homogeneity like those found in machines. At the same time, it is difficult to reconcile this idea with the fact that a machine cannot break down, in and of itself ("objectively").

And it is even more problematic to consider how we might go about measuring or predicting a machine's ability to maintain itself ("subjectively") in relation to its environment. But the implications of all this came across clearly in an early nineteenth-century experiment involving response to pressure: "Please pay close attention. You will occasionally receive a tap on the back of your wrist with a light object. Whenever you sense that you have been tapped, simply say, 'yes.' If you are unsure, just trust your first impression."[26] The experimenters were particularly attentive to "errors resulting from suggestibility or intentional deception"; and, in fact, they themselves resorted to an endless variety of tricks: they asked for a response even when they had not tapped the subject. Clearly, the idea of "objective" techniques must be approached with some reservation; and it should indeed be seen as coloring the entire discourse: language widens the gap separating man and machine, and, moreover, language is at once indispensable and superfluous. Although it is the most basic means of communicating or acknowledging a sensation, it continually insinuates itself into man's every attempt to evaluate his relation with the world, inevitably introducing mistakes, misjudgments. Or worse yet, it results in error or outright deception by virtue of its very structure and status. So whenever we consider the mechanical universe — even that area where natural processes are seen as mechanically determined and capable of a totally objective explanation — the question is always the same: Where do the errors, misreadings, contradictions and negative factors come from?

Modern psychology, as it emerged in the nineteenth century, poses as a way of dealing with the embarrassment of not having absolute certainty; for it suggested how to incorporate the vagaries and unpredictability of "subjectivity" into a set of constants: invariably, the lips are the part of the body most sensitive to weight/pressure, followed by the skin covering the extremities. In almost every instance, a given weight will seem heavier when it is held in the left hand, as opposed to the right. Almost without exception, a person will perceive the difference between ounces and drams even when the standards of comparison vary in quantity and absolute intensity.[27] In short, there is no room for a subject to be mistaken; he can in fact commit an error, but he doesn't have the right to.

Avoiding wasteful or purposeless activity, adjusting the living machine to the lifeless machine, making the living machine function like a lifeless machine — with smooth precision, without an intervening conscience — and, above all, transforming the entire living machine into an efficient and expedient system: these are the desirable accomplishments that might be won through the discipline, before even getting to the problems of "relation" that allow affectivity to enter into the whole question. Sensations of pressure, temperature, physical pain, algesia, electricity;

cutaneous responsiveness, be it caustic, traction, ticklishness; finally subcutane-
ously, vibratory and kinetic: it is unlikely that any investigation of these surfaces
could be carried out as one would carry out geological exploration — for, as we
know, the procedures often take on the character of colonizing invasion.

Next in our catalogue would be the eyes. These precious extensions of the
hands, which they must guide through complex activities, can make judgments
with geometric precision; still, they are subject to error, because of distance and
distraction. Evaluating the visual field, measuring visual acuity, are taken into
account in the approximation of the notion of "reaction time," understood as the
time between the production of an outside stimulation (visual, auditory, olfactory,
taste) and the subject's outward response to the stimulation.[28] The importance
of reaction time attests to the great concern for obtaining precise measurements
while reducing the influence of subjectivity. For Wilhelm Wundt and his school,
the duration of conscious modifications is given more importance than their intensity. In both simple and complex reactions, then, the living machine is placed
under another limitation — one that allows only one way of interpreting the system.
The intensity of productive activity is measured according to the reaction time to
the stimulus, and not the converse; but, reciprocally, the reaction time depends on
the intensity of the stimulation of the sensory organs. The more intense the stimulation, the faster the reaction time. On average, luminous stimulations have a
tendency to produce relatively delayed reactions, while sound and touch produce
faster reactions. In this way, because an increase in stimulation leads to a shortened reaction time, a higher production rate can be achieved. It is all a matter of
setting and maintaining a rhythm — to break it is to risk destroying the entire
machine, for it does not adapt well to sudden changes. The machine produces
more, perhaps less well, as the saying goes; but who cares about quality when quantity is of primary concern? What is more, the instrument is still important and
useful even as absolute surplus production (the longer workday) becomes more
difficult to obtain, by putting the emphasis on relative surplus value (accelerating
the work pace). Marx shows very clearly that if production of absolute surplus
value is derived only from work time, the creation of relative surplus, on the other
hand, completely shakes up "technical processes of labor, and the composition of
society."[29] Such is the case, Marx concludes, "with the Capitalist mode of production properly speaking." But that is not the whole story: the system is perfectible,
and modern psychology has moved closer to fulfilling its destiny, ever since the
middle of the nineteenth century. Make no mistake, psychology is neither simply
an ideological reflection on the capitalist means of production, nor a transparent
effect. Saddled with its dead subject, it has wound along a tortuous path, moving

ever closer to fulfilling the historical project. Slowly but surely, in fits and starts, psychology has accompanied the project. It is always *there*, an indispensable component part of the social machine; yet it follows no set plan of order — since it is there *precisely for that reason*.

The goal of the psychologist in the study of the "two-sided phenomenon," to borrow Théodule Ribot's expression, is first to specify the psychic through arduous research. It is equally necessary to find the causes for the errors and illusions that trip up the senses, but to attribute them less to immediate subjectivity than to the intellectual processes that ordinarily accompany the process. The concept of parallelism,[30] in whatever form it might take (consciousness attributed to all vital phenomena, consciousness reduced to more or less independent physiological syntheses, consciousness accorded to a limited zone of physiological phenomena), either supports the theories of automatism or denies consciousness a role as a controlling, active force (in spite of the attributes with which it is normally invested): consciousness becomes only an epiphenomenon.[31] The most important ramification of parallelism is that, in the guise of scientific proof, it dispenses with the useless and costly — even ruinous — "metaphysical" hypothesis that the body and consciousness must interact. Once a physical phenomenon is relegated to the role of concomitant, any possible immediate causality between the body on the mind is removed, and there is an implied scale of being that must accommodate the possibility that vital phenomena are capable of functioning without consciousness — all of which still does not explain the existence of consciousness, which is ever-present at the highest level of production without having any physical, corporeal presence. The corporeal machine functions without receiving orders through the hierarchy of being; consciousness accompanies without acting: the machine acts on its own; the mind plays only a minor role, that of "logical subject of internal experience."[32] It comes as no surprise, then, that in essence the problem comes down to the relation between the body and the mind: Gustav Fechner, in his *Elements of Psychophysics* (1860), wrote:

> Psychophysics should be understood here as an exact theory of the functionally dependent relations of body and soul or, more generally, of the material and the mental, of the physical and the psychological worlds.... All discussions and investigations of psychophysics relate only to the apparent phenomena of the material and mental worlds, to a world that either appears directly through introspection or through outside observation... briefly, psychophysics refers to the *physical* in the sense of physics and chemistry, to the *psychical* in the sense of experimental psychology, without referring back in any way to the nature of the body or of the soul beyond the phenomenal in the metaphysical sense.[33]

In the end, passing from substance to phenomenon cannot mask the difficulty encountered by the psychologist when he defines the psychic "side"; most energy is devoted to measuring reaction time for psychological phases of so-called elementary intellectual operations.[34] Such efforts translate into operations that are simple in principle but complex and enigmatic in fact: when a precise calculation was made of the duration of the so-called extrapsychological phases, the total obtained was subtracted from the entire reaction time; the difference represented the consciousness phase. In other words, consciousness is the result of a subtraction. Anything that cannot be attributed to the automaton-machine is attributed, quite simply, to consciousness. In any event, no psychologist questions the difficulty of the task. Take the following experiment, for example: The materials used include a black box, twenty-five centimeters long. Affixed to the interior at one end is a blank piece of paper, nine centimeters by eleven; on the opposite end is a circular opening, three centimeters in diameter, which the subject must look through to view the facing panel. A Geissler tube lights up the box and the white panel every time an electrical current is applied; set in the main circuit is a chronoscope whose gauges fluctuate only when the current has passed through the secondary circuit. When the timing mechanism starts up, the noise from the chronoscope signals the subject that the experiment has begun.

The operation procedes as follows: First, the subject closes the circuit halfway; the observer starts the chronoscope, but because the current is still passing through the main circuit at this point, the gauges do not move. Second, the researcher closes the secondary circuit entirely: the Geissler tube lights up, the current is now weakened and the chronoscope gauges oscillate. Third, as soon as the subject notices the white panel, he lifts his hand and interrupts the secondary circuit; the light goes out and the current from the main circuit gains power and immediately stops the chronoscope needles. The result: It was possible to obtain, to the millisecond, the exact time elapsed between the moment the subject "saw" the lighted white background and the moment he signaled his observation by the gesture of his hand. Of course, the visual stimulations could be complicated ad infinitum, or the colors could be varied. The rest is only a matter of subtraction.

Where are the defects in the experiment? In at least two places, (if we leave out the purely technical aspects of the experiment): first of all, individual variations in the reaction of a raised arm are of utmost importance; general psychology cannot do without individual psychology — a psychology of differences, as opposed to one of similarities. Behind the homogeneous beauty of the machine subsists the threatening heterogeneity of the human subjects, for there is no assurance that a subject raises his hand and reacts at the moment he should: whether he hesitates on purpose or involuntarily, the margin accrued to consciousness suddenly increases. And what about the duration of complex conscious phenomena (choice, associations, judgments and so on)? Prudently, the psychologist concludes, "until now, psycho-physiological studies to measure the duration of the phenomena of consciousness have given only indications, not results."[35] The cautious tone is warranted inasmuch as it indicates the true status of psychology: all research into psychophysiological gaps (in other words, research to determine the true nature of gratuitous or "free" acts, or "pure" thought outside any sort of corporeal conditioning) has run into a stumbling block, but tries to get around it by reconsidering the whole system. (What is a "free" act except a kind of "readaptation"?) The substantialist body–mind dualism is replaced by an organism–environment dualism (the Darwinian model conveniently fits things together). The object of study for psychology is not consciousness but the individual subject's dealing with his changing environment. Psychology will first be conceived of as a part of biology, and its essential problem, though not explicitly formalized, will be that of the individual in his social milieu: "In relation to their environment, all organisms are in a state of equilibrium that oscillates with respect to a theoretical point: perfect adaptation."[36]

That is indeed the task of modern psychology: to adapt, as far as possible, the living machine to the social mechanism with which it is in fact integrated during normal, everyday functions. In this way, the machine can carry out its production tasks under optimal conditions, and there is less likelihood that the working parts will squeak and grind. Consciousness has no real specificity outside the dualism, the double-sidedness, that allows us to conceptualize it. It is beyond the realm of science. Only the bodily machine, the organ of transmission and generator of adaptive energy, is the legitimate object of scientific research; yet the status of one element of that concomitance remains enigmatic; and science is hard pressed to explain it without recourse to fiction. "Parallelism consists precisely in this: finding the proper place of the body, that imaginary construct built up over the centuries under the name of the mind, so as to localize the superior functions of the body there."[37] Determining what kind of body we are dealing with, what type of construct it corresponds to and how it sustains itself are precisely the questions to be studied in this work.

The fact that psychology aims to be a "psychology without a soul"[38] is a good indication that it has renounced metaphysics and refuses even to take any stand on the existence of substance. From here, the psychic, which is concomitant, can only be perceived as a function of the subject's capacity to exercise and control its attention. Jean-François Richard has shown decisively the obstructive role that individual variations played in the first attempts at psychological measurement:[39]

once the "personal equation" had been determined in a study of reaction times, the notion of individual variations in attention was taken into account, but, at the same time, there was a displacement that transposed interindividual variations into intraindividual variations. The result was, as Richard puts it, that "what is observed is not reaction time but reaction time as it translates into the time for the aperception process." All that can be obtained from this is the time the process takes; it tells us nothing about the nature of the process itself. It is at this point, obviously, that the psychic concomitance intervenes: if the intensity of the productive activity depends on the time it takes to react to the stimulus, it again follows that attention is susceptible to control by the researcher or to manipulation by the subject himself. The measured time is only the sign of the living machine's capacity for increasing its productivity.

Of course, we must also consider the limitations of individual organs, as Pierre Bouguer demonstrated when searching for the level of light intensity at which the eye can no longer perceive a faint light source. The disappearance of a candle's shadow on a white screen illuminated by another candle requires a distance of seven feet between the two candles: "the distance between the two lights was discernible until the [increment] was about sixty-four times weaker than the first."[40] But these problems, which plague everyone from astronomer to physician, not only constitute "the occasion that makes the thief" but also have special significance for the pioneer psychologist, who declares that what is interesting is not so much the intrinsic limitation of the senses but the variable reactions that lead the living machine to misjudge distances, sizes, sounds and contacts. Psychic concomitance is to be blamed: illusions and errors are not so much the fault of the machine itself but the fault of a defect, albeit a correctable one, in the controlling instruments. The more we deal with the intellect, the greater the chance of error: "certain intellectual operations superimpose themselves onto elementary sensory judgments, often resulting in miscalculations and imprecise perceptions, as in the case of most optical illusions."[41] An example: When two weights with different volumes are compared, the weight with the smaller volume is always underestimated. It is the old story of a kilogram of feathers and a kilogram of lead: "sight only makes it more difficult for the muscles to make judgments of weight."[42] Only the mentally impaired, it seems, do not fall for the optical illusion, as much experimental evidence would have us believe: the less one reflects on the problem (now we see the basis of the metaphor behind the word "reflect"), the faster and quicker the reaction. The senses cannot be fooled. Kant and others were exactly right when they said that the wonderful order and precision of the machine is destroyed only by the faculty of intelligence. The eyes are the most "noble" sense and the paradigm of intelligence, but they are also the organs most closely implicated with psychic concomitance, in that they are the organs of ambivalence: they are the site par excellence of psychic reaction (I see and I raise my arm; I see and I press the button). Hence, within the constraints of the experiment, it is there *in the eyes* that the specificity of the psychic resides, for the eyes determine what will be interpreted as attention span and what will be its duration. The eyes' productive activity is the result of interaction.[43] But the eyes also open the way for misjudgment, and they can trip up otherwise efficient operations. How are these errors rectified? Who will restore the productive circuits that risk being altered by the inevitable but disruptive psychic concomitance? "We are all blind," wrote Diderot, "the eyes are the guide-dogs that lead us" — but he would certainly not fail to add "that the eye would be all the more misleading if its judgments were not constantly corrected by our sense of touch."[44] This remark may well have marked the beginnings of modern psychology, for it acknowledges that only the blind machine can be ideal — not so much an Oedipus-like machine that puts out its eyes in order to attain true sight but, rather, a machine blind from birth. Having been born into a different but complete world in which every problem must be resolved by touch, it would use its robotic claws or grips to carry out each productive task with mechanical precision, over and over again. The question of adaptation would never come up; nor for that matter, would the problem of cataracts! Sightlessness would mean fewer complications, fewer illusions! No eyes to glisten and sparkle, or to look into another's soul only to be disillusioned by the disappointing spectacle of life. Unlike the blank eyes of the statues of antiquity, the eyes of the machine would be completely absent: that is the telos of the living machine. With sight, there is always the danger of error through simple inattentiveness or distraction — errors that cannot be blamed entirely on tricks played on the eyes. Whatever might be said, adaptation is a problem for the life process, but not for the machine: the machine does only what is necessary to keep it functioning. This point is made especially clear with regard to the faculty of sight, because the whole notion of accommodation is as much a question of optics as of biology. Functionalism has come up with an explanation for this. And I am not just talking about a joint critique of "structuralism" and of a psychology of the senses; nor am I aiming to look at all the various means by which the individual interacts with the environment only to replace them all with some substitute theory on individual adaptation or adjustment.[45] More precisely, we need to look at the instrumental theory of the mind, which gave rise to modern operationalism.

In essence, operationalism held that mental activity could be localized in one organ, was susceptible to modification by experience and was capable of being perfected (a codificaton of psychology's concept of conditioning). The mind, which carried out a whole range of activities, from active or passive attention, surveillance, control and decision making to other various functions, is not in fact a guide but, rather, an instrument used by the living machine for the sole purpose of achieving successful adaptation, just like the other sense organs. This description, though, makes it almost impossible to speak of a qualitative difference between mental activity and neural activity; the mind simply represents a qualitatively superior level of the living machine's adjustment process.[46] The concomitant psychicism does not give commands: because it is only one aspect of the living machine, the only order with which it concerns itself pertains to choosing the most efficient techniques for ensuring survival. In other words, the point is not just to live, but to learn how to survive.

In the 1890s, James McKeen Cattell proposed a "test" to measure such an aptitude for survival, involving: dynamometric pressure, speed of movement, sensitive zones, pressure (causing pain), the smallest perceptible difference in mass weight, reaction time to noise, time to recognize color, bisection of a fifty-centimeter line, estimating a ten-second time interval, number of letters remembered after hearing them once.[47] Cattell's entire argument consists in showing that, despite the apparent importance of physiological factors, this kind of research is psychologically significant. As he sees it, "It is impossible to separate bodily energy from mental energy." What is at issue in the case of dynamometric pressure, for example, is the "sense of effort" that reflects "the effects of [volition] on the body." At some maximum point of pressure, a whole set of previously unnoticed forces come into play, offsetting "voluntary control" and "bodily vigor" or "emotional excitation" and "bodily vigor." Moreover, it would be wrong to underestimate the psychological importance of the relation between the speed of executing a movement and the force of that movement: how can one be sure that the force of a movement does not alter either the precision or the force of execution? The answer no doubt lies with "temperament," to the extent that repeated readings of the chronoscope open up the possibility of improved performances, even during the trials when the best subjects are being chosen. Temporal and spatial judgments come into play when measuring a subject's ability to complete certain feats of skill: dividing an ebony ruler (fifty centimeters by three) into two equal parts with a movable cord; tapping on a table with the end of a pencil and waiting ten seconds before beginning again. In both cases, the subject gets only one try. But it all comes down to the subject's judgment, however precise or imprecise it may be; and so, in the end, it is a matter of estimating reaction time.

To consider the body as a machine — as a mechanism that can be evaluated, one that must be maintained and conditioned to remain in good running order — does not quite give the whole picture. Nothing here distinguishes it from an image we might find in classic mechanics. In fact, what such a list describes, in so many words, is essentially the system that merges the living machine and the advanced form of the productive body. The biological body — understood as a unit of organs directly or indirectly interfacing with the outside world — is replaced by a set of tightly interlocked, smooth-running and, hopefully, well-oiled mechanical parts that work together as a component of a larger productive system. On a higher level, the machine is an indispensable part of a greater, primordial production scheme. In other words, the biological body, too, places itself in the service of the productive body (that image a priori the only one possible): the biological body has become the model for both the elemental, constitutive parts, as well as for the total integrated system, of the productive body. Furthermore, if the biological body can place itself in the service of the machine, it is only because the biological body has long been perceived to function like a machine. And since desire has been left out of this schema, the isomorphism is all the more convincing; no symbolic debt will come due and bankrupt the analogy. And so, one of Leviathan's dreams has been realized: the biological body has been well recompensed, having been incorporated into the social body, though it had to fit itself to the supposedly natural limits that had been prescribed for it. Even if the machine cannot think, it can be programmed or, at the very least, stimulated. It's a strange, contradictory machine, devoid perhaps of any true cogitations, but never without ratiocination. With the interest in a new dimension of desire — baptized "motivation" — the system arrives at a form of Taylorism that "managers" and "production supervisors" still contest to this day.[48]

Survival as the Real Theme of Modern Psychology

We can now make some fundamental assumptions about the principles underlying modern psychology, namely, that survival means facing the inevitability of death. For, as we treat the dominant theme of adaptation, we must integrate the living machine in a discussion of the "lifeless mechanism." Survival means putting one's self in the service of death. That is, it is as if life were controlled by some outside organism or force that we will never completely understand; yet all the while we have the impression that we are autonomous. It is undoubtedly at this level that we see the full ramifications of carrying the biological model over into psychology: the survival of the individual subject in his social milieu depends on a selection process that is itself the outcome of the law of competition — "in nine cases out of ten, human life is but a struggle for existence," said William Gladstone.[49]

Adaptation, then, appears as a dynamic and operative part of the life process, although it is not necessarily sufficient for survival. The recurring theme of survival, made familiar by bitterly ironic catchphrases, is far from being a naive concept; it restores to the notion of survival its underlying ambiguity: for there to be survival, there must be victory won in struggle. And so it is for the survivor who, from the earliest moments of his existence, is constantly preoccupied not with life but with its opposite, death, for he is in fact a product of it: basic biological subsistence demands a kind of well-paced rhythm that, through its very repetition, actually marks a gradual loss of energy. This is the paradigm for life's gradual submission to the forces of death, set in motion not so much by technological fatality as by a carefully modulated system for absorbing living work. Adaptation, then, which plays a central role in the system of the productive body, leads us to a consideration of consumption — that being a crucial factor for ensuring not only the "biological" survival of the individual but also for its "social" survival. It is a very delicate matter to introduce a discussion of precedence into this biological-social schema, even if the liberals tend to emphasize the first aspect while the technocrats prefer to deal with the latter. Behind the facade, it is all really a question of a unique process whose elements are interdependent: sometimes the word "abundance" is used to describe "biological" survival (that is, the minimum rate of consumption required to maintain the system), thus making possible the "promotion" of "social" survival henceforth in purely technical terms.

Although the historical destiny of the living machine was to provide, in an immediate vision, a way to reduce the role of the life process and to increase that of the machine, the advent of modern psychology found here a somewhat uneasy foothold. As the evolution of psychology has made all too clear, the discipline's objective was to make it impossible to have a totally mechanical model of life; it is for this very reason that psychology has had to acknowledge the irreducible presence of life in the living machine — hence the recourse to adaptation. Modern psychology, at its high point, represented the ultimate attempt at treating life, scientifically, as a machine — that is, as a working part of the productive body. But that attempt also signaled the failure to remove life from the living machine, and it set the stage for the potential dual definition of life as both conquest and survival. The two concepts shared no common ground, except perhaps a battlefield of the dead and the living. If scientifically oriented psychology undermines the mechanization of life, it is only because its function is to resolve the problem of survival, to reverse the wheels of imagined history, to redirect it toward a point at which cooperation is possible. In a word, it sought to determine the best conditions of adaptation as a way of foreseeing all possible areas of conflict,[50] of doing away with war among the living and replacing it with the peace of machines; and so the image of homogeneous productivity was reinforced by its system of members and organs that carry out their functions according to a fixed plan.

The biological body plays a distinct, separate role within the productive body, but this demarcation does not explain the development of a logical abstraction, which rests on the image of the productive body as an assemblage of parts working together as a self-sustaining and relatively autonomous unit — a unit that, in theory, finds its point of application in automated work. The body is undoubtedly a set of working parts, but this fact brings us no closer to solving the question of the body's apparent autonomy of movement. Quite the contrary: the productive body *requires* autonomy (in the same way that the labor market requires that every individual be "free" to sell his labor). Dependent yet subjugated (separated from the means of production), the body is nevertheless perceived as being autonomous to the extent that it functions as freely as the mechanical parts of any mechanism do, once it is set into movement. Unlike the machine, which is obviously *dependent*, the biological body is shrouded in a complex image wherein mechanical processes are constantly haunted by life forces. And so, at every turn, the productive body presents us with apparently contradictory problems — namely, the needs to increase productivity and to ensure the survival of the individual in a competitive system. On the one hand, the biological body is always reduced to the status of a group of mechanical working parts; on the other hand, though, the biological body is always biological before it is mechanical. In an attempt to accommodate the idea that life entails conquest and risk, old questions about the problem of survival are put in newer terms.

If the producer is separated from the means of production, this certainly does not stem from a vague abstraction but is, rather, the result of a real historical process: the long history of an expropriation. Moreover, it seems that this fundamental separation does not take on vital form except by virtue of a gradual synthesis that eventually pervades the mechanical in general. Which is to say, first and foremost, that there must be a self-regulating biological body, for the biological body is the foundation of the life pyramid and the condition for ensuring the permanence of the system itself. So, if the organism must be machinelike, it is because the machine is itself organic in the way it carries out its normal functions. If this is how life pervades the mechanical universe, it is in order to structure a beautiful, functional totality around sensorial and intellectual potentialities. Each organ is seen as assuming numerous functions — but only those functions facilitating interaction with the outside world are considered. In this way, the organism–environment dualism (already suggested by stimulus–response and excitation–reaction models) must be understood as an adaptative necessity projected into a referential system. Today, this is more properly viewed in the "man–machine" relationship that represents the fusion of the diverse elements of the social mechanism into a fully realized synthesis of the productive body. Undoubtedly, life would have to be entirely extricated from the body in order for life to return, metamorphosed, and without losing any of its substance, in a dominated form; then life energy could be absorbed by the power of dead labor. If such a mechanical conception of life seems to be a renewed effort at promoting a certain epistemological tendency, though, it also appears, within certain limits, as a primary "symptom" of the productive body at its apogee. It is surely the same historical movement that propagates that dual destiny. Science, in this case, does not reflect; it accompanies. Life's resistance must be explained by a special subunit of the body within the man/machine composite; and it is this subunit, at the center of this system, that permits and justifies the discourse on the engineer of souls. Without this separation, there would be no need for scientific psychology. With no function, the discipline would have never progressed beyond those imaginary experiments that marked the first "babblings" of its infancy.[51]

Modern Psychology as a Contributing Factor in Improving Productive Consumption

In order for this separation to be viewed as appropriate and essential to the living machine, though, the machine would have to liberate itself from human power, intelligence and skillfulness. Marx saw such an emancipation as one of the conditions for the development of heavy industry; this, in effect, would be the price of constituting a "completely objective and impersonal organism of production."[52] This hinted at the radical separation of the lifeless machine and the living machine — in spite of the desired homogeneity. The living machine would thus require a specific discipline drawing on substantiated research in physiology and psychology (especially when evaluating sensorimotor skills and intelligence). The productive system requires that the various working parts of the mechanism be set up and made to run with utmost efficiency: each individual becomes a "pieceworker" (as Marx puts it) who works on a machine that itself operates "piecewise," and the worker becomes only one link in a larger, general production process. He is supervised by engineers and mechanics who, in their turn, will also be placed under the scrutiny of psychology. But the whole process becomes intelligible only when viewed from the exterior, from the viewpoint of an overriding capital plan. Seen in this context, the productive body can be said to be comprised of a group of mechanical parts making up the social mechanism: how the biological body is evaluated depends on the subject's position within the division of labor. It is either a question of evaluating how the sense organs can best be adapted to the machine while serving it, or of measuring the sensory or intellectual faculties that permit man to supervise or control the production process, in keeping with its technological evolution. As for the machine itself, it has become an instrument of production, which, as a form of capital, transforms itself into the dead labor that dominates human labor: it depletes the energies of the biological body as it renders it a servant of the "lifeless mechanism."

Psychology insinuates itself into this system by setting itself up as a necessary element of the system: we can best situate this fact by looking at what Marx called "productive consumption" (not to be confused with "individual consumption," which refers to the workers' means of sustenance or whatever is necessary to restore work energy).[53] Between the extremes of individual consumption (the foundation of the biological survival of the individual) and the maintenance (cleaning, repairs and so on) of lifeless machines, there exists another aspect of the individual's survival that bears upon the conditions of the productive body's permanence. Modern psychology, through its various techniques — of selection, detection and development of aptitudes, conditioning and learning, preventing or resolving personality conflicts and so on — is one of the factors, and indeed an important one, of *improving* "productive consumption." It is in this series of separate elements that there resides, for the system as a whole, the true key to mastery: the maintenance of lifeless machines corresponds to the maintenance of the living machine, for, during the production process, the living machine uses automatons as work tools.[54]

The existence of the life machine was oriented more toward conquest, whereas that of the living machine was directed more toward survival. As a consequence,

the coexistence of the two aspects — the body reduced to a mechanical process, the attribution of a vital process to the machine — suddenly began to see life as being always subservient to, or menaced by, death. In the fully developed version of the productive body, not only did machine serve man, but man became a servant of the machine. "Capital," Marx said, "absorbs human labor as if it were the devil in the flesh."[55] It had become a monstrosity.[56] What made it monstrous was the way it deformed and mutilated the body: "Piecework" meant that the body itself was "mutilated," "cut into pieces" and "transformed into an automaton with one, unchanging task." This image had already been described in the fable of Agrippa,[57] but here the body was reduced to a "living appendage of the machine"[58] in which human labor becomes a "simple accessory."[59] Within the larger productive body, the living machine is now no more than a "joint"[60] or a derivative body part; and it also finds itself reduced to an assemblage of mechanical parts that either serve or oversee the machine. The living machine is nothing more than a mechanical system or a surveillance organ forced to obey the strict time-efficiency standards, which are best understood as "quanta of work" and "the sole determining element of production."[61] Far from being a means of production for the living machine, the lifeless machine imposes on the other a threefold task: coordinating the action of the machine with the raw goods, supervising the production process, avoiding problems and mishaps.[62] Therefore, the movement of lifeless machines determines the activity of living machines, and not vice versa. The automaton, inasmuch as it fits into the capital plan and is embodied in the "person of the capitalist" is motivated by one passion alone: "stretching the limits of human elasticity and wearing away all of its resistances."[63] In this view, the discipline of psychology adopts the role reserved for it: the manual or intellectual appendage cannot exceed the dimensions of the construct that brought it into being; and so its criteria of normality are suspended at the furthest limit — but it is a prescribed limit nonetheless. The function of each organ is always sufficiently defined. To exceed the limits is to perform a kind of surgical intervention.

As the productive body appropriates life, it also suppresses knowledge, thus signaling the reinforcement of the division of labor: "the science which obliges inanimate machine parts to be turned into automated tools, by virtue of their construction, is a science that does not apply to the consciousness of the worker. Through the machine, science acts on him as a foreign force, as the very power of the machine."[64] By analogy, this statement can be applied to psychological intervention: the living machine, reduced to an appendage, undoubtedly constitutes a "moment"[65] in the production process, but this "moment" occurs without the participants having a complete understanding of the meaning of the productive activity in which they are engaged. The appendage acts in complete ignorance. One result of psychological intervention and, more generally, of everything that revolves around the idea of a "science of communication" is to restore to the agent a consciousness (after the fact, remote) of its position, by investing it with a kind of self-awareness recentered on the folkloric notion of "participation," of a "feeling of belonging to a group" — that is, of "empathy-spontaneity-creativity," which places the concept of "personality" into a strange union with its indispensable counterpart, the "integration."[66]

Picking up where Andrew Ure left off, Marx defined manufacturing as "a vast automated system comprised of numerous mechanical and intellectual devices that work together, nonstop, in order to produce a given object, with each unit being subordinated to a driving motor that moves of its own accord."[67] This is a compact image of how the advanced productive body functions. "The automaton," Marx said, "is dominated and the workers are simply thinking organs linked to passive, mindless instruments, all of which are subordinated to the central driving force." At the same time, this description seems to provide the ideal model of the productive body, for it gives the illusion of a perfect cooperative interaction among all the organs as they work toward a common goal. Somewhat like the Aristotelian universe, where hierarchical beings that populate the cosmos are motivated only by a strong desire to attain a supreme state of excellence, the leading motor, which runs on its own power in an eternal, circular movement, is driven by pure form, pure acts, pure thought. Psychology, too, will be called on to assume its own particular role in maintaining the illusion — one that allows nothing to disturb the harmonious beauty of the productive body's self-sustaining system. And, to be sure, psychology will respond to its calling.

I have tried to show that, on a certain level, the Galilean–Cartesian myth did nothing more than present a way of introducing production into historical reality. That is one meaning of the theory of the human machine — a theory that always turns in on itself while also suggesting a plausible conception of the productive body. At the other extreme, psychology, as a whole or in any of its various forms, is simply the discourse on production to which economics must take recourse, of necessity, and which allows a certain view of history to become imaginable and to seem inevitable. Or, if one prefers, it is through the discourses on psychology and psychodiagnostics (aptitudes and conditioning, as well as mental pathology personality evaluations) that the productive body itself speaks and reacts, discreetly or overtly disseminating its sometimes contradictory message; and the discourse is continually promoted, reinterpreted and sanitized on other, different frequencies and channels, be they political, ideological, economic, pedagogical and so on. For the productive body is like a message that overrides other transmissions and is broadcast into all sectors of our daily lives. Psychology is *one* of the real discourses on the mastery of the productive body. The subject of psychology is therefore always the productive body itself, as long as the biological body — a fundamental part of the productive body — needs a specific discourse through which to express the entire productive body. The moment that psychology intervenes, it marks everything with its dangerous ambiguity: in spite and because of its premises, psychology presents life as highly mechanized, while also acknowledging that life is not totally mechanized. Psychology did not invent the living machine, but since that machine is *also* living, psychology can only draw on the biological model at the center of psychology itself. The "natural" problem of survival becomes a problem of the living being inside the productive body. In fact, it is a double-sided problem: first, there is the question of individual consumption, and second, that of productive consumption — although psychology considers only one aspect of this couple. The overriding goal of psychology, no doubt unknown to itself, integrates psychology into the general plan of the productive body. The productive body, which cannot account for life, reduces it to the desired mechanical act; still, at every step, it encounters in various forms the very resistance of life that it has sought to avoid or completely discount. In the end, it is the various forms of resistance — local struggles against domination, the resurgence of the aspirations of human creativity or the legitimate alterity that creeps into the sheer fact of day-to-day existence — that remain to be taken into account.

NOTES

1. Edmund Husserl, *The Crisis of European Sciences and Transcendental Phenomenology*, trans. David Carr (Evanston, Ill.: Northwestern University Press, 1970), pp. 49–50 (translation modified).

2. Ibid., p. 54.

3. Ibid., p. 60.

4. Maurice Merleau-Ponty, *Phenomenology of Perception*, trans. Colin Smith (London: Routledge, 1962), p. 92.

5. Ibid., p. 95.

6. This is the well-known theme of the failure of natural finality and spontaneity exalted by the idea of the expulsion of the marvelous and the search for equilibrium. In parallel, simple subsistence was replaced by limitless production, by production for production's sake (a new emphasis on usury; now it was slackness and not avarice that was to be condemned) and so on.

7. The phrase is taken from Robert Lenoble, *Esquisse d'une histoire de l'idée de nature* (Paris: Albin Michel, 1968), p. 326. This image of the organic had several sources: first, it had grown out of the idea that nature is a kind of omnipresent flux, where everything happened by chance, yielding one fortuitous outcome from numerous legitimate possibilities. Still another definition saw nature as a force that blocked off all but one possible outcome, to the exclusion of all others: here, nature was seen as a uniform object susceptible to mathematical analysis. The Galilean revolution was, therefore, less a subversion than a limitation; but that limitation was at the same time a displacement: toward gradually taming the imprecise and irrational forces in nature by inscribing them in a carefully wrought hierarchy of domination, after every life process and task had been prioritized and assigned a specific degree of dignity. In effect, the very notion of the forces of nature disappears, only to be replaced by the idea that objects somehow have unique and eminent qualities, by virtue of their being the privileged outcome of myriad possibilities and combinations. The alternative was to view nature as all waste and confusion. It was necessary, then, to consider each object's uniqueness — first, because in nature it is a matter of all or nothing, and second, because the traditional dualism failed to set down any real guidelines for explaining the way things were. That is, these new qualities could be subjected to invariable and uniform rules, each rationally prescribed and therefore subject to rational analysis (assuming there is a common agreement on the proper methodological tools to be used). What was so radically new in the wake of such limitation-displacement is the idea that scientific-technical production could be entirely rationalistic, that is, explicable, prescribable, justifiable, legitimate and predictable — and therefore efficient, recognizable and, finally, quantifiable.

8. Construction of the image of the body, not as an instrument of knowledge but as a form of mechanical power, implies that corporeal experience not be first understood in its apparently aberrant form: illusions of the senses, phantom members, dreams, madness.

9. René Descartes, "Meditations on First Philosophy," in *The Philosophical Works of Descartes*, vol. 1, trans. Elizabeth Haldane and G. R. T. Ross (New York: Cambridge University Press, 1967), pp. 131–99.

10. Letter to Mesland, February 9, in René Descartes, *Philosophical Letters*, trans. Anthony Kennedy (Oxford: Basil Blackwell, 1981), pp. 154–59.

11. Georges Canguilhem, *La Connaissance de la vie* (Paris: Vrin, 1967), p. 113.

12. See Georges Canguilhem, "Descartes et la technique," in *Travaux du IXᵉ Congrès International de Philosophie*, vol. 2: *Etudes Cartesiennes* (Paris: Hermann, 1937), pp. 77–85: "And since 'we are incapable of making a new body for ourselves' (VII.148), we have to add exterior organs to the interior organs (VII.148). It is basic to needs, appetite and will that we must look for the initiative for technical fabrication (IX, *Principes*, 123)."

13. See Canguilhem, *La Connaissance de la vie*, p. 115: "According to Descartes, a mechanically operated device replaces a directing and controlling power, but God has set the controls once and for all; the maker incorporates movement controls in the mechanical device."

14. See Marx's letter to Engels of Jan. 28, 1863 (Marx and Engels, *Collected Works*, vol. 41: *Marx and Engels, 1860–64* [New York: International Publishers, 1975], p. 451) [All ensuing quotations from Marx correspond to the French text used by the author; citations to the corresponding passages in the English editions are provided when possible — TRANS]: "The industrial revolution began as soon as mechanical means were employed in fields where, from time immemorial, the final result had called for human labor and not therefore — where the actual material to be processed had never, within living memory, been directly connected with the human hand; where, by the nature of things and from the outset man has not functioned purely as power...."

15. It is precisely because of this expansionist and imperialistic image of life-as-conquest (life as aggression in the face of nature) that a certain epistemological myth of the organic machine has taken shape, having been grounded on certain discourses of the physicist, the inventor or the engineer. Although simulation remains on the whole essentially mechanical, some thinkers have gone so far as to use mechanical devices to support their view that man might dispense with "adaptation" as a principal characteristic of the life process (cybernetics as "the art of rendering action more efficient," a definition taken up again by Henri Laborit with regard to biology: "La Cybernétique et la machine humaine," in *Le Dossier de la cybernétique* [Verviers: Gérard et Cie, 1968], p. 195). At bottom, the goal of adapting machine to man is much like the epistemological paradigm of the organic machine, in that in both cases there can only be a mechanical simulation of the life process.

16. Friedrich Engels, "The Condition of the Working Class in England," in Marx and Engels, *Collected Works* (New York: International Publishers, 1975), vol. 4, p 312.

17. English in the original — TRANS.

18. And this very early on, as is attested in Laffemas's attempt to install in his workshop "little children, blind people, armless and crippled old men seated leisurely, without exertion or bodily pain" (see Henri Hauser, *Les Débuts du capitalisme* [Paris: Alcan, 1927], p. 12). Not the least of the system's aspects is that whereby the suffering, pain-ridden and mutilated body and feeble constitution are described as somehow superior to the reductive mechanical gesture of physical effort. In the generalization of competition, capitalism in this way marks the body (it does so in many other ways) in the recuperation of heretofore unsuspected potentialities. As the applications of the productive body expand, so does the range of exploitation of the biological body. (On this subject, see also Marx, *Capital* [New York: International Publishers, 1987], vol. 1, pt. 4, ch. 15, sec. 3, p. 372ff.) The extension of the working/productive body is accompanied by the limitation of the productive activity: "The one-sidedness and the deficiencies of the detail labourer become perfection when he is a part of the collective labourer. The habit of doing only one thing converts him into a never failing instrument, while his connexion with the whole mechanism compels him to work with the regularity of the parts of a machine" (ibid., ch. 14, sec. 3, p. 330).

19. See "Grundrisse," in Marx and Engels, *Collected Works* (New York: International Publishers, 1989), vol. 29, p. 90: "The division of labour increasingly transformed the worker's operations into mechanical ones, so that at a certain point the workers could be replaced by a mechanism."

20. René Descartes, Letter to Régius, Jan. 1642, in *Lettres à Régius* (Paris: Vrin, 1959), p. 89; and *Principles* 4.203. See also G. de Cordemoy, "Des Machines naturelles et artificielles," in *Oeuvres philosophiques* (Paris: P.U.F., 1968), p. 122: "Everything that we admire in works of art, or in Nature, is a pure effect of movement and organization, which, while taking into account their diversities, makes things appropriate for different usages."

21. See *Traité des passions*, arts. 5, 6; see also Georges Canguilhem, *La Formation du concept de réflexe aux XVIIᵉ et XVIIIᵉ siècles* (Paris: P.U.F., 1955), p. 55.

22. See Canguilhem, *La Connaissance de la vie*, p. 108ff.; and Alexandre Koyré, *Etudes d'histoire de la pensée scientific* (Paris: P. U. F., 1966), p. 148, n. 3.

23. The ambiguity subsists by necessity: animal movement, the quintessential mechanical action, can be perceived as the ultimate expression of quickness, precision and efficiency precisely to the extent that it is not the result of conscious deliberation; reasoning is thus characterized as slowness and uncertainty. This is the line of thought pursued in Pierre Chanet, *Considerations sur la sagesse de Charon* (Paris: C. Le Groult, 1643). See J. B. Piobetta, "Au Temps de Descartes: Une Polémique ignorée sur la connaissance des animaux," in *Travaux du IXᵉ Congrès International de Philosophie*, vol. 2: *Etudes Cartesiennes* (Paris: Hermann, 1937), p. 62.

24. This breaking and entering [*effraction*] is, moreover, anchored to the occasion in the form of "naturalism" that gives it justification and limits. These limits are clearly the laws of nature that no one can transgress (see Mersenne, *Les Méchaniques de Galilée* [Paris: P.U.F., 1966], ch. 1). Breaking and entering thus only makes sense in terms of the law.

25. In *De Pulsu, resorptione, auditu et tactu: Annotationes anatomicae et physiologicae* (Leipzig, 1834), E. H. Weber specifies (Prolegomenon 11) that the sense of touch reveals: the force of resistance that bodies exert against the pressure of organs; the form of bodies and the space that spans between them; the force with which bodies compress our organs and, in particular and foremost, their weight; temperatures attained, hot or cold.

26. E. Toulouse and H. Piéron, *Technique de psychologie expérimentale* (2d ed., Paris: Dorin, 1911), vol. 1, p. 34.

27. Weber, *De Pulsu*, Prolegomenon 12.

28. See Jules Jean van Biervliet, "La Psychologie quantitative: La Psychophysiologie," *Revue philosophique de la France et de l'étranger* 63 (June 1907), pp. 565–66.

29. *Capital*, pt. 5, ch. 16, p. 477.

30. For a precise definition of parallelism, see Théodule Ribot, *Introduction à la psychologie allemande contemporaine* (Paris, 1879), pp. ix, xi; and Wilhelm Wundt, *Eléments de psychologie physiologique* [1874], trans. E. Rouvier (Paris: Alcan, 1886), vol. 2, p. 521.

31. See André Godfernaux, "Le Parallélisme psycho-physique et ses conséquences," *Revue philosophique* 58.2 (1904), pp. 329–52, 482–504.

32. See Wundt, *Eléments de psychologie physiologique*, vol. 1, p. 9. See also the definition of the soul or spirit [*l'ame*], vol. 2, p. 526: "the absolute correlation between physical and psychic suggests the following hypothesis: what we call the soul is the internal being of the same entity, an entity which we envision exteriorly as being the body, of which it is a part."

33. Gustav Fechner, *Elements of Psychophysics*, trans. Helmut Adler (New York: Holt, Rinehart and Winston, 1966), esp. p. 67: the hope of devising a law of the senses that would be as important for describing the relationship between the soul and the body as the laws of gravity are for the realm of planetary movement.

34. See van Biervliet, "La Psychologie quantitative," p. 579.

35. Ibid., p. 591.

36. Godfernaux, "Le Parallélisme," p. 343. See also Jean Piaget, "L'Explication en psychologie et le parallélisme psychophysiologique," in Paul Fraisse and Piaget, *Traité de psychologie expérimentale*, part 1: "Histoire et méthode" (2d ed., Paris: P.U.F., 1963), p. 152, which shows how Edouard Claparède formulated a law "according to which a conscious awakening is brought on as the result of maladjustments." For that law itself, refer to Claparède's article, "La Psychologie fonctionelle," *Revue philosophique de la France et de l'étranger* 115 (Jan.–Feb. 1933), p. 14 (see also pp. 5–6: "Psychology...is a part of biology.... The central problem of biology is that of *adaptation*.... And the central problem of psychology is *behavior*. But behavior is nothing more than a certain kind of adaptation").

In a text drawing on the outcome of a direct attack on Auguste Comte, which aims at maintaining the place of "subjectivity," Herbert Spencer writes: "The claims of psychology to rank as a distinct science, are thus not smaller but greater than those of any other science. If its phenomena are considered objectively, merely as neuro-muscular adjustments, by which the higher organisms from moment to moment adapt their actions to environing coexistants and sequences, its degree of speciality even then, entitles it to a separate place. The moment the element of feeling, or consciousness, is used to interpret these neuro-muscular adjustments in the living beings around, objective Psychology acquires an additional and quite exceptional distinction. And it is further distinguished in being linked by this common element of consciousness, to the totally-independent science of subjective Psychology — the two forming a double science, which, as a whole, is quite *sui generis*" (*The Principles of Psychology* [New York: D. Appleton, 1872], p. 141).

37. Godfernaux, "Le Parallélisme," p. 499.

38. See Harald Höffding, *Outlines of Psychology*, trans. Mary E. Lowndes (New York: Macmillan, 1891), p. 14.

39. J. F. Richard, "The Discovery of the Existence of Individual Differences as Obstacles in the First Experiments in Psychological Measurement," a colloquium on "the elaboration of the

concepts and methods of differential psychology in the nineteenth century and at the beginning of the twentieth century," in *Revue de synthèse, colloques, textes des rapports* (Paris: Albin Michel, 1968), pp. 369–82, esp. pp. 375, 381.

40. Pierre Bouguer, *Traité d'optique sur la gradation de la lumière* (Paris: Guerin and Delatour, 1760), bk. 1, sec. 2, art. 1, p. 51. The preceding development points to the category of the average social worker whose never once-and-for-all attained level always entails a permanent dialogue (see, for example, Marx "Materials…" in *Pléiade*, vol. 2, p. 416: "the worker must execute, in a given time, the quantity of work corresponding to the social norm: the capitalist obliges the labourer to furnish a work output which possesses at least the average degree of intensity corresponding to the social norm."

41. Toulouse and Piéron, *Technique de psychologie expérimentale*, vol. 1, p. 214.

42. Ibid., p. 242.

43. See John Dewey's comment: "The ability of the hand to do its work will depend, either directly or indirectly, upon its control, as well as its stimulation, by the act of vision" ("The Reflex Arc Concept," *The Psychological Review* 3.4 [July 1896], p. 359).

44. "Elements de physiologie," in *Oeuvres complètes de Diderot* (Paris: Garnier, 1875), vol. 9, pp. 344, 345.

45. See Dewey, "The Reflex Arc Concept," p. 370.

46. See James Rowland Angell, "The Province of Functional Psychology," *Psychological Review* 14 (1907), pp. 61–91: "The functional psychologist…is interested not alone in the operations of mental process considered merely of and by and for itself, but also and more vigorously in mental activity as part of a larger stream of biological forces that are daily and hourly at work before our eyes." Note equally also William James's remarks: "On the whole, few recent formulas have done more real service of a rough sort in psychology than the Spencerian one that the essence of mental life and of bodily life are one, namely, 'the adjustment of inner to outer relations'" (*Principles of Psychology*, 2 vols. [New York: Dover, 1918], vol. 1, p. 6). This problem of finality is not evaded either by Claparède ("La psychologie fonctionnelle"): "The idea of considering the organic and mental processes in relation to their end purposes and their utility seems deeply infused by finalism"; but first, "functional psychology does not at all contradict mechanistic explications" (p. 7); and second, "the functional viewpoint implies no direct link with finalism. If an explanation can be given in entirely mechanistic terms, so much the better! (Since the mechanistic explanation is always more satisfying to the mind)" (p. 17).

47. See James McKeen Cattell, "Mental Tests and Measurements," *Mind* 15, (1890), pp. 373–81.

48. The most important aspect of Taylorism seems to be "the substitution of a science for the individual judgment of the workman" (Frederick W. Taylor, *Principles of Scientific Management* [New York: Norton, 1967], p. 114). Beyond the manifest motives behind the operation are the following considerations: minimizing distraction; the need to select according to abilities and potential for improvement; a collaboration of the classes seen as "the intimate cooperation of

the management with the workmen, so that they together do the work in accordance with the scientific laws which have been developed, instead of leaving the solution of each problem in the hands of the individual workman" (p. 115); "the accurate study of the motives which influence men" (p. 119); changing from "the state of mind of the shop workers vis-à-vis their work and their employers" in an attempt to bring peace to the workplace, where there was once war. There is also cynicism tinged with naiveté, which comes across quite clearly on every page of *The Taylor and Other Systems of Shop Management*, Hearings before the Special Committee of the House of Representatives to Investigate the Taylor and Other Systems of Shop Management under Authority of H. Res. 90 (Washington, D.C.: Government Printing Office, 1912), as much in Taylor's accession to the head of the team that refused to identify the norm for a "fair day's work" as in the manipulation achieved by means of hopes for salary increases or internal promotion ("incentive") (pp. 1411–1414). Then there are the question of worker–machine interaction: "In working on the average machine tool, of necessity the greater part of the day is spent by the man standing at his machine doing nothing except watch his machine work. I think I would be safe in saying that not more than three hours of actual physical work would be the average that any machinist would have to do in running his machine — not more than three hours' actual physical work in a day. The rest of the time the machine is working, and he simply stands there watching it. So there is no fear of overwork in the machine shop." More instructive, perhaps, is the possibility of treating the manual laborer like a not entirely unintelligent "gorilla" — and considering that, as a result, the correct adjustment to a given job task can be perfectly unintelligible only for whoever carries it out, requiring the operation to be broken down into elementary mechanical activities by a specialist, namely, the one seen as most competent, the engineer of souls (*Principles of Scientific Management*, pp. 124–25). It should come as no surprise, then, that the model on which the "science" in question is based is that of the engineer of bodies, the modern surgeon applying spontaneously, as he carries out his professional duties, the principles of scientific management (p. 126): he is able to use his own abilities and dexterity and combines them with "the best knowledge of the world up to date." Though we need not go into how the surgeon is generally the one who, for therapeutic reasons, removes or replaces, it should be pointed out that on this point science is perfectly integrated into the movement of the working-productive body: its guiding idea is not to be seen so much as a simple ideology of productivity but, rather, as an element of the productive body itself. In this regard, Taylorism merely reinforces the position of modern psychology. As it now happens, that integration was explicitly anticipated and desired: see, for example, the arguments of Andrew Ure from the beginning of the nineteenth century: "By the infirmity of human nature it happens that the more skillful the workman, the more self-willed and intractable he is apt to become, and, of course, the less fit a component of a mechanical system, in which by occasional irregularities he may do great damage to the whole. The grand object of the modern manufacturer is, through the union of capital and science, to reduce the task of his work people to the exercise of vigilance and dexterity" (quoted in J. A. C. Brown, *The Social Psychology of Industry: Human Relations in the Factory* [New York: Penguin, 1986 (1954)], p. 208).

49. Cited in Marx, *Capital*, vol. 1, pt. 7, ch. 25, sec. 5, p. 611.

50. Contemporary psychology does not deny the conflict; on the contrary, it accords it a prominent place. Quite simply, it displaces the idea toward the realms of the inter- and intrapsychic, while universalizing the site to which it is effectively displaced. That idea seems almost banal; whether seen as regression or displacement, though nothing prevents us from calling on it when the occasion warrants, if only to evoke the not too distant time when it was still incongruous.

51. The various "psychometric" projects of Christian von Wolff, Andrew Michael Ramsay, Christian August Crusius, Pierre-Louis Moreau de Maupertuis, Gottfried Ploucquet, Charles Bonnet, Hans Bernhard Mérian, Gottlieb Friedrich Hagen and Christian Albrecht Körber gave only the theoretical outlines, keeping to the "planning stage" without ever really venturing into the realm of experimentation (see Konstantin Ramul, "The Problem of Measurement in the Psychology of the Eighteenth Century," *American Psychologist* 15 [1960], pp. 256–65). In fact, it is imagined experimentation, on two levels, that marks the triumph of "psychology" of the eighteenth century.

The question posed by William Molyneux in his letter to John Locke, dated March 2, 1692 (see *Works of John Locke* [7th ed., London, 1768], vol. 4, p. 282) — which he would include in the second edition of the *Essay* (2.9.8) of 1693 — constitutes a good example of the first level of perception. This facetious, even amusing problem, to borrow Molyneux's expression, brought up a question that called for an immediate response but necessitated no recourse to real experimentation (experiments had been conducted in 1728 by Cheselden — under conditions that supported no definite response — but that doesn't really change anything). First of all, Molyneux's problem was presented as a metaphysical experiment for metaphysicians, a gentlemen's parlor-room experiment not unlike a "riddle" (in the beginning of his letter, Molyneux states that he proposed it to various people almost at random). Even though Molyneux never explicitly states in his letter that he was opposed to real experimentation, at no time did he actually envisage it. Still, the lapidary answer that he gives to the question he himself posed is the clue to the self-imposed limits of the experiment. Molyneux's *query* is, to his view, incontestably a question of pure reasoning, and this is precisely how Locke understands it.

The "metaphysical" experiment, as Molyneux intends it (*Oeuvres de Maupertuis*, vol. 2: *Lettres sur le progrès des sciences* [new ed., Lyon, 1768], para. 17, pp. 426–30), could constitute an example of the second level with which the above-mentioned authors are associated. Whether it's a question of inducing artificial dreams by drugs or of artificially isolating children in order to study language formation, the experiment can be seen as desirable this time, but without the philosopher running any kind of experimental risk, since that is not its objective, at the risk of gaining back a sort of technical success in the context of its polemic. To invoke the Zeitgeist in order to explain this "deficiency" — as does Fraisse via Boring (Fraisse and Piaget, *Traité de psychologie expérimentale*, p. 11) — is simply to avoid the real difficulty.

52. *Capital*, vol. 1, pt. 4, ch. 15, sec. 1, p. 364.

53. *Capital*, vol. 1, pt. 7, ch. 23, p. 536: "The labourer consumes in a two-fold way. While producing he *consumes by his labour* the means of production, and converts them into products with a higher value than that of the capital advanced. This is his *productive consumption*. It is at the same time consumption of his labour-power by the capitalist who bought it. On the other hand, the labourer turns the money paid to him for his labour-power, into means of subsistence: this is his *individual consumption*."

54. See the distinction made by, Edmund Potter, as reported by Marx (ibid., p. 540) between, on the one hand, inanimate machinery, which deteriorates, depreciates every day and is superannuated by constant technical progress; and on the other, the human machinery, which, on the contrary improves thanks to "skill," which is transmitted from generation to generation. Marx states earlier that skill "figures into the capitalist's inventory" (p. 415).

55. "Grundrisse," in *Collected Works*, vol. 29, p. 90.

56. This is an image to which Marx refers time and again; see "Grundrisse," in *Collected Works*, vol. 28, p.398).

57. For man as fragment of his own body, see *Capital*, vol. 1, sec. 4, ch. 14.

58. "Grundrisse," in *Collected Works*, vol. 28, p. 398: "In reality, it is the machine which plays the unifying role. It is not an instrument of the labourer: to the contrary, he himself is tied to the machine. He who once had an individuality endowed with a soul is now but a living supplementary part of the machine." See also *Capital*, vol. 1, sec. 7, ch. 25, p. 472.

59. "Grundrisse," in *Collected Works*, vol. 28, pp. 348–49.

60. Ibid., vol. 29, p. 82.

61. Ibid., p. 85.

62. Ibid., p. 82.

63. *Capital*, vol. 1, pt. 4, ch. 15, sec. 3a.

64. "Grundrisse," in *Collected Works*, vol. 29, pp. 82–88. On the forced acceleration of science as form of production, see this entire chapter of "Grundrisse" (pp. 297-304); see also "Un Chapitre inedit du Capital," pp. 249, 252; *Capital*, pp. 267, 312.

65. "Grundrisse," in *Collected Works*, vol. 29, p. 85: "Capital tends to give production a scientific character and to reduce direct work to the role of a simple moment in the process."

66. For more details, see my article, "Le Philosophe et le psychologue," in *Revue philosophique* (Jan.–March 1971), p. 19ff., as well as the second part of my *La Psychologie: Mythe scientifique pour introduire à la psychologie moderne* (Paris: Robert Laffont, 1969).

67. *Capital*, vol. 1, pt. 4, ch. 15, sec. 4, p. 302.

Translated from the French by Randall Cherry

Artificiality and Enlightenment: From Sociobiology to Biosociality

Paul Rabinow

Worldly Genetics: Artificiality and Enlightenment

Michel Foucault identified the distinctively modern form of power as "bio-technico-power." Biopower, he writes, designates "what brought life and its mechanism into the realm of explicit calculations and made knowledge-power an agent of transformation of human life." Historically, practices and discourses of biopower have clustered around two distinct poles: the "anatomopolitics of the human body," the anchor point and target of disciplinary technologies, on the one hand, and a regulatory pole centered on population, with a panoply of strategies concentrating on knowledge, control and welfare, on the other.[1] My current work turns on a new articulation of the discourses and practices of biopower, currently symbolized by, but not restricted to, the Human Genome Initiative.[2] In this paper, I shall sketch some of the ways in which I believe the two poles of the body and the population are being rearticulated into what could be called a postdisciplinary rationality.[3]

In the annex to his book on Michel Foucault — entitled "On the Death of Man and Superman" — Gilles Deleuze presents a schema of three "force-forms," to use his terminology, which are roughly equivalent to Michel Foucault's three epistemes. In the classical form, *infinity* and *perfection* are the forces shaping beings; beings have a form toward which they strive, and the task of science is to represent correctly the table of those forms in an encyclopedic fashion. In the modern form, *finitude* establishes a field of life, labor and language within which Man appears as a distinctive being, who is both the subject and object of his own understanding, but an understanding that is never complete because of its very structure. Finally, here in the present day, a field of the *surhomme* — which I prefer to call the "afterman" — in which finitude, as empiricity, gives way to a play of forces and forms that Deleuze labels "*fini-illimité*."[4] In this new constellation, beings have neither a perfected form nor an essential opacity. The best example of this "unlimited-finite" is DNA: an infinity of beings can and has arisen from the four bases out of which DNA is constituted. François Jacob, the Nobel Prize–winning biologist,

Polluted New River, Calexico, California, 1989.
Robert Dawson

makes a similiar point when he writes, "a limited amount of genetic information in the germ line, produces an enormous number of protein structures…in the soma.… [N]ature operates to create diversity by endlessly combining bits and pieces."[5] Whether Deleuze has seized the significance of Jacob's facts remains an open question. Still, it is intriguing when something as cryptic as Rimbaud's formula that "the man of the future will be filled with animals" takes on a perfectly material meaning — as we shall see when we turn to the concept of model organism in the new genetics.[6]

Deleuze convincingly claims that Foucault lost his wager that it would be the language of the anthropological triad — life, labor, language — that would open the way for a new episteme, washing the figure of Man away like a wave crashing over a drawing in the sand. Foucault himself acknowledged that his prediction had been wrong when, a decade after the publication of *The Order of Things*, he mocked the "relentless theorization of writing," not as the dawning of the new age but as the death rattle of an old one.[7] Deleuze's claim is not that language is irrelevant but rather that the new epochal practices are emerging in the domains of labor and life. Again, whether Deleuze has correctly grasped the significance of these new practices remains to be seen; regardless, they are clearly important. It seems prudent to approach these terms heuristically, taking them singly and as a series of bonded base pairs — labor and life, life and language, language and labor — to see where they lead.

My research strategy focuses on the practices of life as the most potent present site of new knowledges and powers. The logical place to examine these changes is the Human Genome Initiative (sponsored by the National Institutes of Health and the Department of Energy), whose mandate is to produce a map of our DNA. The Initiative is very much a technoscience project in two senses. Like most modern science, it is deeply imbricated with technological advances in the most literal way, in this case the confidence that qualitatively more rapid, accurate and efficient machinery will be invented if the money is made available (this is already happening). The second sense of technological is the more important and interesting one: the object to be known — the human genome — will be known in such a way that it can be *changed*. This dimension is thoroughly modern; one could even say that it instantiates the definition of modern rationality. Representing and intervening, knowledge and power, understanding and reform, are built in, from the start, as simultaneous goals and means.

My initial stance toward the Initiative and its associated institutions and practices is rather traditionally ethnographic: neither committed nor opposed, I seek to describe what is going on. I follow Foucault when he asks, "Shall we try reason? To my mind nothing would be more sterile. First, because the field has nothing to do with guilt or innocence. What we have to do is analyze specific rationalities rather than always invoking the progress of rationalization in general."[8] My ethnographic question is: How will our social and ethical practices change as this project advances? I intend to approach this question on a number of levels and in a variety of sites. First, there is the Initiative itself. Second, there are adjacent enterprises and institutions in which and through which new understandings, new practices and new technologies of life and labor will certainly be articulated — prime among them the biotechnology industry. Finally, the emergence of bioethics and environmental ethics lodged in a number of different institutions will bear scrutiny as a key locus of discursive reform.

The Human Genome Initiative

What is the Human Genome Initiative? A genome is "the entire complement of genetic material in the set of chromosomes of a particular organism."[9] DNA is composed of four bases that bond into two kinds of pairs wound in the famous double helix. The current estimate is that we have about three billion base pairs in our DNA; the mouse has about the same number, while corn or salamanders have more than thirty times as many base pairs in their DNA as we do. No one knows why. Most of the DNA has no known function. It is currently held, not without a certain uneasiness, that 90 percent of human DNA is "junk." The renowned Cambridge molecular biologist, Sydney Brenner, makes a helpful distinction between "junk" and "garbage." Garbage is something used up and worthless, which one throws away; junk, though, is something one stores for some unspecified future use. It seems highly unlikely that 90 percent of our DNA is evolutionarily irrelevant — but what its precise relevance could be remains unknown.

Our genes, therefore, constitute the remaining 10 percent of the DNA. What are genes? They are segments of the DNA that code for proteins. Genes apparently vary in size from about ten thousand base pairs up to two million base pairs. Genes, or at any rate most human genes known today (1 percent of the presumed total), are not simply spatial units in the sense of a continuous sequence of base pairs; rather, they are regions of DNA made up of spans called "exons," interspersed by regions called "introns." When a gene is activated — and little is known about this process — the segment of DNA is transcribed to a type of RNA. The introns are spliced out, and the exons are joined together to form messenger RNA. This segment is then translated to code for a protein.

We don't know how many genes we have. It is estimated that Homo sapiens has between fifty thousand and one hundred thousand genes — with a rather large margin of error. We also don't know where most of these genes are — neither which chromosome they are found on nor where they are located on that chromosome. The Initiative is designed to change all this: literally to map our genes. This poses two obvious questions: What is a map? And who is the "we" of "our" genes?

For the first question, then: At present there are three different kinds of maps — linkage, physical and sequence. Linkage maps are the most familiar to us from the Mendelian genetics we learned in high school. They are based on extensive studies of family genealogies (the Mormon historical archives provide the most complete historical documentation, and the French have a similar project) and show how linked traits are inherited. Linkage maps show which genes are reinherited and roughly where they are on the chromosomes. This provides a helpful first step for identifying the probable location of disease genes in gross terms — but only a first step. In the hunt for the cystic fibrosis gene, for example, linkage maps narrowed down the area to be explored before other types of mapping completed the task.

There are several types of physical maps: "a physical map is a representation of the location of identifiable landmarks on the DNA."[10] The discovery of "restriction enzymes" provided a major advance in mapping capabilities. These proteins serve to cut DNA into chunks at specific sites. The chunk of DNA can then be cloned and its makeup chemically analyzed and then reconstructed in its original order in the genome. These maps are physical in the literal sense that one has a chunk of DNA and one identifies the gene's location on it (these have been assembled into "libraries"). The problem is to locate these physical chunks on a larger chromosomal map. Cloning techniques involving bacteria were used for a number of years, but new techniques, such as "in situ hybridization techniques," are replacing the more time-consuming cloning techniques.

Polymerase chain reaction reduces the need for cloning and physical libraries. It is necessary to clone segments of DNA in order to get enough identical copies to analyze, but this multiplication can now be done more rapidly and efficiently by having the DNA do the work itself, as follows: first, one constructs a small piece of DNA, perhaps twenty base pairs long, called a "primer" or oligonucleotide, which is then commercially made to specification. The raw material from which one takes the base pairs (to be assembled like Lego blocks) is either salmon sperm or the biomass left over from fermentation processes. A particularly rich source are the by-products of soy sauce (hence the Japanese have an edge in this market). This DNA is refined into single bases, or nucleosides, and recombined according to the desired specifications at a cost of about one dollar per coupling in a DNA synthesizer. The nucleosides could all be made synthetically, but it is currently cheaper given the small quantities needed — most primers are about twenty bases long — to stick to salmon sperm and soy sauce biomass. The current world production of DNA for a year is perhaps several grams, but as demand grows there will be a growing market for the oligonucleotides, custom-made strips of DNA. As Gerald Zon, a biochemist at Applied Biosystems, Inc., put it: The company's dream is to be the world's supplier of synthetic DNA.[11]

Two primers are targeted to attach themselves to the DNA at specific sites called "sequence-tagged sites" (STS's). These primers then simply "instruct" the single strand of DNA to reproduce itself without having to be inserted into another organism — this is the polymerase chain reaction (PCR). So, instead of having physically to clone a gene, one can simply tell one's friends in Osaka or Omaha which primers to build and where to apply them, and they can do the job themselves (eventually including the DNA preparation, which will be automated). The major advantage of the PCR–STS technique is that it yields information that can be described as "information in a database": "No access to the biological materials that led to the definition or mapping of an STS is required by a scientist wishing to assay a DNA sample for its presence."[12] The computer would tell any laboratory where to look and which primer to construct, and within twenty-four hours, one would have the bit of DNA one is interested in. These segments could then be sequenced by laboratories anywhere in the world and entered into a data base. Such developments have opened the door to what promises to be "a common language for physical mapping of the human genome."[13]

Sequencing means actually identifying the series of base pairs on the physical map. There is ongoing controversy about whether it is necessary to have the complete sequence of the genome (after all, there are vast regions of junk whose role is currently unknown), the complete set of genes (what most genes do is unknown) or merely the sequence of "expressed" genes (that is, those genes whose protein products are known). While there are formidable technological problems involved in all this, and formidable technological solutions appearing with the predicted rapidity, the principles and the goal are clear enough. "The technical means have become available to root the physical map of the human genome firmly in the DNA sequence itself. Sequence information is the natural language of physical mapping."[14] Of course, the database is not a language but a computer code, and by "natural" our scientist probably means "currently most useful."

Still, even when the whole human genome is mapped and even when it is sequenced, as Charles Cantor, senior scientist at the Department of Energy, has said, we will know nothing about how it works.[15] We will have a kind of structure without function. Much more work remains to be done, and currently is being done, on the hard scientific problems: protein structure, emergent levels of complexity and the rest. (Remember, the entire genetic makeup of a human being is found in most of our cells, but *how* a cell becomes — and remains — a brain cell instead of a toe cell is not known.) What we will have a decade from now is the material sequence of the *unlimited-finite*, a sequence map of three billion base pairs and between fifty thousand and one hundred thousand genes.

As to the second question: Whose genome is it? Obviously, not everyone has exactly the same genes or, for that matter, junk DNA — if we did, we would presumably be identical (and probably extinct). There was some debate early on in the project as to exactly whose genome was being mapped; there was a half-serious proposal to have a very rich individual finance the analysis of his own genome.[16] The problem is now shelved — literally — in the clone libraries. The collective standard consists of different physical pieces mapped at centers around the world. Cantor has pointed out that given the way genes are currently located on chromosomes (linkage maps), the easiest genome to map and sequence would necessarily be composed of the largest number of abnormal genes. In other words, *the pathological would be the path to the normal*.

Interestingly, all of the sequenced genes need not come from human beings. Genomes of other organisms are also being mapped. Several of these organisms, about which a great deal is already known, have been designated as model systems. Many genes work in the same way, regardless of the living being in which they are found. Thus, in principle, wherever we find a specific protein we can know what DNA sequence produced it. This "genetic code" has not changed during evolution and, therefore, many genes of simpler organisms are basically the same as human genes. Since, for ethical reasons, many simpler organisms are easier to study, much of what we know about human genetics derives from the model genetic systems such as yeast and mice. Fruit flies have proved to be an extremely useful model system. "One DNA sequence, called the 'homeobox', was first identified in the genes of fruit flies and later in those of higher organisms, including human beings."[17] This short stretch of nucleotides (in a nearly regular sequence) appears to play a role in turning genes on and off.

Comparisons with even simpler organisms are useful in the identification of genes encoding proteins essential to life. The elaboration of protein sequences and their differences has led to new classifications and a new understanding of evolutionary relationships and processes. An Office of Technology Assessment report laconically asserts the utility of comparisons of human and mouse DNA sequences for the "identification of genes unique to higher organisms because mice genes are more homologous to human genes than are the genes of any other well characterized organism."[18] Rimbaud's mysterious claim that "the man of the future will be filled with animals" indeed seems sound — if we interpret it to mean that we would know in some detail how we have evolved and what we have retained and added in the process.

From Stigma to Risk: Normal Handicaps

My educated guess is that the new genetics will prove to be an infinitely greater force for reshaping society and life than was the revolution in physics, because it will be embedded throughout the social fabric at the microlevel by medical practices and a variety of other discourses. The new genetics will carry with it its own distinctive promises and dangers.[19] Previous eugenics projects have been modern social projects cast in biological metaphors. Although their social effects have ranged from public hygiene to the Holocaust, none had much to do with the serious speech acts of biology, even if they were all pervaded with discourses of truth.[20] Sociobiology, as Marshall Sahlins and others have shown, is a social project: from liberal, philanthropic interventions designated to moralize and discipline the poor and degenerate, to *Rassenhygien* and its social extirpations, to entrepreneurial sociobiology and its supply-side social sadism, the construction of society has been at stake.[21] Eugenics was frequently professed by reputable, extremely well placed scientists, but — I want to assert here, and I argue the point elsewhere — the specific projects themselves did not emerge from within scientific practice: they were never *dans le vrai*, to use Georges Canguilhem's telling phrase.

In the future, the new genetics will cease to be a biological metaphor for modern society and will become instead a circulation network of identity terms and restriction loci, around which and through which a truly new type of autoproduction will emerge, which I call "biosociality." If sociobiology is culture constructed on the basis of a metaphor of nature, then in biosociality, nature will be modeled on culture understood as practice. Nature will be known and remade through technique and will finally become artificial, just as culture becomes natural. Were such a project to be brought to fruition, it would stand as the basis for overcoming the nature/culture split.

A crucial step in overcoming the nature/culture split will be the dissolution of the category of "the social." By "society" I don't mean some naturalized universal, which is found everywhere and studied by sociologists and anthropologists simply because it is an object waiting to be described; rather, I mean something more specific. In my recent book, *French Modern: Norms and Forms of the Social Environment*, I argue that if our definition is something like Raymond Williams's usage in the first edition of his book of modern commonplaces, *Keywords* — that is, the whole way of life of a people (hence open to empirical analysis and planned change) — then society and the social sciences are the ground plan for modernity.[22]

We can see the beginnings of the dissolution of modernist society happening in recent transformations of the concept of risk. Robert Castel, in his 1981 book, *La Gestion des risques*, presents a grid of analysis whose insights extend far beyond his specific concerns with psychiatry, shedding particular light on current trends in the biosciences.[23] Castel's book is an interrogation of postdisciplinary society, which he characterizes thus: first, a mutation of social technologies that minimize direct therapeutic intervention, supplanted by an increasing emphasis on a preventive administrative management of populations at risk; and second, the promotion of working on oneself in a continuous fashion so as to produce an efficient and adaptable subject. These trends lead away from holistic approaches to the subject or social contextualism and move instead toward an instrumentalized approach to both environment and individual as a sum of diverse factors amenable to analysis by specialists. The most salient aspect of this trend for the present discussion is an increasing institutional gap between diagnostics and therapeutics. Although this gap is not a new one, to be sure, the potential for its widening nonetheless poses a new range of social, ethical and cultural problems, which will become more prominent as biosociality progresses.

Modern prevention is, above all, the tracking down of risks — not in the sense of the result of specific dangers posed by the immediate presence of a person or a group, but rather, the composition of impersonal "factors" that make a risk probable. Prevention, then, is surveillance not of the individual but of likely occurrences of diseases, anomalies, deviant behavior to be minimized and healthy behavior to be maximized. We are partially moving away from the older face-to-face surveillance of individuals and groups known to be dangerous or ill (for disciplinary or therapeutic purposes), toward projecting risk factors that deconstruct and reconstruct the individual or group subject. This new mode anticipates possible loci of dangerous irruptions through the identification of sites statistically locatable in relation to norms and means. Through the use of computers, individuals sharing certain traits or sets of traits can be grouped together in a way that not only decontextualizes them from their social environment but also is nonsubjective in a double sense: it is objectively arrived at, and does not apply to, a subject in anything like the older sense of the word (that is, the suffering, meaningfully situated integrator of social, historical and bodily experiences). Castel names this trend "the technocratic administration of differences." Computerized series dissolve the traditional subject and retain only abstract givens as part of factors in a series. The target is not a person but a population at risk. As an AIDS-advocacy group in France put it: It is not who one is but what one does that puts one at risk. One's practices are not totalizing, although they may be mortal.[24]

Although epidemiological social-tracking methods were first implemented comprehensively in the tuberculosis campaign, they came to their contemporary maturity elsewhere. The distinction that Castel underscores as symptomatic of this change is that between *disease* and *handicap*. A "handicap," according to a French government report authored by the highly respected technocrat François Bloch-Laine, is "any physical, mental or situational condition that produces a weakness or trouble in relation to what is considered normal; normal is defined as the mean of capacities and chances of most individuals in the same society."[25] The concept of handicap was first used officially in England during World War II as a means of evaluating the available workforce in a way that included as many people as possible. Handicaps were deficits to be compensated for socially, psychologically and spatially, not illnesses to be treated — orthopedics not therapeutics. "The concept of handicap naturalizes the subject's history as well as assimilating expected performance levels at a particular historical moment to a naturalized normality."[26] True, this particular individual is blind or deaf or mute or short or tall or paralyzed, but can he or she operate the lathe, answer the telephone, guard the door? If not, what can we do to him or her, to the work or to the environment, that would make this possible? Performance is a relative term. Practices make the person; or rather, they don't — they just make practitioners.[27]

There is a large historical step indeed from the rich web of social and personal significations Western culture inscribed in tuberculosis to the inclusive grid of the welfare state, which has yet to inspire much poetry or yield a celebrated *Bildungsroman*. It has, however, increased life expectancy and produced millions of documents, many of them inscribed in silicon. The objectivism of social factors is now giving way to a new genetics and the beginnings of a redefinition and eventual operationalization of nature.

In a chapter entitled "What Is (Going) To Be Done?" in his book *Proceed with Caution: Predicting Genetic Risks in the Recombinant DNA Era*, Neil Holtzman documents the ways that genetic screening will be used in the coming years when its scope and sensitivity is increased dramatically by such technological advances as PCR, which will reduce cost, time and resistance. There are already tests for such conditions as sickle-cell anemia, and diagnostics for cystic fibrosis and Alzheimer's are on the horizon. These diseases are among the estimated four thousand single-gene disorders. There is a much larger number of diseases, disorders and discomforts that are polygenetic. Genetic testing will soon be moving into areas in which presymptomatic testing will be at a premium. Thus, Holtzman suggests that once a test is available for identifying a "susceptibility-conferring genotype" for breast cancer, earlier and more frequent mammograms would be recommended or even required (for insurance purposes).[28] He adds:

> Monitoring those with genetic predispositions to insulin-dependent diabetes mellitus, colorectal cancer, neurofibromatosis, retinoblastoma, or Wilms tumor for the purpose of detecting early manifestations of the disease might prove beneficial. Discovering those with genetic predispositions could be accomplished either by population-wide screening or, less completely, by testing families in which disease has already occurred.[29]

This remark involves a large number of issues, but the only one I shall underline here is the certain formation of new group and individual identities and practices arising out of these new truths. There will be, for example, neurofibromatosis groups who will meet to share their experiences, lobby for their disease, educate their children, redo their home environment, and so on — and that is what I mean by "biosociality." I am not discussing some hypothetical gene for aggression or altruism. Rather there will be groups formed around the chromosome 17, locus 16,256, site 654,376 allele variant with a guanine substitution. These groups will have medical specialists, laboratories, narratives, traditions and a heavy panoply of pastoral keepers to help them experience, share, intervene in, and "understand" their fate.

Fate it will be. It will carry with it no depth. It makes absolutely no sense to seek the meaning of the lack of a guanine base because it has no meaning. One's relation to one's father or mother is not shrouded in the depths of discourse here, the relationship is material even when it is environmental: Did your father smoke? Did your mother take DES? Rest assured they didn't know what they were doing. It follows that other forms of pastoral care will become more prominent, in order to overcome the handicap and to prepare for the risks. These therapies for the normal will be diverse, ranging from behavior modifications, to stress management, to interactional therapies of all sorts.[30] We might even see a return of tragedy in postmodernist form, although we will likely not simply rail against the gods, but rather be driven to overcome our fates through more technoscience. The nineties will be the decade of genetics, immunology and environmentalism — for, clearly, these are the leading vehicles for the infiltration of technoscience, capitalism and culture into what the moderns called "nature."

Donna Haraway labels these changes "the death of the clinic": "The clinic's methods required bodies and works: we have texts and surfaces. Our dominations don't work by medicalization and normalization any more; they work by networking, communication redesign, stress management."[31] I only partially agree; a multiplication and complex imbrication of rationalities continue to exist. Obviously, older forms of cultural classification of bio-identity such as race, gender and age have no more disappeared than medicalization and normalization have — although the meanings and the practices that constitute them certainly are changing. Postdisciplinary practices will coexist with disciplinary technologies; post–social-biological classifications will only gradually colonize older cultural grids. Thus, Troy Duster has shown how testing for sickle-cell anemia has reinforced preexistent racial and social categories, even though the distribution of the gene is far wider than the African-American community.[32] In complicated and often insidious ways, the older categories may even take on a renewed force as the new genetics begins to spread not only in the obvious racism so rampant today but more subtly in studies of blacks' alleged higher susceptibility to tuberculosis. My argument is simply that these older cultural classifications will be joined by a vast array of new ones, which will cross-cut, partially supersede and eventually redefine the older categories in ways that are well worth monitoring.

Labor and Life

The emergence of modern food, that is, food industrially processed to emphasize uniformity and commodified as part of an internationalization of world agriculture and distribution, can be dated to the 1870–1914 period.[33] Industrial sugar refining and flour milling for the production of white bread was one of the first examples of a constructed consumer need linked to advertising, transportation expansion, a host of processing and preservation techniques — as well as, incidentally, the rise of modernism in architecture (for example, Buffalo's silos and Minneapolis's grain elevators, as Reyner Banham has shown in his *A Concrete Atlantis*[34]). With these changes, agricultural products were on their way to becoming merely an input factor in the production of food and food was on its way to becoming a "heterogeneous commodity endowed with distinctive properties imparted by processing techniques, product differentiation and merchandising."[35] These processes accelerated during World War I, which here, as in so many other domains, provided the laboratory conditions for inventing, testing and improving food products on a truly mass scale. Millions of people became accustomed to transformed natural products like evaporated milk as well as new foods like margarine, in which an industrially transformed product is substituted for a processed "rural" product — vegetable fats instead of butter, for example. Using methods developed in the textile industry, it was now possible not only to produce foods at industrial levels not constrained by "natural rhythms" or inherent biological qualities (even if people had bred for these) but even to get people to buy and eat them.

The cultural reaction against foods classified as "artificial" or "processed" was spearheaded in the years between the wars by a variety of lifestyle reformist groups, satirized by George Orwell. Ecological and environmental campaigns, conducted on a national scale by the Nazis with their characteristic vigor, agitated for a return to natural foods (especially whole-grain bread), the outlaw of vivisection, the ban of smoking in public places and the exploration of the effects of environmental toxins on the human genetic material and so on. Hitler, after all, did not smoke or drink and was a vegetarian.[36] As we have seen in recent decades, not only have the demand for wholesome foods and the obsession with health and environmentalism not meant a return to "traditional" products and processes — although the image of tradition is successfully marketed, few would advocate a return to the real thing with its infected water supplies, low yield and the like — but it has even accelerated, and will continue to accelerate, the improvement, the enculturization of nature drawing on tradition as a resource to be selectively improved.

Once nature began to be systematically modified to meet industrial and consumer norms — a development perhaps embodied best by the perfect tomato, the right shape, color, size, bred not to break or rot on the way to market, missing only the distinctive taste, to the dismay of some and the delight of others — it could be redescribed and remade to suit other biopolitical specifications, like "nutrition." The value of food is now cast not only in terms of how much it imitates whole natural food in freshness and look but in terms of the health value of its component constituents — vitamins, cholesterol, fiber, salt and so on. For the first time we have a market in which processed, balanced foods — whose ingredients are chosen in accordance with nutritional or health criteria — can be presented as an alternative superior to nature. Cows are being bred for lower cholesterol, canola for an oil with unsaturated fats: "once the basic biological requirements of subsistence are met, the 'natural' content of food paradoxically becomes an obstacle to consumption."[37]

Once this cultural redefinition and industrial organization are accepted, then "nature, whether as land, space, or biological reproduction, no longer poses a binding constraint to the capitalist transformation of the production process and the social division of labor."[38] Bernardo Sorj and his coauthors claim that "the rural labor process is now not so much machine-paced as governed by the capacity of industrial capitals to modify the more fundamental rhythms of biological time."[39] This process leads to increased control over all aspects of the food production process and efforts to make it an industry like any other. New biotechnological techniques working toward the industrial control of plant biology increase the direct manipulation of the nutritional and functional properties of crops, accelerating the trends toward rationalization and the vertical integration of production and marketing required for efficiency. Biotechnological advances like nitrogen fixing or the herbicide resistance of newly engineered plant (and eventually animal) species diminish the importance of land quality and the physicochemical environment as determinants of yields and productivity.

Calgene, a leading California agrobiotech company based in Davis, is proud of its genetically engineered PGI Tomato seeds, whose fruit, their 1989 annual report boasted, is superior to a nonengineered control group. Calgene's engineering is no ordinary engineering, though, even by biotech standards: their tomatoes employ an "antisense" technique considered to be one of the cutting-edge achievements in the pharmaceutical and therapeutic fields. Antisense involves disrupting the genetic message of a gene by interfering with either the synthesis of messenger RNA or its expression, that is, before its instructions to make a protein are carried out. While the concept is simple, developing techniques refined and specific enough to achieve the desired results is not. Field trials, according to the annual report, "verified the ability of Calgene's antisense (AS-1) gene to reduce fruit rotting while increasing total solid content, viscosity and consistency."[40] The gene significantly reduces the expression of an enzyme that causes the breakdown of pectin in fruit cell walls and thereby decreases the shelf life.

"This new technology provides a natural alternative to artificial processing, which means that the tomatoes delivered to consumers in the future promise to be closer to home-grown in firmness, color and taste."[41] It looks good, it travels well and it may soon taste like what those who have still eaten old-style tomatoes think they should taste like.

Traditional tastes pose a challenge — not a threat — to technoscience: the more one specifies what is missing from the new product, the more the civilizing process proceeds.[42] Tomatoes aren't what they used to be? But you don't like bugs either? Let's see what can be done. A company in Menlo Park, California, is perfecting a bioengineered vanillin, one of the most complex of smells and tastes. Scientists are approaching museums armed with the PCR technique, which enables them to take a small piece of DNA and amplify it millions of times.[43] This recovered DNA could then, at least in principle, be reintroduced into contemporary products. If eighteenth-century tomatoes are your fancy, there is no reason a priori why one day a boutique biotech company aiming at the Berkeley or Cambridge market couldn't produce one that is consistently pesticide resistant, transportable and delicious for you — and those just like you. In sum, the new knowledges have already begun to modify labor practices and life processes in what Enlightenment botanists called "nature's second kingdom."[44]

In Praise of Artificiality and Enlightenment

What are we to make of all this? Before rushing to judgment, it seems wisest to proceed with both caution and élan in attempting to pose questions in a heuristic fashion. Fredric Jameson's powerful interpretation of the postmodern as the moment when capitalism penetrates into the unconscious and nature, can be supplemented by the insights of Donna Haraway and François Dagognet.[45] In the challenge to the discourse of nature and of the unconscious as the most embedded of givens, both Haraway and Dagognet see a potentially epochal opportunity extending beyond the dreary march of instrumentalization and objectification (although it is that as well). They see present today a Nietzschean potential to free us from some of our most enduring lies.

Haraway concludes her iconoclastic and enlightened 1985 "Manifesto for Cyborgs" by arguing that "taking responsibility for the social relations of science and technology means refusing an anti-science metaphysics, a demonology of technology, and so means embracing the skillful task of reconstructing the boundaries of daily life, in partial connection with others, in communication with all of our parts."[46] She applauds the subversion of "myriad organic wholes (e.g., the poem, the primitive culture, the biological organism)" and proclaims that "the certainty of what counts as nature — a source of insight and a promise of innocence — is undermined, perhaps fatally...." "The cyborg would not recognize the Garden of Eden...."[47] As with nature, so too with culture.

Dagognet, a prolific and fascinating French philosopher of the sciences, a materialist in the style of the eighteenth century — his latest book is in praise of plastics, but he has also written on the extraordinary diversity of leaf forms — identifies three major revolutions in our attitudes toward the world. The first was the possibility of a mechanization of the world, associated with Galileo, and the second was the French Revolution, which showed humanity that its institutions were its own and that, consequently, men could become "masters of the social tie." The third, which is now within our will, concerns neither the universe nor society but life itself.[48]

For Dagognet, the main obstacle to the full exploration and exploitation of life's potentials is a residual naturalism. He traces the roots of "naturalism" to the Greeks. The artisan or artist, it was held, imitates *that which is* — nature. Although man works on nature, he doesn't change it ontologically, because human productions never contain an internal principle of generation. This naturalism has endured. From the Greeks to the present, a variety of naturalisms have held to the following axioms: the artificial is never as good as the natural; generation furnishes the proof of life (life is autoproduction); homeostasis (autoregulation) is the golden rule.[49] Contemporary normative judgments continue to affirm the superiority of the biological, the insecurity of human works, the risks linked to artificiality and the certitude that the initial situation — the Golden Pond or the Rain Forest — was incomparably better.

Dagognet argues that nature has not been natural, in the sense of pure and untouched by human works, for millennia. More provocatively, he asserts that nature's malleability demonstrates an "invitation" to the artificial. Nature is a blind *bricoleur*, an elementary logic of combinations, yielding an infinity of potential differences. These differences are not prefigured by final causes, and there is no latent perfection-seeking homeostasis. If the word "nature" is to retain a meaning, it must signify an uninhibited polyphenomenality of display. Once understood in this way, the only natural thing for man to do would be to facilitate, encourage and accelerate its unfurling — thematic variation, not rigor mortis. Dagognet challenges us in a consummately modern fashion: "Either one adopts a sort of veneration before the immensity of 'that which is' or one accepts the possibility of manipulation."[50] The term manipulation carries with it the appropriate ambiguities implying both an urge to dominate and discipline as well as an imperative to improve on the organic. Confronting this complexity constitutes the challenge of artificiality and enlightenment.

Notes

1. Michel Foucault, *The History of Sexuality*, vol. 1: *An Introduction*, trans. Robert Hurley (New York: Pantheon, 1978), p. 139. Special thanks to Vincent Sarich, Jenny Gumperz, Frank Rothschild, Guy Micco, Hubert Dreyfus and Thomas White.

2. *Mapping Our Genes, Genome Projects: How Big, How Fast?* (Washington, D.C.: Office of Technology Assessment, 1988).

3. For what it's worth, I don't think "postdisciplinary" can be equated with "postmodern."

4. Gilles Deleuze, *Foucault* (Paris: Minuit, 1986): "L'homme tend à libérer en lui la vie, le travail et le language" (p. 140). Foucault's version is found in *The Order of Things: An Archaeology of the Human Sciences* (New York: Vintage, 1966). On natural history in the Classical age, see Henri Daudin, *Cuvier et Lamarck: Les Classes zoologiques et l'idée de série animale* (Paris: Alcan, 1926). On the philosophical understanding of Man, see Jules Vuillemin, *L'Héritage kantien et la révolution copernicienne: Fichte, Cohen, Heidegger* (Paris: P.U.F., 1954).

5. François Jacob, *The Possible and the Actual* (New York: Pantheon, 1982), p. 39.

6. Deleuze, *Foucault*: "L'homme de l'avenir est chargé des animaux" (p. 141).

7. Michel Foucault, "Truth and Power," in Paul Rabinow, ed., *The Foucault Reader* (New York: Pantheon, 1984), p. 127; idem, *The Order of Things*, p. 387.

8. Michel Foucault, "The Subject and Power," in Hubert Dreyfus and Paul Rabinow, *Michel Foucault: Beyond Structuralism and Hermeneutics* (2d ed., Chicago: University of Chicago Press, 1983), p. 210.

9. *Mapping Our Genes*, p. 21.

10. Ibid., p. 30.

11. Interview with author, March 19, 1990.

12. *Mapping Our Genes*, p. 1434.

13. Maynard Olson, Leroy Hood, Charles Cantor and David Botstein, "A Common Language for Physical Mapping of the Human Genome," *Science* 245 (Sept. 29, 1989).

14. *Mapping Our Genes*, p. 1435. Natural languages exist in a context of culture and background practices. Codes are representational but only in the representation degree zero sense of transparency and definitional arbitrariness. I intend to deal with "language" and its relations with "labor" and "life" in another paper.

15. Charles Cantor, Opening Remarks, *Human Genome: I* (San Diego, Oct. 1, 1989).

16. If, as Allan Wilson and his team convincingly argue, there was an "original Eve," the mother of us all, in Africa about 200,000 years ago, there would be an argument to take an African genome as the standard from which other groups have varied: A. C. Wilson, E. A. Zimmer, E. M. Prager and T. D. Kocher, "Restriction Mapping in the Molecular Systematics of Mammals: A Retrospective Salute," in B. Fernholm, K. Bremer and H. Jornvall, eds., *The Hierarchy of Life* (Amsterdam: Elsevier, 1989), pp. 407–19.

17. *Mapping Our Genes*, p. 67.

18. Ibid., p. 68.

19. Both Daniel J. Kevles and John Heilbron agreed with the importance of the social impact of the Initiative. Heilbron: "Oh, a thousand times more important" (Feb. 14, 1990).

20. For this distinction, see Dreyfus and Rabinow, *Michel Foucault*, ch. 3.

21. Marshall Sahlins, *The Use and Abuse of Biology: An Anthropological Critique of Sociobiology* (Ann Arbor: University of Michigan Press, 1976); Robert N. Proctor, *Racial Hygiene: Medicine under the Nazis* (Cambridge, Mass.: Harvard University Press, 1988); Daniel J. Kevles, *In the Name of Eugenics: Genetics and the Uses of Human Heredity* (Berkeley: University of California Press, 1985); and Benno Muller-Hill, *Murderous Science: Elimination by Scientific Selection of Jews, Gypsies, and Others, Germany 1933–45* (Oxford: Oxford University Press, 1988).

22. Paul Rabinow, *French Modern: Norms and Forms of the Social Environment* (Cambridge, Mass.: MIT Press, 1989); Raymond Williams, *Keywords: A Vocabulary of Culture and Society* (New York: Oxford University Press, 1976).

23. Robert Castel, *La Gestion des risques, de l'anti-psychiatrie à l'après-psychanalyse* (Paris: Minuit, 1981).

24. The third term here is genetics. If, as is hinted at, there were a genetic component to AIDS susceptibility, then the equation would be more complex.

25. François Bloch-Laine, *Etude du problème général de l'inadaptation des personnes handicapées, la Documentation française* (1969), p. 111 (cited in Castel, *La Gestion des risques*, p. 117).

26. Bloch-Laine, *Etude*, p. 122

27. Credit is due to James Faubion for clarity on this point.

28. Tom White rightly underlines that all of these developments could be and most likely will be contested.

29. Neil A. Holtzman, *Proceed with Caution: Predicting Genetic Risks in the Recombinant DNA Era* (Baltimore and London: Johns Hopkins University Press, 1989), pp. 235–36.

30. Robert Castel, *Advanced Psychiatric Society* (Berkeley: University of California Press, 1986).

31. Donna Haraway, "A Manifesto for Cyborgs," *Socialist Review* 15.2 (March–April 1985), p. 69.

32. Troy Duster, *Backdoor to Eugenics* (London: Routledge, 1990).

33. A fuller treatment would have to deal with both husbandry and agriculture in evolutionary perspective. Thanks to Tom White for discussions on this and other points.

34. Reyner Banham, *A Concrete Atlantis: U.S. Industrial Building and European Modern Architecture, 1900–1925* (Cambridge, Mass.: MIT Press, 1986).

35. David Goodman, Bernardo Sorj and John Wilkinson, *From Farming to Biotechnology: A Theory of Agro-Industrial Development* (Oxford, Eng.: Basil Blackwell, 1987), p. 60.

36. A good summary can be found in Proctor's *Racial Hygiene*, ch. 8, "The 'Organic Vision' of Nazi Racial Science."

37. Goodman et al., *From Farming to Biotechnology*, p. 193.

38. Ibid., p. 58.

39. Ibid., p. 47.

40. *Planning for the Future*, Calgene 1989 Annual Report, p. 14.

41. Ibid.

42. Keith Thomas, *Man and the Natural World: A History of the Modern Sensibility* (New York: Pantheon, 1983).

43. Norman Arnheim, Tom White and William E. Rainey, "Application of PCR: Organismal and Population Biology," *BioScience* 40.3 (1989), pp. 174–83.

44. François Delaporte, *Nature's Second Kingdom* (Cambridge, Mass.: MIT Press, 1982). I intend to treat animal engineering, transgenic beings and the like in another paper.

45. Fredric Jameson, "Postmodernism, Or the Cultural Logic of Late Capitalism," *New Left Review* 146 (July–Aug. 1984), pp. 53–92.

46. Haraway, "Manifesto," p. 100

47. Ibid., pp. 70, 67

48. François Dagognet, *La Maîtrise du vivant* (Paris: Hachette, 1988), p. 22.

49. Ibid., p. 41.

50. Ibid., p. 12.

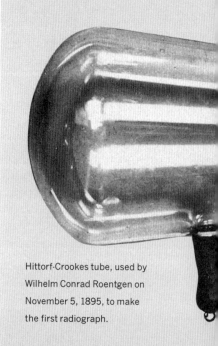

Hittorf-Crookes tube, used by Wilhelm Conrad Roentgen on November 5, 1895, to make the first radiograph.

War and Medicinema
The X-ray and Irradiation in Various Theaters of Operations

A Selected 100-Year Chronology
By Victor Bouillion

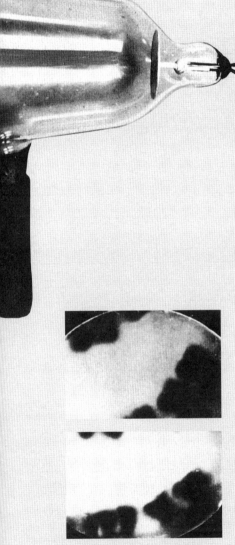

The first dental radiograph made by Dr. Otto Walkhoff, two weeks after Roentgen's experiment.

1845	Birth of Wilhelm Conrad Roentgen at Lennep, Germany.
1869	Hittorf observes properties of cathode rays in vacuo.
	Roentgen receives Ph.D. with thesis on rarefied gases in vacuo.
1879	Crookes experiments with magnetic deflection of cathode rays, further develops the cathode-ray tube.
1895	Roentgen produces X-rays and radiograph.
	Dr. Otto Walkhoff produces dental radiograph.
1896	Lindenthal procures contrast X-ray image of human hand.
	First popular illustrated article on X-rays in *McClure's* magazine.
	First military use of X-rays to irradiate the enemy, Italian-Ethiopian campaign.
	Becquerel observes radioactive emissions in uranium compounds.
1897	X-rays used in hospitals — locating bullets in casualties of the Greco-Turkish War (Tirah campaign) and the Sudan and Boer Wars.
1898	Marie and Pierre Curie discover the radioactive elements polonium and radium.
1899	Cancer treated by irradiation.
1900	Planck and Einstein develop quantum theory.
	Roentgen receives the first Nobel Prize (physics).
1903	Radioactivity explained as the disintegration of the atom.
1906	Barkla observes the polarization of X-rays, proof of their similarity to light.
	Near-perfection of cellulose acetate "safety" film.
1910	Lung disease diagnosed by radiograph.
1913	X-ray mammography used to detect breast cancer.
1914	Developments in X-ray diffraction and crystalline structures lead to the exploration of atomic architecture, particularly in metals.
1919	Rutherford and Bohr develop atomic models for matter and assign energy levels and exchanges.
1921	First practice of X-ray and radiographic inspection of metal castings and ordnance (Watertown Arsenal).
1923	Death of Roentgen.
1924	First comprehensive X-ray laboratory for industrial and military application installed at the Massachusetts Institute of Technology.
1935	Fermi, in atomic experiments with deuteron and uranium bombardment, observes the phenomenon of fission and produces artificial disintegration.
1938	Uranium atom split.
1942	Fermi, Oppenheimer, Compton, Szilard produce controlled nuclear fission chain reaction.
1945	Centennial of the birth of Roentgen.
	Semicentennial of the discovery of X-rays by Roentgen.
	Hiroshima and Nagasaki destroyed by atomic bombs.

Tadeusz Kantor [1915–1991]

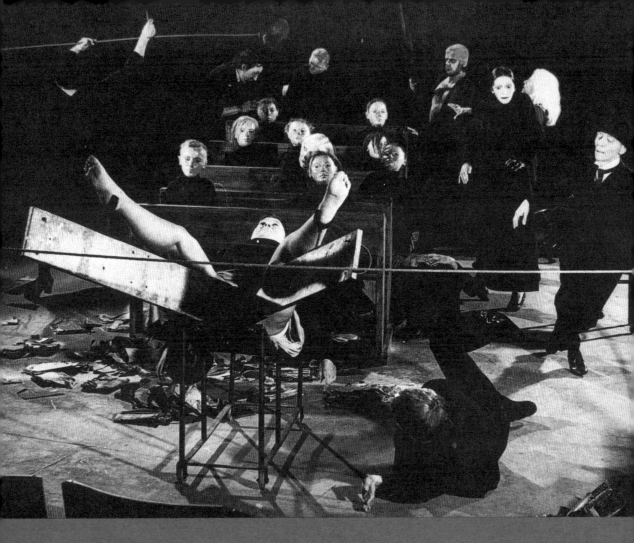

Compilation: Heidi Gilpin

FP-82

Circles, Lines and Bits
Klaus Theweleit

We misunderstand those elaborate formations made from human bodies (mostly women's — especially in the 1920s and 1930s) set in motion and put on display, by seeing them as mere ornaments, as deindividualizations, as luxury-product nature ("flower"- or "wave"-nature), or as indulgent forms of waste. They are also, clearly, technical apparatuses, machines as well as diagrams of an overlapping of the human with a posited "universal harmony," which is reconstructed or anticipated in such forms (whether in the theater, in a revue, in film, in alchemical circle-constructions or in political mass-formations).

The line of dancers in synchronized movement on the stage, or the successively connected hundred women at a hundred pianos, functions like an electric series-connection: the flowing current reaches each leg or each hand simultaneously and causes them to swing high or drop down so as to produce mechanically a movement or a sound: a complicated machinery with several parts moving to the same rhythm, a relatively old-fashioned machinery, used to support the programming of factory- or office-girls to learn such work sequences and thought procedures; also a machine for the structuring and inspiration of mechanical engineers and those other employees whose task is the conversion of human-chaotic work processes into technical-social ones.

The musical rosettes made from bodies of women, as Busby Berkeley produced and described them, are different:

> I built a large kaleidoscope with two mirrors, 18 meters high and 5 meters wide, arranged in the shape of a V. In the middle was a turning platform with a radius of about 6 meters, and when I fixed the camera high above and between these two mirrors, the girls made an infinite pattern of symmetrical forms on the turning glass.[1]

Berkeley's construction with the mirrors, which is in a position to extend such a rosette into infinity, has technically advanced from the electric to the electronic, from wiring to circuitry. The limbs of the dancing women — not sequentially wired but soldered together, as it were — are closer to the ornamentality of an early electronic chip in the interior of a computer (which did not yet exist when Berkeley constructed this rosette) than they are to any part of the mechanical machines that had predominated until then: they are also (in their infinite connection) closer to the modus operandi of a computer: they simulate its split-second execution of mathmatical procedures nearing the "infinite."

Women-ornaments are structures for weak-current procedures.

By contrast, a 220- or 110- volt current pulsates in the chorus line of women and pianists.

The mirror for multiplying rosettes suggests photocopiers and computer monitors.

The legs and hands of the line-series are not saying anything, rather they are performing something: the modus operandi of cogs, mechanical links, belt transmissions (driven by steam, electric, gasoline engines).

The cross section of a plant stem, of a single cell, or the frontal view of opened flower blossoms are not the only forms that yield "ornaments"; the cross section through this telegraph cable (closing in on the Berkeleyan rosette) also does so; fifty years ago, there was nothing *technical* that appeared thus.

Just as this looks like "nerve paths" and "plant capillaries," many parts of a television set — with the traces of their soldering in the colored plastic — when held up to the light look like stained-glass windows (seen only when one holds them up to the light).

Stained-glass windows: *in* them the "ornaments" of the technical performed, but *on* them there weren't yet chorus line revues and electrical-mechanical series-connections (when God was still the television and the churches our amplifiers).

And in the rosettes of stained-glass windows, the "universal harmony" testified to its *modus constructionis*.

The "stained-glass windows" of Giordano Bruno (1588) are "the flowers" of our brains, the drainpipes of our feeling. Not simply an "ornamental representation" of thought procedures; rather, it is a matter of attempting to represent brain activity itself. The "ornamental," the symmetries come into it because Bruno imputes a functional harmony to the brain; "harmony," the "universal" divine, like the human-technical, comes about in circles, is expressed in circles, puts the circle form to use, is reconstructed in circular series-connections.

The figures are supposed to reconstruct the logical and emotional procedures in the human brain/nervous system on the most technical level possible (and are "ornaments" only incidentally)...signs of *universal* harmony, for whose development and promotion in men these representations come about from Bruno's investigations: the Orphic lyre, the "measure of life," or the "lyre" in the world's center, which Bruno, as does Monteverdi, as does Galileo, strikes in like measure — forms of *natural science* in 1600.

This fort over turbulent waters, as well, this fortification surrounded by walls with star-shaped streets, at the center of which stands a tower, is a representation of the human brain (the walls are the skull plates). B. Delbene: "*Civitas veri*," the community, the "City of Truth," the rampart circle of the human brain, Paris, 1609.

The roads driven into the flood are the roads of harmony, of rationalism, of reason. The turbulent parts, the floods, the swamps and seas, the morass are representations of the unbridled human feelings, which are to be bridled, dried up and interlaced with streets and walls in the "civilizing process."

A powerful means for damming them — *architectures*; a circle around men, which a construction-*technic* draws.

Ornament? Only when one limits one's view. A diagram, rather, in which fortress-, town-, dam-constructions and the construction of human brains collapse in one and the same architecture.

What makes this ape in the center of the circle into "homo," who begins, with his head, to stand out from the circle? The sciences and the arts. In Robert Fludd's *Technical History of the Microcosm*.

The circles from the title pages of Fludd's *Technical History of the Microcosm* and *Technical History of the Macrocosm* are less technically developed than are Bruno's "figures." They limit themselves to a symbolic representation of the ascent from ape to HOMO through sciences, arts, technics, human faculties like the "*Ars Memoria*" [Art of Memory], the art of developing a physiognomy,

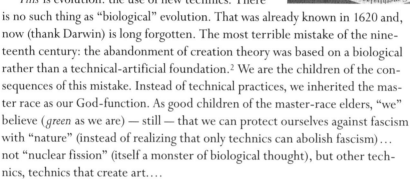

a measure of the world, architecture, alphabetization and so on. (I leave to the reader the pleasure of deciphering the man-making technics in detail — for whom the exposed position of the lyre/organ in the circle of technics will be inescapable.)

Only when he has gazed in all these mirrors, tested all these echoes, taken all these instruments and paintbrushes in hand, brought forth a sound from these strings, will ape Narcissus become man Narcissus.

This is evolution: the use of new technics. There is no such thing as "biological" evolution. That was already known in 1620 and, now (thank Darwin) is long forgotten. The most terrible mistake of the nineteenth century: the abandonment of creation theory was based on a biological rather than a technical-artificial foundation.[2] We are the children of the consequences of this mistake. Instead of technical practices, we inherited the master race as our God-function. As good children of the master-race elders, "we" believe (*green* as we are) — still — that we can protect ourselves against fascism with "nature" (instead of realizing that only technics can abolish fascism)... not "nuclear fission" (itself a monster of biological thought), but other technics, technics that create art....

(The reality: Every second alternative must take astrology seriously — this apecomputer. Amen.)

The man sticking out his tongue, on which the diagram locates "taste," is one of several representations from the sixteenth century in which a localization of the different human faculties in different parts of the human brain is attempted. Very modern. (One of the representations that Bruno put forward.) This is "proof" that people were not simply drawing pretty circles.[3]

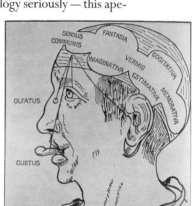

Of all the cogitations one can engage regarding these circles (and many lead far), I think one comes to the fore: clearly, beyond their respective former "symbolic sense," these "ornaments" are building blocks for future apparatuses, constructions, or future men. It is equally clear to me that, in the respective experimental phases of the technical production of "universal harmony," in each respective construction year (when the right cables, bits and relays, the transmissions, fittings, cogs and ducts, the material perfect for its exact plasticity, silicon, had not yet been discovered), the whole of European history — including now women's bodies — is taken to simulate experimentally (in "games," "sports," "arts," "dance") parts of new machines, parts of new human forms; the infinitely malleable, flexible, nimble "sex" allows itself to be spun into all sorts of filaments, to be bent into every "ornament," submits to any current-stream (like Berkeley's technical rosettes, which *follow* the telegraph cable and *anticipate* electronic bits).

This is just as in Giotto's frequent series-connection gazes of women, in which the technic of new social characteristics can be seen — a new kind of participation in social construction, not limited to special women, rather, the installation of an altogether new social gaze (which helps European humanity to see its way out of the Middle Ages).

This procession of images of women formations in a dancing line, in the ballet, in revues, in frescoes, in magazines or on television screens: that they act as the building blocks of new technics has thus far hardly been understood (and it furnishes the key for so many images "of the feminine" — far beyond the respective "meanings" that they have exhibited on one "level of sense").[4]

(The test — the last twenty lines of the *Divine Comedy* undertake to bring into conformity images of women with the circle-form, only to dissolve in a flash, said Dante.)

It is no accident that new machinic technics from the Spinning Jenny to the typewriter and then to the computer were, from the first, allied to the flexible fingers of malleable femininity (especially those technics that lead to a "revolution," that is, a new birth of male-dominated societies).

Especially flexible women were emancipated to a great extent from traditional "women's roles" in these technics, but concomitantly were coded with the advanced practical modes of the masculine birth of reality. Jean-Luc Godard assumes that women would build these machines *differently*. That would be a new *history*, unlike the oldest, the ur-ur-history, which still builds on the (insidious) disconnection of women and technics, women and apparatuses, women and machines — a history that *lives* by this disconnection.

If it is correct that engineers construct society (with their nuclear power plants and Rockets on Top), it won't do the trick to promote God to a woman in order to reconstruct society, women must also become engineers (at least in children building), but also elsewhere. With a technic stuck in a rocket, completely different things can be produced: a new life, a new history.

Exactly what men have not supplicated with "their technics."

They still supplicate for the employment of the "feminine sex." This can always be seen on one of many alternating fronts. What is now called "aerobics" has little to do with "gymnastics" in the sense of mobilizing rusting office-limbs, but rather (its technical side) with drilling these limbs (in a series-mode, as in gym-movement to music) for their annexation to the office computer now ubiquitously deployed throughout the Western world. As a result, the longtime "ideological" resistance that has impeded electronic data-processing pops like a bubble (clearly, pure magic). At the same time, music with a computer-synthesized beat predominates (every day it reinforces the annexation of the Western-feminine employee to the new friend in the workplace).

"His Master's Voice" must be heard differently, as in the gymnastic movements of the girls of the "Eastern Bloc." The unbelievable suppleness in the draining movements of twelve- to fifteen- year-old girl gymnasts from Bulgaria, Romania and the Soviet Union on television screens is a product of the technological backwardness of the East and its more rigid social systems; these girls are making the State-mandated loosening of these characteristic systems and arrested production modes manifestly obvious and even tasteful to the people. It's not for noting that these bodies "grow" in greater quantities in the under-technified East. The bodies of twelve-year-olds are coded with "new mobility." "Glasnost" can also be seen as an "ornament" in functional femininity.

With "us," on the other hand, it is the production of Number-One Figures, World-Toppers (a crack service and reflexes as constant as computers; as stoic-human as Ms. [Steffi] Graf).

The 1988 model of our nervous hamstringing (one of several "Orphic lyres" in use at the moment).

In Billy Wilder's *The Apartment*, a tennis racket served as a strainer for Jack Lemmon's spaghetti (bachelor cooking)…and Shirley MacLaine was bowled over…now the kids measure string tension in pounds…with a "wrong tension" the string breaks…balls hit the net…the game is over…Eurydice isn't caught…not by an out-of-tune lyre…Boris Becker's racket is set at thirty-six kilograms…for *this* lyre he must have a "girlfriend"…in Monte Carlo, or

somewhere…it, something, would be lacking…it wouldn't be *this* history…
Orpheus and *The Ring*…Orpheus and the circles, lines and bits.

In previous centuries, the rosettes were still the terrestrial circle, then the
terrestrial globe, then "the Spirit" draws out of the Waters. With the triumph
of the circle form the world appears in retrospect as if made with compasses,
hence the God-painters put a compass in the Creator's hand; so God has known
all along — only, men just discovered that God is a media man. With the discovery of America, God receives yet another compass in His hand, or (and other
representations — there are dozens) a pen for writing numerical tables. Of the
sciences that fill Robert Fludd's "circles" after 1600, though, He hasn't the
slightest clue.

So God copies, in diminishing intervals. In the year 2000 after Zero He sends
us Creation from the PC (…"and the Angels sing").[5]

NOTES

1. Tony Thomas, Jim Terry and Busby Berkeley, *The Busby Berkeley Book* (New York:
New York Graphic Society, 1937), p. 153.

2. If only men would no longer base it on the foundation out of which children really
come — out of women (even with little children it is not biology that counts but, rather, the
technics through which mothers contrive [*artifiziert*] men — a certainty that States, with
their "doctors" and cultural police, fight tooth and nail to keep from mothers).

3. For more about these images, see the books of Frances A. Yates.

4. I have to laugh a little when I think of old August Kekulé, when in 1865 he discovered the ring structure of Benzene "in a dream." This "ring," this dragon biting its tail, this
circle that closed the formula, this dance of bodies and molecules he had *seen* a hundred
thousand times before he dreamed it — before the dream whispered to him why don't you
test it out on benzene…and organic chemistry was born (of course, Kekulé had been to
the ballet the previous evening).

5. English in the original — TRANS.

Translated from the German by Mark Cohen,
Delphine Bechtel and Ted Byfield

Horror Autotoxicus: Critical Moments in the Modernist Prosthetic

John O'Neill

We love to wear machines — anything from sunglasses to a cigar, from a watch to a car. We even love to carry machines — anything will do, from a walking stick to a boombox, from the *Portable Nietzsche* to a portable computer. We hate to switch off our engines: lest we switch off ourselves, we leave the motors running, the lights on, the radio in the background, the TV over the bar, the refrigerator, or the humidifier.... When we die, there has to be someone willing to switch off the machines that otherwise persist in living for us. We look good to ourselves in machines: they are the natural extensions of our narcissistic selves. They magnify us and at the same time amplify the world we have chosen to create for ourselves — the "man-made" world. There is no escaping our romance with the machines we have created in order to recreate ourselves. At best, we may detect some uneasiness with our future selves.

As we move into an age where the origins and ends of life are increasingly recast in the marriage of biology and technology, the mystery of life may one day surrender to the vision of our laboratories. Once our bodies are entirely machine readable, we may embark on a new edition of the human text. Meanwhile, by means of the telephone and the telescope, by writing and lodging we have left nature's womb forever. In the distance created by our future biotechnologies, we may one day erase our maternal memory and

with it the world's great model of love. Yet, as Freud observed, it is to our very love of those omnipotent parental bodies — which first populated the world's imagination with its gods and furnished our childish minds with such dreams and fairy tales — that we owe our present prosthetic divinity: "Man has, as it were, become a kind of prosthetic God. When he puts on all his auxiliary organs he is truly magnificent; but those organs have not grown on to him and they still give him much trouble at times."[1] Nothing praises our divinity like our own machines; nothing else renders us at once more powerful and more fragile. No holocaust is greater than the one we consecrate to our machines (built to destroy us as much in peace as in war), which we never cease to improve for either end. As prosthetic gods, we lack any perspective on the divinity of our machines. The more they kill us, the more we turn to them for safety; the more they sicken us, the more we turn to them for health; the more they cripple us, the more we turn to them for repairs. Here is the very core of modern *iatrogenesis*, namely, that we have invested a sacred trust in our medical machines and their built-in capacity to repair the troubles they produce in the course of serving us.[2] Rather than subordinate our technologies to the temple and community of the human body, we have abased ourselves in the service of a secular ideology of medicalized life, health and happiness. Moreover, we have recast world history so that it appears to us as a story designed to celebrate and to legitimate our colonial intervention in all "earlier" (older) societies whose technology was less industrialized, less militarized and less medicalized than our own, and whose conquest we now offer to redeem with charitable impositions of technical, medical and military "aid."

Thus, despite the fact that the "advanced" world is choking on its own industrial filth, the globalization of our technoculture and its prosthetic practices quickens its conquest of nonindustrialized cultures. To deal with these issues,

I propose to sketch a "map" of the *prosthetic mythology* that has underwritten our modernity, one that locates "postmodern" exhaustion in two critical moments:

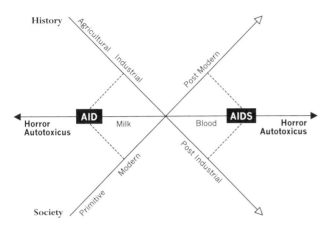

The diagram represents our history through two moments of decisive transformation in the body's relationship to its world, as determined by its inscription in a colonial history of modernization. The mapping of the two bodily events, AID and AIDS, is to be read as a contrastive economy of domination and emancipation in which the exchange of "milk" and "blood" symbolizes two embodied operators, in an *economy of the gift*, that must be "good" if human society is to endure.[3] In other words, in a preindustrial society the social bond may be rendered through the maternal icon — the good gift of the mother's milk — while in an industrial society the social bond may be rendered in terms of the medicalized icon of the gift of blood. Because the gift of blood is necessarily mediated by a medical technology, whereas the gift of milk is not, we may mark the colonization of milk societies by blood societies through such prosthetic devices as bottle-feeding. The latter, of course, represents only a single stage in the colonization of the maternal body.

The power of modern industrial society over itself and its natural environment generates a *myth of autoimmunity*, which society acts out in endless medical interventions upon itself — specularized, for example, in medical soap operas — and in medicalized "AID" to "underdeveloped" countries whose overwhelming hunger and disease weaken their immunity to political and economic conquest. Western medicine saves these countries from themselves and from other political predators. This conception of things, of course, hides the earlier destruction of non-Western medical practices by colonial medicine.[4] The latter intervention is most succinctly dramatized in the African mother who abandons breast feeding in favor of bottle-feeding in response to the iconology of modernization and medicalized progress.[5] However, the scarcity and unpredictable supply of the milk formula increasingly obliges the mother — who has stopped lactating — to dilute it with water so contaminated that she would not otherwise have given it to her infant. The result is that she slowly starves and poisons her own child in the most horrific inscription of maternal love and modernity. The cure here, unfortunately, involves the complete modernization of the social infrastructures presupposed by Western medical practices. "Health" is acquired both at the expense of native and communal medical institutions and through dependence within its political economy and on the diseases it globalizes.

Nothing represents the postmodern moment in our history more sharply than the transformation of our sexuality in its encounter with the HIV virus. Set aside any distinction between heterosexuals and homosexuals, between IV drug users and nonusers: in a blood society, two communities cannot be separated into two immunosystems, one "outside" of, or ghettoized by, the other. Designate as "AIDS" the complex of psychosocial, legal, economic and political responses to persons with HIV and its related diseases. Thus, I prefer to speak not of "persons with AIDS" (PWA's) but rather of a "society with AIDS"

(SWA). The issue here is how such a society is to respond to itself, having discovered that the autoimmunity it believed it enjoyed as an advanced medicalized society is a fiction (the presumption of medicalized immunity had, of course, functioned as the unwritten guarantee of an ideology of sexual emancipation). The civil liberties gradually awarded to the gay and lesbian communities in their struggle with established morality were also required to complete the defamilialization of moral authority in favor of the therapeutic State as the ultimate arbiter of liberal capitalist mores. To the extent that the complex of medicalized immunity and psychosexual freedom reinforce one another, the modern State might appear to have founded itself on the gift of love, in addition to other transfers of health, education and employment. The hazard of HIV, however, destroys this vision of political community, once again dividing us along the lines of a politics of contamination, disease and crime.

The SWA is no longer a society sure of itself. Where once society figured as the agent of missionary and medicalized AID to other societies unable to withstand its colonial penetration, the SWA now stands as a sick image of itself, exhausted by its own mythology of autoimmunity, apparently forsaken by its medical arts and terrorized by its lack of charity toward its own members. HIV completes in the modernist cosmology a series of eruptions which have revealed the fragility of its ecosystem from the upper atmosphere to the seabed, from the rainforests to the food chain. Everywhere there spreads the fear that our technoculture has turned against us, and that it yields only poisonous fruits. This fear, then, is nowhere greater than where our lovemaking

threatens to kill us. For as long as our medical system fails to find a prevention or cure for HIV, we are abandoned to *horror autotoxicus* — the catastrophe of lethal fluids (blood or semen) given to one another in love or in medicalized charity, where the gift of blood has been polluted and now deals death rather than life and love to its trusting recipients.

Yet, in the context of the new global order, our society (*US AIDS*) is still able to construct a political epidemiology in which its own internal Third World of blacks and Hispanics are "objectively" identified as the principal threat to America's immune system.[6] Moreover, this same "map" is deployed to trace the "African" origins of HIV with the intention of sexualizing the transmission of diseases, which historically has followed the trade routes of commerce and war. Once again, the political alliances of Western medicine assume even larger consequences in the framework of the global political economy.

Today, the failure of modernism divides us into celebrants and fundamentalists. Each side will characterize the other according to its own wit, but it will be difficult for either side to ground its own wit in sound institutions. Such is the predicament of postmodernity: the fundamentalists will invoke an arcadian moment and

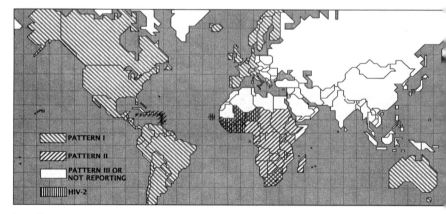

Infection patterns of the AIDS virus. Pattern I: predominantly homosexual males and intravenous drugs users; Pattern II: heterosexual transmission, with equal numbers of infected males and females; and Pattern III: infection through contact with Pattern I or Pattern II countries.

266

the necessary return to the harmony of nature and the human body as the guarantee of any future history, while the celebrants will find nature in a zoo, or in an arcade, where they hunt themselves in video games of digital death. Whether we survive our new barbarism will depend on whether blood societies can restore what is sacred in the gift they still borrow.

Despite the contemporary celebrations of endless exchange value, I claim that there is use value — but "use" means not subject to using, that is, the gift "at par" to be given back. This gift is not good because it is exchanged *but is exchanged because it is good,* for society and for posterity. Life is doubled from the standpoint of collective and intergenerational circulation. These are ecogifts — that is, eco- from *oikos*, as "source of sustainable life" — or better, they are maintainable goods to which we have a right of production as well as a duty to consume. Hence, milk and blood society — and water, "green" — are two garnishes of the sacred. "Sacred" means not appropriable (in mimetic rivalry) because life ought not to be opposed to itself — but repeated here and there — parochially, *per omnia saecula saeculorum*. Therefore, what is "secular" is not opposed to what is sacred — as is assumed by certain Enlightenment rationalisms; rather, the secular is what is given to be continued, to be repeated and to be reproduced within the fold of the sacred. The sacred marks off the clearing, the lightning space, in which there can be a civil domain and from which all other human institutions arise. The sacred is not a vision of things beyond what lies before us; it is the vision that discerns the very realm of thought, an appropriation of reality according to language whose own history will differentiate the realms of law, science, economy, art and literature but from an original matrix of poetry and fable, as Vico demonstrated in the *New Science*. Such is the science of religion but not the religion of science.

In the phenomena of modern contamination we are destroying the capacity of nature to become culture. Hitherto, the function of myth was to reveal a dialectic of reciprocity between society and nature, between cleanliness and dirt, civil and savage, male and female, between the human and the monstrous. To the extent that modern societies destroy nature, with its capacity to become culture, we naturalize our own culture — but at the level of a barbarism from which our myths had once delivered us. The zero point of civilization is achieved where neither nature nor culture can produce *the good gift*, where everything is ruled by incontinence and indifference, where nothing is sacrificed to limit, exchange and the double legacy of present and future generation. Born naked, modern humanity risks dying without the mask of culture, destroyed by impulses that suffer no cultural interdiction. In the meantime, we continue to violate the good differences between humanity with the bad differences of class and colonial power. Unable to see ourselves in these practices, we may yet do so inasmuch as nature's mirror now frightens us with its darkened surface, its cracks and its potential disequilibration before which we may once again stand as the world's primitives.

NOTES

1. Sigmund Freud, *Civilization and Its Discontents*, trans. James Strachey (New York: Norton, 1961 [1930]), p. 43.

2. Ivan Illich, *Limits to Medicine Medical Nemesis: The Expropriation of Health* (New York: Penguin, 1977).

3. Richard M. Titmuss, *The Gift Relationship: From Human Blood to Social Policy* (New York: Vintage, 1971).

4. Dianna Melrose, *Bitter Pills: Medicines and the Third World Poor* (Oxford: Oxfam, 1982).

5. Penny Van Esterik, *Beyond the Breast-Bottle Controversy* (New Brunswick, N.J.: Rutgers University Press, 1989).

6. Jonathon M. Mann, James Chin, Peter Piot and Thomas Quinn, "The International Epidemiology of AIDS," *Scientific American* 259.4 (Oct. 1988), pp. 82–89.

Project for a Glossary of the Twentieth Century

J. G. Ballard

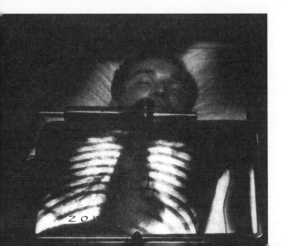

X-ray Does the body still exist at all, in any but the most mundane sense? Its role has been steadily diminished, so that it seems little more than a ghostly shadow seen on the X-ray plate of our moral disapproval. We are now entering a colonialist phase in our attitudes to the body, full of paternalistic notions that conceal a ruthless exploitation carried out for its own good. This brutish creature must be housed, sparingly nourished, restricted to the minimum of sexual activity needed to reproduce itself and submitted to every manner of enlightened and improving patronage. Will the body at last rebel, tip all those vitamins, douches and aerobic schedules into Boston harbor and throw off the colonialist oppressor?

Typewriter It types *us*, encoding its own linear bias across the free space of the imagination.

Zipper This small but astute machine has found an elegant way of restraining and rediscovering all the lost enchantments of the flesh.

Jazz Music's jettisoned short-term memory, and no less poignant for that.

Telephone A shrine to the desperate hope that one day the world will listen to us.

Chaplin Chaplin's great achievement was to discredit totally the body, and to ridicule every notion of the dignity of gesture. Ponderous men move around him

like lead-booted divers trying to anchor the central nervous system to the seabed of time and space.

Trench warfare The body as sewer, the gutter of its own abattoir, flushing away its fears and aggressions.

The pill Nature's one step back in order to take two steps forward, presumably into the more potent evolutionary possibilities of wholly conceptualized sex.

Aerodynamism Streamlining satisfies the dream of flight without the effort of growing wings. Aerodynamics is the motion sculpture of non-Euclidean space-time.

Pornography The body's chaste and unerotic dream of itself.

Time and motion studies I am both myself and the shape that the universe makes around me. Time and motion studies represent our attempt to occupy the smallest, most modest niche in the surrounding universe.

Prosthetics The castration complex raised to the level of an art form.

Biochemical warfare Nerve gases — the patient and long-awaited revenge of the inorganic world against the organic.

Hallucinogenic drugs The kaleidoscope's view of the eye.

The Warren Commission Report The novelization of the Zapruder film.

Genocide The economies of mass production applied to self-disgust.

Phenomenology The central nervous system's brave gamble that it exists.

Crowd theory Claustrophobia masquerading as agoraphobia or even, conceivably, Malthusianism.

AUSCHWITZ I MAIN CAMP
OSWIECIM, POLAND
4 APRIL 1944

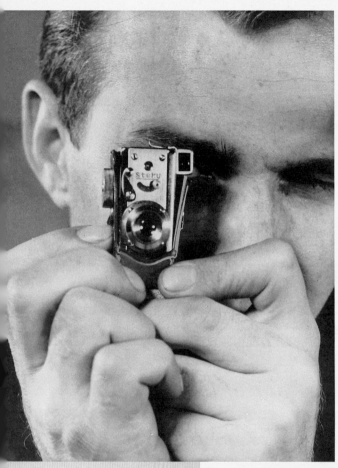

Lysenkoism A forlorn attempt not merely to colonize the botanical kingdom, but to instill a proper sense of the puritan work ethic and the merits of self-improvement.

Robotics The moral degradation of the machine.

Suburbs Do suburbs represent the city's convalescent zone or a genuine step forward into a new psychological realm, at once more passive but of far greater imaginative potential, like that of a sleeper before the onset of REM sleep? Unlike its unruly city counterpart, the suburban body has been wholly domesticated, and one can say that the suburbs constitute a huge petting zoo, with the residents' bodies providing the stock of furry mammals.

Forensics On the autopsy table science and pornography meet and fuse.

Miniaturization Dreams of becoming very small predate Alice, but now the probability grows that all the machines in the world, like the gold in Fort Knox, might be held in one heavily guarded location, protected as much from themselves as from the rest of us. Computers will continue to miniaturize themselves, though, eventually disappearing into a microverse where their ever-vaster calculations and mathematical models will become one with the quarks and the charms.

The Vietnam War Two wholly incompatible martial systems collided, with desperate result. Could the Vietcong, given a little more TV savvy, have triumphed sooner by launching an all-women guerrilla army against the *Playboy*-reading GIs? "First Air Cavalry ground elements in Operation Pegasus killed 350 enemy women in scattered contacts yesterday, while Second Division Marines killed 124 women communists...."

Isadora Duncan The machine had its own fling with her overdisciplined body, the rear wheel of her car dancing its lethal little jig around the end of her scarf.

Furniture and industrial design Our furniture constitutes an external constellation of our skin areas and body postures. It's curious that the least imaginative of all forms of furniture has been the bed.

Schizophrenia To the sane, always the most glamorous of mental diseases, since it seems to represent the insane's idea of the normal. Just as the agnostic world keeps alive its religious festivals in order to satisfy the vacation needs of its workforce, so when medical science has conquered all disease certain mental afflictions, schizophrenia chief among them, will be mimicked for social reasons. By the same token, the great appeal of alcoholism, and the reason why it will never be eliminated, is that it provides an opportunity for honorable and even heroic failure.

Body-building Asexual masturbation, in which the entire musculature simulates a piece of erectile tissue. But orgasm seems indefinitely delayed.

Epidemiology Catastrophe theory in slow motion.

Fashion A recognition that nature has endowed us with one skin too few, and that a fully sentient being should wear its nervous system externally.

Automobile All the millions of cars on this planet are stationary, and their apparent motion constitutes mankind's greatest collective dream.

Skyscraper The eight-hour city, with a tidal population clinging to the foreshore between Earth and the yet to be navigated oceans of space.

Pasolini Sociopath as saint.

Transistor If the wheel is 1 on the binary scale, the transistor is 0 — but what will be 1000001?

Retroviruses Pathogens that might have been invented by science fiction. The greater the advances of modern medicine, the more urgent our need for diseases we cannot understand.

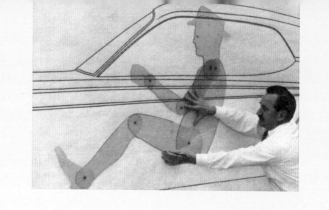

Money The original digital clock.

Abortion Do-it-yourself genocide.

Science fiction The body's dream of becoming a machine.

Answering machines They are patiently training us to think in a language they have yet to invent.

Genetics Nature's linguistic system.

Food Our delight in food is rooted in our immense relish at the thought that, prospectively, we are eating ourselves.

Neurobiology Science's Sistine Chapel.

Criminal science The anatomizing of illicit desire, more exciting than desire itself.

Camouflage The camouflaged battleship or bunker must never efface itself completely, but confuse our recognition systems by one moment being itself, and the next not itself. Many impersonators and politicians exploit the same principle.

Cybernetics The totalitarian systems of the future will be docile and subservient, like super-efficient servants, and all the more threatening for that.

Disease control A proliferation of imaginary diseases may soon be expected, satisfying our need for a corrupt version of ourselves.

Ergonomics The Protestant work ethic disguised as a kinaesthetic language.

Personal computers Perhaps unwisely, the brain is subcontracting many of its core functions, creating a series of branch economies that may one day amalgamate and mount a management buy-out.

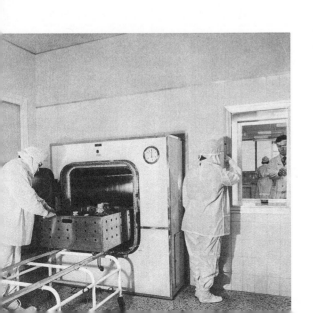

War The possibility at last exists that war may be defeated on the linguistic plane. If war is an extreme metaphor, we may defeat it by devising metaphors that are even more extreme.

International Standard Time Is time an obsolete mental structure we have inherited from our distant forebears, who invented serial time as a means of dismantling a simultaneity they were unable to grasp as a single whole? Time should be decartelized, and everyone should set his or her own.

Satellites Ganglions in search of an interplanetary brain.

Modernism The Gothic of the information age.

Apollo mission The first demonstration, arranged for our benefit by the machine, of the dispensability of man.

Note: The glossary headings were among a list supplied by the editors to Mr. Ballard, who provided their substance.

zone

Radio Antenna, Moscow, 1921.
V. G. Šuchov

Mediators

Gilles Deleuze

If things aren't going well in contemporary thought, it's because there is a return under the name of "modernism" to abstractions, back to the problem of origins and so on. Any analysis in terms of movements or vectors is blocked. We are now in a very weak phase, a period of reaction. Yet, philosophy thought it was through with the problem of origins. It was no longer a question of starting or finishing. The question was rather, what happens "in between"? And it's just the same with physical movements.

For example, in the context of sports and popular habits, movements undergo transformations. We got by for a long time with an energetic conception of movement, which presumes a point of contact or that we are the source of movement. Running, throwing a javelin and so on: effort, resistance, with a starting point, a lever. But nowadays we see movement defined less and less in relation to a point of leverage. Many of the new sports — surfing, windsurfing, hang gliding — take the form of entry into an existing wave. There's no longer an origin as starting point, but a sort of putting-into-orbit. The basic thing is how to get taken up in the movement of a big wave, a column of rising air, to "come between" rather than to be the origin of an effort.

And yet in philosophy we're going back to eternal values, and to the idea of the intellectual as their custodian. We're back to Julien Benda complaining that Henri Bergson was a traitor to his own class, the clerical class, because he tried to think movement.[1] These days, it's the rights of man that provide our eternal values. It's the "constitutional State"[2] and other notions that everyone knows to be very abstract. And it is in the name of all this that thinking is fettered, that any analysis in terms of movements is blocked. Yet, if oppression is so awful, it's because of how it limits movement, rather than because it violates eternal values. In barren times, philosophy retreats to reflecting "on" things. If it doesn't itself create anything what can it do but reflect on something? So it reflects on the eternal or the historical, but can itself no longer produce movement. What we must do, in fact, is take away from philosophers the right to reflect "on" things. The philosopher creates, he doesn't reflect.

Cinema

I have been criticized for going back to Bergson's analyses. To distinguish as Bergson did, though, between perception, affection and action as three kinds of movement is a very novel approach. It remains novel, and I don't think it's ever been quite absorbed; it's one of the most difficult and finest bits of Bergson's thought. But this analysis applies automatically to cinema: cinema was invented while Bergson's thought was taking shape. Movement was brought into concepts at precisely the same time that it was brought into images. Bergson presents one of the first cases of self-moving thought. Because it's not enough to say concepts possess movement; one must also construct intellectually mobile concepts — just as it's not enough to make moving shadows on the wall, one has to construct images that can move by themselves.

In my first book on cinema, I considered the cinematic image as this kind of image that becomes self-moving.[3] In the second book, I considered the cinematic image as it takes on its own temporality.[4] So I'm in no sense taking cinema as something to reflect on. Rather, I'm taking a field in which what interests me actually takes place: What are the conditions for self-movement or autotemporality in images, and how have these two factors evolved since the end of the nineteenth century? For as soon as there is a cinema based on time rather than movement, the image obviously has a different nature than it had in the first period. And only cinema can provide the laboratory to show us this, insofar, precisely, as movement and time have become constituents of the image itself.

The first phase of cinema, then, is the image's self-movement. This happened to take the form of a cinema of narration — but it didn't have to. Noël Burch has argued that narration was not part of cinema from the outset.[5] What led movement-images, that is, the self-movement of the image, to produce narration, was the sensorimotor schema. Cinema is not inherently narrative: it becomes narrative when it takes as its object the sensorimotor schema; someone on the screen perceives, feels, reacts. It takes some believing: the hero, in a given situation, reacts; the hero always knows how to react. And it implies a particular conception of cinema. Why did it become American, Hollywoodian? For the simple reason that this schema was fundamentally American. It all came to an end with World War II, for suddenly people no longer really believed it was possible to react to situations. The postwar situation was beyond them. We thus get Italian Neorealism, which presents people placed in situations that cannot advance through reactions, through actions. No possible reactions — does that mean everything becomes lifeless? No, not at all. We get purely optical and aural situations which give rise to completely novel ways of understanding resisting. We get Neorealism, the French New Wave and an alternate American cinema breaking with Hollywood.

There's still movement in images, of course, but with the appearance of purely optical and aural situations, yielding time-images, movement is no longer specifically what matters, it amounts only to an index. Time-images have nothing to do with before and after, with succession. Succession was there from the start as the law of narration. Time-images are not things happening in time, but new forms of coexistence, ordering, transformation.

What interests me are the relations between the arts, science and philosophy. There is no order of priority among these disciplines. Each is creative. The true object of science is to create functions, the true object of art is to create sensory aggregates and the true object of philosophy is to create concepts. From this viewpoint, given these general heads, however sketchy, of function, aggregate and concept, we can pose the question of echoes and resonances between them. How is it possible — in their completely different lines of development, with quite different rhythms and movements of production — how is it possible for a concept, an aggregate and a function to interact?

An initial example: In mathematics there's a kind of space called "Riemannian" (after Georg Riemann). Mathematically very well defined in relation to functions, this sort of space involves setting up little neighboring portions that can be joined up in an infinite number of ways; it made possible, among other things, the Theory of Relativity. Now, if I take modern cinema, I see that after the war a new kind of space based on neighborhoods appears, the connections between one little portion and another being made in an infinite number of possible ways, and not being predetermined. These two spaces are unconnected. If I say the cinematic space is a Riemannian space, it seems facile, and yet in a way it's quite true. I'm not saying that cinema is doing what Riemann did; but if one takes a space defined simply as neighborhoods joined up in an infinite number of possible ways, with visual and aural neighborhoods joined in a tactile way, then it's Bresson's space. Bresson isn't Riemann, of course, but what he does in cinema is the same as what happened in mathematics, and echoes it.

Another example: In physics there's something that interests me a lot, which has been analyzed by Ilya Prigogine and Isabelle Stengers, called the "baker transformation."[6] You take a square, stretch it out into a rectangle, cut the rectangle in half, stick one half back on top of the other, and go on repeatedly altering the square by stretching it out into a rectangle again, as though you were kneading it. After a certain number of transformations any two points, however close they may have been in the original square, are bound to end up in two different halves. This leads to a whole theory, to which Prigogine attaches great importance in relation to his probabilistic physics.

Or consider Alain Resnais: In his film *Je t'aime, je t'aime* (1967), we see a hero taken back to one moment in his life, and the moment is then set in a series of different contexts, like layers constantly shifted around, altered, rearranged so that what is close in one layer becomes very distant in another. It's a very striking conception of time, very intriguing cinematically, and it echoes the "baker transformation." So I don't feel it's outrageous to say that Resnais comes close to Prigogine, or that Godard, for different reasons, comes close to René Thom. I'm not saying that Resnais and Prigogine, or Godard and Thom, are doing the same thing. I'm pointing out, rather, that there are remarkable similarities between scientific creators of functions and cinematic creators of images. And the same goes for philosophical concepts, for there are distinct concepts of these spaces.

Mediators

Thus, philosophy, art and science come into relations of mutual resonance and exchange, but always for internal reasons. The way they impinge on one another depends on their own evolution. In this sense, then, we really have to see philosophy, art and science as separate melodic lines in constant interplay with one another. And in this, philosophy has no reflective pseudo-primacy, nor, equally, any creative inferiority. Creating concepts is no less difficult than creating new visual or aural combinations, or creating scientific functions. What we must recognize is that the interplay between the different lines is not a matter of mutual monitoring or reflection. A discipline that set out to follow a creative movement coming from outside would itself relinquish any creative role. What counts has never been to go along with some related movement, but to make one's own movement. If no one starts, no one will move. Nor is interplay an exchange: everything happens by giving or taking.

Mediators are fundamental. Creation is all about mediators. Without them, nothing happens. They can be people — artists or scientists for a philosopher; philosophers or artists for a scientist — but things as well, even plants or animals, as in Carlos Castaneda. Whether they're real or imaginary, animate or inanimate, one must form one's mediators. It's a series: if you don't belong to a series, even a completely imaginary one, you're lost. I need my mediators to express myself, and they'd never express themselves without me: one is always working in a group, even when it doesn't appear to be the case. And all the more so when it's apparent — Félix Guattari and I are one another's mediators.

The formation of mediators in a community is well seen in the work of the Canadian filmmaker Pierre Perrault: having found mediators, I can say what I have to say. Perrault thinks that if he speaks on his own, even if he invents fictions, he's bound to come out with an intellectual's discourse, he won't get away from a "master's or colonist's discourse," an established discourse. What we have to do is catch someone else "legending," "caught in the act of legending." Then a minority discourse, with one or many speakers, takes shape. We here come upon the function of Bergson's "fabulation" — to catch someone in the act of legending is to catch the movement of constitution of a people. A people isn't something preexistent. In a way, a people is what's missing, as Paul Klee used to say. Was there ever a Palestinian people? Israel says no. Of course there was, but that's not the point. The thing is, once the Palestinians have been thrown out of their territory, then to the extent that they resist they enter the process of constituting a people. It corresponds exactly to what Perrault calls "being caught in the act of legending." It's how any people is constituted. So, to the established fictions that are always rooted in a colonist's discourse, we oppose a minority discourse, with mediators.

This idea that truth is not something preexistent that we have to discover, but that it has to be created in every domain, is obvious in the sciences, for example. Even in physics, there is no truth that doesn't presuppose a system of symbols, even if they are only coordinates. There is no truth that doesn't "falsify" established ideas. To say that "truth is created" implies that the production of truth involves a series of operations that amount to working on a material — strictly speaking, a series of falsifications. When I work with Guattari, each of us falsifies the other — which is to say, each of us understands in his own way notions put forward by the other. A reflective series with two terms takes shape. And there can be series with several terms, or complicated branching series. This capacity of falsity to produce truth is what mediators are all about.

A Political Digression

Many people expected a new kind of discourse from a socialist government. A discourse very close to real movements and, so, capable of reconciling these movements by establishing arrangements compatible with them. Take New Caledonia, for example.[7] When Edgard Pisani said, "Whatever happens, there'll be independence," that in itself was a new kind of discourse. It meant: Rather than pretending to be unaware of the real movements in order to negotiate over them, we're going to recognize the outcome right away, and negotiations will take place in the light of this outcome set in advance. We'll negotiate ways and means, the speed of change. So there were complaints from the Right, which thought, in line with the old way of doing things, that there should be, above all, no talk of independence, even if we knew it was unavoidable, because it had to be made to depend on very hard bargaining. I don't think that people on the Right are deluded — they're no more stupid than anyone else, but their method is to oppose movement. It's the same as the opposition to Bergson in philosophy, it's all the same thing. Embracing movement or blocking it: politically, two completely different methods of negotiation. For the Left, this means a new way of talking. It's not so much a matter of convincing, as of being open about things. Being open is setting out the "facts" not only of a situation, but of a problem. Making visible things that would otherwise remain hidden. On the Caledonian problem, we're told that at a certain period the territory was treated as a settler colony, so the Canaques became a minority in their own territory. When did this start? How did it proceed? Who was responsible? The Right refuses these questions. If they're valid questions, then by establishing the facts we state a problem that the Right wants to hide. Because once the problem has been set out, we can no longer get away from it, and the Right itself has to talk in a different way. So the job of the Left, whether in or out of power, is to find the sort of problem that the Right wants at all costs to hide.

The Conspiracy of Imitators

How can we define a crisis in contemporary literature? The system of best-sellers is a system of rapid turnover. Many bookshops are already becoming like the record shops that only stock things listed in a top ten or hit parade. This is what *Apostrophes* is all about.[8] Fast turnover necessarily means selling people what they expect: even what's "daring," "scandalous," strange and so on falls into the market's predictable forms. The conditions for literary creation, which emerge only unpredictably, with a slow turnover and progressive recognition, are fragile. Future Becketts or Kafkas, who will, of course, be unlike Beckett or Kafka, may well not find a publisher, and if they don't nobody will notice. As publisher Jerôme Lindon says, "you don't notice that what you don't know isn't there." The USSR lost its literature without anyone noticing, for example. We may congratulate ourselves on the quantitative increase in books, and larger print runs — but young writers will end up molded in a literary space that leaves them no possibility of creating anything. We'll be faced with the monstrosity of a standard novel, imitations of Balzac, Stendhal, Céline, Beckett or Duras, it hardly matters which. Or rather, Balzac himself is inimitable, Céline is inimitable: they're new syntaxes, the "unexpected." What gets imitated is always itself a copy. Imitators imitate one another, and that's how they proliferate and give the impression that they're improving on their model, because they know how it's done, they know the answers.

It's awful, what they do on *Apostrophes*. Technically, the program is very well done, the way it's put together, the shots. And yet it's the zero state of literary criticism, literature as light entertainment. Bernard Pivot has never hidden the fact that what he really likes is football and food. Literature becomes a game show. The real problem with the TV program is the invasion by games. It's rather worrying that there's an enthusiastic audience that thinks it's watching some cultural activity when it sees two men competing to make a word with nine letters. There are strange things going on, summed up by the filmmaker Roberto Rossellini. Listen carefully:

> The world today is too pointlessly cruel. Cruelty is crushing someone else's personality, reducing someone to the state where they'll make a total confession of anything. If there was some reason for the confession, I could accept it, but if it's the act of a voyeur, someone bent, then we have to call it cruelty. I strongly believe that cruelty is always an expression of infantilism. All art these days is becoming daily more infantile. Everyone has the crazy desire to become as childish as possible. Not naive, but childish.... Art these days is either moaning or cruelty. There's nothing else around, either one moans, or one commits some absolutely pointless act of petty cruelty. Look, for example, at all this speculation (for that's what we have to call it) on incommunicability, alienation — I see in it no sympathy whatever, just gross indulgence. And that, as I said, has made me give up cinema.

And it should, still more, make one give up interviews. Cruelty and infantilism are a test of strength even for those who indulge them, and they force themselves even on those who try to get away from them.

Couples Everywhere

We sometimes behave as though people can't express themselves. In fact, though, they're always expressing themselves. The sorriest couples are the ones in which the woman can't be preoccupied or tired without the man saying, "What's wrong? Say something," or the man, without the woman saying...and so on. Radio and television have spread this spirit everywhere, and we're riddled with pointless talk, insane amounts of words and images. Stupidity is never blind or mute. So the problem is no longer getting people to express themselves, but providing little gaps of solitude and silence in which they might eventually find something to say. Repressive forces don't stop people from expressing themselves, but rather, force them to express themselves. What a relief to have nothing to say, the right to say nothing, because only then is there a chance of framing the rare, or ever rarer, the thing that might be worth saying. What we're overcome by these days isn't any blocking of communication, but pointless statements. But what we call the meaning of a statement is its point. That's the only definition of meaning, and it amounts to the same as the novelty of statement. One can listen to people for hours but what's the point ... that's why it's so difficult to discuss anything, that's why there's never any point discussing things. We don't say to someone, "What you're saying is pointless!" We can say, "It's wrong." But the problem isn't that what someone says is wrong, but that it's stupid or irrelevant — that it's already been said a thousand times. The notions of relevance, necessity, point are a thousand times more significant than the notion of truth. Not because they replace it, but because they're the measure of the truth of what I'm saying. It's the same in mathematics: Jules-Henri Poincaré used to say that many mathematical theories are completely irrelevant, pointless. He didn't even bother to say they were wrong — that wouldn't have been much of an indictment.

Oedipus in the Colonies

Maybe journalists are partly responsible for this crisis in literature. Journalists have, of course, often written books. But when writing books, they used to adopt a form different from newspaper journalism — they became writers. The situation has changed, because journalists have become convinced that the book form is theirs by right, and that it takes no special effort to use this form. In one fell swoop and en masse, journalists have taken over literature. And the result is one version of the standard novel, a sort of *Oedipus in the Colonies*,[9] a reporter's travels, arranged around his pursuit of women, or the search for his father. The situation affects all writers: any writer must turn himself and his work into journalism. In the extreme case, everything takes place between a journalist author and a journalist critic, the book being only a link between them, and hardly needing to exist. The book has become an account of activities, experiences, purposes and ends that unfold elsewhere. It has itself become a record. Now everyone seems, and seems to themselves, to have a book in them, just by virtue of having a particular job, or a family even, a sick parent, a rude boss. A novel for everyone in the family or the business…. It's forgotten that for anyone, literature involves a special sort of exploration and effort, a particular creative purpose that can be pursued only within literature itself, whose job is in no way to register the immediate results of very different activities and purposes. Books become "secondary" when marketing takes over.

If Literature Dies, It Will Be by Assassination

Those who haven't properly read or understood Marshall McLuhan may think it's only natural for audiovisual media to replace books, since one assumes these new forms contain all the creative possibilities of a defunct literature or other older modes of expression. It's not true. For if audiovisual media ever replace literature, it won't be as competing means of expression, but as a monopoly of structures that also stifles the creative possibilities in those media themselves. If literature dies, it will have to be a violent death, a political assassination (as happened in the USSR, even if no one notices). It's not a matter of comparing different sorts of media. The choice isn't between written literature and audiovisual media. It's between creative forces (in audiovisual media as well as literature) and forces of domestication. It's highly unlikely that audiovisual media will find the conditions for creation, if they've already been lost in literature. Creative possibilities may be very different in different modes of expression, but they're related to the extent that they must counter the introduction of a cultural space of markets and conformity — that is, a space of "producing for the market" — together.

Style: Qualitative Mediation

Style is a literary notion: a syntax. And yet one speaks of style in the sciences, where there's no syntax. One speaks of style in sports. Very detailed studies have been done on style in sports, but I don't know much about them; they may show that style amounts to innovation. Sports do, of course, have their quantitative scale of records, dependent on improvements in equipment, shoes, vaulting poles…. But there are also qualitative transformations, ideas, which are a matter of style: how we went from the scissor jump to the belly roll and Fosbury flop; how hurdles ceased to present obstacles and came simply to mark a longer stride. Why not start here, why do we have to go through a whole history of quantitative advances? Each new style amounts not so much to a new "move," but a linked sequence of postures, the equivalent, that is, of a syntax, based on an earlier style but breaking with it. Technical advances take effect only by being taken up and incorporated in a new style. This is the importance of "inventors" in sports; they're qualitative mediators. In tennis, for example: When did the kind of return of service in which the returning ball lands on your opponent's feet as he runs to the net, first appear? I believe it was a great Australian player, Bromwich, before the war. Bjorn Borg obviously invented a new style that opened up tennis to a sort of proletariat. There are inventors in tennis, just as there are elsewhere: John McEnroe is an inventor, that is, a stylist — he's brought into tennis Egyptian postures (in his service) and Dostoyevskian reflexes ("if you spend your time voluntarily banging your head against the wall, life becomes impossible"). And then imitators can beat the inventors and do it better than they can: they're sports' best-sellers. Borg produced a race of obscure proletarians, and McEnroe can get beaten by a quantitative champion. We might say that the copiers, by taking advantage of a movement coming from elsewhere, become all the stronger, and that sporting bodies show remarkable ingratitude toward the inventors by whom they live and prosper. It doesn't matter: the history of sports runs through these inventors, who amount in each case to the unexpected, a new syntax, transformations, and without whom the purely technological advances would have remained quantitative, irrelevant and pointless.

AIDS and Global Strategy

One very important problem in medicine is the evolution of diseases. There are, of course, new external factors, new forms of microbe or virus, new social conditions. But there's also symptomatology, the grouping of symptoms: over a very short time scale, symptoms cease to be grouped in the same way, and diseases are isolated that were previously split among various different contexts. Parkinson's disease, Roger's disease and others present major changes in the grouping of symptoms (we might speak of a syntax of medicine). The history of medicine is made up of these groupings, these isolations, these regroupings, which here again become possible with technological advances, but are not determined by those advances. What has happened since World War II in this respect? The discovery of "stress" illnesses, in which the disorder is no longer produced by an attacking agent, but by nonspecific defensive reactions that get out of hand or become exhausted. Medical journals after World War II were full of discussions of stress in modern societies, and the new ordering of illnesses that might be drawn from it. More recently there was the discovery of autoimmune diseases, diseases of the self: defense mechanisms that no longer recognize the cells of the organism they're supposed to protect, or external agents that make these cells impossible to distinguish from others. AIDS comes somewhere between these two poles of stress and autoimmunity. Perhaps we're heading toward diseases without a doctor or patient, as François Dagognet says in his analysis of contemporary medicine: with images rather than symptoms, and carriers rather than sufferers. It's a problem for the welfare system, but it's worrying in other ways as well. It's striking how this new style of disease is like global politics or strategy. They tell us the risk of war comes not only from a specific external potential aggressor, but from our defensive reactions going out of control or breaking down (which is the rationale for properly controlled atomic weapons systems . . .). Now our diseases fit the same pattern — our nuclear policy corresponds to our diseases. Homosexuals are in danger of being assigned the part of some biological aggressor, just as minorities or refugees will fill the role of the enemy. It's one more reason to insist on a socialist government that refuses this dual image of disease and society.

We have to see creation as the tracing of a path between impossibilities. . . . Kafka explained how it was impossible for a Jewish writer to speak German, impossible for him to speak Czech and impossible for him not to speak. Perrault comes upon the same problem: the impossibility of not speaking, of speaking English, of speaking French. Creation takes place in strangled channels. Even in some particular language, even in French, for example, a new syntax is a foreign language within the language. A creator who isn't seized at the throat by a set of impossibilities is no creator. A creator is someone who creates his own impossibilities, and thereby creates possibilities. It's by banging your head against the wall that you find an answer. You have to work on the wall, because without a set of impossibilities, you won't have the line of flight, the exit that is creation, the power of falsity that is truth. You have to be liquid or gaseous, precisely because normal perception and opinion are solid, geometric. It's what Bergson did in philosophy, Virginia Woolf or Henry James with the novel, Jean Renoir in cinema (and experimental cinema, which has gone a long way exploring the states of matter). Not leaving Earth, at all — but becoming all the more earthly by inventing laws of liquids and gases on which the Earth depends. So style needs a lot of silence and work to make a whirlpool at some point, then flies out like a match; children follow beside the water in a gutter. For a style definitely doesn't come about by putting words together, combining phrases, using ideas. You have to open words, rend things, to free Earth's vectors. All writers, all creators, are shadows. How can one write a biography of Proust or Kafka? Once you're writing, shadows come before bodies. Truth is a production of existence. Not something in the head, but something that exists. Writers produce real bodies. With Fernando Pessoa they're imaginary people — but not so very imaginary, because he gives them a way of writing, of operating. The main thing, though, is that it's not Pessoa who's doing what they're doing. You don't get very far in literature with the system, "we saw a lot and traveled a long way," in which the author first does things and then tells us about them. Narcissism in authors is awful because shadows can't be narcissistic. No more interviews, then. What's bad is not having to cross a desert, if one's old and patient enough, but for young writers to be born in a desert, because they're in danger of seeing their venture grounded before it even gets going. And yet, it's impossible for the new race of writers, already engaged in their work and their styles, not to be born.

L'Autre Journal 8 (October 1985)

NOTES

1. Julien Benda, *The Treason of the Intellectuals*, trans. Richard Aldington (New York: Morrow, 1928), pp. 79-80, passim. See also Benda, *Le Bergsonisme, ou une philosophie de la mobilité* (Paris: Mercure de France, 1912); idem, *Sur le succès du Bergsonisme* (Paris: Mercure de France, 1914).

2. "*Etat de droit*" is the French for Schmitt's "*Rechtstaat*" — TRANS.

3. Gilles Deleuze, *Cinema 1: The Movement-Image*, trans. Hugh Tomlinson and Barbara Habberham (Minneapolis: University of Minnesota Press, 1986).

4. Gilles Deleuze, *Cinema 2: The Time-Image*, trans. Hugh Tomlinson and Robert Galeta (Minneapolis: University of Minnesota Press, 1989).

5. Noël Burch, "Narrative/Digesis: Thresholds, Limits," *Screen* 23.2 (Jan.-April 1982), pp. 16–23, reprinted in Burch, *Life to These Shadows*, trans. Ben Brewster (Berkeley and Los Angeles: University of California Press, 1990), pp. 243-66.

6. Ilya Prigogine and Isabelle Stengers, *Order out of Chaos* (New York: Bantam, 1984), pp. 268–79.

7. A French territory in the South Pacific. In the mid-1980s, demands from the indigenous Melanesian population (Canaques) for independence provoked fierce reaction from French settlers, and the repercussions of the resulting disturbances within French politics were reminiscent of the Algerian crisis of the 1950s. Edgard Pisani was the socialist minister given special responsibility for New Caledonia in 1985, and the problem was eventually resolved by an "arrangement" made by a returning socialist government in 1988 — TRANS.

8. A very influential Friday-evening book program on French TV, hosted by the literary journalist Bernard Pivot from 1975 to 1990 (it was voted "best cultural program" in 1985) — TRANS.

9. A play on the title of Sophocles' tragedy, *Oedipus at Colonnus* — TRANS.

Translated from the French by Martin Joughin

zone

Chronophotograph of a standing jump, c. 1882.

Etienne-Jules Marey

The Genesis of the Individual
Gilbert Simondon

When the living being is considered as an individual, there are two ways in which it can be conceived. There is the substantialist viewpoint, which conceives the unity of living being as its essence, a unity that it has provided for itself, is based on itself and is created by itself; a unity that will vigorously resist anything that is not itself. There is also the hylomorphic viewpoint, which regards the individual as having been created from the conjunction of a form and some matter. If we compare these two approaches, we can see there is a clear opposition between the self-centered monism of substantialist metaphysics and the bipolarity depicted by hylomorphism. But despite this oppo-

sition, these two ways of analyzing the real nature of the individual have something in common: in both cases, there is the assumption that we can discover a principle of individuation, exercising its influence before the actual individuation itself has occurred, one that is able to explain, produce and determine the subsequent course of individuation. Taking the constituted individual as a given, we are then led to try to recreate the conditions that have made its existence possible.

However, when the problem of individuation is formulated in terms of the existence of individuals, we find that a presupposition has emerged warranting further explanation. This presupposition points to an important aspect of the solutions that have been given to this problem, and it has surreptitiously determined the course of research dealing with the principle of individuation: that it is the individual qua the already constituted individual that is the most noteworthy reality, the one to be explained. Where this attitude prevails, the principle of individuation is sought only insofar as it is able to account for the characteristics of the individual exclusively, without allowing for this principle's necessary relation to other influences on the being as a whole, which could be equally important to the emergence of this individuated being. *Research carried out under these assumptions accords an ontological privilege to the already constituted individual.* Such research may well prevent us from adequately representing the process of ontogenesis, and from accurately according the individual its proper place in the actual system that results in individuation. *The idea that individuation might have a principle at all is a crucial postulate in the search for a principle of individuation.* The very idea of a "principle" suggests a certain quality that prefigures the sort of constituted individual at which we will arrive, and the properties it will have once the process of constitution is complete.

To a certain extent, the idea of a *principle of individuation* has been derived from a genesis that works backward, an ontogenesis "in reverse," because in order to account for the genesis of the individual and its defining characteristics one must assume the existence of a first term, a principle, which would provide a sufficient explanation of how the individual had come to be individual and account for its singularity (haecceity) — but this does not prove that the essential precondition of ontogenesis need be anything resembling a first term. Yet a term is itself already an individual, or at least something capable of being individualized, something that can be the cause of an absolutely specific existence (haecceity), something that can lead to a proliferation of many new haecceities. Anything that contributes to establishing relations already belongs to the same mode of existence as the individual, whether it be an atom, which is an indivisible and eternal particle, or prime matter, or a form. The atom interacts with other atoms through the *clinamen*, and in this way it can constitute an individual (though not always a viable one) across the entire expanse of the void and the whole of endless becoming. Matter can be impressed with a form, and the source of ontogenesis can be derived from this matter–form relation. Indeed, if haecceities were not somehow inherent within the atom, or matter, or indeed form, it would be impossible to find a principle of individuation in any of the above-mentioned realities. *To seek the principle of individuation in something that preexists this same individuation is tantamount to reducing individuation to nothing more than ontogenesis.* The principle of individuation here is the source of haecceity.

It is clear that both atomist substantialism as well as the theory of hylomorphism avoid giving a direct description of ontogenesis itself. *Atomism* describes the genesis of the complex unit, such as a living body, enjoying only a precarious and transitory unity; it is considered to be the result of a purely chance association, one that will break up into its original elements when overtaken by a force more powerful than the one currently holding it together as a complex unity. Those cohesive forces themselves, which may be taken as the principle of individuation of the complex individual, are in fact negated by the finer structure of the eternal elementary particles, which are the real individuals here. For atomism, the principle of individuation is rooted in the very existence of an infinity of atoms; it is always already there as soon as thought seeks to grasp their essential nature. Individuation is a fact: for each atom it is its already given nature, and for the complex unit it is the fact that it is what it is by virtue of a chance association.

In opposition to this, *hylomorphic theory* decrees that the individuated being is not already given when one comes to analyze the matter and form that will become the *sunolos* (the whole): we are not present at the moment of ontogenesis because we have always placed ourselves at a time before this process of ontogenetic formation actually takes place. The principle of individuation, then, is not grasped at the point where individuation itself occurs as a process, but in that which the operation requires before it can exist, that is, a matter and a form. Here the principle is thought to be contained either in the matter or the form, because the actual process of individuation is not thought to be capable of *furnishing* the principle itself, but simply of *putting it into effect*. Thus, the search for the principle of individuation is undertaken either before or after individuation has taken place, according to whether the model of the individual being used is a physical one (as in substantialist atomism) or a technological and vital one (as in hylomorphic theory). In both of these cases, though, there remains a *region of uncertainty* when it comes to dealing with the process of individuation, for this process is seen as something that needs to be explained, rather than as something in which the explanation is to be found: whence the notion of a principle of individuation. Now, if this process is considered as something to be explained, this is because the received way of thinking is always oriented toward the successfully individuated being, which it then seeks to account for, bypassing the stage where individuation takes place, in order to reach the individual that is the result of this process. In consequence, an assumption is made that events follow a certain chronology: first, the principle of individuation; then, this principle at work in a process that results in individuation; and finally, the emergence of the constituted individual. On the other hand, though, were we able to see that in the process of individuation other things were produced besides the individual, there would be no such attempt to hurry past the stage where individuation takes place in order to arrive at the ultimate reality that is the individual. Instead, we would try to grasp the entire unfolding of ontogenesis in all its variety, and *to understand the individual from the perspective of the process of individuation rather than the process of individuation by means of the individual.*

It is my intention to demonstrate the need for a complete change in the general approach to the principle governing individuation. The process of individuation must be considered primordial, for it is this process that at once brings the individual into being and determines all the distinguishing characteristics of its development, organization and modalities. Thus, the individual is to be understood as having a relative reality, occupying only a certain phase of the whole being in question — a phase that therefore carries the implication of a preceding preindividual state, and that, even after individuation, does not exist in isolation, since individuation does not exhaust in the single act of its appearance all the potentials embedded in the preindividual state. Individuation, moreover, not only brings the individual to light but also the individual–milieu dyad.[1] In this way, the individual possesses only a relative existence in two senses: because it does not represent the totality of the being, and because it is merely the result of a phase in the being's development during which it existed neither in the form of an individual nor as the principle of individuation.

Thus, individuation is here considered to form only one part of an ontogenetic process in the development of the larger entity. Individuation must therefore be thought of as a partial and relative resolution manifested in a system that contains latent potentials and harbors a certain incompatibility with itself, an incompatibility due at once to forces in tension as well as to the impossibility of interaction between terms of extremely disparate dimensions.

The meaning of the expression "ontogenesis" will be given its full weight here if, instead of being understood in the more limited and secondary sense of the genesis of the individual (as opposed to a more extensive idea of genesis, such as that involving the whole species), it is made to designate the development of the being, or its becoming — in other words, that which makes the being develop or become, insofar as it is, as being. The opposition holding between the being and its becoming can only be valid when it is seen in the context of a certain doctrine according to which substance is the very model of being; but it is equally possible to maintain that becoming exists as one of the dimensions of the being, that it corresponds to a capacity beings possess of falling out of step with themselves [*se déphaser par rapport à lui-même*], of resolving themselves by the very act of falling out of step. *The preindividual being is the being in which there are no steps* [phases]. The being in which individuation comes to fruition is that in which a resolution appears by its division into stages, which implies becoming: becoming is not a framework in which the being exists; it is one of the dimensions of the being, a mode of resolving an initial incompatibility that was rife with potentials.[2] *Individuation corresponds to the appearance of stages in the being, which are the stages of the being.* It is not a mere isolated consequence arising as a by-product of becoming, but this very process itself as it unfolds; it can be understood only by taking into account this initial supersaturation of the being, at first homogeneous and static [*sans devenir*], then soon after adopting a certain structure and becoming — and in so doing, bringing about the emergence of both individual and milieu — following a course [*devenir*] in which preliminary tensions are resolved but also preserved in the shape of the ensuing structure; in a certain sense, it could be said that the sole principle by which we can be guided is *that of the conservation of being through becoming.* This conservation is effected by means of the exchanges made between structure and process, proceding by quantum leaps through a series of successive equilibria. In order to grasp firmly the nature of individuation, we must consider the being not as a substance, or matter, or form, but as a tautly extended and supersaturated system, which exists at a higher level than the unit itself, which is not sufficient unto itself and cannot be adequately conceptualized according to the principle of the excluded middle. The concrete being or the full being, which is to say, the preindividual being, is a being that is more than a unit. Unity (characteristic of the individuated being and of identity), which authorizes the use of the principle of the excluded middle, cannot be applied to the preindividual being — which explains why one cannot recreate the world out of monads after the fact, even if one introduces other principles, such as that of sufficient reason, to allow oneself to organize them into a universe. Unity and identity are applicable only to one of the being's stages, which comes after the process of individuation. Now these notions are useless in helping us discover the actual process of individuation itself. They are not valid for understanding ontogenesis in the full sense of the term, that is, for the becoming of the being insofar as it doubles itself and falls out of step with itself [*se déphaser*] in the process of individuating.

Individuation has resisted thought and description until now because we have recognized the existence of only one form of equilibrium: stable equilibrium. The idea of "metastable equilibrium" had not been recognized. A being was implicitly presumed to be in a state of stable equilibrium at all times. Stable equilibrium excludes the idea of becoming because it corresponds to the lowest level of potential energy possible; it is the sort of equilibrium that is attained in a system when all the possible transformations have been achieved and no other force remains to enact any further changes. With all the potentials actualized, and the system having reached its lowest energy level, it can no longer go through any more transformations. The ancients recognized only the states of instability and stability, movement and rest, but they had no clear and objective idea of metastability. In order to define metastability, it is necessary to introduce the notion of the potential energy residing in a given system, the notion of order and that of an increase in entropy. In this way it is possible to define the being in its metastable state, which is very different from stable equilibrium and rest. The ancients were not able to introduce such a concept into their search for the principle governing individuation because no clear physical paradigm could be enlisted to reveal how such notions were to be used.[3] So first I shall attempt to present *physical individuation as a case of the resolution of a metastable system,* beginning with one of the system's *states*, such as those of superfusion or supersaturation, which preside over the genesis of crystals. Crystallization has at its disposal an abundant fund of notions that are well understood, which can be employed as paradigms in other domains; but it does not provide us with an exhaustive analysis of physical individuation.

Now, it can also be presumed that the phenomenon [*la réalité*], in its primitive state, in itself, is like the supersaturated solution and, a fortiori in the preindividual stage, *is something beyond a unity and an identity,* something capable of being manifested as either wave or corpuscle, matter or energy — because any process, and any relation within a process, is an individuation that doubles the preindividual being, pushing it out of step with itself, all the while correlating the extreme values and orders of magnitude without the refinements of mediation. The resulting complementarity, then, would be the epistemological effect of preserving the original and primitive metastability of the phenomenon [*le réel*]. Neither *mechanism* nor *energetism*, both theories of identity, can account for this reality in a comprehensive manner. Field theory, when combined with the theory of corpuscles, and even the theory of the interaction between fields and corpuscles, is still partially dualist, but is well on the way to formulating a theory of the preindividual. By another route, the theory of quanta has perceived the existence of this preindividual *regime*, which goes beyond unity: an exchange of energy is brought about in elementary quantities, as if there had been an individuation of energy in the relation between the particles, which one can consider to be physical individuals in a sense. It would perhaps be in this sense

Serra Pelada gold mine in Para, Brazil.
Sebastiao Salgado

that one could foresee how the two theories (of quanta and of wave mechanics), which had up to now remained impenetrable to each other, might finally converge. They could be envisaged as *two ways of expressing the preindividual state* by means of the various manifestations exhibited when it appears as a preindividual. Underlying the continuous and the discontinuous, it is the quantum and the metastable omplementarity (that which is beyond unity) that is the true preindividual. The necessity both of correcting and of coupling the basic concepts in physics expresses, perhaps, the fact that *the concepts are only an adequate representation of individuated reality,* and not preindividual reality.

Consequently, the exemplary value of the study of the crystal's genesis as a process of individuation would become all the more comprehensible. It would allow us to grasp, on the macroscopic level, a phenomenon that is rooted in those states of the system belonging to the microphysical domain, molecular and not molar. It would manage to grasp that activity which is *at the very boundary* of the crystal in the process of formation. Such an individuation is not to be thought of as the meeting of a previous form and matter existing as already constituted and separate terms, but a resolution taking place in the heart of a metastable system rich in potentials: *form, matter and energy pre-exist in the system.* Neither form nor matter are sufficient. The true principle of individuation is mediation, which generally presumes the existence of the original duality of the orders of magnitude and the initial absence of interactive communication between them, followed by a subsequent communication between orders of magnitude and stabilization.

At the same time that a quantity of potential energy (the necessary condition for a higher order of magnitude) is actualized, a portion of matter is organized and distributed (the necessary condition for a lower order of magnitude) into structured individuals of a *middle* order of magnitude, developing by a mediate process of amplification.

It is the organization of energy in a metastable system that leads to crystallization and subtends it, but the form of the crystals expresses certain molecular or atomic characteristics of the constituent chemical types.

In the domain of living things, the same notion of metastability can be employed to characterize individuation. But individuation is no longer produced, as in the physical domain, in an instantaneous fashion, quantumlike, abrupt and definitive, leaving in its wake a duality of milieu and individual — the milieu having been deprived of the individual it no longer is, and the individual no longer possessing the wider dimensions of the milieu. It is no doubt true that such a view of individuation is valid for the living being when it is considered as an absolute origin, but it is matched by a perpetual individuation that is life itself following the fundamental mode of becoming: *the living being conserves in itself an activity of permanent individuation.* It is not only the result of individuation, like the crystal or the molecule, but is a veritable theater of individuation. Moreover, the entire activity of the living being is not, like that of the physical individual, concentrated at its boundary with the outside world. There exists within the being a more complete regime of *internal resonance* requiring permanent communication and maintaining a metastability that is the precondition of life. This is not the sole characteristic of the living being, and it cannot be seen as an automa-ton that maintains a certain number of equilibria or that seeks to find compatibilities between its various requirements, obeying a formula of complex equilibrium composed of simpler ones. The living being is also the being that results from an initial individuation and amplifies this individuation, not at all the machine to which it is assimilated functionally by the model of cybernetic mechanism. In the living being, *individuation is brought about by the individual itself,* and is not simply a functioning object that results from an individuation previously accomplished, comparable to the product of a manufacturing process. The living being resolves its problems not only by adapting itself — which is to say, by modifying its relationship to its milieu (something a machine is equally able to do) — but by modifying itself through the invention of new internal structures and its complete self-insertion into the axiomatic of organic problems.[4] *The living individual is a system of individuation, an individuating system and also a system that individuates itself.* The internal resonance and the translation of its relation to itself into information are all contained in the living being's system. In the physical domain, *internal resonance* characterizes the limit of the individual in the process of individuating itself. In the domain of the living being, it becomes the criterion of any individual qua individual. It exists in the system of the individual and not only in that which is formed by the individual vis-à-vis its milieu. The internal structure of the organism is brought to completion not only as a result of the activity that takes place and the modulation that occurs at the frontier between the interior domain and the exterior — as is the case with a crystal; rather, the physical individual — perpetually ex-centric, perpetually peripheral in relation to itself, active at the limit of its own terrain — cannot be said to possess any genuine interiority. But the living individual does possess a genuine interiority, because individuation does indeed take place within it. In the living individual, moreover, the interior plays a constitutive role, whereas only the frontier plays this role in the physical individual; and in the latter case, whatever is located on the inside in topological terms must also be thought of as genetically prior. The living individual is its own contemporary with regard to each one of its elements; this is not the case with the physical individual, which contains a past that is radically "past," even when it is in the throes of growth. The living being can be considered to be a node of information that is being transmitted inside itself — it is a system within a system, containing *within itself* a mediation between two different orders of magnitude.[5]

In conclusion, I can put forward the hypothesis — analogous to that of quanta in physics and also to that concerning the relativity between the levels of potential energy — that it is fair to assume that the process of individuation does not exhaust everything that came before (the preindividual), and that a metastable regime is not only maintained by the individual, but is actually borne by it, to such an extent that the finally constituted individual carries with it a certain inheritance associated with its preindividual reality, one animated by all the potentials that characterize it. Individuation, then, is a relative phenomenon, like an alteration in the structure of a physical system. There is a certain level of potential that remains, meaning that further individuations are still possible. The preindividual nature, which remains associated with the individual, is a source of future metastable states from which new individuations could eventuate. According to this hypothesis, it would be possible *to consider every genuine relation as having the status of a being, and as undergoing development within a new individuation.* A relation does not spring up between two terms that are already separate individuals, rather, it is an aspect of the *internal resonance of a system of individuation.* It forms a part of a wider system. The living being, which is simultaneously more and less than a unity, possesses an internal problematic and is capable of being an element in a problematic that has a wider scope than itself. As far as the individual is concerned, participation here means *being an element in a much larger process of individuation* by means of the inheritance of *preindividual reality that the individual contains* — that is, due to the potentials it has retained.

Thus, it now becomes feasible to think of both the internal and external relationship as one of participation, without having to adduce new substances by way of explanation. Both the psyche and the collectivity are constituted by a process of individuation supervening on the individuation that was productive of life. *The psyche represents the continuing effort of individuation in a being that has to resolve its own problematic* through its own involvement as an element of the problem by taking action as a subject. The subject can be thought of as the unity of the being when it is thought of as a living individual, and as a being that represents its activity to itself in the world both as an element and a dimension of the world. Problems that concern living beings are not just confined to their own sphere: only by means of an unending series of successive individuations, which ensure that ever-more preindividual reality is brought into play and incorporated into the relation with the milieu, can we endow living beings with an open-ended axiomatic. Affectivity and perception are seen as forming a single whole in both emotion and science, forcing one to take recourse to new *dimensions*. However, the psychic being is not able to resolve its particular problematic within its own orbit. Its inheritance of preindividual reality allows collective individuation — which plays the role here of one of the preconditions of psychic individuation — to contribute to resolution, at the same time as this preindividual reality is individualized as a psychic being that goes beyond the limits of the individuated being and incorporates it in a wider system of the world and the subject. Individuation in its collective aspect makes a group individual, one that is associated with the group through the preindividual reality it carries within itself, conjoining it to all other individuals; *it individuates as a collective unit*. The two individuations, psychic and collective, have a reciprocal effect on each other; they allow us to define a transindividual category that might account for the systematic unity of internal individuation (psychic) and external individuation (collective). The psychosocial world of the transindividual is neither the social in its raw immediacy nor the interindividual state. It requires that one postulate the previous influence of a veritable process of individuation rooted in a preindividual reality, associated with individuals and capable of constituting a new problematic with its own metastability. It expresses a quantum condition, correlative to a plurality of orders of magnitude. The living being is presented as a *problematic being*, at once greater and lesser than the unit. To say that the living being is problematic means considering its becoming as forming one of its dimensions, and thus that it is determined by its becoming, which affords the being mediation. The living entity is both the agent and the theater of individuation: its becoming represents a permanent individuation or rather *a series of approaches to individuation* progressing from one state of metastability to another. The individual is thus no longer either a substance or a simple part of the collectivity. The collective unit provides the resolution of the individual problematic, which means that the basis of the collective reality already forms a part of the individual in the form of the preindividual reality, which remains associated with the individuated reality. In general, what we consider to be a *relation*, due to the substantialization of the reality of the individual, in fact forms a dimension of the process of

A battalion of farmer-militia prior to its departure for the Chinese front, 1895.
Suzuki Shinichi

山東　途　征　大兵　止七　臨四十明
撮京　中清隊第　田師　時月八治
影青　於軍　從三　步團　第　一年二

individuation by which the individual becomes. In other words, the relation to both the world outside and to the collective is in fact a *dimension of the individuation* in which the individual participates due to its connection with the preindividual reality that undergoes gradual individuation.

Moreover, psychology and group theory are connected, since ontogenesis reveals the nature of the contribution made to the collective unit and also to that of the psychic process conceived as the resolution of a problematic. When we consider individuation to be life itself, then it can be seen as a discovery, in a situation of conflict, of a new axiomatic incorporating and unifying all the various elements of this situation in a system that embraces the individual. In order to understand the role played by psychic activity in the theory of individuation as that which resolves the conflictual character of a metastable state, it is necessary to uncover the true paths by which metastable systems are constructed in life. In this sense, both the notion of an *adaptive relation of the individual to its milieu*[6] and the critical notion of the *relation of the knowing subject to the object known* must be modified. Knowledge is not built up through abstraction from sensations, but through a problematic deriving from a *primary tropistic unity, a coupling of sensation and tropism, the orientation of the living being in a polarized world.* Here once again it is necessary to distance ourselves from the hylomorphic schema. There is no such thing as a sensation that would be the matter constituting a given a posteriori for the a priori forms of the sensibility. The a priori forms are in fact a first resolution, utilizing the discovery of an axiomatic of tensions resulting from the confrontation of *the primary tropistic unities*. The a priori forms of the sensibility are not obtained either a priori or a posteriori by abstraction, but rather must be understood as the structures of an axiomatic that appears in a process of individuation. The world and the living being are already contained in the tropistic unity, but the world here only serves as a direction, as a polarity of a gradient that locates the individuated being in an *indefinite dyad* at whose median point it can be found, and upon which it bases its further exfoliation. Perception, and later Science itself, continue to resolve this problematic, not only with the invention of spatiotemporal frameworks, but also with the constitution of the notion of an object, which then becomes the "source" of the original gradients and organizes them among themselves as if they were an actual *world*. The distinction between the a priori and the a posteriori, an echo of the hylomorphic schema in the theory of knowledge, obscures, with its dark central zone, the true process of individuation that is the seat of knowledge. The very idea of a qualitative or intensive series would do well to be thought along the lines of a theory *of phases* or steps through which a being passes. This theory is *nonrelational* and is not maintained by preexisting polar terms; rather, it develops from a primitive median state that localizes the living being and inserts it in the gradient that confers meaning on the tropistic unity. The series is an abstract vision of meaning by means of which the tropistic unity orients itself. We must begin with individuation, with the being grasped at its center and in relation to its spatiality and its becoming, and not by a realized [*substantialisé*] *individual* faced with a *world* that is external to it.

What I mean by this is that the a priori and the a posteriori are not to be found in knowledge itself.[7] They represent neither the form nor the matter of knowledge — since they themselves are not knowledge — but the extreme poles of a preindividual dyad, and are consequently prenoetic. The illusion that there are a priori forms derives from the preexistence of *prior conditions of totality* in the preindividual system, whose dimensions are greater than that of the individual undergoing ontogenesis. On the other hand, the illusion that the a posteriori applies can be explained by the existence of a reality whose order of magnitude is inferior to that of the individual seen in the light of spatiotemporal modifications. A concept is neither a priori nor a posteriori but a praesenti, because it is an informative and interactive communication between that which is larger than the individual and that which is smaller.

The same method outlined above can be used to explore the affectivity and the emotivity that constitute the resonance of the being in relation to itself, and that connect the individuated being to the preindividual reality associated with it in the same way that the tropistic unity and perception put it in relation with the milieu. The psyche is composed of successive individuations, which allow the being to resolve its problematic states by effectuating permanent communications between that which is larger than it and that which is smaller.

Resolution of the psyche, though, cannot take place at the level of the individuated being alone. It forms the basis of participation in a wider individuation, that of the collectivity. If the individual being puts itself, but nothing else, into question, then it will not be able to move beyond the limits of anxiety, for anxiety is a process without action, a permanent emotion that does not succeed in resolving affectivity, a challenge in which the individuated being explores the dimensions of its being without being able to progress beyond them. *To the collective understood as an axiomatic that resolves the psychic problematic corresponds the notion of the transindividual.*

This set of revised notions is supported by the hypothesis stating that a piece of information is never relative to a unique and homogeneous reality, but rather to two orders that are in the process of "*disparation*." The piece of information, whether it be at the level of the tropistic unity or at the level of the transindividual, is never delivered in a format that can be given in a simple way. It is the tension between two disparate realities, it is *the signification that emerges when a process of individuation reveals the dimension through which two disparate realities together become a system.* If this is the case, then the piece of information acts in fact as an instigation to individuation, *a necessity to individuate;* it is never something that is just given. Unity and identity are not inherent in the information because the information is itself not a term. For there to be information presupposes that there is a tension in the system of the being: the information must be inherent in a problematic, since it represents *that by which the incompatibility within the unresolved system becomes an organizing dimension in its resolution.* The information implies a *change of phase in the system* because it implies the existence of a primitive preindividual state that is individuated according to the dictates of the emerging organization. The information provides the formula that is followed by individuation, and so the formula could not possibly preexist this individuation. One could say that the information always exists in the present, that it is always contemporary, because it yields the meaning according to which a system is individuated.[8]

The conception of being that I put forth, then, is the following: a being does not possess a unity in its identity, which is that of the stable state within which no transformation is possible; rather, a being has a *transductive unity*, that is, it can pass out of phase with itself, it can — in any area — break its own bounds in relation to its *center*. What one assumes to be a *relation* or a *duality of principles* is in fact the unfolding of the being, which is more than a unity and more than an identity; becoming is a dimension of the being, not something that happens to it following a succession of events that affect a being already and originally given and substantial. Individuation must be grasped as the becoming of the being and not as a model of the being which would exhaust its signification. The individuated being is neither the whole being nor the primary being. *Instead of grasping individuation using the individuated being as a starting point, we must grasp the individuated being from the viewpoint of individuation, and individuation from the viewpoint of preindividual being,* each operating at many different orders of magnitude.

I intend therefore to study the *forms, modes and degrees of individuation* in order to situate accurately the individual in the wider being according to the three levels of the physical, the vital and the psychosocial.[9] Instead of presupposing the existence of substances in order to account for individuation, I intend, on the contrary, to take the different regimes of individuation as providing the foundation for different domains such as matter, life, mind and society. The separation, the gradation and the relations of these domains appear as aspects of individuation according to its different modalities. The notions of substance, form and matter are replaced by the more fundamental notions of primary information, internal resonance, potential energy and orders of magnitude.

However, in order to modify our notions in this way, we will have to employ both a new method and a new notion. The method would encourage, on the one hand, a refusal to construct the essence of a given reality by means of a *conceptual* relation between two opposed terms, and on the other, a consideration of any veritable relation as something existing in its own right. The relation, then, represents one of the modalities of the being, since it is contemporaneous with both of the terms whose existence it underwrites. A relation must be understood in its role as a relation in the context of the being itself, a relation belonging to the being, that is, a way of being and not a simple connection between two terms that could be adequately comprehended using concepts because they both enjoy what amounts to an independent existence. It is because the terms are conceived as substances that the relation is seen as a connection between two terms, and the being is divided into these terms because it is first concieved of as a substance, before any questions about individuation have been asked. On the other hand, though, if the being is no longer conceived using the model of a substance, it becomes possible to think of the relation as one of the nonidentity of the being with itself, meaning that the being contains not only that which is identical to itself, with the result that the being qua being — previous to any individuation — can be grasped as something more than a unity and more than identity.[10] This method presupposes a postulate of an ontological nature. The principles of the excluded middle and of identity are inapplicable at the level of the being since at this point individuation has not yet occurred; they only apply to the being after individuation has taken place, and they refer to a rather diminished being due to its having been separated out into milieu and individual. They do not refer to the whole of the being, which is to say, to the totality that will be formed later by the individual together with the milieu, but rather only to that which became the individual, derived from the preceding preindividual being. So one sees that classical logic cannot be used to understand individuation because it forces us to deal with the process of individuation using concepts and their interrelations, which are only valid for the results of the process of individuation, a limited view at best.

A fresh notion, enjoying a great variety of aspects and many areas of application, can be drawn from this method which treats the principle of identity and the excluded middle as being too narrow: *transduction*. This term denotes a process — be it physical, biological, mental or social — in which an activity gradually sets itself in motion, propagating within a given area, through a structuration of the different zones of the area over which it operates. Each region of the structure that is constituted in this way then serves to constitute the next one to such an extent that at the very time this structuration is effected there is a progressive modification taking place in tandem with it. The simplest image of the transductive process is furnished if one thinks of a crystal, beginning as a tiny seed, which grows and extends itself in all directions in its mother-water. Each layer of molecules that has already been constituted serves as the structuring basis for the layer that is being formed next, and the result is an amplify-ing reticular structure. The transductive process is thus an individuation in progress. Physically, it might be said to occur at its simplest in the form of a progressive iteration; however, in the case of more complex domains, such as those of living metastability or psychic problematics, it might progress at a constantly variable rate and expand in a heterogeneous area. Transduction occurs when there is activity, both structural and functional, which begins at a center of the being and extends itself in various directions from this center, as if multiple dimensions of the being were expanding around this central point. It is the correlative appearance of dimensions and structures in a being in a state of preindividual tension, which is to say, in a being that is more than a unity and more than an identity, and which has not yet passed out of step with itself into other multiple dimensions. The ultimate terms at which the transductive process finally arrives do not preexist this process. Its dynamism derives from the primitive tension of the heterogeneous being's system, which moves out of step with itself and develops further dimensions upon which it bases its structure. It does not derive from a tension between the terms that will be found and registered at the furthest edges of transduction.[11] Transduction can be a vital process; in particular, it expresses the sense of organic individuation. It can also be a psychic process and in effect a logical procedure, although one that is in no way restricted to the logical mind-set. In the area of knowledge, it maps out the actual course that invention follows, which is neither inductive nor deductive but rather transductive, meaning that it corresponds to a discovery of the dimensions according to which a problematic can be defined. It is the analogical process insofar as it is valid. This notion can be used to understand all of the different areas of individuation; it applies to all the cases where an individuation occurs and reveals the genesis of a network of relations based on the being. The possibility of using an analogical transduction in order to understand a given area of reality shows that this area is really the place where an analogical structuration has occurred. Transduction corresponds to the presence of those relations created when the preindividual being becomes individuated. It expresses individuation and allows us to understand its workings, showing that it is at once a metaphysical and also a logical notion. *While it may be applied to ontogenesis, it is also ontogenesis itself.* Objectively, it allows us to comprehend the systematic preconditions of individuation, internal resonance[12] and the psychic problematic. Logically, it can be used as the foundation for a new species of analogical paradigms so as to enable us to pass from physical individuation to organic individuation, from organic individuation to psychic individuation, and from psychic individuation to the subjective and objective level of the transindividual that forms the basis of our investigation.

Clearly, transduction cannot be presented as a logical procedure terminating in a conclusive proof. Nor is it not my intention to say that transduction is a logical procedure in the currently accepted meaning of this expression. I see it as a mental procedure, or better, the course taken by the mind on its journey of discovery. This course would be *to follow the being from the moment of its genesis, to see the genesis* of the thought through to its completion at the same time as the genesis of the object reaches its own completion. In this investigation, the above-mentioned course is obliged to play a role that the dialectic is unable to play, because the study of the process of individuation does not seem to correspond to the appearance of the negation that follows as the second step, but rather to an immanence of the negative in the primary state, the precondition for what follows, in the ambivalent form of tension *and* of incompatibility. Indeed, it is the most positive element in the preindividual being — namely, the existence of potentials — that is also the cause of the incompatibility and the nonstability of this state. The negation is primarily an ontogenetic incompatibility, but it is also the other side of the richness of potentials. It is not therefore a negation that is a substance. It is never a step or a stage, and individuation is not synthesis, a return to unity, but rather the being passing out of step with itself, through the potentialization of the incompatibilities of its preindividual center. In this ontogenetic perspective, time itself is considered to be the expression of the *dimensionality of the being as it is becoming individualized.*

Transduction, then, is not only a path taken by the mind, it is also an intuition, since it allows a structure to appear in a domain of problematics yielding a solution to the problems at hand. In the sense contrary to *deduction*, however, transduction does not seek elsewhere a principle to resolve the problem at hand; rather, it derives the resolving structure from the tensions themselves within the domain just as the supersaturated solution is crystallized due to its own potentials and the nature of the chemicals it contains, and not through the help of some foreign body. Nor is it comparable to *induction*, because induction retains the character of the terms of the reality as it is understood in the area under investigation — deriving the structures of the analysis from these terms themselves — but it only retains that which is positive, which is to say, *that which is common* to all the terms, eliminating whatever is singular. On the contrary, transduction represents a discovery of dimensions that are made to communicate by the system for each of the terms such that the total reality of each of the areas' terms can find a place in the newly discovered structures without loss or reduction. The transduction that resolves things *effects the reversal of the negative into the positive:* meaning, that which makes the terms fail to be identical with each other, and that which makes them *disparate* (in the sense in which this expression is understood in the theory of vision), is integrated with the system that resolves things and becomes a condition of meaning. There is no impoverishment in the information contained in the terms: transduction is characterized by the fact that the result of this process is a concrete network including all the original terms. The resulting system is made up of the concrete, and it comprehends all of the concrete. The transductive order retains all the concrete and is characterized by the *conservation of information*, whereas induction requires a loss of information. Following the same path as the dialectic, transduction conserves and integrates the opposed aspects. Unlike the dialectic, transduction does not presuppose the existence of a previous time period to act as a framework in which the genesis unfolds, time itself being the solution and dimension of the discovered systematic: *time comes from the preindividual just like the other dimensions that determine individuation.* [13]

Now, in order to comprehend the transductive process, which forms the basis for individuation at all of its various levels, the notion of form is insufficient. It is part of the same system of thought that substance is, or that in which a connection is considered to be a relation that postdates the existence of the terms. These latter notions have been elaborated based on the results of individuation. They are capable of grasping only an impoverished reality, one that does not take potentials into account, and are therefore incapable of being individualized.

The notion of form must be replaced by that of information, which presupposes the existence of a system in a state of metastable equilibrium capable of being individuated.

Information, unlike form, is never a unique term, but rather the meaning that arises on the heels of a disparation. The old notion of form, as it is given by the hylomorphic schema, is too independent of any notion of system and metastability. That given by the Theory of Form includes, on the contrary, the notion of system, and is defined as the state toward which the system tends when it seeks equilibrium, meaning that it is a resolution of tension. Unfortunately, our reliance on a superficial physical paradigm has meant that the Theory of Form views only the stable state of equilibrium as that state of a system capable of resolving tensions. It has totally ignored metastability. I wish to consider the Theory of Form anew and, by introducing a quantum precondition, show that the problems presented by the Theory of Form can be directly resolved — not by using the notion of stable equilibrium, but only by using that of metastable equilibrium. The True Form, then, is not the simple form, the pregnant geometric form, but the *significant form*, that is, the one that establishes a transductive order within a system of reality replete with potentials. This True Form is the one that maintains the energy level of the system, sustaining its potentials by making them compatible. It is the structure of compatibility and viability, it is the invented dimensionality following which there is compatibility without degradation.[14] The notion of *Form* deserves therefore to be replaced by that of *information*. In the course of this replacement, the notion of information must not be associated with that of the signals or supports [*supports*] or vehicles of information, *as the technological theory of information tends to do, derived by abstraction as it is in the first instance from transmission technology.* The pure notion of form must therefore be retrieved twice over from the evils resulting from a superficial use of a technological paradigm: in the first place, in relation to the culture of the ancients, due to the reductive use made of this notion in the *hylomorphic schema*; in the second place, where it exists as a notion of information, in order to save information as meaning from the *technological theory* of information in modern culture. For in the successive theories of hylomorphism, it is indeed the same aim that we find in the case of the True Form, and then information: the effort to discover the inherence of the given meanings in the *being*. My object is to discover this inherence *in the process of individuation*.

In this way, an investigation concerning individuation can lead to a reform of our fundamental philosophical notions, because it is possible to consider individuation as that which has to be understood before all else in the case of a given being. Even before one asks to what extent it is legitimate or otherwise to make judgments about any being whatsoever, the being can be seen as expressing itself in two senses: the first, fundamental, that the being *is* insofar as it is; but in a second sense, which is always superimposed on the first in the theory of logic, that the being is a being insofar as it is individuated. If it were true that logic is not applicable to any affirmations concerning the being until after individuation has occurred, then a theory of being as it exists previous to any logic ought to be developed. This theory could in fact serve as a foundation for logic, since nothing proves in advance that there is only one possible way for the being to be individuated. If many types of individuation existed, similarly there ought to be many types of logic, each one corresponding to a definite type of individuation. The classification of ontogeneses would allow us to *pluralize logic* relying on a valid basis of plurality. As for the axiomatization of our knowledge of the preindividual being, it cannot be restricted to one of the previously established logics because it is impossible to define any norm or system without taking its content into account. Only the individuation of thought coming to fruition can accompany the individuation of beings that are not thought. Therefore, we cannot have either an immediate or a mediated knowledge of individuation, but only one that is a process parallel to the process with which we are already familiar. We cannot *know individuation* in the common sense of the phrase; we can only individuate, individuate ourselves and in ourselves. On the margins of knowledge proper, this comprehension is an analogy between two processes, which is a specific mode of communication. Individuation of the reality beyond the subject as grasped by the subject thanks to the analogous individuation of knowledge within the subject. But it is *by means of the individuation of knowledge* and not knowledge alone that the individuation of beings that are not subjects is grasped. Beings can be known by means of the knowledge of the subject, but the individuation of beings cannot be understood except by the individuation of the knowledge of the subject.

NOTES

1. Moreover, it is quite possible that the milieu is not to be thought of as a simple, homogeneous and uniform phenomenon, but something that, from its very inception, is characterized by a tension in force between two extreme orders of magnitude that mediatize the individual when it comes into being.

2. And constitution, between the two extremes, of a mediate order of magnitude; in a certain sense, ontogenetic development [*devenir*] itself can be considered as mediation.

3. Normative and intuitive equivalents of the notion of metastability did exist in the ancient world; but since the notion of metastability generally requires the simultaneous existence of two orders of magnitude and the absence of interactive communication between them, this concept owes much to the discoveries made by scientific advance.

4. It is by means of this self-insertion that the living being can be seen as the product of informational exchange, by becoming a node of interactive communication between an order of reality dimensionally superior to its own, and an inferior order whose organization it undertakes.

5. This internal mediation can occur as a continuance of the external mediation that is accomplished by the living individual, thereby allowing the living being to bring two different orders of magnitude into relation with one another: that of the cosmic level (as in the luminous energy of the sun, for example) with that of the intermolecular level.

6. Specifically, the relation to the milieu cannot be envisaged, either before or during individuation, as relation to a unique and homogeneous milieu. The milieu is itself a *system*, a synthetic grouping of two or more levels of reality that did not communicate with each other before individuation.

7. This paragraph appeared as a footnote in the original French — TRANS.

8. This statement is not meant to contest the validity of quantitative theories of information and of orders of complexity, but it works under the assumption that there is a fundamental state — that of the preindividual being — that precedes any duality of sender and receiver, thus any transmitted message. The residue of this fundamental state in the classic example of information transmitted in the form of a message is not the source of the information but the primordial precondition without which there is no information-effect, which means no information. This precondition is the metastability of the receiver, whether it be that of a technical being or the living individual. This information could be called "primary information."

9. *L'Individu et sa genèse physico-biologique: L'Individuation à la lumière des notions de forme et d'information* (Paris: P.U.F., 1964). The present essay forms the introduction to that work — TRANS.

10. Above all, it should be noted that the multiplicity of orders of magnitude and the primordial absence of interactive communication between them forms an integral part of any such understanding of the being.

11. On the contrary, it expresses the primordial heterogeneity of the two levels of reality, one larger than the individual — the system of metastable totality — the other smaller than it, such as a piece of matter. Between these two primordial orders of magnitude the individual develops through a process of amplifying communication of which transduction is the most primitive form, one already present in the physical individuation.

12. Internal resonance is the most primitive form of communication between realities of different orders. It is composed of a double process of amplification and condensation.

13. This process is paralleled by that of vital individuation. A plant institutes a mediation between a cosmic order and an inframolecular order, classifying and distributing the different chemicals contained in the soil and the atmosphere by means of the solar energy obtained from photo-synthesis. It is an interelemental focal point and it develops as an internal resonance of this preindividual sys-

tem composed of two layers of reality that originally had no contact with each other. The interele-
mentary focal point effects an infraelementary function.

14. In this way, the form appears as an active communication, the internal resonance that effects
individuation — it appears with the individual.

Translated from the French by Mark Cohen and Sanford Kwinter

The Reenchantment of the Concrete

Francisco J. Varela

The Disenchantment of the Abstract

Shifts in cognitive science. "Rationalistic," "Cartesian" or "objectivist": These are some terms used in recent times to characterize the dominant tradition within which we have grown.[1] Yet when it comes to a reassessment of knowledge and cognition, I find that the best description of our tradition is "abstract": nothing better characterizes the units of knowledge that are deemed most "natural." It is this tendency to find our way toward the rarefied atmosphere of the general and the formal, the logical and the well-defined, the represented and the planned, that makes our Western world so distinctly familiar.

The main thesis I want to pursue here is this: There are strong indications that among the loose federation of sciences dealing with knowledge and cognition — the cognitive sciences — there is a slowly growing conviction that this picture is upside down, that a radical paradigmatic or epistemic shift is rapidly developing. At the very center of this emerging view is the belief that the proper units of knowledge are primarily *concrete*, embodied, incorporated, lived. This unique, concrete knowledge, its historicity and context, is not "noise" that occludes the brighter pattern to be captured in its true essence, an abstraction, nor is it a step toward something else: it is how we arrive and where we stay.

Perhaps nothing better illustrates this tendency than the gradual transformation of ideas in the very pragmatic field of artificial intelligence. Research in its first two decades (1950–1970) was based on the computationalist paradigm according to which knowledge operates by logic-like rules for *symbolic* manipulation, an idea that finds its full expression in modern digital computers. Initially, efforts were directed at solving the most general problems, such as natural language translation or devising a "general problem solver." These attempts, which tried to match the intelligence of a highly trained expert, were seen as tackling the core issues of cognition. As attempts at such tasks consistently failed, it became clear that the only way to make headway was to reduce the task to something more modest and local. The most ordinary tasks, even those performed by tiny insects, are simply impossible to achieve with a computational strategy. The culmination of these years of research was the realization among those involved that it is necessary to invert the expert and the child on the scale of performance. It became apparent that the deeper and more fundamental kind of intelligence is that of a baby who acquires language from dispersed daily utterances, and who delineates meaningful objects from a previously unspecified world.

As this view has been elaborated, it has revitalized the role of the concrete by focusing on its proper scale: the cognitive activity that occurs in a very special space, which I shall call the "hinges" of the immediate present. For it is in the *immediate present* that the concrete actually lives. But before I go on, I need to revise some entrenched assumptions inherited from the computationalist orthodoxy.

On disunited cognitive agents. There is considerable support for the view that brains are not logical machines, but highly cooperative, nonhomogeneous and distributed networks. The entire system resembles a *patchwork* of subnetworks assembled by a complicated history of tinkering, rather than an optimized system resulting from some clean unified design. This kind of architecture also suggests that instead of looking for grand unified models for all network behaviors, one should study networks whose abilities are restricted to specific, concrete cognitive activities as they interact with each other.

Cognitive scientists have begun to take this view of cognitive architecture seriously in various ways. For example, Marvin Minsky presents a view in which minds consist of many "agents" whose abilities are quite circumscribed: each agent taken individually operates only on small-scale or "toy" problems.[2] The problems must be so because they become unmanageable for a single network when they are scaled up (this last point has not been obvious to cognitive scientists for very long). The task, then, is to organize the "agents" who operate in these specific domains into effective, larger systems or "agencies,"

Fukushima Prefecture,
Shimogo Town, 1990.
Toshio Shibata

and then to turn these agencies into higher level systems. Mind emerges, then, as a kind of "society."

It is important to remember here that, although inspired by a fresh look at the brain, this is a model of the *mind*. In other words, it is not a model of neural societies or networks; it is a model of the cognitive architecture that abstracts (again!) from neurological detail, hence from the "wet" of the living and lived experience. Agents and agencies are, therefore, neither entities nor material processes; they are abstract processes or functions. The point bears emphasizing, especially since Minsky sometimes writes as if he were talking about cognition at the level of the brain. As I shall emphasize, what is missing is the detailed link between these agents and the incarnated coupling, by sensing and acting, which is essential to living cognition. We shall now pause for a moment to look into some of the implications of the notions of fragmented and local cognitive subnetworks.

The model of the mind as a society of numerous agents is intended to encompass a multiplicity of approaches to the study of cognition, ranging from distributed, self-organizing networks to the classical, cognitivist conception of symbolic processing. This encompassing view challenges a centralized or unified model of the mind, be it in the form of distributed networks at one extreme, or symbolic processes at the other. This move is apparent, for example, when Minsky argues that there are virtues not only in distribution, but in insulation, that is, in mechanisms that keep various processes apart. This idea has also been extensively explored, though in a somewhat different context, by Jerry Fodor.[3] The agents within an agency may be connected in the form of a distributed network, but if the agencies themselves were connected in the same way they would, in effect, constitute one large network whose functions would be uniformly distributed. Such uniformity, however, would restrict the ability to combine the operations of individual agencies in a productive way. The more distributed these operations are, the harder it is for many of them to act at the same time without interfering with each other. These problems do not arise, however, if there are mechanisms to keep the various agencies insulated from each other. The agencies would still interact, but through more limited connections.

The details of such a programmatic view are debatable, of course, but the overall picture it suggests (which is not unique to Minsky's formulation of agents and agencies) is that of mind not as a unified, homogeneous entity, nor even as a collection of entities, but as a *disunified, heterogeneous collection of processes.* Such a disunified assembly can obviously be considered at more than one level. What counts as an agency (that is, as a collection of agents) could, if one changes one's focus, be considered as merely one agent in a larger agency. And conversely, what counts as an agent could, if one focuses in greater detail, be seen to be an agency made up of many agents. In the same way, what counts as a society will also depend on one's chosen level of focus.

Having thus set the stage for this key issue in contemporary cognitive science, I want to develop its implications for the question at hand: the present-centeredness of the concrete.

On Being There: During Breakdowns

Readiness-for-action in the present. My present concern is with one of the many consequences of this view of the disunity of the subject, understood as a cognitive agent. The question I have in mind can be formulated thus: Given the myriad of contending subprocesses in every cognitive act, how are we to understand the moment of negotiation and emergence when one of them takes the lead and constitutes a definite behavior? Or, in more evocative terms: How are we to understand the very moment of being there, when something concrete and specific appears?

Picture yourself walking down the street, perhaps going to meet somebody. It is the end of the day and there is nothing very special in your mind. You are in a relaxed mood, in what we may call the "readiness" of the walker who is simply taking a stroll. You put your hand into your pocket and suddenly discover that your wallet is not where it usually is. Breakdown: You stop, your mind-set is unclear, your emotional tonality shifts. Before you know it, a new world emerges: you see clearly that you left your wallet in the store where you just bought some cigarettes. Your mood shifts now to one of concern about losing documents and money, your readiness-for-action is now to go quickly

Miyazaki Prefecture,
Shiiba Village, 1990.
Toshio Shibata

back to the store. You pay little attention to the surrounding trees and passers-by; all your attention is directed toward avoiding further delays.

Situations like this are the very stuff of our lives. We always operate in some kind of immediacy of a given situation: our lived world is so ready-at-hand that we are in no way deliberate about what it is and how we inhabit it. When we sit at the table to eat with a relative or friend, the entire complex know-how of handling table utensils, the body postures and pauses in the conversation, are all present without deliberation. Our having-lunch-self is transparent.[4] We finish lunch, return to the office and enter into a new readiness with a different mode of speaking, different postural tone and different assessments. We have a readiness-for-action proper to every specific lived situation. New modes of behaving and the transitions or punctuations between them correspond to microbreakdowns that we experience constantly. Sometimes the breakdowns become not quite micro, but rather microscopic, as when a sudden shock or danger happens unexpectedly. I shall refer to any such readiness-for-action as "microidentity" and its corresponding situation as "microworld." The way we show up *as* is indissociable from the way things and others show up *to* us. I could go through some elementary phenomenology and identify some typical microworlds within which we move during a normal day, but the point is not to catalogue them but to address their *recurrence*: being capable of appropriate action is, in some important sense, a way in which we embody a stream of recurrent microworld transitions. I am not denying that there are situations in which recurrence does not apply. For example, when one arrives for the first time in a foreign country there is a profound lack of readiness-to-hand and of recurrent microworlds. Many simple actions such as social talk or eating must be done deliberately or learned outright. In other words, microworlds and microidentities are historically constituted. But the pervasive mode of living consists of the microworlds already constituted, which compose our identities. Clearly, there is a lot more that should be explored and said about the phenomenology of ordinary experience — not enough has been done.[5] My intention here is more modest: merely to point to a realm of phenomena intimately close to our ordinary experience.

When we leave the realm of human experience and shift to that of animals, the same kind of analysis applies as an external account. The extreme case is illustrative: biologists have known for some time that invertebrates have a rather small repertoire of behavior patterns, for example, a cockroach has only a few fundamental modes of movement — standing, slow walking, fast walking and running. Nevertheless, this basic behavioral repertoire makes it possible for them to negotiate appropriately *any* possible environment, natural or artificial. The question for the biologist is, then: How does it decide which motor action to take in a given circumstance? How does it select an appropriate behavioral action? How does it have the common sense to assess a given situation and interpret it as requiring running as opposed to slow walking?

In the two extreme cases — human experience during breakdowns, and animal behaviors at moments of behavioral transitions — we are confronted, in vastly different ways, to be sure, with a common issue: at each such breakdown, the manner in which the cognitive agent will next be constituted is neither externally decided nor simply planned. Rather, it is a matter of *commonsensical emergence* of the autonomous configuration of an appropriate stance. Once a behavioral stance is selected or a microworld is brought forth, we can more clearly analyze its mode of operation and its optimal strategy. In fact, the key to autonomy is that a living system finds its way into the next moment by acting appropriately from its own resources. And it is the breakdowns, the hinges that articulate microworlds, that are the source of the autonomous and creative side of living cognition. Such common sense, then, must be examined on a microscale: in the moment *during a breakdown* it actualizes the birth of the concrete.

Knowledge as enaction. Let me now explain how I mean to use the word "embodied" by highlighting two points: first, cognition depends on the kinds of experience that come from having a body with various sensorimotor capacities; and second, these individual sensorimotor capacities are themselves embedded in a more encompassing biological and cultural *context*. These points were introduced above in terms of breakdown and common sense, but I wish to explore further their corporeal specificity and to emphasize that sensory and motor processes, perception and action, are fundamentally inseparable in lived cognition, and are *not* merely contingently linked in individuals.

In adopting what I call an "enactive approach to cognition,"[6] two principles are essential: first, perception consists of perceptually guided action; and second, cognitive structures emerge from the recurrent sensorimotor patterns that enable action to be perceptually guided. (These will become clearer as I proceed.)

Let me begin with the notion of perceptually guided action. For the dominant computationalist tradition, the starting point for understanding perception is typically abstract: the information-processing problem of recovering pregiven properties of the world. In contrast, the starting point for the enactive approach is the study of how the perceiver guides his or her actions in local situations. Since these local situations constantly change as a result of the perceiver's activity, the reference point for understanding perception is no longer a pregiven, perceiver-independent world, but rather the sensorimotor structure of the cognitive agent, the way in which the nervous system links sensory and motor surfaces. It is this structure — the way in which the perceiver is *embodied* — rather than some pregiven world, that determines how the perceiver can act and be modulated by environmental events. Thus, the overall concern of an enactive approach to perception is not to determine how some perceiver-independent world is to be recovered; it is, rather, to determine which common principles or lawful linkages between sensory and motor systems will explain how action can be *perceptually* guided in a *perceiver-dependent* world.

This central concern of the enactive approach stands in contradistinction to the received view that perception is fundamentally a registering of existing environmental information in order to reconstruct a bit of the physical world truthfully. Reality is not cast as a given: it is perceiver dependent, not because the perceiver "constructs" it at whim, but because what counts as a relevant world is inseparable from the structure of the perceiver.

Such an approach to perception is in fact one of the central insights of the phenomenological analysis undertaken by Maurice Merleau-Ponty in his early work. It is worth quoting here in full one of his more visionary passages:

The organism cannot properly be compared to a keyboard on which the external stimuli would play and in which their proper form would be delineated for the simple reason that the organism contributes to the constitution of that form.... "The properties of the object and the intentions of the subject...are not only intermingled; they also constitute a new whole." When the eye and the ear follow an animal in flight, it is impossible to say "which started first" in the exchange of stimuli and responses. Since all the movements of the organism are always conditioned by external influences, one can, if one wished, readily treat behavior as an effect of the milieu. But in the same way, since all stimulations which the organism receives have in turn been possible only by its preceding movements which have culminated in exposing the receptor organ to external influences, one could also say that *behavior is the first cause of all the stimulations.*

Thus the form of the excitant is *created* by the organism itself, by its proper manner of offering itself to actions from the outside. Doubtless, in order to be able to subsist, it must encounter a certain number of physical and chemical agents in its surroundings. But it is the organism itself — according to the proper nature of its receptors, the thresholds of its nerve centers and the movements of the organs — *which chooses the stimuli in the physical world to which it will be sensitive.* "The environment (*Umwelt*) emerges from the world through the actualization or the being of the organism — [granted that] an organism can exist only if it succeeds in finding in the world an adequate environment." This would be a keyboard which moves itself in such a way as to offer — and according to variable rhythms — such or such of its keys to the in itself monotonous action of an external hammer.[7]

According to such an approach, then, perception is not simply embedded in, and constrained by, the surrounding world; it also contributes to the *enactment* of this surrounding world. Thus, as Merleau-Ponty notes, the organism both initiates and is shaped by the environment: he clearly recognized that we must see the organism and environment as bound together in reciprocal specification and selection — a point of which we need to remind ourselves constantly, for it is quite contrary to the received views deriving from the Cartesian tradition.

A classic illustration of the perceptual guidance of action is the 1958 study by Richard Held and Alan Hein, who raised kittens in the dark and exposed them to light only under controlled conditions.[8] A first group of animals was allowed to move around normally while harnessed to a yoke; their gross movements were transferred mechanically to a second group of animals conveyed in gondolas. The two groups shared the same visual experience, but the second group was entirely passive. When the animals were released after a few weeks of this treatment, the first group of kittens behaved normally, but those who had been carried around behaved as if they were blind: they bumped into objects and fell over edges. This marvelous study supports the *enactive* view that objects are not seen by the visual extraction of features, but rather by the visual guidance of action. Similar results have been obtained under various other circumstances and studied even at the single-cell level.

Unless the reader feels that this example is fine for cats, but removed from human experience, let us consider another case. In 1962, Paul Bach y Rita designed a video camera for blind persons that can stimulate multiple points in the skin by electrically activated vibration.[9] Using this technique, images formed with the camera were made to correspond to patterns of skin stimulation, thereby substituting for the visual loss. Patterns projected onto the skin have no "visual" content unless the individual is behaviorally active by directing the video camera using head, hand or body movements. When the blind person does actively behave in this way, after a few hours of experience a remarkable effect emerges: the person no longer interprets the skin sensations as body-related, but rather as images projected into the space being explored by the bodily directed "gaze" of the video camera. Thus, in order to experience "real objects out there," the person must actively direct the camera (using his or her head or hand).

The fine structure of the present. Now that I have situated the emergence of the concrete within the enactive framework for cognition, where it truly makes sense, I can return to the question I started with: How can emergent microworlds arise out of a turmoil of many cognitive agents and subnetworks? The answer I propose here is that in the gap during a breakdown there is a rich *dynamics* involving concurrent subidentities and agents. This rapid dialogue, invisible to introspection, has recently been revealed in brain studies.

Some key aspects of this idea were first introduced by Walter Freeman who, over many years of research, managed to insert an array of electrodes into the olfactory bulb of a rabbit so that a small portion of the global activity could be measured while the animal behaved freely.[10] He found that there was no clear pattern of global activity in the bulb unless the animal was exposed to a specific odor several times. Furthermore, he discovered that such patterns of activity emerged from a background of incoherent or chaotic activity in fast oscillations (that is, with periods of about five to ten milliseconds) until the cortex settles into a global electrical pattern, which lasts until the end of the sniffing behavior and then dissolves back into the chaotic background.[11] The oscillations, then, provide a means of *selectively binding* a set of neurons in transient aggregate that constitutes the substrate for smell perception at that precise instant. Smell appears in this light not as some kind of mapping of external features, but as a creative form of enacting significance on the basis of the animal's embodied history. Most pertinent of all, this enaction happens at the hinge between one behavioral moment and the next, via fast oscillations between neuronal populations capable of giving rise to coherent patterns.

There is growing evidence that this kind of fast resonance transiently binds neuronal ensembles during a percept. For example, it has been observed in the visual cortex of cats and monkeys linked to visual stimulation;[12] it has also been found in radically different neural structures such as the avian brain,[13] and even the ganglia of an invertebrate, *Hermissenda*.[14] This universality is important, for it points to the fundamental nature of resonance binding as a mechanism for the enaction of sensorimotor couplings. Had it been a species-specific process — typical, say, only of the mammalian cortex — it would be far less interesting as a working hypothesis.

It is important to note that this fast resonance is not simply linked to sensorial trigger: the oscillations appear and disappear quite spontaneously in various places of the brain. This suggests that such fast dynamics concerns all the subnetworks that give rise to the entire readiness-at-hand in the next moment. They involve not only sensory interpretation and motor action but also the entire gamut of cognitive expectations and emotional tonality, which are central to the shaping of a microworld. Between breakdowns, these oscillations are the symptoms of very rapid reciprocal cooperation and competition between distinct agents activated by the current situation, vying with each other for differing modes of interpretation constituting a coherent cognitive framework and readiness-for-action. On the basis of this fast dynamics, as in an evolutionary process, one neuronal ensemble (one cognitive subnetwork) finally becomes more prevalent and *becomes the behavioral mode for the next cognitive moment.* By "becomes more prevalent" I do not mean to say that this is a process of optimization: it resembles more a bifurcation or symmetry-breaking form of chaotic dynamics. It follows that such a cradle of autonomous action is forever lost to lived experience since, by definition, we can only inhabit a microidentity when it is already present, but not when it is in gestation. In other words, in the breakdown before the next microworld emerges, there is a myriad of possibilities available until, out of the constraints of the situation and the recurrence of history, a single one is selected. This fast dynamics is the neural correlate of the autonomous constitution of a cognitive agent incorporated at a given present moment of its life.

From temporal fine structure to cognitive action. As noted, the fast resonance of an agent's reciprocity provides the playground for the emergence of a microworld. Evidence indicates that this sensorimotor coupling is linked with other kinds of typically human cognitive performance, which is to say, from the "low"-level event of sensing and acting the true "higher" cognitive levels emerge, enabling action to be perceptually guided.

In fact, this basic idea is at the very core of the Piagetian program.[15] Because it has been argued by George Lakoff and Mark Johnson,[16] I shall present the idea of embodied cognitive structures with special reference to their work. Once again, I must move away from the abstract and emphasize an experientialist approach to cognition. As Lakoff asserts, the central claim of his own and Johnson's approach is that meaningful conceptual structures arise from two sources: from the structured nature of bodily experience, and from our capacity to project imaginatively from certain well-structured aspects of bodily and interactional experience to conceptual structures.

Rational and abstract thought is itself the application of very general cognitive processes — focusing, scanning, superimposition, figure–ground reversal and so on — to such conceptual structures.[17] Basically, embodied (sensorimotor) structures are the substance of experience, and experiential structures "motivate" conceptual understanding and rational thought. As I have emphasized, perception and action are embodied in self-organizing sensorimotor processes; it follows, then, that cognitive structures *emerge* from recurrent patterns of sensorimotor activity. In either case, the point is not, as Lakoff would have it, that experience strictly determines conceptual structures and modes of thought; it is, rather, that experience both makes possible and constrains conceptual understanding across the multitude of cognitive domains.

Lakoff and Johnson provide numerous examples of cognitive structures generated from experiential processes. Reviewing all of these examples would take me too far afield, so I shall discuss briefly just one of the most significant kinds: basic-level categories. Consider the middle-size things with which we continually interact: tables, chairs, dogs, cats, forks, knives, cups and so on. These things belong to a level of categorization that is intermediate between lower (subordinate) and higher (superordinate) levels. If we take a chair, for example, at the lower level it might belong to the category "stool," whereas at the higher level it belongs to the category "furniture." Eleanor Rosch and her co-authors have shown that this intermediate level of categorization (table, chair and so on) is psychologically the most fundamental or *basic* one, for the following reasons, among others: first, the basic level is the most general level on which category members have similar overall *perceived shapes*; second, it is the most general level on which a person uses similar motor actions for interacting with category members; and third, it is the level on which clusters of correlated attributes are most *apparent*.[18] It would seem, therefore, that whether a category belongs to the basic level depends not on how things are arranged in some pregiven world, but rather on the sensorimotor structure of our bodies and the kinds of perceptually guided interactions this structure makes possible. Basic-level categories are both experiential and embodied. A similar argument can be made for image-schemas emerging from certain basic forms of sensorimotor activities and interactions.

Conclusion

I have argued that perception does not consist of the recovery of a pregiven world, but rather of the perceptual guidance of action in a world that is inseparable from our sensorimotor capacities. Cognitive structures emerge from recurrent patterns of perceptually guided action. I can summarize, then, by saying that cognition consists not of representations but of *embodied action*. Correlatively, the world we know is not pregiven; it is, rather, *enacted* through our history of structural coupling. The temporal hinges that articulate enaction are rooted in the fast noncognitive dynamics wherein a number of alternative microworlds are activated; these hinges are the source of both common sense and creativity in cognition.

It is, therefore, the very contemporary quest in cognitive science for the understanding of understanding that points in a direction I consider post-Cartesian in two important ways. First, knowledge appears more and more as built from small domains, that is, microworlds and microidentities. Such basic modes of readiness-at-hand vary but are present throughout the animal kingdom. What all living cognitive beings seem to have in common, though, is knowledge that is always a know-how constituted on the basis of the concrete; what we call the "general" and the "abstract" are aggregates of readiness-for-action. Second, such microworlds are not coherent or integrated into some enormous totality regulating the veracity of the smaller parts. It is more like an unruly conversational interaction: the very presence of this unruliness allows a cognitive moment to come into being according to the system's constitution and history. The very heart of this autonomy, the rapidity of the agent's behavior selection, is forever lost to the cognitive system itself. Thus, what we traditionally call the "irrational" and the "nonconscious" does not contradict what appears as rational and purposeful: it is its very underpinning.

NOTES

1. Portions of this text appear, with modifications, in James Ogilvy, ed., *Revisioning Philosophy* (New York: SUNY Press, 1991); and in Jacques Montangero, ed., *Psychologie génétique et sciences cognitives*, Cahiers de la Fondation Jean Piaget no. 11 (Genève, 1991).

2. Marvin Minsky, *The Society of Mind* (New York: Simon and Schuster, 1986).

3. Jerry Fodor, *The Modularity of Mind* (Cambridge, Mass.: Bradford Books and MIT Press, 1983).

4. The notion of transparency is extensively developed in an unpublished manuscript by Fernando Flores and Michel Graves (Logonet, Inc., Berkeley, Calif., 1990). I am grateful to Mr. Flores for letting me read this ongoing work from which my own ideas have greatly benefited.

5. I am specifically thinking of Martin Heidegger's *Being and Time*, trans. John Macquarrie and Edward Robinson (New York: Harper, 1929), and Maurice Merleau-Ponty's *Phenomenology of Perception*, trans. Colin Smith (New York: Humanities Press, 1962) as prime examples.

6. Francisco Varela, *Connaître: Les Sciences cognitives* (Paris: Seuil, 1989); Varela, "Organism: A Meshwork of Selfless Selves," in Alfred Tauber, ed., *Organism and the Origin of Self* (Dordrecht and Uitgeverij: Reidel Kluwer, 1991); Varela, Evan Thompson and Eleanor Rosch, *The Embodied Mind: Cognitive Science and Human Experience* (Cambridge, Mass.: MIT Press, 1991); and Thompson, Alden Palacios and Varela, "Ways of Coloring: Comparative Color Vision as a Case Study in the Foundations of Cognitive Science," *Behavioral Brain Sciences* 16.1 (forthcoming).

7. Maurice Merleau-Ponty, *The Structure of Behavior*, trans. Alden Fisher (Boston: Beacon, 1963), p. 13 (emphasis added). The first internal quote is from V. F. von Weizsäcker, "Reflexgesetze," in Bethe, ed., *Handbuch der normalen und pathologischen physiologie*, pp. 38–39; the second is from K. Goldstein, *The Organism* (Boston: Beacon, 1963).

8. Richard Held and Alan Hein, "Adaptation of Disarranged Hand–Eye Coordination Contingent upon Re-afferent Stimulation," *Perceptual and Motor Skills* 8 (1958), pp. 87–90.

9. Paul Bach y Rita, *Brain Mechanisms in Sensory Substitution* (New York: Academic Press, 1972).

10. Walter Freeman, *Mass Action in the Nervous System* (New York: Academic Press, 1975).

11. Walter Freeman and Christine Skada, "Spatial EEG Patterns, Nonlinear Dynamics, and Perception: The Neo-Sherringtonian View," *Brain Research Reviews* 10 (1985), pp. 147–75.

12. Charles Gray and Wolf Singer, "Stimulus-Specific Neuronal Oscillations in Orientation Columns in Cat Visual Cortex," *Proceedings of the National Academy of Sciences of the USA* 86 (1989), pp. 1698–702.

13. Serge Neuenschwander and Francisco Varela, "Sensori-triggered and Spontaneous Oscillations in the Avian Brain," *Society Neuroscience Abstracts* 16 (1990).

14. Alan Gelperin and David Tank, "Odour-Modulated Collective Network Oscillations of Olfactory Interneurons in a Terrestrial Mollusc," *Nature* 345 (1990), pp. 437–40. For a recent review, see Steven Bressler, "The Gamma Wave: A Cortical Information Carrier," *Trends in Neuroscience* 13 (1990), pp. 161–62.

15. Jean Piaget, *Biologie et Connaissance* (Paris: Gallimard, 1969).

16. George Lakoff, *Women, Fire and Dangerous Things* (Chicago: University of Chicago Press, 1983); and Mark Johnson, *The Body in the Mind* (Chicago: University of Chicago Press, 1989).

17. George Lakoff, "Cognitive Semantics," in Umberto Eco et al., eds., *Meaning and Mental Representations* (Bloomington: Indiana University Press, 1988), p. 121, provides a concise overview of Lakoff and Johnson's experientialist approach.

18. Eleanor Rosch, Carolyn Mervis, Wayne Gray, David Johnson and Penny Boyes-Braem, "Basic Objects in Natural Categories," *Cognitive Psychology* 8 (1976), pp. 382–439.

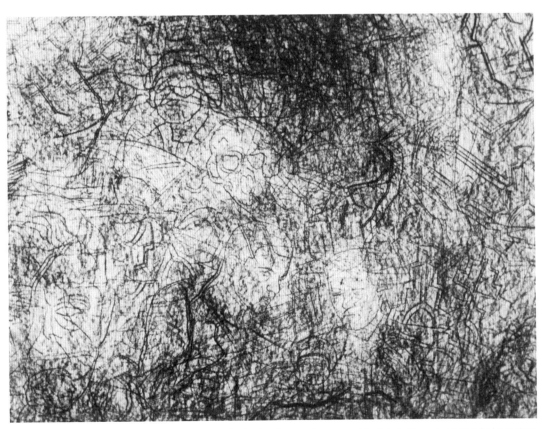

Barbarian Demonology, graphite/photo/board, 18 ½ x 24 ½ inches.
Joseph Nechvatal
Courtesy of Brooke Alexander Gallery

Berlin Wall, Germany, 1990.

Thierry Noir/Elaine Scarry

Arbeit Medallion

Elaine Scarry

Especially in winter on a rainy day, the Kreuzberg section of the Berlin Wall was the brightest thing in the city. Big bands of color — fourteen feet high, four to twenty-four in width — made a steady way from Waldemarstrasse (and before) to Mariannenkirche (and beyond). Its unstoppable stripes gave it a kind of braggadocio sweetness, like a big child balancing on a new bike or a high wall: Watch me, look at me.

Forever showing off, the painted wall signaled and called. Its chattering brightness was its refusal to be camouflaged, to let its own concrete surface blend into the gray-brown masonry of the neighborhoods it divided. Yet the very obdurate surface on which the paint insisted also seemed to dissolve, as though the saturated colors could soak their way into the center and make it disappear. The porousness of the wall was sketched and scrawled all along its 110-mile circumference: line-drawn fists forever punched their way through line-drawn holes and painted steps led upward to doors that had swung open. But the virtuoso Kreuzberg panels were both a tour de force in transparency and a brilliant manifesto on the impulse toward animation that stood at its heart.

If the wall were a string and the Kreuzberg panels were painted beads, the one that might hang at its center is the Arbeit Medallion. In its irregular red border, the unmovable wall became a movable red curtain pulling back on all four sides to reveal a bright blue space behind, inhabited by "*Die 3 Brüder Arbeit*." In the first split second of coming upon them, they seemed to smile, wave, jump off the ground (if they did not jump, they at least levitated slightly, filling them with delight). Behind the actual wall — as one could see by climbing the fifteen steps of the watchtower nearby — there was no bright field of blue filled with luminous people waving, only the empty horizontal expanse of brownish-pink dirt and the white concrete of the second wall in the two-layer construction surrounding West Berlin. But for a moment, back on the ground in front of the Arbeit Medallion, the space behind the curtain had become open, blue, full and alive.

The Arbeit Medallion now appears a precocious anticipation of the November 1989 revolution (open, blue, full and alive) when the working population — not the intellectuals, artists or civic leaders — became the agents of radical transformation, through pacific levitations practiced in the streets in Leipzig, at the exit gates of Czechoslovakia and atop the disappearing wall itself. The prophetic Arbeit siblings lift the wall with their mimesis of aliveness, then go on to reveal how the magic trick is done. They seek not only to animate but to make the act of animation imitable. Their own bodies pass easily back and forth between inanimate and animate. The left arm of the first turns into a rake; the left arm of the second, into a sickle; the left arm of the third, into a hammer. The right arms of all three become blocks of raw material to be worked by the tools of labor — pieces of stone to be reshaped or panels of wall to be broken apart and written on. Their kit of tools includes not just rakes and hammers but pieces of language (*ar, be, it* and a floating arrow), and the effortless continuity with the mental labor of dream and thought is asserted in the giant heap poised in alert reverie nearby.

The Arbeit Medallion is about sentience. Sensation is lopsided in the two outer arbeiters. One, Jürgen, can only hear on his right side; the other, Ralf, only hears what is coming from her left. In between, the two-eared, androgynous Sibylle hears on both sides and hence restores the symmetry of sensation. In the iconography of Berlin wall painting, whatever occupies the spatial geography of "the middle" usually replaces the wall as a topos of mediation. In this panel, the middle sibling's acuity of sentience has become that rival form of mediation.

The first counterfactual wish — to make an impassable object passable — has given way to a second counterfactual wish: to make insensate surface sensate. This loop through transparency to aliveness might be called "Arbeit Magic" or "Arbeit Levitation" or "Arbeit Vivification," and it continually resurfaces in the Kreuzberg panels. The work of sensory perception is unequally distributed across the live body: most of the sensory sites are located on the small surface of head and face. The Arbeit siblings themselves would be mere blockheads (their faces shaped like their concrete block right hands) were it not for all the sensory features concentrated there. Because so many of the Kreuzberg panels were preoccupied with amplifying sentience, they were also preoccupied with the human head — the solitary, ten-foot head of the Arbeit Medallion often reappeared along Waldemarstrasse, now multiplied into painted congregations and assemblies of monolithic heads whose uniform two-foot-high eyes stood exaggeratedly open over protruding noses and lips that sallied forth into the world in surprising variations. Their invitation to heightened sentience was unmistakable: no wonder, then, that when the startled angel in Wim Wenders's *Wings of Desire* acquires permanent color vision, it happens here on the ground in front of these population panels. (The movie shares with the Kreuzberg panels an interest in sustained levitation, as the film's German title, *Himmel über Berlin* [Heaven over Berlin] clearly announces.)

What brought the wall to life was the litheness of the painting, its bright agility, the rapidity of its lines and forms. Above the serene heads of the Waldemarstrasse panels in mercurial script were written the words "Fast Form Manifest," a phrase invented by Thierry Noir to summarize the Kreuzberg school of painting — painting done fast, with the haste manifest in the picture's structure: "Two ideas. Three colors. Quick!" (Marking the wall was dangerous: even the surface facing into West Berlin was owned, surveilled and policed aggressively by the East.) The quickness of the lines gave the panels a fresh, done-on-a-dare look. Fast Form Manifest displayed the readiness to run: the shapes and lines memorialized the skilled rapidity of the motion that produced them, the way the wet streaks of a photograph show the arc of a runner's foot going from 0 mph on the starting block and 50 mph by the time it passes under the knee. Relentlessly good-natured and tense with excitement, the large Kreuzberg panels held within their big patches of color the painter's own state of alertness. Bright nerve endings shimmered beneath the paint of the wall, the way sinews flicker across the silky flank of a large animal, or wind skims along the underside of a flag or sail. Laid edge to edge, the big swatches of color striped the wall like a giant spectrum of light or sound, converting it from inert to supersentient aerial, tremulous with voice and life.

Even faded and covered with graffiti, the Arbeit Medallion was always fresh; now torn down, it seems to have disappeared before its paint was even dry.

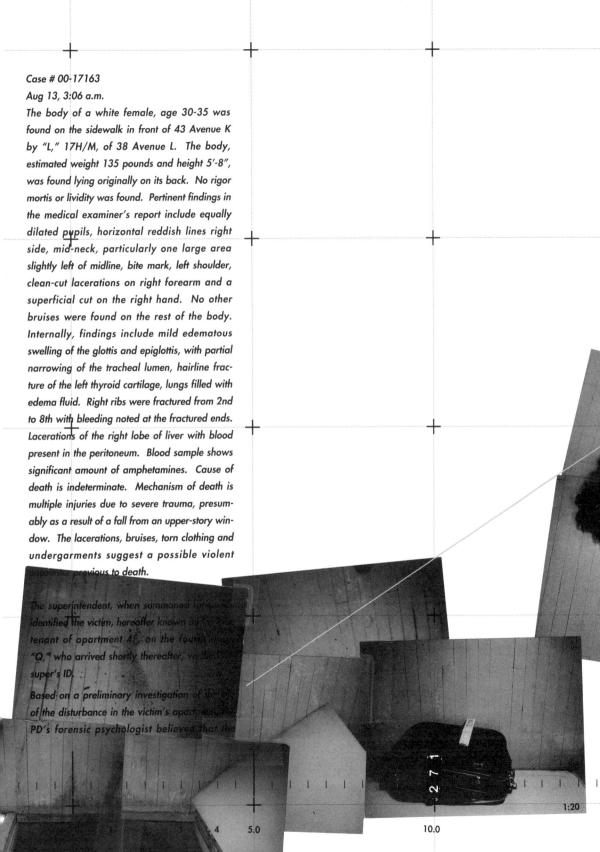

Case # 00-17163
Aug 13, 3:06 a.m.

The body of a white female, age 30-35 was found on the sidewalk in front of 43 Avenue K by "L," 17H/M, of 38 Avenue L. The body, estimated weight 135 pounds and height 5'-8", was found lying originally on its back. No rigor mortis or lividity was found. Pertinent findings in the medical examiner's report include equally dilated pupils, horizontal reddish lines right side, mid-neck, particularly one large area slightly left of midline, bite mark, left shoulder, clean-cut lacerations on right forearm and a superficial cut on the right hand. No other bruises were found on the rest of the body. Internally, findings include mild edematous swelling of the glottis and epiglottis, with partial narrowing of the tracheal lumen, hairline fracture of the left thyroid cartilage, lungs filled with edema fluid. Right ribs were fractured from 2nd to 8th with bleeding noted at the fractured ends. Lacerations of the right lobe of liver with blood present in the peritoneum. Blood sample shows significant amount of amphetamines. Cause of death is indeterminate. Mechanism of death is multiple injuries due to severe trauma, presumably as a result of a fall from an upper-story window. The lacerations, bruises, torn clothing and undergarments suggest a possible violent encounter previous to death.

The superintendent, when summoned to the scene, identified the victim, hereafter known as "V," a tenant of apartment 4F, on the fourth floor. "Q," who arrived shortly thereafter, verified the super's ID.

Based on a preliminary investigation of the scene of the disturbance in the victim's apartment, the PD's forensic psychologist believed that the

1:20

.4   5.0   10.0

[GARBLED] .... EDULED APPOINTMENT   THE DENTIST WILL SEE YOU MONDAY AT NINE THIRTY [BEEP]   REALLY VIOLENT

20.0

30.0

RBLED] I FIGURE YOU'LL LIKE IT [BEEP] THIS IS T— CALL ME TOMORROW AFTER 12   [BEEP]   THIS IS NATIONAL CITY BANK PLEASE CALL ONEEIGHTHUNDRED FIVE FIVE FIVE TWO S

1:320

...ong way with V. Yesterda...

...interesting ...you ask me. ...t ...guy. Yeah. He ...standing there ...long time, lea...

V always goes after ...uys that don't li... ...she ...this yea...

1:220

V'cal... ...un... 9 o'clock. ...he was bore... ...ed me over. Wh...

1:380

277... 279...

40.0   50.0

scene bears certain characteristics of a "disor-
dered" crime scene. Little attempt has been
made to disguise the evidential fragments on
and around the victim's bed, suggesting that the

told me that someone, maybe V's new boyfriend, was threatening her...needed her for some high-income business that seem

crime was an impulsive, violent act, possibly
sexually-motivated and accompanied by little
forethought or planning. The incomplete state in
which parts of the room were left— for example
the interrupted meal— would indicate that the

few times. Every

perpetrator may have experienced the onset of
a hysterical condition during commission of the
crime, inducing in this individual a distorted
sense of time and consequent difficulty organiz-

ver a

tely she was really freaked.... out of control.   M told me that her new boyfriend was a little kinky....dressing up, r

ing thoughts and actions. The psychologist also
expressed concern about the "even" distribution
of the disorder which could be the result of a
highly intelligent power/control killer who
desires to direct the interpretation of the crime.
Suicide has not been ruled out.

An answering machine in the victim's apartment
was largely demolished and tape strewn from

got there we had a few drinks. Then, well... you know.... I was taking care of all her needs   when that total scum M

the machine was found trampled and broken
next to it. According to the forensic psychologist's report, the act seems to have been performed in a heated rage, probably directed
toward a third party not within the room. Partial
decipherable messages recovered from the
remaining tape were subjected to voice print
analysis. Message located at 282.4 on the tape
counter, "I know/no," shows high frequency
nodes framing the "n" of know/no, peaking out
at just over 4000 Hz (fourth line of scan). These
patterns, combined with localized regions of
density in the 2500 Hz and 1500-1900 Hz
areas, confirm a positive match with the supplied print from individual M. The message at
285.7, "nervous," is a positive match with individual R. Speech pattern correlations, for exam-

4:2.4

match

nomatch

KODAK 5053 TMY

281   3   283

60.0   70.0

y shady. R told me that if V said no, he was going to come over and make trouble. R was worried and kept

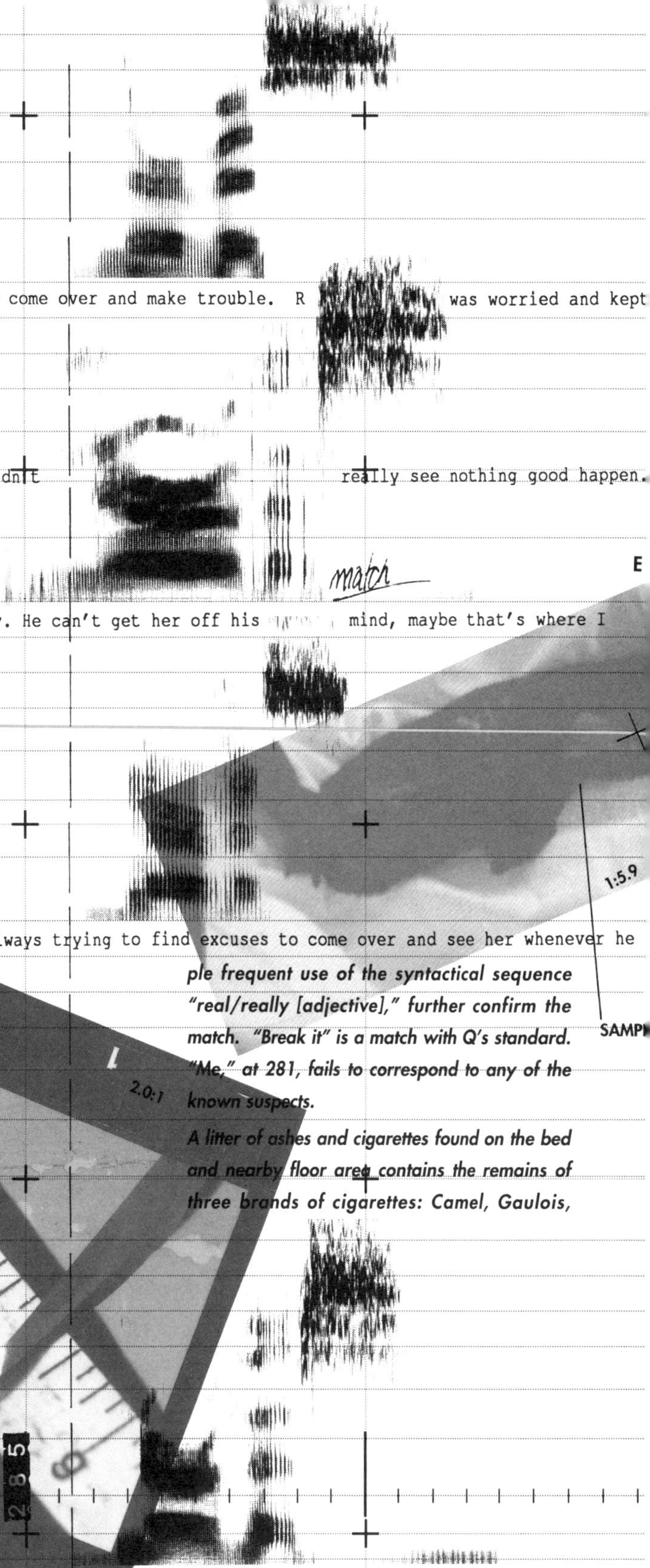

look like something might happen she'd disappear. Didn't really see nothing good happen.

match

E

, you know the type. M didn't like her seeing anybody. He can't get her off his mind, maybe that's where I

ed pushing on the downstairs buzzer. V said he was always trying to find excuses to come over and see her whenever he

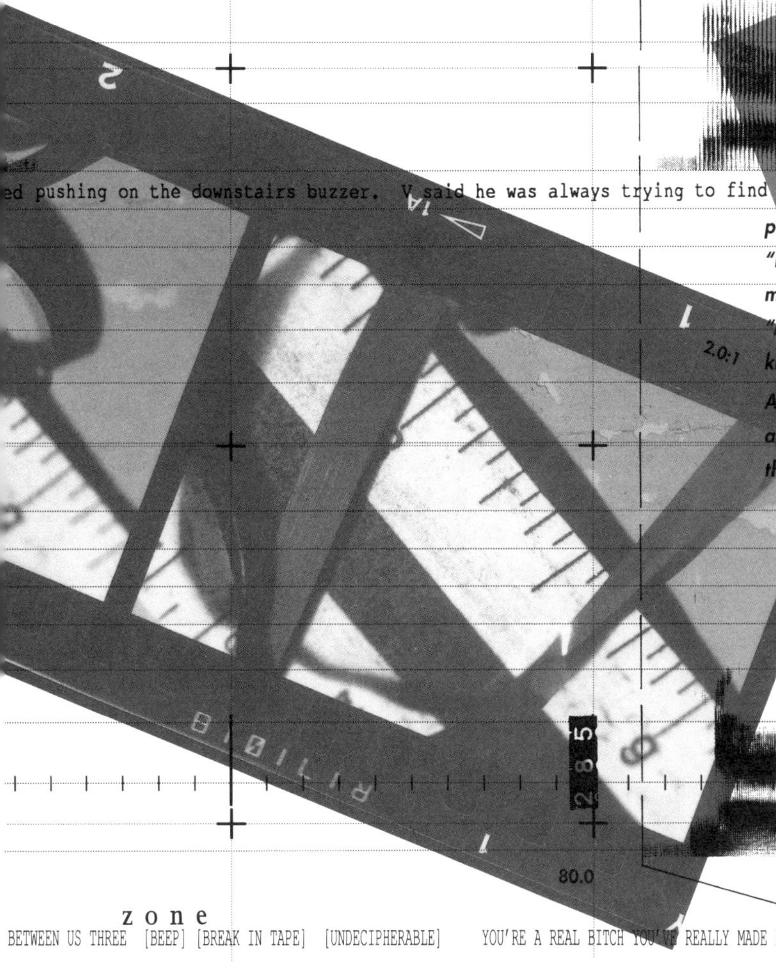

ple frequent use of the syntactical sequence "real/really [adjective]," further confirm the match. "Break it" is a match with Q's standard. "Me," at 281, fails to correspond to any of the known suspects.

A litter of ashes and cigarettes found on the bed and nearby floor area contains the remains of three brands of cigarettes: Camel, Gaulois,

SAMP

zone

BETWEEN US THREE [BEEP] [BREAK IN TAPE] [UNDECIPHERABLE] YOU'RE A REAL BITCH YOU'VE REALLY MADE HIM **NERVOUS** I WON'T GIVE UP THAT EASY I'M COMING OVER

and Marlboro lights, 2 mg of a white powder
(sample 27.2/5.5) and four spent matches.
Subjected to gas chromatographic and IR spec-
trophotometric analysis, the powder substance

gging me to call and see if everything was ok. I tried a few times, you know like around 10, 10:30 **INDIVIDUAL M** or

displays high concentrations of metham-
phetamine, $C_{10}H_{15}N$,. a powerful CNS stimu-
lant, known to produce a disinhibiting and
heightened affect state and inducing intense
behavior relieved of customary intellectual
checks and balances. The IR spectrum revealed
a pair of characteristic simple, broad peaks of
70-95% absorbance between wave number
700 and 740 cm^{-1}, and another cluster of

ndow   wasn't in the right place.   Go ahead take it i

me in-- with V dumping him and his wife talking divorce I thought we could really be a comfort to **INDIVIDUAL R** eac

peaks in the 2800 to 3100 cm^{-1} range. The
distribution of the ashes and other debris sug-
gests the origin of a disturbance roughly locat-
ed at a point on the bed at coordinates
115.5/21.0. The powder distribution, howev-
er, is independent of the ash pattern, promoting
the likelihood that the methamphetamine was
deposited on the bed after the ashtray had
been disturbed.

uld sneak away from his old lady. I didn't want him coming up but he wiggled his way in and started **INDIVIDUAL Q** w

Suspect M showed extreme electrodermal
responses to questions involving drug use and
locational information when voluntarily subject-
ed to polygraphic interrogation. These stimuli
also elicited a rise in baseline on the cardio-
graphic register and a narrowing of the trace
from base to ceiling, confirming a finding of a
deceptive response. Individual R also showed
heightened responses in the area of drug-related
relevancies.

A partial fingerprint developed on one of the
half-smoked cigarettes, the Gaulois, does not
match any of the individuals known to be asso-

D

ASH DISTRIBUTION TRAJECTORY

V(VICTIM)

match

There were noises, uh   sort of a thump

TAPE

90.0   1:2.5   100.0

[BEEP]   [SHORT BEEP]   [BEEP]   [BEEP]   [BEEP]   LOOK HE'LL FUCKING **BREAK IT** ALL BUT I KNOW HE'S WILLING [NOISE]   [BEEP]   [END OF SEGMENT

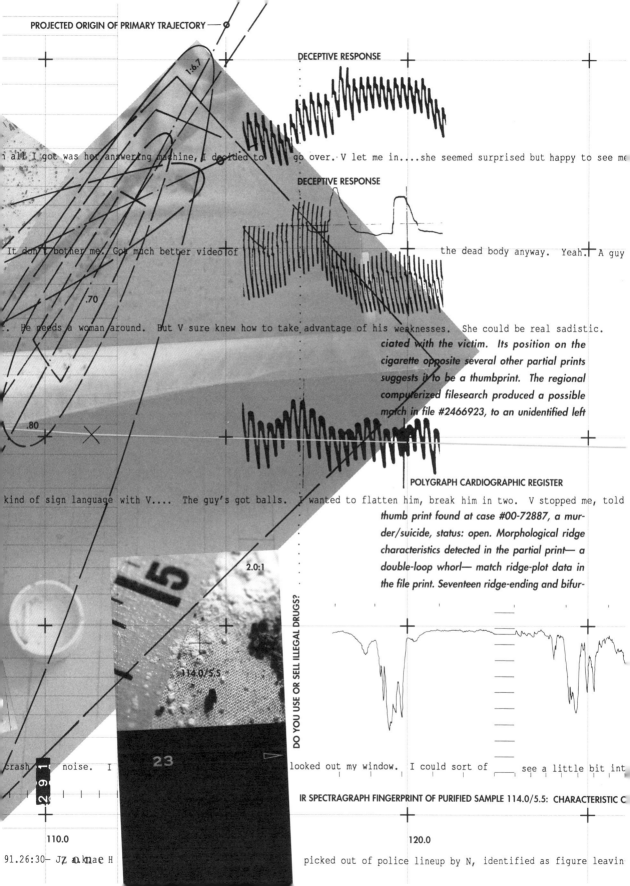

PROJECTED ORIGIN OF PRIMARY TRAJECTORY — Ø

DECEPTIVE RESPONSE

i all I got was her answering machine, I decided to go over. V let me in....she seemed surprised but happy to see me

DECEPTIVE RESPONSE

It don't bother me. Got much better video of the dead body anyway. Yeah. A guy

He needs a woman around. But V sure knew how to take advantage of his weaknesses. She could be real sadistic.

ciated with the victim. Its position on the cigarette opposite several other partial prints suggests it to be a thumbprint. The regional computerized filesearch produced a possible match in file #2466923, to an unidentified left

POLYGRAPH CARDIOGRAPHIC REGISTER

kind of sign language with V.... The guy's got balls. I wanted to flatten him, break him in two. V stopped me, told

thumb print found at case #00-72887, a mur- der/suicide, status: open. Morphological ridge characteristics detected in the partial print— a double-loop whorl— match ridge-plot data in the file print. Seventeen ridge-ending and bifur-

DO YOU USE OR SELL ILLEGAL DRUGS?

2.0:1

114.0/5.5

crash noise. I looked out my window. I could sort of see a little bit int

IR SPECTRAGRAPH FINGERPRINT OF PURIFIED SAMPLE 114.0/5.5: CHARACTERISTIC C

110.0

120.0

91.26:30 JZ aknae H

picked out of police lineup by N, identified as figure leavin

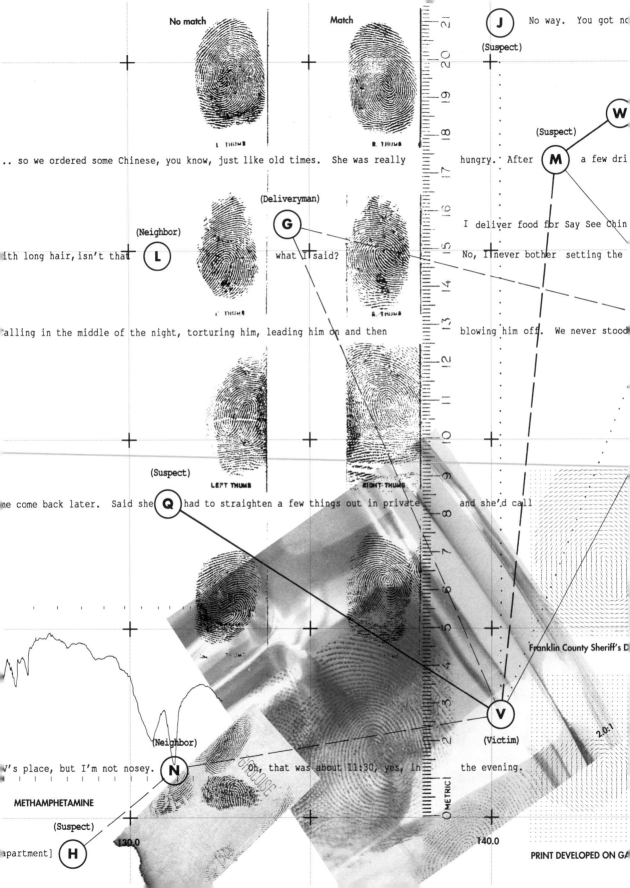

rove I was there on Thursday. Sure we had some business but, you know, business is business. You got a problem

(V Psychiatrist)

(F) V? Well yes, she was a very intelligent woman. She had

cation minutiae matched between file standard and latent prints. A small lipstick sample taken her from the same cigarette did not match any lipstick in the victim's possession. Gene amplifica-

food we all started getting a little loose and friendly when, right out of nowhere, she just went crazy with a pair of

UPDATED SOCIAL NETWORK DIAGRAM

Key:

_____	Acquaintance
_____	Lover/mate
_ _ _ _	Former lover/mate
_ _ _ _	Circumstantial relation
. . . . .	Business relation

A guy called ordered spareribs, spring

It was late...after 2:30. I got

tion detected the existence of repeated DNA sequences located in the Y-chromosome, establishing the saliva on the cigarette as that of a male individual. This pattern did not match M roll or Q. Multiple prints from individuals M, Q and bette V were found on glasses and plates among the partially-eaten food. No other individual's prints were represented on any of the dishes or utensils. It cannot be ascertained whether all three

(R) M and I. Anyhow, when V told me to drop by later that night I knew she was worried about something. When I got

uspect)

ate together. Prints or signs of a struggle at the window could not be accurately determined due to the badly deteriorated condition of the frame and sill.

Droplets on the floor adjacent to the bed, subjected to blood-stain pattern examination and analysis, suggest that the blood sources originated over the lower region of the bed, near

after she got rid of him. I went back to the shop to co

(X)

coordinates 31.0/6.0. Based on the projected origin of blood, which matches (with a probability of at least 98%) the genetic profile of M, showing distinctive loci at five different chromosomes, it can be determined that the documented position of the bed could not have been its position when M was injured. To properly align the bed and floor portions of the M blood stain, the bed must have been located 72cm from its present position along a 95-degree orientation. Blood on the floor attributable to V can be dis-

print sample file #2466923: Left thumbprint of individual X (identity unknown)

Very exciting, yes. Another murder on the news. I alw

150.0   160.0

TTE

z o n e

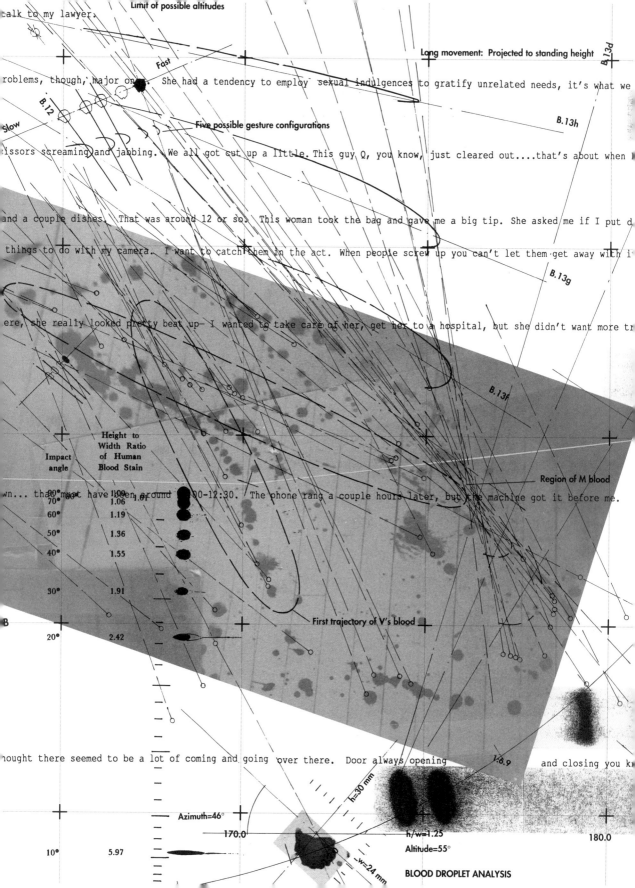

talk to my lawyer.

Limit of possible altitudes

Long movement: Projected to standing height

B.13d

Fast

roblems, though, major one. She had a tendency to employ sexual indulgences to gratify unrelated needs, it's what we

B.12

B.13h

Slow

Five possible gesture configurations

issors screaming and jabbing. We all got cut up a little. This guy Q, you know, just cleared out....that's about when

and a couple dishes. That was around 12 or so. This woman took the bag and gave me a big tip. She asked me if I put d

B.13g

things to do with my camera. I want to catch them in the act. When people screw up you can't let them get away with i

ere, she really looked pretty beat up— I wanted to take care of her, get her to a hospital, but she didn't want more tr

B.13f

Impact angle	Height to Width Ratio of Human Blood Stain		
90°	1.00	1.01	
70°	1.06		
60°	1.19		
50°	1.36		
40°	1.55		
30°	1.91		
20°	2.42		
10°	5.97		

Region of M blood

wn... that must have been around 00-12:30. The phone rang a couple hours later, but the machine got it before me.

First trajectory of V's blood

B

hought there seemed to be a lot of coming and going over there. Door always opening

1:6.9

and closing you k

h=30 mm

Azimuth=46°

170.0

h/w=1.25

180.0

Altitude=55°

w=24 mm

BLOOD DROPLET ANALYSIS

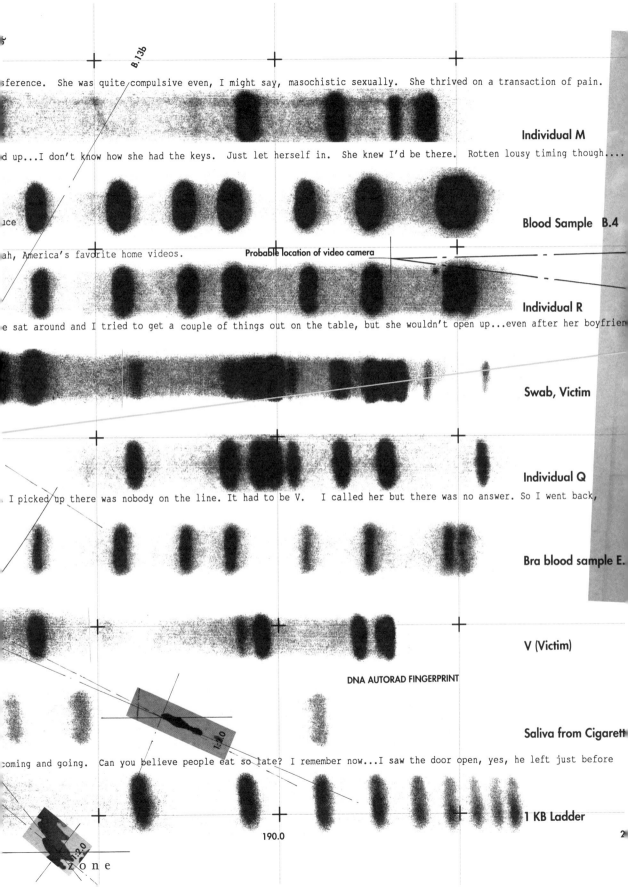

sference. She was quite compulsive even, I might say, masochistic sexually. She thrived on a transaction of pain.

Individual M

d up...I don't know how she had the keys. Just let herself in. She knew I'd be there. Rotten lousy timing though....

Blood Sample B.4

ah, America's favorite home videos.   Probable location of video camera

Individual R

e sat around and I tried to get a couple of things out on the table, but she wouldn't open up...even after her boyfrien

Swab, Victim

Individual Q

I picked up there was nobody on the line. It had to be V.   I called her but there was no answer. So I went back,

Bra blood sample E.

V (Victim)

DNA AUTORAD FINGERPRINT

Saliva from Cigarett

coming and going. Can you believe people eat so late? I remember now...I saw the door open, yes, he left just before

1 KB Ladder

190.0

z o n e

she told tinguished into four trajectories. One of these   me frequently in our sessions that she could only   achieve sexual arou

trajectories shows a continuous alignment from
the bed to the floor only when the bed location
coincides with the site of M's injuries. The other

ure picked the wrong moment. When R saw V she started pounding her head, screaming she wasn't going to put it off any l

three most probably occurred with the bed in its
current location. Using four single-locus probes
as a cocktail, the DNA autorad banding pat-

n for the terns showed that the vaginal swabs taken from   ribs. (I always do that.) I could look into the end room, TV was sure lo

V contained a combination of the profiles of
individuals M and Q. While blood stains found
on the torn brassiere matched the R profile,

ut out. I left after 12:00. M. said he would follow   in a few minutes. V wouldn't let him leave with me.

SCANNING ELECTRON MICROGRAPH:
Acrylic Model of Tooth #7 (Q Standard)

he had to decide, him or me.   That scum.

I.... I should have....

SEM: Bite Print on Left Shoulder of V

Cheers" ended, oh about 9:00, yes. Missed the end.... don't think I'll ever know if Sam got the lottery money. Th

210.0

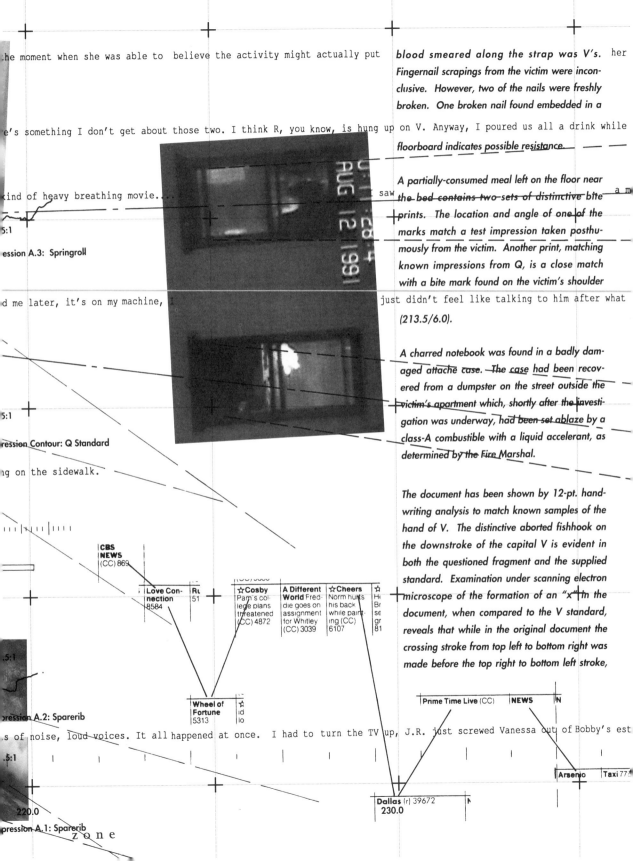

he moment when she was able to believe the activity might actually put

e's something I don't get about those two. I think R, you know, is hung up on V. Anyway, I poured us all a drink while

kind of heavy breathing movie.... saw

5:1

ession A.3: Springroll

d me later, it's on my machine, I

5:1

ression Contour: Q Standard

g on the sidewalk.

CBS
NEWS
(CC) 869

Love Con-	Rι	☆Cosby	A Different	☆Cheers	☆
nection	51	Pam's col-	World Fred-	Norm hunts	Hi
8584		lege plans	die goes on	his back	Bι
		threatened	assignment	while paint-	se
		(CC) 4872	for Whitley	ing (CC)	gι
			(CC) 3039	6107	81

Wheel of	☆
Fortune	id
5313	lo

ression A.2: Sparerib

s of noise, loud voices. It all happened at once. I had to turn the TV up, J.R. just screwed Vanessa out of Bobby's est

5:1

220.0

ression A.1: Sparerib

z o n e

blood smeared along the strap was V's. her
Fingernail scrapings from the victim were incon-
clusive. However, two of the nails were freshly
broken. One broken nail found embedded in a
floorboard indicates possible resistance.

A partially-consumed meal left on the floor near
the bed contains two sets of distinctive bite
prints. The location and angle of one of the
marks match a test impression taken posthu-
mously from the victim. Another print, matching
known impressions from Q, is a close match
with a bite mark found on the victim's shoulder

a m

just didn't feel like talking to him after what
(213.5/6.0).

A charred notebook was found in a badly damaged attache case. The case had been recovered from a dumpster on the street outside the
victim's apartment which, shortly after the investigation was underway, had been set ablaze by a
class-A combustible with a liquid accelerant, as
determined by the Fire Marshal.

The document has been shown by 12-pt. handwriting analysis to match known samples of the
hand of V. The distinctive aborted fishhook on
the downstroke of the capital V is evident in
both the questioned fragment and the supplied
standard. Examination under scanning electron
microscope of the formation of an "x" in the
document, when compared to the V standard,
reveals that while in the original document the
crossing stroke from top left to bottom right was
made before the top right to bottom left stroke,

Prime Time Live (CC)   NEWS   N

Arsenio   Taxi 77

Dallas (r) 39672
230.0

life- threatening situation. She tended to engage ... ships which produce highly co-dependent and ambiva...

the order was reversed in the standard, raising
doubts about the authenticity of the document.

almed R down. When she decided to leave V seemed ... depressed. I stayed behind to talk for a few

A segment of video tape surreptitiously recorded
by "L," 38 Avenue L, during the night of August
12/13 shows distinctly the naked upper torso
ing *of an individual seen through the window of the* on the bed with his shoes on. Well, uh, no actually I only saw the shoes.
victim's fourth-story apartment. Programmatic

Video image, enhanced as female figure

enhancement of the image to determine gender
and location of the individual (from shadow
location) reveals the subject to be not more than
four feet beyond the unshielded ceiling light, ori-

Mask of video camera surveillance

opened. I thought that we could get something going but V kept me at a distance. She had he...

ented roughly square to the camera. This finding
is consistent with results from the camera-angle Vis...
masking analysis. Additionally, the position of
the figure in the frame, when projected to the
zone of possible positions in the room, indicates
that the footage must have been shot after the
bed had moved to its ultimate location. The
enhanced figure is equally plausible as a
female or male.

Video image, enhanced as male figure

10:1

Aborted Fishhook, V Standard #2

10:1

Aborted Fishhook, V Standard #1

Close | Paid

Limit of G's penetration into room, as given by statement

Probable location of Chinese food transaction

don't hear too good. But I saw him through the curtains. She was shaking something, yes, but you know I'm not nosey.

Joe Frank-
lin 56072

10:1

240.0

250.0

Aborted Fishhook, Questioned Document

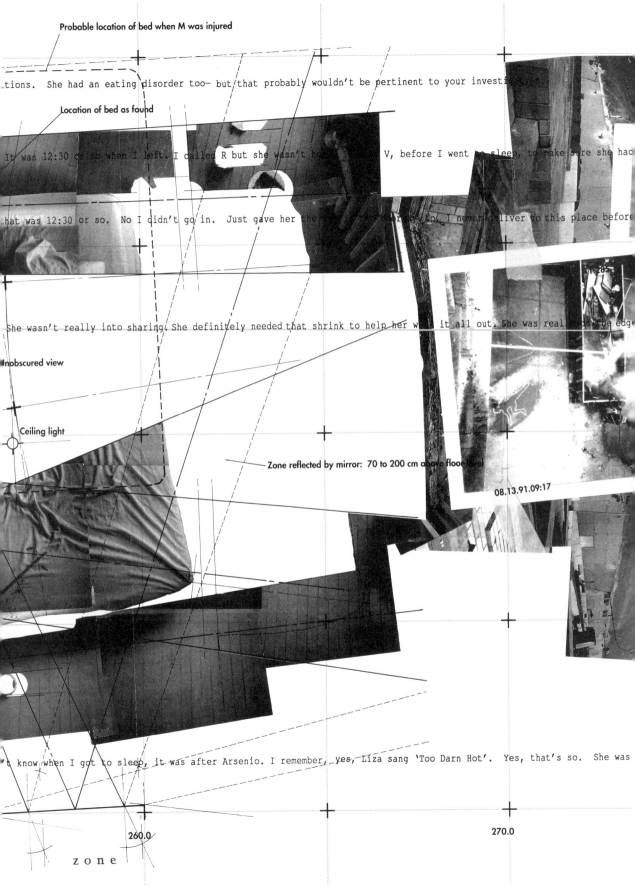

Probable location of bed when M was injured

...tions. She had an eating disorder too— but that probably wouldn't be pertinent to your investigation.

Location of bed as found

It was 12:30 or so when I left. I called R but she wasn't home. V, before I went to sleep, to make sure she had

...that was 12:30 or so. No I didn't go in. Just gave her the ... No, I never deliver to this place before

She wasn't really into sharing. She definitely needed that shrink to help her work it all out. She was really on the edge

Unobscured view

Ceiling light

Zone reflected by mirror: 70 to 200 cm above floor level

08.13.91.09:17

't know when I got to sleep, it was after Arsenio. I remember, yes, Liza sang 'Too Darn Hot'. Yes, that's so. She was

260.0

270.0

z o n e

Project by Elizabeth Diller and Ricardo Scofidio, with Mark Schindler. Assisted by Rafael Berkowitz.

We are grateful to the following persons and firms who generously donated their time and technologies to this project:

Richard Arther, M.A., A.C.P., *Expert Polygraphist, President, Scientific Lie Detection, Inc.*

George Borghi, *Criminalist, Metro-Dade (Florida) Police Department Crime Laboratory Bureau Trace Evidence Unit*

Cellmark Diagnostics, Germantown, Maryland

The Cooper Union Audio-Visual Resource Access Center

Thomas J. David, DDS, *Forensic Odontologist, Georgia Division of Forensic Sciences*

Marcia Eisenberg, Ph.D., *Associate Director, Identity Research and Development, Roche Biomedical Laboratories.*

Fingermatrix, Inc., White Plains, N.Y. (computerized fingerprinting systems)

Jill Frumer, *Criminal Defense Lawyer, Philadelphia, Pennsylvania*

Marc Frumer, *Assistant District Attorney, Philadelphia County, Pennsylvania*

Brian Goldfarb, *Video Enhancement Specialist, Rochester, N.Y.*

Richard Hall, *Certified Latent Print Examiner, ID Supervisor, Metro-Dade (Florida) Police Department Crime Scene Investigation Bureau.*

Dr. Lowell Levine, *Forensic Odontologist, Albany, N.Y.*

Judith Lewis, M.D., *Psychiatric Resident, Columbia Presbyterian Hospital.*

Sgt. Robert Lowe, *Anti-Crime Unit, Plainclothes, Midtown South, New York City Police Department*

E. Mei Shen, MD, *Pathologist, Associate Medical Examiner, Essex County, Massachusetts*

Nancy L. Tegeder, *Trooper I, Examiner of Questioned Documents, New Jersey State Police Document Examination/Voice Identification Unit.*

Voice Identification Inc., Manville, N.J. (voice fingerprinting)

Toby Wolson, M.S., *Blood Stain Pattern Analysis Expert, Criminalist, Metro-Dade (Florida) Police Department Crime Laboratory Bureau Serology Section*

References:

Abrams, Stan. *The Complete Polygraph Handbook.* Lexington, MA: Lexington Books, 1989.

Association of Official Analytical Chemists. *Infrared and Ultraviolet Spectra of Some Compounds of Pharmaceutical Interest.* Washington, D.C.: AOAC, 1985.

Ballantyne, Jack, et al., eds. *DNA Technology and Forensic Science.* Banbury Report 32. Cold Spring Harbor, N.Y.: Cold Spring Harbor Laboratory Press, 1989.

Basu, Samarendra and James R. Millette, eds. *Electron Microscopy in Forensic, Occupational and Environmental Health Sciences.* New York: Plenum Press, 1986.

Bates, Billy Prior. *ISQD: Identification System for Questioned Documents.* Springfield, Ill.: Charles C. Thomas, 1970.

Caldwell, John. *Amphetamines and Related Stimulants: Chemical, Biological, Clinical and Sociological Aspects.* Boca Raton: CRC Press, 1980.

Cunliffe, Frederick and Peter B. Piazza. *Criminalistics and Scientific Investigation.* Englewood Cliffs, N.J.: Prentice Hall, 1980.

Fox, Richard H. and Carl L. Cunningham. *Crime Scene Search and Physical Evidence Handbook.* Boulder, Col.: Paladin Press, 1987.

Gerber, Samuel M., ed. *Chemistry and Crime.* Washington, D.C.: American Chemical Society, 1983.

Goddard, Kenneth W. *Crime Scene Investigation.* Reston, Va.: Reston Publishing Co., 1977.

Holinger, Paul C. *Violent Deaths in the United States.* New York: Guilford, 1987.

Kracauer, Siegfried. *Le Roman Policier: Un Traite' Philosophique.* Paris: Payot, French translation 1981.

MacDonell, Herbert Leon and Lorraine Fiske Bialousz. *Flight Characteristics and Stain Patterns of Human Blood.* National Institute of Law Enforcement and Criminal Justice publication PR 71-4. Washington, D.C.: U.S. Department of Justice Law Enforcement Assistance Administration, November, 1971.

Marx, Gary T. *Undercover Police Surveillance in America.* Berkeley: University of California Press, 1988.

Most, Glenn W. and William W. Slowe, eds. *The Poetics of Murder.* San Diego: Harcourt Brace Jovanovich, 1983.

O'Flaherty, Ellen J. *Toxicants and Drugs: Kinetics and Dynamics.* New York: John Wiley, 1981.

Osterburg, James W. *The Crime Laboratory: Case Studies of Scientific Criminal Investigation.* Bloomington: Indiana University Press, 1968.

Pouchert, Charles. *Aldrich Library of Infrared Spectra.* 3rd edition. Milwaukee, Wis.: Aldrich Chemical Company, 1981 [1970].

Rapp, Burt. *Sex Crimes Investigation—A Practical Manual.* Port Townsend, Wash.: Loompanics, 1988.

Rathbun, Ted A. and Jane E. Buikstra. *Human Identification—Case Studies in Forensic Anthropology.* Springfield, Ill.: Thomas, 1984.

Robertson, J. et al., eds. *DNA in Forensic Science.* Chichester, Eng.: Ellis Horwood, 1990.

Saferstein, Richard. *Criminalistics.* Englewood Cliffs, N.J.: Prentice Hall, 1990.

Soderman, Harry and John J. O'Connell. *Modern Criminal Investigation.* New York: Funk and Wagnalls, 1962.

Swanson, Charles R. Jr. et al. *Criminal Investigation.* New York: Random House, 1988.

Wilson, Colin. *A Criminal History of Mankind.* New York: Carroll and Graf, 1990.

Zonderman, Jon. *Beyond the Crime Lab: New Science of Investigation.* New York: John Wiley, 1990.

settled down....all I got was a busy signal. The next thing I know is what I see on the morning news.

don't know. Maybe suicidal.

Dumpster fire

Location of attache case

SEM: Crossing stroke, questioned document

90:1

re again.

Scanning Electron Micrograph: Crossing stroke, V standard

280.0

65:1

290.0

V 50

Metametazoa: Biology and Multiplicity

Dorion Sagan

How will the body and its life come to be construed by biology? And more important, how will these be construed by a mythopoiesis and popular mythology whose
social birthright now, through the midwife of contemporary biology, may create
the "facts" from which a common future understanding will come? Transformations
of classical models are already underway in contemporary biology, and this essay
shall focus on some of them: Gaia theory, symbiotic evolution and bacterial
omnisexuality.

The Emperor's Imperiled Kingdoms

It is necessary, first of all, to distinguish the tenor of a "new biology," whose theoretical sources are Gaia, symbiosis and gene-trading bacteria, from the tenor of
that more traditional biology for which the paradigm of individuality is the animal body. Modern biology, informed by cellular ultrastructure through electron
microscopy and detailed knowledge of gene sequences, has supplemented or even
negated the long-standing division between plant and animal kingdoms.[1] Although
vying for acceptance and mutually inconsistent, the two most favored current
phylogenies split life into either three domains or five kingdoms. The five-king-
dom classification system still reserves a place for the kingdoms Plantae and
Animalia (both subsumed within the superkingdom Eukaryotae); Carl R. Woese's
three-trunked tree of life, based on typical sequences of RNA in the ribosomes
of cells, contains no separate kingdoms for plants or animals, for it lumps both
within the eucarya (organisms comprised of cells with nuclei), reserving two separate taxa (archaea, which Woese used to call archaebacteria and bacteria, formerly eubacteria) for the rest of life. Molecular and microbiology have not only
confirmed Darwin's paradigm-shattering argument that we are animals but have
also provided evidence that the most fundamental fence in life lies not between

plants and animals but between eukaryotes — cells with nuclei, mitochondria (and, in the case of algae and plants, plastids) — and prokaryotes, also known as monerans or bacteria. *Homo sapiens* clings to its crown as the walls of its kingdom come crumbling down. Moreover, each eukaryotic "animal" cell is, in fact, an uncanny assembly, the evolutionary merger of distinct prokaryotic metabolisms. Strictly speaking, there is no such thing as a one-celled plant or animal. Easily recognizable life forms appear only at the middle range. If we step back from, or come closer to, the living canvas, organisms blend into a pointillist landscape in which each dot of paint is also alive. In short, all previous biology has been grossly zoocentric.

Although psychoanalysis and phenomenology and their popular offshoots have disturbed a monolithic conception of mind, a monolithic notion of "the" body remains largely intact. In classical medicine, the body is considered to be a type of unity. Cancer, paradigmatically, but other diseases as well, are discussed with the rhetoric of war: the body is "attacked" and "invaded," it puts out "defenses" and "fights back." This medical model of the body-as-unity-to-be-preserved, though, of the body proper, is besieged by the new biology.

A radical re-rendering of the body is underway in accordance with three models from the new biology, namely, symbiosis, Gaia and prokaryotic sex. This reformulation augurs a breakdown of the medically proper animal body, which is simultaneously driven in at least two new directions, one poststructural, the other medieval-microcosmic in living environment. Gaia refers to the biosphere understood not as environmental home but as body, as physiological process. Prokaryotic sex, or bacterial omnisexuality, refers to the fluid genetic transfers, by definition sexual, among continuously reproducing bacteria. The consonance with certain poststructuralisms occurs in that the new biology parts company with the unitary self assumed in the zoocentric model. The expression "medieval-microcosmic" is inadequate but suggests the possibility of correspondences among prokaryotic, eukaryotic, zoological and geophysiological (Gaian) levels. It now appears that a type of individuality has appeared at each of these levels. Both spatially and temporally more inclusive, Gaia and animals dwell within a holonomic continuum, superordinating the smaller beings of which they are made.

The Body as Chimera

The body as seen by the new biology is chimerical. Instead of the tripartite division of that mythical creature of antiquity, the chimera, into lion, goat and snake, the animal cell is seen to be a hybrid of bacterial species — although the word "species," as we shall see, is a misnomer when applied to bacteria. Like that many-headed beast, the microbeast of the animal cell combines into one entity bacteria that were originally freely living, self-sufficient and metabolically distinct. Mitochondria populate and energize virtually all eukaryotic cells. These specialized cell parts respire; they take up oxygen and produce carbon dioxide, making ATP (adenosine triphosphate), a kind of molecular capacitor storing energy within cells. It is now widely accepted among biologists that these tiny intracellular power stations were once autonomous respiring bacteria. Eukaryotic cells evolved over a billion years ago, probably when respirers entered and did not kill but, rather, *were incorporated by* larger anaerobic archaebacteria. Over time, the two distinct metabolisms merged and the new incorporated cells produced more and hardier cells than either line of their unincorporated relatives.

Some intriguing signs recall the ancient free lives of mitochondria. Although they lie outside the cell's nucleus, they have their own genetic apparatus, including their own DNA, messenger RNA, transfer RNA and ribosomes enclosed in mito-chondrial membranes. Unlike the DNA of the nucleus, but like bacterial DNA, mito-chondrial DNA is not coated by histone protein. Mitochondria assemble proteins on ribosomes very similar to the ribosomes of bacteria. Both mitochondrial ribo-somes and those of respiring bacteria tend to be sensitive to the same antibiotics, such as streptomycin. Perhaps most telling, mitochondria reproduce on their own timetable and in their own way, foregoing the complex mitosis of the nucleus for a simple bacterium-like division. They engage in the nonsystematic genetic trans-fer that characterizes bacterial sex. All in all, they behave like prokaryotic captives.

As early as 1893, the German biologist A. F. W. Schimper proposed that the photosynthetic parts of plant cells came from cyanobacteria (often still called blue-green algae, but the term is a misnomer since they have no nuclei in their cells). The French biologist Paul Portier believed by 1918 that mitochondria are the descendants of bacteria that had become lodged within the cells of animals and plants. In the first quarter of this century, the American anatomist Ivan Wallin and the Russian scholar-biologist Konstantin S. Mereschovsky had independently come to the same conclusion. In 1910, Mereschovsky, who taught at the University of Kazan, published an essentially contemporary view of the origin of eukaryotic cells from various kinds of bacteria.[2] Experiments at isolating the putative bacterial partners, however, have always failed; the evidence for cooperation rather than parasitism was overlooked and dismissed as "sentimentalism." Herbert Spencer equated the necessary evils of competition with an eminently desirable social progress, and Thomas Huxley referred to the animal world as a "gladiator's show"; Pyotr Kropotkin wrote *Mutual Aid*, and others implicitly linked evolutionary ideas of symbiosis to labor unions, mutualistic societies and socialist ideas.

The animal cell, as well as the cells of plants, fungi and protoctists (a miscellaneous eukaryotic kingdom comprised mainly of algae and what were once called protozoa), combines oxygen-using mitochondria and a larger host cell. Despite its suggestive appearance, the nucleus was probably never autonomous but, rather, the result of interactions among members of cellular communities that evolved into cells. The same cannot be said of the chloroplasts of plants and the plastids of photosynthetic protoctists such as algae. The grass-green photosynthetic organelles of all plants may be the descendants of a single, wildly successful bacterium, now shackled, albeit gently, in its cytoplasmic prison.

A body of behavioral evidence similar to that for mitochondria supports a cyanobacterial origin for the pigmented bodies within algae and plants. The ancestors of all plants were probably cells with mitochondria that ate, but never digested, their live vegetarian dinner. The undigested photosynthetic organisms grew inside their hosts, offering a steady diet of metabolites in return for protective cover and continued life. The red plastids of seaweeds also probably come from autonomous bacteria. If one compares the sequence of nucleotide bases in the ribosomal RNA of red plastids in the seaweed *Porphyridium* with that of RNA in the seaweed's own cytoplasm, the resemblance is less than 15 percent. Making the same comparison with the ribosomal RNA of the cyanobacterium *Synechococcus* and the plastid of the swimming green protist *Euglena* yields similarities of 42 and 33 percent respectively. Indeed, there have always been behavioral clues to the xenic origins of the eukaryotic cell. But the striking likeness between mitochondria and respiring bacteria, on the one hand, and between plastids and photosynthetic bacteria, on the other, has "proved"[3] beyond a reasonable scientific doubt that all cells with nuclei, from a unicellular amoeba to a multibillion-cell anaconda, come from more or less orgiastic encounters (eating, infecting, engulfing, feeding on, having sex with and so on) among quite different types of bacteria. It is now generally agreed, not to mention taught in textbooks, that both mitochondria and chloroplasts derive from bacteria. Like the chimera, the plant cell recombines three distinct and once-separate entities: protective anaerobic host cell, internally multiplying photosynthetic bacterium and respiring bacteria. The evolution of these last was sparked by the accumulation of highly combustible and originally poisonous free oxygen within the atmosphere of the early Earth. Only anaerobic bacteria dwelled on the Earth at this time. The lack of free atmospheric oxygen is attested to, some two billion years ago, by the replacement of banded iron formations (presumed to be the fossil remains of communities of photosynthesizing bacteria) with heaps of rust (representing the accumulation of atmospheric oxygen to near-present concentrations). The buildup of atmospheric oxygen was itself a cyanobacterial phenomenon, since the metabolic waste product of the mutation, which allowed photosynthetic bacteria to use water as a source of hydrogen, was none other than gaseous oxygen, at first an extremely hazardous waste. Those bacteria that did not evolve to tolerate or use oxygen, or team up with cells that did, died. Although the accumulation within the Earth's atmosphere of oxygen was initially catastrophic, it was also an energetic catalyst for organisms such as the oxygen-respiring ancestors of mitochondria, which employed the new abundance of the highly reactive gas to produce intracellular energy reserves at many times the rate of their fermenting bacteria predecessors. Modern fermenting bacteria include anaerobes that, like trolls or elves in a cosmic fairy tale, protect themselves from the hazards of surface oxygen by dwelling underground. Vestiges of the anaerobic environment of the early Earth survive as shoreline stromatolites (rounded bacteria-built stones) and their softer relatives, microbial mats.[4] Human beings belong to the army of mutants that evolved in the aftermath of the oxygen infusion, the greatest pollution crisis the Earth has ever known.

There is less evidence for another player in the symbiotic game whose evolutionary permutations have provided us with all known species of animals and plants: the spirochete. The spirochete's presence has been postulated to persist in ghostly form in all cells possessing the undulating appendages technically known as undulipodia. Undulipodia, whose electron microscopic ultrastructure reveals a characteristic "9 + 2" tubular form, common to the cilia of woman's oviducts and the sperm tails of ginkgo trees (and much else besides), putatively derive from a not-yet-discovered species of spirochete. Ever-squirming anaerobic spirochetes fed not only alone but at the periphery and even inside larger cells. The edges of larger cells, sites of leakage supplying a constant flow of food, were such prime real estate that some spirochetes appear to have renounced their former freedom of movement in order to permanently attach. Later, serving as a means of locomotion and food acquisition to larger cells, the spirochetes would have become increasingly phantomlike as they evolved ever-more harmoniously into the chimerical eukaryotic system. Today, mitosis and the mitotic spindle may be like the smile of Lewis Carrol's Cheshire Cat: the faded remnants of a life form that has all but vanished into symbiotic thin air. Finding evidence for such spirochetes, however, remains a problem.

The human body, too, is an architectonic compilation of millions of agencies of chimerical cells. Each cell in the hand typing this sentence comes from two, maybe three, kinds of bacteria. These cells themselves appear to represent the latter-day result, the fearful symmetry, of microbial communities so consolidated, so tightly organized and histologically orchestrated, that they have been selected together, one for all and all for one, as societies in the shape of organisms.

The wastes of microbial communities, analogous to our garbage dumps and landfills, have also been incorporated as organisms breed together and organismhood appears at spatially more inclusive levels. The mineral infrastructure of our bodies for example, the calcium phosphate of bone, owes its existence to the necessity of eukaryotic cells to keep cytoplasmic calcium concentrations at levels around one in ten million. Because seawater concentrations of calcium are often four orders of magnitude higher than this, ocean-dwelling cells must exude calcium to avoid poisoning. In the full-fathomed sea did the bones of our ancestors and the shells of their eukaryote relatives evolve. Skeletons dramatize an ancient waste, whispering a ghostly testimony to the useful internalization of hazardous waste sites. This gives a good indication of how life within the general economy evolves to deactivate, sacrifice and eventually incorporate the dangerous excesses that accrue from its solar growth.[5]

The implications of a new biology for that identity which arises epigenetically from a single protistlike fertilized egg cell and for the zoocentric, medically proper model are immense. The body can no longer be seen as single, unitary. It is multiple, even if orchestrated by vicissitudes and the need for harmony over evolutionary time. We are all multiple beings. Our chimerical nature is less obvious than *Mixotricha paradoxa*, a species of autonomous nucleated cell (that is, a protist) that seems to be unicellular but, on closer inspection, is seen to consist of several different kinds of cells — among them internal oxygen-respiring bacteria and externally attached spirochetes that serve as oars. In addition, *M. paradoxa* contains its "own" organelles, congenital undulipodia used as rudders that, along with the spirochetes, help propel it through a droplet of water. In the transformation from organism to an organelle cell membranes meld and, ultimately, disappear as the organisms undergo intraorganismic genetic transfers (an example of bacterial omnisexuality) to become organelles.

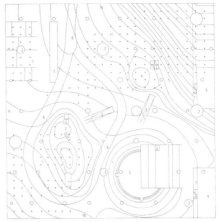

Agadir Convention Center, Morocco 1990.
Urban plaza, level +4–18m.
Office for Metropolitan Architecture
Rem Koolhaas

The brain's neurons, rich in the tubulin proteins that form the walls of the cell fibers known as microtubules, may also be the highly modified remnants of intra- and extracellular spirochetal mobility systems.[6] Undulipodia all consist of microtubules built of tubulin proteins; some spirochetes contain tubulinlike proteins. If the body-brain is not single, but rather the mixed result of multiple bacterial lineage, then health is less a matter of defending a unity than maintaining an ecology. Whereas the zoocentric model causally ascribes diseases to organisms, the emerging biocentric model of the new biology recognizes that many putative disease agents — such as streptococcus bacteria and *Candida albicans* fungi — are normally present in the human biological system. As we move to a new model, the body becomes a sort of ornately elaborated mosaic of microbes in various states of symbiosis. The distinct presences of these microbes become noticeable only when festering and illness throw normal populations and metabolite turnover out of equilibrium. Drugs used to treat bacterial meningitis can kill the bacteria, but in doing so upset the body's internal microbial ecology with the result that fungi, usually held in check, proliferate fatally in the cerebrospinal fluid.

Moreover, disturbances of the body's normal microbial ecology do not, properly speaking, signal sickness so much as the emergence of difference and novelty. Like cataracts or the glaucomous decay of vision, which may lead an artist into new percepts of flowery fields, so the same *Treponema* spirochete associated with deterioration has been linked with remarkable mental feats and artistic productions – here, for example, by the writer Anthony Burgess:

> I became interested in syphilis when I worked for a time at a mental hospital full of GPI (General Paralysis of the Insane) cases. I discovered there was a correlation between the spirochete and mad talent. The tubercle also produces a lyrical drive. Keats had both.... I've been much influenced by the thesis of Mann's *Doctor Faustus*, but... [s]ome prices are too high to pay. There was one man who'd turned himself into a kind of Scriabin, another who could give you the day of the week for any date in

history, another who wrote poems like Christopher Smart. Many patients were orators or grandiose liars.... Some of the tremendous skills that these patients show — these tremendous mad abilities — all stem out of the spirochete.[7]

The body is not one self but a fiction of a self built from a mass of interacting selves. A body's capacities are literally the result of what it incorporates; the self is not only corporal but corporate.

Gaia

Just as the technologies of microscopic apparatus have opened the way toward a view of the human organism as a massive microbial ecosystem, in which eukaryotic waste products such as calcium have been honed into the calcium carbonate architecture of the human skeleton, so also telescopic technologies have opened the way toward seeing the Earth as a living entity, in which animals are not independent actors but organelle-like components within a functioning planetary physiology. Gaia, in its vulgar but succinct version, claims that the Earth is alive. Yet, with greater nuance and accuracy, it can be stated that the largely biogenic surface of the Earth, the biosphere, appears to regulate itself physiologically within the astronomic medium; it behaves *as* a body. Oxygen accounts for about one fifth of our atmosphere, the mean temperature of the lower atmosphere is about 22° centigrade and its pH is just over 7. Although the sun's luminosity is thought to have increased over 30 percent since the first life appeared on the planet and although combustible oxygen instantly reacts with many sorts of molecules nonetheless normally present in the atmosphere (because their concentrations are physiologically replenished), these values (temperature, pH and the distribution of reactive gases) have remained extraordinarily stable for hundreds of millions of years. A major argument here has to do with free oxygen, which once existed only negligibly in the atmosphere: yet, far from the increase in oxygen being a counterexample to Gaian regulation, the switch from a relatively languid anaerobic to a highly energized redox planet can be taken to represent a planetwide metamorphosis, a violent organic homeorrhesis akin to (and in some ways perhaps even formally similar to) developmental changes such as the hormonal floods of puberty or the genetically mediated transformation of a caterpillar. Unlike animal bodies, the living Earth — qua its proximate resources — is one of a kind and thus is not exposed to natural selection. Nevertheless, the global regulation of geophysical values over evolutionary time may be likened to the regulation of the body temperature of a mammal over a period of decades; this allows one to speak meaningfully of a Gaian "physiology," of the surface of the Earth as being alive.[8]

Sociologically, Gaia ties into animism, native Americanism and deep ecologism, and it provides a sort of immanent goddess that for many at last suggests a welcome departure from a transcendent God. Phenomenologically, the switchover to a Gaian worldview, to a perspective in which one inhabits not a static environment but the responsive tissues of a planet-sized complex organism, can hardly be overemphasized. The greatness of the being within which we dwell even provides an explanation for our relative ignorance of it. Gaia theory has also been threatening to philosophers and scientists, for it has occasionally served as a platform for a New Age joy slide into the muck of planetary personification. If biocentrism is currently a prime grove for the culling of noble fictions,[9] then certainly the tree of Gaia, at the very best, bears some of the most tempting fruit.

Gaia theory has been attacked on several fronts: as unscientific, "as either trivial or untestably metaphoric from the viewpoint of analytical philosophy," as an antihuman polemic, mere Green politics, industrial apologetics and even as ecological "Satanism."[10] Yet Gaian theory thrives as a cross-disciplinary science so new the amniotic blood of the mythopoetic still adheres to its newborn skin, announcing its status and making it vulnerable to attacks from the established sciences of geology, biology and atmospheric chemistry.

Seductive and enchanting, Gaia theory had a poetic genesis. It was first put forth by James Lovelock, a British atmospheric chemist and inventor of the mechanism by which minute concentrations of chlorofluorocarbons (said to disrupt the ozone layer) are detected at concentrations as scanty as a few parts per billion. When NASA prepared for the *Viking* mission that landed on Mars in 1976,

scientists were asked to design experiments that could detect life on the red planet. Lovelock, however, suggested that the absence of life on Mars could be detected from Earth. Earth's atmosphere, he pointed out, differs greatly from those of Mars and Venus, which are both more than 95 percent carbon dioxide — that is, stable, unreactive mixtures of gases predictable from laboratory experiments. Earth's atmosphere, by contrast, is inherently unpredictable, containing volatile gases such as methane and hydrogen, which should not normally be found with oxygen. Lovelock reasoned that the atmosphere, far from being a sterile container for life, is inseparable from it, like the shell of a tortoise or the nest of a bird. The atmosphere is at once life's circulatory system and its skin: if life existed on Mars, its natural chemical processes would drive the Martian atmosphere away from equilibrium. But because the gases of the Martian atmosphere are in equilibrium, he argued, there was no need to go to Mars to show it was devoid of life. Needless to say, NASA, on the verge of liftoff, was not overly thrilled.

Lovelock proposed that life on Earth must have monitored its environment on a planetary scale. How else could the gases that comprise it remain in such an unstable situation? The oceans and air of Earth appear to be continuously *physiologically* stabilized, as are the body chemistry, internal temperature, salinity and alkalinity of many organisms. Views of the Earth from space, by astronauts or in kitsch postcards, have literally changed our perspective. Essayist Lewis Thomas, contrasting the Earth seen from space with the dry-as-a-bone Moon, has called Earth the only "exuberant thing in this part of the cosmos," a turquoise orb with the "organized, self-contained look of a live creature, full of information, marvelously skilled in handling the sun."[11] Lovelock asked his country neighbor, the novelist William Golding, for a "good four-letter word" to express the idea that the Earth has, beyond just a physical chemistry, a physiology. Golding proposed the Greek Earth goddess Gaia, mother of the Titans.

The use of a mythological title to describe a serious subject for scientific study is fraught with dangers and opportunities not unlike those of Freud's borrowing of the Narcissus and Oedipus myths for use in elaborating psychoanalysis. Save for the Catholic Virgin Mary, mother goddesses have virtually vanished from the modern West; the unconscious association of the reappearing goddess Gaia with Mother Mary, however — if true, a kind of overcompensation for the transcendent phallogocentrism of Judeo-Christianity — would help account for some of the shrillest among Gaian New Agists, whose moralistic slogans and puritanical admonitions are marshaled to save a (supposedly) pristine Earth. Yet, as Mary Catherine Bateson points out, it is of little use to treat the Earth as a living body while living female bodies themselves still do not command cultural respect. Perhaps considering the Earth a Narcissus-like extension of the human self works better than a neo-Christian feminization. Although satellites had been envisioned as providing us with a view of "the whole Earth," in fact, what has been provided is only one half of the surface, the "face" of the Earth. And although they depend on personification, mythology and the forever unfinished and eroticized nature of human symbolization, such ideographic or iconic chains — Narcissus, Earth, expressive surface — enhance the ethical status of Earth by giving it (a) face. The alternative is to save (this) face by considering the Earth as faceless — inanimate, insensible and unresponsive — and therefore ourselves as unaccountable to it.

It is also possible to argue that "unprovable" Gaia is a species of noble lie, a "narrative integration of cosmology and morality," and that, Western intellectual and moral biases against deception aside, Gaia is simply environmentally useful whether or not it is true. If this is the case, then describing Gaia theory as geophysiology may confer on this infant discipline the nominal equivalent of scientifically correct swaddling clothes. The culturally valuable noble lie (or ironic commentary thereon) dates back at least to Plato's advocacy of a myth of metallic origins in the *Republic*. Like the topology-violating magician who slides a ring onto a knotted loop of string, the well-told noble lie seduces the beholder into believing (in) it despite knowing better. [12]

In my book *Biospheres*, I argue that "artificial" ecosystems — containing humans, technology and the requisite elements for long-term recycling in materially closed environments — are not all that artificial but, rather, the first in a batch of planetary propagules whose proliferation is in keeping with prior epochal evolutionary developments (for example, bacterial spores, animal bodies, plant seeds and so on).[13] Despite the exposure of the scientific inadequacy of the initiators of the world's biggest closed ecosystem,[14] Biosphere II in Oracle, Arizona, other recycling ecosystems — including one planned at the world's biggest cathedral, Saint John the Divine in New York City, which will digitally transmute atmospheric gas measurements into music(!) — will inevitably be built. Already, greenhouses and buildings with central air conditioning represent a step in the direction of closed ecosystems large enough to contain human beings; the next step is the ability to completely recycle gaseous, liquid and solid wastes. Fully recycling self-enclosed ecosystems may first be built by the Japanese, whose limited space, island history and technological prowess are sure to keep them interested in a project whose lucrative applications include pollution control and space station design. Further in the future, functional biospheres may become necessary due to spoilage of the Earth's shared atmosphere. I believe that the pollution-engendered, technology-fostered cropping up of biospheres (already in its initial phase) will have represented the appearance of individuality at the planetary level. This level represents a natural continuation of the microcosmic level of the prokaryote and the eukaryote made from prokaryotes and of the mesocosmic level of animal and plant bodies made from reproducing eukaryotes.

Taking his cue from the maverick Soviet scientist Vladimir Vernadsky (who popularized the term biosphere), Georges Bataille writes:

> Solar radiation results in a superabundance of energy on the surface of the globe. But, first, living matter receives this energy and accumulates it within the limits given by the space that is available to it. It then radiates or squanders it, but before devoting an appreciable share to this radiation it makes maximum use of it for growth. Only the impossibility of continuing growth makes way for squander. Hence the real excess does not begin until the growth of the individual or group has reached its limits.[15]

Vernadsky was a kind of "anti-Lovelock," who, far from imagining the Earth to be alive, considered life to be a kind of mineral. Yet these two scientists, he and

zone   375

Lovelock, are linked by their heuristic dismantling of the boundary between life and its environment, biology and geology — what Lovelock calls scientific apartheid. But from either perspective, the appearance of materially closed ecosystems capable of recycling carbon, nitrogen, sulfur, phosphorus, oxygen and other elements necessary to a total system of life, including human life, merits attention. Supererogatory biospheres, in Bataille's schema, extend the limits of growth. Within that general economy beginning with solar radiation and bacterial photosynthesis, "bonsai" biospheres make use of the solar-driven material surplus generated by what Vernadsky has called the pressure of life. Bonsai biospheres funnel into a new form of life the metabolic reserve whose lavish squandering Bataille has described as a fundamental feature of cultures less acquisitive and profit-oriented than our own. The appearance of closed ecosystems within the general planetary ecosystem makes clear that the biosphere has a fearful symmetry of its own.

Bacterial Omnisexuality

Bacterial omnisexuality refers to the genetic exchanges among bacteria considered to be promiscuous in the sense that they do not delimit these exchanges with species barriers.[16] Theoretically, any bacterium can at any time in its life cycle give a variable quantity (rather than exactly half, as occurs during the meiotic sex of plants and animals) of its genes to any other bacterium, although it may require intermediaries such as plasmids or viruses to do so. Bacterial omnisexuality was the first type of sex to appear on the planet, some three billion years ago. It was always crucial to the biota's ability to react quickly to environmental changes and emergencies, since the *lateral* transfer of useful traits among rapidly reproducing bacteria is of far greater environmental consequence than the slow, vertical inheritance of meiotically reproducing organisms. (Although bacteria are termed asexual, this refers only to their means of reproduction.)

After the evolution of eukaryotic cells from symbiotic bacteria, bacterial omnisexuality became important as a means of genetically "locking" together once-diverse groups of prokaryotes. We are accustomed to thinking of them merely

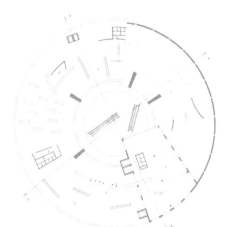

as germs, but most bacteria are harmless to humans. Bacteria are biochemically and metabolically far more diverse than all plants and animals put together. Their natural history is so bizarre that they would have excited huge interest were they discovered in outer space rather than beneath our feet. All things considered, bacteria appear crucial to the upkeep of Gaian systems of sensation, feedback and physiological control. Indeed, Gaia may have appeared on Earth some three billion years ago basically as an emergent phenomenon of bacterial crowding.

As Lynn Margulis has argued, four fifths of the history of life on Earth has been solely a bacterial phenomenon.[17] Moreover, all plants, animals, fungi and the miscellaneous eukaryotic kingdom known as protoctists are bacterial in nature. The nucleated, mitochondria-containing eukaryotic cell on which all nonbacterial forms of life are modularly based is itself the result of symbiosis and bacterial recombination (omnisexuality). The xenic origins of the eukaryotic cell have major implications for the self, the body and a vulgar Darwinism that equates evolutionary success with competition. With respect to the bacterial colonization prerequisite to Gaia and its global metabolism, animals including humans are epiphenomenal. There seems little doubt that even full-scale nuclear war could not destroy the bacterial infrastructure.

Eukaryotic cells evolved through a process known as endosymbiosis. Perhaps the simplest model of endosymbiosis is for one organism to swallow another without digesting it. In microbes especially, thanks to their lack of an immune system, organisms may be eaten that are likely to survive within their hosts. A more complex form of endosymbiosis is bacterial infection: in this case, too, death does not ensue but, rather, the invading organisms successfully reproduce inside, and in some cases may even become absolutely required by, their hosts.[18]

Not only the origin of new species but the origin of the metakingdom Eukaryotae as well, comprising all nonbacterial organisms, occurred not through gradual accumulation of mutations but through endosymbiosis: we may owe our very existence to the ancient "failure" of Lilliputian vampires, oxygen-respiring bacteria similar to modern-day *Bdellovibrio*, to kill the hosts whose bodies they had invaded. This was of course a Pyrrhic victory, since these organelles now energize our entire bodies. They are now generally well behaved, although cancer is noteworthy for the rampant multiplication of the occasionally vampiric mitochondria.

Technogenetic manipulation of bacterial strains, which promises huge financial returns from the biomedical market and, ultimately, a radical refashioning of the human genome into new species, *is* bacterial omnisexuality — bacterial omnisexuality ministered, "engineered" by human hands. If eukaryotes could trade genes as fluidly as do bacteria, it would be a small matter for dandelions to sprout butterfly wings, collide with a bee, exhange genes again and soon be seeing with compound insect eyes. Bacteria are able to trade variable quantities of genes with virtually no regard for species barriers. Indeed, despite a lingering Linnaean nomenclature, bacteria are so genetically promiscuous, their bodies are so genetically open, that the very concept of species falsifies their character as a unique life form.

Bacteria are omnisexual. Genes received by bacteria in one generation are passed down indefinitely thereafter during cell divisions. The discovery that most of the DNA in the genomes of eukaryotic organisms is "redundant," coding for no known proteins, suggests that it may be left over from the merging of stranger bacteria whose incorporation produced supererogatory information, genetic "deadwood." An example of bacterial recombination is the evolution of penicillin-resistant staphylococci. The gene that directs the synthesis of an enzyme that digests penicillin probably arose in soil bacteria. But via phage-mediated omnisexual exchanges staphylococci have incorporated such resistance and survived the hospitalization of their hosts. Omnisexuality makes bacterial boundaries plastic and forces us to view bacterial cells not in isolation but rather as the cells of an extremely diffuse yet continuous Gaian body. Indeed, Sorin Sonea has postulated that such horizontal gene transfer among bacteria qualifies them as a single superorganism whose body coincides with the surface of the planet.[19]

Aside from fictions of Gaians using bacterial omnisexuality to remodel their bodies after the image of beauty or strength or even the demihuman metazoans of Greek myth, where does the confluence of bacterial omnisexuality and evolving notions of the human body lie? Whether discussing the disappearing membranes of endosymbiotic bacteria on their way to becoming membrane-bound organelles, or the current changes within the global human socius, the rectilinear notion of the human self, the bounded, stands challenged today from yet another viewpoint, that of the new biology. This zoological "I" is open to radical revision.[20]

How does a concept of the individual that leans toward the physical model of bacterial omnisexuality and the aesthetic model of a *différance* differ from the "encased self" model of zoocentrism? One example is that used by Burgess — the artist whose production, genius or gift results not from her or his own body, but from the interference patterns generated by a series of symbiotically living forms (spirochetes in this case). The disease that causes discomfort and near-madness is also the symptom of a musical disturbance of former ecological harmony, of what was once environment, *oikos*, but is now neither home *to* nor home *of* but rather body. As an organism's connections to the external environment grow, that environment becomes its body. Like the snail whose house is carried on his back, the "case" of the "self" has been moved, through an incorporation of what once would have been called inanimate matter — admittedly, organically worked and reworked. The boundaries of selfhood are expanding. In microbial ecology, the "I" is literally a figure of large numbers. Pieces of the self — from plasmid and viruses to laboratory-spliced genes and prostheses, from milking machines to mechanical and real hearts — are obvious examples of a circulation of elements of subjective identities always already undergoing active (de)composition. Because the self is not closed but open — for the relations of the elements of physiological identity and psychological subjectivity link up with all matter through all time — it would be hasty to dismiss the general medieval schema of microcosmic correspondence as mere superstition. Nor, of course, is this in any way to suggest a one-to-one linkage or reliably complete mapping for the series prokaryote–protist–person(a)–planet.

Today, for humans, the body and the self are most clearly in a state of fundamental Heraclite change. The proverbial river is recognized as a conduit in the circulatory system of a being that has exerted control over the composition and redox state of its atmosphere for hundreds of millions of years.[21] Ostensibly, human bodies are integrating newly evolved and evolving viruses, only some of them, such as HIV, identifiable due to their pathogenicity. The majority of viruses and bacteria circulate around the biosphere and technosphere harmlessly and unnoticed, joining together genetic fragments in *jamais-vu* combinations. Humans, too, are not merely zoa or metazoa in the sense of mitotically cloned cells differentiated into tissues. We are metametazoa, metazoans whose industrial pollutants, ecological impact and telecommunications have not only altered the shape of life on Earth but forced us to recognize the environment of the sum total of life as a totality with shared destiny, as a single, integrated, sensitive and sensing system.

Life, according to Margulis, is *bacterial*. And this bacterial world, according to Lovelock, has a lifespan. The biggest challenge to life over the long run has little to do with paltry meanderings of human beings. It comes rather from the source of all life, the sun. According to astronomical calculations, the core of the sun is expected to swell as helium begins to fuse with carbon in nuclear reactions, luminosity increases and the sun becomes a "red giant." To forestall a dangerous heating of the Earth attendant with a rise in the surface temperatures of the sun would doubtless involve carbon dioxide. As is widely known, carbon dioxide is a "greenhouse gas" whose presence in the atmosphere heats the Earth by trapping infrared radiation. Gaian scientists believe that (over the long run) life has managed to sequester increasing amounts of carbon dioxide from the atmosphere to counter the effects of a sun that has been growing steadily more luminous since the inception of life on Earth. (Non-Gaian scientists generally believe that geochemical factors account for a lucky decline in atmospheric CO_2 levels.) The carbon dioxide that has vanished from the Earth's atmosphere exists on the terrestrial surface in the form of carbon-containing minerals and carbon-based life forms. If the biosphere has indeed been removing CO_2 to keep itself cool, Gaia's future as a terres-

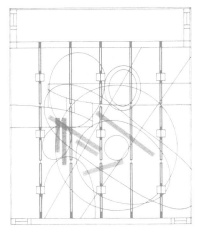

National Library of France, Paris 1989.
Superposition of public spaces.
OMA

trial being extends only some hundred million years: there is only so much carbon dioxide that can be removed from the atmosphere to counter the increasing luminosity of the sun (and this, of course, assumes a total reversal of the recent increase in atmospheric CO_2 due to human industry).[22]

Although imminent from a geological point of view, a hundred million years is about twenty times the average lifespan of a mammalian species. It is almost certain that by this time *Homo sapiens* will have become extinct or speciated. Humanity as a species is no more distinct than animals as individuals, and I have tried in this essay to use the new biology to relativize that zoocentric bedrock, the bounded, autonomous self. In a certain sense, this relativizing represents a preliminary sacrifice to the sun whose red giantism "we" at least will have escaped.

NOTES

1. For supplementary work, see L. Margulis and K. V. Schwartz, *Five Kingdoms* (San Francisco: Freeman, 1982); for negation, see C. Woese, O. Kandler and M. Wheelis, "Towards a Natural System of Organisms: Proposal for the Domains Archaea, Bacteria and Eukarya," *Proceedings of the National Academy of Sciences* 87 (1990), pp. 4576–579. For a popular account, see William Brown, "A New Tree of Life Takes Root," *New Scientist* (August 11, 1990). For Margulis's response to Woese's proposed phylogeny, see L. Margulis and R. Guerrero, "Kingdoms in Turmoil," *New Scientist* 23.1761 (March 1991), pp. 46–50.

2. The acceptance of symbiosis as a scientific fact of life has been championed in this century by Lynn Margulis: see her *Symbiosis in Cell Evolution* (San Francisco: Freeman, 1982) for details. A less technical narrative is presented in her *Early Life* (Boston: Jones and Bartlett, 1982). Margulis has demarginalized symbiosis theory, and the endosymbiotic origins of the eukaryotic cell are now presented as fact in some secondary and college-level biology texts. Nonetheless, the theory of the origin of nucleated (eukaryotic) cells by symbiosis has been around for a century.

3. M. W. Gray and W. F. Doolittle, "Has the Endosymbiotic Theory Been Proven?" *Microbiological Reviews* 46 (1982), pp. 1–42.

4. For a technical treatment of differing views of life's early phase, see J. W. Schopf, ed., *Earth's Earliest Biospheres: Its Origin and Evolution* (Princeton: Princeton University Press, 1983). Most evolutionary narratives are like mystery novels that leave out the beginning of the story. A popular account that does not make short shrift of the first three billion years of evolution is L. Margulis and D. Sagan, *Microcosmos: Four Billion Years of Microbial Evolution* (New York: Touchstone, 1991).

5. Georges Bataille's "general economy" and his constant reflections on the sun are deeply influenced by Vladimir I. Vernadsky: see *The Accursed Share: An Essay on General Economy*, vol. 1: *Consumption* (New York: Zone Books, 1988), esp. pp. 29 and 192, where Vernadsky is explicitly referred to. For Vernadsky in English, see his *The Biosphere* (Oracle, Ariz.: Synergetic Press, 1986), a much-abbreviated and perhaps unreliable "abridged version based on the French edition of 1929." The new uses found for the excess materials produced in the wake of life's growth is a leitmotiv of natural history. The wastes for which uses are found (for example, oil deposits, calcium exudates, oxygen flatulence) produce, in turn, new wastes of their own. Pollution is not new, nor can it be attributed to the development of technology unless by technology we include nonhuman life forms, among them bacteria. For further details on the uses to which wastes generated by rampant growths were put previously, see Margulis and Sagan, *Microcosmos*, pp. 99–114 (for oxygen), 184–87 (for calcium) and 237 (for environmental crises in general).

6. For a recent treatment of the relation between spirochete microbial ecology and human thought, see Margulis's "Speculation on Speculation," in J. Brockman, ed., *Speculations, The Reality Club 1* (New York: Prentice Hall, 1990), pp. 157–66; and *Microcosmos*, pp. 137–54.

7. Interview with Anthony Burgess, "Writers at Work," in George Plimpton, ed., *The Paris Review Interviews*, 4th ser. (New York: Penguin, 1976), pp. 340–41.

8. The idea of a living Earth is not new: "Plato thought the world to be a living being and in the *Laws* (898) stated that the planets and stars were living as well.... During the Renaissance, the idea of Heaven as an animal reappeared in Lucilio Vanini; the Neoplatonist Marsilio Ficino spoke of the hair, teeth and bones of the earth; and Giordano Bruno felt that the planets were great peaceful animals, warm-blooded, with regular habits and endowed with reason. At the beginning of the seventeenth century, the German astronomer Johannes Kepler debated with the English mystic Robert Fludd which of them had first conceived the notion of the earth as

a living monster, 'whose whalelike breathing, changing with sleep and wakefulness, produces the ebb and flow of the sea.' The anatomy, the feeding habits, the colour, the memory and the imaginative and shaping faculties of the monster were sedulously studied by Kepler" (Jorge Luis Borges, *The Book of Imaginary Beings* [New York: Penguin, 1980], pp. 21–22).

9. L. D. Rue, "The Saving Grace of Noble Lies," from a symposium entitled *The Evolution of Deception: A Biocultural Approach*, which took place in Washington, D.C., February 16, 1991. An abstract of Rue's talk is printed in the American Association for the Advancement of Science's *AAAS Annual Meeting Abstracts of Papers*, AAAS Publication 91-02S (Washington, D.C., 1991), p. 92.

10. For Gaia theory as unscientific, see, for example, H. Holland, *The Chemical Evolution of the Atmosphere and Oceans* (Princeton: Princeton University Press, 1984); W. F. Doolittle, "Is Nature Really Motherly?" *CoEvolution Quarterly* 29 (1981), pp. 58–65; and R. Dawkins, *The Extended Phenotype* (Oxford: Freeman, 1982). For Gaia theory as trivial, see J. W. Kirchner, "The Gaia Hypothesis: Can It Be Tested?" *Review of Geophysics* 27 (1989), pp. 223–35. For "Satanism," see C. White, "Mother Earth Marries Satan," *21st Century Science and Technology* 52 (Sept.–Oct. 1989).

11. Cited in James E. Lovelock, *The Ages of Gaia: A Biography of Our Living Earth* (New York: W. W. Norton, 1988). The narcissistic, biocentric Gaian beholds the Earth from space and — through the so-called aha! phenomenon — recognizes her or his macrocosmic body. The astronaut gazes at the baby-blue, cloud-flecked planet from which she or he is now separated. The Earth, spoken of anemically in textbooks as lifeless, a mere geochemical setting for life, no longer appears as mere environment. Before the orbiting astronautical gaze, the planet becomes the unmapped place of all human existence. It mutates from being the home of an ecology or ecofeminism and becomes a giant spherical being. For an interesting synthesis of the effects of the astronautical gaze, see F. White, *The Overview Effect: Space Exploration and Human Evolution* (Boston: Houghton Mifflin, 1987).

12. Although truth may be stranger than fiction, fiction is often truer — if only because its claims to represent truth are less strident. Mythopoetic realities are freely generated within the realm of science fiction. A living planet thrives in Isaac Asimov's book *Foundation and Earth*. In Polish writer Stanislaw Lem's *Solaris*, a planet is inhabited by a giant ocean capable of copying human artifacts and even human beings. In R. A. Kennedy's *The Triuniverse*, Mars divides into

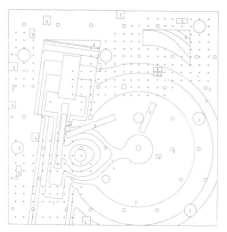

Agadir Convention Center, Morocco 1990.
Roof, level +10–18m.
OMA

two like a giant cell and begins feeding on other planets. In *Born of the Sun*, science-fiction writer Jack
Williamson portrays the planets of our solar system
as eggs laid by the Sun, Earth being the first to hatch.
In my book *Biospheres* (see note 13, below), a putative work of science nonfiction, I extended
the Gaian metaphor of aliveness to the point of reproduction. In this logical extension of the
Gaian trope of a live Earth, I pictured the surface planetary environment as a neuter being
(rather than a "goddess") on the verge of potentially stellar reproduction (but not necessarily
self-conscious of that fact). Such stellar reproduction borders on the incredible and, partly
because of that, illustrates a noble lie of the Gaian kind.

13. D. Sagan, *Biospheres: The Metamorphosis of Planet Earth* (New York: Bantam/McGraw-
Hill, 1990).

14. The group (Space Biospheres Ventures) in charge of the Biosphere II project has recently been exposed to the scrutiny and ridicule of Marc Cooper's investigative journalism.
Space Biosphere Ventures has been characterized as a scientifically pathetic "cult" on a "bogus
journey"; positive articles about the project in *Discover* and *Whole Earth*, among other magazines and the major metropolitan newspapers, have been faulted for taking the project seriously; while Biosphere II itself has been viciously, if accurately, tagged "Planet Velcro." See
Cooper, "Take This Terrarium and Shove It," *The Village Voice* (April 2, 1991), pp. 24–33, and
"Profits of Doom: The Biosphere Project Finally Comes out of the Closet — As a Theme Park,"
The Village Voice (July 30, 1991), pp. 31–36.

15. Bataille, *The Accursed Share*, vol. 1, p. 29.

16. Sorin Sonea and Maurice Panisset, *The New Bacteriology* (Boston: Jones and Bartlett, 1983).

17. For a fun overview of her work — and of the tensions within the new biology as a
whole — see Connie Barlow, ed., *From Gaia to Selfish Genes: Selected Writings in the Life Sciences*
(Cambridge, Mass.: MIT Press, 1991), esp. pp. 47–66.

18. "The Case of the Sick Amoebas," in ibid., pp. 57–62 describes the startling findings of
biologist Kwang Jeon, who witnessed the transformation of infectious bacteria into the needed
organelles of a new species of amoebas. Jeon may be the only person in human history to have
actually witnessed the evolution of a new species in a laboratory (he remains a devout Christian).

19. Sonea and Panisset, *The New Bacteriology*.

20. The Homeric epics never mention a body — the flesh-enclosed entity usually taken for granted as the definable material self — but speak only of what we would think of as body parts, corporeal fragments such as "fleet legs" and "sinewy arms"; see B. Snell, *The Discovery of the Mind*, trans. T. C. Rosenmeyer (New York: Harper Torchbooks, 1960), p. 8. "The idea of the self in a case," Norbert Elias has written, "is one of the recurrent *leitmotifs* of a modern philosophy, from the thinking subject of Descartes, Leibniz' windowless monads and the Kantian subject of knowledge (who from his aprioristic shell can never quite break through to the 'thing in itself') to the more recent extension of the same basic idea of the entirely self-sufficient individual" (*The Civilizing Process: The History of Manners*, trans. E. Jephcott [New York: Urizen, 1978], pp. 252–53).

21. James E. Lovelock, *Gaia: A New Look at Life on Earth* (New York: Oxford University Press, 1979).

22. James E. Lovelock, "Life Span of the Biosphere," *Nature* 296 (April 1982), pp. 561–63.

Beech Tree between Hannover and the Weser, c. 1962.
Albert Renger-Patzsch

Intentionality [1939]

Jean-Paul Sartre

"His eyes devoured her." The expression provides one of
many hints of the illusion, common to both realism and
idealism, that knowing is a sort of eating. This is where
French philosophy is still mired, after a hundred years of
academic development. We've all read our Léon Brunschvicg,
our André Lalande and Emile Meyerson, we've all imagined
a spider-Mind drawing things into its web, covering them
in white saliva and slowly ingesting them, reducing them to
its own substance. What is a table, a rock, a house? A certain collection of "contents of consciousness," an order in
those contents. O, alimentary philosophy! But what could
be clearer: Isn't the table the current content of my perception, and my perception the present state of my consciousness? Nutrition, assimilation. The assimilation, as Lalande
used to say, of things to ideas, of ideas to one another and
of one mind to another. The strong bones of the world were
eaten away by these persistent enzymes: assimilation, unifi-
cation, identification. In vain did the most straightforward
and the crudest among us seek something solid, something,

in other words, that wasn't Mind; everywhere they came only upon that very special fog that was themselves.

Against the digestive philosophy of empiriocriticism and neo-Kantianism, against all "psychologism," Husserl never tires of insisting that things cannot be dissolved in consciousness. Thus, you see this tree. But you see it just where it is: at the side of the road in the dust, alone and twisted in the heat, fifty miles from the Mediterranean coast. It can't enter into your consciousness, for it's of a different nature. You may think you recognize Bergson and the first chapter of *Matter and Memory*. But Husserl is no realist: this tree on its patch of cracked earth is not something absolute, which subsequently comes into relation with us. Consciousness and the world are given together: in its essence external to consciousness, the world is, in its essence, relative to it. For Husserl sees in consciousness an irreducible fact that cannot be conveyed by any physical image. Except, perhaps, the fleeting and puzzling image of breaking apart. To know is to "break out," to escape from moist gastric inwardness and fly out beyond oneself, toward what is not oneself, out there, over by the tree and yet outside it — for it eludes and resists me, and I can no more lose myself in it than it can be dissolved in me — outside it, and outside myself. Don't you recognize in this description what you needed, and suspected? You knew well enough that the tree wasn't you, that you couldn't get it into your dark stomachs, and that knowledge couldn't honestly be compared to possession. At the same time, consciousness has become purified, clear as a gale, nothing is left in it but a flight from itself, a slipping out of itself. If — which is impossible — you entered "into" a consciousness, you'd be caught in a whirlwind and thrown back out, over by the tree, in the dust, for consciousness has no "inside"; it's nothing but its own outside, and it's this absolute flight, this refusal of substance, that makes it a consciousness. Now imagine a linked series of breakings-apart that take us out of ourselves, that don't even leave "ourselves" the time to re-form behind them, but rather throw us beyond them, into the dry dust of the world, onto the rough earth, among things; imagine us thus thrown back out, stranded by our very nature in a stubborn, hostile, indifferent world; then you will have grasped the full meaning of what Husserl expresses in the famous words "All consciousness is consciousness *of* something." This is all it takes to finish with the cozy philosophy of immanence in which everything happens by arrangement, by protoplasmic exchanges, by a tepid cellular chemistry. The philosophy of transcendence throws us onto the open road, in the midst of dangers, in a blinding light. To be, says Heidegger, is to-be-in-the-world. Understand this "being-in" as a movement. To be is to break into the world, it's to go from a void of world and consciousness into a sudden breaking-as-consciousness-into-the-world. If consciousness tries to recover itself, to coincide with itself, all warm inside with the shutters closed, it becomes nothing. This need of consciousness to exist as the consciousness of something other than itself is what Husserl calls "intentionality."

I started by talking about knowledge, the better to be understood: the French philosophy with which we've grown up deals with little but epistemology. But for Husserl and the phenomenologists our consciousness of things is in no sense restricted to knowledge of them. The knowledge or pure "representation" of it is only one of the possible forms of my consciousness "of" this tree; I can also love it, fear it, hate it; and the way consciousness goes beyond itself, which we call "intentionality," is also to be found in fear, hatred and love. To hate someone is another way of breaking out toward him, it's suddenly finding oneself confronting a stranger and experiencing, above all suffering, his objective quality of "hatefulness." And all at once those famous "subjective" reactions of hate, love, fear and sympathy, which were floating in the rancid marinade of Mind, are removed from it; they are just ways of discovering the world. *Things* suddenly reveal themselves to us as hateful, nice, horrible, likeable. It's a *property* of that Japanese mask to be terrifying, an inexhaustible, irreducible property, which is its very nature — rather than the sum of our subjective reactions to a piece of carved wood. Husserl has put horror and delight back into things. He has given us back the world of artists and prophets: frightening, hostile and dangerous, with havens of grace and love. He has cleared the way for a new treatise on the passions based on the simple truth, so completely overlooked by the most subtle among us, that if we love a woman, it's because she's lovable. There's an end to Proust. And an end to the "inner life": it's no good seeking, like Amiel, or like a child stroking its shoulder, for a caressing and fondling of our inmost selves, because ultimately everything is outside, everything including ourselves: outside, in the world, among others. We won't find ourselves in some retreat, but on the road, in the town, in the midst of the crowd, a thing among things, a man among men.

Translated from the French by Martin Joughin

$^1\!/_{100}$ sec. at 70 km/h, 1930.

Anton Stankowski

The Construction of Perception
Leif H. Finkel

We take the world largely for granted. The cozy picture that daily surrounds us, the triumph of the familiar, argues for an inherent order and coherence in our immediate universe. Although we realize that our existence is confined to a small sector of quantum-cosmological space, reality appears to us to be an inherent property of the external world. The vivid detail of this external picture blends seamlessly with our cognitive picture of our place in the universe. And thus, we come to develop a deep trust of our perceptions and an implicit faith in our understanding, or capability of understanding all objects in our survey.

I wish to present an argument to the contrary. I will argue that reality, as we know it, is largely an internally generated construct of the nervous system, and that once constructed it is projected back onto the world through behavioral interactions with objects in our local environments. Much of the consistency and logic of external events is, consequently, a property of the "perceiver" rather than the perceived object. Our view of the world may be more subjective than we realize, even beyond any cultural conventions. What we take to be the basic physical properties of our environment may reflect the structure of our brains more than the structure of the universe.

Such an argument is in some sense philosophical, and it was to overcome specifically this aspect of perceptual relativism and the related metaphysical problems that the scientific method was conceived. Surely the speed of light is not a culturally dependent variable, nor is mitosis a phenomenon open to individual speculation. Yet it may nevertheless be that the scientific view (of classical physics and mathematics) reaches its limits when we approach the domain of cognition: subjective perceptions, what we think, how we feel. And while logical reasoning may be able to order many of the facts of nature, a more "constructionist" view may be necessary to explain the underpinnings of knowledge.

Recent developments in neuroscience, and particularly in computational neuroscience (a new field devoted to theoretical studies of the nervous system), have begun to illustrate how the brain may generate its idiosyncratic perceptions. In fact, a combination of studies in anatomy, physiology, psychophysics and clinical neurology suggest some sobering answers to these basic questions.

Our Bodies, Our Selves: How We Know Where To Scratch

The somatosensory nervous system, which mediates our perceptions of touch, pressure, temperature and pain, provides a good example of the problem. Pain is clearly an internally generated construct, reflecting as it usually does an external insult. Arguing teleologically, pain usually serves as a powerful lesson. However, there are several relatively rare syndromes (chiefly involving the thalamus) in which intense, prolonged pain is perceived in the absence of external stimuli. In conditions such as diabetic neuropathy, in which pain fibers are lost, individuals inflict devastating damage on themselves by senselessly banging their feet against doors, rocks and other stumbling blocks during the course of the day. Yet, since the perception of pain is internally constructed, the question remains: Why is it that when I stub my toe, it feels like my *toe* hurts — as opposed to the whole lower half of my body or even a general malaise? In other words, how does the nervous system manifest the *localized* perception of pain (or touch or heat)?

The answer to this question was first intimated in the findings of a small group of French neurologists in the mid-nineteenth century. Their basic discovery was that function is localized in the cerebral cortex (patients who had had strokes or traumatic lesions in certain regions of their brains were observed to lose specific functions and not others, for example, speech, use of a particular limb and so on). It turns out that function is localized not only in the cortex but throughout much of the nervous system, starting in the spinal cord, and involving most sensory, motor and associative areas. As shown in figure 1, there was actually an antecedent theory of functional localization popularized by the phrenologists, who believed that character traits could be determined by the variegated form of the skull.[1] But the cortex does not directly deal in traits such as "benevolence" or "spirituality" — its concerns are rooted in the tasks of survival.

One might thus presume that localization of perception (for example, that of one's big toe) results from the localization of function within the nervous system, and in the cortex in particular. As it turns out, this is a necessary but not a sufficient condition; however, let me first turn to a brief review of the relevant experimental history.

One of the earliest attempts to systematically map functional domains in the cortex was

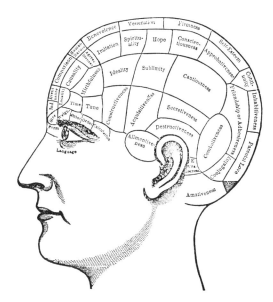

Figure 1. Map of 37 purported brain areas as advanced by the phrenologist Franz Joseph Gall (1825).

performed in 1917 by A. S. F. Leyton and Charles S. Sherrington (the latter being perhaps the greatest neurologist of all time).[2] Their experiment consisted of stimulating different zones of the motor cortex (responsible for controlling movement) in chimpanzees, orangutans and a gorilla. Because stimulation of particular cortical regions elicited particular movements — one site would elicit a hand motion, another a neck movement and so on — motor cortex was found to contain a detailed map. However, the experiment also yielded an insight that would take nearly seventy years to understand: the borders of the motor map were found to be "labile," in other words, over time there were continual macroscopic changes in *what* was represented *where* in the cortex. This plasticity of representation, though, which flew in the face of the emerging concept of ordered maps in the brain, was not pursued.

The major emphasis of somatosensory physiology turned to defining and exploring the detailed maps of the body surface found in cortex. One such map is shown in figure 2. Note that regions of the body are represented roughly according to the precision of touch in that body part (fingers, face and genitalia have large representations, while torso and proximal limbs have small representations). The idea thus took hold that anatomical connectivity established the functionally determined body maps, and that these maps, in turn, were responsible for functional localization.

In 1957, Vernon Mountcastle of Johns Hopkins University initiated the modern era of cortical studies with his discovery of a third dimension to the cortical body maps.[3] When Mountcastle slowly passed a microelectrode through the two-millimeter depth of cortex, he observed that all the cells encountered in a vertical penetration responded to stimulation

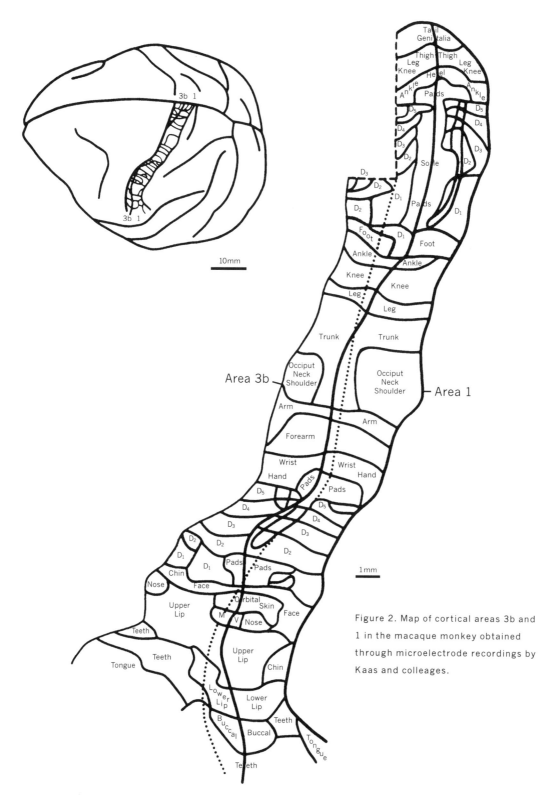

Figure 2. Map of cortical areas 3b and 1 in the macaque monkey obtained through microelectrode recordings by Kaas and colleages.

of a single locus on the skin. Thus, there are "columns" of cells (originally conceived of as solid cylinders, but their shapes are actually more like extended bands), all concerned with representation of a particular body area. These columns organize the input–output connections of a given cortical area to other areas of cortex. Columns thus appear to serve as the functional units of cortical maps, providing the link between structure and function in the brain.

However, the relationship between structure and function occurs at two different levels in the biological domain.[4] At the *physiological* level, structures are usually designed nearly optimally to carry out their functional tasks — witness the aerodynamic properties of avian feathers, the oxygen transport capabilities of the lungs or the optics of the eye. This optimization is the result, however, of a link between structure and function at the evolutionary level — embryonic development generates structure, natural selection evaluates function. The distinction between these two levels is important because one will never find a purely "physiological" explanation for a process that was shaped by an "evolutionary" pressure. It is as if the physiological level provides the mechanism for "how" a function is generated, whereas the evolutionary level explains "why" the process exists. For example, in amphibians, the process of metamorphosis (for example, transformation of a tadpole into an adult frog) occurs when the level of certain thyroid hormones begins to rise. However, the reason metamorphosis exists can only be understood by considering the adaptive advantages it confers, which is to say, from an evolutionary viewpoint.

Thus, to understand the structural basis of brain function, one must be clear as to which level of explanation one seeks. While most attempts to understand cortical processing have quite reasonably focused on the physiological level, the great contribution of Gerald Edelman's new theory of brain function, proposed in his 1987 *Neural Darwinism*, is that it seeks the higher, evolutionary level of explanation.[5]

"Neural Darwinism" proposes that the basic structural–functional unit is a small subset of cortical column known as a "neuronal group." Groups are collections of strongly interconnected cells, which in some ways resemble Mountcastle's (1978) concept of "minicolumns," but for the fact that they are defined functionally rather than structurally.[6] The basic tenet of Neural Darwinism is that the nervous system operates as a selective system, akin to the operation of natural selection in evolution. Neuronal groups serve as the units of selection, analogous to species in evolution. And in place of DNA, genetics and heredity (that is, changes in the frequency of various genes within a population), the nervous system strengthens or weakens the synaptic connections between cells. For example, natural selection operates by changing gene frequencies (genes for blue, brown or green eye color and so on) based on the survival and mating abilities of the individuals' genes. Neural Darwinism proposes that the brain operates by changing the strengths of synapses based on the ability of the neurons connected by those synapses to be activated consistently.

Such a system, with a large population of units operating according to the principles of selection, might be expected to display competitive behaviors analogous to those seen in ecology. Neurons (like animals in the wild) should compete for limited resources, struggle for dominance and attempt to pass on their "phenotype" — that is, characteristics produced by the interaction of genetic makeup and environment — through whatever hereditary mechanism prevails. Such behaviors have been seen in computer simulations of large cortical networks,[7] and have recently been discovered in several in vivo brain systems. Perhaps the most striking of these discoveries is the strange behavior seen in the body maps of somato-sensory cortex.

When Michael Merzenich of the University of California at San Francisco, John Kaas of Vanderbilt University and others began to make very detailed maps of the somatosensory cortex of monkeys (similar effects have been found in the spinal cord by Patrick Wall of University College in London), two interesting observations resulted. First, they discovered that what was previously thought to be a single map of the body is in fact four separate complete body maps, lying side by side in the four architecturally distinct zones of somatosensory cortex (so-called areas 1, 2, 3a and 3b). The four maps represent slightly different sensory modalities — for example, the map in 3b is activated by light touch to the skin, while that in area 2 represents responses of deeper sensors. The existence of multiple representational maps, each concerned with different sets of functional properties, is one of the basic themes of brain organization, and one to which I shall return shortly.

Second, the map in any one of these areas, although grossly similar from animal to animal, displayed a large degree of individual variability. Thus, for example, the amount of cortex devoted to representing the thumb or the precise location within the map of the hand—wrist border differs dramatically among various animals of a single species. More surprisingly, when the same map in the same monkey was determined repeatedly over the course of a year, it was found to vary from month to month by an amount as great as the variation between different animals. The picture thus emerged that these body maps, long thought to be static representations of the underlying anatomical connections, were in fact dynamic structures that change over time. Any particular map determined on any given day is just a snapshot of an evolving dynamic structure. Furthermore, these findings suggest that the body maps are primarily *functional* constructs, not structural or anatomical entities. This is so because, within the constraints imposed by the anatomy, a given body region can be represented anywhere over a relatively large region of cortex. (Representations can move over an area of roughly 10 percent of the map — corresponding on a map of the continental United States to 260-mile shifts in state borders.)

In a series of elegant experiments, Merzenich and Kaas went on to show that the essential parameter regulating map representation was the amount of correlated stimulation to the skin. In other words, there is a competition between skin regions for representation in the brain, and skin regions that are repeatedly and most heavily stimulated (fingers, lips and so on) get the largest representations. Conversely, if a region is deprived of stimulation (by local anesthesia or nerve transection), its representation is competitively diminished, or can be altogether eliminated and replaced by an alternative skin site.[8]

It is possible to recreate these phenomena in a computer simulation of monkey somatosensory cortex based on the ideas of Neural Darwinism.[9] Several colleagues and I have shown that neuronal groups, acting as competitive units, are able to organize a body map similar to that found in monkey cortical area 3b, and that in response to increased or decreased tactile stimulation, the simulated maps show changes remarkably similar to those observed in vivo.

To summarize the argument thus far: Our perception of the world, from a somatosensory viewpoint, depends on an individual's ability to "refer" a particular touch sensation to the correct location on its body. Tactile localization seems to follow in a straightforward manner from the organization of the cortex into body maps. Yet these maps turn out to be dynamic in that they reflect the interaction of the individual with its tactile environment. Furthermore, strange phenomena are easily explained by these considerations. Take the case of "phantom limb": after a limb is amputated, some patients report that they still have sensations that feel like they are coming from the missing arm or leg. These feelings can be tactile, but are most often manifested as tinglings or pain. Phantom limb may result from the fact that although the limb is gone, the cortical and subcortical maps subserving the limb persist for weeks or months until competitive processes lead to their reorganization and rededication. Activation of a map is perceived, as always, as the physical, bodily sensation of "touch" and is referred back to the (missing) limb. In fact, the time course of resolution for a phantom limb closely follows that of map reorganization in monkey cortex.[10]

Here, then, is a case in which the most proximal sensory system, whose domain of survey includes only the surface of the skin, nonetheless appears to construct a picture and project it back onto the world. The perception of the phantom limb is obviously generated internally, by the same cortical maps that generated it internally when the limb was present. And the fact that the somatic perceptions are referred to the spatial location of the (missing) limb most likely reflects the fact that the map dealing with tactile information is still in register with other, higher level maps dealing with position in space and place in the local environment. When we consider sensory systems with more extended domains — for example, the visual system — the constructive abilities of such coupled maps reach an even higher degree of sophistication.

Out of Sight, Out of Mind: The Humpty-Dumpty Phenomenon

When we look at the world we see a picture. The picture is composed of various objects against backgrounds, and each object is characterized by a number of attributes such as shape, color, distance and motion. While the presence of this picture (which to a large degree defines our vision of "reality") is obvious from a psychological viewpoint, the mechanisms by which it is constructed by the brain remain mysterious. In fact, the last thirty years of research on the visual cortex have followed two paths to a remarkable dead end. First, it has been shown that the visual cortex of primates (and other higher vertebrates) is composed of multiple distinct areas — up to two dozen areas in some species of monkeys. These areas are functionally specialized so that, to a large degree, the analysis of color, motion, shape and so on are carried out by different cortical areas. (In fact, each area carries out multiple functions and each function is subserved by several areas; for clarity of argument, though, this degeneracy need not concern us here.) The second startling finding is that, although these multiple areas are exuberantly connected to each other in an intricate and complex scheme, there is no single area that receives connections from every other, or even a majority of other areas. Thus, visual information enters the cortex and is split up according to function (shape and so on), *but there is no place in which the "picture" can be put back together.*

Figure 3. Examples of the visual illusion
known as illusory contours from the Gestalt
psychologist Gaetano Kanizsa.

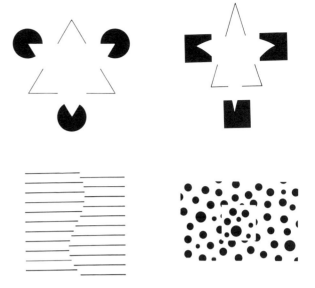

This leaves us with only one option — the picture must result from a dynamic process carried out in a distributed fashion over many cortical areas. In other words, the picture one "sees" does not exist as a single, complete representation somewhere in a brain, rather, it is an emergent property of the system. An analogy can be drawn to *extensive* versus *intensive* processes in thermodynamics. Mass, for example, is an extensive property — if one cuts an object in half, it has half as much mass. Temperature, on the other hand, is an intensive property: cut an ice cube in half and each half still has the same temperature, because temperature results from the statistical properties of large populations of atoms. Based on similar statistical properties, it appears that our picture of the world may emerge from the operations of large neural populations.

In a recent computer model based on the visual cortex of the macaque monkey, Edelman and I were able to show that separate simulated cortical areas, linked by interconnections, can generate integrated, coherent responses to visual stimuli.[11] For example, a picture of a moving "square" against a distant background was shown to a system of three networks: one specialized for "shape," one for "motion" and one for "depth." Each network detects a different aspect of the moving square — the location of the edge, the location of motion and the location of the depth discontinuity between the square and the background. The responses of the three networks are consistent in that these locations are identical. Even more telling, when the networks were shown a number of visual illusions (such as those in figure 3), they responded in much the same manner as humans and animals do. The response to illusions is particularly revealing, because in these cases the response of the system is totally self-generated — there is actually nothing in the physical world corresponding to the perception. For example, the triangle in figure 3 appears "whiter" than the background — yet as can easily be confirmed, there is, in fact, no "triangle" actually present, and the color of the paper is uniform across the page. Thus, illusions may serve as the royal road to uncovering the basis of cortical integration. And toward this end, a number of investigators are beginning to combine physiological, psychophysical and theoretical studies. [12]

Thus, vision demonstrates that even our most cherished view of the world, namely, the organized picture of three-dimensional space, is constructed in an oblique and mysterious way by the brain. In fact, if we look in detail at any one of the component processes that go into constructing this picture, the mystery darkens even further.

Color Constancy and the Cathedral of Rouen

Of all visual features, color is perhaps the most immediate. And despite the unanswerable conundrum of experiential relativism — is my subjective experience of "red" the same as yours — colors evoke a distinct and vivid perception. Furthermore, color appears to have certain mathematical properties that have been apparent since Newton first prismatically decomposed sunlight into its component spectrum.

However, due to a phenomenon known as "color constancy," the situation is not quite so straightforward. Color constancy refers to the fact that the perceived color of an object tends to remain relatively invariant under different illuminating conditions. For example, a stop sign looks red under the midday sun, at dusk and when illuminated by the headlights of a car. If one were to measure the wavelengths of light coming off the stop sign to your eye, one would find that the amount of "red" light (photons with wavelengths around 650 nanometers) varies tremendously between these cases. In fact, Edwin Land (the inventor of the Polaroid system) showed in a remarkable series of experiments that the wavelength of emitted light bears no direct relation to the perceived color of an object. Two objects, one that appears "red" and another "green," for example, can both emit identical spectrums. [13]

The key, as Land showed, is that perceived color depends on the *relative* amount of light of different wavelengths reflected from different parts of the visual scene. In other words, colors are relative — a stop sign looks red because it reflects more "red" light than something that looks green. Only by comparing light received from a large part of the visual world can an accurate perception of color be made. This is an important point, because in our everyday environments the spectrum of ambient light is constantly changing. As one goes from bright sunlight to hazy light, or even in taking a pair of sunglasses on or off, it is imperative that the colors of familiar objects not change drastically.

Thus, the perception of color does not reflect any simple principle of physics, and must instead depend on complex operations carried out by the nervous system. The nature of these operations has been elucidated largely through the work of Semir Zeki at University College in London. When neurons in the first visual cortical area (area V1) are examined, it is found that they directly respond to the wavelength of incident light. Since the nervous system uses a trichromatic system (red, green and blue cones in the retina), one finds cortical cells that respond to the presence of these three colors (the process is actually more complex, in that the neurons also have a spatial component to their responses). These neurons are responding to wavelength but not to *color*, since their responses do not correspond to the perceived color (for example, if the stop sign is made to reflect blue light, the "blue" neurons will be activated even though the sign does not appear blue).

However, when neurons in one of the higher visual cortical areas, namely area V4, are examined, they are found to respond to the *perceived* color rather than to the incident wavelength. This suggests that the neural operations necessary for color constancy are carried out in V4, or at least somewhere between V1 and V4. In fact, Zeki was able to repeat Land's experiments with monkeys, and showed that cells in V4 respond just as would be expected if they were computing relative brightness over the visual field.[14]

The cerebral cortex is, at least grossly, a fairly uniform structure and similar neuronal architectures are found throughout its extent. Thus, the kinds of operations carried out in visual area V4 may be representative of those performed in other visual areas, and indeed in somatosensory, auditory, motor and frontal cortex as well. From this viewpoint, it is particularly illuminating that V4 *constructs* a representation of the (color) world that imposes some sense of order and coherence on a fluctuating and inconstant environment.

The Function of the Cortex: *Solo, Perduto, Abbandonnato*
The cortex, which began its ascendence with the rise of mammals over eighty million years ago, has evolved in an almost exclusive absence of culture, language and civilization. During this period, and as it remains today, the world is a complex and dangerous place, and survival requires vigilance, adaptability and creativity. The cortex came to be responsible for coordinating a growth repertoire of behavioral actions, and was faced with the task of matching

an appropriate action to each situation. Thus, put in the position of both interpreter and forecaster, the cortex adopted a brilliant strategy — the development of a model or representation of the world. This representation had to reflect not just recent history and current events, but the accumulated wisdom of experience. And given the variable, unpredictable and deceptive character of experience, cortical representations became adaptive, multiplex and cross-checking. In short, the cortex was forced to construct a version of the world to be kept inside and used as a basis of comparison to external events. Only by developing this self-consistent version of reality, and constantly refining the representation based on the consequences of its predicted actions, could any semblance of order be arrived at. The elaboration of this internal reality gave rise, by and by, to the emergence of consciousness and the subjective perception that the internal world was, in fact, coextensive with the external.[15] Yet this projection arose from a methodological fallacy. Just as in Plato's allegory of the cave, there would be no way for the denizens of such an internal world to infer the existence or absence of the external. In fact, the rational basis for the notion that we inhabit an ordered, coherent reality can be traced back to the Platonic ideas.

The truth, I fear, lies closer to the Darwinian view. We grope our way, largely in the dark, about our respective caves. The world, to a large extent, is a vision of our own creation. We inhabit a mixed realm of sensation and interpretation, and the boundary between them is never openly revealed to us. And amid this tenuous situation, our cortex makes up little stories about the world, and softly hums them to us to keep us from getting scared at night.

NOTES

1. J. D. Davies, *Phrenology: Fad and Science* (New Haven: Yale University Press, 1955). I would like to thank Mrs. Patricia Kind and the following agencies for supporting my research: the Whitaker Foundation, the Office of Naval Research, the McDonnell-Pew Program in Cognitive Neuroscience and the University of Pennsylvania Research Foundation.

2. A. S. F. Leyton and C. S. Sherrington, "Observations on the Excitable Cortex of the Chimpanzee, Orangutan, and Gorilla," *Quarterly Journal of Experimental Physiology* 11 (1917), pp. 137–222.

3. V. B. Mountcastle, "Modality and Topographic Properties of Single Neurons of Cat's Somatic Sensory Cortex," *Journal of Neurophysiology* 20 (1957), pp. 408–34.

4. E. Mayr, *The Growth of Biological Thought* (Cambridge, Mass.: Harvard University Press, 1982).

5. G. M. Edelman, *Neural Darwinism* (New York: Basic Books, 1987).

6. V. B. Mountcastle, "An Organizing Principle for Cerebral Function: The Unit Module and the Distributed System," in G. M. Edelman and Mountcastle, eds., *The Mindful Brain* (Cambridge, Mass.: MIT Press, 1978), pp. 7–50; and Edelman and L. H. Finkel, "Neuronal Group Selection in the Cerebral Cortex," in Edelman, W. E. Gall and W. M. Cowan, eds., *Dynamic Aspects of Neocortical Function* (New York: John Wiley, 1984), pp. 653–95.

7. J. C. Pearson, L. H. Finkel and G. M. Edelman, "Plasticity in the Organization of Adult Cerebral Cortical Maps: A Computer Simulation Based on Neuronal Group," *Journal of Neuroscience* 7.12 (1987), pp. 4209–23.

8. J. H. Kaas, M. Merzenich and H. P. Killackey, "The Reorganization of Somatosensory Cortex Following Peripheral Nerve Damage in Adult and Developing Mammals," *Annual Review of Neuroscience* 6 (1983), pp. 325–56; and Merzenich, G. Recanzone, W. M. Jenkins, T. T. Allard and R. J. Nudo, "Cortical Representational Plasticity," in P. Rakic and W. Singer, eds., *Neurobiology of Neocortex* (New York: John Wiley, 1988), pp. 41–68.

9. Edelman and Finkel, "Neuronal Group Selection"; Pearson et al., "Plasticity in Organization"; and L. H. Finkel, "A Model of Receptive Field Plasticity and Topographic Reorganization in Somatosensory Cortex," in S. J. Hanson and C. R. Olsen, eds., *Connectionist Modeling and Brain Function: The Developing Interface* (Cambridge, Mass.: MIT Press, 1990), pp. 164–92.

10. Merzenich et al., "Cortical Representational Plasticity."

11. L. H. Finkel and G. M. Edelman, "The Integration of Distributed Cortical Systems by Reentry: A Computer Simulation of Interactive Functionally Segregated Visual Areas," *Journal of Neuroscience* 9 (1989), pp. 3188–208.

12. S. Grossberg and E. Mingolla, "Neural Dynamics of Form Perception: Boundary Completion, Illusory Figures, and Neon Color Spreading," *Psychological Review* 92 (1985), pp. 173–211; M. Livingstone and D. Hubel, "Segregation of Form, Color, Movement, and Depth: Anatomy, Physiology, and Perception," *Science* 240 (1988), pp. 740–49; and E. A. DeYeo and D. C. Van Essen, "Concurrent Processing Streams in Monkey Visual Cortex," *Trends in Neuroscience* 11 (1988), pp. 219–26.

13. E. H. Land, "Recent Advances in Retinex Theory and Some Implications for Cortical Computations," *Proceedings of the National Academy of Science of the USA* 80 (1983), pp. 5163–169.

14. S. M. Zeki, "The Representation of Colours in the Cerebral Cortex," *Nature* 284 (1980), pp. 412–18.

15. See G. M. Edelman, *The Remembered Present: A Biological Theory of Consciousness* (New York: Basic Books, 1989) for a comprehensive theory of consciousness.

Biology and Beauty

Frederick Turner

What was life? No one knew. It was undoubtedly aware of itself, so soon as it was life; but it did not know what it was. Consciousness, as exhibited by susceptibility to stimulus, was undoubtedly, to a certain degree, present in the lowest, most undeveloped stages of life; it was impossible to fix the first appearance of conscious processes at any point in the history of the individual or the race; impossible to make consciousness contingent upon, say, the presence of a nervous system. The lowest animal forms had no nervous systems, still less a cerebrum; yet no one would venture to deny them the capacity for responding to stimuli. One could suspend life; not merely particular sense-organs, not only nervous reactions, but life itself. One could temporarily suspend the irritability to sensation of every form of living matter in the plant as well as in the animal kingdom; one could narcotize ova and spermatozoa with chloroform, chloral hydrate, or morphine. Consciousness, then, was simply a function of matter organized into life; a function that in higher manifestations turned upon its avatar and became an effort to explore and explain the phenomenon it displayed — a hopeful–hopeless project of life to achieve self-knowledge....

What then was life? It was warmth, the warmth generated by a form-preserving instability, a fever of matter, which accompanied the process of ceaseless decay and repair of albumen molecules that were too impossibly complicated, too impossibly ingenious in structure. It was the existence of the actually impossible — to exist, of a half-sweet, half-painful balancing, or scarcely balancing, in this restricted and feverish process of decay and renewal, upon the point of existence. It was not matter and it was not spirit, but something between the two, a phenomenon conveyed by matter, like the rainbow on the waterfall, and like the flame. Yet why not material — it was sentient to the point of desire and disgust, the shamelessness of matter become sensible of itself, the incontinent form of being. It was a secret and ardent stirring in the frozen chastity of the universal; it was a stolen and voluptuous impurity of sucking and secreting; an exhalation of carbonic acid gas and material impurities of mysterious origin and composition. It was a pullulation, an unfolding, a form-building (made possible by the overbalancing of its instability, yet controlled by the laws of growth inherent within it), of something brewed out of water, albumen, salt and fats, which was called flesh, and which became form, beauty, a lofty image, and yet all the time the essence of sensuality and desire....

— Thomas Mann, The Magic Mountain

The title of this essay in itself represents a wholesale questioning of much of the modernist and postmodernist consensus. In order that we shall be quite clear about, first, the extent of our investment in these beliefs, and, second, the painful divestment I believe is necessary if beauty is to be brought back to life, it might be helpful to summarize this consensus as it concerns beauty, and to sketch the main assertions that the reader is asked to consider in this essay.

Few postmodernist thinkers today would disagree with the following propositions: (1) Human beings have no nature; (2) Nature itself is passive before our constructions of it; (3) There is no essence or meaning in things; (4) There is no hierarchy in things other than what is imported into them by our power-seeking constructions of them; (5) There is no progress (modernism began with a triumphant belief in progress, though its contemporary heirs have largely abandoned it); and (6) The past is irrelevant except as a record of mistakes and abuses.

To these we may add two more specifically aesthetic propositions: (7) Beauty is not a reality but a social construction; and (8) The aesthetic consists in the absence of shame.

Finally, four main substitutes for beauty have been offered in the realm of aesthetics, held sometimes together and sometimes in opposition to each other: (7a) The function of the aesthetic is novelty (deconstruction would be the heat-death or final perfected state of this view); (7b) The function of the aesthetic is subjective expressiveness (the interpretation of personal experience in terms of the latest and most prestigious popular psychological theory); (7c) The function of the aesthetic is to demonstrate politically "progressive" attitudes; and (7d) The function of the aesthetic is to demonstrate the absence (Derrida) or presence (Heidegger) of Being-in-the-world, Being conceived of as essentially prior to reflection, culture and the linguistic construction of the world.

To these propositions we may oppose the essential assumptions of this essay: (1) There is a real human nature; (2) There is a real universal nature — partly knowable by appropriate means — that includes us but is not completely determined by our constructions of it; (3) There is an essence and meaning in things; (4) There exist real hierarchical properties in the world, which involve scaling, the organization of living and nonliving systems, and levels of reflexivity and sensitivity; (5) There is such a thing as real progress; and (6) Any significant work in the present must include and be the culmination of the past.

From these assumptions follow the theses of this essay: (7) Beauty is a fundamental reality; (7a) Beauty, though it may be surprising, must also be familiar: it connects past and future, the known and the unknown; (7b) Beauty is culturally universal and goes beyond the subjective self and inner desire: it is a true description of the real world; (7c) Beauty is the guide of politics, as it is the core of morality and speculative understanding; it is not the handmaiden of politics; (7d) Beauty is the defining property of Being, but only if Being is conceived of as complicated, interfered-with, reflexive, epistemological and at least potentially aware in its very essence; and (8) Beauty exists only in the accepted presence of shame.

These assumptions and propositions are not an attempt to turn the clock back. The modernist and postmodernist positions were, in many ways, intellectually honorable and often brilliant attempts to solve major philosophical and social problems bequeathed by the Enlightenment and the history of Europe in general. This legacy included the Cartesian division of the world into mind and matter; the apparent linear determinism of physical nature; the logical, moral and psychological problems generated by the dogma of a single transcendent, immaterial, omniscient and omnipotent deity; a growing unease at the irresponsibility of metaphysics; the experience of apparently irreconcilable multiple frames of reference; and alienating modes of production, unjust social hierarchies and class distinctions, and the increasingly disastrous assumption of Western racial and cultural superiority.

Thus, any revision we make in the postmodern consensus, even in the noble cause of beauty, must also include a satisfactory answer to those problems the consensus has sought to address. I believe such a revision is possible, on the basis of the new set of conditions that is now emerging as we approach the end of the second millennium.

Contemporary sciences of the brain — which embrace fields as diverse as psychology, neuroanatomy, paleoanthropology, ethology, artificial intelligence, genetics and neurochemistry — simply have no use for the mind–matter distinction: the mind–body problem is not a problem any more. Nature turns out to be only partly linear and deterministic; much of the time it is nonlinear, self-organizing, unpredictable, reflexive and stable only through its own feedback processes.

New theologies have appeared, espoused by the followers of Teilhard de Chardin, James Lovelock (of the Gaia hypothesis) and Matthew Fox, and by the Process Theologians and neo-Whiteheadians. They propose an immanent, emerging deity or deities, learning their own natures through the experience of the evolution of the universe and especially through their participation in our existence. Metaphysics in the traditional sense, which sought to find some discussable realm for those entities and qualities we felt sure were real but for which we could find no place in the physical world — the soul, freedom, meaning and so on — is no longer necessary: the physical world now makes generous room for these entities, indeed demands their emergence as new physical features. *Physical science now includes metaphysics.* A whole theory of the interaction of different frames of reference, known as "evolutionary epistemology" or "dramatistics," has arisen; there is no need for a desperate relativism or a defeatist pluralism, and any discourse that can indicate the incommensurability of different frames has already transcended it.

In theory at least, emerging technologies permit us to mechanize inhumanly repetitive and alienating production practices, potentially freeing human beings to devote themselves to more creative and interesting tasks. Clearly, certain economic paradigms based on concepts of production and scarcity no longer suffice to describe emerging conditions and possibilities. The events that have gone under the name "the collapse of communism" have shown us the difficulties of attempting to eliminate hierarchy — which, in Eastern Europe, often resulted only in a dictatorship of the apparat. A democratic ideal may turn out to be not the absence of hierarchy but the ensuring that the hierarchies we construct will be flexible, just, accessible and legitimated by the consent of the governed. The increasing liquidity of all forms of value may lead to a reconfiguring of ossified class systems. Meanwhile, in a number of fields, a natural classicism, panhuman and multicultural, is already emerging as a potential alternative to older, partial and exclusive Eurocentric classicism.

This new view of the world may sound overly optimistic; indeed, it might be objected that it could turn into another attempt to eliminate or at least deny our shame as the inheritors of crime and atrocity, and of an unfinished evolutionary history. On the contrary: I believe that it will remove the obstacles to our recognition of our shame and restore to us the most fundamental and most fertile shame of all, the conscious recognition of ourselves as creatures of matter, animals that feel and think as we eat, breed and die.

Perhaps the finest description of living matter as revealed by the science of biology can be found in the excerpt from Thomas Mann's *The Magic Mountain* that serves as my epigraph. These reflections remain as deep and true today in their broad outlines as when they were written a lifetime ago. The discoveries of the structure of DNA and the function of RNA, and our first groping steps to synthesize new forms of life, have not invalidated any part of Mann's supremely wise and visionary conception. If anything, he does not go far enough: the notion of the physical inorganic universe — that "frozen chastity of the universal" — he inherited from the nineteenth century was still essentially the deterministic, linear and mechanistic one of Newton, Maupertuis and Laplace. In the last few decades, we have seen Mann's description of life as an incontinent, mysterious, self-reflective and self-organizing feedback system — extended by nonlinear chaos theory, fractal mathematics and Prigoginian dissipative systems theory — to every level of material being.

Mann calls life "shameless," and what he means is extremely complex: made capable of shame by its self-consciousness, and helplessly revealing the shameful characteristics of sensuality and desire, yet accepting that shame as the price of its privileged existence — and thus, to an observer, blushingly defiant of its proper modesty. This shameful/shameless beauty and reflexivity have now been found, in a dimmer and simpler form, to be sure, in the turbulence of liquids and gases, in phase changes such as crystallization and partial melting, even in the processes by which the elementary particles and the four forces of physics precipitated out of the primeval cosmic incandescence.

This is not to say that there is nothing linear, predictable and mechanistic in the universe, nothing pure and chaste. Each level of being might rightly regard the lower and earlier levels as more innocent than itself. If there were no *un*self-conscious, honest and straightforward objects in the world, there would be no standard by which to judge the proper degree of modesty (that is, being violated, acknowledged and reaffirmed). In fact, the anguished shame — and beauty — of the world comes not only from self-reflection itself, but from the turbulent and densely enfolded region of contrast between the relatively self-reflective and the relatively unreflective. What is most painfully and delightfully reflected upon is, after all, always the previously unreflected. Certainly there never was an unalloyed purity in the universe; the cosmos hides its privates with a fig leaf, and, if the cosmos is the body of God, then God, coyly, hides Hers too.

Many of the higher animals have, through the feedback process of evolution, added a new twist to this reflexive spiral or helix and have developed a capacity to recognize this beauty in certain limited forms. The colors and shapes of the flowers are a precise record of what bees find attractive, and it would be a paradoxically anthropocentric mistake to assume that, because bees are organisms more primitive than humans — as they indeed are — there is nothing in common between our pleasure in flowers and theirs. The play behavior of many higher species has an irreducible element of pleasure in beauty, a rejoicing in their sheer physical capacities — flight, in the case of the jackdaws (which Konrad Lorenz so lovingly observed), or the speed and power of frolicking horses, or the agility and coordination of cats. Animal communications often seem to be as much for the sake of beauty as for use, as Charles Hartshorne observed in the antiphonal music of tropical songbirds, or as has been recently remarked in the complex individual songs of humpback whales.

Most salient of all is the strong element of beauty in animal rituals, especially mating rituals. It is important to look closely at how such rituals function and evolve, because their implications for our own rituals are very interesting. Generally, when a survival behavior can be accomplished easily, without contradicting other instinctive behaviors, it is done automatically and without fuss and fanfare: breathing, perspiring, sleeping and waking. We do not notice such behaviors as "drives"; they are more a part of what an animal is than what it is driven to do. When two behaviors contradict each other, however, a space between them is sometimes formed that does not belong strictly to either. The animal now must use its nervous system to the utmost; one can see a squirrel or sparrow thinking when its natural and uncomplicated fear of humans is contradicted by its natural and uncomplicated desire for the crust of bread one has put out for it.

When the two contradictory behaviors are both social, their intersection can become the stage for the most elaborate and beautiful displays, dances, songs, even dramas (as when, in the triumph ceremony of the greylag geese that Lorenz describes, the heroic lover attacks an imaginary counterfactual enemy goose as a sign of its exclusive devotion to the beloved). In mating ritual, reproductive behavior is contradicted by territorial or intraspecific aggressive behavior. An area between them is opened in which the linearity of an uncontradicted system will no longer work, and elaborate, nonlinear, highly self-reflexive and mutually reflexive feedback processes take over. Here the linear mathematics of continuous functions no longer applies, and the mathematics of catastrophic and fractal discontinuity comes into its own.

When this immediate individual-to-individual feedback system is supplemented, in turn, by the much larger and slower feedback system of evolution, remarkable changes and developments can take place in a species as a whole. Mating rituals directly affect the reproductive success of an individual: thus, an individual with better ritual pigmentation, better plumage, better looking reproductive organs, better songs and dances, or better antlers with which to stage the gladiatorial games of sexual rivalry, will most likely produce more progeny — and the genes for those qualities can rapidly pervade the gene pool of the species, crowding out the others. Hence the beautiful feathers of the peacock, with their fractal designs, the neon displays of tropical fishes and the extraordinary artistic activities of the blue satin bowerbird, whose courtship involves building an elaborate and useless bower on the ground, which is decorated with colored objects and even painted with the juice of berries. Hence also the development of the elaborate tribal structure and status hierarchy of our close relatives the baboons, chimpanzees and gorillas. The guenon monkeys have differentiated themselves into dozens of microspecies, purely, it would seem, on the basis of their body decoration.

More ominously, as a result of such feedback, some species have developed ritual behaviors, and the structures required for them, to such an extent that their very survival is threatened: the giant elk is thought to have disappeared because the antlers of the male, used for ritual combat, became too large and heavy for its body. The peacock's tail attracts predators no less than potential mates. It is commonplace for individual animals to sacrifice their lives for the opportunity to mate; anyone who has seen the tragic and gorgeous spawning run of the chinook salmon in their brilliant and terrifying nuptial/funereal colors will recognize the kinship with our own bittersweet dramas of passion. Humankind is not the only species that does not live for bread alone, that can risk all for love.

The realm of life groans with the contradictions of sexual reproduction. Sexual reproduction comes in a package that includes programmed individual death. Sex was itself a response to the very theme of life, which is acceleration in the ecological transformation of the world (we must remember that most of the remarkable developments of the higher species of life occurred in the last couple of hundred million years, and that for over three billion years before that, life changed much more slowly). However, even those slow changes and the alterations in the ecology that they brought about would have begun to overload the adaptive capacities of asexually reproducing (self-cloning) organisms. Sex was a biological innovation whose survival value was to increase the extent and speed of adaptation to natural change. Without sex, the enormous recent acceleration in the rate of evolutionary change could not have occurred. However, for sex to work — for there to be room for those sexually produced, monstrous, infantile and protean organisms that might be the progenitors of new species — it required its dark twin, programmed death. An asexually reproducing organism is relatively immortal — that is, it takes an external force or deprivation to kill it; but in a sexually reproducing organism, a cell that turns off its own death-program becomes a cancer cell.

Even earlier, the appearance of life itself might be interpreted as a response to apparently irreconcilable contradictions inherent in matter. (Here I must acknowledge deep debts to J. T. Fraser and the International Society for the Study of Time.) When matter condensed out of energy, it bought a long and stable endurance at the cost of abandoning the uncommitted and flexible quantum indeterminacy of its radiant substance. The trouble with energy is that, left to itself, it flies off radially from itself at the speed of light and dissipates according to the inverse square law; and by thus blowing up the envelope of space-time that it carries with it everywhere, it flattens out the very curvature of space-time from which it derives its being and intensity in the first place. If this was survival, survival was pretty trivial — an unbearable lightness of being.

Matter was more sober. It stayed in one place and took a part in the local history of the universe, recording and reacting to local events, collapsing the indeterminacy of incident bundles of energy into definite events and work, affecting other bodies and thus confirming both its own existence and that of its neighbors. It could act. It took on, like mortgages, many new forms of linear determinism, which we express in the laws of physics and chemistry. But the forms of matter, though enduring, did not possess the immortality of energy: they could be shattered or melted and could not repair themselves, except in the very limited way in which crystals can reform themselves out of a melt along the same planes and angles.

Life solved this problem by means of its power to replicate itself; and thus the form or pattern of life could survive its material substrate, as a sonnet survives when it is copied from an old book, destined for the flames, and given a new printing. And, in solving this problem, life took on all the quivering ambivalence that Mann describes; each new solution to the contradictions of existence raises new contradictions. These contradictions are in fact the general and original forms of which shame is perhaps the latest and most elaborated, most explicitly reflexive development. But these contradictions are also the spurs to the emergence of new and more exquisite forms — and "beauty" is the word we use to describe that emergence.

Before I go on to discuss human ritualization, I would like to present a final, even more speculative note on the history and evolution of the universe (upon which a group of philosophers including Koen de Pryck, Alexander Argyros, Karel Boullart and I have been working). We believe that the pattern I have described — the emergence of a whole new level of existence from a contradiction or insoluble paradox in the previous, more primitive level, and the discovery that the new level itself contains its own peculiar tragic problems — resembles for good reason the concentric nested pattern of transcendent logics generated by Gödel's Incompleteness Theorem.

Gödel proved that for any system of mathematics or logic there would be a permissible proposition of the form of "this statement is not provable," whose truth or falsehood could not be proved within the axiomatic resources of the system itself. There may be a larger system that can decide the truth or falsehood of the proposition — the human mind, for instance, is such a system, and it can easily see that the proposition is both true and unprovable — but such a system would in turn produce paradoxes unsolvable in its own terms. Roger Penrose points out elegantly that a Turing machine — that is, the perfect linear calculator — must, in order to give a complete answer to a problem, be able to tell itself to stop. Problems of this kind are such that a Turing machine can never stop, once it is engaged in their calculation. There must be a level jump — as when we tire of calculating pi to another ten thousand decimal places and turn off the supercomputer, or, more subtly, when we recognize that a mathematical series is converging toward a limit, discontinue the calculation of the series and either obtain the limit by other means or use the limit to whatever decimal place we choose to round it off.

Perhaps the physical universe itself emerged as the new level in which the solution to problems inherent in a primal mathematics might be found — perhaps the world is the only solution of a logical paradox. Perhaps space and time emerged as ways to keep contradictory propositions "artificially" apart, where they could not interfere with each other. Thus, the Pauli Exclusion Principle, which ensures that no two particles can occupy the same state and place and time, may be the only way that the cosmic logic could find to solve certain inherent violations of the law of noncontradiction.

Are we like Turing machines ourselves, then, with some appalling proposition waiting for us, in whose attempted solution we will be unable to turn ourselves off? Or can we contemplate the mandala of being, its concentric circles of more and more fundamental contradictions, and so transcend the system itself? Are we always able to recognize that the calculation is converging toward a limit or an attractor and thus to free ourselves from that final trap? Is not death, inquires the Belgian philosopher Karel Boullart, simply our arrival as organisms at such a problem?

And is not shame, perhaps, the anguish that we feel when we recognize that there may be a viewpoint in which we ourselves are as trapped and helpless as a lower organism, as the living flesh of which our bodily substrate is made, as the wretched Turing machine that goes into the paralysis of not being able to turn itself off? Might we be in some other mind's gaze a comic automaton, another lower organism whose true being is revealed, as David Lindsay put it, in the cheap and vulgar rictus of death? And is not the shame of sexual nakedness precisely its reminder of the ancient double-bind, of the Gödelian paradox itself, that we cannot account for our own existence?

Consider the human body and its remarkable differences from the bodies of other mammals. One of the most obvious is our nakedness; we stand hairless but for odd tufts here and there emphasizing such body parts as the head and face, and the genitals. All other land mammals of our size, and all of our primate relatives (including all tropical primates), are covered with hair. Some much larger tropical species, like elephants and rhinoceroses, are, indeed, also hairless — presumably because their greater size implies a higher ratio of body volume to body surface, and a larger and more stable thermal reservoir, and thus they need no hair. Human beings, however, are more than pantropic in our habitat — we live in all climates — and are much smaller; without clothing and shelter, we would be, in many cases, at a lethal disadvantage.

It is a truism of evolutionary logic that if a given bodily structure (such as hair) is unnecessary and cannot be adapted to another purpose, those individuals that possess it will be at a disadvantage, if only because of the metabolic drain on their resources that the structure's production and upkeep entails. This disadvantage will tend statistically to result in fewer such individuals surviving to reproduce, a thinning out of the genes for that structure in the population, and a preferential rate of increase for genes not specifying that structure. The same applies in reverse: if a species would be better off *with* hair, say, to maintain a constant body temperature, hair will be selected for. As we have seen in the case of the peacock's tail and the elk's antlers, however, sexual ritual can contradict this biological law.

The most plausible explanation for our relative hairlessness — or indeed, nakedness — is that it results from sexual selection in ritual courtship, and that we developed clothing originally both for ritual body decoration and also to replace, for thermal purposes, the hair that we had lost. The invention of clothes, a by-product of our ritual, enabled us to survive even in cool temperate and arctic climates; and so, as hair was no longer necessary for survival, it never came back. Thus, our nakedness is a result of our early culture.

And here we see a new principle of reflexive feedback enter the already tangled, iterative and turbulent process of natural evolution. Cultural evolution — that is, a process of change in behavior that can happen in a single generation and be passed down through imitation and learning to the next — now takes a hand not only in biological evolution but also the iterated cycle of sexually or mutatively generated variation, selection through the preferential survival of useful traits in the population, and genetic inheritance. Biological evolution takes millennia; cultural evolution takes years. Yet the culture of a species, especially in its effect on sexual and reproductive success, is a powerful determinant of which individuals survive to reproduce. The faster process of change — culture — will drive and guide the slower one — biology.

Many of the other peculiar characteristics of the human body can be explained in the same way: its upright stance, its long infancy, its developed vocal chords and otolaryngeal system, its extraordinary longevity (especially in the female), its relatively early menopause, its lack of specialized armaments — big teeth, claws and so on — its opposable thumbs, its superbly refined and coordinated fine motor system, its continuous sexual readiness (most animals are in heat only for a few days in the year), the apparent evolutionary morphology of its brain.

The upright stance reveals the full beauty of one's own and another's primary and secondary sexual organs, and it enables hunters and gatherers to carry the fruits of their labors home (and perhaps then to remember who gets which share) — for which, moreover, it helps us to have a home to carry things home to, thus a ritually charged place, and a kinship system that determines the rules of distribution. The upright stance also enables parents to carry in their arms babies who are helpless because they require a much longer infancy period than the young of other species, a long infancy demanded by the need to inculcate children in the complexities of tribal ritual. The upright stance, moreover, undoubtedly contributed to changing the mating position from mounting to face-to-face, thus encouraging that extraordinary mutual gaze which is the delight of lovers and the fundamental warrant of the equality of the sexes — an equality that was absolutely essential if the human traits of intelligence, communication and imagination were to be preferred and thus reinforced.

Our ritual songs, improved every year, demanded complex voice-production systems, which could then become useful for communication in the hunt and other cooperative enterprises. Our long old age enabled the elders — especially the longer-lived postmenopausal wisewomen — to pass on ritual lore and wisdom. Our lack of bodily armament was compensated for by the development of weapons, which could be wielded by thumbed hands liberated by our upright stance and controlled by an advanced fine motor system — thumbed hands required to enact the ritual actions and paint on the ritual body paint and carry the ritual objects and make the ritual clothing and gather the seeds and roots for our tribal kin. Sexuality was extended and intensified relative to other animals, and was adapted from its original reproductive function into the raw material of an elaborate ritual drama that pervaded all aspects of society.

And the brain mushroomed out, transforming its substructures to the new uses and demands that were being placed on it, pushing out the skull, diminishing the jaws, wiring itself more and more finely into the face, hands and speech organs, specializing particular areas of its right and left sides to handle new linguistic, musical and pictorial-representational tasks, developing a huge frontal lobe to coordinate everything else and to reflect upon itself and its body and its death, and connecting that higher level reflective consciousness by massive nerve bundles to the limbic emotional centers — thus creating a unity of function between the intellectual and the passionate that is close to the heart of our deepest shame, and which has thus been denied by most of our priestly philosophical systems.

From this viewpoint, personal physical beauty perhaps takes on a new importance. Breeders of dogs and horses can tell by very subtle physical signs — the carriage of the head, the set of the eye, the delicacy of proportion — whether the animal is likely to possess psychological characteristics

such as intelligence, heart and concentration. The intangible elements of human beauty as well —
beyond those obviously related to reproductive and survival success — are potentially such external bodily signs of internal neural sophistication. Those intangible elements that we refer to when
we say that someone has beautiful eyes or a beautiful expression, or that we are captured by someone's way of moving — the things that make us watch a great film star — can be quite different from
conventional beauty. They can quickly overwhelm any deficiency in the brute appeal of standardized images of sexual attractiveness. The lovely ambiguity in the word "grace" — divine favor and
excellence in physical coordination — nicely catches this other quality; though, in the context of
the darker price of human excellence, it is significant that grace is also a purifying blessing (from
Old English *blissian*, to wound or make bleed) before meals. When we fall in love, perhaps mate
and have offspring, we do so often because we are captured by such qualities. Thus, we look the
way we do as a species largely because that was the way our ancestors thought intelligent, strong,
loving and imaginative — ritual-ready — animals ought to look. We are the monument to our
progenitors' taste.

Many of our creation myths show an intuitive grasp of the strange process by which the cultural tail came to wag the biological dog. The story of the clothing of Adam and Eve, where (the
awareness of) nakedness is the result of shame, which is in turn the result of self-knowledge,
expresses one aspect of it. Again in Genesis, Eve's punishment for her acquisition of knowledge,
that she must suffer in childbirth, expresses the fact that one aspect of our viviparous species,
whose cranium at birth is large relative to its size at maturity, is the capacity of the female pelvis
to allow the passage of a large skull — hence also the beauty for the male of the female's wide hips.
The larger (and to the heterosexual male, attractive) breasts of the human female, and her dependency upon a protecting male during lactation — also referred to in Genesis — are likewise the
sign of a nurturing power that can deal with a long infant dependency, and thus produce human
beings of intelligence, wisdom and aesthetic subtlety. Infants without protecting fathers must
enter adulthood earlier and cannot be fully instructed in tribal ritual; they thus need smaller
brains, and smaller hipped and breasted mothers to bear them.

Our deep feelings of embarrassment and anger at these facts, the flush that rises to our faces
when we think of our own biology, are the signs of that shame we would deny but whose acceptance is the only gate to beauty. That beauty is summed up in the great pictorial genre of the
mother and child. At present, this tragic contradiction makes itself felt in our society by a conflict
between female roles — of a nurturing that produces the best and noblest and most loving human
intelligence, and of the very exercise of that intelligence. The means and the end of nurturance are
thus perceived as opposed in our society. But we should not deceive ourselves by believing that
were this problem solved, the solution itself would not produce its own contradictions just as
tragic and shameful.

One persistent theme of creation myths all over the world is the presence of a trickster, who
somehow transforms the forces of nature so that they assist rather than hinder the cultural program. The story of Odysseus tricking Polyphemos, the caveman, into rolling away the rock door
of his cave is one such myth; South American jaguar tales, in which fire is adapted to human use,

have the same gist. We find in these myths both the shame of our mistreatment of our mother, nature, and the nostalgia for the beautiful arcadian landscape that we like to imagine as having preexisted the birth of self-consciousness. Polyphemos lives on the slopes of Etna, by the vale of Enna where the fountain of Arethusa rises, mingled with the waters of her pursuer, the arcadian river-god Alpheus; where Proserpina wandered before her rape by Dis; the loveliest arcadian landscape of all, the closest to the volcano and the source of fire, painted by Bellini and sung of in Handel's *Acis and Galatea*.

If the human ritual as I have envisaged it was to have its original evolutionary function, it must have involved a dark and terrible element: for if some members of the tribe enjoyed greater reproductive success, others must have enjoyed less. If some were selected as preferred mates for their intelligence, wit, loving nature, prudence, magnanimity, honesty, courage, depth, sanguine disposition, foresight, empathy, physical health, beauty, grace and strength then others — the dullards, whiners, liars, blowhards, hoarders, spendthrifts, thieves, cheats and weaklings — must have been rejected. The most brutal throwbacks — the rapists, those who grabbed food but did not share, those who could not follow the subtle turns of the ritual and internalize the values that it invented and implied — would be cast out from the tribal cave, into the outer darkness. Defective infants would be abandoned on the mountainside; adults polluted by impiety, crime, incest, madness, disease or their abuse of sacred practices would be led to the borders of the village lands and expelled. Oedipus, who was exposed, though not defective at birth, is among other things a symbol of our guilt at such rejection: when he does return, as all buried shames must, he pollutes the city with his unconscious incest. The old English monster Grendel, that wanderer of the borderlands, the descendant of Cain, is another type of such an outcast and the image of the scapegoat.

But, indeed, the fragile virtues of the human race would have been impossible without this terrible and most shameful selection process. If we consider how morally imperfect we are, it may be a grim satisfaction to reflect how much worse we would be if we had not selected ourselves for love and goodness. Abraham's willingness to sacrifice his son Isaac at God's command (whom we may take, for mythic purposes, to be the evolutionary imperative of the human species, the strange attractor drawing it into being) is necessary, paradoxically, to bring about a more loving and more just humanity. We had better be worth the price.

Indeed, our moral growth has, more recently, caused us to recoil in revulsion from those ancient practices; but that growth was partly their result. The process has not ceased, and we had better face up to that fact. Every time a woman chooses a man to be her husband and the father of her children, for any good personal reason — for his gentleness and his wit, his confident strength and his decent humility — she is selecting against some other man less noble in character, and either helping to condemn him to the nonentity of childlessness or to be the parent, with some less morally perceptive woman, of children who are likely to inherit their parents' disadvantages. It is horribly cruel and shameful, if we think about it, but I believe there is a strange and terrible beauty to the magnitude of the mating choice — and it is at the root of the troubled exaltation we sometimes feel at a good wedding.

The rituals of sacrifice, which survive the European tradition as tragedy or passover or eucharist, are the human way of rendering this ancient horror into beauty. Sacrifice has a peculiar element, which we might call "commutation": every sacrifice commemorates a previous sacrifice, in which some much more terrible act of bloody violence or costly loss was required. Abraham is allowed to sacrifice a ram instead of his son (and instead of a whole firstborn son, only a shred of flesh from the foreskin need be given); the ancient Greeks burned the fat and bones and hide of the bull and ate the flesh themselves. And as the process is transformed into a ritual recognized as such, the sacrificed object can become apparently rather trivial. Cucumbers are sacrificed in some African tribal societies; Catholics and Buddhists burn candles; almost all Christians break bread. Thus, every sacrifice is an act of impurity that pays for a prior act of greater impurity, but pays for it at an advantage, that is, without its participants having to suffer the full consequences incurred by its predecessor. The punishment is commuted in a process that strangely combines and finesses the deep contradiction between justice and mercy.

The process of commutation also has much in common with the processes of metaphorization, symbolization, even reference or meaning itself. The Christian eucharistic sacrifice of bread not only *stands in* for the sacrifice of Christ (which in turn stands in for the death of the whole human race); it also *means*, and in Catholic sacramental theology *is*, the death of Christ. The Greek tragic drama both referred to, and was a portion of, the sacrificial rites of Dionysos — both a mention and a use, as logicians say, or both a metaphor and a synecdoche, in the language of rhetoricians. The word "commutation" nicely combines these senses: in general use, it means any substitution or exchange, as when money in one currency is changed into another or into small change, or when payment in one form is permitted to be made in another; in alchemy it can be almost synonymous with transmutation, as of one metal into another; in criminal jurisprudence it refers to the reasoned lightening of one punishment to another that is less severe but is taken as its juridical equivalent; in electrical engineering it is the reversal of a current or its transformation between direct and alternating current; in mathematical logic it refers to the equivalency of a given operation, such as a multiplied by b, to its reverse, b multiplied by a.

Shakespeare's *The Merchant of Venice* is a profound meditation on the nature of commutation in all these senses: on the commutative relationships between the three thousand ducats, the friendship of Antonio and Bassanio, the pound of flesh, the life of Antonio, the livelihood of Shylock, the wedding ring of Portia and the body of Portia in marriage; between the ducats and the daughter, between inanimate metal, dead flesh, live flesh and the living spirit. The play is most deeply about how sacrifice is the meaning of meaning. What it implies for our own time, I think, is that the death of sacrifice is the death of meaning. The crisis in modern philosophy over the meaning of the word "reference" — and this is the heart of it — has its roots in the denial of shame and thus the denial of commutativeness. For reference and meaning to come back to life, some deep sacrifice is required. Perhaps that sacrifice has been made already, and it is for us to recognize it as such.

The invention of ritual sacrifice, or rather perhaps its elaboration and adaptation from the division of the spoils of the hunt and the disposal of the bodies of the dead, may have begun a process of increasing suppression of the protohuman eugenics I have described. The commutation process gradually took the teeth out of social selection. Instead of the normal expulsion or killing of the polluted, there was occasional human sacrifice; instead of actual human sacrifice, scapegoat animals were killed. More and more egalitarian religious ideas arose, as in the anti-elitist cults of Krishna and of the Buddha in the Hindu tradition, the Greco-Roman myths of the gods in disguise as beggars, the social criticism of the Jewish Prophets and the Christian warning that the last shall be first and the first last. A larger and larger proportion of the population was permitted to have offspring. Tribalism came to be despised. Aristocratic ideas of the inheritance of good blood went into decline. Meanwhile a celibate priesthood came into being in many traditions, clearly and unambiguously signaling that reproductive success was no longer the reward for ritual excellence.

We rightly condemn eugenics and applaud the increasing humaneness — the humanity — of the emerging civilized morality. The word "human" itself means the rejection of the terrible process by which we became human. And if commutation in this sense also means meaning, then meaning is in another way the same thing as sacrifice.

If we think, though, that we can safely suppress the memories of how we became human and of the price of our new freedom, we are quite wrong. To reject such practices should not mean repressing them from our memory; and if we forget them, the basis of our shame and of our beauty as the paragon of animals, we may find ourselves repeating them in some time of terrible stress. And we are indeed at this time trying to repress them. The symptoms of that repression are manifold: our contemporary demonization of technology (while we use it only the more avidly); our attempt to make sexual intercourse shameless by detaching it psychologically from reproduction, family, deep and emotional commitments, and any implication of psychobiological differentiation between the sexes; our bad conscience about racism, animal "rights" and abortion; our inability to face the meaning of the Holocaust, not to mention our willful ignorance of other incidents of genocide; and the element of rabid superstition in our fear that we are destroying Mother Nature. We have few rituals left to enable us to accept and take on the burden of our inescapable impurity.

In giving up *tribal* eugenics, we have irrevocably declared our commitment to technology. As civilization matured, as we have seen, it kept the routine *individual* eugenics implicit in the choice of reproductive partner; in one sense, we could say that the move toward civilization is a move toward an increasing democratization of reproductive choice. Instead of the tribal collectivity deciding who should not have children, we all did, individually, by discriminating against every potential reproductive partner but the one we chose. The selective process was thus rendered weaker, more subtle, less consistent and much more variable.

In contemporary society, where certain sexual practices, medical interventions and birth control tend to frustrate the process of genetic selection through reproductive success, we are in the process of giving up even the individual option for selecting and passing on valued information by genetic means. Still, over the last few thousand years we have been developing other means of passing on such information: oral poetry, writing, the arts, organized social institutions and now computers and other advanced electronic technology. These systems have become the DNA of a new, inconceivably swifter and more complex form of life, a new twist in the evolutionary spiral.

I do not present the foregoing discussion of the complex relations of sacrifice, evolution and meaning as an assertion of a clear moral position — because, as such, whatever moral outcome we chose would involve a tragic revulsion against other moral principles we hold to be of unchallengeable validity. For instance, if we choose the ancient tribal values of the human species, we must also choose collective eugenics, racism and blood sacrifice — or contrive somehow to detach the parts of this package, thus denaturing them of their moral weight. If we choose reproductive freedom, we must also choose advanced informational and biological technology, and find some way of dealing with a human neuropsychological makeup that needs families and primary caregivers. The only proper way to make such an argument is perhaps in a tragic play; but tragic drama requires for its audience a society that has some intellectual grasp of the necessary irreconcilability of our moral and logical conflicts. This essay is intended as a step toward such an understanding; and if it could be a preface to a true tragic drama, it would have fulfilled the true function of criticism, which is to enable beauty to be born out of its own despairing shame.

Two further points about the biology of beauty must be made before I can sum up the argument. The first concerns beauty as a pleasure, the second beauty as analogous to, and a further development of, perception.

The experience of beauty is, among other things, a pleasure. It is now known that such pleasure is mediated by a highly complex brain chemistry involving at least two groups of neuropeptides, endorphins and enkephalins. These molecules are produced as the result of certain activities and experiences in the body or brain; they bind to receptor sites in the neuron and change its activity, either facilitating the transfer of electrochemical information across the synapses or ordering a halt to a completed exchange of stimuli throughout a given system of neural pathways — a completion that we perhaps feel as the satisfaction of coming to a conclusion, as Frank Kermode's "sense of an ending."

These neuropeptides are also known to be implicated in laying down the initial tracks that the dendrites will follow, as they connect the neurons up with each other in the fetal and infant brain. They can also help alter the shape of the synaptic cleft so as to make it permanently more transmissive — in other words, they help lay down memories — and they catalyze the molecular component of memory (part of memory is recorded, much as DNA records biological memory, in complex, long-chain molecules). They seem to have a role in activating and toning up the immune system, and thus pleasure is not only a result of health but a cause of it. They also help to control the hormone system of the body, whereby we mature and attain sexual readiness; and are even subtly implicated in the brain's perception of the passing of time.

Put another way, pleasure, and in particular the pleasure of beauty, is a reward that the brain is designed by evolution to give itself for accomplishing certain creative tasks. Addictive drugs, such as heroin and cocaine, mimic the pleasure peptides in their molecular structure, and thus interfere with the brain's own motivational system: literally stealing the soul, by subverting the purpose of pleasure. The pleasure of eating clearly rewards the effort and concentration of foraging; the pleasure of sex rewards the metabolically expensive process of finding a mate and reproducing the species. What does the pleasure of beauty reward, so very highly developed in human beings, so strongly selected for by human evolution, so subtle and fugitive, so easily suppressed when we deny the shame of our existence, and yet so irresistible when it has us in its power?

Before we can begin to answer this question we need one more piece of the biological puzzle. Let us play with an idea of Kant's and see where we get if we treat the experience of beauty as something analogous to, but higher than, feeling a sensation or perceiving an object.

Imagine dropping a rock on the floor. The rock *reacts*, perhaps, by bouncing and by making a noise, but we would not imagine that the rock feels anything. Now imagine that we drop a worm on the floor; the impact might cause it to squirm, as well as merely bounce and produce a sound of impact. The worm, we would say, *feels a sensation*; but from the worm's point of view, it is not a sensation of anything in particular; the worm does not construct, with its primitive nerve ganglia, anything like an external world filled with objects like floors and experimenters.

Now imagine that we drop a guinea pig. Clearly, it would react as the rock does, and also feel sensations as the worm does. But we would say, in addition, that it *perceives* the floor, the large dangerous experimenter-animal that dropped it and the dark place under the table where it might be safe. Perception is as much beyond sensation as sensation is beyond mere physical reaction: it constructs a precise, individuated world of solid objects, endowed with color, shape, smell, and acoustic and tactile properties. It is generous to the outside world, giving it properties it did not necessarily possess until some advanced vertebrate was able, through its marvelously parsimonious cortical world-construction system, to provide them. Perception is more global, more holistic, than sensation — because it takes into account an entire outside world — and it is more exact, more particular, for it recognizes individual objects and parts of objects.

Now, if both experimenter and subject were not merely humans but, say, dancers, a yet more astonishing capacity comes into play. One could write a novel about how the dance partners experience this drop, this gesture. Whole detailed worlds of implication, of past and future, of interpretive frames come into being; and the table, now a dance floor, does not lose any of the guinea pig's reality, but instead takes on richnesses, subtleties, significant details, held as they are within a context vaster and more clearly understood.

What is this awareness that is to perception what perception is to sensation, and what sensation is to reaction? The answer is the beauty experience. Beauty experience is more constructive, more generous to the outside world, more holistic and more exact and particularizing than ordinary perception, much as ordinary perception is more than mere sensation. Beauty perception is not a vague and touchy-feely thing relative to ordinary perception — quite the contrary. This is why, given an infinite number of theories that will logically explain the facts, scientists will sensibly always choose the most beautiful theory. For good reason: This is the way the world works.

Nor is the dancer, because he or she is a self-aware human being, any the less a perceiving animal like the guinea pig, or a sensing organism like the worm, or a piece of matter subject to, and the source of, the physical effects of electromagnetism and gravitation, like the rock. In fact, part of the richness of his or her experience lies in the dissonances between those levels — the determinism of the world of kinetic energy as against the freedom of the world of dancerly expressiveness, the wormlike solipsism of the bruised cells of the foot as against the mammal awareness of the room, its colors and light and movement. And herein lies the accepted shame of the dancer's art, the athletic body pushed to its limits, the bead of sweat, the straining tendon; the high excitement of mastery almost compromised by the autonomous tremor of a muscle, the unearthly grace given pathos by its mortal animality.

Beauty in this view is the highest integrative level of understanding and the most comprehensive capacity for effective action. It enables us to go with, rather than against, the deepest tendency or theme of the universe: to be able to model what will happen and adapt to or change it. It integrates or focuses the different levels of reality, while recognizing their conflicts, as in the martial arts, where spiritual, mental, emotional and physical energies are concentrated together into the perfect strike or block. Such benefits might well be worth the enormous metabolic expense of the brain, that organ that spends a third of the body's oxygen and sugar, and for which the body will willingly sacrifice itself.

What, then, to conclude, is the pleasure of beauty a reward for? First, for the exercise of the peculiar spiritual skills demanded by the human ritual; second, for the encounter with, acceptance of, and passing-through of the shame of mortal self-awareness; third, for a special integrative sensibility that is partly anticipated in the instinctive preferences of animals, a sensitivity to what is the general tendency or theme of the universe, its self-organizing process; and fourth, for the exercise of the human capacity to continue and deepen that process into new realms of being.

Autobahn bridge near Neanderthal, Rhineland, c. 1936. August Sander

"All strategic roads were built by tyrants and go straight across the country. The other roads wind like processions and waste everybody's time." (Adolph Hitler) The Reichsautobahn Agency, created in 1933, was part of a comprehensive public works program whose real goal was to install the engineering infrastructure that would later sustain the National Socialist military campaign. Conceived as a colossal *Gesamtkunstwerk* expressing both the "German essence" and the harmoniously undulating landscape in which it thrived, the guiding princi- ple behind the autobahn's construction — "uniformity in all aspects" — provided a powerful sensual image that literally laid the foundations for national conformity.

Unfolding Events

Peter Eisenman

In all of the design arts we are experiencing a paradigm shift from mechanical to electronic modes of production; from an age of interpretative techniques to one of mediation. Thus mechanical reproduction (the photograph) differs from electronic reproduction (the facsimile); in the former, transformation — and therefore interpretation — may occur between original and reproduction; in the latter, there is no change, that is, no interpretation, and it is in this sense that one might say the electronic reproduction has no essence. While in both cases the value of an original is thrown into question, mediated reproduction poses a different value system precisely because it involves no interpretation. Contemporary media undermine the essence and aura not only of the original, but of the very nature of reality. Media environments such as advertising and synthetic realities such as Disney World have become so potent that they might be said to form a new reality. Whereas architecture formerly served as a baseline for reality — bricks and mortar, house and home, structure and foundation were the metaphors that anchored our reality — what constitutes reality today is not so clear.

Traditionally, architecture was placebound, linked to a condition of experience. Today, mediated environments challenge the givens of classical time, the time of experience: on any afternoon anywhere in the world, whether at the Prado in Madrid or the Metropolitan in New York, hordes of people pass before artworks, hardly stopping to see, at best perhaps merely photographing their experience. They have no time for the original, even less for the experience of the original. Due to media, the time of experience has changed; the soundbite — infinitesimal, discontinuous, autonomous — has conditioned our new time.

Architecture can no longer be bound by the static conditions of space and place, here and there. In a mediated world, there are no longer places in the sense that we once knew them. Architecture must now address the problem of the event. Today, rock concerts may be considered the archetypal form of architectural event. People go to rock concerts not to listen — because one cannot merely "hear" the music — *but to become part of the environment.* This is a new type of environment, comprised of light, sound, movement, an event-structure in which architecture does not simply stand against media, but is consumed by it. Media deals neither with physical facts nor with interpretation, but rather with the autonomous condition of electronic reproduction. With amplified sound and engineered lighting, the rock concert attempts to deny physical presence. Although architecture cannot accomplish this, it can propose an alternative — some other kind of event, one in which a displacement of the static environment is not merely an electronic one-liner but, rather, an interpretation in which the environment is problematized, in which the event comes between sign and object.

Traditional architectural theory largely ignores the idea of the event. Rather, it assumes that there are two static conditions of object: figure and ground. These in turn give rise to two dialectical modes of building. One mode concerns figure–ground contextualism, which assumes a reversible and interactive relationship between the solid building blocks and the voids between them. A typical exemplar of contextualism would say that in any historical context there are latent structures capable of forming a present-day urbanism. The other mode concerns the point block or linear slab isolated on a tabula rasa ground. Here, there is no relationship between old and new, figure and ground. Rather, the ground is seen as a clear neutral datum, projecting its autonomy into the future. In each case, the terms "figure/object" and "ground" are both determinant and all-encompassing: they are thought to explain the totality of urbanism. As in most disciplines, though, such all-encompassing totalities have come into question; they are no longer thought to explain the true complexity of phenomena. This is certainly true of urbanism.

What is needed is the possibility of reading figure/object and ground within another frame of reference. Such a new reading might reveal other conditions that may always have been immanent or repressed in the urban fabric. Such a reframing would perhaps allow for the possibilities of new urban structures and for existing structures to be seen in a way that they too are redefined. In such a displacement, the new, rather than being understood as fundamentally different from the old, would instead be seen as slightly out of focus in relation to what exists. This out-of-focus condition, then, would permit a blurring or displacing of the whole, which is both old and new. One such possibility of displacement can be found in the form of the *fold*.

It was Leibniz who first conceived of matter as explosive. He turned his back on Cartesian rationalism, and argued that in the labyrinth of the continuous the smallest element is not the point but the fold. From Leibniz, one can turn to the ideas of two contemporary thinkers concerning the fold: one is Gilles Deleuze, the other is René Thom. In the idea of the fold, form is seen as continuous even as it articulates possible new relationships between vertical and horizontal, figure and ground, breaking up the existing Cartesian order of space.

Deleuze says the first condition for Leibniz's event is *extension*, in the sense of a philosophical movement outward along a plane rather than downward into a depth. Deleuze argues that in mathematical studies of variation, the notion of the object is changed: it is no longer defined by an essential form. This new object he calls an "object-event," an "objectile" — a modern conception of a technological object. This new object, for Deleuze, is no longer concerned with framing space but, rather, with a temporal modulation that implies a continual variation of matter, unfolding through the agency of the fold (an idea first defined in the Baroque). He differentiates between the Gothic, which privileges the elements of construction, frame and enclosure, and the Baroque, which emphasizes a matter overflowing its boundaries, and before which the frame eventually disappears. Deleuze states that the fold/unfold are the constants today in the idea of an object-event.

This linking of fold and event also influences work in other disciplines, notably the mathematics of Thom. In his catastrophe theory, Thom defines seven elementary events or transformations, which allow no classical symmetry, hence no possibility of a static object (for there is no privileged plan of projection). Instead, there is a neutral surface formed from a variable curvature or a fold. This variable curvature is the inflection of pure event. For Thom, the structure of the event of change already inheres in the object; it cannot be seen but can be modeled (in the neutral surface of the catastrophe fold). Thus, while a single grain of sand can trigger a landslide, we cannot know which grain or when; but the conditions leading up to the moment of movement can already be seen to be in place in the structure. Thom proposed his seven forms of catastrophe to account precisely for how object-events unfold.

In one sense, then, catastrophe theory can explain abrupt changes in state or form, such as figure to ground, urban to rural, commercial to housing, by means of complex folds that remain unseen. This quality of the unseen folding deals with the fact that it neither stands out from nor looks like the old but is somewhere between the old and the new, an in-between or third figure. It can never be neutral; the fold is neither figure nor ground but contains aspects of both. Architecture can interpret the fold, which is essentially planar in three-dimensional volumes, but not merely as an extrusion from a plan (as in traditional architecture), but rather as something that affects both plan and section. The neutral surface of the catastrophic fold already exists between figure and ground, between plan and section, yet it is homogenous; it is not merely the *appearance* of a third, rather, it *is* a third in its own being.

By introducing the concept of the fold as a nondialectical third condition, one between figure and ground yet reconstituting the nature of both, it becomes possible to reframe what is extant on any site. Such a reframing would express that which was repressed by former systems of authority — analytical or otherwise — and transform it into potentially new interpretations of existing organizations.

The fold, I want to argue, becomes the site of all the repressed immanent conditions of existing urbanism, which at a certain point, like the grain of sand that causes the landslide, has the potential not to destroy existing urbanism but to set it off in a new direction. The fold gives the traditional idea of edge new dimension: what was seen as an abrupt line now has a volumetric dimension, which both mediates and reframes conditions such as old and new, transport and arrival, commerce and housing — the fold is not merely a formal device, but a way of unfolding new social organizations from existing urban environments.

Thus, as we near the end of one era and are about to enter a new one, there is an opportunity to reassess the entire idea of a static urbanism that deals only with objects, not with events. In a media age, static objects are no longer as meaningful as timely events, in which the temporal dimension of the present merges past and future.

Earthquake, 1990
Glass, steel, photographs, lights and motor
69 x 48 1/2 x 15 1/2 inches.
Jon Kessler
Courtesy of Luhring Augustine Gallery

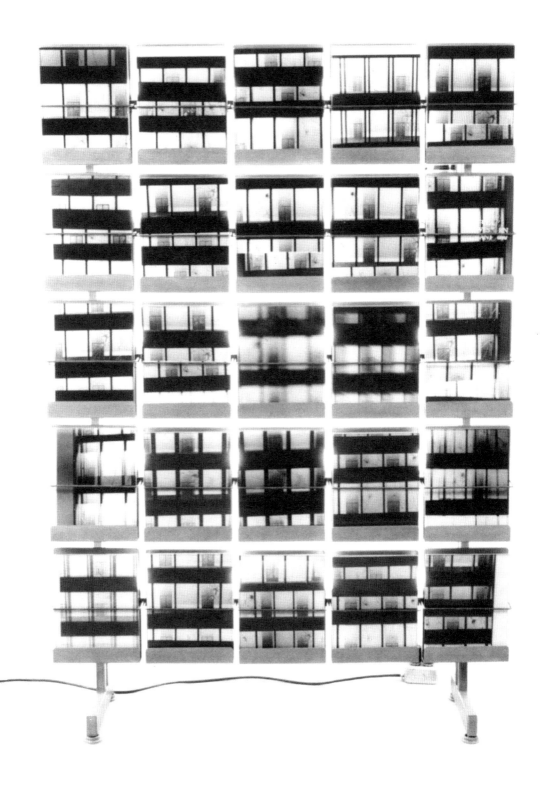

Full Metal Jacket

Bill Krohn

First movement: At a Marine boot camp on Parris Island, a squad of young recruits are brutalized by Sergeant Hartman, a horrifyingly funny drill instructor whose face and voice so dominate the film's first section that only two other characters are permitted to develop a semblance of psychological individuality: a wiseass named Joker and a dumb farmboy named Pyle, whose propensity for screwing up makes him the main target for Hartman's brutality, and that of his own comrades, until he goes mad and shoots his persecutor in the latrine.

Second movement: Cut to Da Nang, where Joker and a gung ho newcomer named Rafter Man have drawn easy duty as correspondents for the Army newspaper Stars and Stripes, and suddenly the tension of the first part dissipates, the structure of the film loosens to the point of entropy and the narrative is set adrift, as if we were watching outtakes from a film whose story we haven't completely understood. We follow Joker and Rafter Man from the placid corruption of Da Nang, broken only by a curiously anemic sequence showing the Tet Offensive, to the countryside around Hue,

where they join a seasoned combat unit called the "Lusthogs" for an assault on Hue, overrun by the Vietcong. The drifting, fragmentary, antidramatic feeling of these sequences is heightened in the aftermath of the assault, when a television crew films the characters speaking in choreographed succession like actors in a bad Broadway play about Vietnam, then addressing the camera directly in interviews that recall a famous episode of TV's "M*A*S*H."

It is only during the last minutes of the film that a sense of narrative progression returns: as the Lusthogs patrol the streets of Hue, they find themselves pinned down by an invisible sniper who turns out, when Joker penetrates her stronghold, to be a teenage girl. Cut down by Rafter Man's bullets, the sniper is slow to die, and only Joker is willing to put her out of her misery with a bullet through the head. Afterward, we see American soldiers marching at night silhouetted against a fiery landscape, singing the "Mickey Mouse Club" theme song, while Joker, barely distinguished from the horde by the last of a sparse series of laconic voiceovers, informs us that he is no longer afraid.

Is Full Metal Jacket an antiwar film, as the critics have assumed, or is it, in the words of an indignant Samuel Fuller, "a recruiting film"? Fuller's reaction did more to point up the slippery quality of Full Metal Jacket for me than all the raves predicated on the notion that Stanley Kubrick had made another Paths of Glory (1957). Since that film and Spartacus (1960), Kubrick has rejected messages in order to purify his art, and Full Metal Jacket (1987), which returns thirty years later to the booby-trapped terrain of the war film, is part of that ongoing process, as we can see by comparing the director's shooting script with the film he finally made. Two scenes were eliminated which would have made the drill instructor a monster: one where he nearly drowns Pyle in a bowl of urine, and one where he orders a recruit who has cut his wrists to clean up the mess he's made before reporting to the doctor. Instead, due in no small part to Lee Ermey's mesmerizing performance, the character remains human-size, believable, by turns outrageous and sympathetic, and seductive.

So it's not difficult to understand Fuller's rage at the way Hartman is portrayed, or his distrust of any film that includes a scene like the one where the recruits, transformed by many sufferings into proud members of the Corps, parade to the strains of the "Marine Corps Hymn," while Hartman's voice tells them they are now part of an indestructible brotherhood. It was just such a scene that the producer of Merrill's Marauders (1962) tacked onto Fuller's film to turn it into the kind of war film described by Roland Barthes in a famous essay in Mythologies:

Take the Army; show without disguise its chiefs as martinets, its discipline as narrow-

minded and unfair, and into this stupid tyranny immerse an average human being, fallible but likeable, the archetype of the spectator. And then, at the last moment, turn over the magical hat, and pull out of it the image of an army, flags flying, triumphant, bewitching, to which, like Sganarelle's wife, one cannot but be faithful although beaten.[1]

In fact, that is a perfect description of what happens in Full Metal Jacket until Pyle shoots Hartman. Then another kind of film begins, and by the time the image of the triumphant army returns at the end, the conventions of the (anti)war film have been transformed into something else altogether.

The best answer I have seen to the perennial critical quarrel about whether Kubrick is a humanist is Gilles Deleuze's observation that all of Kubrick's films portray the world as a brain, one fated to malfunction from both internal and external causes.[2] This surprising insight will at least permit us to do justice to the strangeness of Full Metal Jacket, where the little world of the training camp on Parris Island is portrayed as a brain made up of human cells thinking and feeling as one, until its functioning is wrecked first from within, when a single cell, Pyle, begins ruthlessly carrying out the directives of the death instinct that programs the organ as a whole, and then from without by the Tet Offensive, the external representation of the same force. A double movement is described by the rigorously plotted movements of Kubrick's camera: in the first section, as the camera follows the constant parading of the recruits and their instructor, and movement is almost exclusively from the interior of the screen out, while in the second section, beginning with the striking dolly forward on the miniskirted ass of a Da Nang whore, camera movements into the screen, toward the vanishing point, predominate; but the film's two parts describe a single movement with a single endpoint — the encounter with a fellow human being whose face, in Hartman's memorable phrase, has become a "war face," the face of death.

What is new in Full Metal Jacket is that, for the first time in Kubrick's cinema (although A Clockwork Orange [1971] attempts something similar with its self-effacing boustrophedon structure), the narrative itself begins to malfunction, after Pyle has turned his rifle on Hartman and then on himself, as if eliminating the antagonists whose repeated confrontations made a story possible has condemned the film to wander into regions bordering dangerously on nonsense, until a new antagonist erupts in the encounter with the sniper, which

permits the filmmaker to start turning the screw of suspense again, imparting a linear and dramatic coherence in time to arrest the fatal drift.

Kubrick told Newsweek that he wants to "explode the narrative structure of film," and in Full Metal Jacket the first casualty of the explosion is the conventional notion of character. For Full Metal Jacket is a film without a hero; its sole protagonist is a group-mind whose formation is shown in the boot camp scenes, most of which portray the process of indoctrination, with little reference to combat training per se. Then, in the second section, we follow scattered pieces of the group-mind

as they are set adrift in a world where scene follows scene with no apparent dramatic or thematic necessity, so that even Joker, the protagonist whose acts and motives were starkly delineated by the constricting circumstances of boot camp, seems to withdraw from us, becoming a cipher as the film unfolds — mainly thanks to the unsparing labor of purification, by which Kubrick during the year-long shoot stripped away the elements in his own script that made Joker someone with whom the audience could identify: his voiceovers reduced finally to four or five; the instinctive revulsion that impels him, in a scene that was either cut or never filmed, to kill an Arvin colonel who is murdering prisoners during the helicopter ride from Da Nang to Hue; and his death and burial, which would have concluded the film on an elegiac note — replaced here by the group-shot of soldiers singing the Mousketeer anthem that was originally planned for an earlier scene, after the assault on Hue.

The effect is subtle and at times paradoxical: for example, the mute, expressionless faces in the film's opening sequence, a montage of close-ups of recruits getting their first Marine Corps haircut, seem emotionally much closer to us than the faces in the montage of TV interviews, which distance the characters at the very moment they are being permitted, for the first time, to "express" themselves — with all the method acting, mock hesitations and other signals of sincerity on the part of the actors that "expression" implies. In the second section of Full Metal Jacket, we meet a whole new cast of highly individualistic characters who are imbued with the full range of human emotions, but cut loose from their narrative moorings they appear as opaque

fragments of a larger whole, their acts legible only as behaviors (to borrow a term from the science of operant conditioning) in which are embedded, in a kind of horrible monotony, the traits — racism, misogyny, machismo, homicidal mania — that govern the group-mind, even in its malfunctioning; although this does not prevent us from feeling momentary sympathy for each of the characters. Sympathy, in fact, is necessary if we are to read the subtle, often nearly imperceptible gestures and expressions in which the drama of the group is played out.

One striking effect of Kubrick's narrative experiments in Full Metal Jacket was to force many critics to reconsider their adulation of Platoon (1987), because Kubrick has eliminated every scene or action that might have served as a handhold for the spectator in search of easy edification, choosing instead to construct his film as a parody of all edifying and unifying fictions. It's impossible to watch the last scene, where Joker, made fearless, is swallowed up by the marching throng, without thinking of Stone's proclaimed intention of bringing Americans together and healing the nation's wounds, to which the only proper

reply is Alex's last line in A Clockwork Orange: "I was cured, all right!"

I would also argue that the alienation effects that Kubrick uses in the Vietnam section of his film are a superior form of realism to Platoon's scorched-earth naturalism, which is largely based on effects of déjà vu: Stone, who was there, has portrayed it in images copied from TV coverage of the war and myriad other war films, so that the shock of discovering a new reality is mediated by images that are believable because they are already familiar — as in Salvador (1986), where the photojournalist played by John Savage says not that he wants to take a picture that shows the reality of war, but that he wants to "take one like Capa." Kubrick's formal strategy in Full Metal Jacket — which encompasses every element of his film, and not just the narrative choices I've focused on in this brief description — is to create moments of utter strangeness that have the shock of fresh perception. His motto could be that of the seventeenth-century haiku poet Basho: "I do not seek to follow in the footsteps of the men of old. I seek the thing they sought."

*   *   *

Deleuze discusses Kubrick in the second volume of Cinema, his comprehensive classification of film images and signs, initially assigning him to one of the two stylistic camps into which he divides modern cinema, the cinema of the body (for example, Godard, Cassavetes) and the cinema of the brain (for example, Resnais, Kubrick). Deleuze's description of what is specifically modern in Resnais and Kubrick — as opposed to Eisenstein, who uses a classical model of the brain structured by processes of integration and differentiation — is based on philosopher of science

Gilbert Simondon's speculation that "the properties of living matter are manifested as the maintenance...of certain topological properties, much more than of pure energetic or structural properties," which leads Simondon to propose a non-Euclidian model of living organisms where "the functions of integration and differentiation are a function of a metastable asymmetry between an absolute interiority and exteriority."[3]

Deleuze makes a few adjustments to this speculative model — which seems to be equally applicable to organisms and their parts — when he proposes his own post-classical model of the brain. For example, by "absolute interiority and exteriority" Simondon means simply the organism and its environment, in contrast to the relative relationships of interiority and exteriority which hold between systems of the organism, where the bloodstream may be exterior with respect to a gland that emits secretions into it, and interior with respect to the intestinal walls.[4] Reinterpreted by Deleuze, these topological absolutes become "an inside more profound than any interior milieu, and an outside more distant than any exterior milieu,"[5] both of which are identified with

death in the section on Resnais and Kubrick and, in the conclusion to the volume, with "the unevocable in Welles, the undecidable in Resnais, the inexplicable in Robbe-Grillet, the incommensurable in Godard, the unreconcilable in the Straubs, the impossible in Marguerite Duras, the irrational in Syberberg."[6]

Deleuze's poetic rewriting of Simondon turns out to have many applications: in fact, as that diversified roster of modern filmmakers suggests, Deleuze intends it to be more widely applicable than he first indicates: by the end of the book he is proposing his new model of the brain, which also includes "the irrational cut" and "the black screen," as a model for all the global structures — mainly variations on the series — used in modern films. The new brain model is the "noosign" of modern cine-

ma, just as the spiral was the noosign of classical cinema, based on the classical model of the brain structured by processes of integration and differentiation.[7] Deleuze even says in an interview about the book that the biology of the brain, and not linguistics or psychoanalysis, will furnish the criteria for a new film aesthetics: "The value of all cinema depends on the cerebral circuits it establishes...the richness, complexity and general tenor of its arrangements, of its connections, conjunctions, circuits and short-circuits."[8]

So the cinema of the brain is not just one type of film in Deleuze's taxonomy of modern cinema — it represents the whole terrain to be mapped. This means that the films of Resnais and Kubrick, which take this new organic model as their subject, are exemplary. By dispersing

434

its narrative and making classical narrative one element in a structure that implements another logic, Full Metal Jacket, like any modern film, is exploring the cerebral processes that found the new aesthetic of l'image-temps; but by portraying as parts of a brain the stock characters of a genre that could stand for all of classical cinema ("A film is like a battlefield" — Samuel Fuller, 1965), and having them act out the breakdown of sensorimotor connections that gives rise to "pure optical and aural situations,"[9] Kubrick is staging, in a peculiarly literal way, an allegory of modern cinema.

* * *

I don't want to leave the impression, in concluding, that Kubrick is without masters. He had one, Max Ophuls, who is as present in Full Metal Jacket as he is in an obvious pastiche like Lolita. Hartman's first appearance, for example, visually duplicates the opening sequence of Lola Montès (1955), with Peter Ustinov's ringmaster spieling to the backward-tracking camera as he advances past a line of acrobats standing at attention.

William Karl Guerin, in a recent book on Ophuls, has taught us to be suspicious of this Mephistophelian figure and his twin, the Master of Ceremonies in La Ronde (1950), who subject the other characters and the spectator alike to the seductive rigors of a mise-en-scène designed to illustrate "a sinister conception of man."[10] Traditionally, critics have tended to identify these director surrogates with Ophuls, and Kubrick, who revises his predecessor by killing off Hartman in the middle of the film, might agree with them, but all the ambiguities of Full Metal Jacket are already deployed in Ophuls's late films, where, as Guerin has shown, a single close-up (Simone Signoret in La Ronde, Martine Carol faint and perspiring before her final leap in Lola Montès) is sufficient to derail the Master of Ceremonies' infernal machine.[11] In Full Metal Jacket the

close-up of Pyle, insane, signals the imminent death of Kubrick's Master of Ceremonies, which liberates images and characters from the machine of the narrative; and when the narrative begins to function again during the assault on Hue, the close-up of the young sniper shatters the spell, leaving us with those concluding images of the marauding horde, which recalls the Dionysian mobs at the beginning of "Le Masque" and the end of the "La Maison Tellier" episodes in Le Plaisir (1951): images of a world without a Master of Ceremonies.[12]

Notes

1. Roland Barthes, Mythologies, trans. Annette Lavers (New York: Hill and Wang, 1972), p. 41.

2. Gilles Deleuze, Cinema 2: The Time-Image, trans. Hugh Tomlinson and Robert Galeta (Minneapolis: University of Minnesota Press, 1989), pp. 205–206.

3. Gilbert Simondon, L'Individu et sa génèse physico-biologique (Paris: P.U.F., 1964), p. 261.

4. Ibid., p. 261.

5. Deleuze, Cinema 2, p. 278, (translation modified).

6. Ibid., p. 278, (translation modified).

7. Ibid., pp. 276–78.

8. Deleuze, Pourparlers: 1972–1990 (Paris: Minuit, 1990), pp. 85–86.

9. Deleuze, Cinema 2, p. 18.

10. William Karl Guerin, Max Ophuls (Paris: Cahiers du Cinema, 1988).

11. Ibid., pp. 116, 152.

12. Ibid., pp. 129–30.

RoboCop

Mark Poster

Critical social theory can no longer content itself with the vantage point of the mode of production.[1] Too many things have changed, too many projects have gone awry, too many novelties have been introduced in the means of production, in the relations of production, in the interplay of base and superstructure, in the elements of the superstructure. Theoretical advances in linguistics, structuralism, semiology, poststructuralism, psychoanalytic object-relations theory, feminism, communications theory all take their point of departure outside the concept of the mode of production and find their fruitful developments beyond its perimeters. In this theoretical conjuncture, I introduce the concept of the mode of information to designate a nonunified cluster of electronically mediated communications.[2] Specifically, TV ads, databases and computer writing are symbolic patterns, communications if you will, that require linguistically based theories to explore their operations, their manners of articulation, the forms of domination they incur and the prospects they offer for the project of emancipation.[3]

These elements of the mode of information constitute the subject in new ways. The subject as an agent of history in the form of the liberal autonomous individual or of the socialist class-conscious collective, the subject as a rational, centered, unified point of perspective opposed to a world of objects that is open to its domination, the masculine Western subject of culture during the past two centuries: all of these are being destabilized, threatened and subverted by new communicational patterns. Quite apart from structural changes in the economy and in politics, quite apart from "marginal" political movements like feminism, environmentalism, gay and lesbian activism, antinuclear advocacy, the familiar cultural practices that accompanied the rise of industrial capitalism are rapidly disintegrating in face of the mode of information. Critical theory's sense of the real and the imaginary, the subject and object, the ideal and the material, inside and outside, male and female, mind and body are all open to fluid transformations, the patterns of which are difficult to discern.

It has become a truism that the body is always already culturally inscribed, never a natural object available without mediation for a rational subject (of science). The complication I want to introduce is this: industrial society and now "postindustrial" society, the mode of production and now the mode of information, have inserted into the social space analogues of the human body in the form of increasingly complex tools. Tool-making man makes tools that imitate his own functions, but this process of the machine reproduction of the body has come to the point when it is the brain that is being reproduced, part by part, in computers and more generally in electronically mediated communication systems. An intelligent robot is now a dream of many in the military, industrial, scientific and university communities. As the functions of the brain are progressively added to the robot, the social world progressively includes new species of cyborgs and androids, which confront human beings in a specular relation that deconstructionists tell us is figured as a mise en abîme, a perpetual, infinite mirroring.

Paul Verhoeven's film RoboCop situates itself in the mode of information. Seemingly a film in the cops-and-robbers genre, RoboCop undermines this presentation by extreme stylization and self-conscious references to other Hollywood productions and more especially to TV serials. The action in the film is set against repeated glimpses of people watching television. Everyone in the film — the bad guys, the cops, the idealized victims — watches the same inane game show in which a woman's body is repeatedly displayed and violated by a cake thrown not on her face but on her breasts. Murphy — later RoboCop — wears his gun cowboy-style, in a compartment on the side of his upper leg. After firing, he always twirls it; when asked why he does this, he admits that he wants to impress his son who has seen it done by a TV hero, "T. J. Laser," and he adds, "I get a kick out of it." His gait resembles an exaggerated John Wayne-swagger. Much of the film's mandatory violence, while explicit enough to have summoned the censor's scissors, is exaggerated and funny, rather than frightening. Japanese monster films are cited in the battle between RoboCop and his nemesis ED (Enforcement Droid) 209, the creation of Dick Jones, the film's corporate villain. RoboCop is able to elude and finally defeat ED 209 not through superior strength but through a flaw in the ED's design: it cannot walk down stairs.

The film continuously undermines itself as a film in order to be consumed at the level of a TV serial, in order to take effect at the level of the banal and everyday, in order to refer itself to the viewer's body situated in the intimacy and familiarity of the home.

RoboCop opens with a TV newscast in which life is depicted as dangerous and threatening, with imminent risk of nuclear war and social disorder. But commercials promise to alleviate the problems of the individual (for example, offering a new model Jarvick replacement heart that will end health worries). The viewer is introduced to the film through two interconnected discourses: newscasts figure the body as in danger, and TV ads promise to overcome various threats to it. This double effect is typical of the discursive practice of television, indeed of all discursive practice: the individual is subject to an imposition of power over the body, which is then, in a second maneuver, said to be resolved. In RoboCop, the audience is invited into the discursive game by the familiarity of the introduction: the newscast recasts those probably watched earlier in the evening, before going to the movie. But the commercial, which is part of the verisimilitude of the newscast, is parodic enough to distance and subvert the play of power over the body.

At issue in the newscast is indeed the body, in this case that of a critically wounded (and soon to die) Detroit police officer. In a related story, the anchorman announces that Omni Consumer Products (OCP) has contracted to take over the Detroit Police Department (DPD). The story of the officer's death is the reverse image of the main story of the newscast. The structure of the newscast is binary: nuclear war threat (social chaos)–ad for replacement heart (individual salvation). The structure of the Detroit story is policeman killed by criminals (individual death)/capitalist takeover of the police (social salvation). The common theme in this inverse double discourse is the power of technological capitalism over the body: over the social body of Detroit (by OCP) and over the individual body (by the heart manufacturer).

As the movie develops, it becomes clear that such control over the body is only possible for capitalism through advanced science and technology. Capitalism (OCP) will outperform the State (DPD) only because of its ability to exploit scientific knowledge. The crime problem is defined as the need for a twenty-four-hour cop, one who neither eats nor sleeps, but works relentlessly against crime. The solution to the problem is RoboCop, a cyborg[4] created from another near-dead policeman, Murphy. Advanced technology reworks Murphy into the final crimebuster. Science remodels the human body to suit the needs of capitalism, which, of course, in turn serves to benefit humanity. When the doctors proudly announce that they have saved one of Murphy's arms, the ocp project director angrily tells them to "lose it" — he wants "total body prosthesis" for RoboCop. The surgery on the arm is allowed because Murphy is legally dead and, having signed his bodily integrity away in a release, anything can be done to him. In the gap between the dead and the living, the cyborg will be born.

The shift from the mode of production to the mode of information is directly expressed in RoboCop. The pivotal scenes are two meetings of the ocp board of directors, the sensitive hub of capitalism. In both cases, the themes are violence, capitalism, and the body, and the issue is decided not by brute force but by information technologies. In the first of these scenes, the first episode of violence re-sults, significantly, from an information problem: in a demonstration of ED 209 at an OCP boardmeeting, a young executive is asked to draw a gun on it in order to demonstrate ED's efficient power. But a glitch is revealed in ED's design: ED tells the executive to "put down your weapon," and he does, but ED doesn't register this and annihilates him.

In the second of these pivotal scenes, RoboCop appears at another boardmeeting, intent on arresting Dick Jones. He had been prevented from doing so earlier by a secretly programmed, "classified" directive that forbade him to arrest any OCP officer; on the other hand, though, his cybernetics include an audiovisual recording system, on which he has logged Jones's scoffing announcement that he conspired to murder another OCP executive. Unable to arrest the bad guy, he replays this tape: the head of OCP fires Jones, and Robo-Cop is freed to apprehend the villain. In the mode of information, decisive powers are not mechanical but informational.

Verhoeven gives us a representation of a new field of forces: in the background of the film are capitalism with its relentless search for profits and Hollywood escapist violence. But something new is added that, at one level, reinforces these themes, and, at another level, undermines them: new discursive practices of the mode of information now take the lead in controlling and empowering the body. Science reconfigures the body at will and electronically mediated communication (taped memory) works to undo the forces of evil. The mode of information overlays the traditional themes of capitalism and Hollywood film genres. The outcome of the drama rests with the question of who will best manipulate the capabilities of the mode of information — the bad guys (Dick Jones et al.) or the good guys (Murphy and his partner, Lewis)?

The sacchrymose ending of the film, in which capitalism, romance and morality are aligned and victorious, is partially undermined in two ways: the happy ending is so predictable that it cannot be taken seriously, and the political implications of the film expose the bizarre repositioning of the body in the mode of information. Still, the film is presented in the institutional framework of the "culture industry," and as such its purpose is to make a profit and to divert its audience from attending critically to structures of domination that diminish their lives. RoboCop differs from more conventional films in its genre by subverting, even as it reproduces and celebrates, the banalities of everyday life in the mode of information.

Notes

1. Eric Rentschler was most helpful in suggesting to me relevant studies on film and cultural criticism in general.

2. Bill Nichols, "The Work of Culture in the Age of Cybernetic Systems," Screen 29:1 (winter 1988), pp. 22–47, is very insightful about these processes.

3. There are many ways to formulate these changes; for one different from my own, see Friedrich Kittler, "Gramophone, Film, Typewriter," October 41 (summer 1987), pp. 101–18.

4. Among the interesting studies of the android figure see Donna Haraway, "A Manifesto for Cyborgs: Science, Technology, and Socialist Feminism in the 1980's," Socialist Review 80 (March–April 1985), pp. 65–107; Gabriele Schwab, "Cyborgs: Postmodern Phantasms of Body and Mind," Discourse 9 (spring–summer 1987), pp. 64–84; Patricia Mellencamp, "Oedipus and the Robot in Metropolis," Enclitic 5.1 (spring 1981), pp. 20–42; Janet Bergstrom, "Androids and Androgyny," Camera Obscura 15 (1986), pp. 37–64; and Andreas Huyssen, "The Vamp and the Machine: Technology and Sexuality in Fritz Lang's Metropolis," New German Critique 24–25 (fall–winter 1981–82), pp. 221–37.

Performance

Nina Rosenblatt

Near the end of Performance, a still shot momentarily freezes Mick Jagger's mouth, lips spread and bathed in the greenish white light of the glowing neon tube he brandishes like a space-age erection. Openings, spaces, gaps and holes are the rhetorical elements with which the film describes counterculture, not least because they bluntly assert its surcharged vision of sexuality, of repressed or submerged desires as the forces that move characters and events. But more interesting from the vantage point of two decades later is the way this insistence on derelict spaces and gaps grounds Performance within larger social and cultural ruptures of the sixties and early seventies. The film's historical significance is only partially a function of its (notoriously) flamboyant strategies of sexual perversion. What is more revealing in its vision of counterculture is the recognition that these devices, the kinetic eroticism they describe, are symptomatic of a more pervasive condition of cultural fluidity and indeterminacy — that the types of desire they propose are implicated in a social field within which previous hierarchies and mechanisms of closure have lost much of their relevance.

In considering 1960s culture and counterculture, the phrase "generation gap" inevitably comes to mind — a concept that relates Performance to numerous other films produced during the period, including The Trip (1967), Psych Out (1968), Wild in the Streets (1968), Easy Rider (1969). Interestingly, in most of these (more and less sincere) efforts the breakdown in the transmission of culture from one generation to the next is manifested as conflict, which occurs along familiar lines and within recognizable social landscapes. In the nightmare near-future of Wild in the Streets, for example, antagonism between the generations finds one logical conclusion with the election of a rock star as president of the United States and the consequent internment of everyone over age thirty in camps where they're kept perpetually "medicated" on LSD. While the details of this dystopic world might belong to 1960s counterculture, its vision of power gone haywire is nonetheless drawn according to a previous generation's conventions of politico-militaristic subjectivity and subjugation.

Performance, which marked the 1970 directorial debut of cinematographer Nicholas

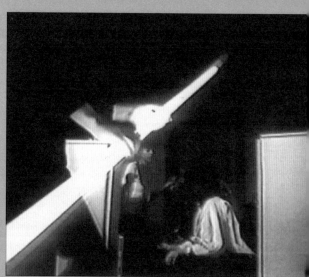

Roeg (codirected by Donald Cammell) retains these models of opposition in outline only, primarily to undermine them, to prove them empty of effective content. One distinctive feature of the film is its use of certain genre conventions to represent two adjacent but ostensibly different realms. The activities of the London mob, which dominate the film's first hour, unfold in the starkly slick settings of a Hollywood thriller, a "mod" gangster film along the lines of John Boorman's Point Blank (1967); the collapse of these cinematic conventions coincides with the introduction of the claustrophobic, densely cluttered setting occupied by the film's hippie drug culture. This deliberate manipulation of genre ultimately has the effect of exposing the structures of the thriller film, though not in the name of parody. Rather, the continual undermining of the genre demonstrates the inadequacy of these stable structures to contain or organize experience in the gangster realm itself. So thoroughly, in fact, is the autonomy and coherence of that realm challenged by the constant intrusion of unexpected objects and events, that by the time the protagonist, Chas (played by James Fox), seeks refuge in the counterculture, he alone seems sufficiently intact to be shocked by the encounter.

In place of rigid opposition, in other words, Performance sets out a dynamic and mutating field, in which genre conventions hold sway only provisionally, and in which the Borgesian theme of identity exchange assumes a peculiar generality. Although the plot traces one specific conjoining, the merging identities of the gangster Chas and Turner (a reclusive ex–rock star played by Mick Jagger), the film as a whole reveals a world whose functioning depends on the instability of subjective states and desires, and their ability to attach to a variety of objects. In a space where different desires, different economies of the body randomly circulate and collide, Chas's exile from the mob is the result of a subtle disruption in that organization's exercise of control. He ceases to be a component in the organization machine ("a cog in the wheel") when he kills the object of his sexual attraction, a fellow mob member, against the orders of his boss. The metonymic relationship between the mob's operations and the logic underpinning the operation of a larger capitalist order takes on resonance in this sense: at issue is not Chas's homosexual desire — since homosexuality proves equally acceptable as a source of productive violence and control — but rather the fact that in this instance his libidinal energy bypasses the regimented paths allowed to it and ends in a nonproductive, even counterproductive exchange of violence.

What distinguishes the counterculture in the film is its renunciation of any particular priority of desire. At this point, the suggestion of unmitigated excess, shaped by the experiences of madness, mysticism, eroticism and hallucinogenic drugs, indicates a world in which the mob's channels of recuperation and organization are rendered inoperative. Here, Roeg's disjunctive camerawork intensifies the impression of a kinetic, deterritorialized existence, contributing perhaps to what one hostile critic called the "promiscuous" construction of the film. The long views and rapid intercutting of the first part give way in the second to a more probing lens and prevailing use of closeups and dissolve shots. Despite the relationship of these strategies to what one might call a formalist cinema, they do not so much emphasize qualities instrinsic to the medium of film as signal an abdication of the camera's "objective," stabilizing function. What raises Performance above a simple narration of countercultural practices, is, in part, the degree to which it refuses to admit limitations, especially the boundaries that normally separate objects and events from their subjective effects. Hence the originality with which Chas's revelatory

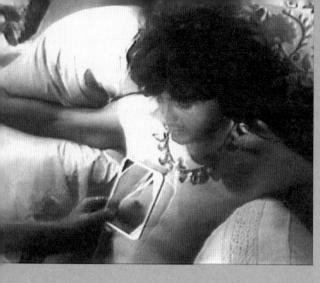

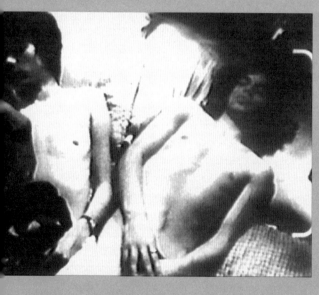

trip scene is conveyed: the effects of hallu-cinogenic mushrooms are registered not with histrionic "psychedelic" effects but by Chas's gradual absorption into the alluring, shifting accumulation of objects, decor and clothing around him.

With the elimination of boundaries comes a sheer surplus of images — a proliferation of camera shots that no narrative can absorb — suggesting the mobile and multilayered func-tioning of desire itself. But the most (at least for the time) transgressive evocation of insur-gent desire in the film is undoubtedly effected by Jagger, whose physical appearance alone strained the limits of description in 1970. A number of writers tried to invoke some unpre-cedented form of androgyny to describe the unexpected fragility of his body and the anom-aly of his made-up face: "a kind of male drag," "an androgynous Pre-Raphealite beauty." The insufficiency of these descriptions of his pres-ence, though, indicates the insufficiency of the bounded, polarized concepts of gender they assume. It may be that the use, by more than one critic, of vaginal imagery to characterize various openings on Jagger's body comes near-er to capturing his condition and that outlined by the movie as a whole: a state of receptivity, accessibility and erotic dissipation.

In the 1990s, however, it is impossible not to find something constrained in the film's vi-sion of dissolution. Its valorization of sexuality as a force meant to oppose dominant models of subjectification seems predicated on a his-torically dated politics of pleasure — that is, an assumption that modes of resistance are defined by the infusion of instinctual energies into the texture and conduct of everyday life. As the crit-ical practice and cultural confrontations of the intervening decades have shown, the produc-tion of these and other new forms of subjec-tivity is increasingly subsumed in the transient indifference of the global marketplace and the disembodied terrain of its technologies.

Within the context of Roeg's own film oeu-vre, this shift is dramatically indicated by the gulf separating Performance from The Man Who Fell to Earth, released in 1976, years after the effective "end of the sixties." In this science-fiction vision of an American waste-land, David Bowie's Newton appears as a numb and desiccated figure of alienation (an interplanetary visitor in search of capital to help his drought-stricken homeland), whose androgyny no longer implies polymorphic pleasure, as it does with Jagger's Turner, but rather the atrophy or short-circuiting of sexual exchange. Thus, Newton's attempt to make love in his natural alien state becomes a gro-tesque parody of excess, in which semen spews from his entire body in a kind of adoles-cent nightmare of sexual malfunction. This image of erotic dehydration, though, is just one symptom of the film's larger subject: the cultural dehydration effected by American global capitalism and its omnipresent powers of recuperation. The real difference between Performance and The Man Who Fell to Earth corresponds to that between the London mob, with its localized effects, and the latter film's "World Enterprises," a government–corporate alliance capable of encompassing all social and desiring operations and trajectories (in-cluding Newton's rise to rock stardom), and of rechanneling all experiences of pleasure back into its own omnivorous network.

Still, the contemporary viewer's sense of nostalgia in the political orientation of Perfor-mance, instead of diminishing the film's im-pact, may well reveal its effectiveness. For the resonance of the film is its evocation of a his-torical threshold, a moment whose contents have since been dispersed. And its vital link to the many countercultural activities of the 1960s is its incarnation of an experience of extreme intensity in which all dissonances momentarily resolve, as in the electrifying dissonances and resolutions of rock and roll.

Aliens

Paul Virilio

Exactly what type of alienation is James Cameron's Aliens all about? We are hell-bound once again, on a punitive expedition disguised as an interplanetary fiction: "colonial marines packing state-of-the-art firepower" sent to rescue "terraforming" colonists who have lost contact with their State-corporate sponsors. The jungles of the Third World are transformed into a planet swarming with pestilential life, to be infiltrated by commandos on a search-and-destroy mission — or a "bug hunt," to use their post–Vietnam Syndrome term that passes off xenophobia as grunt cynicism.

What we have before us is the most recent avatar of the propaganda fiction that has been in vogue for some time in the United States. On one level, we are witnessing the revival of the war propaganda movie: soldiers exploring a Byzantine complex of tunnels inhabited by a seemingly infinite number of aliens who, by their very (and very adaptive) physiology, are indistinguishable warriors. On another though perhaps not so distinct level, the film draws us into a pathological framework of life reduced to warfare: a planet-tumor, an operative field big enough for a conflict in which American soldiers serve at once as cosmic antibodies

and as guinea pigs who, evacuated as "casualties," might happen to return with a specimen of the ultimate biowarfare agent.

In this light, it makes perfect sense that certain sequences shot in the "atmosphere processor," the planet's lung, are reminiscent of an endoscopy, a medical visit into visceral gloom, into the evil incarnate of a celestial object. It also makes sense that the most sophisticated of surveillance and targeting technologies are mobilized in this paramilitary work, the armaments getting equal billing with the actors and special effects, standing as full partners. These machinic actors do battle in a Manichaean combat in which the enemy is no longer an adversary, a fellow creature one must respect in spite of everything; rather, it is an unnameable being that it is more appropriate to exterminate than to examine or analyze: "You're going out there to destroy them, right?" the righteous heroine Ripley (Sigourney Weaver) demands of the expedition's profit-minded corporate overseer. "Not to study, not to bring back, but to wipe them out...."

This, parenthetically, can only lead in the end to the extinction of the talking film, its

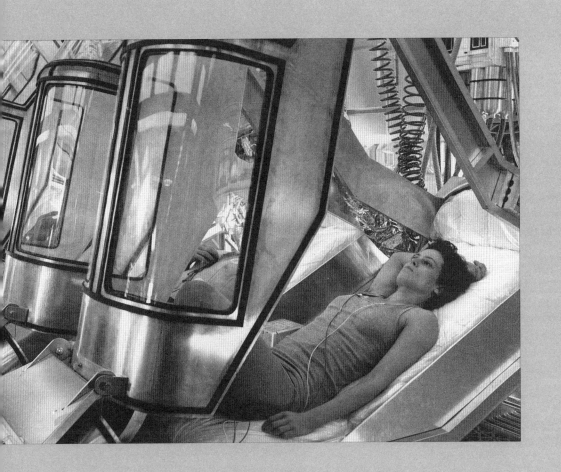

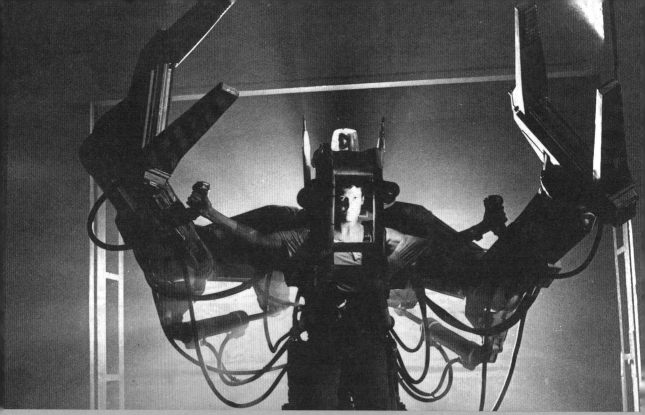

complete replacement by film trailers for hardened militarists.

The only attraction of many recent films is
that they give viewers a chance to detect por-
tents of a misfortune television will later confirm. The arsenal in Aliens is revealing in this
connection. Rather than featuring imaginary
and futuristic technologies, arms or fanciful
costumes, the film celebrates a contemporary
weapons system, a more or less direct descendant of the infamous "electronic battlefield"
first deployed by the U.S. Army in Vietnam,
then brought home to the Mexican border (and
elsewhere) for use against illegal "aliens."
(The film's dialogue explicitly refers to the
problems of border infiltration: a Marine says
of a Hispanic woman soldier carrying a "pulse
rifle" modeled on an M-16 short rifle, "Somebody said 'aliens' — she thought they said
'illegal aliens' and signed up.") Electric eyes
and other sensing devices linked to computers
have long ago made a reality of the biotech-
nical symbiosis extolled by the film's special

effects designers, Giger and Cobb. The armored
command vehicle used on the planet surface
is nothing other than a mobile video control
room permitting a marine patrol to serve as the
sensory and implementary agents of an officer:
the soldiers are war reporters who visualize
for their superiors the trail of danger — and
are scolded the moment the video feed goes
out of focus.

Why would a science-fiction film place
such emphasis on the realism and verisimilitude of the actors' and actresses' equipment
and weaponry? The answer, in the words of the
director: "To make the spectator feel somewhat at home in the midst of the battle." This
is why the film's design elements are calculated to facilitate identification with the fight-
ers — which is probably one of the film's most
original aspects. For the first time, it introduces
into the cinematic spectacle the aesthetic
imperative that is a constant of military pur-
chasing: military design must not age too
quickly, because the awesome appearance of

448

the hardware is part of its military effectiveness.

Now, the classic science-fiction film too often features imaginary high-performance weaponry; this prematurely ages the look of real weapons, helping to discredit them, make their threat obsolete. This discredit immediately transfers to the power of armies, those "forces of order" whose function is primarily dissuasive in nature. (A similar logic figures in the absurdly low "Adjusted Dollar" prices referred to again and again — a planetary colony in the tens of millions and so on.)

To get a better understanding of this very timely question of "military design" in a society where images take precedence over the written word, consider another American production, Top Gun. The film is a veritable air-and-sea military show, spectacular publicity for the swing-wing F-14, which can tear the competition apart on the international market (or could until the "Stealth" bomber, a paradoxical object, hit the selling block).

Let us return to Cameron's Aliens, the nearly eponymous sequel to Alien, yet so different from — almost a caricature of — the 1978 Ridley Scott production in which mystery is emphasized over designating the adversary. The spaceship Nostromo of Scott's film already bore elements of World War II–era battleships, tanks and bombers: Roger Christian remembers, "Ridley showed us Doctor Strangelove and he kept saying, 'what I want, you understand, is not a B-52 floating in space but its military look." Aliens, though, introduces a new "actor," or more precisely, a "double": the "Loader," a humanoid forklift-suit in which Ripley displays her "capability" first to the macho marines, and later to the mother of all the aliens with whom she does final battle. Besides the banal on-duty android Bishop — "I prefer the term 'artificial person'" he flatly states — this robotic Loader, whose operator is named in the credits, is an exemplary object: it is at once a "costume," a machine that multiplies its inhabitant's strength, and a full-fledged actor — the first automotive special effect, a mechanical halo for the heroine's gestures, gaits and stage business.

The reappearance of the Loader at the end of Aliens strikes one more as raising the curtain on a new order of military technology, the pseudo-cyborg, than as the finale of the film's promulgation of familiar military hardware. On the other hand, it really only raises Ripley to a level of brute strength commensurate with the mother alien — who, in any case, gained a vestige of subjectivity, a maternal wrath, when "she" saw Ripley exterminating her young. Thus, the family that formed the pretext of this neocolonial intervention — the "sixty or seventy families" lost, as Ripley states with shock early on — figures as the basis for conflict, once the drama has annihilated every institutional exemplar. And indeed, Aliens, despite its gallery of monstrous morphology, had to invoke the raison d'être of the militarized family, the presence of child-like innocence. For Ripley, it provided moral justification for military feats of valor: little Newt, the orphan who somehow survived the aliens' siege of her colony. She is only an alibi, though, a foil used to justify and stimulate the viewer's jubilation at the extermination of the undesirables. And how could viewers react otherwise when this traumatized innocent re-enters the social sphere in fits and starts — by giving a thumbs-up, saluting, saying "affirmative" and so on?

A bit like a terrorist attack. A psychological war. Women and children are slaughtered in order to create an irreversible situation, an irremediable hatred. The presence of the little victim has no theatrical value other than to dispose us to accept the madness of the massacres, the gruesome carnage of the creepy crawlies designed by Giger. A pity.

Translated from the French by Brian Massumi

My Crasy Life
Jean-Pierre Gorin

"Crasy" with an "s" — gangster's spelling, not Webster's.

I see my film as a slightly insane homage to Flaherty, a *Nanook of Long Beach* of sorts. While the material it covers falls within the documentary genre, *My Crasy Life* is a film scripted, acted, lit and edited along fictional lines. But as fiction, it steers away from melodrama, as it seems to me that gang life is marked in its radical difference by a sense of tragedy, by a refusal/incapacity on the gang members' parts to think their contradiction, their struggle, their resolution in terms of Right and Wrong. Putting an ethnic face on the fifties social-realism à la Stanley Kramer (as so many seem prone to do these days) is a temptation I never had.... It seemed clear to me that these times and this city (L.A.) would not call for a remake of Buñuel's *Los Olvidados* and that the fact a filmmaker is faced with — both aesthetically and politically — is that we are light-years away from the Thirties left-wing melodramatic humanist optimism Buñuel's film is steeped in, despite the bleakness of its conclusion.

So what was to be done? At least attempt a film that would live, so to speak, on gang time and in which the voice of the Boyz would not come through the usual filters (cops, judges, social workers, sociologists, anthropologists, media analysts...and assorted Hollywood filmmakers). Mind you, given that the Boyz are not vying for a Ph.D. in the Queen's English, I knew the enterprise would hurl itself against the ear of a movie-going public. But after all, is it too much to ask the audience to take as music that which it cannot (and

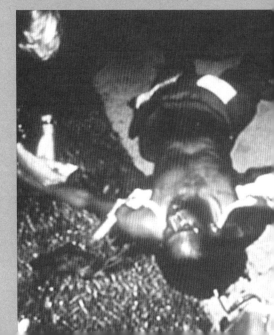

profoundly does not want to) decipher as speech and to hear — the time of a film — this music of survival which plays ever so softly between the harmonics of terror?

Spending time in the hood must have somehow conjured Foucault's ghost and inspired my determination to refuse to treat as a "problem" people who do not live themselves as such or as a "symptom" people who do not cast themselves as a "disease." So, no solution offered here and a film that comes out on the incorrect side of politics with unabashed glee. A purely fictional police computer's voice, which, instead of giving you the sociological scoop, mouths its desire for the soft touch of a cop's finger on its keyboard. And Samoa as flashes of the imagination, a Samoa of the mind that seeps into the discourse for these young men (nobody here beyond twenty four years of age) who talk like old men of their belief in ghosts and their nostalgia for church trips and Island music. And Samoa on the soundtrack as the music of the Unconscious, a music track achieved by mucking up an ethnomusicology tape and altering pitch, slowing down tempo and creating reverse echoes. And a return to Samoa, which is no search for Origins on the part of the filmmaker and is closer to Mr. Hulot's Holiday than to anything else for Spanky, the Long Beach banger. And violence relegated to two sets of police homicide photos, a simple parameter of gang life, less important to the bangers than the love they experience in the imaginary tribe. And a "glossary for the Straights," which piles street slang upon street slang, as if any effort of classification could only turn to farce, and as if the gang could only desire to preserve its identity as a gang. And the refusal by the filmmaker of any individuation that would negate the gang as gang. And raps used not as beats, not as a more taxing form of elevator music, but followed in their trajectory, presented at first as driveway chronicles, studied as rhet-

oric in a recording studio and finally acted out as a slightly out-of-synch playback on a sunny day in the park. And interviews as "arias," repeating endlessly the operatic themes of love, revenge and death, where questions can only be posed by a banger to bangers. And this answer, out of Psycho's mouth, the Westside-32nd-Street-Son-of-Samoa-Gangster-Crip, when asked to choose between "a black crip you say you love and a Samoan Blood ... as far as killing": "I'll take out that Samoan Blood." A "post-Berlin-Wall-demise" Brechtian parable of Americanization, as if becoming American meant going beyond the ethnic protestation of gang life the landscape suggested in the first place and killing your own kind because they have opted for Red (Bloods) over Blue (Crips), because they have chosen to wear Calvin Klein (C.K.=Crip Killer=Bloods) over British Knights (B.K.=Blood Killer=Crips), the true sacrament of one's integration in Sam's — as in Uncle — world.

And ... and ... and ... as Deleuze would hiccup. And I'll stop there. But believe you me or believe me you, there is more....

For those who know Poto and Cabengo and Routine Pleasures they'll see how My Crasy Life qualifies as the third panel of a trilogy, in which I attempt to track down a powerful and "impossible" tribal desire generated and defeated in the same throw of the dice by the Southern California landscape.... For those who come in fresh I hope they'll take it all in, and that they'll hear its static quality as the only possible aesthetic choice for a filmmaker hell-bent on mapping the tragic space in which the banger's life plays itself and as the only political choice for a filmmaker determined to puncture the melodramatic jazzing that is usually imposed upon it. "Westside out!" as they sign off on the corner of 32nd Street in Long Beach.

Techniques of the Body [1934]

Marcel Mauss

Introduction

I use the term "body techniques" in the plural advisedly because it is possible to produce a theory of the technique of *the* body on the basis of a study, an exposition, a description pure and simple of techniques of the body in the plural. By this expression I mean the ways in which, from society to society, men know how to use their bodies. In any case, it is essential to move from the concrete to the abstract and not the other way around.

I want to convey to you what I believe to be one of the parts of my teaching that is not to be found elsewhere, which I have rehearsed in a course of lectures on descriptive ethnology (the books containing the *Summary Instructions* and *Instructions for Ethnographers* are to be published[1]) and have tried out several times in my teaching at the Institute of Ethnology of the University of Paris.

When a natural science makes advances, it does so only in the direction of the concrete and always in the direction of the unknown. Now, the unknown is found at the frontiers of the sciences, where the professors are at each other's throats, as Goethe put it (though he did so less politely). It is generally in these ill-demarcated domains that the urgent problems lie. However, these uncleared lands are marked. In the natural sciences, at present, there is always one obnoxious rubric. There is always a moment when, the science of certain facts not yet being reduced to concepts, the facts not even being grouped together organically, these masses of facts receive that signpost of ignorance: "miscellaneous." This is where we have to penetrate. We can be certain that this is where there are truths to be discovered: first, because we know that we are ignorant, and second, because we have a lively sense of the quantity of the facts. For many years in my course in descriptive ethnology, I have had to teach in the shadow of the disgrace and opprobrium of the "miscellaneous," in a matter in which, in ethnography, this rubric was truly heteroclite. I was well aware that walking or swimming, for example, and all sorts of things of the same type are specific to determinate societies; that the Polynesians do not swim as we do, that my generation did not swim as the present generation does. But what social phenomena did these represent? They were "miscellaneous" social phenomena, and, since this rubric is such a horrible one, I have often thought about this "miscellaneous" — at least as often as I have been obliged to discuss it, and often in between.

Forgive me if, in order to give shape to this notion of body techniques for you, I tell you about the occasions on which I pursued this general problem and how I managed to pose it clearly. It was a series of steps taken consciously and unconsciously.

First, in 1898, I came into contact with someone whose initials I still know, but whose name I can no longer remember (I have been too lazy to look it up). It was the man who wrote an excellent article on swimming for the 1902 edition of the *Encyclopaedia Britannica*, then in preparation.[2] (The articles on swimming in the two later editions are not so good.) He revealed to me the historical and ethnographic interest of the question. It was a starting point, an observational framework. Subsequently — I noticed it myself — we have seen swimming techniques undergo a change in our generation's lifetime. An example will put us in the picture straightaway: us, the psychologists, as well as the biologists and sociologists. Previously, we were taught to dive after having learned to swim. And when we were learning to dive, we were taught to close our eyes and then to open them underwater. Today the technique is the other way around. The whole training begins by getting the children accustomed to keeping their eyes open underwater. Thus, even before they can swim, particular care is taken to get the children to control their dangerous but instinctive ocular reflexes; before all else they are familiarized with the water, their fears are suppressed, a certain confidence is created, suspensions and movements are selected. Hence, there is a technique of diving and a technique of education in diving that have been discovered in my day. And you can see that it really is a technical education and, as in every technique, there is an apprenticeship in swimming. On the other hand, our generation has witnessed a complete change in technique: we have seen the breaststroke with the head out of the water replaced by the different sorts of crawl. Moreover, the habit of swallowing water and spitting it out again has gone. In my day, swimmers thought of themselves as a kind of steamboat. It was stupid, but in fact I still do this: I cannot get rid of my technique. Here, then, we have a specific technique of the body, a gymnastic art perfected in our own day.

But this specificity is characteristic of all techniques. For example, during the war I was able to make many observations on this specificity of techniques, in particular, the technique of *digging*. The English troops I was with did not know how to use French spades, which forced us to change eight thousand spades per division when we relieved a French division, and vice versa. This plainly shows that a manual knack can only be learned slowly. Every technique, properly so called, has its own form.

But the same is true of every attitude of the body. Each society has its own special habits. In the same period, I had many opportunities to note the differences between the various armies. An anecdote about *marching*: You all know that the British infantry marches with a step different from the French — with a different frequency and a different stride. For the moment, I am not talking about the English swing or the action of the knees and so on. The Worcester Regiment, having achieved considerable glory alongside French infantry in the Battle of the Aisne, requested royal permission to have French trumpets and drums, a band of French buglers and drummers. The result was not very encouraging. For nearly six months, in the streets of Bailleul, long after the Battle of the Aisne, I often saw the following sight: the regiment had preserved its English march but had set it to a French rhythm. It even had at the head of its band a little French light infantry regimental sergeant major who could blow the bugle and sound the march even better than his men. The unfortunate regiment of tall Englishmen could not march. Their gait was completely at odds. When they tried to march in step, the music would be out of step, with the result that the Worcester Regiment was forced to give up its French buglers. In fact, the bugle calls adopted earlier, army by army, in the Crimean War, were the calls "at ease" and "retreat." Thus, I often saw, in a very precise fashion, not only in the ordinary march, but also in the double and so on, the differences in elementary as well as sporting techniques between the English and the French. Professor Curt Sachs, who is living here in France at present, made the same observation. He has discussed it in several of his lectures. He could recognize the gait of an Englishman and a Frenchman from a long distance.

But these were only approaches to the subject.

A kind of revelation came to me in the hospital. I was ill in New York. I wondered where I had seen girls walking the way my nurses walked. I had the time to think about it. At last I realized that it was in movies. Returning to France, I noticed how common this gait was, especially in Paris; the girls were French and they too were walking in this way. In fact, American walking fashions had begun to arrive over here, thanks to the movies. This was an idea I could generalize. The positions of the arms and hands while walking form a social idiosyncrasy — they are not simply a product of some purely individual, almost completely psychic, arrangements and mechanisms. For example, I think I can also recognize a girl who has been raised in a convent. In general, she will walk with her fists closed. And I can still remember my third-form teacher shouting at me: "Idiot! Why do you walk around the whole time with your hands flapping wide open?" Thus, there exists an education in walking, too.

Another example: There are polite and impolite *positions for the hands* at rest. Thus, you can be certain that if a child at table keeps his elbows in when he is not eating, he is English. A young Frenchman has no idea how to sit up straight; his elbows stick out sideways; he puts them on the table and so on.

Finally, in *running*, too, I have seen, you all have seen, the change in technique. Imagine, my gymnastics teacher, one of the top graduates of Joinville around 1860, taught me to run with my fists close to my chest — a movement completely contradictory to all running movements. I had to see the professional runners of 1890 before I realized the necessity of running in a different fashion.

Hence, I have had this notion of the social nature of the habitus for many years. Please note that I use the Latin word — it should be understood in France — "*habitus*." The word translates infinitely better than "*habitude*" (habit or custom), the "*exis*," the "acquired ability" and "faculty" of Aristotle (who was a psychologist). It does not designate those metaphysical *habitudes*, that mysterious memory, the subjects of volumes or short and famous theses. These "habits" do not vary just with individuals and their imitations; they vary especially between societies, educations, proprieties and fashions, types of prestige. In them, we should see the techniques and work of collective and individual practical reason rather than, in the ordinary way, merely the soul and its repetitive faculties.

Thus, everything tended toward the position that we in this society are among those who have adopted, following Auguste Comte's example: the position of Georges Dumas, for example, who, in the constant shuttlings between the biological and the sociological, leaves but little room for the psychological mediator. And I concluded that it was not possible to have a clear idea of all these facts about running, swimming and so on, unless one introduced a triple consideration instead of a single consideration — be it mechanical and physical, like an anatomical and physiological theory of walking, or on the contrary psychological or sociological. It is the triple viewpoint, that of the total man, that is needed.

Finally, another series of facts impressed itself upon me. In all these elements of the art of using the human body, the facts of *education* are dominant. The notion of education could be superimposed on that of imitation. For there are particular children with very strong imitative faculties, others with very weak ones, but all of them go through the same education, such that we can understand the continuity of the concatenations. What takes place is a prestigious imitation. The child, the adult, imitates actions that have succeeded, which he has seen successfully performed by people in whom he has confidence and who have authority over him. The action is imposed from without, from above, even if it is an exclusively biological action, involving his body. The individual borrows the series of movements of which he is composed from the action executed in front of him, or with him, by others.

It is precisely this notion of the prestige of the person who performs the ordered, authorized, tested action vis-à-vis the imitating individual, that contains all the social element. The imitative action that follows contains the psychological element and the biological element.

The whole, the ensemble, though, is conditioned by the three elements indissolubly mixed together.

All this is easily linked to a number of other facts. In a book by Elsdon Best that reached here in 1925, there is a remarkable document on the way Maori women in New Zealand walk. (Do not say that they are primitives, for in some ways I think they are superior to the Celts and Germans.)

> Native women adopted a peculiar gait [the English word is delightful] that was acquired in youth, a loose-jointed swinging of the hips that looks ungainly to us, but was admired by the Maori. Mothers drilled their daughters in this accomplishment, termed *onioni*,

and I have heard a mother say to her girl: "*Ha! Kaore koe e onioni*" ("you are not doing
the *onioni*") when the young one was neglecting to practise the gait.[3]
This was an acquired, not a natural way of walking. To sum up, there is perhaps no
"natural way" for the adult. A fortiori when other technical facts intervene: to take
ourselves, the fact that we wear shoes to walk transforms the positions of our feet:
we certainly feel it when we walk without them.

On the other hand, this same basic question arose for me in a different region,
vis-à-vis all the notions concerning magical power, beliefs in the not only physical
but also moral, magical and ritual effectiveness of certain actions. Here I am perhaps even more on my own terrain than on the adventurous terrain of the psychophysiology of modes of walking, which is a risky one for me in this company.

Here is a more "primitive" fact, Australian this time: a ritual formula for both
hunting and running. As you well know, the Australian manages to outrun kangaroos,
emus and wild dogs. He manages to catch the opossum at the top of its tree, even
though the animal puts up a remarkable resistance. One of these running rituals,
observed a hundred years ago, is that of the hunt for the dingo, or wild dog, among
the tribes near Adelaide. The hunter constantly shouts the following formula:

Strike [him, i.e., the dingo] with the tuft of eagle feathers [used in initiation, etc.]
Strike [him] with the girdle
Strike [him] with the string round the head
Strike [him] with the blood of circumcision
Strike [him] with the blood of the arm
Strike [him] with menstrual blood.
Send [him] to sleep, etc.[4]

In another ceremony, that of the opossum hunt, the individual carries in his
mouth a piece of rock crystal (*kawemukka*), a particularly magical stone, and chants
a formula of the same kind, and it is with this support that he is able to dislodge the
opossum, that he climbs the tree and can stay hanging on to it by his belt, that he
can outlast and catch and kill this difficult prey.

The relations between magical procedure and hunting techniques are clear, too
universal to need to be stressed.

The psychological phenomenon I am reporting at this moment is clearly only too easy to grasp and understand from the normal viewpoint of the sociologist. But what I want to get at now is the confidence, the psychological *momentum* that can be linked to an action that is primarily a fact of biological resistance, obtained thanks to some works and a magical object.

Technical action, physical action, magicoreligious action are confused for the actor. These are the elements I had at my disposal.

All this did not satisfy me. I saw how everything could be described but not how it could be organized; I did not know what name, what title, to give it all.

It was very simple, I had just to refer to the division of traditional actions into techniques and rites, which I believe to be well founded. All these modes of action were techniques, the techniques of the body.

I made, and went on making for several years, the fundamental mistake of thinking that there is technique only when there is an instrument. I had to go back to ancient notions, to the platonic position on technique, for Plato spoke of a technique of music and in particular of a technique of dance, and I had to extend these notions.

I call "technique" an action that is *effective* and *traditional* (and you will see that in this it is no different from a magical, religious or symbolic action). It has to be *effective* and *traditional*. There is no technique and no transmission in the absence of tradition. This, above all, is what distinguishes man from the animals: the transmission of his techniques, and very probably their oral transmission.

Allow me, therefore, to assume that you accept my definitions. But what is the difference between the effective traditional action of religion, the symbolic or juridical effective traditional action, the actions of life in common, moral actions on the one hand, and the traditional actions of technique, on the other? It is that the latter are felt by the author as *actions of a mechanical, physical or physicochemical order* and that they are pursued with that aim in view.

In this case, all that need be said is quite simply that we are dealing with *techniques of the body*. The body is man's first and most natural instrument. Or more accurately, not to speak of instruments, man's first and most natural technical object, and at the same time his first technical means, is his body. Immediately, this whole broad category of what I classified in descriptive sociology as "miscellaneous" disappeared from that rubric and took shape and body: we now know where to file it.

Before instrumental techniques there is the ensemble of techniques of the body. I am not exaggerating the importance of this kind of work, the work of psychosociological taxonomy. But it is something: order imposed on ideas where there was none before. Even inside this grouping of facts, the principle made possible a precise classification. The constant adaptation to a physical, mechanical or chemical aim (for example, when we drink) is pursued in a series of assembled actions, and assembled for the individual not by himself alone but by all his education, by the whole society to which he belongs, in the place he occupies.

Moreover, all these techniques were easily arranged in a system that is common to us, the notion basic to psychologists, particularly Rivers and Head, of the symbolic life of the mind; the notion we have of the activity of the consciousness as being, above all, a system of symbolic assemblages.

I would never stop if I tried to demonstrate to you all the facts that might be listed to make visible this concourse of the body and moral or intellectual symbols. Here let us look for a moment at ourselves. Everything in us all is under command. I am a lecturer for you; you can tell it from my sitting posture and my voice, and you are listening to me seated and in silence. We have a set of permissible or impermissible, natural or unnatural attitudes. Thus, we should attribute different values to the act of staring fixedly: a symbol of politeness in the army, and of rudeness in everyday life.

Principles of the Classification of Body Techniques

Two things were immediately apparent given the notion of techniques of the body: they are divided and vary by sex *and* by age.

Sexual division of body techniques (and not just sexual division of labor). This is a fairly broad subject. The observations of Robert Mearns Yerkes and Wolfgang Köhler on the position of objects with respect to the body (and especially to the groin) in monkeys provide inspiration for a general disquisition on the different attitudes of the moving body in the two sexes with respect to moving objects. Besides, there are classical observations of man himself on this point. They need to be supplemented. Allow me to suggest this series of investigations to my psychologist friends, as I am not very competent in this field and also my time is otherwise engaged. Take the way of *closing the fist*. A man normally closes his fist with the thumb outside, a woman with her thumb inside; perhaps because she has not been taught to do it, but I am sure that if she were taught, it would prove difficult. Her punching, her delivery of a punch, are weak. And everyone knows that a woman's throwing, of a stone for example, is not just weak but always different from that of a man: in a vertical instead of a horizontal plane.

Perhaps this is a case of two instructions. For there is a society of men and a society of women. However, I believe that there are biological and psychological things involved as well. But there again, the psychologist alone will be able to give only dubious explanations, and he will need the collaboration of two neighboring sciences: physiology and sociology.

Variation of body techniques with age.
The child normally squats. We no longer know how to. I believe that this is an absurdity and an inferiority of our races, civilizations, societies. An example: I lived at the front with Australians (whites). They had one considerable advantage over me. When we made a stop in mud or water, they could sit down on their heels to rest, and the "*flotte*," as it was called, stayed below their heels. I was forced to stay standing up in my boots with my whole foot in the water. The squatting position is, in my opinion, an interesting one that could be preserved in a child. It is a very stupid mistake to take it away from him. All mankind, excepting only our societies, has so preserved it.

It seems, besides, that in the series of ages of the human race this posture has also changed in importance. You will remember that curvature of the lower limbs was once regarded as a sign of degeneration. A physiological explanation has been given for this racial characteristic. What even Rudolf Virchow still regarded as an unfortunate degenerate, and is in fact simply what is now called "Neanderthal" man, had curved legs. This is because he normally lived in a squatting position. Hence, there are things that we believe to be hereditary, but which are in reality physiological, psychological or sociological in kind. A certain form of the tendons and even of the bones is simply the result of certain forms of posture and repose. This is clear enough. By this procedure it is possible to classify not only techniques, but also to classify their variations by age and sex.

Having established this classification, which cuts across all classes of society, we can now glimpse a third one.

Classification of body techniques according to efficiency.

Body techniques can be classified according to their efficiency, that is, according to the results of training. Training, like the assembly of a machine, is the search for, the acquisition of, an efficiency. Here it is a human efficiency. These techniques are thus human norms of human training. These procedures that we apply to animals men voluntarily apply to themselves and to their children. The latter are probably the first beings to have been trained in this way, before all the animals, which first had to be tamed. As a result, I could to a certain extent compare these techniques, them and their transmission, to training systems and rank them in the order of their effectiveness.

This is the place for the notion of dexterity, so important in psychology as well as in sociology. But in French we have only the poor term "*habile*," a bad translation of the Latin word "*habilis*," which far better designates those people with a sense of the adaptation of all their well-coordinated movements to a goal, who are practiced, who "know what they are up to." The English notions of craft or cleverness (skill, presence of mind and habit combined) imply competence at something. Once again we are clearly in the technical domain.

Transmission of the form of the techniques.

One last viewpoint: The teaching of techniques being essential, we can classify them according to the nature of this education and training. Here is a new field of studies: masses of details that have not been observed, but should be, constitute the physical education of all ages and both sexes. The child's education is full of so-called details, which are really essential. Take the problem of ambidextrousness, for example: our observations of the movements of the right hand and of the left hand are poor, and we do not know to what extent they are acquired. A pious Muslim can easily be recognized: even when he has a knife and fork (which is rare), he will go to any lengths to avoid using anything but his right hand. He must never touch his food with his left hand, or certain parts of his body with his right. To know why he does not make a certain gesture and does make a certain other gesture, neither the physiology nor the psychology of motor asymmetry in man is enough; it is also necessary to know the traditions that impose it. Robert Hertz has posed this problem correctly.[5] But reflections of this and other kinds can be applied whenever there is a social choice of the principle of movements.

There are grounds for studying all the modes of training, imitation and especially those fundamental fashions that can be called the "modes of life," the *modes*, the *tonus*, the matter, the manners, the way.

Here is the first classification, or rather, four viewpoints.

Biographical Lists of Body Techniques

Another quite different classification is, I would not say, more logical, but easier for the observer. It is a simple list. I had thought of presenting to you a series of small tables, of the kind American professors construct. I shall simply follow more or less the ages of man, the normal biography of an individual, as an arrangement of the body techniques that concern him, or that he is taught.

Techniques of birth and obstetrics.
The facts are not very well known, and much of the classical information is disputable.[6] Among the best is that of Walter Roth on the tribes of Queensland and on those of British Guiana.[7]

The forms of obstetrics are quite variable. The infant Buddha was born with his mother Māya upright and clinging to the branch of a tree. She gave birth standing up. Indian women in the main still give birth in this position. Something we think of as normal, like giving birth lying on one's back, is no more natural than doing so in other positions, such as on all fours. There are techniques of giving birth, both on the mother's part and on that of her helpers, of holding the baby, cutting and tying the umbilical cord, caring for the mother, caring for the child. Here are quite a number of questions of some importance. And here are some more: the choice of the child, the exposure of weaklings, the killing of twins are decisive moments in the history of a race. In ancient history and in other civilizations, the recognition of the child is a crucial event.

Techniques of infancy

Rearing and feeding the child: Attitudes of the two interrelated beings, mother and child. Take the child — suckling, carrying and so on. The history of carrying is very important. A child carried next to its mother's skin for two or three years has a quite different attitude to its mother from that of a child not so carried;[8] it has a contact with its mother utterly unlike our children's. It clings to her neck, her shoulder, it sits astride her hip. This remarkable gymnastics is essential throughout its life. And there is another gymnastics for the mother carrying it. It even seems that psychic states arise here that have disappeared from infancy with us. There are sexual contacts, skin contacts and so on.

Weaning takes a long time, usually two or three years. The obligation to suckle, sometimes even to suckle animals. It takes a long time for the mother's milk to run dry. Besides this, there are relations between weaning and reproduction, suspension of reproduction during weaning.[9]

Mankind can more or less be divided into people with cradles and people without. For there are techniques of the body that presuppose an instrument. Countries with cradles include almost all the peoples of the two northern hemispheres, those of the Andean region and also a certain number of Central African populations. In these last two groups, the use of the cradle coincides with a cranial deformation (which perhaps has serious physiological consequences).

The weaned child can eat and drink; it is taught to walk; it is trained in vision, hearing, in a sense of rhythm and form and movement, often for dancing and music.

It acquires the notions and practices of physical exercise and breathing. It takes certain postures that are often imposed on it.

Techniques of adolescence.

To be observed with men in particular. They are less important with girls in those societies to whose study a course in ethnology is devoted. The big moment in the education of the body is, in fact, the moment of initiation. Because of the way our boys and girls are brought up, we imagine that both acquire the same manners and postures and receive the same training everywhere. The idea is already erroneous about ourselves — and it is totally false in so-called primitive cultures. Moreover, we describe the facts as if something like our own school, beginning straightaway and intended to protect the child and train it for life, had always and everywhere existed. The opposite is the rule. For example, in all black societies, the education of the boy intensifies around the age of puberty, while that of women remains traditional, so to speak. There is no school for women. They are at school with their mothers and are trained there continuously, moving directly, with few exceptions, to the married state. The male child enters the society of men, where he learns his profession, especially the profession of arms. However, for men as well as women, the decisive moment is that of adolescence. It is at this moment that they learn definitively the techniques of the body that they will retain for the whole of their adult lives.

Techniques of adult life.

To list these we can run through the various moments of the day among which coordinated movements and suspensions of movement are distributed.

We can distinguish sleep and waking, and, in waking, rest and activity.

Techniques of sleep: The notion that going to bed is something natural is totally inaccurate. I can tell you that the war taught me to sleep anywhere, on heaps of stones, for example, but that I have never been able to change my bed without a moment of insomnia: only on the second night can I go to sleep quickly.

One thing is very simple: it is possible to distinguish between those societies that have nothing to sleep on except the "floor" and those that have instrumental assistance. The "civilization of latitude 15°" discussed by Fritz Graebner is characterized by, among other things, its use of a bench for the neck.[10] This neckrest is often a totem, sometimes carved with squatting figures of men and totemic animals. There are people with mats and people without (Asia, Oceania, part of America). There are people with pillows and people without. There are populations that lie very close together in a ring to sleep, around a fire or even without a fire. There are primitive ways of getting warm and keeping the feet warm. The people of Tierra del Fuego, who live in a very cold region, cannot warm their feet while they are asleep, because they have only one skin blanket (*guanaco*). Finally there is sleep standing up. The Masai can sleep on their feet. I have slept standing up in the mountains. I have often slept on a horse, sometimes even a moving horse: the horse was more intelligent than I was. The old chroniclers of the invasion picture the Huns and Mongols sleeping on horse-back. This is still true, and the riders' sleeping does not stop the horses' progress.

There is the use of coverings, people who sleep covered and uncovered. There is the hammock and the way of sleeping while suspended.

Here are a large number of practices that are both techniques of the body and that also have profound biological echoes and effects. All this can and must be discovered.

Waking: techniques of rest: Rest can be perfect rest or a mere suspension of activity: lying down, sitting, squatting and so on. Try squatting. You will realize the torture that a Moroccan meal, for example, eaten according to all the rituals, would cause you. The way of sitting down is fundamental. You can distinguish squatting mankind and sitting mankind. And, among the latter, people with benches and people without benches and daises; people with chairs and people without chairs. Wooden chairs supported by crouching figures are widespread, curiously enough, in all the regions at 15° of latitude north and along the equator in both continents.[11] There are people who have tables and people who do not. The table, the Greek trapeza, is far from universal. Normally, it is still a carpet, a mat, throughout the East. This is all complicated, for these forms of rest include meals, conversation and so on. Certain societies take their rest in very peculiar positions. Thus, the whole of Nilotic Africa and part of the Chad region, all the way to Tanganyika, is populated by men who rest in the fields like storks. Some manage to rest on one foot without a pole, others lean on a stick. These resting techniques form real characteristics of civilization, common to a large number of them, to whole families of peoples. Nothing seems more natural to psychologists: I do not know if they would quite agree with me, but

I believe that these postures in the savannah are due to the height of the grasses there and the functions of shepherd or sentry; they are laboriously acquired by education and are preserved.

You have active, generally aesthetic, rest; thus, even dancing at rest, for instance, is frequent. I shall return to this.

Techniques of activity, of movement: By definition, rest is the absence of movement, movement the absence of rest. Here is a straightforward list:

Movements of the whole body: climbing, trampling, walking.

Walking: The *habitus* of the body being upright while walking, breathing, rhythm of the walk, swinging the fists, the elbows, progression with the trunk in advance of the body or by advancing either side of the body alternately (we have grown accustomed to moving all the body forward at once). Feet turned in or out. Extension of the leg. We laugh at the goose-step. It is the way the German army can obtain the maximum extension of the leg, given in particular that all northerners, high on their legs, like to take as long a step as possible. In the absence of these exercises, we Frenchmen remain more or less knock-kneed. Here is one of those idiosyncrasies that is simultaneously a matter of race, of individual mentality and of collective mentality. Techniques such as those of the about-turn are among the most curious. The about-turn "on principle," English-style, is so different from our own that it takes considerable study to master it.

Running: Position of the feet, position of the arms, breathing, running magic, endurance. In Washington, I saw the chief of the Fire Fraternity of the Hopi Indians who had arrived with four of his men to protest against the prohibition of the use of certain alcoholic liquors in their ceremonies. He was certainly the best runner in the world. He had run 250 miles without stopping. All the Pueblos are accustomed to prodigious physical feats of all kinds. Henri Hubert, who had seen them, compared them physically with Japanese athletes. This same Indian was an incomparable dancer.

Finally, we reach techniques of active rest that are not simply a matter of aesthetics, but also of bodily games.

Dancing: You have perhaps attended the lectures of Erich von Hornbostel and Curt Sachs. I recommend to you the latter's very fine history of dancing.[12] I accept their division into dances at rest and dances in action.[13] I am less prepared to accept their hypothesis about the distribution of these dances. They are victims of the fundamental error that is the mainstay of a whole section of sociology. There are supposed to be societies with exclusively masculine descent and others with exclusively uterine descent. The uterine ones, being feminized, tend to dance on the spot; the others, with descent through the male, take their pleasure in moving around.

Sachs has better classified these dances into extrovert and introvert dances.[14] We are plunged straight into psychoanalysis, which is probably quite well founded here. In fact, the sociologist has to see things in a more complex way. Thus, the Polynesians and in particular the Maori, shake vigorously, even on the spot, or move around very energetically when they have the space to do so.

Men's dancing and women's dancing should be distinguished, for they are often opposed.

Finally, we should realize that dancing in a partner's arms is a product of modern European civilization, which demonstrates that things we find natural have a historical origin. Moreover, they horrify everyone in the world but ourselves.

I move on to the techniques of the body that are also a function of vocations and part of vocations or more complex techniques.

Jumping: We have witnessed a transformation of jumping techniques. We all jumped from a springboard and, once again, full-face. I am glad to say that this has stopped. Now people jump, fortunately, from one side. Jumping lengthways, sideways, up and down. Standing jump, pole-vault. Here I return to the objects of the reflection of my friends Köhler, Paul Guillaume and Ignace Meyerson: the comparative psychology of man and animals. I won't say anything more about it. These techniques are infinitely variable.

Climbing: I can tell you that I'm very bad at climbing trees, though reasonable on mountains and rocks. A difference of education and hence of method.

A method of getting up trees using a belt encircling the tree and the body is of prime importance among all so-called primitives. But we do not even have the use of this belt. We see telephone workers climbing with crampons, but no belt. They should be taught this procedure.[15]

The history of mountaineering methods is very noteworthy. It has made fabulous progress in my lifetime.

Descent: Nothing makes me so dizzy as watching a Kabyle going downstairs in Turkish slippers (*babouches*). How can he keep his footing without the slippers coming off? I have tried to see, to do it, but I can't understand.

Nor can I understand how women can walk in high heels. Thus, there is a lot even to be observed, let alone compared.

Swimming: I have told you what I think. Diving, swimming; use of supplementary means; air-floats, planks and so on. We are on the way to the invention of navigation. I was one of those who criticized Louis de Rougemont's book on Australia, demonstrated plagiarisms, believed he was grossly inaccurate.[16] Along with so many others, I held his story for a fable: he had seen the Niol-Niol (northwest Australia) riding cavalcades of great sea turtles. But now we have excellent photographs in which these people can be seen riding turtles. In the same way, Robert Rattray noted the story, among the Ashanti, of pieces of wood on which people swim.[17] Moreover, it has been confirmed for the natives of almost all the lagoons of Guinea and of Porto-Novo, Dahomey, in our own colonies.

Forceful movements: Pushing, pulling, lifting. Everyone knows what a back-heave is. It is an acquired technique, not just a series of movements.

Throwing, upward or along the ground and so on; the way of holding the object to be thrown between the fingers is noteworthy and undergoes great variation.

Holding. Holding between the teeth. Use of the toes, the armpit and so on.

This study of mechanical movements has gotten off to a good start. It is the formation of mechanical "pairs of elements" with the body. You will recall Franz Reuleaux's great theory about the formation of these pairs of elements.[18] And here the great name of Louis-Hubert Farabeuf will not be forgotten. As soon as I use my fist and, a fortiori, when a man had a "Chellean hand-axe" in his hand, these "pairs of elements" are formed.

This is the place for conjuring tricks, sleight of hand, athletics, acrobatics and so on. I must tell you that I had and still have a great admiration for jugglers and gymnasts.

Techniques of care for the body:

Rubbing, washing, soaping: This dossier is hardly a day old. The inventors of soap were not the ancients, they did not use it. It was the Gauls. On the other hand, independently, in the whole of Central America and the northeast of South America they soaped themselves with *quillaia* bark or "brazil," hence the name of the empire.

Care of the mouth: Coughing and spitting technique. Here is personal observation: a little girl did not know how to spit and this made every cold she had much worse. I made inquiries. In her father's village, and in her father's family in particular, in Berry, people do not know how to spit. I taught her to spit. I gave her four sous per spit. As she was saving up for a bicycle, she learned to spit. She is the first person in her family who knows how to spit.

Hygiene in the needs of nature: Here I could list innumerable facts for you.

Consumption techniques:

Eating: You will remember the story Harald Høffding repeats about the shah of Persia. The shah was the guest of Napoleon III and insisted on eating with his fingers. The emperor urged him to use a golden fork. "You don't know what a pleasure you are missing," the shah replied.

Absence and use of knives. An enormous factual error is made by W. J. McGee, who believed he had observed that the Seri (Indians of the Madeleine Peninsula, California), having no notion of knives, were the most primitive human beings. They did not have knives for eating, that is all.[19]

Drinking: It would be very useful to teach children to drink straight from the source, the fountain and so on, or from puddles of water and so on, to pour their drinks straight down their throats and so on.

Techniques of reproduction: Nothing is more technical than sexual positions. Very few writers have had the courage to discuss this question. We should be grateful to Friedrich Krauss for having published his great collection of *Anthropophyteia*.[20] Consider, for example, the technique of the sexual position consisting of this: the woman's legs hang by the knees from the man's elbows. It is a technique specific to the whole Pacific, from Australia to lower Peru, via the Behring Straits but very rare, so to speak, elsewhere.

There are all the techniques of normal and abnormal sexual acts. Contact of the sexual organs, mingling of breath, kisses and so on. Here sexual techniques and sexual morals are closely related.

Techniques of the care of the abnormal: Massages and so on. But let us move on.

General Considerations

General questions may perhaps be of more interest to you than these lists of techniques that I have paraded before you at rather too great a length.

What emerges very clearly from them is the fact that we are everywhere faced with physio-psycho-sociological assemblages of series of actions. These actions are more or less habitual and more or less ancient in the life of the individual and the history of the society.

Let us go further: One of the reasons why these series may more easily be assembled where the individual is concerned is precisely because they are assembled by and for social authority. This is how I taught, as a corporal, the reason for exercise in close order, marching four abreast and in step. Once I ordered the soldiers not to march in step drawn up in ranks and in two files, four abreast, and I obliged the squad to pass between two of the trees in the courtyard. They marched on top of one another. They realized that what they were being made to do was not so stupid. In group life as a whole, there is a kind of education of movements in close order.

In every society, everyone knows and has to know and learn what he has to do in all conditions. Naturally, social life is not exempt from stupidity and abnormalities. Error may be a principle. The French navy only recently began to teach its sailors to swim. Example and order, though, that is the principle. Hence, there is a strong sociological causality in all these facts. I hope you will accept that I am right.

On the other hand, since these are movements of the body, this all presupposes an enormous biological and physiological apparatus. What is the breadth of the linking psychological cogwheel? I deliberately say cogwheel. A Comtian would say that there is no gap between the social and the biological. What I can tell you is that here I see psychological facts as connecting cogs and not as causes, except in moments of creation or reform. Cases of invention, of laying down principle, are rare. Cases of adaptation are an individual psychological matter. In general, though, they are governed by education, and at least by the circumstances of life in common, of contact.

On the other hand, there are two big questions on the agenda for psychology: the question of individual capacities, of technical orientation, and the question of salient features, of biotypology, which may concur with the brief investigations I have just made. The great advances of psychology in the last few years have not, in my opinion, been made vis-à-vis each of the so-called faculties of psychology, but in psychotechnics, and in the analysis of psychological "wholes."

Here the ethnologist comes up against the big questions of the psychic possibilities of such a race and such a biology of such a people. These are fundamental questions. I believe that here, too, whatever the appearances, we are dealing with biologico-sociological phenomena. I think that the basic education in all these techniques consists of an adaptation of the body to their use. For example, the great tests of stoicism, which constitute initiation for the majority of mankind, have as their aim to teach composure, resistance, seriousness, presence of mind, dignity and so on. The main utility I see in my erstwhile mountaineering was this education of my composure, which enabled me to sleep upright on the narrowest ledge overlooking an abyss.

I believe that this whole notion of the education of races selected on the basis of a determinate efficiency is one of the fundamental moments of history itself: education of the vision, education in walking, ascending, descending, running. It consists especially of education in composure. And the latter is, above all, a retarding mechanism, a mechanism inhibiting disorderly movements; this retardation subsequently allows a coordinated response of coordinated movements setting off in the direction of a chosen goal. This resistance to emotional seizure is something fundamental in social and mental life. It separates, it even classifies, the so-called primitive societies according to whether they display more brutal, unreflected, unconscious reaction or, on the contrary, more isolated, precise actions governed by a clear consciousness.

It is thanks to society that there is an intervention of consciousness. It is not thanks to unconsciousness that there is an intervention of society. It is thanks to society that there is the certainty of pre-prepared movements, domination of the conscious over emotion and unconsciousness. It is right that the French navy is now to make it obligatory for its sailors to learn to swim.

From here we easily move on to much more philosophical problems.

I don't know whether you have paid attention to what my friend Marcel Granet has already pointed out in his great investigations into the techniques of Taoism, its body techniques, and breathing techniques in particular.[21] I have studied Sanskrit texts of Yoga enough to know that the same things occur in India. I believe precisely that at the bottom of all our mystical states there are body techniques that we have not studied, which were studied fully in China and India, even in very remote periods. This socio-psycho-biological study should be made. I think that there are necessarily biological means of entering into "communication with God." Although, in the end, breath technique and so on is only the basic aspect in India and China, I believe this technique is much more widespread. At any rate, on this point we have the methods to understand a great many facts that we have not understood hitherto. I even believe that all the recent discoveries in reflex therapy deserve our attention, ours, the sociologists', as well as that of biologists and psychologists…much more competent than ourselves.

NOTES

1. Marcel Mauss, *Manuel d'ethnographie*, ed. Denise Paulme (Paris: Payot, 1947).

2. See Sydney Holland, "Swimming," *Encyclopaedia Britannica* (10th ed. [supp. to the 9th], Edinburgh: Encyclopaedia Britannica, 1902–1903), vol. 33, pp. 140–41 — TRANS.

3. Elsdon Best, *The Maori: Memoirs of the Polynesian Society*, 2 vols. (Wellington: Board of Maori Ethnological Research, 1924), vol. 1, p. 408 (cf. p. 135). [The latter reference seems to be a mistake of Mauss's; could he have been referring to vol. 1, p. 436, or vol. 2, p. 556, which refer to the gait of men and women respectively? — TRANS.]

a mistake of Mauss's; could he have been referring to vol. 1, p. 436, or vol. 2, p. 556, which refer to the gait of men and women respectively? — TRANS.]

4. Christian Gottlieb Teichelmann and Clamor Wilhelm Schurmann, *Outlines of a Grammar, Vocabulary, and Phraseology, of the Aboriginal Language of South Australia, Spoken by the Natives in and for Some Distance around Adelaide* (Adelaide: published by the authors at the native location), xerographic facsimile, South Australian Facsimile Editions no. 39, 1962, p. 73; quoted in Edward John Eyre, *Journals of Expeditions of Discovery into Central Australia and Overland from Adelaide to King George's Sound in the Years 1840–41*, 2 vols. (London: T. and W. Boone, 1845), vol. 2, p. 241.

5. Robert Hertz, "La Prééminence de la main droite: Etude sur la polarité religieuse," *Revue philosophique de la France et de l'étranger* 68 (1909), pp. 553–80 [Hertz, "The Pre-eminence of the Right Hand: A Study in Religious Polarity," in *Death and the Right Hand*, trans. Rodney and Claudia Needham (London: Cohen and West, 1960), pp. 87–113, 155–60].

6. Even the latest editions of Hermann Heinrich Ploss, *Das Weib* (Bertel's editions, etc.) leave something to be desired on this question. [See Hermann Heinrich Ploss, *Das Weib in der Natur- und Völkerkunde, Anthropologische Studien*, 2 vols. (Leipzig: Grieben, 1884); Ploss and Max Bartels, *Das Weib in der Natur- und Völkerkunde*, 2 vols. (8th ed, Leipzig: Grieben, 1905); and Ploss, Max Bartels and Paul Bartels, *Woman: An Historical, Gynecological and Anthropological Compendium*, 3 vols., ed. and trans. Eric John Dingwall (London: Heinemann, 1935) — TRANS.]

7. Walter Edmund Roth, *Ethnological Studies among the North-West-Central Queensland Aborigines* (Brisbane: Government Printer, 1897), pp. 182–83; idem, "An Introductory Study of the Arts, Crafts, and Customs of the Guiana Indians," *Thirty-Eighth Annual Report of the Bureau of American Ethnology to the Smithsonian Institution, 1916–17* (Washington, D.C., 1924), pp. 693–96.

8. Observations are beginning to be published on this point.

9. Ploss's large collection of facts, supplemented by Bartels, is satisfactory on this point. [See Ploss, Bartels and Bartels, *Woman*, vol. 3, p. 183 — TRANS.]

10. Fritz Graebner, *Ethnologie in die Kultur der Gegenwart*, ed. Paul Hinneberg (Leipzig: Teubner, 1923), pt. 3, sec. 5.

11. This is one of the useful observations in Graebner, *Ethnologie in die Kultur*.

12. Curt Sachs, *World History of the Dance*, trans. Bessie Schonberg (London: Allen and Unwin, 1935).

13. Curt Sachs uses the term "close dance" and "expanded dance" — TRANS.

14. Sachs, *World History of the Dance*, pp. 54–61.

15. I have just seen it in use at last (spring 1935).

16. Louis de Rougemont [pseudonym for Henri-Louis Grin], *The Adventures of Louis de Rougemont as Told by Himself* (London: Newnes, 1899), p. 86.

17. Robert Sutherland Rattray, *Ashanti* (Oxford: Clarendon Press, 1923), pp. 62–63, figs. 8–12, 15–16.

18. Franz Reuleaux, *The Kinematics of Machinery: Outlines of a Theory of Machines* (London: Macmillan, 1876), p. 43: "The kinetic elements of a machine are employed singly, but always in pairs; or in other words…the machine cannot so well be said to consist of elements as of pairs of elements [*Elementenpaare*]. This particular manner of constitution forms a distinguishing characteristic of the machine."

19. W. J. McGee, "The Seri Indians," *Seventeenth Annual Report of the Bureau of American Ethnology to the Smithsonian Institute for the Year 1895–96* (Washington, D.C., 1898), p. 152. [In fact, the Seri live on the island of Tiburon and the adjacent mainland of Sonora Province, Mexico, on the Gulf of California — TRANS.]

20. Friedrich Saloman Krauss, ed. *Anthropophyteia: Jahrbücher für folkloristische Erhebungen und Forshungen zur Entwicklunggeschichte der Geschlechtlichen Morala* (Leipzig: Deutsche Verlagaktiengesellschaft, 1904–1909; Ethnologischer Verlag, 1910–1913).

21. Marcel Granet, *Chinese Civilization* (New York: Knopf, 1930).

Johann Cruyff, 1975.

Spine, City, Form
Peter Fend

PERSONS
BALANCE

THEY
FALL
BOTH
WAYS
EACH
TIME

SKELETONS
KEEP FALL
ING DOWN;
ONE WAY &
THE OTHER

SECTION
OF CORE

FROM
CORE
EXTE
NDSA
BODY

ARMS
LEGS
RIBS

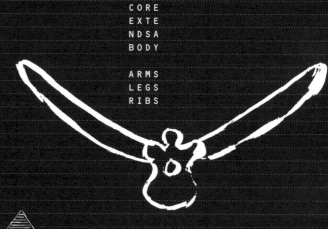

BUILD
NOTAS
ERECT
HUMAN
BUTAS
SPINE
WITHA
SETOF
WINGS

STANDARD
BUILDING
ASITSITS

SPLITOF
FULCRUM
PAIRSON
RAWSITE

FALL
DOWN
BOTH
WAYS

SPLITHE
BUILDING
INHALVES
SOTHATIT
CANHOIST
UPWEIGHT
ANDLEAVE
SITEFREE
FORBEAST

TWIN
FALL
BALA
NCES

478

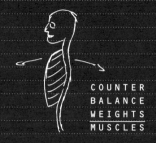

COUNTER
BALANCE
WEIGHTS
MUSCLES

STUDY OF
BACKBONE
AND RIBS

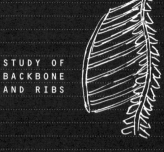

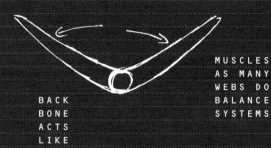

MUSCLES
AS MANY
WEBS DO
BALANCE
SYSTEMS

BACK
BONE
ACTS
LIKE
A FUL
CRUM

ONESPINE
CITYFORM

VIEW   LOFTS

SHOPS

GROUND NOW
EXPOSED TO
SUN & WIND

INDUSTRY   CAISSON

CANTILEVERED
LOFTS HOLD A
MODULE SKEIN

TWOSPINE
CITYFORM

THE CITY
IMITATES
SKELETON
SO LIFTS
OVER THE
WILDLIFE

COUNTER-SWUNG
AQUADUCT MASS
TRANSIT SETUP

CABLES HOIST
MODULE ROOMS
AND OFFICES—
HOLD BALANCE
OF STRUCTURE

Dancing Bodies
Susan Leigh Foster

If you are asked to describe an object, you answer that it is a body with a surface, impenetrable, shaped, coloured, and movable. But subtract all these adjectives from your definition and what is left of that imaginary being you call a body?
— Denis Diderot, "Letters on the Deaf and Dumb"

As a dancer working with, in and through the body, I experience it as a body-of-ideas. I believe it is, as Diderot observed, the sum of all the adjectives that can be applied to it. I know the body only through its response to the methods and techniques used to cultivate it.

When I read recent critical writing about the body, I am, on the one hand, delighted at this new interest in it, and on the other, dismayed by the tendency to treat it as a symbol for desire or sexuality, for a utopia, for that which is unique to woman or for the elusive nature of the text. These writings seldom address the body I know; instead, they move quickly past arms, legs, torso and head on their way to a theoretical agenda that requires something unknowable or unknown as an initial premise. The body remains mysterious and ephemeral, a convenient receptacle for their new theoretical positions.

Alternatively, these writings scrutinize and analyze the body, but only as a product of the various discourses that measure it. Here it exists as the referent for genres of calculation that concern the historian of science or sexuality: we learn intriguing details about the significance of sundry anatomical parts and how they have been subjected to study — and, by extension, incorporated into the larger workings of power.

What I miss in both approaches — the synecdochic substitution of the body for a theoretical topos or its metonymic replacement by a set of measurements — is a more meat-and-bones approach to the body based on an analysis of discourses or practices that *instruct* it. Roland Barthes refers to it in this way when he describes Bunraku puppet performances or the involvement of his own body in the physical organization of his desk and chair, his daily routines and habits of writing.[1] Michel Foucault delineates aspects of the instructable body when he describes the disciplinary procedures, the lines, hierarchies and spatial organizations that bodies are asked to maintain as part of the disciplinary lineaments of culture.[2]

These two examples hardly suffice, though, when one considers what might be done toward studying methods of cultivating the body — whole disciplines through which it is molded, shaped, transformed and, in essence, created. Such disciplines include all sports and physical-culture pursuits; regulations governing posture, etiquette and comportment, and what is dubiously titled "nonverbal communication"; habits in the workplace or place of worship; conduct in the performing arts; patterns of standing, lying, sitting,

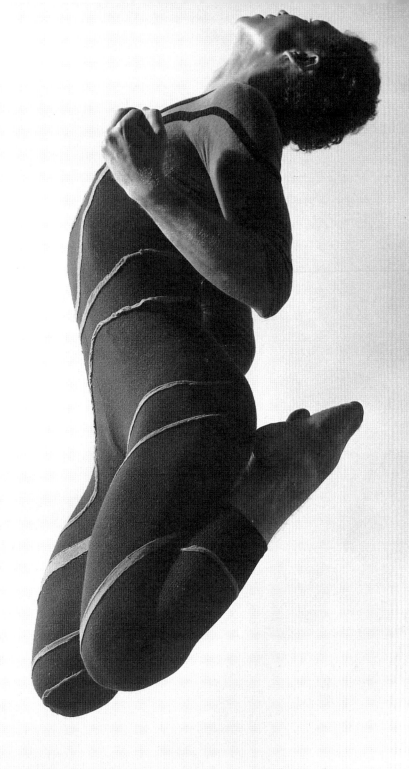

Merce Cunningham, *Totem Ancestor*, 1942.
Barbara Morgan

eating, walking, as well as all practices that contribute to the development of what Marcel Mauss has called "techniques of the body."[3] Such practices, Foucault has demonstrated, are part of the fabric of culture itself. They "invest, mark, train and torture the body; they force it to carry out tasks, to perform ceremonies, and to emit signs."[4]

The daily practical participation of a body in any of these disciplines makes of it a body-of-ideas. Each discipline refers to it using select metaphors and other tropes that make it over. These tropes may be drawn from anatomical discourse or the science of kinesiology; or they may liken the body to a machine, an animal or any other worldly object or event. They may be articulated as verbal descriptions of the body and its actions, or as physical actions that show it how to behave. Whether worded or enacted, these tropes change its meaning by re-presenting it.

In what follows, I shall attempt to describe one such body-of-ideas, that of the theatrical dancer. I have imagined that I am addressing someone who has seen but never participated in theatrical dance. My comments fall into two sections: the first focuses on the formation of dancing bodily consciousness, and the second situates this bodily consciousness in a cultural and aesthetic moment. Both are firmly rooted in a Western framework for considering the purpose and value of dance; they cannot avoid, even as they try to provide a perspective on, Western assumptions about the body, the self and the expressive act.

The Perceived and Ideal
Dancing Bodies

Typically, a dancer spends anywhere from two to six hours per day, six to seven days per week for eight to ten years creating a dancing body. During the course of this travail, the body *seems* constantly to elude one's efforts to direct it. The dancer pursues a certain technique for reforming the body, and the body seems to conform to the instructions given. Yet suddenly, inexplicably, it diverges from expectations, reveals new dimensions and mutely declares its unwillingness or inability to execute commands. Brief moments of "mastery of the body" or of "feeling at one with the body" occur, producing a kind of ecstasy that motivates the dancer to continue. Clear sensations of improvement or progress — the result of a momentary matching of one's knowledge and awareness of the body with a developing physical capacity — also provide encouragement. The prevailing experience, however, is one of loss, of failing to regulate a miragelike substance. Dancers constantly apprehend the discrepancy between what they want to do and what they can do. Even after attaining official membership in the profession, one never has confidence in the body's reliability. The struggle continues to develop and maintain the body in response to new choreographic projects and the devastating evidence of aging.

Training thus creates two bodies: one, perceived and tangible; the other, aesthetically ideal. The dancer's perceived body derives primarily from sensory information that is visual, aural, haptic, olfactory and, perhaps most important, kinaesthetic. Dancers see large portions of their own bodies, a vista that changes as they move. They hear the sounds produced by locomotion, by one body part contacting another, by the breath and by joints and muscles creaking, popping and grinding as they flex, extend and rotate. They feel the body's contact with the ground, with objects or persons and with parts of itself and they sense its temperature and sweat. They smell sweat and breath. They sense kinaesthetic indications of the tension or relaxation, tautness or laxness, and degree of exertion for every muscle, the action of any joint and, consequently, the proximity of one bone to another, the relationship of any part of the body to gravity and the entire body's equilibrium. Any of this information about the perceived body may be incorporated into the dancer's ideal body, where it combines with fantasized visual or kinaesthetic images of a body, images of other dancers' bodies and cinematic or video images of dancing bodies. The dancer's ideal body may specify size, shape and proportion of its parts as well as expertise at executing specific movements. Both bodies, the perceived and the ideal, consist of the skeletal, muscular and nervous systems and any fat tissue of the biological body. The lungs, stomach, sense organs, circulatory systems exist only minimally; other organs and the endocrine system not at all.

Both bodies are constructed in tandem; each influences the development of the other. Both result from the process of taking dance classes, as well as watching dance and talking about it. Cumulatively, these activities help the dancer to develop skills at attending to, duplicating, repeating and remembering bodily movement. A third kind of body, the demonstrative body, mediates the acquisition of these skills by exemplifying correct or incorrect movement. Where the ideal body eludes the dancer with its perfection, the demonstrative body didactically emphasizes or even exaggerates actions necessary to improve dancing: it isolates moments in a movement sequence or parts of the body in order to present an analysis of the ideal. The demonstrative body displays itself in the body of the teacher, and sometimes in one's own image in the mirror and in the bodies of other students in the class and their mirror images. For example, when I look at another student in the class, I see her or his body not as that of a friend or an acquaintance, but as the bodily instantiation of desired or undesired, correct or incorrect, values.

Several systematic programs of instruction, known as "dance techniques," exist for studying the perceived body, organizing the information it presents and correlating it with demonstrative and ideal bodies. Each technique cultivates bodily strength, flexibility and alignment, the shapes made by the body, the rhythm of its movement and the quality and amount of tension through-

out it. Most techniques offer both a body topography, a mapping of key areas on or in it, as well as principles governing the proper relations of these areas. In dance technique classes, this topography is put in motion by performing sequences of movement usually designated by the demonstrative body of the teacher.

Unlike the private classes offered in the technique of playing a musical instrument, dance classes are usually attended by fifteen to fifty students at a time. They occur daily, rather than weekly or monthly, and they rarely present for study and performance an entire dance composition. Phrases or sections of dances may be taught, but the issues of interpretation, development, coherence or style of performance are more often addressed in rehearsal for a specific work rather than in technique class. Furthermore, dancers are not expected to practice extensively on their own. Their training is communal and highly regimented, but it is also context specific. As students learn to duplicate the correctly demonstrative body and to avoid the mistakes of the incorrect body, they present (and are presented with) endless new variations on right and wrong. The demands of both the perceived and the ideal bodies are thus redefined by each teacher with each group of students.

Each dance technique relies on an extensive nomenclature, sometimes literal and sometimes metaphoric, for designating key areas of the body and their relations. A dancer may be asked to "rotate the head of the femur in the hip socket," "lift the floating ribs" or "increase the space between the skull and top cervical vertebra"; alternatively, to become "a balloon expanding with air" or "a puppet." Techniques might visualize the body as a set of abstract lines running close to the bones, as a set of points or regions of the surface and interior, as a set of forces that lift, descend, expand or condense specified areas of the body. Dancers pull, tuck, extend, lift, soften and lengthen areas of the body throughout the duration of the technique class. They learn the curves or angles that body parts can form, and to place these in a particular shape at a given time. They learn to delineate rhythmic structures, to regulate the flow of effort from one part to another, to sculpt, trace and imprint these parts in space.

Both the exercises themselves and any directives offered by the teacher are usually highly repetitive. Drilling is necessary because the aim is nothing less than *creating the body*. With repetition, the images used to describe the body and its actions *become* the body. Metaphors that are inapplicable or incomprehensible when first presented take on a concrete reality over time, through their persistent association with a given movement. For example, it may at first seem impossible to lift the leg forward using the back thigh muscles, but continued attempts to execute the movement with this image in mind subtly reorganize muscular involvement so as to produce the clear perception that precisely this is happening.

Over months and years of study, the training process repeatedly reconfigures the body: it identifies and names aspects or parts that were previously unrecognized, and it restructures the whole in terms of dynamic actions that relate the various parts. Neither the perceived body nor the ideal body remains constant throughout this process: definitions of both are altered and refined. The mastery of one area of the body's topography enables the dancer to comprehend new images and to reconsider familiar ones from a new perspective. Once one can "lift" the leg from "underneath," one can appreciate anew how to avoid "leaning into the hip" of the "supporting" leg.

Metaphors open out into related metaphors, leading the dancer further into a given system for conceptualizing the body. The daily routines of training consolidate metaphoric knowledge and thereby produce bodily habits, some "good" and some "bad." Good habits form the basis for the newly perceived body, and they allow the student to attend to assimilating additional information.

Bad habits (only recognizable as such once they already exist) indicate problems that require special attention. If the metaphoric system in use proves ineffective in eliminating bad habits or in preventing or curing injury, the dancer may discard it in favor of alternative systems. The dancer must decipher each new interpretive framework, however, using as reference the body of metaphors built up through prior training.

As dancers labor to meet the standards for the ideal body — determined sometimes by themselves, at others by a choreographer, style or tradition — they inevitably encounter areas of bodily resistance or incapacity. These deficits are exaggerated by the intensity of training, and they produce highly distorted, often obsessive images of the perceived body. The training regimen reveals the perceived body to be horribly deficient in the size and proportion of its parts. Its areas of inflexibility and lack of strength or endurance can take on grotesque dimensions. Its inability to imitate shapes, to hear rhythms or to relax or tense appropriately become an aberrant inadequacy.

Working to correct bad habits, to modify the body's aberrations and to increase its capabilities, the dancer frequently incurs pain and learns quickly to distinguish between several kinds: constructive pain that will lead to greater strength or flexibility; destructive pain caused by the incorrect positioning or use of a part of the body; chronic pain, the cumulative result of bad habit; pain resulting from too much tension, too little strength, activities other than dance, overambition, inattentiveness and so on. Some pains remain consistent and reliable, and the dancer carries them around as constant features of bodily topography. Others, intermittent and unpredictable, cause the dancer to chase after them in search of a diagnosis that could prevent their recurrence.

As both the perceived and the ideal bodies develop, they increasingly occupy the dancer's consciousness. Over time, dancers increasingly monitor their alignment, the quality of their movement and their bodily pain — not only in the dance studio but in quotidian situations as well. They may or may not apply technical principles learned in the dance class to daily chores and routines, but they certainly attend more fully to these activities. They also retain kinaesthetic information from past performances of these activities so as to begin to acquire a historical sense of their own bodily movements.

Most dance classes emphasize seeing a movement and then performing it, which further heightens the dancer's kinaesthetic awareness of others. Dancers, more than those who do not dance, strongly sense what other persons' bodily movements feel like. Walking down the street, they register the characteristic posture and gait of passers-by; in conversation, they sense the slouch, strain and gesticulations of others. This capacity for kinaesthetic empathy, however, rarely includes erotic feelings. The metaphors used to train the dancing body seldom, if ever, refer to the sexual body. The frequent use of mirrors in learning to dance promotes a form of narcissistic enthrallment with the body, but this is usually mitigated by the tendency to focus on, and criticize, bodily inadequacies. The musculoskeletal empathy developed by dancing usually involves an appraisal of the other's and one's own perceived bodies. The sexual bodies, perhaps adjacent to, and informed by, the dancing bodies, remain clearly separate.

A dancer's daily consciousness of the body thus ranges between her or his perceived body — with all its pains and distortions — and images, both fantasized and real, of other bodies. Dancers alternate between, or sometimes fuse together, images from all these bodies as they objectify, monitor, scan, regard, attend to and keep track of bodily motion throughout the day. The metaphors learned during instruction serve as both markers and interpreters of developing bodily consciousness. They also integrate the training of the body with aesthetic, social and moral be-

liefs about dance. The repertoire of metaphors learned in class functions not only to define the dancer's body but also to establish the epistemological foundation for performing dance.

The Body of Dance Techniques

I have tried to describe the development of dancing bodily consciousness in a way that would apply to most programs of instruction. Each dance technique, however, constructs a specialized and specific body, one that represents a given choreographer's or tradition's aesthetic vision of dance. Each technique creates a body that is unique in how it looks and what it can do. Generally, the style and skills it imparts can be transferred only partially to another technique; thus, ballet dancers cannot assume the bearing or perform the vocabulary of movements found in contact improvisation, and vice versa. Training not only constructs a body but also helps to fashion an expressive self that, in its relation with the body, performs the dance. Aesthetic expression can result when a self uses the body as a vehicle for communicating its thoughts and feelings, or when the self merges with the body and articulates its own physical situation. Body and self can also coexist, enunciating their own concerns and commenting on each other's. Many other relations are also possible, each producing a specific aesthetic impact on dancer, dance and viewer.

In order to illustrate the different forms that expression, both felt and enacted, can take, I have compiled brief descriptions of five twentieth-century techniques that formulate distinct bodies and selves. These descriptions, which emphasize the differences among the techniques, derive from choreographers' and critics' writings about the techniques, as well as from observations I have heard or have made as a student in class. Far from comprehensive, they present only a few key features of each technique in order to suggest possible relationships between body and self that result from instructing the body in a given dance technique.

Ballet Technique. The dominant and most familiar of all theatrical dance techniques is ballet. Of the five bodies to be considered here, it is the only one with requirements for the dancer's physique. Success in this technique depends in part on thin, long limbs capable of displaying the formal geometric features of the tradition. The ideal body — light, quick, precise, strong — designates the linear shapes, the rhythm of phrases, even the pantomimed gestures, all with lyrical effortlessness. Success also requires the promising student to make an early and dedicated commitment to intensive training. The perceived body, never sufficiently thin or well proportioned, must mold itself repeatedly into the abstract forms presented in class and then on stage. The dancer's self exists to facilitate the craftlike acquisition of skills: it serves the choreographer and, ultimately, the tradition by ordering the body to practice and then to perform ideals of movement.

Classes, organized into several levels of competence, measure the student's progress through a standardized set of physical skills. As with the levels of classes, the exercises in a given class progress from simple to more complex. Dancers begin a standard daily sequence with one arm stabilizing the body by holding a barre. They perform movements, announced (in French) by the teacher, originating in, and returning to, basic positions — first on one side and then, switching arms at the barre, on the other. The movements work the legs (always in a turned-out position) and, to a lesser extent, the arms to create variations and embellishments on circular and triangular designs. The torso provides a taut and usually erect center connecting the four appendages and the head. Approximately one half of a class session takes place at the barre. Students then move to the center of the room for longer, more intricate combinations at varying tempos. Class ends with sequences of leaps and turns in which dancers travel across the room diagonally, two or three at a time. Descriptions of movements and corrections are phrased so as to ask parts of the body to conform to abstract shapes; they place the pelvis or head in specific locations, or extend the limbs along imaginary lines in space. Additional criteria based on the precision of timing, clarity of shape and lightness of quality all measure the student's performance.

The teacher illustrates the correct approach by performing a small excerpt from the phrase — seldom, if ever, an entire sequence. The ideal body glimpsed in performances of the premier dancers thus remains distinct from the demonstrative body that models proper practice. From the teacher's unchallenged authority, students assimilate the system of values and internalize the impulse to evaluate and rank their own and others' performances. Competition, although quiet, is fierce — in part because standards for perfection are so clearly defined. The aesthetic

San Francisco Ballet.
Garry Sinick

rationale based on the pursuit of classical beauty offers dancers no alternative conceptions of dance: inability to succeed at ballet implies failure at all dance.[5]

Duncan Technique. Reacting in part against the artificial and hierarchical organization of ballet, Isadora Duncan and several other early twentieth-century choreographers and performers pioneered a radically new dance aesthetic and a concomitant approach to training the body. Claiming for the body an intrinsic freedom and merit, Duncan transported those for whom she danced into an evanescent realm of feeling-filled forms. Her work has been reconstructed by a number of companies that currently perform and teach regularly throughout the United States. It has also been preserved in the practices of dance camps that offer summer study, primarily to women, in interpretive dancing.

For Duncan and those following in her tradition, the dancing body manifests an original naturalness. Unadorned by the contrived distortions of movement that modern society incurs, the ideal body inheres in a primal experience of integration both within one's self and within society. Its harmonious passages for the limbs and graceful phrasing emanate from the protean ductility of the respiring central torso. It is here, in the region of the solar plexus, that soul and body meet and converse. The ideal body resides within every body but deforms at an early age in response to social pressures. By requiring dance study of all young children, it is thought, society will make itself over, for dance is a revolutionary force that evokes noble and pure motives in all its participants.

In order to cultivate the natural body and to allow it to relinquish affected habits, Duncan's approach advocates the study of "basic" human movements such as walking, running, skipping, lying down, standing, turning and jumping — all performed with a graceful, relaxed fullness, initiated by patterns of breath. These basic movements form sequences practiced to music of

Isadora Duncan, *Rubyaiyat* of Omar Khayyam, 1899. Jacob Schloss

great nineteenth-century classical composers. Dancers also act out simple imaginary scenarios guided by the music's meter and harmonic development. Since music is considered to be the truest expression of the human soul, dance, which replicates its compositional structure, can likewise indicate the soul's ephemeral but fervent states of being. When students are asked to "retreat, shielding themselves from an evil force moving toward them," or to "fall to the earth, lie quietly and then rise to greet the sun," they are participating, body and soul, in primordial human situations.

Students imitate the unpretentious intent and full-bodied commitment of the teacher, who frequently dances alongside them. The actual shape of the limbs is less important than the degree of involvement in the dance, evident in the face, the quality of movement and the graceful connections among areas of the body. These criteria for success discourage critical

Martha Graham, *War Theme*, 1941.
Barbara Morgan

evaluation of one's own or others' bodies (such as a pronounced distance between perceived and ideal bodies could only result in pretentious performance). Instead, through repetition in a communal setting, movement and music work their elevating, liberating charm. The ideal body, then, one that has achieved simplicity in its movement and harmony with the self, issues from a nurturing collective of bodies.[6]

Graham Technique. For Martha Graham, the dancing body must possess the strength, flexibility and endurance necessary to provide the expressive self with a fully responsive instrument. The goal of dance, to represent in archetypal form the deep conflicts of the human psyche, can be realized only through a rigorous training program. As with Duncan, the body functions as a perfect index of the self's feelings. The self's ability to express those feelings, though, like the body's ability to manifest them, shares none of Duncan's exuberance — the self is too dark and repressed, the act of expression too tortured for movement to be light and free-flowing. The ideal body, then, even as it manifests an agile responsiveness, also shows in the strained quality and definition of its musculature the ordeal of expression.

Graham's technique coalesced out of the vocabulary she developed in her earliest dances. The basic set of exercises, which became routine by the 1950s, dominated the American university dance curriculum for many years, and it continues to provide a coherent and viable alternative to ballet training in dance schools around the world. The first half of a class — as much time as the ballet student spends at the barre — consists of exercises performed in a sitting or lying position; students then practice sequences standing and, finally, traveling across the floor. The exercises privilege movements originating in the torso and radiating out with restrained tension to the periphery of the body. The slow progression from sitting to standing to traveling,

Erick Hawkins and Martha Graham, "Puritan Love Duet" from *American Document*, 1939.
Barbara Morgan

The principal metaphor explored in these exercises, that of contraction and release, promotes a connection between physical and psychological functioning. Students introspectively delve into the interior body as they contract and relate internal to external space through various pathways of release. Unlike Duncan's classes, in which the student is cast into imagined situations, the comments made in Graham's classes refer only indirectly to psychological experience: they allude to the self's condition by contextualizing physical corrections within the larger and arduous project of becoming an artist. Just as the choreographer must submit to constant self-interrogation concerning the validity of the dance's message, so the dancer scrutinizes self as well as body in a search for the causes of the body's unresponsiveness. The dancer's perceived body, always lacking either in integration or articulation, must struggle to become more than it is — a quest that, in turn, strengthens and sensitizes the self.[7]

Cunningham Technique. Merce Cunningham, a member of the third generation of American modern dancers, left Martha Graham's company in the late 1940s to develop his own approach to choreography and technique.

Cunningham's method presents the physicality of multiple bodies inscribing complex spatial and temporal patterns. His conception of the dancing body fuses body and self by immersing the self in the practical pursuit of enhancing the body's articulacy. The self does not use the body for its own expressive purposes as in Graham or Duncan; rather, it dedicates itself, as in ballet, to the craftlike task of preparing and presenting movement. Unlike ballet, however, a radically nonhierarchical definition of competence and distinctive value prevails. Cunningham's approach celebrates unique physiques, quirkiness and the unanticipated. This is, in part, the open-ended message his dances convey.

Exercises for the technique class vary from

and the tensile successions from central to peripheral body, affirm both the possibility and the difficulty of bodily expression. Exercises, repeated with slight variations composed by the teacher each day, cause the body to spiral around a spinal core, extending out and then pulling back into dynamic positions. The body, galvanized into action as much by its own potential energy as by the dissonant textures of the musical accompaniment, arrives on the downbeat, but then surges almost immediately in a new direction. Although the precise metric requirements for these miniature cycles of attraction and withdrawal give the class an almost military appearance, tensile elasticity predominates over visual pattern in the overall movement.

day to day as they systematically explore the body's segments and their possible range of movement. They present spinal curves, arches and twists, leg lifts, knee bends, brushes of the foot — all using quotidian names for parts of the body and their actions. Sequences of these moves, complex in duration, meter and rhythm, form subtle relations with the surrounding space. Students focus on accomplishing clear bodily enunciations of these spatiotemporal relations. The dancer is asked to enhance bodily accomplishment by remaining alert and concentrated, to be "quick on his or her feet." Where ballet's ideal body privileges certain joint actions over others, Cunningham's ideal body is imbued equally throughout with animated alertness.

The teacher presents movement sequences as problems to be solved. Students are asked to focus on and to demonstrate, through their articulacy, the choreography inherent in the movement sequences. The height of a jump or extended leg matters less than the clear presentation of complex directives — quick changes of weight or focus, polyrhythmic patterns in different body parts, carefully patterned paths of movement across the floor. The accompanist reinforces the emphasis on composition by experimenting with different tonal and timbral frameworks, even for the repetition of a given exercise. Such a strong and contrasting musical presence affirms the autonomy of dance and music as expressive media. Students must attend to the two distinct forms simultaneously and to their unpredictable relationships, rather than to fuse one with the other.[8]

Contact Improvisation Technique. If the Cunningham body is a jointed one, the body cultivated in contact improvisation is weighted and momentous. This technique, developed collaboratively in the early 1970s by Steve Paxton, Nancy Stark Smith, Lisa Nelson and others, explores the body's relations to gravity and to other bodies which result from its ability to flow as a physical mass. Contact improvisation gained popularity rapidly in the United States during the 1970s and early 1980s as an artistic and social movement. Its technique classes were complemented by frequent informal practice sessions known as "jams," which allowed dancers to learn from, perform for, and socialize with, one another. Its lyrical athleticism has been incorporated into the movement style of many dance companies in the United States and also in Europe, where it offers one of the few alternatives to ballet training.

Unlike any of the other techniques discussed here, contact improvisation sets parameters for how to move but does not designate a set vocabulary of movements for students to learn. Students explore through improvisation the movement territory established by the stylistic and technical rules of the form. Classes include practice at simple skills of weight transfer as well as opportunities to use them through improvisation with others. Exercises present ways to "drain weight" out of one area of the body, to "collect" it in another and to transfer weight across any of the body's joints. Certain lifts or rolls are practiced again and again; other exercises direct students to experiment for several minutes at a time with methods of regulating and channeling the body's weight on their own or with a partner. As in Duncan's approach, the body is believed to have its own intelligence — though one encumbered by its artificial and ungainly habits. Dancers can be advised on how to roll, jump into another's arms or land from a great height, but they are also encouraged to "listen" to the body, to be sensitive to its weight and inclinations and to allow new possibilities of movement to unfold spontaneously by attending to the shifting network of ongoing interactions.

The teacher's guidance, like the students' participation, is based on an assessment of the needs of the moment. Rather than specifying a series of preconceived forms, both teacher and students must determine what movement is appropriate for the group at a given time. In this

Nancy Stark Smith and Alan Ptashek,
Contact Improvisation, 1979.
Erich Franz

democratic, unpredictable and highly physical situation, the dancer's self becomes immersed in the body, as it does for Cunningham. The body, however, is not invested with an ongoing identity: its definition is constantly renegotiated in the changing context of the improvised dance. Ideally, its strength should be sufficient to bear the weight of another; but even more important, it must manifest an ability to go with the flow.[9]

Both contact improvisation and Duncan technique cast the teacher in the role of facilitator, and both ask students to appreciate and encourage one another. Each of these techniques embraces all participants in the class, whatever their age or level of expertise, as members of a com-

munity of dancers. In ballet, by contrast, the hierarchy of values evident in the levels of classes and companies, in the choreography itself and in its viewers' responses all incite competition among students. Teachers, as they introduce the tradition's standards for success and rank the students' performance against them, embody the authority of the tradition's abstract ideals. Graham's technique, on the other hand, places dancers in competition with each other but also with themselves. Criteria for success revolve around the dancer's ability to perform fully Graham's vocabulary of movement, but the dancer is also asked to fuse inner motivation with physical form. The teacher encourages the student to measure this psychological and physical participation through comments that question one's commitment to discipline. Cunningham's technique, with its emphasis on composition, encourages dancers to interest themselves in making dance as well as in performing. Students take from class whatever insights may be relevant to their own careers as choreographers and dancers.

The structure of authority developed in each class helps to connect the dancing body to its aesthetic project. Ballet's prescribed pairings of positions and steps, and its emphasis on outwardly rotated legs and arms, constructs a flexible, elegant, lifted body that displays the classical linear and aerial forms that are the hallmarks of that tradition. The teacher's concise directives place the student within that tradition. Duncan's walks and skips, different from the quotidian in their rhythm and quality, embody an ideal of naturalness. Their graceful, grounded litheness seeks to render the body transparent to the luminous inclinations of the soul. The teacher's enthusiasm and conviction help to incorporate the student into the dancing community. The restrained successive movements of Graham's contraction and release build a sinewy, tensile, dynamic body that symbolizes a self full of turbulent feelings and the struggle inherent in expressing those feelings. The teacher's intimation of the arduous training ahead warns students of their need for commitment as it summons them to the dance. Cunningham's matter-of-fact inventory of the body's structural capabilities produces a lanky, intelligent, alert body that eloquently declaims its own physicality. Cunningham teachers tend to approach their students as junior colleagues, instructing them while preserving their autonomy as potential artists. Contact improvisation's athletic, fleet body realizes itself through the act of contact with others. Its teachers must consistently empower students with the ability to improvise an innovative and sensitive response to the collective gathering of dancers.

Much more could be said about each of these techniques — how each elaborates a set of relations among parts of the body, and among dancing bodies, and how each develops the body within a sonoral and architectural environment. Ballet dancers, for example, have insisted on practicing before a mirror since the middle of the eighteenth century, whereas Duncan preferred teaching outdoors on a carefully groomed lawn. Through choices such as these, reiterated daily in distinctive routines, each technique introduces students to the set of metaphors out of which their own perceived and ideal bodies come to be constructed. It also instructs them in the rhetorical relations that bind body to self and to community.

Trisha Brown, *Water Motor*, 1978.
Babette Mangolte

The "Hired" Body

Prior to the last decade, each of these techniques was considered to be unique. Not only did each mark the body so deeply that a dancer could not adequately perform another technique, but each aesthetic project was conceived as mutually exclusive of, if not hostile to, the others. Recently, however, choreographic experimentation with eclectic vocabularies and with new interdisciplinary genres of performance has circumvented the distinctiveness of these bodies. A new cadre of dance makers, called "independent choreographers," has emerged; their aesthetic vision can be traced to the experimental choreography of the early 1960s and 1970s, a period when choreographic investigation challenged boundaries between dance and day-to-day movement and claimed any and all human movement as potential dance. Because these choreographers' work neither grows out of, nor is supported by, any of the academies of dance, classical or modern, their success depends largely on their own entrepreneurial efforts to promote their work. New institutions of "arts management and administration" have grown to meet the needs of producing their work. Issues of fashion and fundability have increasingly influenced their aesthetic development.

These choreographers have not developed new dance techniques to support their choreographic goals, but instead encourage dancers to train in several existing techniques without adopting the aesthetic vision of any. They require a new kind of body, competent at many styles. The new multitalented body resulting from this training melds together features from all the techniques discussed above: it possesses the strength and flexibility found in ballet necessary to lift the leg high in all directions; it can perform any movement neutrally and pragmatically, as in Cunningham's technique; it has mastered the athleticism of contact improvisation, enabling a dancer to fall and tumble, and to support another's weight; it articulates the torso as a Graham dancer does; it has the agility of Duncan's dancers.

This body exists alongside others that remain more deeply involved in, and consequently more expert at, the techniques I have outlined. It does not display its skills as a collage of discrete styles but, rather, homogenizes all styles and vocabularies beneath a sleek, impenetrable surface. Uncommitted to any specific aesthetic vision, it is a body for hire: it trains in order to make a living at dancing.

The hired body has been shaped partly by contemporary practices of physical education whose goals for such activities as sports, aerobics and individual exercise programs — jogging, swimming, weight lifting and so on — have been set by the scientization of the body's needs. Like the ideal body promoted by these activities, this hired body should achieve a certain heart rate, a general level of strength and flexibility and a muscular tonus. The criteria for evaluating its training share physical education's specialized and scientific orientation. They use the language of biology and kinesiology to appraise the strength, flexibility and endurance of the body's muscle groups. Through this scientific language of the body, the body's character is reduced to principles of physics: it can be enlarged here, elasticized there. This body, a purely physical object, can be made over into whatever look one desires. Like one's "lifestyle," it can be constructed to suit one's desires.

Of equal influence on the hired body is the video dancing body, which is as familiar to "dancercize" and MTV enthusiasts as to theatrical dance choreographers, performers and viewers. The video dancing body is often constructed from the edited tapes of dance movement filmed from different angles and distances. Its motion can be slowed, smeared or replicated so that it performs breathtaking feats, and yet it projects none of the tensile qualities of movement, the body's situation in space or the charisma of a live performance. Nonetheless, it offers to performers, choreographers and scholars the irresistible promise of a "permanent" record of the

dance, which can be viewed and reviewed indefinitely. This record, helpful as a tool in the choreographic process, has become increasingly mandatory as a promotional device required by all dance producers and funding agencies as an unproblematic simulacrum of live dance.

Although the video body bears little resemblance to any of the bodies perceived in the dance class, it shares with the hired body certain ideals. Both feature a rubbery flexibility coated with impervious glossiness, and both are equally removed from the aesthetic vision that implements them. Training to construct it primarily takes place standing behind the camera and sitting in the editing room. The techniques it manifests, along with the aesthetic orientation it supports, belong properly to the medium of video, not to dance as a performing art. Training to construct the hired body occurs in rooms full of bodybuilding machines or in dance classes whose overall aesthetic orientation may hold little appeal. Still, both video and hired bodies appear as the products of an efficient and "unbiased" training program, assumed to be neutral and completely adaptable; as a result, they mask the process through which dance technique constructs the body.

Of course, there is nothing new about the assertion of a normative or original body, or an efficacious way to instruct the body. Duncan and the other early modernists, for example, obscured their approach to constructing the body by insisting on the "naturalness" of their training. Their "natural" body, however, contravened prevailing aesthetic ideals and presented a profoundly different alternative, whereas the multipurpose hired body subsumes and smooths over differences. The modernist approach to dance making, even as it promoted the body's movement as material substance to be worked into art, assumed an irrevocable connection to a self. The hired body, built at a great distance from the self, reduces it to a pragmatic merchant of movement proffering whatever look appeals at the moment. It not only denies the existence of a true, deep self, but also proscribes a relational self whose desire to empathize predominates over its need for display. The hired body likewise threatens to obscure the opportunity, opened to us over this century, to apprehend the body as multiple, protean and capable, literally, of being made into many different expressive bodies.

Notes

1. See, for example, Roland Barthes, *The Empire of Signs*, trans. Richard Howard (New York: Hill and Wang, 1978); and *Barthes by Barthes*, trans. Richard Howard (New York: Hill and Wang, 1977). Barthes, however, also uses the body as a symbol for desire and the unconscious. I am indebted to Cynthia Novack and to Kim Benton for their insightful comments on this paper.

Trisha Brown, *Man Walking Down Side of Building,* 1970. Carol Gooden

2. Michel Foucault, *Discipline and Punish: The Birth of the Prison*, trans. Alan Sheridan (New York: Pantheon, 1978).

3. His essay is included in this volume, pp. 454–477 — EDS.

4. Foucault, *Discipline and Punish*, p. 25.

5. Descriptions of the ballet class can be found in Merrill Ashley and Larry Kaplan, *Dancing for Balanchine* (New York: Dutton, 1984); Cynthia Lyle, *Dancers on Dancing* (New York: Drake, 1977); and Joseph Mazo, *Dance Is a Contact Sport* (New York: Saturday Review Press, 1974).

6. For more detailed accounts of Duncan's approach to dance technique see Irma Duncan, *Duncan Dancer* (Middletown, Conn.: Wesleyan University Press, 1966); *The Technique of Isadora Duncan* (Brooklyn, N.Y.: Dance Horizons, 1970); and Isadora Duncan, *The Art of the Dance* (New York: Theatre Arts, 1928).

7. Graham's philosophy of dance technique is summarized in her article, "The American Dance," in Merle Armitage and Virginia Stewart, eds., *Modern Dance* (New York: Weyhe, 1935), pp. 101–106; idem, "A Dancer's World" (transcript of the film *A Dancer's World*) *Dance Observer* (Jan. 1958), p. 5; and in Alice Helpern, "The Evolution of Martha Graham's Technique," Ph.D. Dissertation, New York University, 1981.

8. Cunningham describes his approach to dance technique in his article "The Function of a Technique for Dance," in Walter Sorell, ed., *The Dance Has Many Faces* (New York: World Publishing, 1951), pp. 250–55; and, in conversation with Jacqueline Lesschaeve, *The Dancer and the Dance* (New York: Boyars, 1985).

9. For a comprehensive and insightful analysis of the development of contact improvisation, see Cynthia Novack, *Sharing the Dance: An Ethnography of Contact Improvisation* (Milwaukee: University of Wisconsin Press, 1990); and *Contact Quarterly*, a journal featuring articles on contact improvisation.

The Metropolitan Museum of
Art invited several industrial
designers to assist the architects participating in the 1934
contemporary Industrial Art
Exhibition. Lee Simonson
worked with Raymond Loewy
(shown here) to create this
mockup of an ideal industrial
designer's office. Note the
three-line motif.

Hygiene, Cuisine and the Product World of Early Twentieth-Century America

Ellen Lupton and J. Abbott Miller

Viewed through the categories of traditional art history, "modernism" is a visual style characterized by geometry, simplification, the rejection of conventional types and the invention of new sculptural or graphic forms. "Modernism" also manifested itself in relation to the massive changes that swept through the fields of hygiene and cuisine in the early twentieth century. Modern design has two faces: its public front equates "modernism" with a reduced, elemental style that embraces the imagery and rationality of the Machine Age, while a more private, hidden side may be linked to a reorganization of the human digestive system, enabled by the creation of new products, environments and civic structures.

An art historian might compare a piece of furniture with abstraction and the aesthetics of the machine in art and architecture. Take, for example, Raymond Loewy's model interior for an industrial designer's office, erected in the Metropolitan Museum of Art in 1934.[1] A standard stylistic analysis of Loewy's ideal office might note the reduction of decorative elements to a simple vocabulary of circular and rectilinear forms. The curving structure of the chairs and tables is articulated by a black metal outline, echoing the graphic bands applied to the wall surface. Geometric light fixtures pierce the tabletops, suggesting roots anchored to the floor and stems growing up-ward to the ceiling. The room allusively suggests an elegant ocean liner, a scientific laboratory or a futuristic spacecraft.

Loewy's ideal workshop, however, has sources in a "modernism" of a more domestic sort: not the ocean liner's glamour or the laboratory's rigor but the mundane, familiar and feminized space of the bathroom and kitchen. Loewy has replaced the carved paneling, heavy drapery and rich carpets of the traditional executive suite with built-in cabinets, stationary fixtures, nonporous surfaces and curved forms — typical features of the modern bathroom and kitchen. Hard, seamless linoleum has replaced dust-collecting wood and carpets, concealed storage has replaced open shelving and stationary fixtures have replaced free-standing tables and movable cabinets. Like plumbing pipes, the lamp stems penetrate the floor and counters, apparently integrated into the structure of the building itself. The rounded corners of walls, tables and storage units suggest an easy-to-clean surface harboring no dust or germs.

Modernizing the Bathroom and Kitchen

The modern American bathroom is an invention of the late nineteenth century, arising from the establishment of new urban systems for water supply and waste disposal.[2] Although water supplies were instituted as early as the 1790s

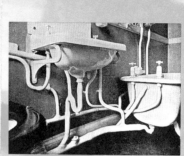

1. American Compact Bathroom, 1908. Around 1908 catalogues show the compact bathroom as the new hotels were beginning to install it. Fixtures are still supplied from different walls: the tub is still raised on feet. Its position along the short wall contrasts with what was hitherto normal. 2. American Compact Bathroom, 1915. Before the one-piece double shelled tub could be mass produced leading American firms were already propagating the compact bathrooms with recessed tub. 3. British bathroom plumbing, 1935. 4. Giuseppe Terragni, Casa del fascio, Como, 1932–1936. 5. "House of the Future" bathroom, Alison and Peter Smithson, Ideal Homes Exhibition, 1956. 6 & 7. Biosphere 2 bathroom, Oracle, Arizona.

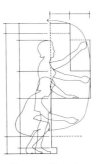

and developed unevenly from then on, the physical and bureaucratic integration of such resources did not begin until the late nineteenth century. Water *supply* technology advanced ahead of water and waste *drainage*, though, resulting in new sanitation and health problems. The actions of health reformers led American cities to frame health codes and plumbing standards in the 1880s.[3] Indoor plumbing, toilets and bathtubs did not become part of an "American standard" of middle-class living until the 1920s.[4]

Prior to the advent of modern plumbing, sanitary devices were used in various areas of the house. Bathing took place in small tubs, easily moved and emptied, which might be found in the bedroom or kitchen, near the hearth for warming water; bowls for more casual bathing rested on washstands. Outhouses were constructed away from the home, and chamber pots were kept most often in small cupboards near the bedside, or disguised with amusing trompe l'oeil techniques.[5]

With the spread of indoor plumbing, the washbasin and the toilet with flushed water drainage assumed a *fixed* position in relation to the plumbing. Accordingly, the "bathroom" became a fixed location in the home, tied to the structure of the building by pipes for water and waste: the pot chamber replaced the chamber pot. When bathrooms with running water

were incorporated into existing homes, they were either assigned marginal spaces such as stairwell landings or, at the other extreme, were allowed to take over bedrooms. In middle- and upper-class Victorian homes, early plumbing devices mingled with the furniture, decorative schemes and rich drapes and carpets of bedrooms and parlors: the bathroom was a kind of hybrid space containing the latest in technology and sensual comforts.

It was at the turn of the century that the bathroom was more strictly defined as a site of sanitary care. As promotional images show, aesthetically and technically coordinated fixtures replaced the loose accumulation of chamber pots, portable tubs, washstands and "running water appliances." White porcelain and bright, polished metals were favored because they revealed the presence of dirt: they were proof of their own cleanliness. The bathroom became a test for the hygiene of the entire house and of the family living there; as a 1917 essay in an architectural journal remarked, "The bathroom is an index to civilization. Time was when it sufficed for a man to be civilized in his mind. We now require a civilization of the body."[6]

The differences between a bedroom or stairwell landing populated with "hygienic furniture" and the bathroom designed as a fully industrialized ensemble of porcelain-enameled fixtures reflect a larger development in health and hygiene: the gradual acceptance of the germ theory of disease, which was the basis for much nineteenth-century health reform. Germ theory, proven in the 1880s with the identification of the disease-producing bacteria of typhus, tuberculosis and cholera, postulated that disease could be transmitted by germs living in dust, dirty clothing, unwashed hands, houseflies, ice — virtually any unclean substance. The entire domestic terrain was animated by potential disease. Germ theory made the thick carpeting, drapery and even

 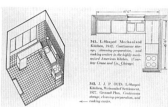  

1. J. J. P. Oud, Weissenhof
Settlement, Stuttgart, 1927.
2. J. J. P. Oud, L-Shaped Kitchen,
Weissenhof Settlement, 1927.
Ground Plan. Continuous
storage, cleaning-preparation
and cooking center. 3. Grete
Schütte-Lihotzsky, Variant of
the Frankfurt Kitchen, Leipzig,
1930. 4. Demonstration Kitchen
of Brooklyn Borough Gas Co.,
based on motion study, 1930
5. Reconstruction of the
Frankfurt Kitchen by Haags
Gemeentemuseum, 1982.
6. Kitchen, Eileen Gray.

the wallpaper of Victorian bathrooms incompatible with "modern" hygienic standards.[7]

Following the bathroom, the middle-class kitchen also underwent technological and aesthetic changes in the early twentieth century. The adoption of nonporous materials for flooring, shelving and work surfaces in the first decades of this century reflected the same ethos of hygiene — as did the gradual disappearance of legs from stoves, refrigerators, sinks and storage units in the 1920s and 1930s. The modern kitchen, like the bathroom, came to favor *fixtures* over *furniture*: the enclosed, cubic forms of modern appliances and cabinets were apparently integrated into the structure of the room, and they eliminated the dust-collecting space beneath them.[8]

Built-in kitchen cabinets are seen in linoleum ads as early as 1921. In addition to reflecting new standards of household cleanliness, built-in cabinetry embodied contemporary theories of how housework should be organized. The widely circulated book *American Woman's Home*, written by Catharine Beecher and Harriet Beecher Stowe in 1869, features a kitchen design with sink and work surface integrated by a single cabinet base; the surrounding walls are lined with shelves.[9] Their model is the "cook's galley in a steamship [which] has every article and utensil used in cooking for two hundred persons, in a space not larger than this stove

room, and so arranged that with one or two steps the cook can reach all he uses."[10] This ideal kitchen, however, was not widely adopted by builders.

The idea of analyzing the kitchen into an efficient work space was promoted again by Christine Frederick, a domestic theorist retained by the *Ladies Home Journal* in the years after 1910. Frederick's 1920 book *Household Engineering* applied the Taylorization of factory labor to housework.[11] As the historian Dolores Hayden has pointed out, the Taylorizing of housework is logically untenable: unlike the factory management on which it was modeled, which presupposes the division of labor into discrete, repetitive motions, the modern housewife works alone on a wide range of tasks.[12] Nevertheless, Frederick's "new housekeeping" attracted considerable publicity — including notice from Taylor himself — and she and other theoretically minded housewives were hired as consultants to the appliance industry.

Frederick focused on the arrangement of kitchen labor rather than the design of individual appliances. Her theories were advanced in the 1920s by German designers and architects, who based on them the redesign of the kitchen's physical units — eventually developing the standard of the built-in, continuous assemblage of cabinets and appliances.[13] No less a personage than architect Bruno Taut took interest in her irrational and rationalized kitchen plans.[14]

The stove designed by Norman Bel Geddes for the Standard Gas Equipment Company in 1932 helped establish the ideal of the modern appliance as an enclosed box sitting on a low base. Geddes's design quickly became the paradigmatic modern stove: an interior framework to which metal panels are clipped. (Such a modular system allowed the manufacturer to assemble a variety of models from one kit of parts.) The stove occupies a single level, with an oven underneath; next to the oven is a concealed compartment for storing pots and pans.

1 & 2. A&P Supermarket. 3. Point
of sale display, 1952. 4. Package
of Bird's eye quick frozen green
peas. 5. Detergents and soap
flakes packaged in standard sized
boxes with front panels used for
sale inducements, and side and
back panels for instructions and
coupons, 1953.

A metal lid covers the stove when not in use, protecting it from dust and unifying it with the other work surfaces of the kitchen. Geddes's stove has been compared to the modern skyscraper, which was also constructed out of modular panels fixed to a steel frame,[15] but there is another source as well — less monumental but more familiar to the kitchen: packaged food.

This type of merchandise, which began to proliferate rapidly in the 1880s, soon dominated urban and suburban grocery sales across the United States. As a primary object of exchange in the rapidly rising consumer economy, packaged food made its mark in industry as well: in 1900, food processing accounted for 20 percent of U.S. manufacturing, and in 1901, food advertising accounted for nearly 15 percent of the business of N. W. Ayer, America's largest advertising agency. Food remained the single most advertised commodity until the 1930s, when it was surpassed by the automobile.[16]

Packaging was a major force in the shift from locally based agriculture to the dominance of corporate food production around the turn of the century. By 1910, many brand names that remain "household words" today were the trademarks of nationally distributed products, including Quaker Oats (1901) and Kellogg's Toasted Cornflakes (1903). Paperboard boxes served to package and advertise dry foods such as crackers and grains, which formerly had been sold in bulk by wholesalers to grocers — conventional products distributed in a new way. This was by no means the rule, though: the first "continuous-process canning" factories — which cooked, preserved and packaged meats and vegetables in a single process — were operated by H. J. Heinz and the Campbell's Soup Company, beginning in the 1880s.[17]

The food package encloses the product in a smooth, uninterrupted skin, giving the organic, shapeless substance inside a clear geometric shape; and it seals the product not only from the elements but from view as well — much as the shells of modern kitchen cabinetry and appliances would later hide the tools and materials of the kitchen. Unlike them, though, modern packaging becomes useless garbage at the end of the consumer cycle: this built-in wastefulness was extended to durable goods in the 1920s and 1930s, when advertising and marketing publicists sought to justify the inherent wastefulness of the modern "consumer economy." Such an economy sells industrial products to a large populace through high-volume production, making individual items cheaper by selling a greater number. The consumer economy was frequently contrasted with traditional European manufacture, in which a smaller quantity of goods, costing more individually, was sold to a smaller and wealthier group. American mass manufacture staked its success on the idea that the working class was a *consuming* class: the capital invested in mass-production ventures required that vast quantities of products be sold to the largest market of all, the wage-earning population.[18]

Because such a consumer economy would fail when the market reached a saturation point, *waste* became an essential component of the *production* cycle. Industry, then, needed to shorten the natural "lifespan" of "durable" products, so that people would buy them not once but several times, thereby stabilizing the production cycle. The most powerful engine of planned obsolescence was stylistic change, an impetus for replacing objects that were not yet physically worn out. Raymond Loewy's 1930 "Evolution Chart of Design" depicts objects in a Darwinian cycle of perpetual transformation: the final product in the series is the female body, a primary marketing site for the expanding consumer economy.

Although designers and advertisers used the term "consumption" in reference to durables such as radios, furniture and clothing, the term's more literal reference was to the food cycle: *to consume* means to devour, to eat in a voracious, gluttonous manner. To consume an object is to destroy it in the process of implementing it, as fire consumes a forest. The advertising executive Ernest Elmo Calkins wrote in 1922, "Goods fall into two classes, those which we use, such as motor cars and safety razors, and those which we use *up*, such as tooth paste or soda biscuit. Consumer engineering must see to it that we use *up* the kind of goods we now merely use."[19] The continual movement of goods through the consumer economy — figured as a kind of "body," whose health depends on continual production and waste, ingestion and excretion — was thus made analogous to human digestion by the promoters of planned obsolescence. "Waste" was conceived not merely as an incidental by-product of the consumption cycle, nor even as an essential moment in it, *but as a generative force.*

Advertising raised the cost of products but was defended as a necessary lubricant for the continual flow of goods through the system: it created desire for new goods (and generated emotional distinctions between things otherwise indistinguishable). It was a major force, moreover, in spreading the new standards of hygiene, housekeeping and nutrition, by promoting the products that promised to make these ideals attainable and describing them in tones of moral urgency.[20]

Giving voice to the ethos of disposal, Christine Frederick employed the oxymoron "creative waste" to describe the housewife's moral and social obligation to buy and discard products rhythmically. The phrase "creative waste" elevated garbage to a form of positive production, valuing the destruction and replacement of objects as a pleasurable and socially instrumental act.[21] In 1841, Catharine Beecher had already described the consumerist ethos: "The use of superfluities…to a certain extent, is as indispensable to promote industry, virtue, and religion, as any direct giv-

ing of money or time."[22] Thus, just as consumption had pervaded the logic of production in the consumer economy, "production" found its place in the process of consumption — a cycle paralleled by the body's most conspicuous and original product, its most "creative" form of waste: excrement.

As the settings for physical sustenance and hygienic care, the kitchen and bathroom — and the product "worlds" they frame — are crucial to intimate bodily experience, helping to form the individual's sense of cleanliness and filth, taste and distaste, pleasure and shame. These rooms are the home's most heavily invested "objects" of domestic labor: failure to meet the high standards of hygienic maintenance attached to them is a source of guilt and embarrassment. Freud wrote that a major domain of infantile sexual experience is the mother's constant attention to the mouth, anus and genitals: feeding, wiping, washing, powdering.[23] By extension and association, the "erogenous zones" of the home are its kitchen and bathroom, which require continual maternal maintenance and are the locale of oral pleasure and personal care for the whole family. The symbolic entrance of the typical suburban home is located at its facade (its "face"), but the home's functioning entrance is more often its back door or "service entry": this aperture — at once mouth and anus — receives and expels a myriad of goods and services. As one architectural writer explained in 1922, "The butcher, the baker, the grocer all deliver their wares at the [service] entry door, and most of the waste must find its way through [this] entry before being removed from the house."[24]

The evolution of industrial methods and economic sectors, domestic spaces and hygienic and culinary concerns were all tied together by across-the-board changes — some as practical as plumbing, others as "subtle" as Frederick's "new housekeeping," the invention of the modern bathroom, and the discovery of ubiquitous

germ-infested surfaces. Given these developments, it is not untenable to speak of the home
as a "disciplinary" site in the Foucauldian
sense.[25] The home as we have described it, in
particular through the modern bathroom and
the modernized kitchen, determines yet another form of docility: *consumerism*, a physical
realization of the logic of the market economy
and its cycles of ingestion and waste.

While Foucault's disciplinary institutions
(school, hospital, prison, factory) are objects of
state, municipal or corporate control, the modern home presents itself as a locale for "private"
experience: private property, private leisure
and private sexual and familial life. This sense
of privacy is epitomized by the sealed-off space
of the bathroom, lodged at the core of home:
the bathroom door can be locked even against
other family members. The ideology of the
home as a "private" place was exploited and
reinforced by the marketers of domestic appliances in the early twentieth century, who dis-
couraged the formation of centralized laundry
and cleaning services by appealing to the sense
that such work should be done at home — that
is, *house*work — and that every home should
have its own mechanical appliances.[26] While
many standard histories of industrial design
describe the mechanization of the home as the
progressive liberation of women from domestic
drudgery, feminist historians have argued that
the appearance of modern appliances was accompanied by ever-more rigorous standards of
cleanliness and maternal duty, and a schedule
increasingly committed to consumption activities.[27] The private "inside" of the household is
continually penetrated by external goods, services and media.

Housework — food preparation, home
maintenance, childcare and so on — has traditionally had a peculiar relation to the money
economy. Typically, it does not create goods
or services sold for cash in the marketplace;
rather, it involves *spending* rather than *earning*

money. Twentieth-century housework, in particular, has largely consisted of managing
consumption and waste: the intake of goods,
services and utilities and their expulsion from
the home in the form of packaging, sewage,
bills and discarded objects.[28] Thus, because it
does not constitute "production" as it is typically understood, housework has been margin-
alized in the discourses of both capitalism and
Marxism.[29]

Industrialized food was a primary model
for the production and consumption of durable
goods. Package design, product design, advertising and market research were all services
offered by major advertising agencies in the
1920s and 1930s, such as Ernest Elmo Calkins'
firm Calkins and Holden — one indication of the
fact that product design was in great part an
extension of the advertising business. Many
industrial designers did in fact begin their
careers with advertising and packaging, and
there are numerous product designs that primarily engage the exterior shell of an object
but not its working parts. For example, Loewy's
redesigns of the Gestetner duplicating machine (1929) and the International Harvester
cream separator (1937) both involved the creation of external casings for an aggregate of
mechanical parts. Similarly, Loewy's Sears
Coldspot refrigerator designs, produced yearly
between 1935 and 1938, were merely modifications of the external box.[30] Loewy explained
his process:

> I believe that when a given product has
> been reduced to its functional best and
> still looks disorganized and ugly, a plain,
> simple shield, easily removable, is aes-
> thetically justified. This shield itself ac-
> complishes something, and it becomes
> functional, the specific function being to
> eliminate confusion.[31]

The continual stylistic modification of consumer goods such as refrigerators, toasters
and cars of course shortened their life span

1. International Harvester cream
separator before redesign by
Raymond Loewy, 1936. 2. International Harvester cream separator, Raymond Loewy, 1936.
3. Streamlined tricycle. 1940.
4. Streamlined pencil sharpener,
Raymond Loewy, 1934.
5. Kitchen cabinet, c. 1930.
6. Stainless-steel flatware for
Krupp Italiana, Milan, Sixth
Milan Triennale.

and ensured their eventual replacement by new models.

A central structure of Marx's thought, according to Elaine Scarry, is the reciprocity between object and body: every manufactured object "recreates" the body, and the body itself becomes a kind of manufactured object.[32] In the most primitive subsistence economy, "consumption" amounts to little more than food to fuel the body and provide for tissue regeneration. As economies advance, a "production" emerges that merely supplements more bodily functions with material objects: tools extend the hand, clothing augments the skin and so on. From this perspective, there is no qualitative difference between the most elementary consumable object, food, and the most technically sophisticated prosthetics, for they all relate to the body as a permeable, manipulable surface, ingesting, incorporating and expelling an expanding range of objects. Yet this openended circulation does not occur in some pure or open space; rather, as various bodily functions are extended "outside" the body, so the spaces of these extensions are embodied, in every sense of the word.

The study of "streamlining" began in the late nineteenth-century research into aerodynamics, and it was originally applied to the design of aircrafts, ships, locomotives and automobiles in a way that reduces the friction encountered in motion ("streamline" referring literally to the path of a particle in a fluid medium as it passes a solid body).[33] The verb "to streamline" (dating from 1913) means, in one sense, to design or construct with a "streamline," in another, to modernize, to organize, to make more efficient or simple — hence the use of "streamlining" to describe the curvaceous, aerodynamic styling typical of 1930s mass-produced objects.

Because such imagery evoked "speed" and "modernity," streamlining evolved into a set of stylistic mannerisms useful for stimulating sales of all kinds of goods, including stationary objects such as Loewy's 1934 pencil sharpener, an object lesson in the misapplication of streamlining.[34] The usefulness of streamlining as a laxative for the consumer economy was eloquently registered by a marketing executive thus: "Streamlining a thing strips it for action, throws off impediments to progress.... [S]treamlining a product and its methods of merchandising is bound to propel it quicker and more profitably through the channels of sales resistance."[35]

That "streamlining" was interchangeable with "cleanlining" points up how it was seen as a technique for modernizing objects totally — gracing them with the "cleaner" lines associated with modern design, on the one hand, and efficiency, hygiene and style on the other.

Characteristic of streamlined design is the production of continuous, sculptural forms that minimize mechanical joints and eliminate hinges, bolts and screws. This aspiration toward seamlessness in streamlined design is usually achieved through the processes of stamping, molding and extrusion — each of these processes requires a "body" from which, or into which, the finished product will take its shape: sheet material is struck against the exterior of the body, a liquid material is poured into the interior of the body or a malleable substance is forced through a shaped aperture.[36] A less technical means of streamlining is evident in a 1935 girdle advertisement that portrays a woman whose garment has the metallic sheen and rigid definition of stamped metal. The ad copy boasts that Flexees "actually streamline the figure, transforming wayward curves and bulges into smart and flattering lines." As with Loewy's evolution chart of design, the female form is represented as yet another raw material upon which industrial culture will leave its stamp.

Unlike traditional industrial products, which were bolted together out of discrete parts, such

1. Dymaxion Bathroom, interior
view. 2. Dymaxion Dwelling
Machine, top interior view.
3. Wichita House, view of central
masthead, 1945. 4. Wichita
House, full assembly, 1945.
5. View of Main Assembly floor
of Beech Aircraft where the
Wichita House was to be produced, 1945.

Buckminster Fuller.

stamped or molded forms took their shape from a negative. As in a photograph, a potential infinity of copies can be cast from a single negative, and the uniform surface of the object is unbroken by such syntactical connectors as bolts, rivets and joints. Laszlo Moholy-Nagy, director of the "New Bauhaus" in Chicago in the late 1930s and early 1940s, was fascinated by the seamless, organic character of streamlining, although he was critical of its decorative, emotional application to mass consumer goods.[37] Moholy proposed the manufacture of stamped objects from continuous pieces of material: for example, "furniture, molded without joints" and "clothing, cast, pressed or molded in one piece."[38] Such objects complemented Moholy's interest in indexical signs as the basis for a "language of vision" grounded in material phenomena: a tire track in the snow, a smear of light on photosensitive paper, the cracks and bubbles of peeling paint.[39]

Streamlining generalizes a machine, concealing its constituent moving parts inside a continuous, sculpted shell, which renders them, thereafter, "internal" components and initiates a distinction between inside and outside. Such industrial skins discourage the user from intervening in a machine's inner regions, and thereby domesticate and anthropomorphize it. As Paul Frankl asserted, "Simple lines tend to cover up the complexity of the machine age. If they do not do this, they at least direct our attention and allow us to feel master of the machine."[40] Similarly, the package and product designer Ben Nash wrote in 1945:

> The automobile designers and manufacturers have achieved the task of making it possible for consumers to practically live in a vehicle of transportation, almost unconscious of its being a piece of complicated mechanism. In brief, the mechanical aspects have been made entirely unobtrusive....[41]

The machine with which people traveled between architectural spaces had itself become a naturalized element of the domestic environment, a machine for living in.

Not surprisingly, machines and objects also took on bodily aspects. Loewy was certainly aware of the anthropomorphic quality of his design: his autobiography invokes the body of Betty Grable, "whose liver and kidneys are no doubt adorable, though I would rather have her with skin than without."[42] Loewy courts a coy Freudianism by titling a chapter of his autobiography "Sex and the Locomotive," and he reveals that it was on a train that he was first kissed. Loewy also rhapsodizes on the Coke bottle:

> Even when wet and cold, its twin-sphered body offers a delightful valley for the friendly hold of one's hand, a feel that is cozy and luscious. It is interesting to watch the almost caressing, affectionate way with which the average teenager fondles his Coke bottle.[43]

Such innuendos are reiterated by publicity shots of Loewy astride his steam engines.

In the literature of streamlining, phallic imagery is a commonly accepted subtext: for example, in the first chapter of his recent book *The Streamlined Decade*, "The Science of Penetration," Donald Bush frequently mentions the predominance of tapered, conical and cylindrical forms in the vocabulary of 1930s design.[44] Yet the reduction of streamlined imagery to a phallic theme overlooks another corporeal process, a surreal conflation of the man-made and the natural: the finely wrought industrial object whose complex curvature conforms to notions of the "organic" rather than to the mechanical. This organicism was supported by the production/waste ethos of modern marketing: product lifespan, decay and obsolescence were critical to the "health" of the economic cycle.

The accelerated "production" of modern consumer culture was accompanied by a renewed attention to all forms of waste. A concern with wasted labor, time and space in the form of purportedly labor-, space- and time-saving devices and procedures masked a

1. Bathroom. 2. Toilet articles.

3. Metallic shower curtain.

4. Ceiling storage space.

Eileen Gray, architect,

1876–1976.

rapidly expanding regime of bodily and domestic caretaking; while new products promised to "save" time, they were part of an increasingly demanding routine of housekeeping and grooming chores. The cleanliness imperative was mirrored by the rhythmic accumulation and disposal of new products — from "durables" such as vacuum cleaners and garbage disposals to expendables such as soap, mouthwash, deodorant, floor polish, air freshener and tissues. Just as socially valued character traits like orderliness and cleanliness drew upon sublimated excremental pleasures, the unprecedented cleanliness promoted by the emerging consumer culture was complemented by a secondary preoccupation with waste. The attention to dust, sweat, bad breath, cooking odors and the innumerable germs hiding in the cracks and crevices of the home was as much a process of *objectification* as of elimination — making visible what had once been invisible, bringing to the surface that which had been "hidden."

Christine Frederick's injunction "creative waste" was a succinct formulation of the emerging "logic" that brought together the contradictory imperatives of production and elimination by figuring waste as a mode of making; the period's euphoric elevation of garbage was complemented by the emergence of rigorous new standards of hygiene. The psychoanalytic literature on anal eroticism has theorized the coexistence of these apparent oppositions — production and waste, cleanliness and filth — as part of the process of socializing individuals: a child fascinated with his or hers own excrement learns to sublimate this urge into character traits such as orderliness, fastidiousness and cleanliness.[45]

As has recently been shown, the marketing and advertising industry was familiar with Freud's *Civilization and Its Discontents*. Egmont Arens notes in his 1932 manifesto, *Consumer Engineering*, that touch is one of the "sublimated" senses of modern culture, and that product and package designers can profit from subtle appeals to the forgotten pleasures of tactility.[46] Designers of the 1920s and 1930s generated products and packages with skins alluringly soft or hard, crisp or curved, glossy or grained, slippery or matte, convex or concave. Unlike the "objective" senses of sight and hearing, tactility involves immediate contact between body and product; it is akin, rather, to taste and smell, which involve the incorporation of the object by the body.

The "sublimated" sense of touch exploited by modern design was one form of a large and even more deeply sublimated aesthetic of anal eroticism. Tactility is part of the child's pleasure in handling his or her own excrement, a forbidden pleasure gradually displaced to progressively abstracted substances: from sand, clay and rubber to pebbles, marbles and coins.[47] An analogous progression from soft to hard — and with it an entry into the economy — is embodied in the organically curved yet hard, enclosed forms of streamlined products, whose models typically were molded out of soft clay and then cast or stamped out of metal or plastic — rigid, nonporous substances impervious to change and resistant to grime.

These contradictory reactions to human waste find their common ground in anal eroticism: in disgust, manifested in stinginess, fastidiousness, organizational compulsiveness, and a general "withholding" or "holding in"; and a delight, manifested in artistic production, generosity and a general "giving out."[48] Objects like Loewy's streamlined pencil sharpener embody an attenuated form of just such a contradictory aesthetic of waste; their molded, sculptural forms reflect the pleasure in manipulating plastic materials as well as a fastidious interest in concealing a messy interior behind a clean, "streamlined" body. And while contemporary and recent discussions of streamlining have revealed a sophistication about "Freudian" symbolism, the referent is assumed to be phallic.[49] These objects, though, also re-semble the biologically extruded forms of feces, the child's first work of art. This additional ref-erent, summarized by the phrase "creative waste," better accounts for the coexistence of a fetishized cleanliness and an economy that values the rhythmic disposal of products as an almost biological imperative.

The nexus of hygiene, waste and efficiency, conflated in streamlining, as an aesthetic and an ideology, is expressed well in a 1937 ad for the laxative Petrolagar. The text describes a modern metropolis where "high speed living" and "unfavorable eating and working conditions" make unhealthy demands on the human body: "The bowel, like a modern railway, must have a regular schedule of operation." This is a com-parison that Raymond Loewy never invited.

Notes

1. For monographic studies of Loewy's career, see Raymond Loewy, *Industrial Design* (Woodstock, N.Y.: Overlook Press, 1979), and Angela Schonberger, ed., *Raymond Loewy: Pioneer of American Industrial Design* (Munich: Prestel, 1990).

2. For a review of sewage and sanitation in urban America, see Stanley K. Schultz and Clay McShane, "To Engineer the Metropolis: Sewers, Sanitation, and City Planning in Late-Nineteenth-Century America," *Journal of Ameri-can History* 65.2 (Sept. 1978), pp. 389–411. Schultz and McShane explain that the compar-atively late development of urban services such as sanitation and water supply is attributable to the decentralized structure of municipal government, whose authority was undercut by real estate speculators who parceled territory and land use.

3. The late and uneven development of water supply is also attributable to the fact that before municipal control, it was often available only to individuals or neighborhoods able either to influence local politicians or to pay companies and individuals for the use of private water supplies. See May Stone, "The Plumbing Paradox," *Winterthur Portfolio* 14.3 (1979), pp. 283–309.

4. As late as 1940, 93.5 percent of the dwellings in urban America had running water, 83 percent were equipped with indoor toilets, and 77.5 percent had bathing arrangements. Of the more than 40 percent of Americans liv-ing in rural areas, 17.8 percent of the homes had running water and 11.2 percent had toilets and bathtubs. Gail Caskey Winkler, *The Well-Appointed Bath* (Washington, D.C.: Preservation Press and The National Trust for Historic Preservation, 1989), p. 11.

5. Histories of the bathroom include, in addition to those cited above, Lawrence Wright, *Clean and Decent: The Fascinating History of the Bathroom and Water Closet and of Sundry Habits, Fashions, and Accessories of the Toilet Principally in Britain, France and America* (New York: Viking, 1960); Sigfried Giedion, *Mechanization Takes Command: A Contribution to Anonymous History* (New York: W. W. Norton, 1975); Alexander Kira, "Sanitation: A Historical Survey," *The Architect's Journal* (April 3, 1937); Reginald Reynolds, *Cleanliness and Godliness or The Further Meta-morphosis* (Garden City, N.Y.: Doubleday, 1946); and Bernard Rudofsky, "Uncleanliness and Ungodliness," *Interior Design* (June 1984), pp. 212–21.

6. "Bathrooms and Civilization," *House and Garden* 30.2 (Feb. 1917), p. 90.

7. Adrian Forty describes the relationship between hygiene and germ theory in his chap-ter "Hygiene and Cleanliness," in *Objects of Desire* (New York: Pantheon, 1986), pp. 156–81. For a more extensive overview, see Daniel M. Fox, *Health Policies and Health Politics: The British and American Experience, 1911–1965* (Princeton: Princeton University Press, 1986). Studies of the popular reception of health and hygiene reform include Andrew McClary, "Germs Are Everywhere: The Germ Threat as Seen in

Magazine Articles, 1890–1920," *Journal of American Culture* 3.1 (Spring 1980), pp. 33–46; and John C. Burnham, *How Superstition Won and Science Lost: Popularizing Science and Health in the United States* (New Brunswick, N.J.: Rutgers University Press, 1987).

8. A history of domestic appliances that focuses on design is Penny Sparke, *Electrical Appliances, Twentieth Century Design* (New York: Dutton, 1987). The impact of domestic technology on housework is chronicled by Ruth Schwartz Cowan, *More Work for Mother: The Ironies of Household Technology from the Open Hearth to the Microwave* (New York: Basic Books, 1983); Giedion, *Mechanization Takes Command*; Susan Strasser, *Never Done: A History of American Housework* (New York: Pantheon, 1982); and Christina Hardyment, *From Mangle to Microwave: The Mechanization of the Household* (Cambridge, Mass.: Polity Press and Basil Blackwell, 1988). A schematic history of the American kitchen, documented with contemporary advertisements, is Jane Celehar, *Kitchens and Kitchenware* (Lombard, Ill.: Wallace Homestead, 1985). On kitchen ranges, see Jane Busch, "Cooking Competition: Technology on the Domestic Market in the 1930s," *Technology and Culture* 24.2 (April 1938), pp. 222–45. American domestic architecture, including its kitchens, is chronicled in two books by Gwendolyn Wright: *Moralism and the Modern Home: Domestic Architecture and Cultural Conflict in Chicago, 1873–1913* (Chicago: University of Chicago Press, 1980), and *Building the American Dream: A Social History of Housing in America* (Cambridge, Mass.: MIT Press, 1981).

9. Works by Catharine Beecher on home economy include *Treatise on Domestic Economy, for the Use of Young Ladies at Home, and at School* (Boston: Marsh, Capon, Lyon, and Webb, 1841), and "How To Redeem Woman's Profession from Dishonor," *Harper's New Monthly Magazine* (1865), pp. 710–16. Catharine Beecher and Harriet Beecher Stowe collaborated on the 1869 *American Woman's Home, or, Principles of Domestic Science, Being a Guide to the Formation and Maintenance of Economical, Healthful, Beautiful, and Christian Homes* (Hartford, Conn.: Stowe–Day Foundation, 1985).

10. Beecher and Beecher Stowe, *American Woman's Home*, p. 34.

11. Christine Frederick, *Household Engineering: Scientific Management in the Home* (Chicago: American School of Home Economics, 1920). Other "scientists" of domestic labor of the period include Lillian Gilbreth and Ellen Richards. See Gilbreth, *Management in the Home: Happier Living through Saving Time and Energy* (New York: Dodd, Mead, 1959); and Richards, *Euthenics: The Science of Controllable Environment* (Boston: Barrows, 1929). Domestic work is compared to factory labor in Mary Ormsbee Whitton, "The Eight Hour Kitchen," *House and Garden* 38.2 (Aug. 1920), pp. 19–21, 81. Anson Rabinbach evaluates the time-and-motion movement in the European context, in *The Human Motor: Energy, Fatigue, and the Origins of Modernity* (New York: Basic Books, 1990).

12. Dolores Hayden, *The Grand Domestic Revolution: A History of Feminist Designs for American Homes, Neighborhoods, and Cities* (Cambridge, Mass.: MIT Press, 1981), p. 285.

13. Penny Sparke discusses Frederick's theories in relation to German design in *Electrical Appliances* (New York: E.P. Dutton, 1987). John Heskett also suggests that the continuous-surface kitchen originated in Germany, inspired in part by American motion studies, in *Industrial Design* (New York and Toronto: Oxford University Press, 1980), pp. 80–84. The concept of a coordinated, fully built-in kitchen was part of the literature, if not the reality, of American domestic design, as shown by the prophetic designs of the Beecher sisters and by articles in the early 1920s such as Kate Hammond, "The Permanent Kitchen," *House and Garden* 38.2 (Aug. 1920), p. 51; and Ethel R. Peyser,

"Furnishing Your Kitchen," *House and Garden* 38.3 (Sept. 1920), pp. 56–57, 76, 78, 82.

14. Bruno Taut, *Die Neue Wohnung, Die Frau als Schoüpferin* (Leipzig: Klinkhardt and Biermann, 1926).

15. Jeffrey L. Meikle, *Twentieth Century Limited: Industrial Design in America, 1925–1939* (Philadelphia: Temple University Press, 1979), p. 102; and Arthur Pulos, *American Design Ethic: A History of American Design to 1940* (Cambridge, Mass.: MIT Press, 1983), p. 358.

16. Harvey A. Levenstein, *Revolution at the Table: The Transformation of the American Diet* (New York and Oxford: Oxford University Press, 1988), pp. 35, 37.

17. Afred D. Chandler describes the rise of the modern food corporation in *The Visible Hand: The Managerial Revolution in American Business* (Cambridge, Mass.: Belknap Press, 1977), chs. 7 and 9. A pictorial catalogue of American brandnames is Hal Morgan, *Symbols of America* (New York: Penguin, 1987). On food processing, see Samuel C. Prescott and Bernard E. Proctor, *Food Technology* (New York: McGraw-Hill, 1945). An early report on quick-freezing, noting its packaging benefits, is Allan Shephard, "The Quick-Freezing Process and the Distribution of Frozen Foods," *Harvard Business Review* 8.3 (April 1930), pp. 339–45. On changes in grocery store design, see Chester L. Liebs, *Mainstreet to Miracle Mile: American Roadside Architecture* (Boston: Little, Brown, 1985). Textbooks on package design include Richard Franken and Carroll B. Larrabee, *Packages that Sell* (New York: Harper, 1928); and Carroll B. Larrabee, *How To Package for Profit: A Manual for Packaging* (New York: Harper, 1935).

18. The ideology of consumerism is summarized and celebrated in Daniel J. Boorstin, "Welcome to the Consumption Community," *Fortune* 76 (1967), pp. 118–38.

19. In Roy Sheldon and Egmont Arens, *Consumer Engineering, A New Technique for Prosperity* (New York: Harper, 1932), p. 32.

20. See Roland Marchand, *Advertising the American Dream* (Berkeley: University of California Press, 1985).

21. Frederick uses the term "creative waste" in *Selling Mrs. Consumer* (New York: The Business Bourse, 1929). Numerous texts written in the 1920s and 1930s voiced this ethos: for example, "It's up to the Women: The Movement Started by the Journal Is Sweeping the Country," *Ladies Home Journal* (April 1932), compares the shopping habits of "Mrs. Depression" and "Mrs. Prosperity." The social historian Winifred Wandersee has demonstrated that women were indeed spending a great deal during the Depression, often struggling to maintain the "standards of living" that emerged during the 1920s. Many married women went to work in order to support new "necessities" such as electric appliances and automobiles. See Wandersee, *Women's Work and Family Values, 1920–1940* (Cambridge, Mass.: Harvard University Press, 1981).

22. Beecher, *Treatise on Domestic Economy*, p. 161.

23. *The Standard Edition of the Complete Psychological Work of Sigmund Freud*, ed. James Strachey, (London: Hogarth, 1953), vol. 7, pp. 173–200.

24. Verna Cook Salomonsky, "Putting the Service Entry To Work," *House and Garden* 41.1 (Jan. 1922), p. 51.

25. Michel Foucault, *Discipline and Punish: The Birth of the Prison*, trans. Alan Sheridan (New York: Vintage, 1979).

26. See Fred DeArmond, *The Laundry Industry* (New York: Harper, 1950).

27. For mechanization as liberation, see Giedion, *Mechanization Takes Command*, Pulos, *American Design Ethic*, and Heskett, *Industrial Design*; for mechanization as intensified drudgery, see Cowan, *More Work for Mother*, and Strasser, *Never Done*.

28. Works discussing the role of consumption in American housework include Cowan,

cited above, and her earlier essay "The 'Industrial Revolution' in the Home: Household Technology and Social Change in the Twentieth Century," *Technology and Culture* 17.1 (Jan. 1976), pp. 1–23. See also John Kenneth Galbraith, *Economics and the Public Purpose* (Boston: Houghton Mifflin, 1973); and Christine Kleinegger, "Out of the Barns and into the Kitchens: Transformations in Farm Women's Work in the First Half of the Twentieth Century," in Barbara Drygulski et al., eds., *Women, Work, and Technology: Transformations* (Ann Arbor: University of Michigan Press, 1987), pp. 162–81.

29.   For a review of the literature on the economic status of housework, see Nona Glazer-Marlbin, "Housework," *Signs: Journal of Women in Culture and Society* 1.4 (1976), pp. 905–22. For a discussion of the status of housework in Marxist terms, see Terry Fee, "Domestic Labor: An Analysis of Housework and Its Relation to the Production Process," *Review of Radical Economics* (Spring 1976), pp. 61–68. Phyllis Palmer's book *Domesticity and Dirt: Housewives and Domestic Servants in the United States, 1920–1945* (Philadelphia: Temple University Press, 1984) asserts that more middle-class women had servants during the interwar period than is commonly thought, and that the high standards of housekeeping inherited from that period are based on the ideal of a house with servants.

30.   Meikle, *Twentieth Century Limited*, pp. 104–107.

31.   Raymond Loewy, *Never Leave Well Enough Alone* (New York: Simon and Schuster, 1951), p. 219.

32.   Elaine Scarry, *The Body in Pain: The Making and Unmaking of the Material World* (New York and Oxford: Oxford University Press, 1985).

33.   See Donald J. Bush, *The Streamlined Decade* (New York: Braziller, 1975), pp. 4–14.

34.   Pulos, *American Design Ethic*, p. 395.

35.   Quoted in Meikle, *Twentieth Century Limited*, p. 72.

36.   For a brief history of plastic, see E. G. Couzens and V. E. Yarsley, *Plastics in the Modern World* (Baltimore: Penguin, 1968). For a discussion of industrial plastics forming techniques, see Clark N. Robinson, *Meet the Plastics* (New York: Macmillan, 1949).

37.   Laszlo Moholy-Nagy, *Vision in Motion* (Chicago: Paul Theobold, 1969).

38.   Ibid., pp. 51–54.

39.   See Ellen Lupton, "Visual Dictionary," in Lupton and J. Abbott Miller, eds., *The Bauhaus and Design Theory* (New York: The Cooper Union and Princeton Architectural Press, 1990), pp. 22–33.

40.   Quoted in Meikle, *Twentieth Century Limited*, p. 153.

41.   Ben Nash, *Developing Marketable Products and Their Packaging* (New York: McGraw-Hill, 1945), p. 87.

42.   Loewy, *Never Leave Well Enough Alone*, p. 220.

43.   Loewy, *Never Leave Well Enough Alone*, p. 297.

44.   See also Karal Ann Marling and Donald J. Bush, "Autoeroticism," *Design Quarterly* 146 (1989).

45.   Sigmund Freud, *Civilization and Its Discontents*, ed. and trans. James Strachey (New York: W. W. Norton, 1961), pp. 43–45.

46.   Stuart Ewen, *All Consuming Images: The Politics of Style in Contemporary Culture* (New York: Basic Books, 1988), pp. 49–50.

47.   Sandor Ferenczi, "The Ontogenesis of the Interest in Money," in Ferenczi and Otto Rank, *Sex in Psycho-Analysis* (New York: Dover, 1956), pp. 269–79.

48.   Ernest Jones, *Papers on Psychoanalysis* (Boston: Beacon, 1961).

49.   Richard Pommer acknowledges the sexual, yet strictly phallic, implications of streamlining in "Loewy and the Industrial Skin Game."

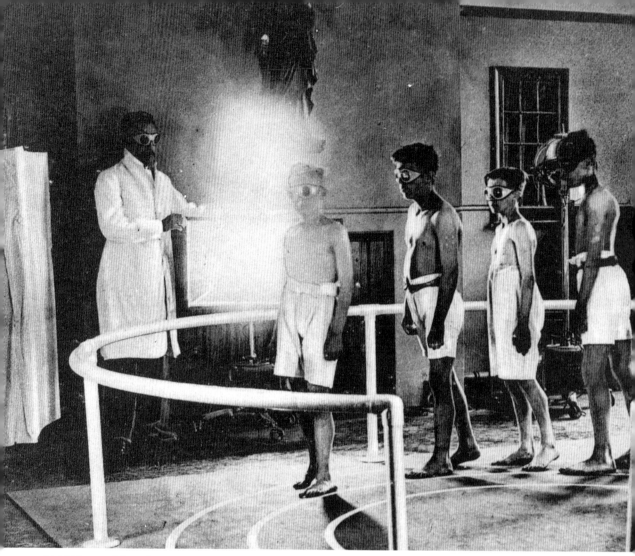

Light Therapy Clinic, Bedford Court College, Worcestershire, c. 1920.

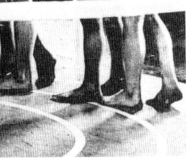

Toward a Biopsychiatry

François Dagognet

Before one can read the marks of a troubled mind on the sensitive and polyphonic body, one must first understand how the body effectively encloses and reveals the psyche. Two powers affect us all, gradually giving us shape: on the one hand, the sum of our instinctual drives (notably the sexual and oral, the need for food, sleep and so on); on the other, society supervising those drives, tolerating them as long as they remain within limits, otherwise persecuting and suppressing them. We are born where the currents of desire and forces of order meet. The somatic arises from their confrontation or reconciliation.

This is why looking at the body can reveal the conflict of these powers at their intersection or interface. Thus, what I shall provisionally call the "anthropologist" must necessarily take an interest in appearance and a full range of physical manifestations (such as posture, bearing, gestures, the voice and its timbre, facial expressions). Isn't a key element of his art to externalize buried psychomotility as much as affectivity (which he apprehends during the act of transference)? In effect, the psychomotorial has been obliged to become "virtual" to such an extent that it has almost disappeared from view. One must learn to represent it, to convert the interior to the exterior. Then it will be possible to put the "mind" outside, to lay it bare.

No one can accomplish this kind of "visualization" or projection without instruments (oscilloscopes, telemetric devices and so on). Success is possible because the mind is unable to withdraw completely into its inner recesses. It continues to "disperse" or to percolate to the surface. As vigorously as one tries to constrain it — and it is indispensable that one should — at every turn one encounters signs of its presence. It emerges just as markedly in a furtive sideways motility as in apparently insignificant acts, which unexpectedly take on meaning. These minor details become "symptoms." Indeed, I have affirmed elsewhere that the body *is* the unconscious. We must not imagine desires or drives as submerged in some vague, black night: they never cease, however indirectly, to reveal themselves. Let's abandon the dangerous idea of an ego that is interior or hidden.

In his unpublished lectures, Georges Canguilhem remarks that the word "secret" must be compared to "secretion" (that which flows) and "secretary" (documents preserved and made public, depositions, records). Certainly, a gland must remove from circulation those substances it needs to produce its secretions. It sets aside and hoards accordingly. Likewise, an administration keeps its archives locked up. In both cases, something is isolated; this meaning, however, is masked by the other meanings, namely that of discharging (the gland) or informing (the secretariat). In short, language never lies. We are (just barely) in the presence of an ambivalent term. Through words, one knows that what claims to be hidden is not. It is no different with the corporeal, which hides less than it reveals. The interior overflows; mental energy always spills over. Let us learn to recover and interrogate that overflow.

In "The Purloined Letter," Edgar Allan Poe demonstrates that one conceals most effectively by not concealing at all: a minister has purloined a letter with which he plans to blackmail the queen; the police, though they rigorously search both his person and his premises, cannot find it — because he has left it out in the open. "The more I reflected...the more satisfied I became that, to conceal this letter, the Minister had resorted to the comprehensive and sagacious expedient of not attempting to conceal it at all."[1] The comment applies equally to the psyche. Doesn't the ego betray itself by being too dishonest and secretive? Don't violent thoughts occasionally overflow the boundaries that are supposed to contain them, don't they aspire to show themselves by whatever means they can? In short, the surface always betrays what lies below.

Freud addressed this "externalization" of deep-seated conflicts, if only in terms of transference. The subject appears not to know what perturbs him: it must be brought to consciousness, thereby exposing a confused "formation" (rebellion, division). The patient must be reconciled with herself. Freud also finds the "vicissitudes of the repressed" in daily life, proof that the unconscious demands at least symbolic satisfactions and accomplishments. We know that Freud initially turned to "dream images" in order to grasp more fully the patient's crises, but he was forced to pull back and admit that the goal of such a quest is unattainable. The dream is always narrated by a psyche that rearranges, that necessarily distorts the order and content of the imaginary scenes. Eventually, Freud came to understand that an individual continues to dream, even when she is fully awake. Throughout life, the subject is a sleepwalker.

Let me briefly note that an eminent specialist of the nervous system, Michel Jouvet (whose work with psychoelectric procedures I shall draw on later), conclusively demonstrated the existence of "waking sleepers." It had been thought that humans divide their lives between two states (sleep and waking), whereas in fact a third state invades and is nourished by the first two. Thus, the subject's reveries continue during the day in a different mode. This fact explains the frequently observed difficulties in attention of the apparently alert child (it is sleeping on its feet).[2] This also explains the more conspicuous phenomenon of strange states in adults who have been prevented from sleeping:

> If a subject is kept awake by whatever methods (coffee, cold water and so on), a syndrome that can be characterized as a waking sleep appears by the end of the second day. An electroencephalograph registers very brief episodes of sleep during which the subject is unable to focus his attention, is incapable of distinguishing true from false, and is no longer able to control his actions.... If lack of sleep is prolonged, by the end of the third day a very pronounced syndrome appears, accompanied by both objective and subjective symptoms. Objectively, the subject's features are drawn and haggard; he has what the Anglo-Saxons call the mindszenty look (after Cardinal Mindszenty). The fingers and forehead show signs of confused sensory perceptions....[3]

This proves that the adult whose rest is disrupted plunges squarely into that middle state.

Lacking such means or proofs, Freud was nonetheless able to turn his attention from the patient's nocturnal life to his "daytime" life, punctuated by spells of gloom and sudden nightmares. On the one hand, he turned to involuntary witticisms: these are inspired by the inhibited energies they bring into focus; the satisfactions they give rise to are intense, yet brief. Below the tightly controlled and slow-moving surface of language, a second language lurks, testifying to our principal desires. On the other hand, daily life is rife with actions corresponding to the least-tolerated tendencies. When the subject gives in to an activity that takes center stage and marshals his attention, tiny, inconsequential movements — a flurry of tics, gestures like "scratching, fidgeting, rubbing, turning to manipulate objects in his fingers, even brandishing useless implements" — cannot be prevented. It is impossible to overemphasize the importance of these gestural symptoms. Both diffuse and minute, they constitute an implicit challenge to our exterior persona. Through them, what was prohibited is revealed or at least allowed to surface. "There are a thousand unnoticed openings," notes Freud, "which let a penetrating eye at once into a man's soul."[4]

From the outset, the educative process of "mentalization" constricts and obstructs the underlying, primary activity, because the latter is fraught with explosive risks. Reflection is well named, insofar as the indistinctly motor-emotive current turns back on itself, only gradually producing a vague outline. And it is this circuit that constitutes the psyche, opening the way for consciousness. The immediate and the concrete give way to the possible (a virtual, increasingly internalized picture). This metamorphosis, however, does not descend upon us as a sudden miracle. Verbalization, speech, the ability to "represent" intervenes between the two poles. Words lighten a burden that, in their absence, would be hard to either "carry" or hold on to: they welcome "incorporation and assimilation." Thus, the orator is allowed to try the speech out on himself before delivering it in public. Thanks to this mirror effect, he is able to shift from listener and speaker to actor-spectator. Thus divided, contemplation and leisurely preparation make ready for every eventuality. From now on, his way is well lit. I freely grant to this transformation all the importance it deserves. It defines "true subjectivity." This indispensable cerebral labor, though, so often analyzed by anthropologists from Condillac to Pierre Janet, does not altogether eliminate the accompaniment or participation of the motorial. To acknowledge how imperceptible and virtual this may be is not to deny that it exists: the ego has never been unfettered from the corporeal in which it is "inscribed."

Let me recall now a particularly well-known and well-documented process. It evolves in three stages. First, a child, spectator to some external activity, initially joins in and pantomimes it with hands, legs or, if possible, the entire body. The child's fidgeting is tireless, even exhausting. She must be trained to repress this motor participation, to moderate this waste of energy. Second and later, the spectator limits herself to less blatant imitations. The spectator's pupils openly follow moving objects, and her head turns as needed to keep up with them, hiding neither the act of looking nor object of attention. Her actions are still emphatic (the look is frank and open). Finally, the subject gradually learns not to call attention to herself: the eyes appear to be fixed, even as they track moving objects. This dance, during the course of which we gain self-control — let us mark the movements — withdraws into the realm of the cerebral. All the while, the eyelashes continue to flutter, the eyes to turn in place, the hands to fidget, the lips to move. But this fibrillation is perceptible only by means of instruments that record and amplify neuropsychic vibrations. The body does not stop entering into the external scene; it still participates, becomes unsettled (frenzied), but society requires it to maintain apparent immobility. No one moves as much as a child, and nothing is more intolerable than the motion, the instability of an adult who externalizes himself, expending this degree of energy. We find it difficult to tolerate because it constricts us (impoliteness consists of stretching out, occupying space, ignoring others) and above all because such excess reminds us of our own sacrifices, the suffering that accompanies our self-restraint. "Why have I given up this freedom," we protest inwardly, "while so-and-so refuses to?" Partial petrification, rigidity: that is what our early education accomplishes, aided by the storm of cerebromotor activity that compensates for relative paralysis. Initially, a child does not know how to sit down or keep still. It wants to get up, run around, explore, gesticulate freely. We make it "do nothing," force it to "wait" (at the dinner table, for example, when the food is late in arriving). "Active inaction" is one of the first burdensome tasks a child faces. "To think is to refrain from acting," has been repeated often enough. Classical psychology has clearly analyzed this process of mentalization.

Psychology apparently has illuminated one side of the process at the expense of the other. It has contemplated the "death of the body," eliminated and replaced by increasingly disembodied "images," some of which may even cross over into the unreal. But the body has been refined rather than actually expelled. The psychomotorial continues to maintain and sustain inner life, even if we ignore what continues to indicate its presence (a new set of apparently cortical gestures).

Let me delineate some of the methods and instruments that make it possible to bring the interior life out into the open. We know how to make it visual. We become aware of its essential role as much with respect to the recognition and detection of aptitudes (the instrumental aspect) as to attitudes (the investigation of so-called personality, its system of "demands and inhibitions"). It is worthwhile to distinguish these two axes of analysis, even if they ultimately intersect.

Perhaps I will be reproached for "violating" the personality: it digs in, and one dislodges it; it slips away (with every justification), and one tracks it down. Why such zeal to unveil it? To be sure, subjecting individuals to psychological "X-rays" is an ill-conceived project unless the goal is therapeutic; otherwise one is exploring for perverse, voyeuristic ends or to fulfill a sociopolitical objective (the subordination of a scholarly and professional orientation to a technocratic whole is also dangerous, especially inasmuch as it fails: too much planning leads to inertia, pigeonholing and squeezing patients into systems that are simply not large enough and break down). I am not unaware of all these perils, but eventually I shall justify these techniques of transference or exteriorization. Let me limit myself to the following double comment by Marcel Jousse, a theoretician of gestures. First, he affirms, "Anything that cannot be recorded represents an imperfection in our present microscopic or macroscopic methods. More or less makes no real difference to the nature of a gesture. A microscopic internal gesture is just as much a gesture and just as measurable as a macroscopic external gesture."[5] Another comment by Jousse to which I subscribe fully: "For too long, we have neglected to study human gestures under the microscope. When someone says, 'To think is to refrain from acting,' he makes a profound mistake. On the contrary, it is to tighten the human composition so the interplay will be more intense."[6] I shall remember these useful warnings; now let me turn to a description of three of the practices that permit a psychological laboratory to conduct its investigations.

The first is that of Carl Jung, who wanted to explore the hidden (motor) dimension. Instead of collecting surface symptoms, he employed devices to measure body tensions. The most notable of these devices is the pneumometer. His cunning technique of "word induction," is familiar to many. Hearing a particular word, the subject is invited to respond by free association with what are called "induced words." It is true that the subject is an imperfect participant: he employs stratagems to elude this trap, mentioning any word or even resorting to conventional tricks, while what is really called for is a spontaneous response. Jung took precise measurements of verbal discharges or the volume of air exhaled. Why? First of all, words are heavy and evocative, loaded with meaning; they reverberate in the mind, which means they affect breathing. They may perturb the mind a little or momentarily daze it. This technique of word induction also deploys a chronometer to measure the elapsed time between stimulus and response. Not living in tenths of a second, an individual cannot control these slight delays. The delay of the response already proves that we are in the presence of a "vocable" with emotional overtones. Conversely, strictly neutral, anonymous terms — carriers of information associated with no memories — proceed rapidly and produce a cascade of suggestions. But the pneumometer goes further: as I have noted, it records and measures respiration. One's body does not form a homogeneous whole: it allows for tightly controlled zones (the glance, facial muscles, especially utterances, bearing and so on) as well as, by necessity, less controlled zones. But why bother about things that escape the best observers just as they elude the subject?

How can we monitor what escapes us (microtensions)? "At the critical moment," notes Jung, "the volume of air exhaled decreases, respiration is diminished...."[7] By itself, the voice, slightly tense or disguised, externalizes the psyche in a similar fashion, but to a greater degree it externalizes the "this-sidedness" of the psyche, the discharge of air, an opening up to the outer atmosphere, to the environment (whether or not the body is constrained). What one exhales one must inhale. Measuring the latter is tantamount to measuring the behavior of the subject in full interface (at the mind–body juncture). Starting from such psychophysiological measurements, Jung unearthed complexes or dramatic scenes that otherwise never would have come to light. The psychologist is thus comparable to a geologist. The latter also relies on minute signs, insignificant, sometimes almost invisible, in order to determine where minerals and other underground riches are deposited. The earth's crust reveals the depths below. Doubtless, it is better to work with direct samples, to bore beneath the surface, but one can gather information just by looking at the surface. The same applies to psychopathology. Wasn't the essence of Hippocrates' art to diagnose the patient by examining demeanor, facial expressions and such?

Thus, we can distinguish at least three sorts of peripheral action: first, actions that escape our consciousness, such as breathing, certain voice intonations and modulations; second, minute, imperceptible actions, such as eye and lip movements, a multitude of microgestures, which accompany or give play to the psyche — their economy as well as their waste; finally — and we cannot forget the most explosive of these actions, which burst through the surface but also dissemble, as Freud demonstrated, springing up in ambivalence, if not false neutrality — blunders, spasms, poorly channeled outbursts and tics.

In brief, a discreet restlessness (of the eyes, the mouth, the hands) interprets and betrays us. In effect, the psychomotorial never ceases to emerge to a greater or lesser degree: it is never totally quelled. Through it, or because of it, we reproach physiognomy with having followed too closely the human frame, the marks, the morphology (facial contours, thickness of features, architecture and partition of regions, even of the skeleton, the length of its joints and circumference of its sockets and so on). This is not to say that we must disavow the substratum, which we hold as our inheritance, the instinctual sediment of generations (often at odds, resulting in breaks and irregularities); but we must not cut off organs from their stimulation and functions, nor the human anatomy from its potentialities, nor the body from its incessant and furtive movements.

The second practice I'd like to describe is that of an existential and physical anthropology. As a general rule, external methods are deceptive, because of both their archaic nature and their poverty (thus, "man is the measure," as long as one can illuminate with this examination). Just as "symptoms" reveal the pathology and facilitate its interpretation by the doctor, so the psychologist must train herself to discover and interpret "signs," peripheral and superficial ones as well as functional ones.

It is already clear that some visual signs — slackness, rigidity, various postures (and I leave aside dress, which is so revealing, and speech, which is rich with stylistic turns, not to mention vocabulary) — do not require subtle interpreters. So it is in the case of the adolescent with the protruding stomach (as for young children with doll-like faces and slender limbs) who openly slides back into the past and sinks into hieratic immobility, as if he were occupied with preventing any evolution. Or an even clearer case: How can one doubt, as Sandor Ferenczi remarks, the meaning of a sudden blush? Such uncontrolled vascular dilation signifies both (erotic) desire and its refusal. Everything happens, moreover, up above (extreme displacement), far from the concerned (sexual) regions, the precise result of the attempt to establish excessive self-domination, which brings, as its shadow, its unmasking:

Through the language of the body, blushing magically brings about what is forbidden to conscious thought. Vessels dilate as if to absorb some object, and this organic fiction becomes the symbol of repressed desire. Thus, we use our bodies for making symbols, just as the artist uses his materials to create a work of art. Both cases involve materializing repressed desires as if by magic. And this is possible, because our body functions from the outset as a language.

In every case, according to Jean-Paul Sartre, this coloring expresses uneasiness, the alienation of the body caught in another's glance. The subject attempts to struggle against that which reveals, against a body that escapes control — a fruitless undertaking because opposition to the body merely increases its presence. One wants to forget the body or bracket it; the body takes its revenge.

By focusing primarily on methods, one can learn from Jouvet's elegant analysis and procedures concerning the science of sleep and dreams. On the one hand, he records the electroneural activity of the cortex. On the other, he measures muscular relaxation and diverse motor functions, less of accompaniment than of actualization (valid in their own right, not performing just as an auxiliary or doubling function): eye movements, mute groans, mimicry (the face is animated); one could add grimaces, smiles and small finger movements. I include all these microkinetic elements.

Let me eliminate one objection right away, namely, that one can only gather effects, never the experience — sometimes anguished — of the dreamer, which is akin to the idea that only crumbs can be gathered from the feast. Once again, I hear recriminations against the external and its mechanical substitutions (recording disjointed, minimal movements). Philosophy is obliged to belittle what happens on the outside, still more to obscure bodily perturbations. But first, it is possible when we examine the results carefully (cerebral or otherwise) — head, eye, hand movements — to know what unreal objects haunt animals, in their so-called paradoxical sleep. For example, if the animal moves incessantly, it is likely pursuing imaginary prey. If it freezes into immobility, even stops breathing, then it is hiding. Jouvet ascribes to cats dreams of hunting (mice and rats) or, more rarely, dreams expressing an infraprimary narcissism: a grooming session. If the cat licks the walls of its cage instead of its paws, we can infer that it is quenching a symbolic thirst. In short, one notes either a predatory behavior (extended claws, lowered ears, slightly arched back) or active self-interest. Jouvet set out to trace the general lines of the repertory (endogenous unfolding), and without a doubt he exposed it, as much in eye movement and the hallucinations that apparently result as in various releases or expressive facial play. But let me be clear: no "sexual scenes" for carnivores!

But does that which applies to an animal (the cat) also hold for man? I do not doubt the differences, beginning with the "interior screenplay," but nonetheless, the dream offers this opportunity in both cases: the individual, removed from society and the external world, entirely self-absorbed (a dangerous state, moreover, in slightly different circumstances), gives in to half-real, half-unreal behavior, sketched out in very broad strokes. Waves and graphs inform an observer of the number of these "image" patterns (four in principle), their length (from a few seconds to several minutes) and even their intensity. The parallel recording of the mimicry (with the eyes, fingers, entire body and, if possible, the storm of generalized sensations) reveals the tragedy underway. The sleeping individual does not fall into complete immobility. On the one hand, he is stirred by internal sensations. On the other (and Maury marvelously analyzed it), he stirs outwardly, finally speaks, even cries, grimaces or smiles. Through this sequence of gesticulations, resting on profound motor apathy, how can one fail to glimpse the scene this individual is traversing? Dreams have been too much the preserve of the depth psychologist, whereas they are actually the mechanism by which the body rejects its tutelage and regains a little (imaginary) freedom. We have seen sleep too much as a state of complete rest, a momentary "beheading." In reality, during the night the senses are out on a spree (entry) and are answered by a multitude of virtual actions (exit), which are only barely comprehensible. Nonetheless, some will insist that the "content" escapes us. The essential remains unknown: only the dreamer knows it (through the personal history of his phantasms and desires). And even the dreamer is not completely certain — the process of psychological deformation never ceases — that these experiences correspond to particular desires (or this or that desire). If those experiences give full play to basic drives, the circumstances count less than the structure of the drama. Likewise, the cat does not stalk or catch a particular mouse but mouse in general.

I should not overglorify the night, though, during which the subject regresses to the most archaic and darkest places for the most ancient of acts. Above all, one should respect that method which approaches the dreamer not through her accounts — they are fictitious and rearranged, or they impose a false logic on the original "screenplay" — but her textuality — kinesia and minute jerks, concrete even though incomplete (the mouth protrudes, the eyes turn, the fingers grasp). Even if these notions are rejected, one must still admit that the inner dream cannot fail to express itself outwardly in a riot of postures and microtremors. It is also appropriate to concede the significance of "inner meaning" free from monitoring. It is likely, therefore, that the "inner screenplay" serves less to promote sleep than to compensate for the many frustrations resulting from social life and to claim immediate reparation for oppressed mankind (that is, the oldest instincts). This also explains why birds "dream," but reptiles and amphibians do not. The capacity to dream develops at the same pace and rhythm as social organization and the harshness or violence of the duties it imposes. On the other hand, though, one must sleep in complete tranquillity to be able to dream, which presupposes a tightly knit social group. Ultimately, humanity sets out during the night to liberate forbidden gestures and do some writing on an "anti-daytime" novel.

It goes without saying that as soon as electroencephalography revealed "a torrent of images," neuro-anthropology was able to achieve some elegant experimental successes, such as enabling a cat to sleep but preventing it from "dreaming," thus dissociating what had always been profoundly linked. Jouvet has drawn the appropriate conclusions. We know better what dreams "are good for," or what happens if they are suppressed (the psychotic cat and its incurable disequilibrium). But I want to evoke only the method (electric and anti-interiorizing), not its results.

The third investigative practice I shall examine is a subtler act than bearing or posture: material writing, handwriting itself, which may act as the mirror of the mind, revealing the irregular rhythms of psychomotor activity. This has already been recognized, from Ludwig Klages to Alfred Binet, from Paul Guillaume to Maurice Merleau-Ponty, but no one has advanced much beyond at least the last two. Why? Doubtless because of the charlatanism that surrounds the endeavor and also because of the misinformation promoted by scholarly books — the improbable and wretched naiveté they bring to bear in uncovering the psyche on the basis of the minute strokes and flourishes that make up handwriting.

We have no assurance that we can escape this risk. Nonetheless, the expert jurist reassures us a little. Since civilization assigns ever-increasing significance to signatures and written documents, it has been obliged to analyze closely this kind of transcription of ourselves. Now, if someone can be identified by these physical marks, does that not prove that he bestows something of himself in them? Recognition necessarily implies a kind of "knowledge." The parallel between handwriting and the psyche serves first to authenticate, but it must also permit the writer to depict himself. One cannot have one without the other. If writing conveys personality to this degree, it is because we inscribe ourselves in it.

In this regard, let us consider the success of Edmond Locard, renowned detector of forgers (imitations, disguises), and examine one of the methods on which his work was based, graphometry. Suppose, in effect, that the letter a has been written in many, even thousands of ways. Enlarging samples makes analysis easier. The letter is made up of one or more elements, called "grammas": in this case a_1, the circle, then a_2, the second stroke. For this a_1, systematically note the elliptical or oval shape of the circle, the presence of a downstroke or upstroke, whether the circle is closed, the presence or absence of a preparatory stroke; then note the relative height of the two grammas, the angle they form, the ligature between them and that with the following letter. In short, subdivide into as many elements as possible, bring into relief all the variations with which the letter can be written. Finally, code the information, which makes it possible to summarize it. The result? A person can be mapped to a grid of usages. This person doesn't realize that she conforms in spite of herself to a set of writing particularities, consistently preferring one stroke to another. We count the frequency of each variety, from dominant to rare, and note the correlative exclusions. At the most, in the Roman alphabet, we have at our disposal twenty-six capitals, twenty-six lowercase letters, and ten digits, or a total of sixty-two characters. All of these could never be taken into account; it is sufficient to choose some and to draw up for them a table of groupings and a table of variants. A given handwriting can be reduced to a formula of these combinations. Thus, a person can be identified in this linear construction all by itself. Even a signature ultimately seems double. Not only is it the effective, psychological and ethically binding mark of the person who affixed it, but its form in turn bears witness to the existence of the person who wrote it.

To this first examination, we can add a second, qualitative investigation of the idiomatic or particular (vestiges of an upbringing, signs of a group and so on):

Such a manner of eliding the t or z or the double s may surprise a southerner; it seems quite natural to anyone accustomed to corresponding with Germans. A barred l replacing the double l in a manuscript is not really idiomatic; it is an ethnic letter: it reveals that the author is Polish or knows Polish. Other less noticeable anomalies reveal a school, an association, a race....[8]

We take as much trouble with the whole writing sample: the placement of the text, its direction (slanted, swerving, rising), the spacing (tight or far apart), dimensions (foreshortened or elongated), intensity (animated or even) and so on. We neglect nothing in the pattern, and through this nonanalytic, nonquantitative, even inexact investigation, we try to seize the bearing, the style of a writing sample.

This double task of identification opens the way to another, anthropological task, because writing renders motility visual: through it, one projects desire or mental energy. Thus, we can discern impatience, impetuous greed, inadequate self-regulation, no less than playful disinterest, or even mastery, calculation, concentration. We exclude neither apathy nor happy liveliness, in short, no behavior that translates either a heightening or lowering of tension. The psyche projects itself. We are stunned by that assertion insofar as we want to keep the mind enclosed in itself, protect it from anything that gives it spatial dimension, while the movement of eyes, hands and voices, all that delicate musculature, endlessly reveals it. Likewise, a body of writing encourages the discovery, the identification of the person who composed (marked) it, and knowledge about that person.

It is true that several factors compromise this reading. First is habit, which flattens and smooths out the pattern but also gives it freedom of movement, an undeniable celerity, thus a little life. Conversely, the individual who rarely writes will lack sureness, will grope; with this person we risk mistakes. A second error derives from our attention to the content of the text: we should concentrate solely on the structure, but it is hard to read without picking up a little on the meaning. This obstructs what should be an observation strictly of pattern. In a third error, the reader-interpreter often gets mired in difficulties because of extreme naiveté. On the basis of documents or samples that are too short, one thinks one can answer simple questions concerning age, upbringing, sex, even nationality. Nothing is more slippery and deceptive: one must remember the existence of "mannish woman" and vice versa — some women produce "virile" and strongly accented writing; some men produce so-called effeminate writing — so that one can avoid falling into this trap and thereby disqualifying the investigation. Binet did not fail, moreover, to forewarn us on just this point: "We find three distinct kinds of writing: first, writing samples for which the sex of the writer is very clear; second, writing samples for which the sex of the writer is ambiguous; third, rare samples which carry the signs of the opposite sex."[9]

How can one doubt that reserve, restraint, perseverance, even fatigue would not reveal themselves in writing samples, as would emotional, even impetuous outbursts? I have emphasized that the psyche is born of two energies, one associated with multiple and untamed desires, the other with the discipline that restrains those desires. Is it not possible to detect this confrontation in handwriting? According to Klages, "Proportion in writing reflects the degree to which an individual lacks emotions. Someone with an ill-proportioned handwriting has a very emotional character."[10] We can go beyond these rather bland remarks to discern in writing the micro-kinetic melody, its distribution, its grace or rigidity (without amplitude or connections, since it is almost totally cut off from the body). In the text, by which I mean the material transcription, one can detect subtle exchanges. The two realms of which I have been speaking take over by turns, or neutralize each other, or compose between them (among other compromises) what is called a "scalar disposition," in the sense that when one word or phrase falls (descending writing), the following word or phrase compensates by rising. Now, this regular rhythmic pattern, which balances the lines, makes the text scannable, and thus gives it a degree of animation. If too many flourishes signify a "mannerism" (autistic vector), the lack of alternatives or of slight contrasts introduces monotony, even inertia, a collapse (the weight of controls). In this respect, Klages makes some remarks that are perhaps too vague, although picturesque, concerning the frequency of peaks and curves:

> The world of clouds and water never shows angular contours; the world of rocks almost always does. The proof is that an artist can impress us by drawing masses of storm clouds and imposing boulders on a postcard format, whereas his endeavor would remain incomprehensible if he set out to represent angular clouds and rounded boulders, even on a large canvas.... The style of Western Antiquity is characterized by the straight line; the Romanesque style that is closest to it is distinguished by its curved lines; and the Gothic style displays a completely different meaning with its broken lines. And throughout all these, we find the original principle that informs productions of the Mind: dress, arms, utensils, and especially writing, whether Romanesque, uncial, or Gothic.[11]

In any case and in spite of the oddities that have always surrounded it, the analysis of handwriting, that fragile psychokinesis, appears to us as a privileged world of *impressions*. In fact, it is comparable neither to a purely virtual motility, hard to grasp and externalize, nor to a concrete, embodied motility. It belongs instead to the realm of the specular and corresponds to a true mirror effect that both brings into focus and reduces. Moreover, what we want and can coax out of it is not the particular that it records (meaning), but the manner, which does not vary; not the matter, through which it disappears as means, but the style, thus a gait, the movement or the microdance proper to the writer. Balzac — theoretician of the expenditure of energy, attentive to the symbiosis of the mental and the material — maintained in 1830 that one can judge an individual by his gait: "Is it not horrifying to think that a careful observer can discover a vice, a twinge of remorse, a disease, just by looking at a man walking?" Or: "A glance, the voice, breathing, a man's gait: all these are identical; but since it has not been given to us to be able to monitor these four diverse and simultaneous expressions of his thought at the same time, look for the one that declares the truth: you will know the man in his entirety." If he is right, one can a fortiori recognize a man still better through his written meanderings, which represent a kind of autoinscription.

In the preceding discussion, then, I have outlined three sensitive biomaterial regions: respiration or breaths of air; numerous tentative movements, some in our inner dreams or reverie; and finally, handwriting. The list certainly does not end with these, but I needed only to establish the diversity of registers where the personality inhabits and expresses itself. I have not entered into detail concerning their possibilities — that would require another work — but I have attempted to specify the extent and the significance of the psychographical (and sometimes electropsychic) field. Victor Egger has examined the unchanging "interior speech" that for him defined the psyche: if speech reveals the thought that accompanies it, then it is also true that thought is made up of speech babbling incessantly, trying ever in vain to escape. All the same, he wrote, "one would say that the mind came into existence with an innate hatred of extensions."[12] Thus, we proceed toward the thesis whereby the mind is only the sanctified name of a particular body, an idea — not one's real body, but the virtual body, which overlaps the first, renders it possible, encourages it, even assures its mobility, and reveals itself in the process.

Classical psychology did not fail to recognize all these tentative movements that race through the body and agitate the brain, this inner micro-kinesis; instead it recognized them in order to minimize their importance. This is notably the case with Maine de Biran, Ravaisson, Bergson and, without question, Merleau-Ponty. But even they never really preserve that tight solidarity between the organic and the mental that constitutes reality. They are more concerned with the spontaneous ego (the substantial and instigative ego), and they lay the foundation for an anthropology of consciousness. "Will" transcends "movement" or the phenomenology of the body, which they refer to only as a starting point. The organic substratum ultimately provides ballast for the mental, plays the role of guardrail (or mediator), because it prevents rapid ascension into an overly ethereal, delocalized and impersonal reverie. It serves as both springboard and anchorage. In short, it fulfills various roles but is only valid as foundation. Without reverting completely to the Antique-Christian tradition colored by the neoplatonism of Plotinus, which considers the psychophysiological as contemptible (the fall, degradation), these thinkers perpetuate the myth of a "mental inwardness" that is slowly acquired at the expense of the body. Maine de Biran relates valuable observations, but motility quickly gives way to pure reflection. We must reverse "Biranism," itself heir to an immaterializing philosophy. In this respect, Bergsonism should be worth yet another sleight of hand: first, no one understood as well as Bergson the subtlety of the cerebral dance, but second, if he praised the sensorimotorial and the schematization of the psychophysiological, he immediately reduced the latter to the level of a means. It only serves (negative power) to sort out or impede the flood of inopportune memories. *Matter and Memory* contains, it is true, elegant documents gleaned from the medical literature, designed to explain recognition or attention, the sense of the present. "Stage by stage we shall be led on to define attention as an adaptation of the body rather than of the mind...."[13] He does not hesitate to recopy Théodule Ribot. He makes concessions on the one hand in exchange for what is essential on the other. Praise of the cerebral prefaces its devaluation at the expense of the mental, of pure memory and of ego freed from space. He grants only servile tasks to psychomotility. This is why organic degeneration (sickness then death) has no effect on the mind (which is beyond immaterialism and the supernatural), even to the point that memory cannot be diminished or impaired during aphasia. Only the faculty of pronunciation is affected. Apraxia *appears* to entail amnesia or the loss of the meaning of limits, but that is only as illusion, and, moreover, it is easily explainable (the superposition of two insufficiencies). Pure memory, constituted over time, paradoxically escapes erasure over time, as well as every other factor of erosion, protected as it is by its immateriality. The brain illuminates only an apparent forgetting, not memory.

Working against the current of the *pura mens*, it is very fitting to restore the multiplicity of bodies (first the real body, then the virtual, even representations of the body) their infinite potentialities, or else to restore what we have sought throughout to reduce and erase: the break between function (in this case, memory [*mnesia*]) and its substratum, between the depths and the surface, the outer and the inner, between a practice and its scope of possibilities.

Certainly, the human subject lays claim to a particularity that differentiates her (the problem of individuation) and does not expect to find anything in the insignificant play of muscles or neurons on which to base personal singularity, her uniqueness. Would anyone dare to reduce this subject to a collection of physical tensions, spasms or relaxations? But we imagine just such an anatomical and fragmented representation of the body. This kind of representation cannot perform a personalizing function. We withhold what is alive — sexuality, aggression and so on — from biological structures (neutralized or degraded morphology). We cannot free the self that we have just sought to uproot. We cannot reconnect consciousness, its movements and desires, with anatomy, nor even with a physiology intended only to give life to an inert substratum. Why not proceed in the opposite direction? We take the mysterious mind for a psychomotility that has not yet disappeared, that continues to surround its operative possibilities with complexes, that has refined and inhabited ever-more completely a body rendered virtual. A quasi-cellular inscription should not be seen as a degradation, but as the reverse side of the right side. Even the imagination cannot function and play a part without the (perhaps orgiastic) participation of the brain. I shall return to this point — but, here and now, I believe that even a poem is an extension of the muscles. Valéry confirms this. In one of his narrations, for example:

As I went along the street where I live, I was suddenly *gripped* by a rhythm which took possession of me.... It was as though someone were making use of my *living-machine*. Then another rhythm overtook and combined with the first, and certain strange *transverse* relations were set up between these two principles.... They combined the movement of my walking legs and some kind of song I was murmuring or rather which was being murmured through me.... Notice that everything I have said, or tried to say, happened in relation to what we call the *External World*, what we call *Our Body*, and what we call *Our Mind*....[14]

Valéry — who I argue is the lucid poet of a frank metapsychophysiology (all the arts are forms of action and must be analyzed in terms of action, he said repeatedly) — dispelled dreams and habitual lies, in order better to define the poetic act: it consists in recovering the power of gesture (dance) and sounds (musicality) — quite simply, the highest degree of the sensorimotorial.

Let the psychologist work with the neurologist to study that "without which" we do not exist — our tremors, our postures, our bearing and our secret impulses. That is why, but in the opposite sense, psychopathological maladjustments imply "a body in difficulty." The worst of these, moreover, consists of imagining that one is leaving the body behind, or that one can abandon it, or again to endow it in too archaic and obstinate a fashion (the orally fixated body). "The ego that loses its body," writes Gisela Pankow, "loses reason at the same time." Instead of taking on a free and virtual body, the sick patient effectively becomes a body that he suffers, that invades him where he is lodged in a manner as excessive as it is clumsy. He must learn to make it work, not to live it — to have it, not to be it. And the task of psychology is without a doubt to lead us to accept the body while liberating us from it.

Exteriorization, nonetheless, leads to another exterior, to the famous *partes extra partes*. One can understand, therefore, the anthropologist's reluctance to allow it the capacity to secure the ego's foundation and its equilibrium. We always come back to the same difficulty, to the same philosophical objection. But what initially seems to be rarefied in "space" actually reveals itself there. Moreover, the "ego" does not scatter in a hostile outside so much as it inhabits its own body, an integrated and even focused cohesion. It completely escapes all risk of fragmentation. Does extension in space serve as a means of "self-manifestation" or even as a means of our existence? It is important to get beyond this conception, which is too restrictive and more or less Aristotelian in origin. The material (corporeal) does not individualize a form that is prior to it. We must strike down this last bastion of dualism, and the sooner the better. The slightly hypocritical cleverness in this reply is quite clear: Grant much to the body, but in order to take away everything (that is, the mind) from it. The body is good only for concretizing.

Now, just as life is fully characterized by the biochemical architecture that defines it, so the psyche emerges from the most complex corporeal structures; it expresses itself entirely through these structures. Desire coincides with the body that it invigorates. Thought springs from half-real, half-unreal cerebral displacements, just as sensibility results from our expressive and energizing systems. This is why one need not fear that the procedures for a biomaterial examination are inevitably inadequate. Just as we have learned to read the movements of the heart through electrical signals, it must be possible to perceive emotions or flashes of intellect through delicate interactions difficult to project, linked to our most highly differentiated cells, to our newest tissue.

Is this a materialist profession of faith? Not at all, for I have been careful to underscore the different stages, the discontinuities and the growing complexity between them. It remains true that life defines the most analyzable and the most determinant stage (the body). And that is why sedatives or other drugs can render the patient more accessible to the psychiatrist, just as they magnify cerebral capacities (lowering barriers, overcoming hesitation, removing obstacles, even enlarging perspectives and heightening sensations). The classical psychologist can never come to terms with this transformational potency, which fascinates the poet or artist. That is precisely her Achilles' heel. This psychologist cannot acknowledge it without becoming an accomplice and even identifying individuality with the body. These comments may appear reckless, so much so that I should be more explicit. Fortunately, a number of psychologists have blazed trails in the examination of gesture where I am now walking. I shall limit myself to a rapid survey.

Jousse, referred to above, devoted his work, rich in observations and data, to this endeavor. For him, one activity characterizes and singularizes humankind: language, or more accurately, speech. Thanks to speech, humankind preserves messages and "memorizes" them. Jousse labored to describe how we begin our history by "pantomiming" a reality that reverberates in us (intussusception). We act out or imitate this reality by means of various movements that permit us to incorporate them. They serve to encourage our domination of the world, but to the degree they are able to carry out their task, the correlative is also true: "things" must succeed in slipping past their own requirements (the law of equilibrium, for example, which appears later in Jousse's most learned formulations).

But where does this concern we have for the universe "reflected" in us come from? What gives birth to this original act of understudy? A rather rudimentary comment, but suggestive: Jousse highlights a "natural photoengraving" that must have inspired us. Thanks to it, he remarks, we are better able to grasp the grand lines, the canvas and the large movements that surround us (animation, projection of images, reduction, possession):

It has been said that in Egypt, the god Toth revealed writing, but we are the god, or rather the god is human pantomime. We need to study the shadow phenomenon which has played, among some peoples, such an important role.... Shadows spontaneously invent writing. As soon as the sun rises or a fire is lit, the invention of writing has already taken place. My shadow extends along the wall as I make an offering? I trace my offering on the wall. In all pictographic writings, we find this grand gesture of the offering. Primordial man struggles with his moving shadow, dominates it, traces it, and makes it endure. It is through pantomime that the subject springs forth and achieves stability.[15]

Sound, however, accords even better with this scheme. Rather than reflecting an object, sound characterizes it. Above all, sound provides humankind a way to make an impression (by expressing itself) on the object and thereby to assimilate it. In sum, the domain of the vocal is our primary handle on reality, more so than the gestural, which requires too much physical expenditure. The mobile mouth outpaces the hands, even though it is doing no more than carrying out their displacements, just as they celebrate and simulate actions, desires, even events. And so we proceed from transposition to transposition. We pass from a global theater of mime to theater of the vocal organs, which is no less a transcription, only more concise. That is why the term "reproduction" must be partially desexualized: humankind first succeeds in "seizing power" from the universe thanks to the labor of a corporeal transcription. With the joy of domination and appropriation, a human "reflects" in himself, by a kind of echo, that which envelops him (thanks to the physical act of vocalization-naming).

Now we see how firmly psychophysical this anthropology is. The text in front of you now is consumed and retained only because of certain rhythmic patterns that facilitates its conveyance and conservation. (The mnesial interiorization is primarily oral.) We should avoid making that split between the activity of "mere" musculature, on the one hand, and the melody of pure memory, on the other. Just as our most important habits enter into body movements, which they fully "inhabit" and facilitate (the mind materializing), certain rhythmic uses of language are likewise fully immanent to the vocal organs, to respiration and the body as a whole. Only a balanced pedagogy establishes an accord between breathing and its own oscillation. Looking from this angle at the Eastern or ancient texts of chants that have been preserved, it is clear that they contain, in addition to their literal message, information about how to recite or vocalize them. This information consists of their division into equal fragments, an internal movement that traverses the text. They are divided, for example, into relatively short "phrases" (not exceeding the length of a breath, the octosyllabic) or, better yet, the classical alexandrine, but subdivided into two hemistiches (favorable to parallelism and the heartbeat).

> The Greek philosopher said "man thinks because he has a hand." In our French language, we could say with more truth and more anthropological wealth: "Man thinks because he has two hands." And we mean think [*penser*] in its etymological sense: *pensare–pendere*–to weigh, to balance. Bilateralism is truly the spontaneous law of human balance, and it is omnipresent.[16]

Because bilateralism constitutes the prerequisite for grasping and walking, it must also permeate declamatory speech (assonance, regular rhyme and phrasing at fixed intervals matching our own rhythms). The mental — even the sacred and liturgical — cannot disdain the gestures that sustain it, permit it and in which it is inscribed. This is Ariadne's thread, which makes it possible to reconstitute incomplete fragments or to detect apocryphal passages. We know a passage is inauthentic when the body's shadow is missing: without that relation to the pulsings of the body it could never have been committed to memory. Within a phrase, we should find "systolic–diastolic" alternations, a sequence of violent explosions or consecutive relaxations (which is the necessary precondition to bringing the catechistic back to life).

Later, writing in its turn must submit to the same injunctions and rules of articulation:

Our contemporary typefaces seem to try to outdo each other in cramming and jamming Hebrew phrases into the minimum of pages and space. Whereas a typeface should do its best to distribute the text with ample white space on large pages, in symmetrical and logical clauses, which would enable those mechanisms of spontaneous equilibrium and those mechanisms of voluntary ordering to flourish and achieve their full value. [17]

Thus speech, the phrase or text, far from ignoring or dismissing the human body, imply its physicality and come into being through it. Before settling into words or lines, meaning bends to the physiology of our gestures. The better the body functions, the more it participates, and the more thought will be preserved from erosion (or forgetfulness) and retained inwardly (archived). Primary schooling may have obliterated or repressed this mute base of rhythmic motility and regulated it for the sake of immobility and thought, but that is a practical problem beyond the framework of this study.

To convince any who are still in doubt, I shall fall back on the biopsychiatry of Wilhelm Reich, the spirit of which is as well known as its content. It is sharply opposed to psychoanalysis on the grounds that psychoanalysis opened only one register — the language of modesty and its garrulous prolixity — which is full of misleading turns and dead-end traps. It forsook others, notably those concerning demeanor and bodily tensions. But inhibition and repression do not operate in a vacuum. Forces do not exist without a fulcrum. That is why the disciplinarian marks the body with a red-hot iron — to stiffen and straighten it out. Thus, the muscles either brace themselves to restrain mounting desires (armoring the character) or they become anemic and collapse. According to Reich, the very notion of mental illness has become an aberration and a source of mystification, because we no longer know where to situate the disorder, whereas it is incontestable that a neurosis fractures gestures (the beginnings of genitality, the most varied expressions of our impulses). This conception is too well known, even indelicate, to dwell on. I turn to it only to strengthen my conclusions in favor of a reading and therapy that are kinetic and psychophysiological. I am ignoring, in effect, the properly sexual side, even though I take it as axial and even decisive that our difficulties have orgasmic origins. I am limiting myself to the revealing study of somatic appearances. There, at least, shelter can be found from the cathartic mania that affects so many theoreticians, including Freud. If Freud did not disregard the physiological and gestural, he certainly overemphasized a limited area of the organic — mainly orifices: mouth, anus, sexual organs.

But first, what are the visible signs of neurosis, and how can we localize it, that is, place it in the body? No one answers these questions as well as Reich: Stop divorcing the "ego" from its musculature, learn to detect minimal tensions, barely perceptible defenses, grosser spasms, as well as excessive self-restraint — in short, give as much weight to a physical examination, that is, the most psychological examination possible. In everyday life, we make do without oscilloscopes and optical and acoustic devices of the investigator (which are capable, as we know, of detecting otherwise imperceptible movements, registering one's inner voice, so feebly whispered, and of discerning eye movements that sweep over and lightly stroke, so to speak, what they look at), and thus we fasten onto "manners." But in fact we might do well to rely on, as needed, devices of fine discrimination, like the electromyographic recorder (electroneuromyometry), which measures minute muscular contractions, very weak spasms that in turn signal psychological difficulties, obstructions, genuine blockages. We can then better recognize those beleaguered and tense places where the body is besieged than we could with purely psychological or projective investigation (for example, of the Rorschach type).

In his writings, Reich repeats tirelessly:

Clear-cut experiences…show that the behavior of the patient, his look, manner of speech, facial expression, dress, handclasp, etc., that all these things are not only underestimated in their analytic significance, but usually completely overlooked…. This view of the psychic surface puts a different face on the rule that "one should always proceed from the surface." Analytic experience shows that behind this politeness and niceness there is always hidden a more or less unconscious critical, distrustful or deprecatory attitude….[18]

Or else:

The character resistance expresses itself not in the content of the material [all that psychoanalysis takes into account, according to Reich], but in the *formal* aspects of the general behavior, the manner of talking, of the gait, facial expressions and typical attitudes such as smiling, deriding, haughtiness, over-correctness, the manner of the politeness or of the aggression, etc.[19]

In at least three regions, the biosemiologist has an even better understanding of the body language that exposes, in a public manner, genital deformations and disorders, or through these, violent conflicts between societal and parental forces and sexual impulses. The first of these is breathing, which should be no surprise. Since the patient has not achieved true psychosomatic integration, since he is split between a higher realm, which he supervises or invests himself in, and a lower realm that is rejected, leaving it to its own devices — so there is no energizing circulation between the two levels: the patient cannot breath deeply or bring his diaphragm into play and is restricted to a partial, weak breathing confined to the thorax. In effect, the schizophrenic contracts the abdomen and sucks in air (victory of regressive orality), rather than swallowing (chest and belly separated by a border, the phrenic ring). Unconstrained oxygenation implies open self-display — not withdrawal, operator of insensibility and stasis — acknowledgment of the bowels, firm entry into a world that can, with full reciprocity, penetrate us. The neurotic, in another way, immobilizes his chest protectively, partially rejects the undulation that should traverse the body from bottom to top, is disconnected and slow in his movements. In this respect, we should examine the nomenclature and the bio-mythology of the Greeks: we know that the ancients granted a decisive role to the diaphragm, where madness, the passions and mental difficulties are concerned (the suffix -*phrenia* survives in the words "schizophrenia" and "oligophrenia" as a vestige of that explanation). Was this prophetic, in light of our current understanding of the significance of a blocked thorax? Or did the Greeks simply reiterate thereby their hatred of the body, source of frenzy and unreason? Was it an expression of their morbid pathogenesis? They tended to separate the inferior (the shadowy and the infernal) from the superior (the dominant, bright logos). Perhaps they believed in a disease, in a process of mingling, in an effort that is powerless to prevent rising desires. Overwhelmed, the diaphragm struggles in vain. Contemporary psychiatry, though, seeks to overcome this split and work toward integration. It restores to the body its lost unity, which for the divided patient is broken, even sectioned (emerging from signs related to the ancient metameric segmentation).

Another locus for expression: The most diverse spasms, the anti-instinctual armor that limits gestures and gives to the patient a borrowed air, and nervous, slow or artificial bearing, a studied mimicry.

Without reviewing here the rich analyses of Reich or Alexander Lowen, we know that, according to them, the patient has to anesthetize the body in order to avoid living fully. He has suffered frustration and disillusion (usually in childhood), which leads toward a protective therefore advantageous regression. For its part, society pushed the patient to this veiled suicide — who owes it to himself, therefore, to repress desires through the sensorimotor realm where expression, communication and animation take place. His behavior becomes cold, conservative. Above all, the patient moderates and lowers emotional tonality and enters into a behavior inhabited by contradiction (in effect, wanting life, but still more denying it in himself, which is translated, in the body, by defenses and a constricted economy of gestures).

Better yet, against this astonishing and almost visceral background of rejection and profound apathy appears the very thing that conceals it: arrogant outbursts, forced exuberance, hysterical actions. And there we discern a new rupture, the contrast between false passivity and resignation and that which only partially hides it beneath the inverted excesses of bravado or psychomotor excitation. Conduct is thus inspired by pretense, as is self-deception, but in the midst of this confusion one learns to recognize restless and spasmodic movements. The body's interface cannot altogether suppress those contrivances that result in both (muscular) erection and its concomitant inhibition, necessarily and psychophysiologically the source of tensions, plates or bands of immobility, of a visible locking, or muscular contractions.

Moving out from the diaphragm (from the respiratory), let us consider, with more precision, the Rachidian axis (the osteotendinous). We can envisage the tip of the toes as well as the shaft of the spinal column, even the principal hinge joints (the occipitocervical, the dorsolumbar, the lumbosacral), because bearing and posture reveal a troubled self-affirmation, the sense of security as well as of solid footing. One need only think of the lowered head of the guilty person, or the slightly inclined forehead of the obsessed one, of the sunken neck associated with Damocles' syndrome, of the stooped back of the cenesthopath. An individual's balance or fossilized perturbations (scoliosis, lordosis, kyphosis), the equilibrium of legs and feet, how the feet are planted on the ground and the weight distributed, are all expressive, and the modalities of this expression reveal to a degree corporeal or existential capacities — or at the other extreme, a sense of being overwhelmed or even of collapse (the Atlas syndrome). There is no neurosis without a secret corporeal disorder or transformation that organizes it. One of the most common disorders, although little researched, comes from the patient who experiences difficulty holding herself steady without digging in, or remaining upright without excess (stiffness) or excessive expenditure of energy. And if the patient carries the weight of the body on her heels or extremities (equine posture), if she is *genu valgum* (bowlegged) or *varum* (knock-kneed), or even subject to a slight slope or curvature in posture, one can guess the fragility, the lack of stability that causes complications for her bearing, movement or consciousness of her body — which is to say, in the final analysis, the patient's consciousness of herself. The whole is obviously linked, according to Reich, to orgasmic (low) disorders and congestion.

Psychic difficulty always comes from the fact that one's body is punished, forced to submit to physical constraints, or is unstably grounded (the patient betrays a ponderous manner of implanting herself). Reich discerns illnesses of the mind primarily in somatic manifestations, because he discovers hidden therein indications of violence, of rejection, even of authoritarian domination. Not only does he teach us to read the pace of a gesture, the position of the shoulders and the Rachidian axis, but also to listen to the voice, to examine its rhythm and delivery (not the content of what is named, as with the Freudians, but the melody itself). Such a patient is striking because of his frozen expression, lifelessness, conventional mimicry, all products of a castrating superego. Others, conversely are notable for their overflowing, even autoerotic gesticulation, demonstrating an excess of ego. But in both cases, psychophysiology is enough to expose and reveal the mind that spreads itself before our eyes. We apprehend it not through behavior, but through appearances alone.

Thus, it is appropriate to take everything into account, to ignore no physical detail — above all those that seem irrelevant or spontaneous — the smallest spasms, glances, capacities for sensation, impulsive or inhibited movements, a gait, anything that participates in the symbolic economy of the libido. We pay special attention to motility (motion as the means of seizing hold) because it displays the profound need that it clarifies. An individual's grip on the world — reflected, for example, in mute speeches and rapid eye movement — this is comparable, as we have already noted, to the enticing demands and violent acts of genitality (reproduction). And if sex effectively plays an essential role, we track it down first of all in signs that are "manifest" and open. The phenomenological alone forewarns us, but it escapes us because it is furtive, rapid, apparently insignificant.

A final question after the investigation of the most revelatory zones (the respiratory, the muscular, the Rachidian): How do we struggle against all these deformations? I shall confront this question, albeit very briefly and as if by caricature, in order to be able to dismiss the objection that has already been raised concerning the uselessness and the dangers of psychographic practices. In reality, they help heal. How?

First of all, they direct us toward self-hypnosis (for example, Schultz's self-generated training). It is necessary to reconcile the subject with himself, by which we mean with his own body, the psycho-architecture of which is understood. Thus, stretched out prone, relaxed, eyes shut, he will lie in wait, first completely still, for the first coenesthetic sounds, a warm, sensation that gradually washes over the (uncrossed) hands, then the numbed legs. Then he slides toward wider disconnections, in the direction of the osteotendinous, before experiencing the impossibility of movement (motion abolished, weightlessness, imaginary flight through a body of lead). The tranquilization or relaxation advances further, reaches the cardiovascular, the respiratory. Progressive self-soothing finally decomposes the stable organic structures that enfold one another. Thus, he succeeds in provoking a state of coolness in the rhinopharynx, and helps relieve light mucous edemas (some asthmatics recover from psychosomatic disorders). In every case, according to Schultz's schema, the patient learns to progress by stages: reduces hypertension, frees himself of spasms and constrictions and introduces a state of sedation in the limbs.

It is appropriate to prevent by means of this psycho-organic maneuver what lies at the base of the psychiatric: the rupture between the human being and her organs. We rediscover a unity in the process of erasure. It is less a matter of monitoring muscles (of which we have lost control or consciousness) than of initiating a dialogue between the body and itself (without the interposition of any other entity), even to initiate a relative narcissism, revitalization of the libidinal relations between oneself and oneself. This is the price for cementing the hoped-for reconciliation. This difficult reeducation of the body runs into two obstacles, however: first, social entreaties, violently hostile to self-attention, and everyone sees why;

second, our organic mechanisms, which slide down the slope of autonomy and end by working for separatist ends (indurate and uncontrolled spasms). Division, fracturing, isolation are everywhere. The descent into self is followed by a slow reascent, which facilitates pacification, recovery, harmony. This leads to the full enjoyment of a mobile body. On the whole, a human being finishes by being able to inhabit the body that she reinvests. But such a treatment — I freely acknowledge — is only valid for minor neuroses in their early stages (cracks, so to speak, in the body's outer shell). It is the function of instruments to render these microfissures visable, to reveal their location as much as their magnitude.

To pursue a more Reichian approach, we know how to take more drastic measures: then we can break the peripheral rigidities that oppose an explosion; we can break through defensive barriers and liberate overly compromised instinctual energies. Thus, we oblige the patient to break out of his reserve and paralysis. How? Sometimes it can suffice, in order to break down the wall, to teach him to breath deeply, to open the lungs and use the abdominal muscles in the breathing process. This prevents withdrawal and restriction motivated by the desire for security. Likewise, we can facilitate a return from self-disavowal and self-repression by paying unexpected attention to the quasi visceral: "What parts of your body are you conscious of?" We try to open affective and sensorial possibilities. We teach the individual to feel emotions that he had rejected. We can also help the patient to reeducate gestures and overcome hesitation, as well as avoid precipitous action. We attempt to rebuild motility, since we hope to dissolve arrogance, presumption, even compunction. We attack indirectly whatever sustains or consolidates a "defense." But for Reich, the essential consists in struggling against social rules, especially those that demand adherence to a sexual ethic or the regulation of either of the fundamental character deformations: contentiousness or confusion. Reich aims at reestablishing the rights of the body, most notably sexual freedom. The bourgeois or monogamous family — in its concern to preserve and increase its inheritance — has intensified its controls. If the body defines personality, then it is necessary to oppose everything that degrades it or bends it to political and economic interests.

We don't need to examine the foundations or even the ultimate outcome of a therapy that is as determined as it is global. It suffices to note the difficulties that accompany any attempt to free the body from its prison, to "demummify" it. It has been obstructed and constrained. However, we must also expedite and cultivate the process of interiorization (virtualize what is expelled). We seek a difficult harmony, free from the rigidity of self-surveillance or self-condemnation on the one hand, and uncontrolled self-liberation (psychomotor incoordination) on the other. It is rare that one can satisfy both of these opposing demands: not to give too much free rein, and (even more critical) not to brutalize the body. But the process of exteriorization can destroy just as effectively as paralyzing anger can.

I am less interested in what mobilizes and rescues the body than what defines it as a witness, sediment of a history, indicator, collection of marks or traces. I have on several occasions alluded to the function of the skin, generally transferred to clothing, which displays social rank and bears various adornments. But if psychology cannot neglect dress, finery or even tattoos, it must especially consider and scrutinize the body itself: the body is its object, its field, its stage.

In the body can be read not only consciousness, but what is usually called the unconscious. The latter is neither beyond nor within; it is simply on the surface, where it is difficult to read, albeit spread out on display. The process of "seeing it" is arduous. We generally search in the distance for what is at hand and sometimes even mocks us. Everything is visible, barely disguised, but we fail to recognize it. We are held back by the clamor of "meaning," by what is fixed and stationary. The object of our quest twists and turns, passes in and out of the shadows, but remains throughout on the exterior, beneath our confused gaze.

Notes

1. Edgar Allan Poe, *Collected Works* (Cambridge, Mass.: Harvard University Press, 1978), vol. 3, p. 990.

2. Michel Jouvet, "Les Etats de vigilance: Bilan et perspectives," *Perspectives et santé* 14: "From the social viewpoint, the discovery of a good nontoxic and nonaddictive mood elevator would be very useful. In some Asian countries, it is normal to give children green tea" (p. 75).

3. Ibid., p. 77.

4. Sigmund Freud, "Symptomatic and Chance Actions," in *The Psychopathology of Everyday Life*, ed. James Strachey and trans. Alan Tyson (New York: W. W. Norton, 1965), p. 194. [Freud is citing Laurence Sterne's *Tristram Shandy*, vol. 6, ch. 5.]

5. Marcel Jousse, *L'Anthropologie du geste* (Paris: Resma, 1969), p. 50. Jousse continues: "Even one's inner life is sustained by motor complexes." It could not be said any better.

6. Ibid., p. 50.

7. Carl Jung, "*The Experience of Association*," in Herbert Read, Michael Fordham and Gerhard Adler, eds., *The Collected Works of C. G. Jung*, vol. 2: *Experimental Researches* (Princeton: Princeton University Press, 1973).

8. Edmond Locard, *Les Faux en écriture* (Paris: Payot, 1959), p. 25.

9. Alfred Binet, *Les Révélations de l'écriture, d'après le contrôle scientifique* (Paris: Alcan, 1906), p. 12 (ch. 3, "Le Sexe apparent, le sexe dissimulé, le sexe falsifié").

10. Ludwig Klages, *Expression à caractère dans l'écriture* (1947), p. 34 [*Handschrift und Charakter* (Leipzig: Barth, 1921)].

11. Ibid., p. 124.

12. Victor Egger, *La Parole intérieure* (Paris: G. Baillière, 1881), p. 96.

13. Henri Bergson, *Matter and Memory*, trans. Nancy M. Paul and W. Scott Palmer (New York: Zone Books, 1988), p. 100.

14. Paul Valéry, *The Art of Poetry*, trans. Denise Folliot (New York: Pantheon, 1958), pp. 61–63.

15. Jousse, *L'Anthropologie du geste*, pp. 101–102.

16. Ibid., p. 203.

17. Ibid., p. 240.

18. Wilhelm Reich, *Character Analysis*, trans. Theodore P. Wolfe (New York: Orgone Institute Press, 1949), p. 29.

19. Ibid., p. 47.

Translated from the French by Donald M. Leslie

Faces, Surfaces, Interfaces Paris: J. Vrin, 1982

The Influencing Machine [1919]

Victor Tausk

I

Methodological Observations. The following considerations are based on a single example of the Influencing Machine complained of by a certain type of schizophrenic patient. Although in this particular case the structure of the machine differs materially, to the best of my knowledge, from all other varieties of apparatus of this sort, it is hoped that the present example will nevertheless facilitate psychoanalytic insight into the genesis and purpose of this delusional instrument.

My example is a variant — a very rare variant — of the typical influencing machine. The objection can, of course, be made that it is rash to draw general conclusions from the study of a single case; and further, that generalizations to be regarded as scientifically valid should be based on a larger mass of material. My justification is that I have simply not encountered any further case material in support of my conclusions, and that, to the best of my knowledge, psychiatric literature contains no descriptions of individual cases of the influencing machine phenomenon, such as would make my paper superfluous. There exist only general descriptions of the apparatus, and its regular features and functions are given only as perfunctory, clinical illustrations. Clinical psychiatry, interested only in general descriptions, lays no stress on the significance of individual symptoms for the study of the dynamics of psychoses. Psychiatry has not hitherto sufficiently investigated the origin, the meaning and the purpose of a symptom because, not employing the psychoanalytical method, it does not even postulate such problems. Yet, in principle, it is permissible to derive general conclusions from exceptional types. Variants and mixed forms stimulate inquiry into general types. The conformity of typical cases may have the ultimate effect of an impenetrable barrier, while a deviation from type, on the other hand, may be a window in the wall through which a clear view is to be obtained.

Deviations from the rule and ambiguous types compel the assumption that a given phenomenon may be of diverse origin. It is only when an unexpected departure from the accustomed occurs that one feels the necessity of investigating the uniformity that had previously characterized the phenomenon or, at least, had seemed to do so. Inquiry into extraordinary causative factors has often stimulated inquiry into those ordinarily encountered.

It is to be hoped only that the example taken as a basis for the following conclusions will prove to justify them, and that the origin and significance of this variant example have been correctly conceived and formulated.

II

The schizophrenic influencing machine is a machine of mystical nature. The patients are able to give only vague hints of its construction. It consists of boxes, cranks, levers, wheels, buttons, wires, batteries and the like. Patients endeavor to discover the construction of the apparatus by means of their own technical knowledge, and it appears that with the progressive popularization of the sciences, all the forces known to technology are utilized to explain the functioning of the apparatus. All the discoveries of mankind, however, are regarded as inadequate to explain the marvelous powers of this machine, by which the patients feel themselves persecuted.

The Patients' Complaints Understood as "Effects" of the Influencing Machine. The main effects of the influencing machine are the following:

First: It makes the patients see pictures. When this is the case, the machine is generally a magic lantern or cinematograph. The pictures are seen on a single plane, on walls or windowpanes; unlike typical visual hallucinations, they are not three-dimensional.

Second: It produces, as well as removes, thoughts and feelings by means of waves or rays or mysterious forces, which the patient's knowledge of physics is inadequate to explain. In such cases, the machine is often called a "suggestion apparatus." Its construction cannot be explained, but its function consists in the transmission or "draining off" of thoughts and feelings by one or several persecutors.

Third: It produces motor phenomena in the body — erections and seminal emissions — that are intended to deprive the patient of his male potency and weaken him. This is accomplished either by means of suggestion or by air currents, electricity, magnetism or X-rays.

Fourth: It creates sensations that, in part, cannot be described, because they are strange to the patient himself, and that, in part, are sensed as electrical, magnetic or due to air currents.

Fifth: It is also responsible for other occurrences in the patient's body, such as cutaneous eruptions, abscesses and other pathological processes.

The machine serves to persecute the patient and is operated by enemies. To the best of my knowledge, the latter are exclusively of the male sex. They are predominantly physicians by whom the patient has been treated. The manipulation of the apparatus is likewise obscure, the patient rarely having a clear idea of its operation. Buttons are pushed, levers set in motion, cranks turned. The connection with the patient is often established by means of invisible wires leading into his bed, in which case the patient is influenced by the machine only when he is in bed.

The Same Complaints without Influencing Machine. However, it is noteworthy that a large number of patients complain of all these ailments without ascribing them to the influence of a machine. Many patients consider the cause of all these alien or hostile sensations, of physical or psychic change, to be simply an external mental influence, suggestion or telepathic power, emanating from enemies. My own observations and those of other authors leave no room for doubt that these complaints precede the symptom of the influencing apparatus, and that the latter is a subsequent pathological development. Its appearance, as many observers state, serves the purpose of an explanation for the pathological changes that are felt as alien and painful, which dominate the patient's emotional life and sensations.

According to this view, the idea of the influencing machine originates in the need for causality inherent in man; and the same need for causality will probably also account for the persecutors who act not through the medium of an apparatus but merely by suggestion or telepathy. Clinical psychiatry explains the symptom of an influencing machine as analogous to the ideas of persecution in paranoia (which, it is known, the patient invents in order to justify his delusions of grandeur), and calls it "*paranoia somatica*."

However, there is a group of patients that dispenses completely with any gratification of the need for causality, and complains simply of emotional changes and strange apparitions within the physical and psychic personality, without the intervention of foreign or hostile power. It is particularly declared by some patients that their visions are not foisted upon them in any way but that, to their great astonishment, they simply see them. There also occur other strange sensations for which there is no evidence of an originator — especially, for instance, the complaint of a loss or change of thoughts and feelings, without the thoughts or feelings being "drained" from them or foisted upon them. Complaints of a change of sensations in the skin, face and extremities are of a similar nature. This group of patients does not complain of influences originating from a foreign, hostile force, but of a feeling of inner estrangement. They become strange to themselves, no longer understand themselves: limbs, face, facial expression, thoughts and feelings have become estranged. These symptoms are clearly part of an early stage of *dementia praecox*, although they may also be observed in advanced stages.

Influencing Machine Terminal in a Symptomatology, Beginning with Feelings of Alienation. In some cases, it may be stated with certainty, and in others with strong probability, that the sense of persecution originates from the sensations of change accompanied by a sense of estrangement. These feelings of persecution are ascribed to a foreign, personal interference, suggestion, or telepathic influence. In other cases, the ideas of persecution or influence may be seen entering into the construction of an influencing apparatus. It is necessary to assume, therefore, that the influencing apparatus represents the terminal stage in the evolution of the symptom, which started with simple sensations of change. I do not believe that heretofore the entire sequence in the development of the symptom could have been studied completely from a single case; but I have observed the connection between at least two stages (of which I shall present an example later), and I have no hesitation in maintaining that under especially favorable circumstances it may be possible to observe the entire series of developmental stages in a single patient. Meanwhile, I am in the position of the observer of plasmodia who notes various pathological forms in the blood cells as developmental stages of a continuous cycle of growth, although he is never able to observe, in any one blood corpuscle, more than a single phase.

Recognition of the various symptoms as stages of a unified developmental process is rendered difficult not merely by inaccurate observation but by other factors as well. Patients conceal single stages behind secondary and correlative symptoms — each patient in accordance with his morbid disposition. Changes of feeling are covered up by a simultaneously or consecutively produced psychosis or neurosis belonging to another clinical group, such as depression, mania, paranoia, compulsion neurosis, anxiety hysteria or amentia. These clinical pictures, advancing to the foreground, conceal from the observer the more subtle elements in the development of the delusion of reference. It is very likely, moreover, that in many cases not every stage of development reaches consciousness, and that one stage or another runs its course in the unconscious and thus leaves gaps in the conscious psyche. Finally, depending on the rapidity of the pathological process and on the individual disposition, some of the stages may be missing altogether.

Ideas of reference in schizophrenia develop equally with or without the influencing apparatus. In but one case[1] have I been able to observe electrical currents in the absence of the influencing apparatus to which those are usually ascribed — in the absence, in fact, of any hostile powers whatsoever.

Discussion of Cases. The above observation was made in the case of a thirty-four-year-old man, Josef H., an inmate of insane asylums at frequent intervals throughout his life. He felt electrical currents streaming through him, which entered the earth through his legs; he produced the current within himself, declaring with pride that that was his power! How and for what purpose he did this he refused to disclose. On discovering these currents in himself for the first time, he was (he admitted) somewhat astonished, but he soon came to the conclusion that this manifestation had a special significance — that the currents served a mysterious end, regarding which he refused to give any information.

I shall now cite another instance, a singular case of *paranoia somatica*, having, as will later be seen, a significance of its own in substantiating the developmental process that I have assumed. The same example has already been cited by Freud in another connection. Miss Emma A. felt herself influenced by her lover in a singular manner: she maintained that her eyes were no longer properly placed in her head but were entirely twisted out of position, and this she attributed to the fact that her lover was an evil, deceitful person who twisted eyes. At church one day, she suddenly felt a thrust, as if she were being displaced; this was caused by the fact that her lover disguised himself,[2] and that he had already ruined her and made her as evil as himself.

This patient did not merely feel herself persecuted and influenced; hers was a case of being influenced by identification with the persecutor. If we take into consideration the view held by Freud and myself — that in object-choice the mechanism of identification precedes the cathexis proper by projection — we may regard the case of Miss Emma A. as representing the stage in the development of the delusion of reference preceding the projection (namely, onto a distant persecutor in the outer world). The identification is obviously an attempt to project the feelings of the

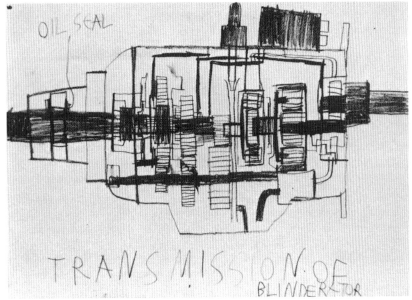

Joey, the "mechanical" boy was an autistic child successfully treated by Dr. Bruno Bettelheim at the University of Chicago Orthogenic School. Fluent in machinic terminology, Joey constructed a series of elaborate and fantastic electrical machines that, for a period, mediated all human contact and daily activity including eating, sleeping and defecation.

Pictured above is the car machine which drove Joey during sleep. This battery powered machine, included a speaker which allowed him to talk and to hear. Shown in one of Joey's drawings is the machine that ran him by remote control. Note the "oilseal" that protected him from total disembowelment, and the "Transmission of Blinderator" which prevented seeing and understanding.

inner change onto the outer world. It constitutes a bridge between the feelings of an inner change without external cause and the attribution of these changes to the power of an external person — a kind of intermediary position between the feeling of self-estrangement and the delusion of reference. This rounds out especially well, and substantiates psychoanalytically, the concept of the development of the symptom, up to its crystallization in the influencing machine. We are here concerned with the discovery, or rather the invention, of a hostile object; for the intellectual process, though, it is unimportant whether the objects observed are hostile or friendly, and the psychoanalyst, at least, will certainly have no objection to the equating of love and hate in this instance. Among the illustrations that may be given of the various forms or stages of the delusion of reference, the case of Staudenmayer (whose autobiography was presented before the Vienna Psychoanalytic Society some years ago) may be mentioned.

Staudenmayer — who, if I am not mistaken, was declared to be a paranoiac and is at any rate considered to be one by me — described his sensations during his bowel movements from the beginning of the movement to its conclusion, and attributed every single peristaltic motion coming to his awareness to the activity of special demons allegedly located in the intestines and entrusted with the performance of each separate motion.

The Complete Symptomatology. We may now summarize and describe schematically the phenomena that, in some cases, appear to be produced by the influencing machine and, in other cases, occur without it.

First: We note simple sensations of inner change in the beginning devoid of, and later accompanied by, a sense of estrangement, without awareness of an originator. The sensations are of changes in the psychic and physical functions within various parts of one's own body. In many cases, this stage of the illness probably occurs at a very early age, before puberty. Because at this age no exact reports can be obtained on inner conditions, and because, moreover, pathological changes are not infrequently compensated by infantile peculiarities of character (such as naughtiness, aggressiveness, concealed fantasies, masturbation, seclusiveness, dullness and so forth), this stage either remains unrecognized or else is misnamed. It is only at puberty, when special adjustments to the environment are required of the individual, who is compelled to relinquish all crude expressions of his abnormality, that the illness comes to the surface; it is at this time, too, that further development of symptoms is stimulated.

Second: Feelings of inner change in the form of abnormal sensations, with awareness of an originator — in this instance the patient himself (case Josef H.).

Third: Feelings of inner change accompanied by awareness of an originator, who, although existing within the patient, is nevertheless not the patient himself (case Staudenmayer).

Fourth: Feelings of inner change accompanied by hallucinatory projection of the inner occurrence to the external world, without awareness of an originator; at first, feelings of estrangement are not present, but later on they appear (seeing pictures).

Fifth: Feelings of inner change accompanied by awareness of an external originator as a result of identification (case Emma A.).

Sixth: Feelings of inner change accompanied by projection of the inner occurrence onto the outer world and belief in an originator produced by the paranoid mechanism (causing pictures to appear, influencing by suggestion, hypnotism, electricity, producing or draining off thoughts and feelings, effecting bodily motions, weakening potency, producing erections, seminal emissions and so forth).

Seventh: Feelings of inner change attributed to the workings of the influencing machine manipulated by enemies. At first, the enemies are usually unknown to the patient and only vaguely discerned by him; later on, he is able to make them out, knows who they are and enlarges their circle after the pattern of the paranoid conspiracy. Similarly, the patient is at first completely unable to explain the construction of the influencing apparatus, but he familiarizes himself with it gradually.

Having solved the relation between ideas of reference and the influencing apparatus, we may proceed to an examination of the latter without reference to its effects.

The Construction of the Influencing Machine. It is not necessary to discuss the magic lantern that produces pictures or images, because its structure harmonizes perfectly with the function attributed to it, and because it does not reveal any error of judgment beyond the fact of its nonexistence. This rational superstructure is absolutely impenetrable. We must, at the start, use structures less solidly built, the walls of which reveal gaps through which it is possible to look inside.

The ordinary influencing machine has a very obscure construction; large parts of it are completely unimaginable. In cases where the patient believes he understands the construction of the apparatus well, it is obvious that this feeling is, at best, analogous to that of a dreamer who has a feeling of understanding, but has not the understanding itself. This characteristic may be discovered whenever an accurate description of the apparatus is demanded of the patient.

Also, the apparatus is, as far as I know, always a machine — a very complicated one.

The "Machine" — A Symbol of Individual's Genitals (cf. Dreams of Machines). The psychoanalyst cannot for a moment doubt that this machine must be a symbol — a view recently emphasized by Freud in one of his lectures, in which he stated that the complicated machines appearing in dreams always represent the genitalia. Having studied machine dreams analytically over a long period of time, I can fully confirm Freud's statement; I may add, moreover, that the machines always stand for the dreamer's own genitalia and that the dreams are of a masturbatory character. I can state further that these dreams are dreams of escape, of the type described in my paper on alcoholic delirium.[3] In this paper it is shown that whenever an urge to masturbate, or rather a readiness to ejaculate semen, leads to a dream fantasy that is favorable to discharge, another fantasy is hastily substituted, by means of which a new state of inhibition is induced momentarily, and the ejaculation of semen is made difficult, if not impossible. The dream reacts to the repudiated wish for discharge with a successive alteration of symbols.

The machine dream possesses an analogous mechanism, except that the introduction of single components of the machine is not accompanied by the simultaneous disappearance of the other components for which they are substituted — the new components are simply added to the old ones. This is how the hopelessly complex machine originates. In order to strengthen the inhibition, the symbol has been made complex, instead of being displaced by another one; but the result is the same. Each complexity draws the attention of the dreamer to himself, rouses his intellectual interest, reciprocally weakens his libidinal interest and effects in this manner inhibition of instinct.

In machine dreams, the dreamer awakens, more often than not, with his hand on his genitalia, after having dreamed of manipulating the machine. It may, therefore, be assumed that the influencing apparatus is a representation of the patient's genitalia projected onto the outer world, analogous in origin to the machine in dreams. The frequent complaint of the schizophrenic that the apparatus causes erection, drains off semen and weakens potency only confirms this view. At any rate, the analogy of the symptom to a dream production, as well as the accessibility of the symptom to psychoanalytic dream interpretation, is a step beyond the rationalizations and the demand for causal connections that underlie the usual clinical interpretation of the influencing machine in schizophrenia. I can now present my example, which will not only strengthen my hypothesis, but will enlarge it materially.

The Case of Natalija A.: Report. The patient is Miss Natalija A., thirty-one years old, a former student of philosophy. She has been completely deaf for a great number of years, due to an ulcer of the ear, and can make herself understood only by means of writing. She declares that for six and a half years she has been under the influence of an electrical machine made in Berlin, though this machine's use is prohibited by the police. It has the form of a human body, indeed, the patient's own form, though not in all details. Her mother, like her male and female friends, is also under the influence of this machine or similar machines. Of the latter she gives no explanation, describing only the apparatus to which she herself is subjected. She is certain that for men there is a masculine machine representing the masculine form and for women a female one. The trunk (torso) has the shape of a lid, resembling the lid of a coffin, and is lined with silk or velvet. Regarding the limbs, two significant explanations are given. At the first interview, she described them as entirely natural parts of the body. A few weeks later, these limbs were not placed on the coffin lid in their natural form, but were merely drawn on it in two dimensions, in the position they would occupy in the natural state of the body. She cannot see the head — she says that she is not sure about it and does not know whether the machine bears her own head. She has practically nothing to report about the head. The patient does not know definitely how this machine is to be handled, or how it is connected with her; but she vaguely thinks that it is by means of telepathy. The outstanding fact about the machine is that it is being manipulated by someone in a certain manner, and everything that occurs to it happens also to her. When someone strikes this machine, she feels the blow in the corresponding part of her body. The ulcer (lupus) now present on her nose was first produced on the nose of the machine, and some time later the patient herself became afflicted with it. The inner parts of the machine consist of electric batteries, which are supposed to represent the internal organs of the human body. Those who handle the machine produce a slimy substance in her nose, disgusting smells, dreams, thoughts, feelings, and they also disturb her while she is thinking, reading or writing. At an earlier stage, sexual sensations were produced in her through manipulation of the genitalia of the machine; but now the machine no longer possesses any genitalia, though why or how they disappeared she cannot tell. Ever since the machine lost its genitalia, the patient has ceased to experience sexual sensations.

She became familiar with the apparatus — about which she had previously heard — through all kinds of occurrences, especially through conversations among people, that is, through auditory hallucinations. The man who utilizes the apparatus to persecute her, her rejected suitor, a college professor, is prompted by jealousy. Very soon after she had refused his courtship she felt that he was trying, by means of suggestion, to bring about a friendship between his sister-in-law, her mother and herself — his obvious purpose being to use this influence to make her accept him. When, however, suggestion failed, he subjected her to the influence of the machine; not only the patient herself but also her mother, her physicians, her friends and all those who had her welfare at heart, came under the influence of this diabolical apparatus, with the result that the physicians submitted a mistaken diagnosis to her: the apparatus deluded them into diagnosing ailments other than those with which she was afflicted. She could no longer get along with her friends and relatives: she aroused everyone's animosity and felt compelled to run away. It was impossible to obtain any further details from the patient. On her third visit, she became inaccessible and only stated that the analyst, too, was under the influence of the apparatus, that he had become hostile to her and that they could no longer understand each other.

The Case of Natalija A.: Interpretation. This case provides a definite reason for believing that the influencing machine represents a stage in the development of a symptom that can also appear without this stage, as a delusion of reference. The patient clearly stated that her persecutor had recourse to the apparatus only when his attempt to influence her by suggestion failed. The fact that she seems to have previously heard about the machine is also enlightening. This vague recognition obviously awakened in the patient old familiar sensations that she had experienced before she was subjected to the apparatus; this is analogous to the well-known fact that persons in a state of infatuation have the feeling of having always known the beloved one — though in reality, they are merely rediscovering one of their old libidinal imagos. We shall later hear just how remote was the past in which she had first experienced sensations similar to those caused by the influencing apparatus.

The peculiar construction of the machine substantiates my assumptions to a great extent, especially with regard to the significance of the machine as a projected symbol of the genitalia. I may add that the apparatus represents not only the patient's genitalia but, obviously, her whole person. It represents the projection of the patient's body onto the outer world. At least the following results are unquestionably obtained from the patient's report: the apparatus is distinguished above all by its human form, easily recognized despite many nonhuman characteristics. In form, it resembles the patient herself, and she senses all manipulations performed on the apparatus in the corresponding part of her own body and in the same manner. All effects and changes undergone by the apparatus take place simultaneously in the patient's body, and vice versa. Thus, the apparatus loses its genitalia following the patient's loss of her genital sensations;

it had possessed genitalia for as long a period as her genital sensations had lasted.

Applying the technique of dream interpretation to this case, it may be said that the patient's inability to provide any detailed description of the head of the apparatus, and especially her inability to decide whether it was her own head or not, proves conclusively that it is her own head. We know from analytic observations that the person not recognized in a dream is actually the dreamer himself. In my analysis of the *Dream of the Clinic*,[4] it was clear that the dreamer meant herself when she dreamed of a person whose head she could not see.

A further detail in the description of the apparatus — namely, that the lid is lined with silk or velvet — may substantiate this opinion. Women very frequently describe the feelings evoked by caressing their own skin in such terms. That the intestines appear in the form of batteries is only of slight significance here, although it will assume a more profound meaning later on. This superficial interpretation may be associated with the information given directly or indirectly to schoolchildren, to the effect that the viscera resemble a very complicated machine. In this case, the tendency seems to be toward a verbal interpretation of this infantile conception. This conclusion, regarding its ontogeny, is arrived at with the help of the patient's description of her influencing apparatus.

Initially, the patient reported that the limbs of the apparatus appeared in their natural form and position. Several weeks later, she declared that the limbs were drawn on the lid. This is obviously a manifestation of the progressive distortion undergone by the apparatus, which, consequently, eventually loses all human characteristics and becomes a typical, unintelligible influencing machine. First the genitalia, then the limbs are eliminated in this process. The patient, to be sure, is unable to report how the genitalia are removed. She states, however, that the limbs are removed in the following manner: they lose their three-dimensional human form, flattening to a two-dimensional plane. It would not have been surprising if, after a lapse of several weeks, the patient had declared that the apparatus did not possess any limbs at all. Nor would it have been astonishing had she stated that the apparatus had never had any limbs. A failure to recall the developmental stages of the apparatus has obviously the same significance as that of forgetting the origins of dream pictures. It is not too bold to draw the conclusion that the coffin lid of the machine is a product of such successive distortions, and that originally it had represented a human being — namely, the patient herself.

Psychoanalytic experience brings to light the causative factors in such distortion. Underlying every distortion of a psychic phenomenon there is a defense mechanism that has as its aim the protection of the conscious ego against the appearance or reappearance of undisguised fantasies. The patient obviously seeks not to recognize herself in the influencing machine, and thus, in self-protection, she divests it of all human features; in short, the less human the appearance of the delusion, the less does she recognize herself in it. The origin of this rejection will be examined later.

When the influencing machine of Miss Natalija A. first came to my attention, it was in a special stage of development; I was fortunate, moreover, in observing the machine in the process of development as concerned the limbs, and also in obtaining specific information from the patient herself regarding the genitalia. I assume that this process will end with the production of the typical influencing apparatus known to clinical observation, but I cannot affirm that this apparatus will pass through all the stages of development to the very end. It is very possible that it will stop at a middle point, without proceeding further.

III

In the meantime, I shall consider a second hypothesis that may have suggested itself to the reader. It must be taken into consideration that, notwithstanding all that has been said above, the influencing machine of Miss Natalija A. may be merely an inexplicable exception to the general rule. The complex, unintelligible machine, as fantastically described and interpreted by other patients, would perhaps first have to be studied and defined before an explanation of Miss Natalija A.'s influencing machine could be undertaken. For want of other material at hand to substantiate my hypothesis, except the machine dream, I shall start with the assumption that the influencing apparatus is a projection of the patient's genitalia. In presenting this second hypothesis together with, or in lieu of, the first, I realize how much indulgence is exacted from the reader, and I should not be surprised if I were reproached with levity or legerdemain. I myself was unpleasantly surprised to discover that this second hypothesis was probably as valid as the first, and that consequently both became improbable or worthless, for their content differs and each leads to quite a different theory. Fortunately, another theory suggests itself, one that brings into immediate harmony both interpretations of the influencing apparatus. This problem will be touched on again toward the end of this paper.

Regressive Loss of Ego Boundaries. Attention may be called now to a symptom in schizophrenia, which I have named "loss of ego boundaries." This symptom is the complaint that "everyone" knows the patient's thoughts, that his thoughts are not enclosed in his own head, but are spread throughout the world and occur simultaneously in the heads of all persons. The patient seems no longer to realize that he is a separate psychic entity, an ego with individual boundaries. A sixteen-year-old patient in the Wagner-Jauregg Clinic indulged in gay laughter whenever she was asked for her thoughts. Catamnesis revealed that for a long while when being questioned, she believed I had been jesting; she knew that I must be familiar with her thoughts, because they occurred at the same time in my own head.

We are familiar with this infantile stage of thinking, in which a strong belief exists that others know of the child's thoughts. Until the child has been successful in its first lie, the parents are supposed to know everything, even its most secret thoughts. Later on, in the event that the child has been caught lying, this conception may be formed again, now caused by the feeling of guilt. The striving for the right to have secrets from which the parents are excluded is one of the most powerful factors in the formation of the ego, especially in establishing and carrying out one's own will. The developmental stage observed in the above-mentioned case falls into this period when the child does not yet sense this right to privacy and does not yet doubt that the parents and educators know everything.[5]

Patients deduce subsequently from their own thoughts the symptom whose content is that "thoughts are given to them." This must be attributed to the infantile impression originating in an earlier period in life, when the child knows nothing through its own efforts but, rather, obtains all its knowledge from others: how to make use of its limbs, its language, its thoughts. In that period, all is "given to" the child, all joy and all sorrow, and it is difficult to evaluate what share the child itself has in its accomplishments.[6] The sudden discovery that it is able to accomplish a task without the help of others is greeted by the child with a great deal of surprise and excitement. It is probable, therefore, that this symptom represents a regression to this particular stage of infancy. This special period of infancy, though, presents a problem: How far back does it go? What causes the formation of the ego and, as a reaction to the outer world, the ego boundaries? What arouses the realization of individuality, of self, as a distinct psychic unit?

Theoretically, we cannot assume that the ego begins to take form earlier than the time of object finding. The latter comes with gratification and renunciation of instinctual drives, whereas an awareness of the outer world, independent of the infant's drives and desires, is established only gradually. It is hardly possible that the sex instincts should have a greater influence on the development of this awareness than the drive to be nourished. To be sure, the sex instincts will soon take on a special significance that must not be underestimated. But, for the time being, it should be stated that there is a stage when no objects of the outer world exist, and therefore there is no realization that one has an ego.

In that period there exist, nevertheless, desires and drives, and a specific urge to obtain mastery over whatever stimulates the sex organs is observable.

Some Theoretical Speculations. The developmental stage that precedes the stage of object finding has been recognized as that of *identification*. This became evident from the analysis of neurotics, in whom the inability to obtain possession of objects of gratification, or to reach goals of pleasure, was seen to be due to their identification with the objects. The neurotic himself simply stands for what attracts him in the outer world; he has not found his way to the outer world and, therefore, is unable to develop an adequate ego in his stunted, exclusively libidinal relationships. This peculiar organization of libido has been termed "narcissistic." The libido in such cases has been directed toward the neurotic's own personality; it is attached to his own ego and not to the objects of the outer world. Observations and theoretical considerations, especially those of Freud, have led to the assumption that this libido organization characterizes the beginning of psychic development, the "objectless" period, and that this libido organization must be considered a correlate, if not a cause, of the "objectlessness." This organization of libido corresponds also to the stage of intellectual development in which the person considers all the sensory stimuli he receives as endogenous and immanent. At this stage of development the psyche does not yet perceive that intervals of time and space exist between the object from which the stimulus emanates and the sensory response.

The next stage of development is, then, that of an outward projection of the stimulus and the attributing of this stimulus to a distant object, hence a stage of distancing and objectification of the intellect, and along with this a transfer of libido to the discovered, or rather, self-created, outer world. As a safeguard to this psychic achievement, and as a kind of critical authority for objectification, there evolves at the same time the faculty of distinguishing between objectivity and subjectivity, an awareness of reality, which enables the individual to recognize his inner experiences as distinct from the outer stimuli — in other words, to regard inner experiences as internal and not to confuse them with the objects of sensory response.

This correlative developmental process, however, is apt to meet with inhibitions. There are inhibitions from the intellectual side, or as we say, from the ego — the chief weapon of which is the intellect; and there are inhibitions that arise from the transference of libido in various stages of development, and with various results, depending on the relation of the ego to the libido. These points of inhibition are called, after Freud, "fixation points." In most cases, the factor that causes ego disturbances seems to lie in lesions of the libido. Thus, it is clear from Freud's interpretation that paranoia is a reaction to repressed homosexuality. The prohibition against finding an object for the homosexual drive, which results in an inhibition of the transference of homosexual libido organization, should be recognized as originating from within and remaining within. This projection is a defensive measure of the ego against the renounced homosexual libido that emerges with onrushing force out of repression. Libidinal inhibition leads to intellectual inhibition, which may be manifested in impaired judgment or in insanity. An internal psychic process due to displacement and projection is mistaken for an external one, which leads to more or less marked "affective weakness of judgment," with the accompanying reactions of the psyche quantitatively and qualitatively determined by the morbid process.

One may say that in the case of impaired libido organization, the ego finds itself faced with the task of mastering an insane outer world, and hence behaves insanely.[7]

In the neuropsychoses that usually appear in later life, with a history of previous relative psychic health, it is not difficult to observe that the impairment of the ego is caused by an impairment of the libido. However, in cases of psychosis that develop gradually and insidiously, beginning with earliest infancy, we may assume not so much a successive impairment of libido and ego as a correlative inhibition, primarily, of the entire development of the individual. The one group of instinctual drives does not develop normally, and this is paralleled by an arrest of the functions of the other group of drives, and by a simultaneous development of secondary relations, which are to be regarded as attempts at self-cure and at adaptation to the functional disturbance by means of compensations and overcompensations. Furthermore, regressions occur on the part of functions that have developed normally but, whenever there is a marked discordance between the diseased and the normal portions of the psyche, abandon their normal level and retreat, for the purpose of adaptation, to the lower level of the impaired functions. During this retreat, there may arise various temporary or permanent symptom formations of different clinical types; and from these develop mixed psychotic formations. The existence of these partial processes, and their great variety with regard to levels of regression at a given moment, require careful consideration. In considering inhibitions of instinctual drives, one must constantly keep in mind that all inhibited drives are capable of being transformed into, or being discharged as, anxiety. To quote Freud, "It may be said that, in a certain theoretical sense, symptoms are formed only in order to forestall an otherwise inevitable development of anxiety."

IV

We have learned from Freud that the projection of the homosexual libido in paranoia is to be regarded as a defensive measure of the ego against an inopportune and socially reprehensible sexual urge pressing from the unconscious. Is it possible to regard the projection of the patient's own body in the case of Miss Natalija A. as an analogous situation? Naturally, the projection would have to subserve the defense of that libido which belongs to the patient's own body, and which has become either too extensive or too inopportune in its demands for the patient to be able to tolerate it as her own. It is also necessary to assume that this projection pertains only to the libido of the body and not to the libido of the psychic ego as well; that, moreover, the libido of the psychic ego[8] has facilitated the defense against the bodily libido because it was, so to speak, ashamed of it. That a projection mechanism has been chosen for the purpose of defense — a mechanism belonging to the primary functioning of the ego in the process of object finding — gives reason to believe that one is here dealing with a libido position that is coeval with the beginnings of intellectual object finding and achieved either by regression or by the persistence of a vestigial phenomenon (*Resterscheinung* — Freud), which has been for years, and up to the onset of the illness, effectively compensated or concealed. In regressions, however, there is always an effort to reach the formerly uninhibited libido positions. In paranoia, regression reaches a stage when homosexual object choice has not yet come under the prohibition of the ego and there is free homosexual libido, which is only later subjected to repression at the behest of the cultural demands of the ego.

The libido directed toward a person's own self, which the ego tries to get rid of by projecting its own body, is, naturally, characteristic of a period when it was still free from conflict with the demands of other love-objects. This period must coincide with the developmental stage of the psyche in which object finding still occurs within the individual's own body, and when the latter is still regarded as part of the outer world.

I am intentionally differentiating between object choice and object finding. By the former, I mean only libidinal cathexis; by the latter, the intellectual awarenesses of this cathexis. An object is found by the intellect, and *chosen* by the libido. These processes may occur either simultaneously or in sequence, but for my purpose they are to be regarded as distinct.

The projection of one's body may, then, be traced back to the developmental stage in which one's own body is the goal of the object finding. This must be the time when the infant is discovering his body, part by part, as the outer world, and is still groping for his hands and feet as though they were foreign objects. At this time, everything that "happens" to him emanates from his own body: his psyche is the object of stimuli arising in his own body but acting on it as if produced by outer objects. Later, these disjecta membra are pieced together and systematized into a unified whole under the supervision of a psychic unity that receives all sensations of pleasure and pain from these separate parts. This process takes place by means of identification with one's own body. The ego, thus discovered, is cathected with the available libido; in accordance with the psychic nature of the ego, narcissism develops; and in accordance with the function of individual organs as sources of pleasure, autoeroticism results.

But if the psychoanalytic theories previously employed are correct, this object finding within one's own organs, which can be regarded as parts of the outer world only by projection, must be preceded by a stage of identification with a narcissistic libido position,[9] and it is necessary to assume two successive stages of identification and projection.

The projection that participated in the object finding within one's own organs would, then, be the second phase of the preceding stage — although the part that depends on the postulated identification has yet to be discovered.

I am, then, assuming the existence of these two successive phases of identification and projection in object finding and object choice within one's own body.

I do not run counter to psychoanalytic conceptions in contending that the individual comes into the world as an organic unity in which libido and ego are not yet separated, and all available libido is related to that organic unity which does not deserve the name "ego" (that is, a psychic self-protective organization) any more than does the cell. In this situation, the individual is equally a sexual and an individual being, simultaneously performing ego and reproductive functions — like the cell that takes nourishment up to the time when it divides. This stage of the newly born child is biological up to the time of conception, but must be regarded as psychological from the time when — at an indeterminable stage of fetal life — cerebral development takes place. From the viewpoint of libido, we may say that the newly born child is a sexual being. I am in accord with Freud's assumption that the individual's first renunciation is the renunciation of the protection of the mother's body, imposed upon the libido and accompanied by that expression of anxiety, the birth cry. However, once this first trauma is over and no discontent arises to bring the infant into a clash with itself and with the environment, it is in complete possession of its own libido and knows nothing of the outer world, not even that part of the world it will soon discover within itself. This is the stage of identity that precedes the first projection for the purpose of object finding within one's own body. This stage did not come about because of that psychic activity which may be called "identification," but is present from the beginning. Nevertheless, the result is the same as in actively established identity — absolute self-satisfaction, no outer world, no objects. I shall designate this stage as "innate narcissistic" — a situation in which the libido, directed outward, first cathects the subject's own body by the indirect way of projection, and returns by way of self-discovery to the ego. In the meantime, the ego has undergone a decided alteration under the influence of these first psychic stirrings, which one may call "experience," and is now again cathected by libido. I shall call this stage "acquired narcissism"; it finds a considerable quantity of innate narcissism already present and is superimposed on it. The condition of innate narcissism normally remains attached for all time to the organs and their functions, and is in constant conflict with the various further stages of ego development, which, with the assistance of anxiety and judgment, take place under the aegis of all the faculties that have been gradually acquired in the meantime. The struggle is carried on, at first, chiefly in the spheres of excretory functions and of the autoerotic sources of pleasure, since these are the spheres that give rise to the greatest difficulties in the individual's relation to the environment. Nevertheless, we must definitely understand that throughout life the ego develops with constant shiftings in the narcissistic libido position —

that man, in his struggle for existence, is constantly compelled to find and recognize himself anew — and that the acquisition of narcissism is immanent in culture and is conceivable only on the basis of an intact inborn narcissism that serves as a source of nourishment and regeneration. This constant struggle revolving around the self occurs in various degrees in relation to various instinctual drives; it concerns homo- and heterosexuality and every libido component in different degrees at different times, and provokes various reactions, compensations, superstructures and eliminations. These secondary psychic formations then enter again into combination and produce insoluble dynamic, qualitative, relative and modal relations, resulting in a great variety of charac-ter types and symptoms. The development of both the ego and the libido — either alone or in their relation to each other — may become arrested and may set up goals of regression at as many points as there are primary, secondary, tertiary (and so on) factors of relationship and development.

Pathological Projection as a Defense against Narcissistic Regression of Libido. The entire prob-lem is further complicated by the elements of time and space, and so made insoluble. Suppose that the projection of one's own body is a pathological repetition of that psychic stage when the individual was endeavoring to discover his body by means of projection. It would not be too much to say that just as the projection in normal primary development has been successful because the innate narcissistic libido position had to be renounced under the attack of outer stimuli, so also pathological projection takes place because there has developed an accumulation of narcissistic libido analogous to the primary narcissism — although here it is anachronistic, regressive or fix-ated, yet resembles it in character insofar as it isolates the individual from the outer world. Hence, projection of one's own body may be regarded as a defense against a libido position correspond-ing to the end of fetal existence and the beginning of extrauterine development. Freud, indeed, has not hesitated to declare, in his Introductory Lectures, that psychological problems are to be traced back to intrauterine existence.[10]

Explanation of Several Psychotic Phenomena on This Basis. These considerations may be used as a starting point for the explanation of various schizophrenic symptoms. Is it not possible that catalepsy (*flexibilitas cerea*) corresponds to the stage when man senses his own organs as foreign, as not belonging to himself, as being dominated by an outside force? A similar instance is the symptom of having one's limbs moved by someone. This symptom reproduces especially well the situation in which one's own body becomes strange and, so to speak, part of an outer world dom-inated by outer forces. May we not say that catatonic stupor, which represents a complete rejec-tion of the outer world, is a return to the uterus? May not these severest catatonic symptoms be the ultimate refuge of a psyche that has given up even the most primitive ego functions and, in toto, has retreated to the fetal and nursing stages, because it cannot use in the present state of its libido even the simplest ego functions that maintain the relation to the outer world? The cata-tonic symptom, the negativistic stare of the schizophrenic, is nothing else than a renunciation of the outer world expressed in "organ language." Does not also the "nursing reflex" in the terminal stages of general paralysis indicate such a regression to infancy?[11]

The psychic correlate of *flexibilitas cerea* and that stage in which man regards himself as a part of the outer world, lacks consciousness of his own volition and of his own ego boundaries, is the patient's feeling that his thoughts are known and possessed by everyone else. In the period here duplicated pathologically, there are indeed no thoughts, but even thoughts are subjected, as already stated above, to the same process of being regarded at first as coming from the outer world before they are counted among the functions of the ego. Thoughts must first be assimilated into the consciousness of ego unity before they can be an automatic ego function; and this cannot occur before the intellect has advanced to the stage of memory perceptions. Freud has taught that this, too, is a later process, preceded by the stage of hallucinations of memory pictures — that is, a stage when the perceptions actually appear in the outer world and are not regarded as internal occurrences. Moreover, this stage of hallucinatory perceptions, in itself representing a kind of objectification, object finding and object choice, also belongs to the first period of life. The regression, of course, does not occur equally in all psychic faculties and relationships. The capacity for thinking with memory perceptions is still intact, but the libido is already degraded to the nursing stage and sets up a relation with the thinking faculty as it exists. The consciousness of personality has been lost, and this loss is shown in the patient's inability to locate his intact psychic inventory. The patient who declares that his thoughts and feelings are in all people's minds merely declares, in words and concepts derived from the memory reserve of a later developmental stage, that his libido finds itself at the stage where it is still identical with the outer world, still has no ego boundaries set up against the outer world; and his libido is now compelled, therefore, to renounce the normal intellectual object relations insofar as these depend on the degraded libido position.

These feelings and this mode of expression depend on the intactness of the psyche's ability to operate with memory perceptions. This faculty, too, may undergo regression,[12] in which case the patient hallucinates. The libido has retreated behind the stage of identification, the intellect no longer knows how to establish a relation to the outer world, even by means of identification. The psyche is approaching closer and closer to the mother's womb.

Furthermore, may not perhaps "picture-seeing in planes" represent a stage of the development of the visual sense still earlier than the hallucinatory stage?

V

I have stated that narcissistic self-discovery and self-choice repeat themselves with every new acquisition of the ego, to the effect that, under the guidance of conscience and judgment, each new acquisition is either rejected or cathected with libido and attributed to the ego. I shall call this "narcissism," or "psychic narcissism," and contrast it with the organic narcissism that guarantees in the unconscious the unity and functioning of the organism. There is nothing new in calling attention to the great dependence of physical health, and even of life itself, on what is called "love of life," or in the reminder that one can actually die of a "broken heart," and that, as Wilhelm Ostwald mentions in his book on *Great Men*, university professors emeritus often die soon after they have been absolved of their duties, even when they have previously been in the best of health.[13]

They die not of old age but because they lose the love of life when they can no longer perform the duties they have loved. Freud tells of a famous musician who succumbed to his illness because of the discontinuation of his creative work.

The Distribution of Narcissistic Libido and Its Significance for Hypochondriasis, "Entfremdung" and Projection. We must assume that the libido flows through the entire body, perhaps like a substance (Freud's view), and that the integration of the organism is effected by a libido tonus, the oscillations of which correspond to the oscillations of psychic narcissism and object libido.[14] On this tonus depends the resistance to illness and death. Love of life has saved many a man whom physicians had given up as incurable.

Whenever there occurs an influx of organic narcissism to a given organ as a site of predilection,[15] there may also occur a consciousness of organ relations and organic functions that, in normal life, are relegated to an unconscious and vegetative role. Analogously, objects cathected by psychic narcissism and object love come to consciousness wherever the cathexis has reached a sufficient degree of strength. This influx of libido directs attention to the organ and provides the consciousness of a transformation of the organ or its functions, that is, the feeling of estrangement. This is the mechanism described by Freud as hypochondria. This influx of libido is followed by the turning away of the ego from the organ pathologically overcharged with libido, or from its functions — that is, by estrangement.[16] This is to be considered a defensive measure against the anxiety associated with hypochondria. The feeling of strangeness is a defense against libidinal cathexis, no matter whether it concerns objects of the outer world, one's own body or its parts. Of course, the estrangement does not cause the giving up of the unconscious libido position. The estrangement is not a destructive force but merely a denial of the pathological cathexis; it is an instance of the ostrich tactics of the ego, which may be very easily reduced ad absurdum, and which must ultimately be supplanted by other or more effective measures of defense.

When, in paranoia, the feeling of estrangement no longer affords protection, the libidinal drive toward the homosexual object is projected onto the latter and appears, by a reversal of direction, as aggression toward the loving one (the patient himself) in the form of a sense of persecution. Strangers become enemies. The enmity is a new and more energetic attempt at protection against the rejected unconscious libido.

The narcissistic organ libido in schizophrenia may undergo a similar transformation. The estranged organ — in our case, the entire body — appears as an outer enemy, as a machine used to afflict the patient.

Three Stages in the History of the Development of the Influencing Machine. Three principal stages in the history of the influencing machine should be distinguished, then:

First: The sense of internal alteration produced by the influx of libido into a given organ (hypochondria).

Second: The feeling of estrangement produced by rejection, whereby the pathologically altered organs or their functions are, so to speak, denied and eliminated as something alien to the wholly or partially sound organs and functions accepted by the ego.

Third: The sense of persecution (*paranoia somatica*) arising from projection of the pathological alteration onto the outer world, by attribution of the alteration to a foreign hostile power, and by the construction of the influencing machine as a summation of some or all of the pathologically altered organs (the whole body) projected outward. Note that among these organs the genitals take precedence in the projection.

The assumption of an influx of libido into specific organs, in the physiological sense of the word, should receive proper consideration. On the basis of this assumption, transient swellings of organs, often observed in schizophrenia without inflammation and without an actual edema, may be interpreted as equivalents of erection, produced like erections of the penis and clitoris by an overflow of secretion resulting from libidinal charging of organs.[17]

VI

Differentiation of Two Types of Projected Objects in Their Relation to the "Machine." It is not at all surprising that the hostile apparatus is handled by persons who, to an objective observer, cannot but appear as love-objects — suitors, lovers, physicians. All these persons are associated with sensuousness, deal with the body and demand a transfer of libido to themselves. This is what actually occurs in normal situations. But the narcissistic libido, whenever too strongly fixated, cannot but regard this demand made by love-objects as inimical and looks on the object as an enemy. It should be noted, however, that another group of love-objects — mother, the patient's present physician, close friends of the family — are counted not among the patient's persecutors but among the persecuted, compelled to share his fate in being subjected to the influencing machine. In contrast to paranoia, the persecuted and not the persecutors are organized into a passive conspiracy, and this conspiracy is of a passive nature. Of this phenomenon the following explanation may be offered:

It is noteworthy that the persecutors are all persons who live at some distance from the patient, whereas the persecuted belong to the closest circle of acquaintanceship and — including the physicians who are images of the father and hence also family members — represent a kind of constantly present family. Now, the family members are those love-objects who, because of their presence from the beginning of the patient's life, are subjected to the narcissistic object choice by identification. To these persons our patient still applies this form of object choice insofar as he subjects them to his own fate, identifying himself with them. Normally, the demand for transfer of libido with respect to members of the family is not felt as requiring either the overcoming of any great distance or any substantial sacrifice of narcissism. In establishing an identification with these persons, the patient follows a well-trodden path, which does not appear sufficiently inimical to the patient to force him to revolt against the cathexis of these objects and to regard them as hostile. It is different with lovers and suitors. These threaten a narcissistic position with their substantial demands for object libido and are, therefore, repulsed as enemies. The fact that these persons are spatially distant evokes a feeling of distance on the part of the libido. The transfer of libido *par distance* is felt as an extraordinarily strong demand for the acknowledgment of an object position, as a demand for self-denial. This also holds for normal conditions. Spatial distance separating the beloved threatens the object libido; it even leads people, ultimately, to withdraw themselves and give up the object. To have to love at a distance is a difficult task, only unwillingly performed. Our patient, however, cannot simply give up love-objects in a normal way, because he has not cathected them normally. To those demanding much from him, he can only react with the paranoid mechanism; to those demanding less, only with identification. I do not know why the persons who work the influencing machine are in my observation exclusively male. This may be due to faulty observation or to chance. Further investigations must clarify this point. However, that heterosexual objects can appear as persecutors, in contradiction to Freud's theory of the exclusively homosexual genesis of paranoia, may be explained by the fact that the influencing machine corresponds to a regressive psychic stage in which the important distinction is not between the sexes but between narcissistic and object libido, and every object demanding a transfer of libido is regarded as hostile, irrespective of its sex.

VIII

After this long digression — which, I hope, will not be regarded as superfluous — I shall return to the question of how even the ordinary, clinically familiar influencing machine in its typical form can be a projection of the patient's body, as was true in the case of Miss Natalija A. The answer should not be difficult to discover. If one does not want to assume that the machine has been established by successive substitutions of the parts of the patient's idea of his own body picture ("*wie Fuchs aus alopex*"),[18] and if one makes use, rather, of the genitality of the machine as previously established to explain the typical influencing machine, one should avail oneself of the following considerations:

The regression of libido to the early infantile stage determines the retransformation of the meanwhile genitally centralized libido into the pregenital stage, in which the entire body is a libidinal zone — in which the entire body is a genital. Such fantasies are also found in cases of narcissistically strongly cathected, sexually extremely infantile, neurosis. I have myself observed such cases. The fantasy originates in the intrauterine (mother's body) complex and usually has the content of the man's desire to creep completely into the genital from which he came, refusing to content himself with any lesser satisfaction. The entire individual is, in this case, a penis. Further, the road of identification with the father (the penis of the father) is overdetermined in the symptom formation of male patients. The symptom is also to be conceived as regression to a stage of diffuse, narcissistic organ libido and is, in most cases, associated with genital impotence. The genital, too, is renounced.[19] The same situation is revealed by the lack of genitalia in the influencing machine of Miss Natalija A. The intrauterine fantasy and the identification[20] with mother probably find expression in the domelike lid of the trunk, which perhaps represents the patient's mother during pregnancy. The enclosed batteries are perhaps the child, which is the patient herself. The fact that the child is equated with the batteries, that is, with a machine, lends further support to

Early television transmission, c. 1929.

the supposition that the person feels himself to be a genital — all the more so because the machine's lack of genitalia stands for the pregenital, in a certain sense, nongenital stage.

The construction of the influencing apparatus in the form of a machine, therefore, represents a projection of the entire body, now wholly a genital.

The fact that the machine in dreams is nothing but a representation of the genital raised to primacy in no way contradicts the possibility that it is, in schizophrenia, a symbol of the entire body conceived as a penis, and hence a representative of the pregenital epoch. The patient has indeed not lost the ideational content of his past life. The picture of the genital as a representation of sexuality has been retained in the psychic apparatus. It is, therefore, used as a means of representation, a mode of expression, a language in which phenomena existing prior to this means of expression are communicated. Here, the genital is merely a symbol of a sexuality older than the symbolism and than any means of social expression. The picture, then, is in the language of the later genital period nothing but: "I am sexuality." But the context is, "I am wholly a genital." This test has, of course, to be translated into the language suited to the actual libido conditions.

It is possible that the ordinary influencing apparatus, in the form of the machine, owes its existence simply to the fact that its early stages were not formed gradually, because the pathological process seized too precipitately on remote phases of existence. It is also possible that the early stages were not noticed by observers and not reported by the patient, or not recognized and evaluated as early stages. Thus, the connection between the influencing apparatus of Miss Natalija A. and the ordinary influencing machine has been lost to science.

But the contradiction between the two concepts — on the one hand, that the machine form of the influencing apparatus originated through successive distortions of the influencing apparatus that represents the projection of the body, and on the other, that the machine form of the influencing apparatus represents, like the machine in a dream, a projection of the genitalia — is now abolished. The evolution, by distortion of the human apparatus into a machine, is a projection that corresponds to the development of the pathological process that converts the ego into a diffuse sexual being — or, expressed in the language of the genital period, into a genital, a machine independent of the aims of the ego and subordinated to a foreign will.[21] It is no longer subordinated to the will of the ego, but dominates it. Here, too, one is reminded of the astonishment of boys when they become aware for the first time of erection. The fact, moreover, that the erection is shortly conceived as an exceptional and mysterious feat supports the assumption that erection is felt to be a thing independent of the ego, a part of the outer world not completely mastered.

NOTES

1. At the Belgrade Neuropsychiatric Division.

2. Taken literally, this patient's words, "*Sich verstellt*," mean "moves oneself from one place to another" — TRANS.

3. Victor Tausk, "Zur Psychologie des alkoholischen Beschäftigungsdelirs," *Internationale Zeitschrift für Psychoanalyse* 3 (1915) [trans. Eric Mosbacher and Marius Tausk, as "On the Psychology of the Alcoholic Occupation Delirium," *The Psychoanalytic Quarterly* 38.3 (July 1969), pp. 406–31].

4. Published in *Internationale Zeitschrift für Psychoanalyse* 2 (1914), p. 466. Miss N. dreams: "I am seated on an upper bench in the surgical amphitheater. Below, a woman is being operated on. She lies with her head toward me, but I cannot see the head, as it seems to be concealed by the lower benches. I see the woman only from her chest down. I see both thighs and a heap of white towels and linens. I see nothing else clearly."

Analysis of the dream reveals that the dreamer sees herself as the woman operated on. A few days before the night of the dream, the dreamer called on a young physician who made advances to her. On this occasion she was reclining on a couch. The physician raised her skirts and while he operated "below," she perceived the heap of white underclothes overhead. Just as she saw of herself in this situation, she sees of the woman in the dream, and the woman's head remains invisible to her just as she could not see her own head in the actual situation. According to Freud, the "woman without a head" in a dream represents the mother. The basic reason for this interpretation will not be discussed here, but will be treated in another section of this paper.

5. This would fall into the period before the first successful lie, which occurs very early in infancy. Lies fabricated in the first year of life are nothing unusual; they can be observed especially in children who resist the regular elimination of bodily wastes when, by means of grimaces, gestures and inarticulated words, they mislead the training person into believing that they have had a satisfactory evacuation. The educator who allows herself to be deceived by the child must ultimately look to divine guidance in order to keep the child within the truth, when the latter, to gain forbidden pleasure, begins to enjoy the practice of lying. Very soon, the time arrives when recourse to the highest authority of omniscience becomes necessary. The introduction of the omniscient God in the educational system becomes, indeed, a necessity because, de facto, children learn to lie from parents and upbringers, who by misrepresentations and unkept promises make the child obey and teach him to disguise his true purposes. In order to safeguard the success of education, teachers cannot but transfer the power of omniscience to God — an authority that they themselves have abandoned. The incomprehensible nature of this deity precludes the possibility of practicing deception on him. Nevertheless, many children do not submit even to this authority, continually test their God with regard to His omniscience and not infrequently actually succeed in unmasking Him as a phantom of the dethroned parental, specifically paternal, power.

6. In the discussion of this paper at the Vienna Psychoanalytic Society, Freud emphasized that the infant's conception that others know its thoughts has its source in the process of learning to speak. Having obtained its language from others, the infant has also received thoughts from them; and the child's feeling that others know his thoughts, as well as that others have "made" him the language and, along with it, his thoughts, has therefore some basis in reality.

7. The cases in which inhibition endangers the intellect primarily are to be attributed to dementia.

8. The projection of the libido position of the psychic ego produces the symptoms of simple paranoia, the mechanism of which was discovered by Freud. In what follows, I shall omit from consideration the fact that ego-libido is necessarily homosexual in its strivings, that is, attracted by the sex that the ego itself represents. I shall describe briefly only one mechanism, which appears to be out of harmony with object-libido and which is exemplified by the symptomatology of our patient, Miss Natalija A.

The patient reports: After she had rejected her suitor, she felt that he suggested that her mother and she strike up a friendship with his sister-in-law, so that the patient might be more amenable to a later proposal on his part. What appears here as suggestion on the suitor's part is nothing more than the projection of the patient's own unconscious inclination to accept the proposal of marriage. She had rejected the proposal not without inner conflict and had vacillated between accepting and rejecting her suitor. She gave realization in action to the rejection, while she projected her inclination to accept the proposal onto the object of her conflicting desires and made it appear as the sensory effect of an influence on the part of the object, or in other words as her symptom.

The patient was ambivalent toward her suitor, and projected one side of the conflict, the positive libidinal one, while manifesting in action the negative side, the rejection, because this procedure was in conformity with her ego. The choice, which in this instance has projection as its outcome, may in other cases be the reverse one. Here, I am merely calling attention to the mechanism of partial projection of ambivalent tendencies.

A special contribution to the subject of the projection mechanism, which also made me aware of this principle, was made by Dr. Helene Deutsch in her discussion of this paper at the Vienna Psychoanalytic Society. A schizophrenic patient had the feeling that her friends always laid down their work when she herself began to work, and that they sat down whenever she stood up — in brief, that others were always performing the opposite of what she herself was doing. The patient merely felt this; she could not possibly see it, since she was blind. Dr. Deutsch regarded the symptom as a projection of one of two tendencies present in every one of her patient's actions — namely, the tendency to do and the tendency not to do. This interpretation was confirmed by cases presented by other commentators. On this occasion, Freud proposed the formulation that ambivalence makes the projection mechanism possible. Once expressed, this thesis appears self-evident. It has its corollary in another of Freud's contentions, to the effect that ambivalence produces repression. This has as its natural consequence the formulation mentioned above, since only what is repressed is projected, insofar as boundaries between the unconscious and the conscious still obtain. The entire problem furnishes special justification for Bleuler's term "schizophrenia," and at the same time corroborates Pötzl's views discussed in note 16, below.

The present paper shows how, albeit unconsciously, I had been demonstrating Freud's formulation.

9. Freud has already indicated in his paper on the Schreber biography ["The Psychotic Doctor Schreber," in *Three Case Histories* (New York: Collier, 1963), p. 163 — TRANS] that the libido in schizophrenia is located at a stage even earlier than autoeroticism. I arrive at the same conclusion by a different route, and I take the liberty of presenting this fact as proof of the correctness of Freud's contentions.

10. Sigmund Freud, *Introductory Lectures on Psychoanalysis*, ed. James Strachey (New York: W. W. Norton, 1966), "Some Thoughts on Development and Regression — Aetiology," pp. 339–57.

11. Many patients are actually aware of this regression to infancy and to the embryonic stage — the latter, though, only as a threat of further illness. A patient said to me: "I feel that I am constantly becoming younger and smaller. Now I am four years old. Shortly I shall get into diapers and then back into mother."

Dr. Helene Deutsch, during the discussion of this paper, reported the case of a thirty-one-year-old female schizophrenic who wet and soiled her bed and stated as her justification that "they were making a baby of her."

On the same occasion, Freud, referring especially to the influencing machine of Miss Natalija A., and to the interchangeability of sexuality and death, called attention to the significance of the mode of burial of the Egyptian mummies. To place the mummies in a case resembling the human body suggests the idea of the return to "mother earth," the return to the mother's body in death. Freud's reference shows how, as a compensation for the bitterness of death, men take for granted the bliss of existence in the uterus. The fantasy of return to the uterus is, then, an atavistic one, a preformed fantasy; and as such it may be added to the "primal fantasies" postulated by Freud. This fantasy appears symptomatically in schizophrenia as the pathological reality of the regressing, disintegrating psyche. The mummy returns to the mother's body by physical death, and the schizophrenic by psychic death. ("*Mutterleibsphantasie*" — an expression, as far as I know, first used by Gustav Grüner.)

12. For further discussion of this subject, see Sigmund Freud, "Metapsychological Supplement to the Theory of Dreams" [1916–17], in *Collected Papers*, ed. Joan Riviere (New York: Basic Books, 1959), vol. 4, pp. 137–52. This work appeared while the present paper was in proofs. I am pleased to be able to refer to the many points of agreement between my own contentions and those of Freud in his paper, of which I had no knowledge at the time.

13. Wilhelm Ostwald, *Grosse Männer* (Leipzig: Akademische Verlagsgesellschaft, 1909).

14. Melancholia is the illness the mechanism of which consists in the disintegration of psychic narcissism, in the renunciation of love for the psychic ego. Melancholia, in pure culture, is the paradigm of the dependence of the organic on the psychic narcissism. The separation of libido from the psychic ego, that is, the rejection and condemnation of the raison d'être of the psychic person, brings with it the rejection of the physical person, the tendency toward physical self-destruction. There occurs a consecutive separation of the libido from those organs that guarantee the functioning and the value of the physical individuality, a separation by means of which the organs' function is impaired or given up. Hence appetite is lost, constipation occurs, menstruation ceases and potency is lost — all as a result of unconscious mechanisms. This failure of function is to be traced to the destruction of the respective organic libido positions that are essentially vegetative, that is, unconscious; it is thus to be strictly differentiated from the conscious, deliberate suicidal tendency expressed in refusal of nourishment or in activities inimical to life.

Melancholia is the persecution psychosis without projection; its structure is due to a specific mechanism of identification. (Further discussion on this point can be found in my paper, "Diagnostische Erörterungen auf Grund der Zustandsbilder der sogen. Kriegspsychosen," *Wiener medizinische Wochenschrift* 37–38 [1916]. While this paper was in proof, Freud's article "Mourning and Melancholia" [1917], in *Collected Papers*, vol. 4, pp. 152–70, appeared, to which I refer in this connection.)

15. This involves the Freudian principle of the erotogenicity of organs, that is, of the erotogenic zones.

16. Dr. Otto Pötzl suggested on a certain occasion (I do not remember whether it was in connection with a thesis of his own or as an addendum to theories of others) that the catatonic stare is an expression of the patient's inability to apportion his motor impulses, disintegrated by the split of his volition into agonistic and antagonistic elements, so that a purposeful action may again be performed. (In Meyrinck's story, *Der Fluch der Kröte* ["The Curse of the Toad"], the millipede is unable to move a limb the moment he focuses his attention on the activity of any one of his thousand legs.)

Theory of catatonia: Pötzl's conception is in harmony with the psychoanalytic theory that the regressive narcissistic libido undergoes a pathological division with the cathexis of the individual functions of the psyche and the organs, such that agonistic and antagonistic portions of the purposefully directed antithetical pair of forces are brought into the reach of awareness by the disturbance of the equilibrium between their respective libido quantities and are deprived of automatic functioning. This would be a special case of hypochondria and estrangement related to the antithetical pairs of forces with their respective specific consequences.

Pötzl's view does not contradict the assumption that the outer world may be eliminated as a result of regressive narcissistic libido, and it actually allows the application of the theory of hypochondria to further special points in the psychophysical makeup of men. Pötzl's concept even suggests the hypothesis that there was, in the life of man, a period — not a definitely determinable period, it is true, and perhaps only potential — in which the activity of the antagonistic pair of forces was still automatic and had to be discovered and learned by the person himself as if from an alien outer world. This period may well be present in ontogenesis only as an "engram" of phylogenetic stages that comprised the origin of the now-complex motor organs from the simplest single-tracked active formations. Regression in schizophrenia would then be traceable to those "engrams" of the oldest era of the race, and the theory would demand that these phylogenetic traces of function retain their capacity for being reactivated. We must not shrink from this hypothesis. It provides us with another idea to use in investigating problems in schizophrenia: perhaps this remarkable disease consists in just this — that the phylogenetic vestiges of function retain in many individuals an extraordinary capacity for being reactivated. Psychoanalysis would have to make room for this conception, since psychoanalysis has already in many instances uncovered the roots of symptoms in the history of the species. From this it may perhaps be possible, via ontogenesis, to proceed to an explanation of the mysterious "electrical currents" complained of by patients. This paresthesia may once have been a sensation that accompanied the first nerve and muscle functions. It is perhaps a reminiscence of the sensation of the newly born being who enters the strange air of the external world out of the comfortable covering of the mother's womb, or for whom the latter is replaced by its first garments. The bed he first lays in is perhaps the one that comes in the patient's consciousness when he feels himself, while lying in bed, electrified by invisible wires.

17. These psychological assumptions are strongly supported from the organological standpoint by a report made some years ago by Fauser at Stuttgart on the presence of sexual secretion in the blood of dementia praecox patients, as demonstrated by Abderhalden's dialytic method. New and important findings in this connection are to be expected from Stemach's experiments. When the present paper was completed, there appeared in the *Müenchener medizinische Wochenschrift* 6 (1918), under the title, "Umstimmungen der Homosexualität durch Austausch der Pubertätsdrusen" ["Transformation of Homosexuality by Exchange of Puberty Glands"], a very interesting and significant article by Steinach and Lichtenstern, which realized these expectations. After the completion of this paper there also appeared in the *Internationale Zeitschrift für ärztl. Psa* 4 (1917), an article by Sandor Ferenczi, "Von Krankheits und Pathoneurosen" ["Disease or Patho-Neuroses," in *Further Contributions to the Theory and Technique of Psychoanalysis* (London: Hogarth Press and the Institute of Psychoanalysis, 1926), pp. 78–79], in which the assumption of the libidinal cathexis of individual organs in the sense above described appears to be applied with notable success.

18. "Like fox from alopex" — a student parody on etymological derivations consisting of the stringing together of rhyming and nearly rhyming words — TRANS.

19. This renunciation of the genitalia is felt by the male schizophrenic as a loss of virility, which is "drained off" from him, or else as a direct transformation into a woman, corresponding to the infantile notion of boys that there is only one kind of genital, namely their own, and that those of women are the result of castration and really represent a loss of the genital. The castration complex is often combined with the infantile identification of semen with urine, resulting from urethral eroticism. I have observed an attack of castration anxiety while catheterizing a schizophrenic who refused to empty his bladder. He maintained that I was practicing coitus with him by means of the catheter and that I had emptied him of all his semen. Thus, his retention of urine appears as a refusal to yield semen, representing his virility. The patient's playing with excrement is explicable by the narcissistically rooted conception that feces and urine are parts of the body. Coprophagia is not inhibited by the thought that the excreta are nothing else than the body from which they come.

20. The proof of this identification derived from symbolic language has already been given in the dream of "the woman without a head," note 4, above.

21. Indeed, the machines produced by man's ingenuity and created in the image of man are unconscious projections of man's bodily structure. Man's ingenuity seems to be unable to free itself from its relation to the unconscious. See Hanns Sachs, "The Delay of the Machine Age," *The Psychoanalytic Quarterly* 2 (1933).

Translated from the German by Dorian Feigenbaum

A way station for launching an obsolete power. (A thought collision factory in pursuit of journey.) (*A clip in a rifle — a weapon.*) Project for P.S.1, N.Y., 1979.
Dennis Oppenheim

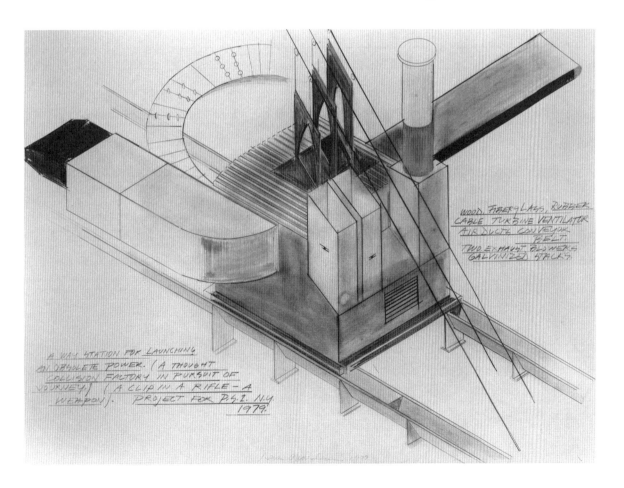

Mappings — A Chronology of Remote Sensing

Judith Barry

1859 Félix Nadar takes the first known aerial image, a daguerreotype of Paris, from a balloon.

1861 Thaddeus Lowe, a meteorologist, is arrested as a spy by the Confederate Army when his balloon is blown off-course into South Carolina. After his release, Lowe demonstrates an ascent for Abraham Lincoln and sends the first air-to-ground telegraph message. Lincoln subsequently sets up an Army Balloon Corps with Lowe in command.

1906 17 kites flown from a ship in San Francisco Bay carry a large-format camera that records the earthquake aftermath.

1909 In Italy, the first photos taken from an airplane are shot from in a plane piloted by Wilbur Wright.

1911 A recon flight makes observations of Turkish positions during the Italian invasion of Tripolitana.

The U.S. Army Signal Corps establishes the first flight training school at College Park, Md. Aerial photography is on the curriculum from the outset.

1913–16 The United States makes recon flights in the Philippines and in Mexico, where they are used in the pursuit of Pancho Villa.

1916 The effectiveness of the spy planes during WWI results in the creation of "scout" planes.

1918 During the Meuse-Argonne offensive, 56,000 aerial photographs are delivered to U.S. Army units within a 4-day period. By war's end, the process is so efficient that only 20 minutes are needed for photos to be brought to ground, printed, interpreted, and used to range artillery fire.

1927 The first "real-time" photos: George Goddard's photos of Fort Leavenworth Federal Prison are transmitted over telegraph wires.

1939–45 During WWII, British RAF Mosquitos are the first to use radar recon cameras that penetrate darkness and clouds. Color and infrared films are used to detect camouflage.

1946 RAND publishes a plan for the first artificial satellite.

1947 The Long Range Detection Program authorizes the U.S. Air Force to develop a recon system able to determine the time and place of a nuclear explosion anywhere in the world. The first rocket-based images of earth are taken by a V–2.

1949 Recon planes on a routine mission from Japan to Alaska detect the fallout of the first nuclear bomb detonated by the Soviet Union at Semipalatinsk.

1952 President Truman creates the National Security Agency to handle the increasingly vast amounts of Signals Intelligence.

1956 The first U–2 spy plane flies a mission over Moscow, Leningrad and the Baltic coast.

1957 Sputnik is lifted into orbit by an SS–6.

1958 The National Advisory Committee for Aeronautics is transformed into NASA; although it has strong ties to the air force, its ostensible mission is to advance the peaceful uses of space while championing freedom of travel.

Control of the U.S. satellite recon program is handed to the CIA.

1959 On February 28, Discoverer I is launched, and East Germany denounces the U.S. for espionage. On April 13, Discoverer 2 is launched but recovered by the Soviet Union. In September, Luna 2 is lifted by an SS–6. In October, Luna 3 circles the moon and returns with photos of its far side.

1960 A U–2 piloted by Francis Gary Powers is shot down over the Soviet Union. NASA launches the first space-based observation platform, the TIROS–1, a meteorological satellite. The National Reconnaissance Office is formed to manage space recon.

1961 The National Photographic Interpretation Center is established. On January 31, SAMOS–2 is successfully placed in orbit.

1962 On February 27, the last publicly acknowledged Discoverer is launched. On March 23, a directive from the Defense Department classifies all military space activity. Henceforth, all photographic intelligence satellites are designated as KEYHOLE spacecraft; SAMOS satellites are retroactively dubbed KH–1s, and Discoverers, KH–2s.

In October, the Cuban missile crisis is precipitated by American U–2E spy photos.

1963 On May 18, a new camera system (KH–4A) for CORONA is launched. On July 12, the GAMBIT program (KH–7), destined to provide close-look photos, is initiated. President Johnson announces air force plan to develop a Manned Orbiting Laboratory (MOL).

1964 Manned space programs collect photos from near-equator orbits. The first meteorological polar orbiting satellites are deployed; they either store images until they move into the range of a ground station or relay images directly in real time.

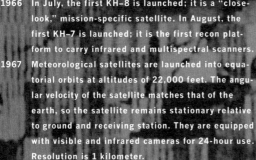

1966   In July, the first KH–8 is launched; it is a "close-look," mission-specific satellite. In August, the first KH–7 is launched; it is the first recon platform to carry infrared and multispectral scanners.

1967   Meteorological satellites are launched into equatorial orbits at altitudes of 22,000 feet. The angular velocity of the satellite matches that of the earth, so the satellite remains stationary relative to ground and receiving station. They are equipped with visible and infrared cameras for 24-hour use. Resolution is 1 kilometer.

1969   Strategic Arms Limitations Talks (SALT).

1971   In June, the KH–9 is launched.

1972   The Anti-Ballistic Missile Treaty. NASA launches the first Earth Resources Technology Satellite (Landsat I); its imagery, of coarser resolution than that of Pentagon recon satellites, is accessible to the public.

1975   Landsat II is put into orbit.

1976   On December 19, the first KH–11 is launched. It no longer uses film to produce imagery but an electro-optical system that allows data to be relayed back to a ground station almost instantaneously.

1978   William Kamplies, a former CIA employee, sells KH–11 secrets to the Soviet.

1979   SALT II

1980   After the failed mission to rescue American hostages in Iran, KH–11 photos are left behind at Desert One.

1982   Landsat IV is put into orbit.

1983   In March, President Reagan announces "Star Wars" or Strategic Defense Initiative (SDI). Analysts at NPIC, using recon imagery provided by KEYHOLE satellites, discover that the Soviet Union is building a phased-array radar at Krasnoyarsk. The radar, used to detect ballistic missiles, is said to violate the ABM treaty.

1984   The Landsat Commercialization Act transfers control of the Landsat program to the Earth Observation Satellite Company (EOSAT), a private corporation subsidized by the U.S. government. Landsat V is put into orbit. Challenger Space Shuttle Mission 41-C practices refueling in preparation for KH–12. First retrieval of broken satellites.

1986   In January, the Challenger shuttle explodes. In February, France launches SPOT (Système Probatoire d'Observation de la Terre), a commercial satellite offering black and white imagery with a 10-meter resolution. In April, the United States uses KH–11 imagery to plan its air attack on Libya and to assess damage afterward.

1987   Congressman George Brown resigns in protest of the almost exclusive use of satellite technology for recon purposes and the ban on speaking of it.

1988   In September, space shuttle launches resume with the successful voyage of the Discovery. In December, the Atlantis shuttle deploys a radar spy satellite dubbed "LaCrosse."

1989   On February 11, the first component of the Global Positioning System (GPS) is launched. The GPS, a radio satellite network, will enable troops, aircraft, and ships to pinpoint their position within 10 feet anywhere on earth.

1990   On February 14, a Delta rocket launches two laser test satellites for SDI. On February 28, the shuttle Atlantis launches a classified Pentagon spy satellite that breaks up and reenters the atmosphere. On April 24, the shuttle Discovery launches the Hubble Space Telescope (HST). On May 17, a team of U.S. scientists reports that a small sensor can distinguish between nuclear and nonnuclear cruise missiles by detecting the output of gamma rays from the warhead. On May 29, a U.S. recon satellite gathers the first photographic evidence of the deployment of ballistic missiles in North Korea. On November 12, a satellite is put into orbit to enable continuous observation of the Persian Gulf.

1991   SPOT sells imagery for use in Desert Storm.

Biological Ramparts

Ronald Jones

Decontamination methods can reduce the number of viable organisms almost to zero, but since they are based on the logarithmic order of death, it is both mathematically, and in practice, impossible to reach zero.

— *Conference on Potential Hazards of Back Contamination from the Planets*

After entering the *Eagle*, *Apollo 11*'s lunar module, following their first "extra-vehicular activity" around Tranquility Base on July 22, 1969, Neil Armstrong and Buzz Aldrin worked through the checklist of the measured choreography that would resettle them in their lunar spacecraft. But when they removed their space helmets the reassuring order of the procedures was shattered: a pungent odor struck their nostrils. Something distinctly alien hung in the air, an anomaly had engulfed the tiny cockpit. Their astonishment and shock dissolved once it dawned on them that the stench was the Moon itself.

Think about it: At that moment, some 112 hours into the *Apollo 11* mission, it would have been impossible to ignore that they were the first humans to smell literally another world and to roll its powdery soil between their fingers.

This unparalleled moment in history immediately withered into a disruptive annoyance. Like powdered graphite, the odious lunar dust clung to everything in the cockpit. A speck floated into Armstrong's eye and momentarily blinded him; he flushed it out as he would have a grain of sand. They stripped and then soaked towels in hot water, but even a sponge bath did little to alleviate the inescapable dust pervading the air they breathed. Armstrong and Aldrin, focusing their attention, resisted thinking of the contaminated air:

ARMSTRONG: We cleaned up the cockpit and got things pretty well in shape. This took us a while and we planned to sleep with our helmets and gloves on for a couple of reasons. One is that it's a lot quieter with your helmet and gloves on, and then we wouldn't have any mental concern about the ECS [Environment Control System] and so on having two loops working for us there.

ALDRIN: We wouldn't be breathing all that dust.

Inhaling the gray dust was their first opportunity to meditate on the real possibility that lunar pathogens were permeating their organs, weaving through the tracery of their nervous systems. No one could guarantee that life did not exist on the Moon, that microorganisms weren't living on or just beneath the lunar surface. Five years before Armstrong set foot on the Moon, the National Academy of Sciences had concluded that "negative data will not prove that extraterrestrial life does not exist; they will merely mean that it has not been found." These were not sci-fi daydreamers but highly placed officials in the space agency who had considered the possibility that destructive extraterrestrial biological agents could be introduced into Earth's biosphere by returning astronauts. Armstrong and Aldrin had been specifically warned about breathing the dust by the Bioscience Panel of the NASA Apollo Science Team: "Lunar organisms," they reported, "even if not inherently pathogenic, could, acting in conjunction with a terrestrial organism in the nose and throat of an astronaut, produce disease." Like condemned men, Armstrong and Aldrin were left alone that night to contemplate how much time would pass if indeed the toxins took effect.

Moon Life

Figure 12-3 from NASA's *Apollo 11 Mission Report* records Armstrong's heart rate for the two hours and fourteen minutes during which he first walked the moon and returned to the *Eagle*'s cockpit. Unfortunately, we do not know if his heart rate jumped when the Moon's odious smell surprised him as his helmet came off (no official record of this moment survives). The Apollo missions produced so many physiological effects that it was impossible to anticipate them all or to monitor very many of them. Even school-age kids knew that space travel's

most exaggerated and spectacular effects on the body happened during the G-forces at liftoff and during reentry; but between them zero-G intervened, creating a subtext of less interesting, not-so-legendary effects — muscle atrophy, a loss of bone density and a space sickness that one quarter of the time culminated in gravity-free vomiting.

Apollo 11's epic technology not only imposed unparalleled stress on the astronauts, getting them to the Moon and back to Earth, but it also *delivered* their bodies into *being* on the Moon. In the years before the Apollo astronauts left Earth, the Lunar Topographical Simulation Area was constructed in Houston at the Manned Space-craft Center. It was a physical rehabilitation center where astronauts struggled to overcome the handicaps of being Earthbound and reconditioned their bodies for an extraterrestrial modus vitae. Suspended beneath a contraption that resembled oversized space-age training wheels, 80 percent of an astronaut's Earth weight was lifted from his back so that he could learn to walk on the Moon. This and other techniques reframed the body on Earth so the astronauts could learn to live "normal" Moon lives.

For all the rehearsals, actual life on the Moon was unlike mock-ups, simulators and dry runs. Unsteady as the town drunk, the astronauts would stumble and twist, rotating really, then fall in a freakish slow motion, only to bounce back like an actor in a film running in reverse. It made for spectacular TV. They looked like toddlers on a barren gray playground, righting themselves after each tumble, filthier than before but always OK.

Watching them prancing across the screen like video ghosts, we could envy their boyish

INTRAVEHICULAR
PRESSURE GLOVE

zone

spirit, and long for the freedom of this idyllic dusty playground. It was the purest form of entertainment — never would it have occurred to us that one of them might not rebound, that after a pratfall, he would just lie there, like Lee Harvey Oswald, Officer Tippett, Martin Luther King or RFK, so quiet and still. Before NASA could have interrupted the lunar telecast with a ghastly black, we would have seen the dust kicked up by the accident gently settle atop the lunar suit. Dr. Charles Berry, the Apollo Program's Flight Surgeon speculated on the outcome after such an incident: "If the victim were unconscious and totally unable to help himself, it would be very difficult — perhaps impossible — for the other astronaut to get the crewman back to the spacecraft." Even before the 1967 Apollo spacecraft fire that killed Grissom, White and Chaffee, *Soyuz 11* (the 1971 Soviet space disaster) or the space shuttle *Challenger* debacle, we always sensed the heroic peril of each astronaut and cosmonaut. The hot allure of courageous adventure always cools when exposed to the clouds of hazard. One thing about entertainment is that danger is always vicarious — but *Apollo 11* wasn't just entertainment.

1,191,600,000

And yet, there was a moment a quarter century ago when each of us shared fully in the astronaut's gamble, when a kind of freakish pathological adventure was as much ours as theirs. Flash back to the view from Michael Collins's window as the *Eagle* fell slowly from view, beginning its gyrating lunar orbit that would gradually decay into a silent crash on the lunar surface. The mission accomplished, Armstrong, Aldrin and

Collins began preparations for the ride that would sling them out of lunar orbit and set them on their sixty-hour glide path back to Earth. The twenty-two kilograms of rocks and cores of the regolith, in sealed evacuated containers, were stowed at their feet.

As expected, the Command Module (CM) ended up face down in the Pacific Ocean. Collins, straining against Earth's gravity, the rocking waves and the harnesses that suspended him in his seat, reached to flip the switch that would deploy three large ocher-and-white balloons to right the craft. The CM lurched over, sending the astronauts onto their backs, and bobbed gracefully. The recovery began: four members of a U.S. Navy underwater demolition team leaped from a helicopter, though only one approached the spacecraft. He positioned his orange raft *upwind* of the CM and donned a biological isolation garment (BIG), the kind of suit we now associate with toxic chemical spills and nuclear disasters. With measured precision, he opened the CM's hatch, threw in three BIGs, then closed it tight, all in a single gesture. Those few seconds, when the dusty interior of the cockpit was open to the warm Pacific air, were as stirring as when Armstrong and Aldrin first smelled the Moon, breathed its dust into their lungs, tasted its grit in their mouths and felt its chalky texture on their skin. When the CM's hatch cracked open, the risk of global contamination instantly multiplied by 1,191,600,000 — factored by the sum of the world's population.

Microbe Reservations in the Dakotas

In 1964, five years before the launch of *Apollo 11*, the War on Poverty was declared, Miss Arizona Donna Axum became Miss America, the Warren

Previous pages:

Pressurized moon glove;

Moonboot, Apollo mission.

Photos by Albert Watson

Commission's report was released, the Tonkin Resolution was passed by Congress, Julie Andrews won an Oscar for her performance as Mary Poppins and thirty-one men gathered at the National Academy of Sciences to discuss the possibility that Earth would be fatally contaminated by extraterrestrial microbes brought back from other planets. Their meeting became known as the *Conference on Potential Hazards of Back Contamination from the Planets*. The succinct and unnerving centerpiece of their conclusion was "the logarithmic order of death." In simple language, they determined that the technology of the Apollo mission (which could trigger the fatal logarithmic order by returning extraterrestrial fragments to Earth) was not matched by a reciprocal technology that could prevent destructive lunar microbes from finding their way into Earth's biosphere, or even halt an epidemic should one begin.

Without the slightest idea of *what* to expect, NASA blindly planned for the moment in the Pacific when Apollo would threaten to alter life forever, when Earth might fall victim to extraterrestrial pestilence. For all the millions of research dollars spent at the Manned Spacecraft Center, not one of the experts could tell the others what to expect. The best they could do was respond as they would to an earthly epidemic: strict quarantine. Quarantine, like that imposed on patients with highly infectious respiratory diseases, was to be our defense against Moon plague. But why assume that the conventional quarantine, which presupposes known diseases, symptoms and incubation periods, would be the appropriate response to an unknown lunar organism? Dr. David E. Price, the Deputy Surgeon of the U.S. Public Health Service was ambivalent: "We must make an arbitrary approach to quarantine," he said, "but must also realize that quarantine is a crude concept and a crude approach to problems of this sort. I would not feel safe in placing a large part of my faith in it as a security method." Set against the logarithmic order of death, the quarantine defense went pale, then collapsed, while the unflinching desire to hold a Moon rock on Earth intensified.

Though it was never originally conceived of as a facility for quarantine, the Lunar Receiving Laboratory was redesigned as the barrier between Earth and the returning astronauts, their spacecraft and the lunar samples. At the moment the decision was made that quarantine would serve as the biological rampart against lunar pathogens, uncertainty spiraled out of control and questions spun away three and four deep — no one knew what questions to ask. Bert King, the former administrator of the Lunar Receiving Laboratory, sketched the heart of the problem:

> [I]n order to ascertain the length of the quarantine period, we had to estimate the incubation period of the mythical microbes. Similarly, in case of a break in the biological barrier, we needed to know how to sterilize the potentially contaminated area. Should we saturate the area with sodium hypochlorite, fuming nitric acid, or Scotch whiskey?

Introducing the astronauts into quarantine was a ballet between men and chemicals. The crew emerged from the CM, dressed in their isolation suits, and crawled into the waiting orange raft. The hatch was closed behind them, ending the second unscreened exposure to Moon matter. The navy diver sprayed the area around the hatch with Betadine, an iodine solution, before wiping himself, the astronauts and the raft with

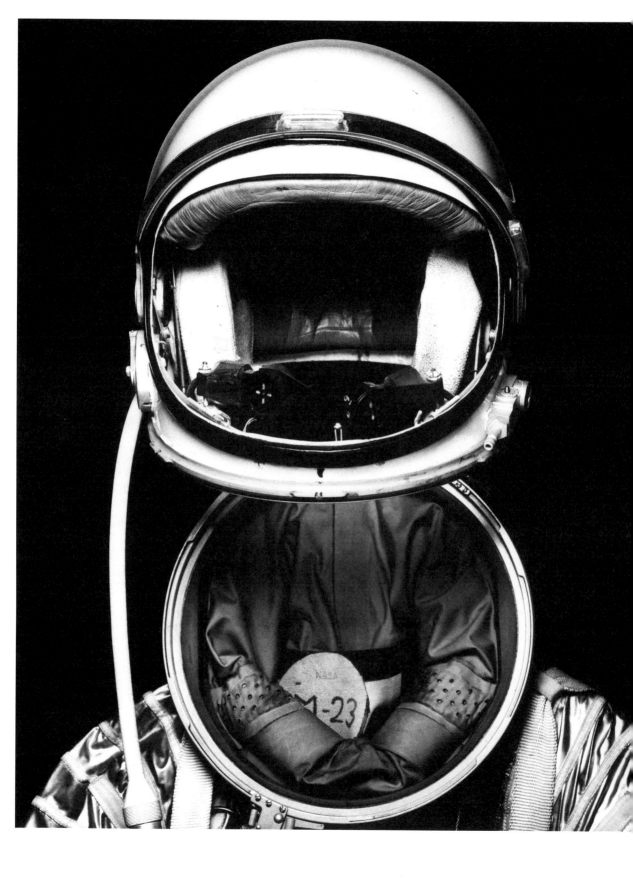

sodium hypochlorite. Once the astronauts were lifted into the helicopter for the twelve-mile flight to the USS *Hornet*, the diver bathed the CM and the raft with Betadine, emptied the rest of the chemical onto the floor of the raft, stepped out of his BIG and — after a thirty-minute contact time with the "disinfectant" — the raft and remaining equipment were sunk. Onboard the *Hornet*, the path on which the astronauts walked toward the Mobile Quarantine Facility (a converted Air Stream trailer) was "decontaminated" with formaldehyde and a glutaraldehyde solution.

Think back to the sinking raft: speckled with lunar dust, drenched in chemicals, responding to the ocean's shifting currents, ever so slowly it made its way to the cold depths of the Pacific. With its swaying movement as a murky backdrop, let the history of pandemics gently scroll like movie credits: *Small pox decimated the Native Americans after it was introduced by Europeans. Hundreds of thousands died from malaria in Brazil after the* Anopheles gambiae *mosquito was introduced there from Africa. The 1918 influenza epidemic. AIDS.* Let the underwater dance of the raft swirl like a free-form rhapsody, so that the rationalizations of the scientists and technicians who, five years before had pondered the logarithmic order of death, can play its hard counterpoint:

> Even non-pathogenic organisms might constitute a serious hazard. An organism, innocuous when in the hostile environment of a planet might, when transported to earth, overgrow terrestrial life forms or alter the physical or chemical characteristics of the biosphere. For example, the exotic soil organisms with unfamiliar metabolic capabilities conceivably could sequester a nutrient, such as fixed nitrogen, in a stable form which could not be attacked or utilized by terrestrial organisms. In time, the terrestrial flora would experience nitrogen starvation.

> Despite the advanced state of preventative technology, present day control of epidemics usually depends heavily on the availability of some specific, effective weapon, such as a vaccine. Lacking the proper techniques, which usually are the result of many years of intensive research, epidemics generally run their course, ending only when natural forces intervene. It is most unlikely that effective weapons would be immediately available to control an extraterrestrial.

> Policies of defense against back contamination must be based on the proposition that if infection of the earth by extraterrestrial organisms is possible, it will occur. Decontamination methods can reduce the number of viable organisms almost to zero, but since they are based on the logarithmic order of death, it is both mathematically, and in practice, impossible to reach zero. Therefore, the objective of defensive measures cannot be to prevent for all time the introduction to the earth of extraterrestrial organisms but rather to protect the earth from *immediate* infection. Over the longer term, as the nature of the exotic organisms becomes familiar, devices such as vaccines or some means to destroy the microbes can be developed. Ultimate protection against possible savages of exotic life may be in some sense their domestication.

The final sentence is stunning. Knowing that any attempt to prevent global infection would require canceling the Moon landing, NASA scientists were left to consider domesticating the savages of exotic interplanetary life. Flying the colors of a bizarre and anachronistic colonialism, they planned to revive the tactics once familiar to the Spanish explorers and the U.S. Cavalry in combating the "savages of exotic" Native American life.

Previous pages:

Helmet of the *Apollo 15* mission, 1976;

Neil Armstrong's space suit. First walk on the Moon, 1969.

Photos by Albert Watson

Futuromantic Desire/Futuromaniac Risk

In 1978, I touched a Moon rock, tacitly confirming for myself the general feeling at NASA in 1964 regarding lunar pathogens. Few in the Apollo Program ever believed a biological threat existed. The prevailing sentiment was that if one wanted to create a sterile environment one would, in fact, make it as much like the Moon as possible. Dr. Harold Urey, a Nobel laureate in chemistry, offered to eat a piece of a lunar rock if it would help to dispense with the quarantine. The day the *Apollo 11* crew reached the Lunar Receiving Laboratory to begin their quarantine, the director of the laboratory said: "The chance of bringing anything harmful back from the Moon is probably one in a hundred billion." In the minds of many at NASA, the quarantine, from the $20.00 worth of Betadine to the $15.8 million Lunar Receiving Lab, was largely an exercise in public relations. The Betadine *might as well* have been whiskey.

The scientific community either realized that no baffle of biological screens would make a difference if pathogens were present in the returning Moon rocks, or simply didn't believe in lunar organisms, pathogenic or otherwise. By the time *Apollo 11* was launched, the purpose of the quarantine had been neatly but ironically reversed: if it couldn't shelter Earth from extraterrestrial microbes, it would instead protect returning astronauts from contracting a terrestrial infection, and thereby avoid inciting a 1960s version of Orson Welles's *War of the Worlds* mass hysteria. One NASA official said: "We don't want someone coming down with Asian flu two weeks after he returns and starting a moon plague panic."

An intricate network of ideas weaves the spectacle of Apollo into the history of the human body. Whispering within the nave of this complex architecture are the voices of an elaborate rapprochement between futuromantic desire and futuromaniac risk. Twenty years ago, in the minds of a handful of NASA officials, a compromise was reached between the irresistible desire to go to the Moon and the risk that Earth's biosphere would be transformed into a fouled chamber, an environment with a finite quantity of uncontaminated air.

This human *being* on the Moon was astonishing, but somehow familiar — a moment when desire and mortal danger coincide irreversibly. When Kennedy committed the United States to beating the Soviets in the race to the Moon — in 1961, at the height of the Cold War — the image of a Moon rock cradled in American hands was too powerful to resist. But Neil Armstrong did not fulfill this imperative until that July day in 1969, two weeks after Nixon ordered troop withdrawals from Vietnam and three days before the possibility of defeat was codified as the politically prophylactic Nixon Doctrine. America's footing slipped in Saigon even as it was regained at Tranquility Base, and Americans were left not with a political cure but a pure spectacle: *an American rolling lunar dust between his fingers, gazing past his rigid flag toward the blue planet whose Cold War demarcations had given way to effluvial atmospheric swirls*. Whatever was left of Kennedy's visionary politics when the *Eagle* landed was submerged beneath a vicious nostalgia for his era, the damp entanglements of Vietnam and the hot urban brutality of race riots in Harlem, Watts, Detroit. And the simple act of touching the alien Moon, which held forth the promise of radical change in the course of the history of the body's primal senses, hinted as well that this very history might end unceremoniously.

Epidemics of the Will

Eve Kosofsky Sedgwick

Once upon a time, the story goes, back in the old country, some people sometimes took opium.[1] For many of these people, opium use functioned as a form of control: it brought into realistic conformity with the material exactions of their lives their levels of concentration, their temporality or their alertness to stimuli such as pain. For some it may have been a source of pleasure — if a vice, then a commonplace one. For all of these people, it was a behavior among other behaviors.

Then, according to the Foucauldian narrative offered by Virginia Berridge and Griffith Edwards in their important book, *Opium and the People*,[2] something changed. Under the taxonomic pressure of the newly ramified and pervasive medical-juridical authority of the late nineteenth century, and in the context of changing class and imperial relations, what had been a question of acts crystallized into a question of identities. To paraphrase, in relation to *the addict,* Michel Foucault's famous account of the invention of *the homosexual:* as defined by early nineteenth-century norms, opium-eating

> was a category of…acts; their perpetrator was nothing more than the juridical subject of them. The nineteenth-century [addict] became a personage, a past, a case history, and a childhood…. [His addiction] was everywhere present in him: at the root of all his actions because it was their insidious and indefinitely active principle; written immodestly on his face and body because it was a secret that always gave itself away…. The [opium-eater] had been a temporary aberration; the [addict] was a species.[3]

In the taxonomic reframing of a drug-user as an addict, what changes are the most basic terms about her. From a situation of relative homeostatic stability and control, she is propelled into a narrative of inexorable decline and fatality, from which she cannot dis-implicate herself except by leaping into that other, even more pathos-ridden narrative called "kicking the habit." From being the *subject* of her own perceptual manipulations or indeed experimentations, she is installed as the proper *object* of compulsory institutional disciplines, legal and medical, which, without actually being able to do anything to "help" her, nonetheless presume to know her better than she can know herself — and indeed, offer everyone in her culture who is *not* herself the opportunity of enjoying the same flattering presumption.

The assignment of a newly pathologized addict identity to users of opium-derived substances was not, however, the end of the story. To the gradual extension of addiction-attribution to a wider variety of "drugs" over the first two thirds of the twentieth century there has been added the startling coda of several recent developments: in particular, the development that now quite explicitly brings not only every form of substance ingestion, but more simply every form of human behavior, into the orbit of potential addiction-attribution. Think of the telling slippage that begins by assimilating food ingestion perceived as excessive with alcoholism — in the founding of, say, Overeaters Anonymous as an explicit analogue to Alcoholics Anonymous. From the pathologizing of food consumption to the pathologizing of food refusal (anorexia), or even of intermittent and highly controlled food consumption (bulimia), is a short step, but a consequential one. For the demonization of "the foreign substance" that gave an ostensible coherence to the new concept "substance abuse" is deconstructed almost as soon as articulated: if addiction can include ingestion *or* refusal *or* controlled intermittent ingestion of a given substance, and if the concept of "substance" has become too elastic to draw a boundary between the exoticism of the "foreign substance" and the domesticity of, say, "food," then the locus of addictiveness cannot be the substance itself and can scarcely even be the body itself, but must be some overarching abstraction that governs the narrative relations between them.

That abstract space where substances and behaviors become "addictive" or "not addictive" — shall we call it the healthy free will? The ability, let us say, *to (freely) choose health?* We could, after all, argue that what still unites the overeater, the anorexic and the bulimic as substance abusers is, if not anything poisonous about the substance, still the surplus of mystical properties with which the addict/abuser projectively endows it: consolation, repose, beauty or energy that can "really" only be internal to the addicts themselves are delusively attributed to the magical supplement which can then — whether consumed or refused — operate only corrosively on the self here self-construed as lack. In that case, *healthy free will* would belong to the person who had in mind the project of unfolding these attributes (consolation, repose, beauty, energy) out of a self, a body, already understood as containing them in potentia. In this view, which indeed is by now a staple of medicalized discourse both lay and clinical, not the dieter but the exerciser would be the person who embodied the exact opposite of addiction.

But then what are we to make of the next pathologized personage to materialize out of the taxonomic frenzy of the early 1980s: the exercise addict? In the absence of any projective hypostatization of a "foreign" substance, the object of addiction here seems to be the body itself. More accurately the object of addiction is the exercise of those very qualities whose *lack* is supposed to define addiction as such: bodily autonomy, self-control, will power. The object of addiction has become, precisely, enjoyment of "the ability to choose freely, and freely to choose health."

It seemed logically clear from the moment of this development that if exercise was addictive, nothing couldn't be; the exercise addict was really the limit case for evacuating the concept of addiction, once and for all, of any necessary specificity of substance, bodily effect or psychological motivation. (The brain-chemical markers invoked by scientists to "explain" addiction, of course, never had more than a tautologically explanatory or diagnostic force.) And this isn't only a theoretical aperçu from outside the newly efflorescent community of people interested in defining addiction. To the contrary: What is startling is the rapidity with which it has now become a commonplace that, precisely, any substance, any behavior, even any affect may be pathologized as addictive. Addiction, under this definition, resides only in the *structure* of a will that is always somehow insufficiently free, a choice whose volition is insufficiently pure.

Yet, like exercise, the other activities newly pathologized under the searching rays of this new addiction-attribution are the very ones that late capitalism presents as the ultimate emblems of control, personal discretion, freedom itself: beyond the finding of a custom-made telos in work ("workaholism"), there is the telos of making ostentatiously discretionary consumer choices ("shopaholism"); of enjoying sexual variety ("sexual compulsiveness"); or even of being in sustained relationships ("codependency" or "relationship addiction"). As each assertion of will has made volition itself appear problematic in a new area, the assertion of will itself has come to appear addictive. Recently, there has even been a spate of journalism on the theme that the self-help groups and books that popularize this radical critique of addiction and promote themselves as the only escape may themselves be addictive. Typically, the headlines of these articles present the suggestion as if jokingly; but the substance of most of them, to their credit, takes seriously the self-help proposition that, understood logically, addiction-attribution is nowhere to be circumscribed.

The self-help analysis proceeds to this conclusion with an admirable clarity and rigor that, at best, enable very trenchant descriptive and analytic work to proceed against the grain of many contemporary ideologies. For example, while by no means is all of the codependency literature feminist, and while there are limits (individualism, ahistoricity) to the political leverage of even the most ambitious, the codependency paradigm nevertheless represents an incisive deconstructive tool rendered remarkably accessible to "commonsense" experiential narratives. As such it has, as numerous self-help authors have shown, a formidable feminist descriptive salience.

Bigger Than Life,
Nicholas Ray, 1956.

The analytic work that these addiction paradigms cannot do, however, is to question or interrupt their own implication in an apparently unidirectional historical process: the propaganda of free will. By "propaganda" I mean something grammatically specific: the imperative that the concept of free will be propagated. The demand for its propagation seems to require, however, not only that it spread and circulate but that it be continually displaced — and even that the concept of free will withdraw eternally across a network of contiguities to constitute, at the last, a horizon of absence whose pressure on what is present then approaches the absolute. If the epidemic of addiction-attribution constitutes, in some ways, a crisis in this propaganda, in other ways it represents its direct and inexorable continuation.

So long as an entity known as "free will" has been hypostatized and charged with ethical value — a situation whose consolidating moment in the Reformation already revealed the structure of its dramatic foundational fractures and their appropriability to the complex needs of capitalism — for just so long has an equally hypostatized "compulsion" had to be available as a counterstructure always internal to it, always requiring to be ejected from it. The scouring descriptive work of addiction-attribution is propelled by the same imperative: its exacerbated perceptual acuteness in detecting the compulsion behind everyday volition is driven, ever-more blindly, by its own compulsion to isolate some new, receding but absolutized space of *pure* voluntarity. The late writing of Nietzsche is an excellent example of this contradiction: all that there is to learn from, and to recognize in, Nietzsche's rendering of human psychology qua an exquisite phenomenology of addiction — *all* tied to the bizarrely moralized imperative for the invention of a Will whose value and potency seem to become more absolute as every grounding possibility for its coming into existence breathtakingly recedes and recedes.

It is striking how deftly we have taught ourselves and each other to manipulate these apparently unwieldy absolutes in the lived world of addiction and addiction-attribution. In twelve-step and similar programs, the heroics of sobriety (and I don't mean to diminish the sense of a heroism to whose value and difficulty I am strongly attuned) involves a skill, paradoxically, in the micromanagement of absolutes. Under the accumulated experiential pressure and wisdom of many people's lived addictions, the loci of absolute compulsion and of absolute volition are multiplied in twelve-step programs. Sites of submission to compulsion figured as absolute include the insistence on a pathologizing model ("alcoholism is an illness") that another kind of group might experience as disempowering or demeaning; the subscription to an antiexistential rhetoric of unchangeable identities ("there are no ex-alcoholics, only recovering alcoholics"); and the submissive recourse to a receding but structurally necessary "higher power." At the same time, sites of a volition figured as absolute are also procured and multiplied by fragmentation — in rituals of taking responsibility for past damages; in the decentralized and highly egalitarian, if very stylized, structure of group experience; and especially through a technique of temporal fragmentation, the highly existential "one day at a time" that severs every moment of choice (and of course they are infinite) from both the identity-history and the intention-futurity that might be thought to constrain it. Among these sites of subtle negotiation among reduplicated absolutes, many people seem able to create for themselves a workable way out of the deadly system of double binds where an assertion that one can act freely is always read in the damning light of the "open secret" that the behavior in question is utterly compelled — while one's assertion that one was, after all, compelled, shrivels in the equally stark light of the "open secret" that one might at any given moment have chosen differently.

If will and compulsion are, necessarily, mutually internal categories; if the nineteenth-century isolation of addiction "itself" must therefore be seen as part of the same historical process as the Nietzschean hypostatization of Will "itself"; if this pressure of overlapping classifications does nothing more than chisel a historically specific point of stress into the centuries-old fault line of free will; then we must ask, what are the specifying historical coordinates of the present crisis of addiction-attribution? The simplest answer, I think, to the question, *Why now?* — why the twentieth century, and most of all its final quarter, should turn out to be the site of this epidemic of addiction and addiction-attribution — must lie in the peculiarly resonant relations that seem to obtain between the problematics of addiction and those of the consumer phase of international capitalism. From the Opium Wars of the mid-nineteenth century up to the current details of U.S. relations with Turkey, Colombia, Mexico and Peru, the dramas of "foreign substances" and of the new imperialisms and the new nationalisms have been quite inextricable. The integrity of (new and contested) national borders, the reifications of national will and vitality, were readily organized around these narratives of introjection. From as far back as Bernard de Mandeville, moreover, the opium product, the highly condensed, portable, expensive, commerce-intensive substance, the cartel-vulnerable commodity crop for export par excellence (as opposed to the subsistence crop for home use), was seen as having a unique ability to pry the potentially unlimited trajectory to demand, in its users, conclusively and ever-increasingly

"M",
Fritz Lang, 1930.

apart from the relative homeostasis of need. With the advent of the age of advertising, then, the addictive substance was spectacularly available *to be brought back* home as a representation for emerging intuitions about commodity fetishism.

Furthermore, the paraphrase from Foucault's *History of Sexuality* with which I begin this paper suggests that, because the emergence of the addict identity and the homosexual identity have so closely coincided both structurally and temporally, their historical interimplications may have been deep indeed. In *The Picture of Dorian Gray*, as in *Dr. Jekyll and Mr. Hyde*, drug addiction is both a camouflage and an expression of the dynamics of male same-sex desire and its prohibition: both books begin by looking like stories of erotic tensions between men, and end up as cautionary tales of solitary substance-abusers. The two new taxonomies of the addict and the homosexual condensed many of the same issues for late nineteenth-century culture: the old anti-sodomitic opposition between something called "nature" and that which is *contra naturam* blended with a treacherous apparent seamlessness into a new opposition between substances that are *natural* (for example, "food") and those that are *artificial* (for example, "drugs"), and hence into the characteristic twentieth-century way of distinguishing desires themselves between the natural, called "needs," and the artificial, called "addictions." Perhaps the reifying classification of certain particular, palpable substances as unnatural in the (artificially stimulating) relation to "natural" desire must ultimately throw into question the naturalness of any desire. (Thus Wilde writes in *Dorian Gray*: "Anything becomes a pleasure if one does it too often.") And of course one of the many echoes resounding around the terrible accident of HIV and the terrible nonaccident of the overdetermined ravage of AIDS is the way that it seems "naturally" to ratify and associate — as unnatural, as unsuited for survival, as the appropriate objects of neglect, specularized suffering and premature death — the notionally self-evident "risk group" categories of the gay man and the addict.[4]

Even apart from AIDS, some of the different connections in which addiction-attribution today brings up the question of the "natural" are illustrated in the "Opinion" pages from a 1987 *USA Today* (see figure) focusing on the controversies around steroid use by athletes.[5] The very definition of addiction is up for grabs here: Ron Hale says steroids are not addictive (and hence should not be banned) because they "aren't uppers, they're not downers, they don't alter the mind, and it's not a habit that can't be broken"; William N. Taylor says they *are* and therefore *should*, because "self-users exhibit tolerance to the drugs and withdrawal phenomena so that personality changes and addiction are common." In the all-American voices cited in this debate, the Natural is invoked to ward off bogies that hover around us on several different axes: the cyborg axis that stretches between people and machines ("If athletes have to turn to steroids, they are trying to build up a machine and not a human being"); the narrative evolutionary axis that stretches between people and animals, only glancing at that intermediate space of inter-breeding, the "era of monstrous athletes"; the axis that extends from the autoerotic to the alloerotic (since "muscular bodies are usually the result of years of anabolic steroid-induced narcissism"); the puritanical axis between a moralized "health" and the deprecated "enhance-ment of a person's body"; the axis between satiable and "insatiable" drives, whether for sex or for substance ingestion; the axis between immanent "natural ability" and the extrinsic additive ("individuals should compete with their bodies' resources rather than relying on some unnatural chemical"); and of course the axis between the "free world," where steroid use in amateur com-petition is absolutely prohibited, and "Russia," where, the editorial speculates, it "might" be absolutely compulsory. Steroids, moreover, by inducing " 'roid rage" have the dangerous property of blurring the should-be-obvious distinction between heterosexuality and male violence against women. Worse, even though steroids ought to be easy to situate on the axis between male and female gender — they are, after all, "man-made versions of the male hormone testosterone" — they actually seem to have unpredictably destabilizing effects on gender attributes. If their gen-erally virilizing tendency leads to "women built like men and men built like the Carpathian Mountains," if they cause "growth of facial hair, baldness, and shrunken breasts" in women and "overly aggressive and violent behavior" in men, they also induce in women a "nymphomania" that can't be so securely categorized as a *masculinity* effect; and, most damagingly to the gender schema that always seems to underlie hormonal models, they cause men to "develop...female characteristics like breasts." The chilling editorial cartoon summarizes the worst news about the foreign substance of steroids: the bulked-up body of absolute volition, scared as it is scary, is haunted by a memento mori, the X-ray skeleton of its own absolute compulsion; between the two images, however, the supposedly self-evident place of the desirable, "natural" outlines of just-plain-boy has already corroded away beyond remembering or restoring.

It is not so hard, then, to come up with a proliferation of if not causal *explanations* for the present epidemic of addiction-attribution, then at least aspects of the present historical moment — aspects that seem to solicit the addiction model into politically fraught, discursively productive mutual relations of representation and misrepresentation. I'd like to end, though, by asking a much more difficult question than *Why now?* — namely, *How could it have been otherwise?* What shards of outdated cognitive resources may we still find scattered by the roadside of progress, resources by which it might be, or might once have been, possible to think volition and compulsion differently — to resist simply repropelling the propaganda of a receding "free will"? I have to say that I do not find the concept of the unconscious, whether individual or historical, to be of much help in approaching this particular question: both psychoanalytic and Marxist thought seem to have the modern heroics of volition/compulsion already inscribed too deeply at the source of their narrative and analytic energies. When I look, on the other hand, at the work — from which I've learned a lot — of Thomas Szasz, whose deconstructive analyses of concepts like addiction have been so vigorous that they might better be called debunking, I also see that his salutary leverage on the pathologizing mythologies of compulsion owes everything to a tropism toward the absolute of punishable free will that itself more than verges on the authoritarian.

I'll just suggest briefly that the best luck I've had so far in reconstructing an "otherwise" for addiction-attribution has been through a tradition that is not opposed to it or explanatory of it but rather one step to the side of it. This is the tradition of reflecting on *habit*, a version of repeated action that moves not toward metaphysical absolutes but toward interrelations of the action and the self acting with the bodily habitus, the appareling habit, the sheltering habitation, everything that marks the traces of that habit on a world that the metaphysical absolutes would have left a vacuum. Though perpetuated and fairly intensively moralized from at least Cicero up to at least William James, with an especially acute psychologizing currency around, for instance, the eighteenth-century and Romantic origins of the English novel, the worldly concept of habit has dropped out of theorized use with the supervention in this century of addiction and the other glamorizing paradigms oriented around absolutes of compulsion/volition. And indeed, I can understand the mistrust of modern versions of "habit," such as ego psychology, whose dependence on a metaphorics of *consolidation*, and whose consequent ethicization of the unitary self, seem to render it peculiarly vulnerable to moralistic hijacking. Yet the unmoralized usage of the language of habit in, for instance, Proust is as scouring as any version of contemporary addiction-attribution — without at all requiring the hypostatization of a ghostly, punitive free will on the receding horizon. Proust treats habit as, in the first instance, a perceptual matter, which means that his wealth of resources for denaturalizing the polarities "active" and "passive" in perception is at work in all his discussion of habit, the human faculty that can "change…the colour of the curtains, silence…the clock, [bring] an expression of pity to the cruel, slanting face of the glass."[6] Habituation is "that operation which we must always start afresh, longer, more difficult than the turning inside out of an eyelid, and which consists in the imposition of our own familiar soul on the terrifying soul of our surroundings."[7] A banal but precious opiate, habit makes us blind to — and thus enables to come into existence — our surroundings, ourselves as we appear to others and the imprint of others in ourselves.

Habit also, however, demarcates the space of perceptual and proprioceptive reversal and revelation — revelation at which introspection itself can never arrive. As on the narrator's receipt of Albertine's letter saying she has left him for good:

> Yes, a moment ago, before Françoise came into the room, I had believed that I no longer loved Albertine, I had believed that I was leaving nothing out of account, like a rigorous analyst; I had believed that I knew the state of my own heart…. I had been mistaken in thinking that I could see clearly my own heart. But this knowledge, which the shrewdest perceptions of the mind would not have given me, had now been brought to me, hard, glittering, strange, like a crystallized salt, by the abrupt reaction of pain. I was so much in the habit of having Albertine with me, and now I suddenly saw a new aspect of Habit. Hitherto I had regarded it chiefly as an annihilating force which suppresses the originality and even the awareness of one's perceptions; now I saw it as a dread deity, so riveted to one's being, its insignificant face so incrusted in one's heart, that if it detaches itself, if it turns away from one, this deity that one had barely distinguished inflicts on one sufferings more terrible than any other and is then as cruel as death itself.[8]

Habits in Proust, like lies and foolish sorrows, resemble "servants, obscure and detested, against whom one struggles, beneath whose dominion one more and more completely falls, dire and dreadful servants whom it is impossible to replace and who by subterranean paths lead us towards truth and death."[9] And yet it is also they, the habits " — even the meanest of them, such as our obscure attachments to the dimensions, to the atmosphere of a bedroom — that take fright and refuse, in acts of rebellion which we must recognize to be a secret, partial, tangible and true aspect of our resistance to death."[10]

It is extraordinarily difficult to imagine an analytically usable language of habit, in a conceptual landscape so rubbled and defeatured by the twin hurricanes named Just Do It and Just

Say No. I most feel the vertigo of this scene of denudation when I learn that Philip Morris has bought, or at least rented from the National Archives, sponsorship of the Bill of Rights to the U.S. Constitution — involving, in a series of ads to promote the abstraction Freedom, both the Freedoms already articulated in that document and others, it is more than hinted, that may yet be specified. A recent ad, for instance, features a handsome black-and-white photograph of a smiling but dignified Barbara Jordan whom it quotes as saying, "The Bill of Rights was not ordained by nature or God. It's very human, very fragile." The ad is short on specifics, however. The rest of the text: "The Bill of Rights had been a source of comfort for me. While I was born into poverty, I knew it didn't have to be a permanent condition. I was free to do whatever I wanted to do. And the liberating force throughout my life and career has been the Bill of Rights. It's where the United States of America comes to life. Without it, this country as we know it would cease to exist."

I won't even discuss the hideousness of the "irony" of this propaganda for Freedom coming from an industry whose fully owned and paid-up senator, Jesse Helms of North Carolina, murders constitutional freedoms as lavishly and recklessly as he allows the lives of gay men and addicts to be extinguished.

I assume that this advertising campaign represents more than an attempt to associate tobacco advertising, at present itself very embattled, more intimately with the First Amendment protections on which it battens whenever it is threatened with further regulation. Beyond the issue of Freedom to advertise, it alludes to past and future tobacco-company campaigns on the theme of smokers' rights, campaigns (including publication of a glossy new magazine just for smokers) that are attempting to mobilize and organize smokers as a potent lobbying and advocacy group on the model of the National Rifle Association. Now, in terms of the addiction/free will paradigm, the bright idea of crystallizing a smoker-advocacy community is obviously volatile indeed: while, on the one hand, the tobacco companies cherish the vision of a population united to claim the right to smoking as a high exercise of individual freedom (in solidarity with their good friends at the tobacco companies to whom not only the articulation but in fact the setting of these assertive "rights" agendas is meant unquestionably, even abjectly, to be surrendered); on the other hand, this Philip Morris wet dream must be shadowed by a nightmare in which smokers could unite to claim rights, not as embodiments of that ultimate freedom, the freedom to smoke, but rather *as addicts*, as people who define themselves as *not* having freedom with respect to smoking. It is, of course, only by claiming the latter identity, by a willingness to stigmatize themselves further by making common cause with the most disempowered of social groups in demands for, shall we say, reliable, unpunitive access to the addictive substance; for affordable or free, high-quality, nonjudgmental health care available to all who have been, still are or will be at risk of becoming addicts (that is, to everyone); and for freedom from economic exploitation by traffickers in the addictive substance — it is only by making something like this claim to, or acknowledgment of, the pathologized addict identity that smokers as a body could paradoxically empower themselves in legal, economic and ideological contestation against the tobacco companies, as well as in areas where their interests may coincide with the companies'. (The latter areas might include, for instance, limiting workplace prohibitions on smoking and resisting victim-blaming insurance surcharges against smokers.)

There is plenty of evidence that what tobacco companies most fear is official and legal recognition of the open secret that, behind a facade of volition, smoking "is really" addictive. If the operation of that open secret is, at present, disempowering to smokers, so at the same time is the dynamic of the countervailing open secret: that anyone who claims to be compelled to smoke is actually, with every cigarette she lights, making "a free choice" not to do otherwise. I see these ads as most effectually performing, at some level, the warning taunt of a blackmailer, aimed at smokers, at driving ever in and against them the ugly twisting point that in the present discursive constructions of consumer capitalism the powers of our "free will" are always already vitiated by the "truth" of compulsion, while the powers attaching to an acknowledged compulsion are always already vitiated by the "truth" of our free will. No wonder then that, as Proust suggests, acts of refusal and rebellion in this wasting landscape need to muster real rhetorical and political cunning to remain secret, partial, tangible, true.

NOTES

1. This paper was written for a conference on "Epidemics" held at MIT in October 1990; I am grateful to the organizers of that conference, especially David Halperin, for the instigation to try to pull together into one train of argument the somewhat fragmentary reflections on addiction and addiction-attribution that had lately been punctuating almost all of my writing. I have been indebted in my thinking on the subject to the great encouragement of Andrew Parker. I have profited even more from the exciting opportunity, over many years, of sharing with Joshua Wilner his meditations on it. His writing about substance ingestion and Romanticism

The steroid hormone cortisone is a naturally occurring hormone of the adrenal cortex. It was isolated from adrenal extracts in 1936 and introduced in synthetic form for treatment of rheumatoid arthritis in 1948. Corticosteroid drugs act as anti-inflammatory agents by suppressing immune-response through altered carbohydrate metabolism. The therapeutic dose, when used as an anti-inflammatory, is much larger than the amount normally present in the body, with the result that the functions of the hormone become exaggerated. Cortisone dependency is associated with suppression of normal adrenal gland function, diminished sensitivity to pain, feelings of intense well-being and euphoria and a disposition to psychosis.

includes "Autobiography and Addiction: The Case of De Quincey," *Genre* 14 (winter 1981), pp. 493–503, and "The Stewed Muse of Prose," *MLN* (Dec. 1989), pp. 1085–1098.

2. Virginia Berridge and Griffith Edwards, *Opium and the People: Opiate Use in Nineteenth-Century England* (2d ed., New Haven: Yale University Press, 1987).

3. *History of Sexuality*, vol. 1: *An Introduction*, trans. Robert Hurley (New York: Pantheon, 1978), pp. 42–43.

4. Issues mentioned in the preceding two paragraphs are contextualized more fully in my *Epistemology of the Closet* (Berkeley: University of California Press, 1990), ch. 3, and "Nationalisms and Sexualities: As Opposed to What?" in Andrew Parker, Mary Russo, Doris Sommer and Patricia Yaegger, eds., *Nationalisms and Sexualities* (New York: Routledge, forthcoming).

5. All quotations are from *USA Today*, Monday, Jan. 6, 1987, p. 10A.

6. Marcel Proust, *Remembrance of Things Past*, trans. C. K. Scott Moncrieff and Terence Kilmartin, 3 vols. (New York: Vintage, 1982), vol. 1, p. 9.

7. Ibid., vol. 2, p. 791.

8. Ibid., vol. 3, p. 426.

9. Ibid., vol. 3, p. 948.

10. Ibid., vol. 1, p. 722.

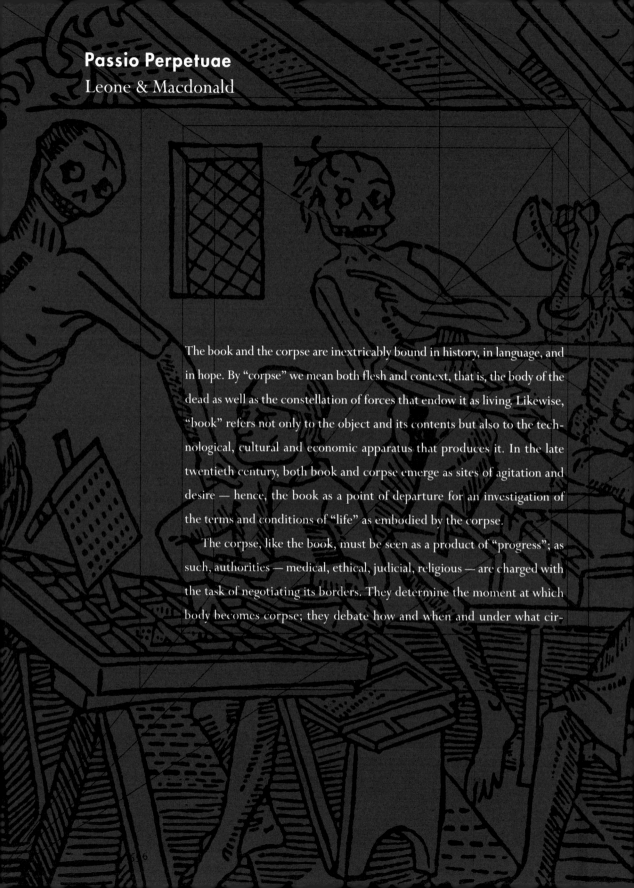

Passio Perpetuae
Leone & Macdonald

The book and the corpse are inextricably bound in history, in language, and in hope. By "corpse" we mean both flesh and context, that is, the body of the dead as well as the constellation of forces that endow it as living. Likewise, "book" refers not only to the object and its contents but also to the technological, cultural and economic apparatus that produces it. In the late twentieth century, both book and corpse emerge as sites of agitation and desire — hence, the book as a point of departure for an investigation of the terms and conditions of "life" as embodied by the corpse.

The corpse, like the book, must be seen as a product of "progress"; as such, authorities — medical, ethical, judicial, religious — are charged with the task of negotiating its borders. They determine the moment at which body becomes corpse; they debate how and when and under what circumstances we should employ or deny life-prolonging medical technologies; they make fine distinctions between the living and the dead. The authorities provide answers, albeit conflicting ones.

We locate the corpse on the site of the classical book page, rendering its contour in relation to the conventions of the grid. Derived from a diagram by Jan Tschichold, the geometry of the grid functions as a cartographic intervention, a fractured narrative mobilized by its own resistance to completion. Traditionally, the grid demarcates a live area, a region beyond which essential elements cannot be positioned. An invisible bleed line borders the region on all sides, marking the zone of our inquiry: the area necessarily present but never reproduced.

The body copy is set in Perpetua, a twentieth-century revival of a classic roman alphabet, designed by Eric Gill in 1928. Named for the medieval martyr who, in the sacred moments after her baptism, prayed for "endurance of the flesh," Perpetua, as type, embodies the urge to endure. Her prayer for eternal life has become our legacy, recontextualized by the forces of modernity.

Our classical page is black, a reverse book, a multiple surface stained by the faint and partial traces of authority. To render the corpse visible in the late twentieth century, then, is to dust for prints, to draw to the surface the indefinite, shifting lines that distinguish the living from the dead.

Sedit and the Two Brothers Hus

Sedit is Coyote; the brothers Hus are buzzards. Olelbis, about to create
men, sends the brothers to earth to build a ladder of stone from it to
heaven; half way are to be set a pool for drink and a place for rest; at the
summit shall be two springs, one for drinking and the other for bathing —
internal and external purification — for these are to be that very Fountain
of Youth whose rumour brought Ponce de Léon to Florida. When a man or
a woman grows old, says Olelbis, let him or her climb to Olelpanti, bathe
and drink, and youth will be restored. But as the brothers build, Coyote,
the tempter, comes, saying, "I am wise; let us reason"; and he pictures con-
temptuously the destiny which Olelbis would bestow: "Suppose an old
woman and an old man go up, go alone, one after the other, and come back
alone, young. They will be alone as before, and will grow old a second time,
and go up again and come back young, but they will be alone, just the same
as at first. They will never have any friends, any children; they will never have
any pleasure in the world; they will never have anything to do but to go up
this road old and come back young again." "Joy at birth and grief for the
dead is better," says Coyote, "for these mean love." The brothers Hus are
convinced, and destroy their work…. (Curtin, "Sedit and the Brothers
Hus" in Hartley Burr, *Mythology of All Races* [Boston: Marshall Jones, 1916],
vol. 10, p. 234)

Cultures that live by the values of self-realization and self-mastery are not especially good at dying, at submitting to those experiences where freedom ends and biological fate begins. Why should they be? Their strong side is Promethean ambition: the defiance and transcendence of fate, material, and social limit. (Michael Ignatieff, "Modern Dying," *The New Republic*, Dec. 2, 1988, p. 32)

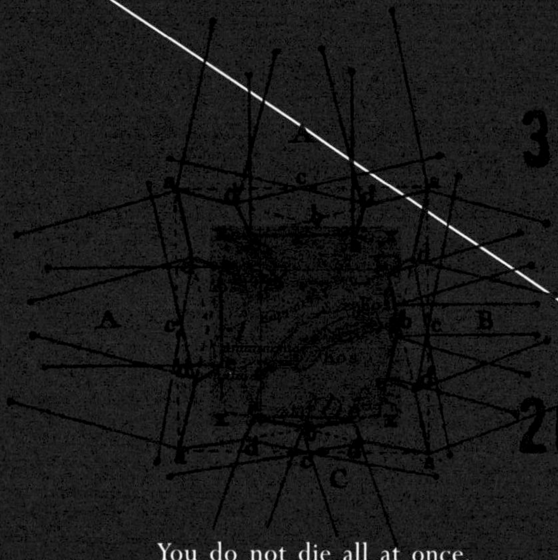

300

200

100

You do not die all at once. Some tissues live on for minutes, even hours, giving still their little cellular shrieks, molecular echoes of the agony of the whole corpus. Here and there a spray of nerves dances on. True, the heart stops; the blood no longer courses; the electricity of the brain sputters, then shuts down. Death is now *pronounceable*. But there are outposts where clusters of cells yet shine, besieged, little lights blinking in the advancing darkness. Doomed soldiers, they battle on. Until Death has secured the premises all to itself. (Richard Selzer, *Mortal Lessons* [New York: Touchstone, 1987], p. 136)

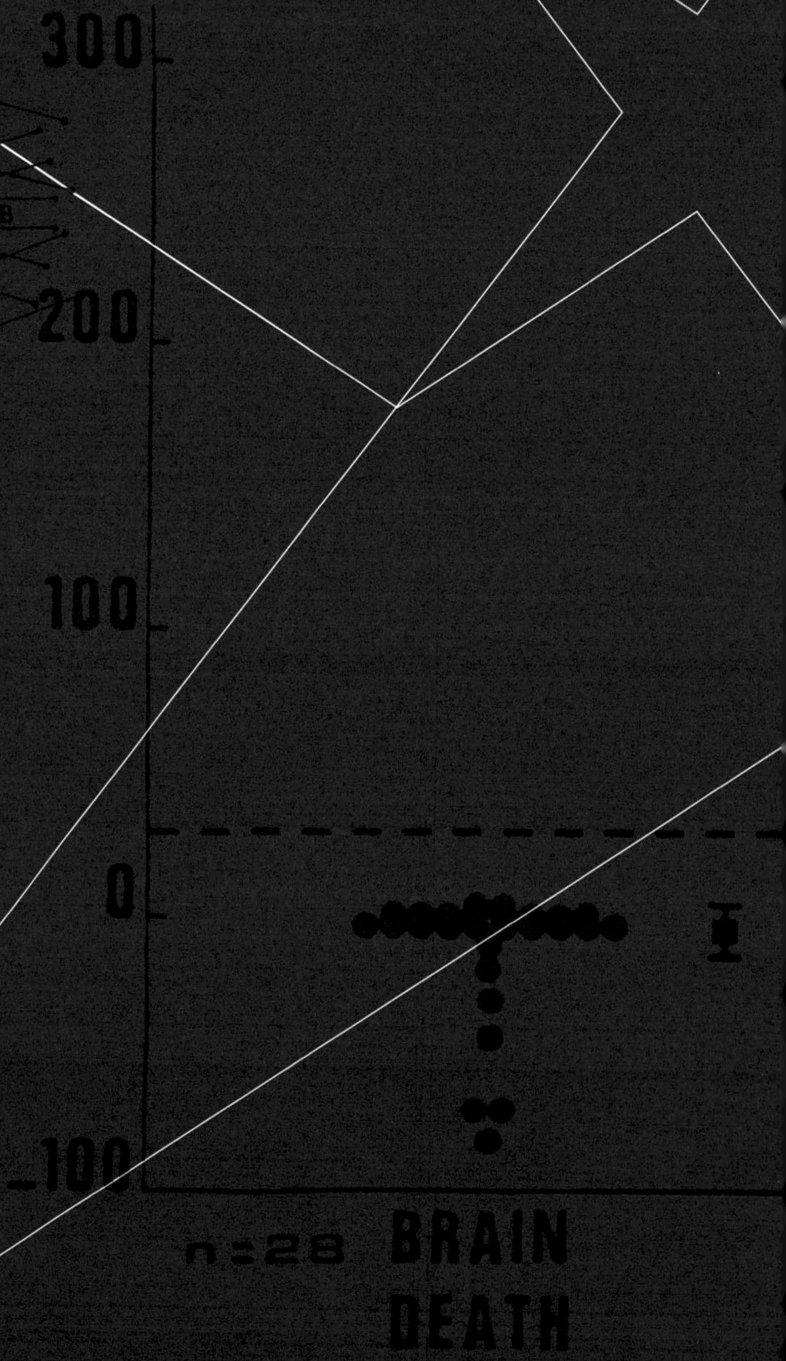

0

−100

n=28 BRAIN
DEATH

Reichsleiter Bouhler and Dr. Brandt, M.D., are charged with the responsibility of enlarging the authority of certain physicians, to be designated by name, in such a manner that persons, who according to human judgment, are incurable can, upon more careful diagnosis of their condition of sickness, be accorded a mercy death. (Letter signed by Hitler, dated Sept. 1, 1939. Mitscherlich and Mielke, *Doctors of Infamy* [New York: H. Schuman, 1949] pp. 93–94)

SEVERE   n=28
COMA

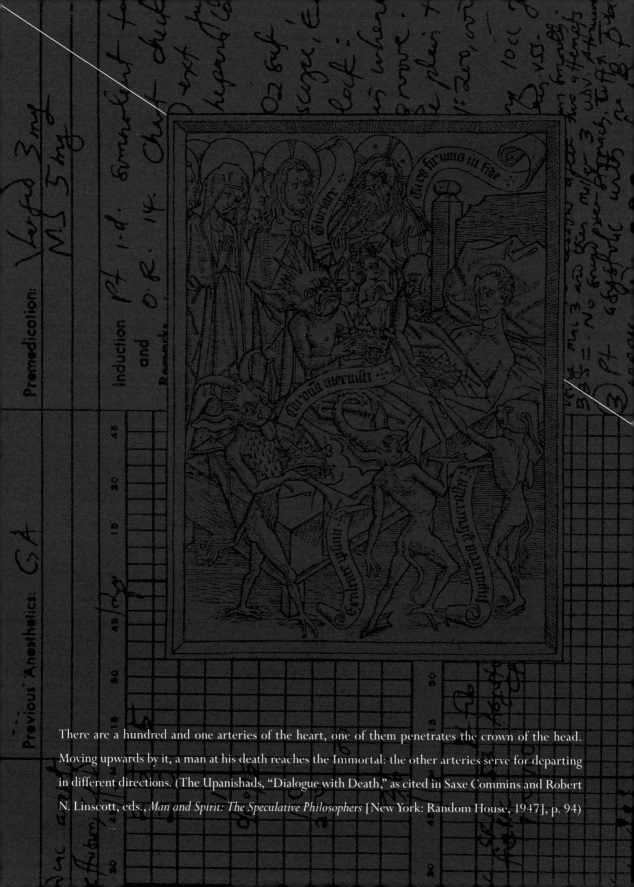

There are a hundred and one arteries of the heart, one of them penetrates the crown of the head. Moving upwards by it, a man at his death reaches the Immortal: the other arteries serve for departing in different directions. (The Upanishads, "Dialogue with Death," as cited in Saxe Commins and Robert N. Linscott, eds., *Man and Spirit: The Speculative Philosophers* [New York: Random House, 1947], p. 94)

From the point of view of death, disease has a land, a mappable territory, a subterranean, but secure place where its kinships and its consequences are formed;
local values define its forms. Paradoxically, the presence of the corpse enables us
to perceive it living — living with a life that is no longer that of either old sym-
pathies or the combinative laws of complications, but one that has its own roles
and its own laws. (Michel Foucault, *The Birth of a Clinic* [New York: Vintage
Books, 1975], p. 149)

Who is so fond of this body
that he would drag it about
with him through all eternity
if he could get on without it.
(Immanuel Kant)

The State Supreme Court, adopting much of the trial court findings, described Nancy Cruzan's medical condition as follows: "…(1) [H]er respiration and circulation are not artificially maintained and are within the normal limits of a thirty-year-old female; (2) she is oblivious to her environment except for reflexive responses to sound and perhaps painful stimuli; (3) she suffered anoxia of the brain resulting in a massive enlargement of the ventricles filling with cerebrospinal fluid in the area where the brain has degenerated and [her] cerebral cortical atrophy is irreversible, permanent, progressive and ongoing; (4) her highest cognitive brain function is exhibited by her grimacing perhaps in recognition of ordinarily painful stimuli, indicating the experience of pain and apparent response to sound; (5) she is a spastic quadriplegic; (6) her four extremities are contracted with irreversible muscular and tendon damage to all extremities; (7) she has no cognitive or reflexive ability to swallow sufficient [sic] to satisfy her needs. In sum, Nancy is diagnosed as in a persistent vegetative state. She is not dead. She is not terminally ill. Medical experts testified that she could live on for thirty years." (*Cruzan v. Harmon*, 760 S.W.2d 408, 411 Mo.1988, in "Cruzan v. Director, Missouri Dept. of Health," *Supreme Court Reporter* 110, p. 2845)

It was becoming clear that there wasn't simply death on one side and life on the other, but rather a frontier so ungraspable that one could lose oneself in the night, wearing a smile. (Edmond Jabes, *From the Desert to the Book* [New York: Station Hill Press, 1990], p. 7)

Image References

Pages 596–597

Earliest known representation of the printing press appeared in an edition of *The Dance of Death* produced in Lyons, France in 1500. (Douglas C. McMurtrie, *The Book: The Story of Printing and Bookmaking* [New York: Covici-Friede, 1937], p. 235)

Jan Tschichold's diagram of classical book page, in black. Fragments of grid appear in reverse throughout the dossier. (Rauri McLean, *Jan Tschichold: Typographer* [Boston: Godine, 1975], p. 117)

Pages 598–599

Cryonic suspension is a method to prevent physical deterioration after death, based on principles of hypothermia. Advocates believe scientists of the future will have the capability and inclination to revive, cure and rehabilitate the dead. The large storage unit holds one or two corpses; the small unit holds up to four heads. (Robert Kastenbaum and Beatrice Kastenbaum, eds., *Encyclopedia of Death* [Phoenix: Oryx Press, 1989], pp. 61–66)

Biopsy of hippocampus shown at two different planes of focus. Section reveals pyramidal neuron containing neurofibrillary tangle, a disorganized bunch of neurofilaments commonly seen in the brains of Alzheimer's patients. (Photo courtesy of Dr. Barbara McGuire)

Pages 600–601

Diagram of military field fortifications. (J. G. Heck, *The Complete Encyclopedia of Illustration* [New York: Park Lane, 1979], p. 355)

The Greek physician Hippocrates, born on the Island of Kos, is credited with formulating the Hippocratic oath, an ancient code of medical ethics. Although written in the fourth century B.C., the oath continues to inform contemporary principles of medical ethics. (*Philips' International Atlas* [Chicago: Rand McNally, 1941], 4th ed., pp. 65–66)

Results of a study to evaluate a technique for early, low-cost diagnosis of brain death. The dotted line represents the cutoff point for brain death diagnosis. (D. Payen, C. Lamer, A. Pilorget, T. Moreau, S. Beloucif, and E. Echter, "Pulsed Doppler Common Carotid Blood Flow as a Noninvasive Method for Brain Death Diagnosis: A Prospective Study," *Anesthesiology* 72.2 [Feb. 1990], p. 225)

"The two best methods of self-deliverance from a terminal illness — lacking the direct help of a doctor — are from the use of selected prescription drugs, aided by a plastic bag. There are two possible situations: (a) you have barbiturate drugs such as secobarbital (Seconal) and pentobarbital (Nembutal); or (b) you have non-barbiturate drugs such as diazepam (Valium) and propoxyphene (Darvon)." (Derek Humphrey, *Final Exit: The Practicalities of Self-Deliverance and Assisted Suicide for the Dying*, [Oregon: The Hemlock Society, 1991], p. 110–11)

Pages 602–603

Anesthetic record of patient during surgery.

Woodcut illustration representing the dying man's temptation to impatience, printed in the block book *Ars Moriendi* (Art of Dying) Netherlands, c. 1450. (*The Book: The Story of Printing and Book Making*, p. 118)

The White Rose was a resistance movement formed at the University of Munich in 1942 to protest Nazi atrocities. It was later adopted as the symbol for the International Anti-Euthanasia Task Force as a means to link Hitler's "mercy killing" with current efforts to legalize euthanasia. ("Perpetual Flowering Bedding Rose", *Autumn Planting* catalogue [Mentor, Ohio: Wayside Gardens, 1948], p. 84)

Pages 604–605

Tollund Man, one of the best naturally preserved mummies ever found, dates from the Iron Age. (P. V. Glob, *The Bog People: Iron-Age Preserved* [New York: Cornell, 1969], p.26)

Radiograph of Dobbhoff tube knotted in the stomach. Feeding tube is used for prolonged nasoenteric hyperalimentation. (G. Ghahremani and R. Gould, "Nasoenteric Tubes: Radiographic Detection of Complications," *Digestive Diseases and Sciences* 31.6 [June 1986], p. 579)

Page 606

Physician using cardiopulmonary resuscitation to revive heart attack victim; patient died. *New York Times*, May 30, 1982.

Radio Listener, c. 1929.
Alexander Rodchenko

Virtual Systems

Allucquère Roseanne Stone

Near the close of the mechanical age, the evolution of the space and character of human social interaction has thrice been radically altered. This transformation was produced by a succession of prosthetics: the development of prosthetic speech in the form of disembodied voices heard through acoustic transducers; by prosthetic writing as text on monitor screens; and by prosthetic proxemics in the form of interactive video. As a result, but in quite different ways for each, the locus and character of the social arenas of Western industrialized societies shifted. Overall, in character this has meant a change from individual or group interaction, which implied physical presence, to decentered and fragmented communication whose nature and quality took on rapidly shifting and fundamentally novel forms. In locus, it meant a shift from a physical space whose geographical coordinates resist traditional modes of representation.

The kind and quality of human interactions created by these shifts — interactions of a character quite unrecognizable from the standpoint of geographically located agoras — have been described in many different ways. Usually they are referred to as networks, whether local or globally distributed. Science fiction writers have for some time been interested in such spaces and their potential for redefining social interaction. In the science fiction world they have still more names — mirror worlds, the net, consensual loci, the matrix, cyberspace. In fictional form they have served as rallying points and working metaphors for widely various organizations, theoreticians and experimenters.

In "real" form, as interactive computer systems and the possibilities that such systems imply for novel sociality, they have acted as powerful attractors for a broad spectrum of interests that includes the military, big (and small) business, psychology and education, as well as computer, social and cognitive science.

Perhaps the best-described of these worlds of phantasmic social interaction is cyberspace, a term that has quickly passed from provocative literary fantasy to a hotly contested financial, cultural and ethical frontier. I find the vast amounts of energy (and hard cash) expended on computer systems designed around the metaphor of cyberspace to be particularly intriguing — because cyberspace itself does not yet even exist.

Cyberspace is a physically inhabitable, electronically generated alternate reality, entered by means of direct links to the brain — that is, it is inhabited by refigured human "persons" separated from their physical bodies, which are parked in "normal" space. The physical laws of "normal" space need not apply in cyberspace, although some experiential rules carry over from normal space — for example, the geometry of cyberspace is, in most depictions, Cartesian. The "original" body is the authenticating source for the refigured person in cyberspace: no "persons" exist whose presence is not warranted by a physical body back in "normal" space. But death in either normal space or cyberspace is real, in the sense that if the "person" in cyberspace dies, the body in normal space dies, and vice versa.

To some extent, though, cyberspace already exists as a metaphor for late twentieth-century communications technologies (databanks, financial systems, ATMs). Many of us already live at least part-time in cyberspace, but call it "computer conferencing," "phone sex," banking, or "virtual" this or that. Insofar as these activities involve communicating with other people through narrow-bandwidth media, though, it may be understood in terms of negotiating the tensions between individual subjects, virtual collectivities and the physical bodies in which they may or may not be grounded. Proto-cyberspace has been around for many years in various forms — visually as *dioramas* and *botanical gardens*, aurally as radio dramas, kinesthetically as carnival rides and textually, perhaps, as novels.

Cyberspace has achieved visibility in the context of late capitalism, in the historic moment of "biosociality" — Paul Rabinow's term for the collapse of the distinctions between biological observation, construction and control (as in the Human Genome Project) — or "technosociality," the state in which technology and nature are the same thing, as when one inhabits a network as a social environment. Cyberspace is a social environment: the networks are elsewheres where we can observe new collective structures risking themselves in novel conditions. These structures take the form of organized and moderated conferences, multiuser groups, anarchic chats, clandestine assignations. Some are trivial, but some are definitely not trivial and have real effects outside the nets. Some of the interactions are gendered, stereotypical, Cartesian, reifying old power differentials whose workings are familiar and whose effects are well understood; but some of the interactions are novel, strange, perhaps transformative.

This essay is about science fiction, in the sense of emerging technologies, shifting boundaries between the living and the nonliving, optional embodiment — in other words, the everyday world as cyborg habitat. It is not about cyberspace, but rather social systems arising in phantasmic spaces enabled by, and constituted through, communication technologies. To some extent, they exist in the cultural milieu suggested by recent cyberspace metaphors; but they also considerably predate the last decade.

I am not a neutral observer — I am interested in the nets for what they make visible about the "real" world,

things that might otherwise go unnoticed. I am interested because of their potential for emergent behavior, for new social forms that arise in a circumstance in which "body," "meeting," "place" and even "space" mean things quite different from our accustomed understanding. How tenacious are these new social forms in the face of adversity, and what can be learned from them about social problems outside the worlds of the nets? How do groups of friends evolve when their meeting room exists in a purely symbolic space? How does narrowing the bandwidth — that is, doing without customary modes of symbolic exchange such as gesture and tone of voice — affect sharing and trust, and how do inhabitants of virtual systems construct and maintain categories such as gender and race? How do people without bodies make love?

This trek into the mysterious depths of technology — which in the case of computer technology is ultimately the binary — in search of the natural is a familiar classical trope. Of course there is an ironic twist to this Conradian search: I am suggesting a venture not into the heart of "nature" in search of redemption, but rather into the heart of "technology" in search of nature — and not nature as object, place or originary situation, but in Donna Haraway's sense nature as Coyote, the Native American trickster — diversity, flexibility, irruption, danger, playfulness — put briefly, nature as actant, as process, a continual reinvention and encounter actively resisting representation.

By entering into technology we tacitly agree to view certain imaginary movements as literal. This action activates the extreme permeability of boundaries between a politically authorized social entity and a technical prosthetics that characterizes the technosocial. In the space we find there, at once technological and social, we become aware of new kinds of beings who inhabit the phantasmic spaces of technology. They are at home in an environment whose existence has not even been recognized by those not deeply immersed in an age of instantaneous communication — they are beings for whom technology is nature, for whom elsewhere is geography, for whom the problematic tie between unitary awareness and unitary physical body has political consequences. Frequently, we see them juxtaposed with more familiar social beings, and the contrast is jarring. We are used to encountering legally and epistemologically validated social units that are fixed in place by a dense network of location technologies. Interpreting them as such is by now a reflex, from "true names" (a persistent obsession of governments) to "legal addresses." In these efforts to fix the location of the political subject, other problematic couplings, such as the tie between body and the located self, pass almost unnoticed. I have proposed the idea of fiduciary subject as a useful way of articulating the (always political) tie between what our society defines as a single physical body and a single awareness of self.

In contrast, I have juxtaposed the mode of the technological, which is in many of its aspects the mode of the computer nets — which, in turn, evoke fragmentation and multiplicity as an integral part of social identity. The multiple personality is a preexisting example of such a social mode. In the language of the computer programmers who inhabit the frontiers of the techno-social, multiple personality is a mode that is already in place, fairly debugged in the current release; multiples exist around us, here and now — and regardless of the bad press accorded to Multiple Personality "Disorder," many remain invisible, living their lives quietly and gracefully. The multiple is the enantiomorph, the opposite of the socializer within the networks who exists in the mode of multiplicity outside a unitary physical body located at a terminal in another elsewhere.

The cyborg, the multiple personality, the cyber-space cowboy suggest radical rewritings in the techno-social space — in which everything is writing (computer code) — of the definition of body, the cultural meaning of bodies, and of the bounded individual as the standard social unit and validated social actant. As, for example, with the well-known multiple Truddi Chase, who consists of ninety-two supposed "functions," Thyrza Goodeve points out that

> Truddi's troops (who, for the most part, significantly, do not go by conventional "names," but by what we might call "functions" — The Interpreter, The Gate Keeper, The Buffer, The Recorder, for example) — explain their origin as "an intellectual reproduction system." The in-

dividual, imploding under the pressures of her material conditions, disappears, and the emergent construction, developing from the ashes of violence, seems something much closer to the population of a "small town," or an ever flickering series of switching television channels — but never that embattled Cartesian cogito so often presumed by the pronoun "I."

Such fractured identities call attention to alternatives, always multiple, always in tension. Just as changes in complex "real-world" political economies presage a radical simplification of biological diversity, the ramifications of complex social systems in the alter-space of communications technologies suggest a war between simplification and multiplicity ... an explosion of actors and actants that includes the almost-living, the not-living and the never-living arising in the boundaries between technology, society and "nature," in the architectures of multiple embodiments and multiple selves. We already have a considerable industry built around these possibilities, although we never say so. There is, of course, nothing fortuitous about this. Never has so much money and attention been paid to a phenomenon that originated as science fiction no more than seven years ago. A look at the origins of virtual systems may suggest that the effort is driven by more than either defense needs or market forces can explain. We might begin not with the multiple subjectivities of the inhabitants of a computer network, but rather with an example of multiple personality from a recent newspaper article:

> On July 23, 1990, a 27-year-old woman filed a complaint in Oshkosh, Wisconsin, charging that Mark Peterson, an acquaintance, raped her in her car. The woman had been previously diagnosed as having Multiple Personality Disorder (MPD). She claimed that Peterson raped her after deliberately drawing out one of her personalities, a naive young woman who he thought would be willing to have sex with him.

Such a story is situated in a tangle of multiply nested assumptions. One thread of this tangle is that subjectivity is invariably constituted in relation to a physical substrate — that subjects must be associated with bodies. Another is that we know unproblematically what "body" is. We have been raised with the social imperative that there is one primary persona or "true identity" and that in the offline world — the "real world" — this persona is firmly attached to a single physical body by which our existence as a social being is authorized, and in which it is grounded.

There can be productive interventions into our cultural belief that the unmarked social unit, besides being white and male, is a single self in a single body. Multiple Personality "Disorder" (MPD) is one. MPD is generally considered to be pathological, the result of trauma. But we can look to the medicolegal construction and management of pathology for the circumstances that constitute and authorize the unmarked, in order to take the pathologization of MPD — and generally the management and control of any manifestations of body-self other than the one body-self norm — to be useful tools for taking apart discourses of the political subject. There are other interventions to be made, and I will interrogate the elsewhere of virtual space, that new phantasmic "structure" within which real social interactions take place.

★ ★ ★

Let me tell you a boundary story, a tale of the nets, as a means of anchoring one corner of the system of discourse within which this discussion operates. This story is about a totally disabled older woman who could still push the keys of a computer with her headstick. The personality she wore on the net was huge, though, and her disability was invisible and irrelevant. Her standard greeting was an expansive "HI!!!!!!" She was sympathetic and intelligent, and in the intimate electronic companionships that can develop during online conferencing between people who may never physically meet, her women friends shared their deepest troubles, and she offered them advice that helped make significant changes in their lives.

After several years, something happened that badly shook the conference's participants. We learned that she was only an online persona; that in her offline life she was a middle-aged male psychiatrist. How had this come about? Logging on to the conference for the first time, he had accidentally begun a discussion with a woman who mistook him for another woman. "I was

stunned at the conversational mode," he said later. "I hadn't known that women talked among themselves that way. There was so much more vulnerability, so much more depth and complexity. Men's conversations on the nets were much more guarded and superficial, even among intimates. It was fascinating, and I wanted more."

He spent considerable time carefully choosing and then developing the right persona. A totally disabled, single older woman seemed perfect for his purpose: he assumed that she wouldn't be expected to have a social life offline. It worked for years, until one of her devoted admirers, bent on finally meeting her in person, tracked her down. The news of their meeting and the discovery of the woman's offline male persona traveled quickly through the conference. Reactions varied from humorous resignation to blind rage. Those most deeply affected were the women who had shared their innermost feelings with her. "I felt raped," one said. "I felt that my deepest secrets had been violated." Several went so far as to repudiate the gains they had made in their personal and emotional lives, which they felt to be predicated on deceit and trickery. But the computer engineers, the people who wrote the programs by means of which the nets exist, just smiled tiredly. They had understood from the beginning that the nets presaged radical changes in social conventions, some of which would go unnoticed until such an event brought them to the foreground. Some of these engineers, in fact, wrote software for the utopian possibilities it offered. Young enough to react and adjust quickly in the first days of the net, they had long ago taken for granted that many of the pre-net assumptions about the nature of identity had quietly vanished.

There is a subtext here, which relates to what I have been calling the online persona. Of course we all change personae all the time to suit the social occasion, although with online personae the act is more purposeful. The actively multiple, situational and fragmented character of the online persona calls into question commonsense notions of the relationships between communities and the individuals that constitute them. We take as starting points that communities are made up of aggregations of individual "selves," and that each "self" is equipped with a single physical body. I tell inquiring scholars that at the Group for Study of Virtual Systems we refer to this assumption as BUGS — a Body Unit Grounded in a Self. The notion of the self as we know it, called in various studies the "I" and in others the "subject", that tenacious just-so story that goes on to assure us that there exists an "I" for each body and that while there can be more than one "I" on tap there can only be one present at any time, seems a natural and inevitable part of life. It was just this kind of story that we told each other to hide the complexities of gender and of what we call "race," until theoreticians of gender and culture made the practices visible and showed how their invisibility authorized and anchored a system of oppression.

★ ★ ★

What social groups does communications technology bind? What groups escape or cannot be bound? What treaties are enforced in these settlements? What can we learn from examining such treaties?

Let us regard the history of communications technologies as an account of dissociation and integration — of the tensions between selves and bodies and the play of their interactions, separations and fusions. By mediating these interactions, communications technologies serve specific functions as creators and mediators of social/phantasmic consensual bodies, consensual spaces and consensual groups.

Social spaces and social groups do not spring into being only as concomitants of technology. Some workers study technologies as crystallizations of social networks, the technologies and the networks cocreating each other in an overlapping multiplicity of complex interactions. Technologies can be seen simultaneously as causes of, and responses to, social crisis. Consider the history of communication technologies as the study of social groups searching for ways to enact and to stabilize a sense of presence in increasingly diffuse and distributed networks of electronically mediated interaction, and thus also as ways to stabilize self/selves in shifting and unstable fields of power.

Let us consider bodies and selves in relation to communications technology in three ways:

First: As structures that mediate cultural legibility for the biological substrates to selves, substrates that legally authenticate political action; that is, as an apparatus for the production of body.

Second: As selves and relationships between selves constituted and mediated by technologies of communication; that is, as an apparatus for the production of community.

Third: As technologies mediating between bodies and selves, which may or may not be within physical proximity; that is, as interfaces.

Implicit in many of these accounts are assumptions about what bodies should be or do, what form bodies should take, and what conditions relationships between bodies and selves should require.

Over time, the relationship between bodies and their attendant "selves" has undergone a slow process of change. Strictly speaking, the classical bourgeois worldview, which incorporated a mechanistic view of the universe or nature and an egoistic view of "man" (with its implications for the ways in which body and self might be coupled under specific political and epistemological constraints), was a preeminent factor in the production of knowledge for a period of only about 150 years. Its influence began to be felt perhaps in the late 1600s, signaled, for example, by the publication of Newton's *Principia*; it ended around the 1840s about the time, for example, of the discovery of non-euclidean geometry and the development of critical psychology.

The subsequent deployment of knowledge structures — that is, the classical sciences, evolving under the primary influence of capital — was accompanied by improvements in systems of measurement in the realms of both the physical and the symbolic (as in cartography and psychology). In part, this was a complex expression of the political need to order the relationships between the emerging "subject" and its presumed associated body in ways that assured the maintenance of a social order that was already in dangerous disequilibrium. Social order, in this sense, implied spatial accountability — that is, knowing where the subject under the law was.

Traditionally, accountability referred to the physical body and most visibly took the form of laws that fixed the physical body within a juridical field whose fiduciary characteristics were precisely determined: the introduction of street addresses, passports, telephone numbers — in other words, the invention and deployment of documentations of citizenship in all their forms. This fine-tuned surveillance and control was developed in the interests of producing a more "stable," manageable citizen. The subtext of this activity is an elaboration and amplification of spatiality and presence — a hypertrophy of the perception of where, that is, what physics calls velocity and position.

The symmetry implied by the increasing precision with which both velocity and position could be determined in the macro- and microworld was ruptured in the 1920s and 1930s by the theoretical work of Niels Bohr and, later, Werner Heisenberg. The deep ontic unease that these proposals generated was perhaps not entirely different from the increasing preoccupation on the part of political apparatuses with precisely determining action and position in everything from satellite ranging to postal codes. Implicit in this elaboration of the concepts of spatiality and presence is the development of the fiduciary subject, in other words, a political, epistemological and biological unit that is not only measurable and quantifiable but also understood as being essentially in place. The individual social actor became fixed with respect to geographical coordinates that determine physical locus — a mode that ontically privileges the physical body (in an unusual invocation of a metaphysics of presence) rather than being located in a virtual system — that is, in relation to a social world of an information network, a social world whose primary mode of interaction is that of narrow-bandwidth symbolic exchange. In the context of this research, by "metaphysics of presence" I mean that a (living) body implies the presence within the body of a socially articulated self that is the true site of agency. It is this coupling, rather than the presence of the body alone, that privileges the body as the site of political authentication and political action.

* * *

On a high-resolution color computer screen appear images of a man and woman being married in an elab-

orate ceremony. They, their wedding party, a few presents and the surrounding landscape appear on the screen as detailed drawings, like a cartoon movie. Some of the guests appear to be animals, while others are invisible, signaling their presence by a small cloud at the top of the screen. Each bodylike form on the screen is an avatar, a body-representative for a physical person. The mainframe that makes their social interaction possible is located in Yokohama, but each person's physical body is seated at a terminal somewhere in the world; and the geography of the landscape that surrounds their wedding party is "elsewhere."

Many recent theorists view individuals' experiences of their own bodies as socially constructed — over and against other approaches that hold the body to be ontologically present to itself and to the experiences of the (always unitary) "self" inhabiting it. If we consider the physical map of the body and our experience of inhabiting it as socially mediated, then it should not be difficult to imagine the next step in a progression toward the social, to imagine the location of the self inhabiting the body as similarly socially mediated — not in the usual terms of position within a social field or of capacity to experience, but in terms of the physical location of a subject independent of the body, within a system of symbolic exchange — that is, information technology.

Theorizing a self in this way — in a spatiality of a different order, vectors different from those by which the body moves, a self moving in a spatiality from which the body is excluded — allows us to interpret the world of high-speed communications technology as a cultural framework within which social interaction can be understood as "normal" and can be studied in the same way as other social systems. Having said this, however, I must immediately add that interactions in virtual systems are, after all, a bit different. The chief difference is the effect of a changed density of the communication, the bandwidth.

* * *

"Bandwidth," as I use the term here, refers to the amount of information exchanged in unit time. "Reality" is wide-bandwidth, because people who communicate face to face in real time use multiple modes simultan-ously — speech, gestures, facial expression, and so on. Certain critics have commented wryly that the current standard for bandwidth by which we judge visual com-munication is that of reality…a high bandwidth indeed. Computer conferencing is narrow bandwidth, because communication is restricted to lines of text on a screen.

The cultural history of communication is, in part, a history of exponentially increasing bandwidth. The effect of a narrowing bandwidth, then, is to engage more of the participants' interpretive faculties. This makes communication more difficult when we need the information conveyed precisely. On the other hand, for symbolic exchange originating at, and relating to, the surface of the body, narrowing the bandwidth has startling effects: a deep need to create extremely de-tailed images of the absent and invisible body, of human interaction and of the symbol-generating artifacts that are part of such interaction. Frequently, in narrow-bandwidth communication, the interpretive faculties of one or the other participants are powerfully, even obsessively, engaged.

A typical example of the extent to which partici-pants in narrow-bandwidth communication engage their own interpretive faculties, and of the extent to which their interpretations are driven by engaging structures of desire, is indicated by studies of client-provider interactions in phone sex. Phone sex is the process of constructing desire through a single mode of communication, the human voice. The communica-tion bandwidth between client and provider is further narrowed because the voices are passed through the telephone network, which not only reduces the audio bandwidth but also introduces relatively high levels of distortion.

Technically speaking, the effect of distortion on the intelligibility of the human voice has been thoroughly studied (as one might expect, mostly by the military in an effort to find standards of intelligibility for battle communications). These studies have shown that the human auditory system has an extremely wide toler-ance for distortion and bandwidth limitation in voice communication. On the other hand, they have failed to note that even small amounts of distortion change

interactive styles. It seems reasonable to speculate that these changes are caused by the participants' engaging their interpretive faculties in an effort to provide closure to a set of symbols perceived as in-complete. But closure in regard to what?

In phone sex, once the signifiers begin to "float" loose from their moorings in a particularized physical experience, the most powerful attractor becomes the client's idealized fantasy. In this circumstance, narrow bandwidth becomes a powerful asset because extreme-ly complex fantasies can be generated from a small set of cues. In enacting such fantasies, participants draw on a repertoire of cultural codes to construct a scenario that compresses large amounts of information into a very small space. The provider verbally codes for ges-ture, appearance and proclivity, and expresses these as verbal tokens, sometimes compressing the token to no more than a single word. The client decompress-es the tokens and constructs a dense, complex inter-actional image.

Because tokens in phone sex are presented only verbally, the client employs verbal cues to construct a multimodal object of desire, with attributes of shape, tactility, scent — in other words, all the attributes of physical presence — from his or her own experiential or phantasmic schema. This act is thoroughly individ-ual and interpretive: from a compressed token of de-sire the client constitutes meaning that is dense, locally situated and socially particular.

Narrow-bandwidth interactions are useful in analyz-ing how participants construct desire, because the in-teractions are both real and schematized. While they cannot provide information about the vast and complex spectrum of human sexuality across societies, they do provide a laboratory that is large, moderately diverse and easily accessible for a detailed study of desire. But one need not engage in desire-mobilizing interactions to experience the attraction of virtual systems. An in-formant at an organization that tracks high-technology businesses reports that large public databases are ex-periencing difficulty in becoming profitable:

> What's happening is that users don't find the services, like online ticketing, electronic shopping and stock re-ports, very interesting. On the other hand, the online

conferences are jammed. What commercial online information services like Prodigy don't realize is that people are willing to pay money just to connect. Just for the opportunity to communicate.

★ ★ ★

Virtual systems imply particular understandings of space, time, proximity and agency. When we contrast the unease early users of the telephone felt — speaking "to" another person "through" the telephone — with easy familiarity with which early users of the computer seized upon computer conferencing, we can see that people have become comfortable with the idea that there are agencies — by which I mean politically authorized personae — on the other end of a wire, and indeed, eventually that it is unnecessary to be assured that there is an "other end."

Prior to prosthetic communication, an agent maintained proximity through texts bearing the agent's seal, and the agency the texts implied could be enforced through human delegates; but in the era of electronic speech, proximity is maintained through technology, and agency becomes invisible. Users of the telephone eventually took for granted that they were speaking to another person "on" the telephone. It is this sense of assurance in the presence of a specific, bounded, unitary agency, grounded by a voice, that undergirded a gradual refiguration of the meaning of proximity. With the advent of electronically mediated speech, agency is grounded not by a voice but by an iconic representation of a voice compressed in bandwidth and volume as well as distorted by the limitations of the early carbon-granule transducers. It becomes something more than a signature or seal on a text but far less than an embodied physical vocalization. Agency is proximate when the authorizing body can be manifested through technological prosthetics. This, in turn, implies that as these prosthetics become more complex, the relationship between agency and authorizing body becomes more discursive.

While there are bodies produced in virtual systems, physically they are isolated bodies (though within a refigured phantasmic public space, one needs to redefine "public" and "private"). The interactions of the virtual body within fields of power is complex; uncoupled, the subject produced in these stories is multiple, ungrounded, and it is constituted through technologies of communication.

In this regard, I have been conducting a study of two groups who seemed to instantiate productive aspects of this idea. One is phone sex workers, the other is computer scientists and engineers working on Virtual Reality (VR) systems that involve making humans visible in virtual space. I was interested in the ways in which these groups, which seem quite different, are similar. The work of both is about representing the human body through limited communication channels: both groups code cultural expectations as tokens of meaning.

Computer engineers are fascinated by VR because they not only program a world but somehow inhabit it; and virtual worlds can be inhabited by communities. Thus, in the process of articulating a virtual system, VR engineers make templates for communities (as with George Lucas's Habitat); and because communities are inhabited by bodies, VR engineers model bodies as well. Although cheap and practical systems are years away, many workers are debating the form and character of the communities they believe will spring up in their quasi-imaginary cyberspace. In doing so, they are articulating their own assumptions about bodies and sociality and projecting them onto the codes that define cyberspace systems. For example, since programmers, in interaction with workers in widely diverse fields, create the codes by which VR is generated, how these heterogeneous groups understand cognition, community and bodies will determine the nature of cognition, community, and bodies in VR.

Bodies in VR are constituted by descriptive codes that "embody" expectations of appearance. Many of the engineers currently debating the form and nature of cyberspace are young men in their late teens and twenties, and they are at times preoccupied with the things that have always preoccupied the postpubescent. This group will generate the codes and descriptors by which bodies in cyberspace are represented. Because of practical limitations, some of their discussion is concerned with data compression and tokenization; but as

A salesman demonstrates camera designed to aid
tailors in making better and quicker fits. 1948.

with phone sex, VR is a relatively narrow-bandwidth representational medium, visual instead of aural, and the ways bodies will be represented will involve the mechanisms of recognition.

One of the most active sites for speculation about how recognition might work in cyberspace is the work of computer game developers, particularly in the area known as interactive fantasy (IF). Workers in (and critics of) interactive fantasy have been speculating about how it will be deployed in VR scenarios. For example, how people will make love in cyberspace — a space in which everything, including bodies, exists as a metaphor, is coded.

* * *

Using this necessarily brief account as background, I want to use studies of virtual systems as an entry point for understanding the prosthetic quality of electronic communication and to search for apparatuses for the production of community and of body. I do not intend to present a detailed analysis here, but rather to show some of the things I treat at length elsewhere.

First: Members of prosthetic virtual communities act as if the community met in a physical public space. The number of times that online conferencees refer to the conference as a place is overwhelming: "This is a nice place to get together" or "This is a convenient place to meet." This sense increases with time, as online multiple-user environments describe inhabitable spaces in increasingly complex ways. For example, an experimental environment (MUD) at Xerox consists of a multi-roomed house and surrounding grounds, the appearance and character of which are described in considerable detail. A visitor "hears" the conversations taking place among other inhabitants nearby.

Second: Virtual space is most frequently visualized as Cartesian. Online conferencees tend to visualize the conference system as a simple three-dimensional space; some branches of the conference are "higher up" and others "lower down." In multiple-user environments this quality is explicit. This virtual space is frequently laid out with respect to the cardinal compass

points: directions are expressed as east, west, north, south, and in some systems as up and down; others will use left, right, forward and back.

Third: Conferencees act as if the virtual space were inhabited by bodies. Conferencees construct bodies online by describing them, either spontaneously or in response to questions, and articulate their discourses around the assumed presence of bodies.

Fourth: Bodies in virtual space have complex erotic components. As in "real" life, conferencees place a high value on unambiguously identifying the gender of their fellow conferencees. Having made this determination, they frequently flirt with each other. Some may engage in "netsex," constructing elaborate erotic mutual fantasies. Erotic possibilities for the virtual body are a significant part of the discussions of some of the groups designing cyberspace systems. The consequences of virtual bodies are considerable in the local frame, in that conferencees mobilize significant erotic tension in relation to their virtual bodies. In contrast to the conferences, the bandwidth for physicalities in phone sex is quite limited. One worker said ironically, "On the phone, every female sex worker is white, five feet four, and has red hair." It is significant that almost without exception a binary gender system is ontologized in virtual space; there have been a few experiments in creating alternative gender constructs, but so far participants have not shown a high level of sophistication at doing so.

Fifth: The meaning of locality and privacy is not settled. The legal status of communication within the networks is a subject for continual debate. One ongoing problem is the meaning of inside and outside. Traditionally, when sending a letter one ensures privacy by enclosing it in an envelope. But in electronic mail, for example, the message is part of the address. The design of electronic mail systems erases the distinction of inside and outside, together with the idea of privacy — although no one has given up on encryption. A side effect of encryption will be to enable those engaged in electronic communication to reinstate the inside-outside dichotomy, and with it the notion of privacy in the virtual social space. Some early conferences experimented with private "areas" in which conversation was restricted to specific individuals, but to be truly private those areas had to be off-limits to the system operator as well — a situation that led to problems for the system as a whole. This is another example of how the evolution of virtual systems discloses many typical problems of emergent social order, as well as many of the same conflicts between the interests of the individual and the group, as do "real" social systems.

Sixth: Names are local labels. Conferencees (or their avatars that is, their delegated virtual personae) develop satisfyingly complex relationships with other conferencees. These remain stable through considerable variation in frequency and quality of interaction, including when one or another of the conferencees decides to change names. Conferencees may have several avatars, with a separate constructed personality for each, and move between them. These may sometimes be on the same conference. For friends who may know more than one avatar there is an intriguing persistence of identity — they treat the new avatar as as if it were still partly the old one. Which characteristics are most likely to persist is still under study.

★ ★ ★

The situation of women vis-à-vis technology in the "real" world — that is, the relatively fewer numbers of women who have had the encouragement or opportunity to deeply engage with complex computer systems, or who have found their way into top jobs in the high-technology industries — is mirrored in virtual systems, in which the participants are more likely to be male. This may be due to the ways that men and women are taught to respond to the sign of power. The sense of power that the ability to interactively influence the simulation provides is itself gendered, and may help to explain the gender imbalance among participants. In psychoanalytic terms, power for the young male is first associated with the mother figure. The experience of power that the mother figure represents is fraught with an unresolvable need for reconciliation with an

always absent structure of personality, and it is the peculiar quality of the interface itself to mimic the same structure. As Sherry Turkle first suggested, an "absent structure of personality" is also another way of describing the peculiarly seductive character of that vague but palpable sentience, the computer. Turkle characterizes this aspect of computer interaction as producing the quasi-personality complex that she calls the "second self." Danger, the sense of threat as well as seductiveness which the computer can evoke, comes from both within and without. It derives from the complex interrelationships between human and computer, and thus partially from within the human; and it exists partially within the simulation. It simultaneously constitutes erotic pleasure and a sense of loss of control over the body. This mobilizes a constellation of responses to the simulation which deeply engage fear, pleasure, and also, perhaps, the simultaneous desire for and possibility of control. This experience has a protean character. The quality of mutability that virtual interaction promises is expressed as a sense of dizzying, exciting physical movement occurring within a phantasmic space — again an experimental mode psychoanalytically linked to primal experiences. It is no wonder, then, that inhabitants of virtual systems seem to experience a sense of longing for a space that is simultaneously embodied and imaginary, such as cyberspace suggests. This longing is frequently accompanied by a desire, inarticulately expressed, to penetrate the interface and merge with the system — what I have humorously referred to elsewhere as "cyborg envy."

The origin of the warranted self, safe in its politically authorized coupling with a biological body, is linked to the cultural production of bourgeois modernity. At the close of the twentieth century this linkage is dissolving, and the bounded social individual is engaged, willfully or otherwise, in a process of translation to the refigured and reinscribed agencies of virtual systems. "Sex and death among the disembodied" is an apt expression for the generous permeability of boundaries between the biological and symbolic, which this translation signifies. But as with everything else in the postmodern, the meanings of both sex and death have undergone translation. Sexuality refers to desire, but virtual desire is figured in terms of bandwidth and internal difference, leading to unexpected results. Death has many meanings, politically and personally. The personal body dies, coterminously with the juridically warranted subject. But the avatar within the virtual system does not die: it decouples — an act with an unsettlingly spiritual resonance.

Virtual systems and the social worlds they imply are examples of the flexible and lively adaptations that persons seeking community are beginning to explore. These new kinds of communities are part of a range of innovative solutions to the need for social interaction — a need that is frequently thwarted by the geographical and cultural realities of modern cities. Increasingly structured according to the needs of powerful economic interests, rather than in ways that encourage and facilitate habitation and social interaction in the urban context, the modern city thwarts rather than fosters social space and social interaction. Virtual systems and the redefinitions of the social that they imply may prefigure a wide variety of complex and ingenious strategies for survival in what many critics term the urban wasteland. The deepened split between the physical realities and dangers of urban life and the phantasmic world of online sociality is a both hopeful and cautionary sign, a new opportunity and a flight from responsibility, a chance to circumvent a world that many see as out of control and also a way of avoiding a complex and dangerous role in reclaiming the world from the forces that threaten to destroy it. Because of the power and potential of virtual systems there is a temptation to think of them as easy fixes. We must be wary of this attitude even as it emerges, encouraged by some of the brightest of the advanced system designers. Whether virtual systems can sustain the depth and complexity necessary for durable social structures that can withstand time and disruptive circumstances as yet unknown, remains to be seen.

As virtual systems burgeon, it is critical to remember that decoupling the body from the subject is an act that is politically fraught. As we enter the era of electronic virtual systems we should be acutely aware of whose agendas we serve. At the close of an era of a particular definition of individuality, consciousness still remains firmly rooted in the physical; the bounded subject is a refractory construct, quite difficult to dislodge, and it remains the object of force in a time when political agencies are as enamored of force as they have been at any time past. Before we can allow ourselves to forget this, the decoupled subject must possess a different order of agency from that of the name of a "disappeared" Central American, called back to momentary life by a graffito on a public wall.

The imagery of cyberpunk authors, and of a few virtual world builders, echoes with images of purely phantasmic bodies, freed from the constraints that flesh imposes. They take for granted that the human body is "meat" — obsolete, as soon as consciousness itself can be uploaded into the network. This, too, has unsettling religious resonances. Because of the ways that power works, it is important to remember that forgetting about the body is an old Cartesian trick, one that exacts a price from those bodies rendered invisible by the act of forgetting — those on the lower end of the social scale by whose labor the act of forgetting is made possible. Remembering the body may help us to prevent virtual systems from becoming unwitting accomplices in new exercises of social control. Remembering that bodies, selves, technologies and cultures constitute each other suggests a broad range of questions and unsettled debates from which to interrogate the burgeoning virtual communities.

Collective structures risking themselves in novel circumstances, reworking the structure of sociality, inventing a geography of elsewhere — and in the process, reinventing the links and tensions between bodies, selves, and communities. The alter-space within the vast electronic webs by means of which most of the symbolic exchange of the world already takes place is the first of many such elsewheres. This (un)real estate, supporting a different mode of existence from face-to-face sociality but nevertheless evincing a kind of tenacious Cartesianism that infects all attempts to describe it, is already home to thousands of communities whose impact outside the nets is only just beginning to be appreciated. The inhabitants of these virtual communities thoroughly internalize the Homo ludens mode of sociality — working from narrow-bandwidth cues, acting as if they inhabited common social territory.

The mode of interaction that this milieu fosters — congeries of personae whose greatest commonality is a single physical substrate in which they are loosely grounded, collective structures whose informing epistemology is multiplicity and reinvention — makes transformation as reflexive as it is transitive, and it is one of the "schizo" modes that Gilles Deleuze and Félix Guattari describe. Perhaps in virtual systems we can make out the lineaments of Coyote laughing at the metrics of classical physics by means of which science attempts to make and stabilize a world, collapsing and reinventing the terms by which spatiality, and consequently the ontology of articulating social spaces, is understood. It is not necessary to give up classical physics to step into the social world of virtual systems, but it is necessary to bracket it…that is, to open another reality window. This is social multitasking on the macro level — a mode we enter when we switch personae for each social world we enter — and to the extent that it is reflexive, it is an entry point to the dangerous multiple perspectival mode of Haraway's cyborg or the disruptive experiential bricolage of Deleuze and Guattari's schizo. It is both the challenge and the promise of virtual systems.

The Myth of the Clean War

Paul Rogers

Six months after the end of the Gulf War, reports began to emerge in the press about a tactic used widely by United States armored units that involved the deliberate collapsing of Iraqi infantry trenches as the U.S. forces moved into Kuwait at the end of Operation Desert Storm. Initial press reports that Iraqi troops had been buried alive during the U.S. ground assault gave the impression that these actions had been incidental to the assault. The full account made it clear that the tactic was part of a systematic large-scale action to destroy the Iraqi front-line trenches and their occupants. Abrams tanks, fitted with bulldozer blades, drove parallel to the trenches, filling them in and burying the Iraqi infantry alive, even as some were still trying to fire their weapons. The action had been extensively rehearsed and was used as a tactic to minimize U.S. casualties.

An estimated seventy miles of Iraqi trenches were attacked in this manner. United States soldiers reported seeing the flattened trenches with arms and legs sticking out through the surface of the sand. According to one report, up to seven thousand Iraqis were killed in this way.

This report sits uneasily alongside the impression given to the media throughout the Gulf War that it was a precision war against physical targets and not against people. Unlike the Vietnam War, there was no recourse to "body counts," only to tank counts and artillery counts. This was, at least for the military's public relations purposes, a "war against real estate." The media was given plentiful access to video footage showing deserted bridges and bunkers being destroyed with great accuracy. Any footage showing people being killed was carefully withheld from view.

This myth of a clinically clean war, carefully nurtured by the military throughout the conflict, was initially contradicted by reports of the massacre of fleeing Iraqis on the Basra road just before the cease-fire. But even that action formed just part of a much more general process of direct and precise targeting of people throughout the war. The Basra road carnage and the burying tactics of the First Mechanized Infantry Division were no more than the tail end of a process that was a key part of the entire war.

In the early stages of the air war, most targets were military facilities, such as command bunkers, missile sites, munitions dumps and barracks. Dual-use targets such as bridges, power stations and telephone exchanges were also destroyed. Ultimately, this targeting did so much damage to the Iraqi civil infrastructure that there has been a huge postwar increase in ill-health and, especially, infant mortality.

As the war progressed, the coalition forces began the process of systematically destroying the Iraqi forces in Kuwait and southeastern Iraq. These forces were comprised of mainly peasant conscripts and reservists, as the elite forces were generally kept away from the most dangerous zones. They were exposed to the latest generation of area-impact munitions — weapons designed specifically to kill and to maim humans over the widest possible area.

Many of these weapons were developed during the Vietnam War. They include the successors to napalm and similar fuel-air explosives and slurry bombs. While both of these weapon types were used during the Gulf War, most of the casualties were caused by two other area-impact weapons: the cluster bomb and the Multiple Rocket Launch System.

An example of a cluster bomb is the Rockeye 11, which weighs about five hundred pounds. It acts as a dispenser for 247 grenade-sized bomblets that explode together to produce a hall of half a million antipersonnel shrapnel fragments. Such bombs will kill or severely injure anyone within the space of an acre. One plane can carry up to sixteen such bombs. The U.S. Navy alone dropped 4,400 cluster bombs, and the U.S. Air Force many thousands more. The British equivalent, the BL755 made by Huntings, was also used extensively, especially by Jaguar strike aircraft.

The Multiple Launch Rocket System (MLRS) is even more devastating. It was used operationally for the first time in the Gulf War by both the U.S. and British armies. The launcher is a tracked vehicle carrying twelve missiles with a range of over twenty miles. The missiles can all be fired within a minute and can be aimed to spread out over a target area of sixty acres. As they detonate, they release nearly eight thousand antipersonnel fragmentation grenades. During the closing stages of the war, the U.S. forces fired ten thousand MLRS missiles and the British army another 2,500.

Many other antipersonnel weapons were employed, including a fragmentation version of the Tomahawk cruise missile. Their cumulative effect on the Iraqi troops was devastating. Within days of the war's end, unofficial Saudi military sources were reporting Iraqi casualties of sixty five to one hundred thousand. More recently, a report leaked from the U.S. Defense Intelligence Agency put the figures at one hundred thousand killed and three hundred thousand injured. It is probable that many of the injured subsequently died for lack of medical care.

The antipersonnel attacks were concentrated in the last two weeks of the war and led one analyst to use the term "hyper-war." To find a historical instance of a similar intensity of killing in such a brief time period, one must go back to Hiroshima or Dresden, or to the mass land battles of World War I.

The Gulf War is, therefore, an example not so much of a precise, high-tech war, but a vivid demonstration of the other military revolution — the steady development of "higher forms of killing." Over the past twenty years there have been major developments in the science of killing and maiming people in wartime. These new antipersonnel weapons make conventional war far more devastating and likely to cause much greater suffering and death than we could have previously imagined. They were demonstrated with remarkable effect during the Gulf War, even as strenuous efforts were made to give an altogether different impression. The reality of Desert Storm — killing and maiming on an extraordinary scale — is a very long way from the image of clean war so carefully nurtured in those military briefings from Saudi Arabia.

Jakob Halip, 1937.

Ethology: Spinoza and Us
Gilles Deleuze

"Spinoza and us" — this phrase could mean many things, but among other things, it means "us in the middle of Spinoza." To try to perceive and to understand Spinoza by way of the middle. Generally one begins with the first principle of a philosopher. But what counts is also the third, the fourth or the fifth principle. Everyone knows the first principle of Spinoza: one substance for all the attributes. But we also know the third, fourth or fifth principle: one Nature for all bodies, one Nature for all individuals, a nature that is itself an individual varying in an infinite number of ways. What is involved is no longer the affirmation of a single substance, but rather the laying out of a *common plane of immanence* on which all bodies, all minds and all individuals are situated. This plane of immanence or consistency is a plan, but not in the sense of a mental design, a project, a program; it is a plan in the geometric sense: a section, an intersection, a diagram.[1] Thus, to be in the middle of Spinoza is to be on this model plane, or rather to install oneself on this plane — which implies a mode of living, a way of life. What is this plane and how does one construct it? For at the same it is fully a plane of immanence, and yet it has to be constructed if one is to live in a Spinozist manner.

How does Spinoza define a body? A body, of whatever kind, is defined by Spinoza in two simultaneous ways. In the first place, a body, however small it may be, is composed of an infinite number of particles; it is the relations of motion and rest, of speeds and slownesses between particles that define a body, the individuality of a body. Second, a body affects other bodies, or is affected by other bodies; it is this capacity for affecting and being affected that also defines a body in its individuality. These two propositions appear to be very simple; one is kinetic and the other dynamic. But if one truly installs oneself in the midst of these propositions, if one lives them, things are much more complicated and one finds that one is a Spinozist before having understood why.

Thus, the kinetic proposition tells us that a body is defined by relations of motion and rest, of slowness and speed between particles. That is, it is not defined by a form or by functions. Global form, specific form and organic functions depend on relations of speed and slowness. Even the development of a form, the course of development of a form, depends on these relations, and not the reverse. The important thing is to understand life, each living individuality, not as form or a development of form but as a complex relation between differential velocities, between deceleration and acceleration of particles. A composition of speeds and slownesses on a plane of immanence. In the same way, a musical form will depend on a complex relation between speeds and slownesses of sound particles. It is not just a matter of music but of how to live: it is by speed and slowness that one slips in among things, that one connects with something else. One never commences; one never has a tabula rasa; one slips in, enters in the middle; one takes up or lays down rhythms.

The second proposition concerning bodies refers us to the capacity for affecting and being affected. You will not define a body (or a mind) by its form, nor by its organs or functions, and neither will you define it as a substance or a subject. Every reader of Spinoza knows that for him bodies and minds are not substances or subjects, but modes. It is not enough, however, merely to think this theoretically. For, concretely, a mode is a complex relation of speed and slowness, in the body but also in thought, and it is a capacity for affecting and being affected, pertaining to the body or to thought. Concretely, if you define bodies and thoughts as capacities for affecting and being affected, many things change. You will define an animal or a human being not by its form, its organs and its functions and not as a subject either; you will define it by the affects of which it is capable. Affective capacity, with a maximum threshold and a minimum threshold, is a constant notion in Spinoza. Take any animal and make a list of affects, in any order. Children know how to do this: Little Hans, in the case reported by Freud, makes a list of affects of a draft horse pulling a cart in a city (to be proud, to have blinders, to go fast, to pull a heavy load, to collapse, to be whipped, to kick up a racket, and so on). For example, there are greater differences between a plow horse or a draft horse and a racehorse than between an ox and a plow horse. This is because the racehorse and the plow horse have neither the same affects nor the same capacity for being affected; the plow horse has affects in common, rather, with the ox.

It should be clear that the plane of immanence, the plane of Nature that distributes affects, does not make any distinction at all between things that might be called natural and things that might be called artificial. Artifice is fully a part of Nature, since each thing, on the immanent plane of Nature, is defined by the arrangements of motions and affects into which it enters, whether these arrangements are artificial or natural. Long after Spinoza, biologists and naturalists will try to describe animal worlds defined by affects and capacities for affecting and being affected. For example, Jakob von Uexküll will do this for the tick, an animal that sucks the blood of mammals. He will define this animal by three affects: the first has to do with light (climb to the top of a branch); the second is olfactive (let yourself fall onto the mammal that passes beneath the branch); and the third is thermal (seek the area without fur, the warmest spot). A world with only three affects, in the midst of all that goes on in the immense forest. An optimal threshold and a pessimal in the capacity for being affected: the gorged tick that will die, and the tick capable of fasting for a very long time.[2] Such studies as this, which define bodies, animals or humans by the affects they are capable of, founded what is today called *ethology*. The approach is no less valid for us, for human beings, than for animals, because no one knows ahead of time the affects one is capable of; it is a long affair of experimentation, requiring a lasting prudence, a Spinozan wisdom that implies the construction of a plane of immanence or consistency. Spinoza's ethics has nothing to do with a morality; he conceives it as an ethology, that is, a composition of fast and slow speeds, of capacities for affecting and being affected on this plane of immanence or consistency. That is why Spinoza calls out to us in the way that he does: you do not know beforehand what good or bad you are capable of; you do not know beforehand what a body or a mind can do, in a given encounter, a given arrangement, a given combination.

Ethology is first of all the study of the relations of speed and slowness, of the capacities for affecting and being affected that characterize each thing. For each thing these relations and capacities have an amplitude, thresholds (maximum and minimum) and variations or transformations that are peculiar to them. And they select, in the world or in Nature, that which corresponds to the thing; that is, they select what affects or is affected by the thing, what moves or is moved by it. For example, given an animal, what is this animal unaffected by in the infinite world? What does it react to positively or negatively? What are its nutriments and its poisons? What does it "take" in its world? Every point has its counterpoints: the plant and the rain, the spider and the fly. So an animal, a thing, is never separable from its relations with the world. The interior is only a selected exterior, and the exterior, a projected interior. The speed or slowness of metabolisms, perceptions, actions and reactions link together to constitute a particular individual in the world.

Further, there is also the way in which these relations of speed and slowness are realized according to circumstances, and the way in which these capacities for being affected are filled. For they always are, but in different ways, depending on whether the present affects threaten the thing (diminish its power, slow it down, reduce it to the minimum), or strengthen, accelerate and increase it: poison or food? — with all the complications, since a poison can be a food for part of the thing considered.

Lastly, ethology studies the compositions of relations or capacities between different things. This is another aspect of the matter, distinct from the preceding ones. Heretofore, it was only a question of knowing how a particular thing could decompose other things by giving them a relation that was consistent with one of its own or, on the contrary, how it risks being decomposed by other things. But now it is a question of knowing whether relations (and which ones?) can compound directly to form a new, more "extensive" relation, or whether capacities can compound directly to constitute a more "intensive" capacity or power. It is no longer a matter of utilizations or captures, but of sociabilities and communities. How do individuals enter into composition with one another in order to form a higher individual, ad infinitum? How can a being take another being into its world, while preserving or respecting the other's own relations and world? And in this regard, what are the different types of sociabilities, for example? What is the difference between the society of human beings and the community of rational beings?... Now, we are concerned not with a relation of point to counterpoint, nor with the selection of a world, but with a symphony of Nature, the composition of a world that is increasingly wide and intense. In what order and in what manner will the powers, speeds and slownesses be composed?

A plane of musical composition, a plane of Nature, insofar as the latter is the fullest and most intense Individual, with parts that vary in an infinity of ways. Uexküll, one of the main founders of ethology, is a Spinozist when first he defines the melodic lines or contrapuntal relations that correspond to each thing, and then describes a symphony as an immanent higher unity that takes on the breadth and fullness ("natural composition"). This musical composition comes into play throughout the *Ethics*, constituting it as one and the same Individual whose relations of speed and slowness do not cease to vary, successively and simultaneously. Successively: the different parts of the *Ethics* are assigned changing relative velocities, until the absolute velocity of thought is reached in the third kind of knowledge. And simultaneously: the propositions and the scholia do not proceed at the same pace, but compose two movements that intercross. The *Ethics*, a composition whose parts are all carried forward by the greatest velocity, in the fullest movement. In a very fine text, Lagneau spoke of this velocity and amplitude, which caused him to compare the *Ethics* to a musical work: a lightning "speed of thought," a "wide-ranging power," a "capacity for discerning in a single act the relationship of the greatest possible number of thoughts."[3]

In short, if we are Spinozists we will not define a thing by its form, nor by its organs and its functions, nor as a substance or a subject. Borrowing terms from the Middle Ages, or from geography, we will define it by *longitude* and *latitude*. A body can be anything; it can be an animal, a body of sounds, a mind or an idea; it can be a linguistic corpus, a social body, a collectivity. We call longitude of a body the set of relations of speed and slowness, of motion and rest, between particles that compose it from this point of view, that is, between *unformed elements*.[4] We call latitude the set of affects that occupy a body at each moment, that is, the intensive states of an *anonymous force* (force for existing, capacity for being affected). In this way we construct the map of a body. The longitudes and latitudes together constitute Nature, the plane of immanence or consistency, which is always variable and is constantly being altered, composed and recomposed, by individuals and collectivities.

There are two very contrary conceptions of the word "plan," or of the idea of a plan, even if these two conceptions blend into one another and we go from one to the other imperceptibly. Any organization that comes from above and refers to a transcendence, be it a hidden one, can be called a theological plan: a design in the mind of God, but also an evolution in the supposed depths of nature, or a society's organization of power. A plan of this type can be structural or genetic, and both at the same time. It always involves forms and their developments, subjects and their formations. Development of forms and formation of subjects: this is the basic feature of this first type of plan. Thus, it is a plan of organization or development. Whatever one may say, then, it will always be a plan of transcendence that directs forms as well as subjects, and that stays hidden, that is never given, that can only be divined, induced, inferred from what it gives. It always has an additional dimension; it always implies a dimension supplementary to the dimensions of the given.

On the contrary, a plane of immanence has no supplementary dimension; the process of composition must be apprehended for itself, through that which it gives, in that which it gives. It is a plan of composition, not a plan of organization or development. Perhaps colors are indicative of the first type of plan, while music, silence and sounds, belong to this one. There is no longer a form, but only relations of velocity between infinitesimal particles of an unformed material. There is no longer a subject, but only individuating affective states of an anonymous force. Here the plan is concerned only with motions and rests, with dynamic affective changes. It will be perceived with that which it makes perceptible to us, as we proceed. We do not live or think or write in the same way on both plans. For example, Goethe, and even Hegel in certain respects, have been considered Spinozists, but they are not really Spinozists, because they never ceased to link the plan to the organization of a Form and to the formation of a Subject. The Spinozists, rather, are Hölderlin, Kleist and Nietzsche, because they think in terms of speeds and slownesses, of frozen catatonias and accelerated movements, unformed elements, nonsubjectified affects.

Writers, poets, musicians, filmakers — painters too, even chance readers — may find that they are Spinozists; indeed, such a thing is more likely for them than for professional philosophers. It is a matter of one's practical conception of the "plan."

It is not that one may be a Spinozist without knowing it. Rather, there is a strange privilege that Spinoza enjoys, something that seems to have been accomplished by him and no one else. He is a philosopher who commands an extraordinary conceptual apparatus, one that is highly developed, systematic and scholarly; and yet he is the quintessential object of an immediate, unprepared encounter, such that a nonphilosopher, or even someone without any formal education, can receive a sudden illumination from him, a "flash." Then it is as if one discovers that one is a Spinozist; one arrives in the middle of Spinoza, one is sucked up, drawn into the system or the composition. When Nietzsche writes, "I am really amazed, really delighted...I hardly knew Spinoza: what brought me to him now was the guidance of instinct,"[5] he is not speaking only as a philosopher. A historian of philosophy as rigorous as Victor Delbos was struck by this dual role of Spinoza, as a very elaborate model, but also as a secret inner impulse.[6] There is a double reading of Spinoza: on the one hand, a systematic reading in pursuit of the general idea and the unity of the parts, but on the other hand and at the same time, the affective reading, without an idea of the whole, where one is carried along or set down, put in motion or at rest, shaken or calmed according to the velocity of this or that part. Who is a Spinozist? Sometimes, certainly, the individual who works "on" Spinoza, on Spinoza's concepts, provided this is done with enough gratitude and admiration. But also the individual who, without being a philosopher, receives from Spinoza an affect, a set of affects, a kinetic determination, an impulse, and makes Spinoza an encounter, a passion. What is unique about Spinoza is that he, the most philosophic of the philosophers (unlike Socrates himself, Spinoza requires only philosophy...), teaches the philosopher how to become a nonphilosopher. And it is Part Five — not at all the most difficult, but the quickest, having an infinite velocity — that the two are brought together, the philosopher and the nonphilosopher, as one and the same being. Hence, what an extraordinary composition this Part Five has; how extraordinary is the way in which the meeting of concept and affect occurs there, and the way in which this meeting is prepared, made necessary by the celestial and subterranean movements that together compose the preceding parts.

Many commentators have loved Spinoza sufficiently to invoke a Wind when speaking of him. And in fact no other comparison is adequate. But should we think of the great calm wind the philosopher Delbos speaks of? Or should we think of the whirl-wind, the witch's wind spoken of by "the man from Kiev," a nonphilosopher par excellence, a poor Jew who bought the *Ethics* for a kopek and did not understand how everything fit together?[7] Both, since the *Ethics* includes both the continuous set of propositions, demonstrations and corollaries, as a grand movement of concepts, and the discontinuous sequence of scholia, as a launching of affects and impulses, a series of whirlwinds. Part Five is the extreme extensive unity, but this is because it is also the most concentrated intensive peak: there is no longer any difference between the concept and life. But in the preceding parts there was already the composition or interweaving of the two components — what Romain Rolland called "the white sun of substance" and "the fiery words of Spinoza."

NOTES

1. The French word *plan*, used by the author throughout this essay, covers virtually all the meanings of the English "plan" and "plane." To preserve the major contrast that Deleuze sets up here, between *plan d'immanence ou de consistance* and *plan de transcendance ou d'organisation*, I use "plane" for the first term, where the meaning is, roughly, a conceptual-affective continuum, and "plan" for the second term. The reader should also keep in mind that "plan" has the meaning of "map" in English as well. — TRANS.

2. Jakob von Uexküll, *Mondes animaux et monde humain* (Gonthier).

3. Jules Lagneau, *Célèbres leçons et fragments*, (2d ed., Paris: P.U.F., 1964), pp. 67–68. This is one of the great texts on Spinoza. Similarly, Romain Rolland, when he speaks of the velocity of thought and the musical order in Spinoza: *Empédocle d'Agrigente, suivi de l'Eclair de Spinoza* (Editions du Sablier, 1931). As a matter of fact, the theme of a velocity of thought greater than any given velocity can be found in Empedocles, Democritus or Epicurus.

4. See what Spinoza calls "the simplest bodies." They have neither number nor form nor figure, but are infinitely small and always exist as infinities. The only bodies having a form are the composite bodies, to which the simple bodies belong according to a particular relation.

5. See Nietzsche, letter to Overbeck, July 30, 1881.

6. Delbos, *Le Problème moral dans la philosophie de Spinoza et dans l'histoire du spinozisme* (Paris: Alcan). This is a much more important book than the academic work by the same author, *Le Spinozisme* (Paris: Vrin).

7. "Let me ask you what brought you to Spinoza? Is it that he was a Jew?"

"No, your honor. I didn't know who or what he was when I first came across the book — they don't exactly love him in the synagogue, if you've read the story of his life. I found it in a junkyard in a nearby town, paid a kopek and left cursing myself for wasting money hard to come by. Later I read through a few pages and kept on going as though there were a whirlwind at my back. As I say, I didn't understand every word, but when you're dealing with such ideas you feel as though you were taking a witch's ride. After that I wasn't the same man..."

"Would you mind explaining what you think Spinoza's work means? In other words, if it's a philosophy, what does it state?"

"That's not easy to say.... The book means different things according to the subject of the chapters, though it's all united underneath. But what I think it means is that he was out to make a free man of himself — as much as one can according to his philosophy, if you understand my meaning — by thinking things through and connecting everything up, if you'll go along with that, your honor."

"That isn't a bad approach, through the man rather than the work. But...."

From Bernard Malamud, *The Fixer*, 1966.

Translated from the French by Robert Hurley

GIOVANNI ANSELMO
ART & LANGUAGE
LOTHAR BAUMGARTEN
CHRISTIAN BOLTANSKI
MARCEL BROODTHAERS
JAMES COLEMAN
TONY CRAGG
RICHARD DEACON
GER VAN ELK
DAN GRAHAM
REBECCA HORN
ANSELM KIEFER
JUAN MUÑOZ
MARIA NORDMAN
GIULIO PAOLINI
GIUSEPPE PENONE
GERHARD RICHTER
THOMAS SCHÜTTE
THOMAS STRUTH
NIELE TORONI
JEFF WALL
LAWRENCE WEINER

MARIAN GOODMAN GALLERY

24 WEST 57TH STREET   NEW YORK. NY 10019   212 977-7160   FAX 212 581-5187

VINCENT WAPLER   COMMISSAIRE PRISEUR

18 RUE DE MARIGNAN 75008 PARIS   TÉLÉPHONE (033 1) 42 25 58 78   FACSIMILE (033 1) 42 56 11 21

Antony Gormley *Earth Above Ground II* , 1986-1989

salvatore ala 560 broadway new york 10012

LEO CASTELLI

420 WEST BROADWAY
578 BROADWAY
NEW YORK

ARTFORUM

INTERNATIONAL CONTEMPORARY ART

SUBSCRIBE 1•800•341•1522

TERRY ALLEN
MASSIMO ANTONACI
ALICE AYCOCK
JAMES BIEDERMAN
ALIGHIERO E BOETTI
BRUCE BOICE
JOE BREIDEL
DANIEL BUREN
VICTOR BURGIN
THOMAS JOSHUA COOPER
HAMISH FULTON
CHARLES GAINES
MARCO GASTINI
JACK GOLDSTEIN
HANS HAACKE
NANCY HOLT
MAGDALENA JETELOVA
BARBARA KASTEN
MEL KENDRICK
SUSAN LEOPOLD
SOL LEWITT
ALLAN MCCOLLUM
ROMAN OPALKA
PAPUNYA TULA ARTISTS
ADRIAN PIPER
THE ESTATE OF ROBERT SMITHSON
FRANZ ERHARD WALTHER
KES ZAPKUS

JOHN
WEBER
GALLERY

142 GREENE STREET NEW YORK 10012 TEL.212.966.6115 FAX.212.941.8727

CULTURE LAB

Book Release

Princeton Architectural

Press Forthcoming

Edited by Brian Boigon

+

Symposium Series
1992–1993

Sponsors

University of Toronto
School of Architecture
+ Landscape Architecture

Stephen Bingham Company

Susan McKenna

SL Simpson Gallery

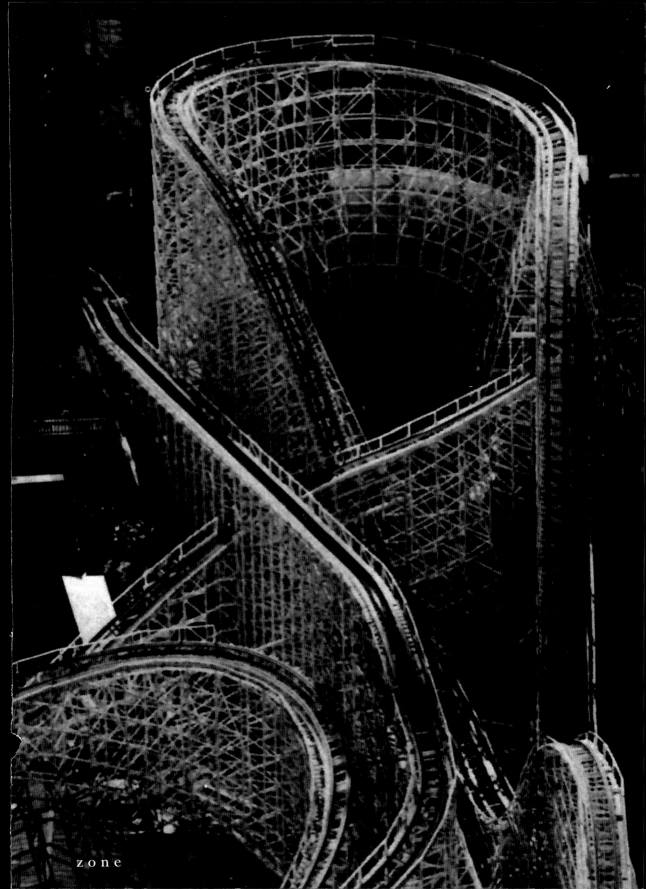

zone